Lexical Ambiguity Resolution:

Perspectives from Psycholinguistics, Neuropsychology, and Artificial Intelligence

Contributors

Geert Adriaens
Curt Burgess
Claudia Brugman
Cristiano Castelfranchi
Garrison W. Cottrell
Kurt P. Eiselt
Dan Fass
Ilene M. France
Dedre Gentner
Helen Gigley
Richard H. Granger, Jr.
Graeme Hirst
Jennifer K. Holbrook
Alan H. Kawamoto

Marta Kutas
George Lakoff
Steven L. Lytinen
Edward H. Matthei
Robert Milne
Domenico Parisi
P. A. Prather
Mark Seidenberg
Greg B. Simpson
Steven L. Small
David A. Swinney
Patrizia Tabossi
Michael K. Tanenhaus
Cyma Van Petten

Edited by

Steven L. Small,
Department of Computer Science, University of Rochester
Garrison W. Cottrell,
Institute for Cognitive Science, University of California, San Diego
Michael K. Tanenhaus,
Department of Psychology, University of Rochester

Morgan Kaufmann Publishers, Inc.
San Mateo, California

Editor and President *Michael B. Morgan*
Production Manager *Jennifer M. Ballentine*
Copy and Technical Editor *Lee Ballentine*
Text Design *Michael Rogondino*
Composition *Ocean View Technical Publications*
Text Programming *Bruce Boston*
Technical Illustrations *Terry Earlywine*
Cover Design *Scott Kim and David Healy*
Index *Elinor Lindheimer*
Mechanicals *Beverly Kennon-Kelley*
Manufacturing *R.R. Donnelley & Sons*

This book was produced from electronic media provided by the contributors. Design programming and composition was performed using MKS Toolkit™ and Ventura Publisher™. Technical illustrations were hand rendered and dropped-in. MKS Toolkit is a trademark of Mortice Kern Systems Inc. Ventura Publisher is a trademark of Ventura Software Inc.

Library of Congress Cataloging-in-Publication Data

Lexical ambiguity resolution.

    Bibliography: p.
    Includes index.
    1. Ambiguity. 2. Semantics. 3. Linguistics--Data
processing. 4. Psycholinguistics. 5. Artificial
intelligence. I. Small, Steven Lawrence, 1954-   .
II. Cottrell, Garrison Weeks, 1950-   . III. Tanenhaus,
Michael K.
P325.5.A46L4 1988   401.41   87-33939
ISBN 0-934613-50-8

Morgan Kaufmann Publishers, Inc.
2929 Campus Drive, Suite 260
San Mateo, CA 94403
Order Fulfullment: PO Box 50490, Palo Alto CA 94303

93 92 91 90 89 5 4 3 2 1

Foreword

Yorick Wilks
New Mexico State University

This is an important book, one that focuses on problems in language understanding by computer that many, in traditions other than that of the present editors, would prefer to forget.

They are close to a tradition (though they may not agree with this characterization!) I shall call "computational semantics" in a sense fairly well understood in artificial intelligence and computational linguistics but one not beyond dispute by other users of the term "semantics." I shall just state the sense intended, because my purpose here is not to defend the use, which has been done often enough, but to use it to introduce the chapters in this book.

What is "Computational Semantics?"

As is often the case, a position can best be described by contrasting it with others, and in this case I can contrast Computational Semantics usefully with three positions: syntactic analysis, logical semantics, and expert systems. There are refinements and subtleties in all those positions but, speaking broadly, Computational Semantics is opposed to any claims as to the necessity or sufficiency, for computational language understanding, of logical semantics or syntactic analysis. To say that is not to deny, in certain cases, the usefulness of a syntactic analysis, nor the aesthetic pleasures of a subsequent formal axiomatization. Computational Semantics holds, however, that, for the solution of practical and enormous problems like lexical ambiguity resolution, the real theories of language understanding, which is to say, the substantive algorithms and the right level of analysis, lie elsewhere.

The comparison with natural language interfaces to expert systems is rather different: There exists a position, for which it is difficult to give textual sources (in a way that it is all too easy for the above two positions), which claims that, if the appropriate "expert" knowledge structure is adequate, then practical problems of language semantics (lexical ambiguity, etc.) do not arise since the knowledge base contains only appropriate word senses. This claim is simply false, unless (a) the domain chosen is trivial, or (b) the domain chosen includes language itself, as in Small's Word Expert parsing system [Chapter 1, this volume]. However, to say that is not to mark computational semantics off from knowledge realms and their formal expression: on the contrary, it is to suggest that knowledge of language and "the world" are not separable, just as they are not separable into databases called, respectively, dictionaries and encyclopedias.

Computational Semantics and Connectionism

No introduction to anything these days would be complete without some reference to connectionism: the current cluster of artificial intelligence theories around the notion of very simple computing units, connected in very large numbers, and "learning from experience" by means of shifting aggregated weights in a network. This development may offer a way forward in many areas of artificial intelligence, including computational semantics. Two of the chapters in this book follow this line; Kawamoto's excellent model of the acquisition of lexemes and Cottrell's model of lexical access. Connectionism shares many of the differences that computational semantics has with the approaches noted above: an emphasis on the integration of semantics and syntax, continuity between linguistic and other forms of world knowledge, and a type of inference that is not reconcilable with the kind offered by logic-based approaches. Moreover, connectionism has stressed notions such as that of active competition between representational structures, with the tendency of the more strongly connected representations to "win," a notion to be found explicitly in computational semantics systems such as Preference Semantics, and Small's Word Expert approach [Chapter 1, this volume].

An important difference, as regards lexical ambiguity resolution in particular, arises here between so-called sub-symbolic approaches within connectionism [Smolensky 1988] and those usually called localist [Cottrell, 1985; Waltz and Pollack, 1985]. This difference, which is yet in no way settled, bears very much on the subject matter of this book: in a sub-symbolic approach to computational semantics one would not necessarily expect to distinguish representations for particular word-senses, they would be simply different patterns of activation over a set of units representing sub-symbolic features, where similar senses would lead to similar patterns. On the other hand, localist approaches [Waltz and Pollack, 1985; Cottrell, 1985] to computational semantics have assumed real distinguished word senses in their symbolic representations at the outset and have then given weighting criteria for selecting between them.

The difference between these two notions of connectionism, as they apply to issues of word sense in computational semantics, captures precisely the issue at the heart of lexical ambiguity resolution—namely, are there, in any real sense, discrete word senses, or is it all just a matter of fuzzy, numerical-boundary classifications of individual examples of use? That this issue is a serious one can be seen from the consequence that, if there is no real basis, psychological or computational, to word-sense classes, then there is no topic to be called lexical ambiguity resolution, and this book should be on the same library shelf as alchemy, phrenology, and the Greek myths. Before going on to reassure the reader on this issue, let me complete the historical introduction by setting the contrasts above in an earlier context.

Some Brief History of Computational Semantics

What is the historical origin of computational semantics, as defined above? In some broad sense nearly all the work in the early 1970s on artificial intelligence approaches to natural language understanding can be said to fall under the description computational semantics: the two approaches that fit most straight forwardly were Schank's Conceptual Dependency [1975] and Wilks's Preference Semantics [1975], but in a yet broader sense Winograd's SHRDLU [1972] was also within the description given above, since his own emphasis at the time was not on reference (to the limited number of blocks on his simulated table) but on "procedural semantics." Very much the same can be said of Simmons's networks [1973] and Charniak's inferential system [1972].

Versions of these systems all still appear in systems under development today: the emphasis in the Conceptual Dependency group has shifted from describing their work as natural language processing to describing it as human memory research, but the change is largely cosmetic, since at Yale the approach is still applied to machine translation [see Lytinen, Chapter 4, this volume] and database front-ends, among other things. A recent paper by Lehnert [1986], although its title suggests a continuing concern with memory, is very much a return to early Conceptual Dependency concerns and is certainly computational semantics: in fact a fusion of Conceptual Dependency and Preference Semantics approaches.

More recent work in the computational semantics tradition has been concerned with the central issue, isolated above and discussed below, of the discreteness of word-senses (as opposed to a model of continuity between them, as connectionism prefers) and the question of how, if distinctions are to be made between senses, this can be done at the appropriate time, as information enters the system, rather than on the basis of early all-or-nothing commitment, in the way earlier computational semantics systems all did. Key work here has been by Small [Adriaens and Small, Chapter 1, this volume], Hirst [Chapter 3, this volume] and Mellish [1985].

The emphasis there is on the boundaries between word-senses, continuity and vagueness [Lytinen, Chapter 4, this volume] and the ways in which sense decisions can be made appropriately if the phenomena are less discrete than was once supposed. These are the real concerns of human and machine understanders, and ones about which logic-based semantics has little or nothing to say.

Are Word-Senses Real?

Let us now, in conclusion, review the issue itself rather than its research history, and do so by asking the basic question this way: is it right to assume a notion of "word sense," unexamined, and direct from traditional lexicography? What evidence have we that a serious computational semantics can be based on such a notion?

To put the matter another way: Many have claimed that the inability of programs to cope with lexical ambiguity was a major reason for the failure of early computational linguistics tasks like machine translation. Yet, does it follow from that that the lexical ambiguity distinguished by conventional dictionaries, or even LDOCE (*Longman's Dictionary of Contemporary English*, [Proctor 1979]) has any real significance for that task? LDOCE is worth a special mention here. It is a real dictionary, on sale as a book, but which has also, in electronic form, been used by computational linguists (e.g., [Wilks et al., 1987]) as a knowledge base for English. It is peculiarly suitable for this because it is written complete with fine grammar codes, with word-sense entries in a restricted English (of about two thousand "primitives") and in a restricted English syntax. What all such documents do, as we all know, is to set out for each word of English, such as "play," a claim that it has, say, eight senses that are then described and distinguished. What, we are asking now, is the status of such a claim; is it more than the arbitrary segmentation of the word's usage by a lexicographer or a small team of them?

The point can be put most clearly with the suggestion that there never was any lexical ambiguity until dictionaries were written in roughly the form we now have them, and that lexical ambiguity is no more or less than a product of scholarship: a social product, in other words. Translation between languages, as well as more mundane understanding tasks had, however, been going for millenia before such scholarly products and therefore cannot require them. If any reader finds this position bizarre, even as a discussion point, let them ask what empirical evidence they have that there were word senses before the publication of dictionaries.

A certain kind of cognitive psychologist may find this position tempting. It is also very much to the taste of certain formal semanticists who have never found the idea of lexical ambiguity interesting or important. For them, it is a peripheral phenomenon, one that can be dealt with by subscripting symbols into play1, play2 etc., (as Wittgenstein first did in his *Tractatus* [1922]) and claiming that there is, in any case, no real ambiguity in the world itself: symbols indicate disjoint classes of things and that fact can best be captured by disjoint (subscripted) symbols.

The answer to this position is that, however well people translated "ambiguous words" before the advent of dictionaries, the processes they went through cannot be modelled by computer without some representation of lexical ambiguity. All practical experience for 25 years has confirmed that, and it is at precisely this point that the psychological research on the reality of word-sense ambiguity is so important [Petten and Kutas; Gigley; Burgess and Simpson; Simpson and Burgess; Prather and Swinney; Tanenhaus, Seidenberg, and Burgess, all this volume].

But other problems still remain to be faced by those who, like the present author, reject the opposition in this way and still intend to construct a lexical ambiguity database for computation. One is what we might call the arbitrariness factor: different dictionaries may give 1, 2, 7, 34, or 87 senses for a single word and they cannot all be right. Worse yet, those different segmentations of usage into discrete senses may not even be inclusive: sometimes different dictionaries will segment usage into senses for a given word in incommensurate ways: perhaps "play3" (the third of three) in dictionary A could not be associated with any one of the eight senses of "play" in dictionary B.

Giving Word-Senses an Empirical Foundation

There are two answers to this last objection. One is extensibility: a dictionary and lexical ambiguity resolution algorithm are plausible only if they can extend so as to capture new senses, not already in the dictionary, on the basis of textual material presented. In that way differing dictionaries could, in principle (though it might serve no practical purpose) be tuned to "sense compatability," just as people can be if exposed to the same texts. Such a position is not far from the one Dreyfus [1979] has defended over the years: that modelling intelligence must inevitably be by means of extensible, or learning, systems. In the case of natural language understanding, that task is often subcontracted out to "metaphor understanding." The position defended here is that that phenomenon, whatever it is called (and "metaphor" has always tended to marginalize it) is utterly central: to language understanding itself and even to the possibility of reliable, compatible, machine dictionaries that start from different databases. Fass's system [Chapter 6, this volume], called Collative Semantics, seeks to put Preference Semantics on a firmer representational foundation, while at the same time tightly linking lexical ambiguity resolution to metaphor understanding: the detection of new senses in context.

The second answer to the last mentioned attack on the "reality of word senses" is itself empirical and computational. Researchers such as Sparck Jones [1966; republished 1986] attempted many years ago to give a computational clustering of word usages, such that what we think of as word senses would fall out naturally as nonarbitrary groups or clusters. However, such research was almost impossible to carry out on the computers of that time, involving, as it did, the inversion of very large matrices. More recently, Plate (see [Wilks et al., 1987]) has established networks of words, by means of such large matrix inversions, based on occurrence and contiguity frequency, within the 2000 "defining primitives" of the LDOCE dictionary. The networks are very intuitively appealing with, for example, the "financial" and "river" senses of "bank" separating out quite clearly as decomposable subnetworks. It might be objected that this is no proof at all, since the text analyzed for the associations is LDOCE, that is to say, not a normal text but a dictionary, one that assumes the very sense distinctions we are setting out to establish empirically!

But this objection fails, and an empirical basis for word senses is saved, because it is easy to show that most usages of any given word in the whole LDOCE (and the computation ranges over the whole dictionary) occur not in its own definition (where its senses are indeed distinguished a priori) but in examples and in the definitions of other words. Hence, LDOCE is, in effect, just a text, and its empirical separation of lexical senses by classification techniques is real evidence of their existence.

Word senses are certainly here to stay, and so therefore will be computer programs that can distinguish them in context, as the researches of the authors in this book do. No problem in computational linguistics is more practically pressing or more intellectually challenging.

References

Charniak, E. 1972. Towards a model of children's story comprehension. Technical Report No. MIT-AI-TR266.

Cottrell, G. 1985. Connectionist parsing. In *Proc. Seventh Annual Cognitive Science Conference*, Irvine, CA.

Dreyfus, H. 1979. *What Computers Can't Do*, 2nd edition. New York: Harper and Row.

Lehnert, W. 1986. *Utilizing Episodic Memory for the Integration of Syntax and Semantics.* Unpublished ms., University of Mass., CS Dept.

Mellish, C. 1985. *Computer Interpretation of Natural Language Descriptions.* Chichester: Ellis Horwood.

Proctor, P. 1979. *Longmans Dictionary of Contemporary English.* London: Longmans.

Schank, R. 1975. *Conceptual Information Processing.* Amsterdam: North Holland.

Simmons, R. 1973. Semantic networks: Their computation and use for understanding English sentences. In Schank and Colby (eds.), *Computer Models of Thought and Language.* San Francisco: Freeman.

Smolensky, P. 1988. On the proper treatment of connectionism. *Behavioral and Brain Sciences 11.*

Sparck Jones, K. 1986. *Synonymy and Semantic Classification.* Originally Cambridge Ph.D. thesis 1967. Edinburgh: Edinburgh University Press.

Waltz , D., and Pollack J. 1985. Massively parallel parsing: A strongly interactive model of natural language interpretation. *Cognitive Science 9.*

Winograd, T. 1972. *Understanding Natural Language.* New York: Academic Press.

Wilks, Y. 1975. A preferential pattern-seeking semantics for natural language inference. *Artificial Intelligence 6.*

Wilks, Y., Fass, D., Guo, C-M., MacDonald, J., Plate, T. and Slator, B. 1987. A tractable machine dictionary as a basis for computational semantics. Technical Report No. MCCS-87-105.

Wittgenstein, L. 1922. *Tractatus Logico-Philosophicus.* London: Routledge and Kegan Paul.

Contents

PART II: EMPIRICAL STUDIES

Preface

Steven L. Small

Department of Computer Science
University of Rochester

Garrison W. Cottrell

Institute for Cognitive Science
University of California at San Diego

Michael K. Tanenhaus

Department of Psychology
University of Rochester

The goal of this book is to bring together current research from several disciplines on the problem of lexical ambiguity resolution in the processing of natural language. This research spans psychology, computer science and linguistics, providing an interdisciplinary, Cognitive Science perspective. The aim is to provide a sourcebook for cognitive scientists and those interested in lexical ambiguity, whether they be working primarily in artificial intelligence, psycholinguistics, neurolinguistics, or theoretical linguistics. This volume includes papers that would otherwise require a search through the journals and conference proceedings of many disciplines to find. Furthermore, the authors have described their research goals and results in such a way that cognitive scientists of different fields can comprehend their general import. Along the way, perhaps some consensus on the important problems may emerge. This book is at least the starting point for such a consensus.

Some readers may feel that lexical ambiguity resolution is too narrow a topic for a book. Hence a look at the scope of this problem from the point of view of a discipline (Artificial Intelligence) that is trying to resolve it is in order. Lexical ambiguity was rarely attacked directly in early work on Natural Language Understanding (NLU) in Artificial Intelligence. However, it is perhaps the most important problem facing an NLU system. Given that the goal of NLU is understanding, correctly determining the meanings of the words used is fundamental. This is not an issue limited to strange sentences devised by linguists. In an informal study, Gentner [1982] found that the 20 most frequent nouns have an average of 7.3 word senses each; the 20 most frequent verbs have an average of 12.4 senses each. Small [1978] lists 57 senses for the word "take." Not to be outdone, Hirst [1984] reports that "go" has 63 meanings listed in the Merriam Webster Pocket Dictionary. It is remarkable that people rarely notice this degree of ambiguity in their most frequently used words. An important premise underlying the work in this book is that it is important to understand how people resolve the ambiguity problem, since whatever their approach, it appears to work rather well.

A Taxonomy of Lexical Ambiguity

Lexical ambiguity is of two types, syntactic and semantic. Syntactic lexical ambiguity simply refers to ambiguity of *category*, e.g., noun vs. verb. For example, **fish** can be either the act performed by an angler or the target of his activity. This is to be distinguished from *structural* ambiguity, which refers to sentences which have more than one phrase structure tree assignable to them. Winograd's famous example is *Put the block in the box on the table*, which can be assigned two structures depending on whether "in the box" modifies "block" or not. In general, we will not address problems of structural ambiguity in this book.

Semantic lexical ambiguity is of two types. *Polysemy* refers to words whose several meanings are related. For example, the two uses of **fell** in *Chile's democracy* **fell** *to CIA backed generals* and *John* **fell** *and hurt himself* are similar in meaning, but not literally the same. Polysemy, as pointed out by Hirst [1984], often blends into metaphor. *Homonymy* refers to words whose various definitions are unrelated, as in the two uses of **ball** in *They danced till dawn at the* **ball** versus *This dog can be entertained all day with a* **ball**.

Semantic and syntactic ambiguity are orthogonal, since a single word can have related meanings in different categories (as in **can** *of fruit* vs. *to* **can** *fruit*), or unrelated meanings in different categories (as in **I saw** *the carpenter's* **saw**), or both (**I saw** *the carpenter* **sawing** *with the rusty* **saw**).

In order to resolve ambiguity, an NLU system (human or otherwise) has to take into account many sources of knowledge. For example, categorial ambiguity can often be resolved on syntactic considerations alone, as in **I can** *do it*, where the only possible syntactic class of **can** is auxiliary. Some sentences are *globally ambiguous* in this respect, e.g., in *His* **will** *be done*, the category of **will** is either auxiliary or noun, depending on who is speaking and where, i.e., a minister in church, or a mechanic in a garage. This also illustrates how categorial and structural ambiguity can interact.

People appear to use semantic sources of information for categorial disambiguation as well, although this sometimes leads them astray, as in *The old* **man** *the boats* (the old people operate the boats). Although there is a syntactic frequency argument as well, one explanation for the "garden path" nature of this sentence is that the semantic representation of "old man" overrides the proper syntactic interpretation. The fact that such semantic garden path sentences exist is some evidence that the semantic representation of a word can influence decisions concerning its syntactic representation.

Semantic ambiguities often require global context for their resolution as well. For example, *She looked at her* **pupils** could mean either her eyes or her students, depending on the situation. However, often all that is required is *local context*, specifically, the context provided by the rest of the sentence. For example, in *Bob* **threw** *the fight*, whether **threw** refers to "propelling" something or "intentionally losing" something is determined by the presence of **fight**.

Now we can see that lexical ambiguity is a difficult problem. Not only are there several kinds of lexical ambiguity,[1] but they can interact in complex ways, both with each other and with other types of knowledge. Consideration of these problems leads us willy-nilly into the mysteries of understanding language. The fundamental mystery is why understanding seems so simple for humans. The puzzle for cognitive scientists is to try and unravel the means by which this trick is accomplished. Two major approaches are represented in this book. The first might be termed "top-down"—try to build a language understanding device in order to discover the functions necessary, and to determine how they should interact. The other is bottom-up—examine the phenomena in the laboratory and try to induce the nature of the processes being used. In the next section we briefly summarize the goals of each paper.

A Tour of the Book

The papers collected here represent most of the current approaches to the study of lexical ambiguity resolution in many disciplines. The articles from artificial intelligence (AI) provide computational data regarding the nature of the knowledge and processes found to be *necessary* to perform lexical disambiguation

---

1 We have not even covered all of the types. For the most part, we ignore in this book the problem of *referential ambiguity*, that is, the problem of determining which conceptual entity a word (especially pronouns) refers to.

computationally. This research describes certain formally defined mechanisms (i.e., algorithms) that can account for this computation. Some of these articles suggest how well such algorithms correspond in their functional characteristics to the available data on human processing. Computer programs provide valuable specificity in modeling the processes, yet the assumptions they make in formulating this specification are often incorrect as models of human processing. In contrast, psychological models of ambiguity resolution have generally been somewhat vague in their processing and representational assumptions. However, using a variety of newly developed chronometric techniques, psychologists have been able to provide preliminary answers to some of the important questions about how human language users process lexical ambiguity. In particular, a detailed picture is emerging of the time course of meaning access and ambiguity resolution. The psycholinguistic papers in this volume sample the spectrum of current experimental work on lexical ambiguity resolution, including pioneering neurolinguistic studies.

Although the experimental results demonstrate that multiple levels of processing appear to be involved in lexical ambiguity resolution, the interactions among these levels and the time course of knowledge application within and between levels is not well understood. Just as experimental studies of ambiguity resolution can guide and constrain computational theories, the computational literature may provide ideas that will shape the next generation of experimental studies.

AI Models

Many approaches to various parts of the ambiguity problem are represented by these works. In an interesting extension to Word Expert Parsing, **Adriaens and Small** consider not only lexical ambiguity but other lexical effects in parsing, most notably, long distance dependencies. **Milne** gives a clear account of how many form class ambiguities may be accounted for by top down expectations in a Marcus-style deterministic parser. This is an important first cut in the search for the "meaning" of a word. Picking up where Milne leaves off, **Hirst** assumes that the category of the word has already been selected, and tries to determine the proper meaning of a word. As in the Word Expert Parser, each word has a process associated with it (called a *Polaroid Word*) that interacts with the processes for other words and a knowledge base. Unlike WEP, it uses a uniform set of rules for each form class and uses marker passing through a frame system to select the proper frame for disambiguation purposes. Frame selection is a hard problem for frame-based systems, often solved by using a lexically based approach. **Lytinen** points out problems with this approach in the case of polysemous words, and gives an alternative algorithm for frame selection via a process of concept refinement in a hierarchical frame system. **Parisi and Castelfranchi** identify various decision points from a processing point of view in their lexically based parsing system. They display several procedures for resolving the ambiguities presented depending on the type of choice point.

Many researchers have said that there is a scale of lexical ambiguity from words with unrelated meanings to words with related meanings to metaphorical usage. This view is complicated by other types of usage, such as metonymy, a figure of language in which a part stands for the whole (e.g., "nice set of wheels"). **Fass** demonstrates a new algorithm for matching semantic structures occurring in "is a" sentences that recognizes instances of metonymy and metaphor in the service of building an appropriate semantic representation.

Turning to systems that attempt to mimic human mechanisms, **Cottrell** describes a simple connectionist model for the access of word meanings that aims to account for some of the psychological data on that process. **Kawamoto**'s model goes further describing how such knowledge can be learned in a connectionist framework. Finally, **Gigley**'s system hypothesizes processing deficits that may account for aphasic performance in processing sentences.

Empirical Studies

Experimental studies of lexical ambiguity resolution have primarily been concerned with tracing the time course of lexical access and ambiguity resolution. Lexical access is the process of accessing all of the information about a word, usually from visual or auditory input. Three questions have been of primary interest: (1) Does lexical access make available one or more than one meaning of an ambiguous word? (2) Does prior context constrain lexical access such that only the contextually biased sense is initially accessed? (3) Does the relative frequency (dominance) of the different senses affect access, and interact with the effects of biasing sentential context? In the late 1970s and early 1980s a number of studies used "cross-modal" priming paradigms in which experimental subjects listened to a sentence and made a rapid response to a visually presented target word displayed at some point during the sentence. Facilitation in responding to a target word that is related to a particular sense of an ambiguous word provides evidence for that sense having been active at the time that target was presented. For example, facilitation to the target word MONEY following the ambiguous word BANK indicates the "financial institution" sense of BANK was active. The consensus that emerged from these studies was that all common meanings of an ambiguous word are accessed regardless of contextual bias, with contextually inappropriate senses becoming rapidly unavailable.

The papers in this volume add considerable detail to this story and in some cases argue that it is fundamentally incorrect. **Simpson and Burgess** provide a general introduction to experimental studies of lexical ambiguity, and to their role in addressing fundamental issues of word recognition and its development.

They also present some recent experiments demonstrating that word senses are accessed in the order of their relative frequencies. **Prather and Swinney** offer a spirited defense of the hypothesis that the early stages of lexical processes operate as an autonomous processing module. They also discuss "backward priming," the priming of a word by a following target word and its implications for the cross-modal ambiguity literature. Backward priming is the focus of the paper by **Tanenhaus, Burgess, and Seidenberg**. They present experiments that challenge a recent paper by Glucksberg, Rho, and Kreuz which concluded that only contextually biased senses of ambiguous words are accessed when backward priming is eliminated by the use of special targets. **Tabossi** discusses some recent experiments demonstrating that contexts emphasizing salient features of the dominant sense of an ambiguous word result in only the biased sense being activated. These experiments offer the strongest challenge to modularity hypotheses, and emphasize the importance of focusing on the properties of different types of biasing contexts. **Gentner and France** use the clever device of varying the semantic plausibility of sentences, setting up a competition between nouns and verbs for domination of the resulting sentential meaning. The relative strength of nouns and verbs are assessed in a paraphrase task, and the results used to infer the properties of the system.

Holbrook, Eiselt, Granger, and Matthei address the neglected problem of how readers retrieve the correct sense of an ambiguous word when the context biases the sense that eventually turns out to be incorrect. For example, *He made the medical students examine the tiny **cell** so that they would be aware of the consequences of malpractice.* They argue that only the contextually biased sense is active, whereas other senses are conditionally retained. **Burgess and Simpson** address the same issue from a different perspective. They present an experiment that suggests that multiple senses for ambiguous words are retained longer in the right hemisphere than the left hemisphere, and they conjecture that the right hemisphere may play a fundamental role both in recovery from initial misassignment, and more broadly, in the interpretation of non-literal meaning.

Progress in understanding ambiguity resolution and other rapid unconscious processes in language understanding depends crucially on methodologies that can track the time course of comprehension processes. In pioneering work, **Van Petten and Kutas** use event-related potentials produced by brain waves to track ambiguity resolution. They argue that their results challenge the conclusions drawn from other experimental techniques. In particular, they suggest that the pattern of EEG activity supports a backward priming explanation for multiple access. Although the interpretation of these results is likely to be controversial, this experiment represents an important extension of an exciting methodology.

Most of the experimental work represented here is concerned with the core meaning of nouns having unrelated senses. The important issue of polysemy is confronted by **Brugman and Lakoff** in a case study of the word *over*. They show that there are many regularities to be discovered in the relationships between the meanings of polysemous words, relationships which could be exploited by a natural language understanding system. Similar analyses of other polysemous words are likely to uncover systematic patterns in the way core meanings are extended.

Conclusion

We believe that progress in understanding natural language must depend on integrating ideas drawn from artificial intelligence, cognitive psychology, linguistics, and the neurosciences. Lexical ambiguity has served as something of a case study in cognitive science, an area in which researchers from different disciplines have already significantly benefited from each others' work. As. the articles in this volume clearly illustrate, there is room for more interaction. If it helps to encourage further interdisciplinary work, this book will have served its purpose.

Acknowledgments

We would like to thank, first of all, the contributors to this volume for their patience during the seemingly endless process of completing this book and for their time in cross-reviewing each other's work. Additional reviewers included Yves Chauvin, David Corina, Mark Fanty, Susan Garnsey, Cathy Harris, Kerry Kilborn, Michael Mozer, and Jay Weber, who took valuable time away from their own research to help us.

This book would not have been possible without the administrative acuity of Peggy Meeker who managed the paperwork through the first half of the publishing process. Thanks for moral and other support go to Jerry Feldman, George Miller, and Yorick Wilks, who each in his own way lent encouragement to this project. The beauty of the final product is the result of the tenacity of our excellent production manager, Jennifer Ballentine.

Steven L. Small
Gary Cottrell, and
Michael Tanenhaus
May 1988

PART

I

COMPUTER MODELS

1

Word Expert Parsing Revisited in a Cognitive Science Perspective

Geert Adriaens
Siemens AI Research
Leuven, Belgium

Steven L. Small[1]
Department of Computer Science
University of Rochester

1 *Introduction*

The Word Expert Parser (WEP) [Small, 1980] was an early AI model of natural language understanding to make a serious attempt at handling multiple senses of the words in its vocabulary.[2] WEP was a semantic parsing program in which lexical ambiguity resolution was considered the essence of language understanding. This view led to a radical departure from other parsing models, and a system architecture based upon disambiguation mechanisms, which will be discussed in the next section of this chapter. Besides being a working AI

---

1 Current address: Decision Systems Laboratory, University of Pittsburgh, 1360 Scaife Hall, Pittsburgh, Pennsylvania 15261
2 See also [Wilks, 1973; Hayes, 1977; Boguraev, 1979].

program, WEP also claimed to be a model of the process of language comprehension in the human being. Although at the time little was done to confront these claims with results of linguistic, psychological, and neurological research, the growing importance of cognitive science has inspired such a confrontation. The third (and main) section of this chapter directly addresses this issue; we shall put WEP in a broader cognitive science perspective, discussing its flaws and merits through a confrontation with linguistics and psycholinguistics (for a confrontation with neurolinguistic research, see [Adriaens, 1986b]). The final section briefly discusses some issues for future research.

2 Lexical Ambiguity Resolution

2.1 General Principles

When we look at the words of a natural language (by skimming through a dictionary, or by introspection), we find that they are objects with a very rich and highly idiosyncratic content. Some help tie other words together (e.g., "a," "the," "in"), while others display a great number of different meanings (e.g., "deep," "throw," "pit"), from among which the human being is capable of picking the contextually appropriate one during comprehension.

A large number of existing parsing systems ignore this richness of individual words and the entirety of the sense selection problem. They advocate instead an approach that captures generalities about language in syntactic and/or semantic rules, treating the words as tokens that simply participate in comprehension by virtue of their inclusion in these rules (see [Rieger and Small, 1981]).

The apparent incompatibility of the sense selection problem and the rule-based approaches led to a radically different model organization. Instead of having a number of components (e.g., morphological, syntactic, semantic), consisting of static rule structures spanning sentence constituents or complete sentences, with some central interpreter taking care of the application of these rules to the input, the words themselves are considered as active agents, or word experts. They trigger processes that idiosyncratically control the whole parsing process. This process involves continuous interaction of a word with a number of knowledge sources in memory: the words in its immediate context, the concepts processed so far or expected locally, knowledge of the overall process state, knowledge of the discourse, and real-world knowledge. These knowledge sources are not invoked uniformly by a general interpreter, but are accessible at all times by the word expert processes throughout the overall process of sense discrimination. They help the experts to eventually agree on a context-specific semantic interpretation of a fragment of text. This overall parsing process makes crucial use of word-based expectations guiding the word experts in their sense discrimination.

In summary, word expert parsing is seen as a data-driven (word-by-word), expectation-based, highly interactive process coordinated by the individual words that are viewed as active knowledge sources (word experts). We will now take a closer look at matters of representation and implementation that turn these principles into a working program.

2.2 Representation

Informally, word experts can be viewed as sense discrimination networks consisting of nodes of context-probing questions and arcs corresponding to the range of possible answers. Each of the leaves of the network represents a specific contextual meaning of the word in question reached after network traversal during sentence processing. Figure 1.1 shows such an informal network for the highly ambiguous word "deep." The left half of the net represents its adjectival usages ((1) through (4)), the right half its nominal ones ((5) through (7)). Meaning (1) would be arrived at in a context like "The deep philosopher

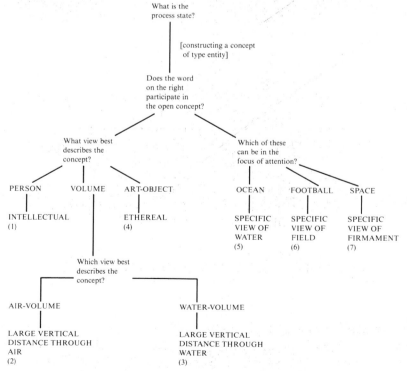

Figure 1.1 A sense discrimination network

likes Levinas," (2) in a context like "He throws the ring into the deep pit"; meaning (5) would be chosen in the context "The giant squid still lives in the deep," etc. for the other usages.

These nets form the basis for the design and development of word experts, but have to be translated into a formal declarative representation used procedurally by the WEP process. Such a representation is a graph composed of designated subgraphs without cycles. Each subgraph (an "entry point") consists of question nodes that probe the multiple knowledge sources mentioned above and action nodes that build and refine concepts, keep track of their lexical sequences, etc. These questions and actions constitute the formal representation language for word experts. We will not give a full description of the syntax and semantics of the word expert representation language here, but briefly mention the most important questions and actions that deal specifically with sense discrimination (excluding bookkeeping actions that keep track of lexical sequences, and internal expert control actions). The actions that deal with expert interaction are discussed in Section 2.3, the subsection about implementa-

---

QUESTIONS

?SIGNAL: Probe incoming control signals (which are either the process state or idiosyncratic signals from other experts).

?BINDC: Probe different memory sources.

?BINDC MEMORY ACTIVE/EXPECT: Try to find a specific concept in active memory or expected by it.

?BINDC DISCOURSE FOCUS/EXPECT: Ask memory whether a specific concept is in focus or expected by the discourse.

?BINDC REAL-WORLD PLAUSIBLE/BELIEF: Probe real-world knowledge

?VIEW: Probe the conceptual proximity of two concepts.

?LITERAL: Probe the word of some expert.

?IDIOM: Probe the lexical sequence of a concept to see if it is an idiomatic expression.

ACTIONS

BUILDC: Construct a concept.

REFINEC: Refine a concept.

STOREC: Store a concept in active memory.

ROLEC: Specify a concept role (e.g., c1 is object to c2).

ASPECTC: Specify the slots of a concept.
           (e.g., c2 takes c1 as an object)

Figure 1.2 Sense discrimination questions and actions

tion. The Appendix contains an example word expert (the expert for "deep" that implements part of the network of Figure 1.1). A full description can be found in [Small, 1980], and partial descriptions in [Small and Rieger, 1982], [Small and Lucas, 1983], and [Adriaens, 1986b]. Figure 1.2 shows the questions and actions performing sense discrimination within the word experts.[3]

The actions build concept structures as a side effect of the course of the overall parsing process. In WEP, these structures have received much less attention than the processing issues (how to control the expert interactions). Hence, not much will be said about them here. Nouns build entity concepts, that are refined by their modifiers; verbs assign roles to the entities, deciding on the contextually appropriate caseframe (the ROLEC action and its counterpart ASPECTC—see also Section 3.4). The result is a kind of dependency structure linking together all the concepts built up during the process.

The questions deserve a little more attention, since they direct the sense disambiguation process. An example of the SIGNAL question can be found in the word expert for "deep" in the Appendix. In order to find out at what point it enters the process, "deep" probes its incoming signal (if it is *entity-construction*, "deep" simply participates in the current lexical sequence and goes on to its subprocess at entry1. If not, it first opens a sequence). The BINDC question is probably the most important probing question since the process of disambiguation depends fundamentally on interactions between word experts and memory mechanisms. An expert can probe the active memory containing the concepts processed so far, it can look at the concepts expected by other experts, it can probe elements of the discourse (e.g., what is in focus?), and it can appeal to real-world knowledge. The VIEW question completes the memory interactions: it reflects the relative ability of memory to view one memory object as another, i.e., it tries to determine the conceptual closeness (proximity) of two memory objects.

The understanding of "My friends throw a get-together" depends on the ability of memory (probed by "throw" in this sentence) to view "a get-together" as most closely related to "a party." Thus, the "throw" expert asking the VIEW question (can the concept fulfilling the object role in my frame best be viewed as a physical object, a person, a contest, etc., or a party?) can continue its sense refinement accordingly. Finally, the LITERAL and IDIOM questions look for particular lexical elements. The "throw" expert, for instance, looks at the word to its right (with the LITERAL question) and takes appropriate actions if it happens to be one of the possible particles it can take

---

3 In a recent application of WEP to Dutch [Adriaens, 1986a; 1986b], some questions and actions were removed, and others added. In order not to complicate matters here, the original questions and actions from [Small, 1980] are discussed. The only thing changed here is that the BINDC nodes were considered action nodes in [Small, 1980], whereas they all "query" some memory mechanism, and as such are better viewed as question nodes.

("away," "up," "in," or "out"). Supposing it was "in," and a concept was processed after "throw in," "throw" probes the lexical sequence of this concept (with the IDIOM question) to see if it is e.g., "the towel," which leads to a concept refinement "give up."

Since this completes our overview of the sense discrimination part of the WEP representation language, a word is in order about the implementation of all the memory mechanisms discussed. The answers to the real-world, discourse and view probes are currently provided by interaction with the WEP user. This is mainly a matter of clean design: the inter-expert interactions have been the focus of attention. Access mechanisms to the knowledge sources in memory are provided, but we have chosen to assume the existence of a fully developed central semantic network scheme (along the lines of Fahlman [1979]), which we shall eventually integrate with the language system.

2.3 *Implementation*

So far we have discussed the general principles behind WEP, and the representation issues following from those principles. In this last subsection we will discuss the overall system implementation. How is it that the experts can communicate with each other throughout the disambiguation process to finally agree on the meaning of a fragment of text?

The decentralized representation of parsing knowledge in word experts leads to an overall model organization which supports exchange of information and distributed decision-making (i.e., agreement on overall meaning). Every word expert is implemented as a LISP coroutine. A coroutine is a process that runs for a while (in our case: coordinating the entire parsing process when it does), suspends itself when it needs a piece of information (letting another coroutine take over control), runs again when this information arrives, etc. until it stops executing. Thus, the lexical interaction among the expert coroutines consists first of providing information, and second, waiting for needed information.

Figure 1.3 contains the WEP actions that are used by individual word experts to perform these tasks. This set of actions was called the *Lexical Interaction Language* by Small [1980].

Providing information happens through the WEP actions REPORT and SIGNAL, making a concept or signal available for use by other experts respectively. Awaiting and receiving information requires a more complicated protocol, involving suspension of execution while waiting for a piece of information from another expert and resumption of execution when that information becomes available. This basic aspect of distributed control is taken care of by "restart daemons," data structures created automatically by the WEP action AWAIT which specifies the nature of the awaited information (a SIGNAL,

Providing information

SIGNAL: Make a message about the process state
            available for use by other experts.

REPORT: Make a concept structure available
            for use by other experts.

Awaiting information

AWAIT SIGNAL: Awaits the SIGNAL action.

AWAIT CONCEPT: Awaits the REPORT action.

AWAIT WORD: Awaits arrival of a specific word.

Figure 1.3 Lexical Interaction language

CONCEPT or specific WORD) and the point at which to continue execution upon arrival of the awaited data.

It should be noted that execution of the AWAIT action does not necessarily imply "complete" suspension of a word expert, since the different entry points of an expert are designed to be executed in parallel. One part of the process may temporarily be suspended, but other parts can go on, even initiating other restart daemons in turn (several outstanding AWAITs are possible). Yet, an expert cannot wait forever for some piece of information as there is no certainty about arrival. Therefore, each restart daemon is accompanied by a "timeout daemon" which specifies how long the expert is willing to wait for the information it desires[4] and the point at which to continue processing if the restart daemon times out (see [Small, 1981] for a full discussion of timeouts). An interesting aspect of this intricate machinery is that WEP does not contain some finite fixed length buffer to represent working memory, but models memory limitation with "processes" that have a strictly limited life span.

Figure 1.4 illustrates by way of a cartoon the overall WEP control flow resulting from the coroutine environment. This flow of control can be viewed as the movement of a window across the input stream. Inside the window, control passes from word expert to word expert and back again. Reading new words and the termination of old experts causes the overall processing window to move ahead, expanding its right side and contracting its left side. Eventually, the window includes the last word of the input text, and the process terminates.

---

4 In the current system the units of measurement for timeouts are based on certain model events, including (a) the number of syntactic groups created, (b) the number of words read, and (c) the number of sentence breaks encountered. It is our intention to change these units to semantically more interesting ones, such as the number of concepts of specific types processed (e.g., "wait for one concept of type action to be processed before timing out").

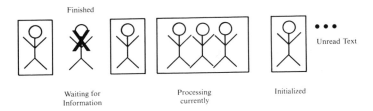

Figure 1.4 Word expert parser control flow

Note that attempts to create a fully distributed implementation of the word expert parser, with parallel execution of entry points in word experts, have not been successful. Some of the reasons for this are discussed in [Small et al., 1982], [Cottrell and Small, 1983] and in another context by [Fahlman, 1982]. This has led to the (massively parallel) connectionist approach to parsing (see [Cottrell and Small, 1983], [Cottrell, 1985], and chapters in this volume by Gigley, Cottrell, and Kawamoto). However, this failure has not resulted in the complete abandonment of WEP but rather in the relaxation of its claims as a fully distributed system. In the sections to come we will see that the system has a number of interesting aspects that motivate continued research. Moreover, an attempt is being made to redefine WEP in such a rigid way that implementation in a parallel version of PROLOG should become possible.

3 *Word Expert Parsing and Psycholinguistics*

3.1 *Introduction*

In the last several years, interest in the lexicon and its organization has grown substantially. At the same time the study of processes has become a fundamental element unifying the field: computational processes in AI, cognitive processes in psychology, neural processes in the neurosciences (see [Arbib et al., 1982] or [Winograd, 1983]). Since WEP integrates both lexicon and process into one model, it may be considered a cognitive science approach from an AI perspective. Thus, it is interesting to look at the model from the perspective of some of the other disciplines, which we do in this section.

Since much recent psychological research deals with the way or ways access and further processing of the mental lexicon are done during sentence comprehension, we will now confront the findings of this research with the WEP model. First, WEP will be situated within general models of sentence processing. Next, we will go into specific research topics.

3.2 *General Models*

Currently, there seem to be two kinds of global psycholinguistic models of language processing. One kind is the autonomous component model [Forster, 1979], both for spoken and written language), the other is the interactive model [Marslen-Wilson and Tyler, 1980] for spoken language, [Just and Carpenter, 1980] for written language).

In Forster's model the language processor consists of a linear chain of three separate and autonomous processing systems: a lexical processor locating the input elements in the lexicon, a syntactic processor assigning syntactic structures to the input and a semantic processor (called "message processor") building conceptual structures. (Note the correspondence between levels of processing and levels of linguistic description.) Thus, the input enters the lexical processor, whose output enters the syntactic processor, whose output in turn enters the message processor; no other communication among the processors is allowed. All three processors have access to a "language-oriented data storage," the lexicon. In this model, the resolution of ambiguities happens in the message processor; however, to achieve this the processor has no access to general conceptual knowledge (e.g., real-world knowledge).

It will be clear from this description that this model is incompatible with WEP. The lexicon is a vaguely defined data storage, hardly any interaction among processing components is allowed, and ambiguity resolution is relegated to a message processor allowed to access the input only "after" it has been processed syntactically. Moreover, the message processor is forced to do this without access to knowledge sources considered indispensable in WEP for disambiguation.

Marslen-Wilson and Tyler's model of spoken language understanding (partly a critique of Forster's model) starts from the claim that a listener tries to fully interpret the input as he hears it, on a word-by-word basis. The processing (i.e., recognition) of the words is directly influenced by the contextual environment in which they occur. Lexical, structural (syntactic) and interpretative knowledge sources are seen as communicating and interacting freely in an optimally efficient and accurate way during language comprehension, without any delays in availability of information. The same view of the comprehension process is held by Just and Carpenter in their model of written language understanding: their "immediacy assumption" posits that all knowledge sources in working and long-term memory aid undelayed interpretation of the words of a textual fragment as they are read. Both interactive models also stress that the words themselves are the primary information sources the language user has. Bottom-up processes triggered by the words are more important than the top-down ones that further aid interpretation.

WEP appears to be compatible with these interactive models. The current system only analyzes written text, and as such it comes closer to Just and Carpenter's model. A full comparison of this model and WEP would lead us too far here. We will come back to Just and Carpenter's results with eye-fixation research in Section 3.6 when we discuss research into the distinction between content and function words. An interesting topic for future WEP research suggested by their model is also the relation between eye movements during reading and the way control is passed back and forth between the experts as they execute and suspend within the coroutine regime.

3.3 *Lexical Access*

A question that has been the subject of a lot of psycholinguistic research in the last decade is the following: Does context restrict lexical access so that only the contextually appropriate meaning of a word is accessed (the Prior Decision Hypothesis) or do we access all meanings temporarily, with the context aiding selection of the appropriate meaning after access (the Post Decision Hypothesis)? Whereas early research yielded mixed results[5] recent work has produced results that support the post decision hypothesis[6] for noun-noun ambiguities (e.g., "bug" = insect or microphone) as well as for noun-verb ambiguities (e.g., "rose" = flower or "stood up") it was found that "all" meanings were accessed. Cases in which prior decision showed up in the results [Seidenberg et al., 1982]—i.e., with noun-noun ambiguities in a highly constraining context— were more readily explained by automatic intralexical network priming (i.e., a word occurring before the target was strongly semantically related to one reading of the ambiguous word) instead of contextual influence. Moreover, attempts to induce priming based on other types of contextual information (syntactic or pragmatic) have failed.

WEP operates in accordance with the post decision hypothesis: the interactive disambiguation process starts after retrieval of all the word's meanings. (An earlier attempt at constraining word experts by prior pruning [Rieger and Small, 1981] was abandoned. That prior pruning proved very hard to do helps us understand why human beings access all meanings of a word: exhaustive access with pruning after is less resource-consuming than the use of information to restrict access.) However, WEP cannot account for intralexical priming effects, since the experts are not connected into a semantic network through

---

5 See [Lackner and Garrett, 1972; Foss and Jenkins, 1973; Conrad, 1974; Swinney and Hakes, 1976; Holmes, 1977].
6 See [Swinney, 1979; Tanenhaus et al., 1979; Seidenberg et al., 1982, 1984].

which these effects could be spread. The introduction of such a network is a high priority issue in future research (see also Chapter 3, in this volume, by Hirst).

3.4 Lexical Expectation

Since word-based expectations play a central role in the WEP understanding process (through the AWAIT action), we shall examine the psycholinguistic research into this topic. It has repeatedly been suggested that during understanding people use lexical information about the possible syntactic or thematic frames of words (especially verbs). Anticipation of verb complements can guide understanding of words and phrases in a sentence [Fodor and Garrett, 1967, 1968] [Clark and Clark, 1977]. Fodor and Garrett [1968] have shown that the existence of possible alternative frames of a verb influences the ease with which complex sentences are paraphrased or sentence anagrams are solved. Lexical expectation has also been related to the understanding of filler-gap constructions (e.g., "Who < = filler> do you think I like <gap>?"). Fodor [1978] has suggested that the relative ranking of subcategorization options for verbs plays an important role in understanding filler-gap constructions. Clifton et al. [1984] have shown that grammaticality judgements about certain filler-gap sentences were quicker when sentence structure matched the preferred verb frame (viz. transitive or intransitive), which was interpreted as possible evidence for the use of verb frame information to guide gap postulation. Finally, Clifton et al. [1984] have also suggested that for gap-finding and -filling pragmatic information about the plausibility of the filler as an object for a (transitive) verb is also important. Ford et al. [1982] have further demonstrated that preference for specific verb frames shows up in a task like sentence meaning paraphrasing: the ambiguous sentence "The woman wanted the dress on that rack," for instance, was usually interpreted as subject-verb-objectNP and not as subject-verb-objectNP-complementPP.

None of the above findings or suggestions are the result of experiments with on-line comprehension and as such can only give indirect evidence for on-line use of lexical expectations. Luckily, experiments testing lexical expectations (especially the transitive/intransitive distinction) during comprehension are starting to emerge [Clifton et al., 1984; Tanenhaus et al., 1985]. Since they are not numerous, we will take a closer look at them, especially at Clifton et al.

Clifton et al. had subjects read sentences of the types illustrated in Figure 1.5, which was adapted from their Table I [1984; p. 698]. The idea of the experiment was the following: verbs like "read" have a preferred transitive frame, whereas verbs like "sing" have a preferred intransitive one. At the same time

	verb preference	sentence form	sentence
(1)	transitive	transitive	The babysitter read the @ story to the sick child.
(2)	transitive	intransitive	The babysitter read to @ the sick child.
(3)	intransitive	intransitive	The babysitter sang to @ the sick child.
(4)	intransitive	transitive	The babysitter sang the @ story to the sick child.

Note: sentence presentation interrupted at @ for lexical decision task.

Figure 1.5 Sentences used by Clifton et al. [1984]

they can also be used intransitively and transitively respectively, but this is the less common reading of the verb.[7]

A prediction that follows from this is that sentences with transitive verbs used transitively (case (1) in Figure 1.5) should be easier to understand than when the verbs are used intransitively (case (2)) (the same reasoning applies for intransitives (cases (3) and (4)). To test this prediction, the subjects were given a lexical decision task at point @ (see Figure 1.5) during the word-by-word presentation of the sentence. In the "easy" sentences ((1) and (3)) reaction times should then be shorter for the secondary task than in the "difficult" ones ((2) and (4)), reflecting difficulty of sentence processing. The results confirmed the hypothesis: subjects were faster on the lexical decision task when the phrase following the verb matched its preferred frame than when it did not. The final interpretation by Clifton et al. is that "lexical information can have an effect at a stage of sentence processing prior to combining the meanings of the words in a sentence into a coherent representation" [1984, p. 699]. They motivate the "prior to" by observing that the secondary task was presented before the semantic content of the NP or PP which followed the verb was available to

---

7 Both Clifton et al. [1984] and Tanenhaus et al. [1985] used the norms for verb frame preferences determined by Connine et al. [1984]. The latter asked subjects to write sentences about specified topics with a number of verbs and counted the frequency of each of a variety of syntactic constructions, defined in terms of the syntactic categories of the complements of the verb (i.e., NP, PP, NP PP, inf-S, etc.; cp. the strict subcategorization frames in the Chomskyan tradition).

the readers. Thus, readers could only determine that a (syntactic) NP or PP would follow. When we discuss how lexical expectations are encoded in verbs in WEP below, we will criticize this "syntax-first" biased interpretation.

Tanenhaus et al. [1985] tested lexical expectations with transitive/intransitive verbs in filler-gap constructions, looking at the same time for the possible influence of pragmatic information (i.e., the plausibility of the filler). Their results confirmed those of Clifton et al. in that lexical expectation (i.e., about (in)transitivity) was found to control gap detection and gap filling. Plausibility effects also showed up in the results, but more clearly with transitive verbs than with intransitive ones.

In WEP lexical expectations associated with verbs are encoded in what we call "dynamic caseframes" (used especially in the application to Dutch), that are much more elaborate than the strict subcategorization frames used in the experiments above. This does not imply any kind of a priori correctness.[8] Dynamic caseframes are a processual[9] encoding of the attempt of a verb to "catch" concepts processed before it (if any) and to be processed after it into possible frames (though "frame" is not such a good term here, since it suggests a fixed structure). As an example we take the verb "eten" ("to eat"—one of the Dutch verbs implemented). Figure 1.6 gives the possible ordering of constituents in simple sentences in Dutch. The number of each sentence type is then used in Figure 1.7 to show (informally) what happens when the verb from each example sentence enters the comprehension process.

There are a number of interesting observations to be made about this approach:

1. It is semantic in nature, i.e., the binding attempts as well as the expectations refer to semantically refined concepts (i.e., AWAIT an "animate agent" or an "edible object," not just "wait for an NP"). We admit that no attempt has yet been made at specifying features or any other semantic device (cf. the absence of a semantic network, or the user-provided answers to the VIEW question), but this is not of great

---

8 As such they come closer to the specification of verbs in lexical-functional grammar, in which the lexical structure of the verb includes the subject of the sentence and not merely its object(s) (as in strict subcategorization). However, in LFG the syntactic specification of the verb (in terms of grammatical functions) is much more important than the semantic specification (in terms of cases) and phrase-structure rules play a crucial role in determining the surface location of the subject, object, etc. In WEP no phrase-structure rules are involved. The verb looks dynamically for its semantic cases and derives syntactic information from the time-course of the semantic analysis process (see further in the text).

9 We prefer using this neologism to using "procedural" or "computational" since we want it to reflect the neutrality of the noun "process" (procedures and computations are terms that too easily suggest computer implementations).

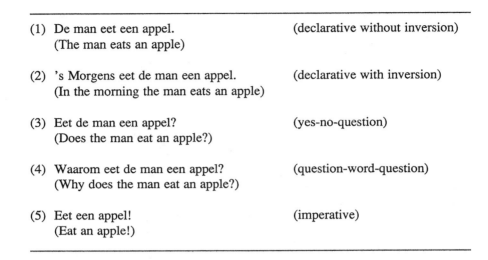

(1) De man eet een appel.   (declarative without inversion)
    (The man eats an apple)

(2) 's Morgens eet de man een appel.   (declarative with inversion)
    (In the morning the man eats an apple)

(3) Eet de man een appel?   (yes-no-question)
    (Does the man eat an apple?)

(4) Waarom eet de man een appel?   (question-word-question)
    (Why does the man eat an apple?)

(5) Eet een appel!   (imperative)
    (Eat an apple!)

Figure 1.6 Example sentences in Dutch

importance here. The statement is that lexical expectation is semantic, with syntactic form (NP, PRO, etc.) being less important.

2. Dynamic caseframes do not assume structurally fixed positions (as put down in rules, for instance) for the different cases revolving around the verb. The verb is seen as an active case catcher that finds its cases at specific points in the process (i.e., time-bound processes dominate over space-bound structures). That "eten" looks for an agent first and an object after, is inspired by observed sentence structures (and their relative frequencies), but these structures are in no way encoded in the semantically driven process. On the contrary, they can be retrieved as a static side-effect of the process. Though this observation may have more implications for linguistics with its static view of subcategorization/caseframes, it is also important for the lexical expectation research, since it implies an indirect criticism of the use of filler-gap sentences. Sentences like "Who do you think I despise <gap>?" are never seen as sentences in their own right, but are always related to some other (normative) structure, the deep structure from transformational grammar [Fodor, 1978] or a fixed subcategorization frame that assumes an object to follow its verb. The filler-gap view of those sentences rests on an assumption of movement of constituents from some place where they "ought to be." This critique is partly based on the difficulty of positing a "gap" in Dutch sentences of the type above. Whereas in English verbal

i) **if** no concepts have yet been processed (3 and 5)
> **then** refine sentence structure as question or imperative;
> **else** if the concept is an interrogative word group (4)
>> **then** refine sentence structure as question;
> **else** refine sentence structure as declarative.

ii) Try to find a concept of type entity in active memory (i.e., an animate entity) that can fill the agent role.
> **if** found (1)
>> **then** refine sentence structure as declarative without inversion and try to find a concept of type entity in active memory that can fill the object role (i.e., something edible);
>
> **if** found
>> **then** refine sentence structure as imperative (5) unless it was refined as declarative with inversion earlier (2);
>> **else** wait for such a concept.
>
> **if** it arrives
>> **then** OK;
>> **else** if it does not arrive before the end of the sentence refine "eten" as having an implicit object (e.g., "De man eet").

else (i.e., agent not found (2, 3, 4, 5) wait for a possible agent
> **if** agent arrives in time (2, 3, 4)(2) (3) (4))
>> **then** refine sentence structure as declarative-with-inversion unless it was refined as a question earlier (which it remains) and then continue from (b) above.

Figure 1.7 Dynamic caseframe process of a verb

groups are always found nicely together—with objects following the verb group, part of the typical structure of Dutch is that the verb group is often split with objects and complements occurring obligatorily "between," for example, an auxiliary and the past participle[10] When a present perfect is used, for instance, an object can "never" follow the meaning-bearing past participle, but is always somewhere before it. It can be between the auxiliary—with many possible functions—and the participle, or even in front of the auxiliary. Compare the following sentences.

---

10 This is called the "pincers construction" in Dutch, because the two parts of the verb group act like a pair of pincers holding other constituents in between them. (For the importance of discontinuous constituents in Dutch and their implications for WEP, see [Adriaens, 1986a; 1986b].

   1. Ik heb een man gezien
      "I have a man seen"   (I have seen a man)
   2. Ik heb gisteren een man gezien
      "I have yesterday a man seen"   (Yesterday I saw a man)
   3. Gisteren heb ik een man gezien
      "Yesterday have I a man seen"   (Yesterday I saw a man)

3. With these sentences in mind, it is hard to see where "gaps" for objects
    are to be located in sentences like "Wie heb je <gap>? gisteren <gap>?
    gezien <gap?>?" (Who did you see yesterday?). Moreover, Dutch does
    not have the "stranded preposition" construction used for the intransitive
    cases in the filler-gap experiments. The preposition occurs together with
    the "moved" NP: "Met wie was je <gap>? aan het praten <gap?>?" (Who
    were you talking to; "Met" = "to"). Since going into these differences in
    detail would lead us too far here, we only stress the point we want to
    make about the non-fixation of objects in specific positions in WEP:
    finding objects is something that happens in the "time" course of the verb
    process and is not necessarily related to assumed positions in sentence
    structure.

4. Note also that in WEP the different caseframes are related to each other.
    For "eten" the transitive frame and the implicit-object frame are related
    through the AWAIT for the object. If the object does not arrive in time,
    the implicit-object frame is automatically chosen. Thus, the application of
    the latter frame depends on the failure of application of the former.

In summary, note that lexical expectation in WEP is a semantic phenomenon, and combined with the dynamic caseframe notion it is considered a very
important element in sentence comprehension with implications for overall interpretation of a sentence

It will be clear then, that this implies a critique of the interpretation of
their results by Clifton et al. As mentioned above, they try to make their results
fit their belief in a syntax-first comprehension process (see Section 3.2) in a
way that is not convincing to us. They take their results to show that lexical expectation for transitive/intransitive verbs is a matter of expecting syntactic constituents (NPs or PPs), supporting this claim by the observation that the lexical
decision task came "before" the arrival of the semantically important noun
(phrase). However, it is clear that this noun (phrase) is not needed for lexical
expectation to be of a semantic kind. It is the verb itself that may easily project
a semantically determined object expectation, with the syntactic realization as
an NP, pronoun, or some other construction of secondary importance. The verb
had been processed even before the arrival of the determiner/preposition fol-

lowing it, thus its possible semantic expectations were active before the arrival of the noun (phrase) later on. In short, their results can just as well be interpreted as showing "semantic" lexical expectations (cf. WEP). The distinction implied in a syntax-first approach between "prestored preferences for linguistic structures" (influencing comprehension above and before all) and "preferences for analyses computed on line" [Connine et al., 1984, p. 318] looks like an artificial one from the standpoint of the dynamic caseframe notion in WEP. Understanding goes straight for the meaning in a dynamic way.

Of course, these comments are more easily made than tested. They do suggest at least that using strict syntactic subcategorization frames to test lexical expectations, or using the pragmatic plausibility of the filler in filler-gap constructions, may be insufficient to find lexical preferences for verb frames. This is certainly the case if one favors an interactive model in which meaning determination is the driving force.

3.5 *Idioms*

Idiomatic expressions have long been the object of study by linguists (see [Fraser, 1976; Makkai, 1972; Fernando and Flavell, 1981; Gross, 1984]). To what extent are idioms still flexible? What syntactic operations do they allow? How are they used in word play, e.g., through a subtle interplay of their possible literal interpretation and their more or less frozen idiomatic interpretation? This last question implies that certain lexical sequences can be ambiguous between a literal meaning, composed of the meanings of its parts, and a more or less frozen idiomatic one.

In psycholinguistics too, idioms have been studied, but from a different perspective. The question is whether idioms are processed in a manner similar to other lexical sequences or instead require a special processing mode. Here again, as with lexical access, two hypotheses are put forward, with one of the two getting most of the support from experimental research. The Idiom List Hypothesis [Bobrow and Bell, 1973] holds that idioms are stored in (and accessed from) a special list which is not part of the normal lexicon, and that a literal analysis is always attempted on a word string before an idiom mode of processing is undertaken. The Lexical Representation Hypothesis (supported by most of the results; see [Swinney and Cutler, 1979; Estill and Kemper, 1982]). Glass [1983], on the contrary, holds that idioms are stored in and retrieved from the lexicon in the same manner as any other word, and that both the literal and idiomatic meanings are computed upon occurrence of the first word (with contextual disambiguation choosing the appropriate one, compare the Post Decision Hypothesis above). However, some results by Ortony et al. [1978] and Gibbs [1980] showed that idiomatic interpretations are reached more quickly than literal ones. Although Estill and Kemper [1982] failed to replicate these results and attribute them to post-retrieval processes (contextual integration and postcomprehension paraphrasing abilities), they suggest that there may be a bias towards idiomatic interpretation in cases where a literal one seems highly improbable or rare. An example would be "let the cat out of the bag" in modern usage.

One of the linguistic ideas behind WEP was that all fragments of language are more or less idiomatic [Bolinger, 1979]. This view is closely related to the stress on idiosyncrasy in language, disputing the sharpness of the idiom notion. As a consequence, WEP portrays idiom processing as an instance of normal comprehension where the degree of idiomaticity is reflected in the relative importance of idiosyncratic interactions (e.g., the LITERAL question) that dominate for highly idiomatic expressions on the one hand, and more global interactions (e.g., the BINDC question) that play a more important role for less idiomatic linguistic units. Thus, WEP does not assume any type of special mode of access and further processing of idioms. They are treated by the same overall disambiguation process as any other input but the types of interactions involved during comprehension/integration with the context may vary. This is in accordance with the Lexical Representation Hypothesis. However, assuming that it exists, a bias towards the idiomatic interpretation of expressions is not incorporated in the model.

Future research will try to incorporate frequency of occurrence of particular meanings of linguistic elements over others, as observed in large corpora or obtained by giving subjects specific tasks, such as constructing sentences with certain verbs to check their preferred caseframes (compare [Connine et al., 1984]) into the disambiguation process. As a result we will also consider giving priority to idiomatic interactions over literal ones in specific cases.

3.6 *Function Words and Content Words*

Linguists have often made a descriptive distinction between function (closed class) words and content (open class) words.[11] Function words do not have a strong semantic content, but mark the beginning of syntactic constituents ("a," "in,"...) or tie constituents together ("and," "but,"...); content words do not usually fulfill those roles but contribute mainly to meaning ("good," "house," "eat,"...).

---

11 See [Carlson and Tanenhaus, 1984] for a short historical overview of the distinction in linguistics, and a detailed characterization of the differences between the two classes.

In psycholinguistics[12] the question has been whether there are differences in the way function and content words are stored and processed during language comprehension. Studies by Garrett [1976] provide evidence that function and content words are processed differently. Analysis of speech error data showed that the two classes do not typically interact in the production of errors, for example, where an exchange would involve two content words, not a content and a function word. Moreover, they seem to have their own kind of errors, shifts and exchange errors respectively. Since these data pertain specifically to speech production, and WEP is a model of written language comprehension, we will not go into them any further, concentrating instead on lexical access and eye-fixation research. We assume here that the production and comprehension modalities differ to a large extent. Though both modalities undoubtedly make use of the same knowledge sources, we believe that the "processes" involved in production and comprehension differ substantially in a way that is more complex than mere "reversal of the machinery." (See [Arbib et al., 1982, Chapter 4] for a discussion of these matters.)

Bradley [1978] looked at frequency effects in recognizing function versus content words. While the usual finding in psycholinguistic research is that higher frequency words are recognized faster, Bradley found this frequency effect only with content words, not with function words. Her conclusion was that there is a separate non-frequency-sensitive accessing mechanism for function words—stored outside the general lexicon—in linguistic processing. However, recent research [Gordon and Caramazza, 1982; Garnsey and Chapman, 1985] has failed to replicate Bradley's results. By implication, there would be no differences between function and content words in initial access, but rather in post-access processing. It is interesting to note that these results, taken together with the lexical access (Section 3.3) and idiom processing (Section 3.5) ones seem to converge on a view of human information accessing as a uniform, automatic, exhaustive and independent processing mechanism.

WEP again appears in accord with the research findings: function and content words are stored and accessed in the same way, but post-access processing differs for the two classes. Content words require significant processing of the sense discrimination variety (building and refining concepts), whereas function words and inflectional or derivational morphemes aid correct functional interpretation of those concepts through their "concept catching" actions, and through the sending and receiving of control signals.

---

12 In neurolinguistics too the dichotomy of function and content words has received a lot of attention. The way WEP (as an explicitly lexically-based model) can easily be "lesioned" in accordance with research findings in aphasia, the predictions it yields, and the view it inspires of how the internal lexicon is organized in normals (and disrupted in aphasics) is discussed in [Adriaens, 1986b].

Just and Carpenter [1980] (also see Section 3.2) have looked at eye-fixations during reading of scientific text. They found that almost all content words are fixated (with considerable variations in fixation duration), whereas short function words ("of," "the," "a") are not always fixated. Within their model of written language understanding, they propose that gaze durations reflect the time to execute comprehension processes, longer fixations implying longer processing. Though they extensively discuss processing associated with content words, they do not talk about the strange result that function words are hardly fixated. Within their framework, this probably implies that function words are processed very fast and do not strain the comprehension mechanisms, which are more concerned with semantic processing of the content words. WEP cannot account for these results since the model is not precise about the relationship between the time course of its operations and that of real-time processing. Moreover, traces of sentence parses show that the executions of function words and inflectional or derivational morphemes constitute a large part of the process. This may be a flaw in the model, but we also suggest that not fixating a word does not necessarily mean that it plays no significant role in processing.

3.7 *Morphology*

Most (and probably all) natural language analysis programs that analyze a fairly large subset of a natural language contain a morphological component consisting of affix-stripping rules applied to the input at an early stage of the analysis. The algorithm for the application of these rules roughly works like this:

Look for the word in the lexicon.
   If present, then task completed.
   If absent, then try to find base and affixes by using affix-stripping
      rules (implying the presence of base forms and possibly affixes
      in the lexicon).
      If successful, then task completed.
      If failure, then signal trouble.

More often than not, the morphological component is considered unimportant, and nothing much is said about it in the description of the system. WEP is hardly an exception to this: the above algorithm looks for the presence of the word in the list of monomorphemic experts ("eat," "in," etc.) or in the list of irregular experts. In the latter case the component elements listed with the word are returned as a result of the analysis (e.g., "throw" is listed as "throw plus -en"). Otherwise, rules are applied to the word to find its component parts. Thus, words are morphologically segmented as soon as they are read. However, the exact nature of the relationship between stems and affixes is determined by lexical interaction, with affixes like "-en" or "-s" modelled as word experts just like potential stems ("eat," "peach," etc.). For the whole of the morphological process, this means that segmentation and interpretation are implemented as two independent processes. It will be clear that this approach—though it works for a small subset of language—is insufficient for a correct treatment of complex morphological phenomena.

Assuming that segmentation works correctly, WEP can handle possible ambiguities of interpretation fairly easily through lexical interaction. "Works," for instance, leads to an execution of "work" first. This expert will determine from the context whether it is a noun or a verb, and signal the result to "-s," which will choose between the "noun plural" and "verb 3rd person singular" refinements accordingly. In theory, even more complex cases like "walker" (person) versus "cooker" (instrument) versus "cleaner" (person or instrument) could be dealt with through interactions with the context, encoded in "-er." However, these cases raise the question of the usefulness of segmentation plus interpretation as compared to a full listing of the words, which means less complex processing. Full listing even becomes a necessity for multiply segmentable words, where knowledge of the context is necessary to make the correct segmentation. A nice example from Dutch is the word "kwartslagen" that means "quarter beats" if segmented as "kwart plus slagen" and "quartz layers" if segmented as "kwarts plus lagen." Correct segmentation is only possible through interaction with the context. The obvious solution here is again to simply consider "kwartslagen" as a word in its own right and to disambiguate it without an attempt at undecidable segmentation first.[13] Listing a huge number of words in a lexicon may look like a poor solution, especially to linguists more concerned with generality than idiosyncrasy. However, if one recognizes the dominance of idiosyncrasy over generality for natural languages, the view held by WEP, there is nothing strange about such an approach. It may even prove to be the only viable one, since lexical elements behave very idiosyncratically as far as their derivational morphology is concerned [Taylor, 1980; Butterworth, 1983b]. Moreover, it calls for a closer examination of a phenomenon that has been largely neglected in linguistics, and even in psycho-

---

[13] Another solution, certainly not an easy one to implement, would be to somehow allow interaction between the segmentation knowledge source (modelled as an active process coroutine) and the other knowledge sources "over the heads" of the experts, the only active processes in the current model. This would allow the former to decide among ambiguous cases of segmentation. However, such an approach is incompatible with the decentralized process view of WEP.

linguistics, the internal organization of the lexicon, the representation of its elements and the way they are related; see also [Adriaens, 1986b].

In his overview of the literature, Butterworth [1983b] deplores the lack of convincing research in the area of lexical representation and on-line morphological analysis. Two of the topics he discusses are of particular interest in the context of WEP and morphology. The first is the rule/list controversy: are inflected and derived forms listed explicitly in the lexicon (the Full Listing Hypothesis of FLH) or are only the base forms listed, and all other forms derived or interpreted by rules (the classical linguistic approach)?

No solid evidence for either hypothesis seems to emerge from research into these matters. As with function and content words, errors in speech production suggest that stems and bound morphemes lead separate lives in the production process, in that the bound morphemes are selected independently of their stems and added to them at a relatively late stage in production [1983b, 266–269]. Butterworth challenges this "evidence" for the base form plus rule hypothesis by suggesting that a supporter of the FLH can easily accommodate these results: the FLH does not exclude the knowledge of rules by language users. The assumption that completes the FLH is that those rules are not routinely used by people. Anything not available via a rule "must" be separately listed, but availability via a rule does not necessarily imply that there is no other way of finding some morphologically complex form (i.e., in a list). This is related to his view of rules as "fall-back procedures." Rules are probably known to language users to varying degrees, but not used in normal verbal behavior where much information is routinely accessed. This is one of the many expressions of dissatisfaction with a direct mapping of rule-based approaches to processing models [Marin, 1982; Rumelhart, 1984]). Evidence from the other modalities (hearing/reading) hardly yields any evidence for either hypothesis, and Butterworth concludes (prematurely) that the lack of evidence for the reigning view of base form plus rule application leaves us with the "weaker" alternative of the FLH, provided it is supplemented with some grouping together of morphologically related forms, though not necessarily with a base form or other abstract representation as a heading.

This proviso brings us to the second issue discussed by Butterworth: What is the type of unit proposed for lexical representations? Words without internal morphemic structure? Words with morphemic boundaries marked? Abstract underlying representations? Morphemes? We will not go into the many possibilities proposed by linguists and psychologists, since there seem to be as many proposals as researchers. To complete the discussion of Butterworth, however, we simply mention his conclusion about these matters, which is similar to the one above. Butterworth supplements his bias towards FLH with a view of full words as unit type. For the problematic data with this view—people sometimes produce errors that are morphologically well-formed but non-existing words—

he suggests rules as fall-back procedures, with full words being the input to those rules.

WEP does not operate in accordance with the FLH, but uses a "segmentation first, interpretation after" approach as discussed above. If we assume this approach to be correct, the following view of on-line morphological analysis suggests itself: segmentation happens automatically (like lexical access, see Section 3.3) with post-segmentation processes (i.e., lexical interaction) interpreting morphemes in context. To make the parallel with the lexical access research complete, in cases of ambiguity, all possible segmentations would have to be made, with the context choosing the correct one. As we saw above, WEP does not and cannot operate in accord with the latter part of this view. Also, problematic segmentation cases seem to imply the necessity of fully listing certain words, with the presence of these words in the lexicon blocking the segmentation process (see the algorithm above). Thus, this view has its problems and may be incorrect. Listing everything, on the other hand, may not have these problems, but it creates others. It is unclear how the lexicon has to be organized internally, and there is a danger of massive duplication of information.

If we try to combine the best aspects of all the views discussed, the following non-uniform treatment of morphology suggests itself for WEP. The segmentation-rule component can be removed, and all the morphemes (words plus affixes) are "listed," be it in different ways. Stems and affixes trigger their processes as they do now. In cases where lexical interaction can handle the relationship between stem and affixes of complex words, disambiguating multiple possibilities if necessary, these words are listed with their component parts (i.e., morphology is present in the lexicon). This avoids the enormous duplication of processual information that would occur if every word had its own process associated with it. However, in cases where segmentation is problematic, or where lexical interaction between stem and affixes may look like "processual overkill," the words are listed without internal morphemic marking. They have their own process associated with them. For example, "kwartslagen" could then easily disambiguate itself through contextual interaction. Even though this non-uniform treatment solves many problems, it does not solve the one of the internal organization of the lexicon in WEP. However, it suggests that this organization will not only have to consider the semantic relatedness of words, but also their morphological relatedness. And of course, the cognitive validity of this treatment remains to be seen.

4 Conclusions and Further Research

We have described the general principles, representations and implementation of a computational model of natural language understanding—the Word Expert Parser—that attaches great importance to lexical ambiguity resolution. Next, we have confronted the model with experimental evidence from psycholinguistics to assess its flaws and merits as a model of human language understanding.

Its greatest flaws are: the absence of an implemented large-scale semantic network (long-term memory) and of the important psychological concept of spreading activation ([Collins and Loftus, 1975] and others) within that kind of network, and the impreciseness of the relationship between the time course of its operations and that of human language processing, together with an absence of true parallelism. Yet, it has a number of merits as well. Its stress on the lexicon fits in with the general lexicalist approach in linguistics. It is one of the few models that tries to implement the interactive view of language processing, and the way it works is in accordance with a number of important results in psycho- and neurolinguistics, see Adriaens [1986b]. At the same time, it yields interesting predictions about normal and aphasic behavior. This makes the model a valuable computational tool for cognitive science research in human natural language understanding. Future research will include the following topics:

1. Development of a processual account of linguistic facts, for example, what processes do linguistic elements trigger in language understanding? Examples are: Processing a noun or prepositional phrase can be formally described in terms of specific outstanding awaits (a WEP notion) and their resolution. A verb triggers the application of a dynamic caseframe that handles sentential semantics with elementary syntax as a by-product (see Section 3.4);

2. Attempting to organize the expert networks in accordance with the observed relative frequencies of the different meanings of a word. Thus, frequency could influence network traversal when no other information forces choosing a specific path (see Section 3.4);

3. Attempting to determine what parts of the word expert process are independent of each other, possibly across the entries as defined now. "If" such parts can be found, the nets could be reorganized in a more "semantic" way and a limited form of parallelism could be introduced;

4. Further refinement of the expert representation language through extended application of WEP to broader samples from natural languages;

5. Experimentation to test on-line morphological processing, the full listing hypothesis, eye-movements, and eye-fixations during reading (what happens to the function words?), further experiments dealing with function and content words to check the status of specific subclasses of both types.

This list could probably be extended with other topics[14] but these may suffice to show that the Word Expert Parser remains an interesting model inspiring a wide range of cognitive science research.

Appendix: An Example Word Expert

```
<word-expert deep

<entry0[n0:q signal s0
        [*entity-construction* n1]
        [* n2]]
    [n1:a [declareg]
        [continue entry1]]
    [n2:a [openg *entity-construction*]
        [declareg]
        [continue entry1] ]
>
<entry1[n0:a [buildc concept0 entity
        [oneof PERSON ARTISTIC-OBJECT VOLUME ANYTHING]]
        [await concept entity
        [filter concept0]
        [bindconcept concept1]
        [report here]
        [wait group 1]
        [continue entry2]
        [else entry3]]]
>
<entry2[n0:q view concept1
        [ANYTHING n4] [PERSON n1] [ARTISTIC-OBJECT n2]
        [VOLUME n3]]
    [n1:a [refinec concept1 INTELLECTUAL]
    [report concept1]]
```

---

14 We should also mention that interesting research is being conducted into the usefulness of the WEP approach for the understanding of text cohesion at the University of Konstanz, Germany (see [Hahn, 1986]).

```
        [n2:a [refinec concept1 ETHEREAL]
           [report concept1]]
        [n3:a [refinec concept1 VERTICALLY-SPACIOUS]
           [report concept1]]
        [n4:a [refinec concept1 DEEP]
           [report concept1]]
>
<entry3[n0:a [buildc concept2 entity]
           [refinec concept2 DEEP-ENTITY]
           [link concept2]
           [closeg *complete-entity*]
           [report concept2]]
>
```

References

Adriaens, G. 1985. Process linguistics: Missing link between linguistics, psychology and artificial intelligence. Cognitive Science Technical Report No. 28s, University of Rochester.

Adriaens, G. 1986a. Word expert parsing: A natural language analysis program revised and applied to Dutch. In *Leuvense Bijdragen* 75(1):73–154.

Adriaens, G. 1986b. *Process Linguistics: The Theory and Practice of a Cognitive-Scientific Approach to Natural Language*. Ph.D. Thesis, University of Leuven, Department of Linguistics.

Arbib, M. et al. (eds.). 1982. *Neural Models of Language Processes*. London: Academic Press.

Bobrow, D.G. and A. Collins (eds.). 1975. *Representation and Understanding. Studies in Cognitive Science*. London: Academic Press.

Bobrow, S. and S. Bell. 1973. On catching on to idiomatic expressions. *Memory and Cognition* 1:343–346.

Boguraev, B.K. 1979. Automatic resolution of linguistic ambiguities. Technical Report No. 11, Computer Laboratory, University of Cambridge.

Bolinger, D. 1979. Meaning and memory. In Haydu (ed.), *Experience Forms,* pp. 95–111.

Bradley, D.C. 1978. *Computational Distinctions of Vocabulary Type*. Ph.D. Thesis, Department of Psychology, MIT.

Bresnan, J. 1978. A realistic transformational grammar. In Halle et al. (eds.), pp. 1–59.

Butterworth, B. (ed.). 1983a. *Language Production Volume 2. Development, Writing and Other Language Processes.* London: Academic Press.

Butterworth, B. 1983b. Lexical representation. In Butterworth (ed.), *Language Production Volume 2. Development, Writing and Other Language Processes*, pp. 257–294. London: Academic.

Cairns, H.S. et al. 1981. Effects of prior context upon the integration of lexical information during sentence processing. *Journal of Verbal Learning and Verbal Behavior* 20:445–453.

Caplan, D. (ed.). 1980. *Biological Studies of Mental Processes.* Cambridge: MIT Press.

Carlson, G. and M.K. Tanenhaus. 1984. Lexical meanings, structural meanings, and concepts. In Testen et al. (eds.), pp. 39–52.

Chomsky, N. 1965. *Aspects of the Theory of Syntax.* Cambridge: MIT Press.

Clifton, C. et al. 1984. Lexical expectations in sentence comprehension. In *Journal of Verbal Learning and Verbal Behavior* 23:696–708.

Cogen, C. et al. (eds.). 1975. *Proceedings of the First Annual Meeting of the Berkeley Linguistic Society*, Berkeley, California.

Collins, A.M. and E.F. Loftus. 1975. A spreading-activation theory of semantic processing. *Psychological Review* 82(6):407–428.

Connine, C. et al. 1984. Verb frame preferences: Descriptive norms. *Journal of Psycholinguistic Research* 13:307–319.

Conrad, C. 1974. Context effects in sentence comprehension: A study of the subjective lexicon. *Memory and Cognition* 2(1a):130–138.

Cooper, W.E. and E.C.T. Walker (eds.). 1979. *Sentence Processing: Psycholinguistic Studies Presented to Merrill Garrett.* Hillsdale: Erlbaum.

Cottrell, G.W. 1985. *A Connectionist Approach to Word Sense Disambiguation.* Ph.D. Thesis, University of Rochester Department of Computer Science, Rochester, New York.

Cottrell, G.W. and S.L. Small 1983. A connectionist scheme for modelling word sense disambiguation. *Cognition and Brain Theory* 6(1):89–120.

Devos, M. In press. *A Parallel Implementation of a Theoretically Improved Version of the Word Expert Parser in Prolog.* Engineer's Thesis, Department of Computer Science, University of Leuven.

Dresher, B.E. and N. Hornstein. 1976. On some supposed contributions of artificial intelligence to the scientific study of language. *Cognition* 4:321–398.

Dresher, B.E. and N. Hornstein. 1977a. Reply to Schank and Wilensky. *Cognition* 5:147–149.

Dresher, B.E. and N. Hornstein. 1977b. Reply to Winograd. *Cognition* 5:379–392.

Estill, R.B. and S. Kemper. 1982. Interpreting idioms. *Journal of Psycholinguistic Research* 11(6):559–568.

Fahlman, S.E. 1979. *NETL: A System for Representing and Using Real-World Knowledge.* Cambridge: MIT Press.

Fahlman, S.E. 1982. Three flavors of parallelism. In *Proceedings of the Canadian Society for Computational Studies of Intelligence,* pp. 230–235.

Feldman, J. and D.H. Ballard. 1982. Connectionist models and their properties. *Cognitive Science* 6:205–254.

Fernando, C. and R. Flavell. 1981. On idiom: Critical views and perspectives. University of Exeter, Exeter.

Fodor J.D. 1978. Parsing strategies and constraints on transformations. *Linguistic Inquiry* 9:427–474.

Ford M. et al. 1982. A competence-based theory of syntactic closure. In Bresnan (ed.), *The Mental Representation of Grammatical Relations,* pp. 727–796.

Forster, K.I. 1979. Levels of processing and the structure of the language processor. In Cooper and Walker (eds.), pp. 27–85.

Foss, D. and C. Jenkins. 1973. Some effects of context on the comprehension of ambiguous sentences. *Journal of Verbal Learning and Verbal Behavior* 12:577–589.

Fraser, B. 1976. *The Verb-Particle Combination in English.* London: Academic.

Garnsey, S.M. and R.M. Chapman 1985. *Function and Content Word Reaction Times and Evoked Potentials During Lexical Decision.* Unpublished manuscript, Department of Psychology, University of Rochester, Rochester, New York.

Garrett, M.F. 1976. Syntactic processes in sentence production. In Wales and Walker (eds.), pp. 231–256.

Gazdar, G. et al. 1985. *Generalized Phrase Structure Grammar.* Oxford: Blackwell.

Gibbs, R.W. Jr. 1980. Spilling the beans on understanding and memory for idioms in conversation. *Memory and Cognition* 8:149–156.

Glass, A.L. 1983. The comprehension of idioms. *Journal of Psycholinguistic Research* 12(4):429–442.

Gordon, B. and A. Caramazza. 1982. Lexical decision for open- and closed-class words: Failure to replicate differential frequency sensitivity. *Brain and Language* 15:143–160.

Gross. M. 1979. On the failure of generative grammar. *Language.* 55(4):859–885.

Gross, M. 1984. Lexicon-grammar and the syntactic analysis of French. In *Proceedings COLING,* pp. 275–282.

Hahn, U. 1986. A Generalized Word Expert Model of Lexically Distributed Text Parsing. In *Proceedings Seventh ECAI* I:203–211.

Halle, M. et al. (eds.). 1978. *Linguistic Theory and Psychological Reality.* Cambridge: MIT Press.

Haydu, G.G (ed.). 1979. *Experience Forms. Their Cultural and Individual Place and Function.* The Hague: Mouton.

Hayes, P.J. 1975. Semantic markers and selectional restrictions. In Charniak and Wilks (eds.), *Computational Semantics*, pp. 41–54.

Hoekstra, T. et al. (eds.). 1980. Lexical grammar, publications in language sciences 3. *Glot* 2(3–4). Dordrecht: Foris.

Holmes, V.M. 1977. Prior context and the perception of lexically ambiguous sentences. *Memory and Cognition* 5:103–110.

Just, M. and P. Carpenter. 1980. A theory of reading: From eye fixations to comprehension. *Psychological Review* 87(4):329–354.

King, M. (ed.). 1983. *Parsing Natural Language*. London: Academic.

Lackner, J.R. and M.F. Garrett. 1972. Resolving ambiguity: Effects of biasing context in the unattended ear. *Cognition* 1:359–372.

Lakoff, G. 1978. Some remarks on AI and linguistics. *Cognitive Science* 2:267–275.

Lehnert, W.G. and M.H. Ringle (eds.). 1982. *Strategies for Natural Language Processing*. Hillsdale: Erlbaum.

Le Ny, J.-F. and W. Kintsch (eds.). 1982. *Language and Comprehension. Advances in Psychology 9*. Amsterdam: North-Holland.

Makkai, A. 1972. *Idiom Structure in English*. The Hague: Mouton.

Marin, O.S.M. 1982. Brain and language: The rules of the game. In Arbib et al. (eds.), pp. 45–69.

Marslen-Wilson, W.D. and A. Welsh. 1978. Processing interactions and lexical access during word recognition in continuous speech. *Cognitive Psychology* 10:29–63.

Marslen-Wilson, W.D. and L.K. Tyler. 1980. The temporal structure of spoken language understanding. *Cognition* 8:1–71.

Minsky, M. (ed.). 1968. *Semantic Information Processing*. Cambridge: MIT Press.

Norman, D. (ed.). 1970. *Models of Human Memory*. London: Academic.

Norman, D. (ed.). 1981. *Perspectives on Cognitive Science*. New Jersey: Ablex.

Ortony, A. et al. 1978. Interpreting metaphors and idioms. Some effects of context on comprehension. *Journal of Verbal Learning and Verbal Behavior* 17:465–477.

Rickheit, G. and M. Bock (eds.). 1983. *Psycholinguistic Studies in Language Processing*. Berlin: de Gruyter.

Rieger, C.J. and S.L. Small. 1981. Toward a theory of distributed word expert natural language parsing. *IEEE Transactions on Systems, Man, and Cybernetics* 11(1):43–51.

Rumelhart, D.E. 1984. The emergence of cognitive phenomena from sub-symbolic processes. In *Proceedings of the 6th Annual Conference of the Cognitive Science Society*, pp. 59–62. Boulder, Colorado.

Schank, R.C. 1972. Conceptual dependency: A theory of natural language understanding. *Cognitive Psychology* 3(4):552–631.

Schank, R.C. and K.M. Colby (eds.). 1973. *Computer Models of Thought and Language.* San Francisco: Freeman.

Schank, R.C. and R. Wilensky. 1977. Response to Dresher and Hornstein. *Cognition* 5:133–145.

Schank, R.C. and C.K. Riesbeck (eds.). 1981. *Inside Computer Understanding. Five Programs Plus Miniatures.* Hillsdale: Erlbaum.

Seidenberg, M.S. et al. 1982. Automatic access of the meanings of ambiguous words in context: Some limitations of knowledge-based processing. *Cognitive Psychology* 14:489–537.

Seidenberg, M.S. 1984. Pre- and postlexical loci of contextual effects on word recognition. *Memory and Cognition* 12(4):315–328.

Small, S.L. 1980. *Word Expert Parsing: A Theory of Distributed Word-Based Natural Language Understanding.* Ph.D. Thesis, Department of Computer Science, University of Maryland, College Park, Maryland.

Small, S.L. 1981. Demon timeouts: Limiting the life span of spontaneous computations in cognitive models. In *Proceedings of the 3rd Annual Conference of the Cognitive Science Society,* Berkeley, California.

Small S.L. and M.M. Lucas. 1983. Word expert parsing: A computer model of sentence comprehension. Cognitive Science Technical Report No. 1. University of Rochester, Rochester, New York.

Small, S.L. and C.J. Rieger. 1982. Parsing and comprehending with word experts (a theory and its realization). In Lehnert and Ringle (eds.), *Strategies for Natural Language Processing,* pp. 89–147.

S.L. Small, G.C. Cottrell, and L. Shastri. 1982. Toward connectionist parsing. In *Proceedings of the National Conference of the American Association for Artificial Intelligence.* Pittsburgh, PA. Los Altos: Morgan Kaufmann.

Sparck Jones, K. and Y. Wilks (eds.). 1985. *Automatic Natural Language Parsing.* Chichester: Horwood.

Starosta, S. 1978. *Lexicase II: Lexicon.* Unpublished manuscript, University of Hawaii.

Swinney, D. 1979. Lexical access during sentence comprehension: [Re]consideration of context effects. *Journal of Verbal Learning and Verbal Behavior* 18:645–659.

Swinney, D. 1981. Lexical processing during sentence comprehension: Effects of higher order constraints and implications for representation. In Myers et al. (eds.), pp. 201–209.

Swinney, D. and D.T. Hakes. 1976. Effects of prior context upon lexical access during sentence comprehension. *Journal of Verbal Learning and Verbal Behavior* 15:681–689.

Swinney, D. and A. Cutler. 1979. The access and processing of idiomatic expressions. *Journal of Verbal Learning and Verbal Behavior* 18:523–534.

Tanenhaus, M.K. et al. 1979. Evidence for multiple stages in the processing of ambiguous words in syntactic contexts. *Journal of Verbal Learning and Verbal Behavior* 18:427–440.

Tanenhaus, M.K. et al. 1985. The interaction of lexical expectation and pragmatics in parsing filler-gap constructions. In *Proceedings of the 7th Annual Conference of the Cognitive Science Society,* pp. 361–365. Irvine, CA.

Taylor, S.M.H. 1980. *Lexical Idiosyncrasy in English: An Argument for a Lexically Based Grammar.* Ph.D. Thesis, University of Oregon, UMI, London.

Thompson, H. 1985. Natural language processing: A critical analysis of the structure of the field with some implications for parsing. In Sparck Jones and Wilks (eds.), pp. 22–38.

Wales, R.J. and E. Walker (eds.). 1976. *New Approaches to Language Mechanisms.* Amsterdam: North-Holland.

Wilks, Y. 1973. An artificial intelligence approach to machine translation. In Schank and Colby (eds.), pp. 114–151.

Winograd, T. 1972. *Understanding Natural Language.* London: Academic.

Winograd, T. 1977. On some contested suppositions of generative linguistics about the scientific study of language. A response to Dresher and Hornstein's On some supposed contributions of artificial intelligence to the scientific study of language. *Cognition* 5:151–179.

Winograd, T. 1983. *Language as a Cognitive Process. Volume I: Syntax.* Reading: Addison-Wesley.

2

Lexical Ambiguity Resolution in a Deterministic Parser

Robert Milne

Intelligent Applications Limited
Kirkton Business Centre
Livingston Village, Scotland

1 *Introduction*

Lexical ambiguity and especially part-of-speech ambiguity is the source of much non-determinism in parsing. As a result, the resolution of lexical ambiguity presents deterministic parsing [Marcus, 1980] with a major test. If deterministic parsing is to be viable, it should be shown that lexical ambiguity can be resolved deterministically for many situations in which people do not have trouble. In this paper, it is shown that Marcus's "diagnostics" can be handled without any mechanisms beyond what is required to parse grammatical sentences and reject ungrammatical sentences and that many other classes of ambiguity can be easily resolved as well. This result is possible because of the constraints on English from word order and number agreement.

Although many high-level constituents can be "moved" in English, the lower-level structure of some constituents is relatively fixed. For example, after a determiner, one expects a noun rather than a verb. In this paper we also wish to ask, "How might this low-level fixed order assist in the resolution of ambiguity?" We will not give a definite answer to this question, but will see that it is extremely useful in the resolution of ambiguity.

The examples of ambiguity shown in this paper seem to cause no apparent problems to a person reading them. That is, all of these examples read easily and certainly do not exhibit the garden path effect, except, of course, the examples that are intended to be difficult. If a parser is to be psychologically plausible, then it is desirable that it handle these examples in such a way as to explain why people have no apparent difficulty with most sentences, despite the inherent ambiguity in them.

In parsing English, one of the major causes of non- determinism is part-of-speech ambiguity. If a word can be two parts of speech, then a non-deterministic parser may have to explore both possibilities. If one claims to be able to parse English deterministically, then the resolution of part-of-speech ambiguity is a very important area.

It should be noted that a non-deterministic parser does not need to tackle the problem of local part-of-speech ambiguity. If it should make an error, then it can backtrack and correct it. Alternatively, it could maintain all possible parses at once and throw some of them away. In deterministic parsing we are not allowed to use either backtracking or parallelism. Although this problem has been investigated for many non-deterministic parsers, it has not been the critical problem that it is for deterministic parsing. To handle ambiguity deterministically, we must never make an error. As a result, our methods of disambiguation must be reliable. We will see that many cases of ambiguity can be resolved using standard techniques which have been applied to non-deterministic parsers.

If it is possible to handle all the examples of local ambiguity presented here, with no additional mechanism, device or feature than is needed for ordinary sentence parsing, then our goal above can be considered met. One possible explanation for the fact that people do not notice local ambiguities may be that there is no special mechanism needed for them, so that nothing differing from normal parsing is necessary. Conversely, if it is necessary to add special mechanisms and routines to the parser just to handle these examples of ambiguity, then this will not explain how people can understand these examples so well and it can be considered a weakness in the model.

To say part-of-speech ambiguity can be handled deterministically, but with the use of special mechanisms, would be no surprise and not very important. To say one can handle part-of-speech ambiguity deterministically with no special mechanisms is a more significant claim. In this paper it is indeed suggested that many cases of part-of-speech ambiguity can be handled by the parser with no special mechanisms.

This paper is a summary of a section of the author's Ph.D. thesis [Milne, 1983] with the same title, and describes work done at the University of Edinburgh. In that thesis, a deterministic parser, ROBIE, is presented which is able to resolve lexical ambiguities. That parser is fully implemented in PROLOG. ROBIE has two lookahead buffers and does not use Marcus's Attention Shift mechanism. This means that ROBIE scans the current item and one more of lookahead. Marcus's parser (PARSIFAL) scanned the current item and two lookahead items. Each of these items could be a word, or any single constituent represented by a single node. In this paper, only local ambiguities are addressed, that is, ambiguities which can be resolved within the sentence. Global ambiguities, which require context to resolve, are not discussed. That is, sentences in which, with no help either from intonation or context, more than one analysis is possible. Given just the sentence, there is not enough information to determine a unique interpretation.

For this paper, it is assumed that the reader is familiar with deterministic parsing. No other understanding of specific parsing mechanisms is assumed.

In the rest of this paper, we will look at lexical ambiguity from simple examples to more complex ones. We will start with how words are defined within the parser to be ambiguous and how the morphology can be used to resolve ambiguities. Next we will look at how word order, and finally, various types of agreement can be used to resolve most remaining ambiguities.

2 Syntactic Context

2.1 Word Data Structures

As a first approach to handling ambiguity, it was asked, "If we construct a compound lexical entry for each word composed of the features of each part of speech the word can have and make no alterations to the grammar, how wide a coverage of examples will we get?"

This approach was used by [Winograd, 1972] and was found to be very effective for the following reasons. Each word has all the possible relevant features for it. Therefore, the test will succeed for each possible part of speech with which a word can be used. In this way, all applicable rules will match. It may be that often only one rule will match, or that the first rule tried is the correct rule. The question is, how often will the rule which matches be the correct rule?

All words in ROBIE are defined in the syntactic dictionaries. Each word has a compound lexical entry incorporating all the features for all the possible parts of speech which the word could have. This is exactly as was done by [Winograd, 1972]. For example, "block" is defined as a noun and a verb, "can" is defined as a noun, auxiliary verb, and verb, and "hit" is defined as a noun and a verb. The features for each of these parts of speech are kept in the dictionary and, when the word is looked up, they are returned as a single ordered list of features. These features are sub-grouped according to the part of speech they are associated with. Hence, when the word "block" is looked up, the result returned is both the noun and the verb definition. In this way, all possibilities are returned.

In the English language, most words can have several parts of speech. This fact must be reflected in a parser of English and we do this with the multiple meanings above. When the parser has enough information to decide which is the correct part of speech, it ignores (removes) the other possibilities. In this way, we have not built structure which is later thrown away. Although some may argue that this is a form of parallelism, it seems necessary since it reflects the inherent parallelism of language.

2.2 *Morphology*

The first part of the disambiguation process takes place in the morphology. When ROBIE identifies a word which has a morphological ending, the morphology must adjust the features of the word. For example, when "blocked" is identified, the feature "ed" must be added to the list of features for "block." At the same time, a portion of the disambiguation takes place. If "block" is defined as both a noun and a verb, then "blocked" is not a noun. The morphology causes some features to be added, such as "ed, past" and some features to be removed such as "tenseless." As features which are no longer applicable are removed, so also are parts of speech and their associated features which are no longer applicable. For "blocked," the features "noun, ns, n3p" will be removed and the features "adjective, ed, past" will be added.

The morphology will identify words such as adverbs, adjectives and verbs in a similar way. The morphology which is used is very similar to that of [Winograd, 1972], [Deward, Bratley, and Thorne, 1969] and the part-of-speech additions and deletions are taken from [Marcus, 1980]. Although this technique may seem obvious, it is included to point out that a majority of the occurrences of part-of-speech ambiguity can be resolved or reduced on the basis of the morphology alone.

2.3 *Disambiguation*

Now that we have allowed words to have multiple parts of speech and the morphology can be used to trim some of the ambiguity, we need a simple technique for disambiguating words to a single part of speech. Again, referring to Occam's Razor, what is preferable is a simple and general technique for all types of disambiguation.

In ROBIE each rule matches the features of one or two buffer cells. A buffer cell can contain either a word, or any single constituent represented by a single node. If the word "block" is in the first buffer cell, then a pattern (noun) or a pattern (verb) will match. These patterns do not relate to the other possible definitions of a word. If a rule pattern has matched on the feature "noun" in the first buffer cell, then ROBIE assumes that this word is a noun. It would then be appropriate to disambiguate the word as a noun. This is exactly as in [Winograd, 1972].

In a non-deterministic parser it is not essential to find the correct rule first. If the parser runs an incorrect rule, the parser may backtrack and change the category assignment. But in a deterministic parser, there will never be any backtracking and this solution cannot be used.

Since ROBIE does not backtrack, disambiguating the word when the pattern matches will always result in the same disambiguation as if the word were disambiguated in the grammar rule. Once a rule runs assuming a buffer contains an item as a certain part of speech, it must be used as such in the parser. The general disambiguation scheme is: if a full pattern matches a word as a certain part of speech, then it is disambiguated as that part of speech.

The compound lexical entries and pattern-matching disambiguation alone will handle many examples of ambiguity. In the rest of this paper we will see just what this can do for us.

2.4 *An Example*

Given the above mechanisms—multiple definition and disambiguation by the pattern matching, let us see how a few simple examples are handled. Consider:

(1) The falling block needs painting.

We will look only at the words "falling" and "block" in this example. The word "falling" is defined as a verb and an adjective in the dictionary and "block" is defined as a noun and a verb.

While parsing this example, after the word "the" has initiated an NP and been attached to it as a determiner, the rules to parse adjectives are activated. The rule ADJECTIVE has the pattern: (adj), and matches the word "falling." "Falling" is then attached and disambiguated as an adjective. Recognition of "falling" as a verb does not occur. As there are no more adjectives, ROBIE will activate the rules to parse the headnoun. (ROBIE's grammar assumes that all words between the first noun and the head noun of an NP are nouns; see Section 2.6.) The rule NOUN with the pattern (noun) will match on the word "block" and it will be attached as a noun. Hence "block" will also be disambiguated without the verb use being considered by ROBIE.

Other ambiguities inside the noun phrase will be handled in a similar way. This approach will usually cover the situation of singular head nouns, verb/adjective ambiguity and many other pre-nominal ambiguities. This works because the noun phrase has a very strict word order. When an ambiguous word is found, only one of its meanings will be appropriate to the word order of the noun phrase at that point. This approach can be thought of as an extension of the basic approach of the Harvard Predictive Analyzer [Kuno, 1965].

This strategy will also often disambiguate main verbs. For example, consider the following sentences:

(2) Tom hit Mary.

(3) Tom will hit Mary.

(4) The will gave the money to Mary.

In (2), "hit" is the main verb. In the dictionary, "hit" is also defined as a noun, (as in card playing). The parser will attach "Tom" as the subject of the sentence and then activate the rules for the main verb. Since "hit" has the feature "verb," it will match that rule and be attached and disambiguated as a verb. Again other possible parts of speech are not considered.

The word "will" could be a noun or a model as sentences (3) and (4) demonstrate. In (3), "will" cannot be part of the headnoun with "Tom," so the NP will be finished as above. The rules for the auxiliary will then be activated and the word "will" then matches the pattern (modal) and is attached to the AUX.

In (4), the word "will" is used as a noun. Since it follows the determiner, the rules for nouns will be activated. The word "will" then matches the pattern (noun) and attaches to the NP as a noun.

The same approach will also disambiguate "stop" and "run" in the following sentence. Since "stop" is sentence initial and can be a tenseless verb, the rule IMPERATIVE will match and it will be disambiguated as a verb. The word "run," which can be a noun or a verb, will be handled as "will" in (4).

(5) Stop the run.

2.5 *The Word TO*

Now let us consider a more difficult example, the word "to." "To" is defined as an auxiliary verb and a preposition in ROBIE, as illustrated by these sentences:

(6) I want to kiss you.

(7) I will go to the show with you.

In (6), "to" is the infinitive auxiliary, while in (7) "to" is a preposition. This analysis is based on that of [Marcus, 1980, p. 118]. Our two buffer cell lookahead is sufficient to disambiguate these examples.

The buffer patterns for the above sentences are:

```
[to][tenseless]  ⇒ embedded VP
[to][ngstart]  ⇒ PP
```

By looking at the following word, "to" can be disambiguated. In (7), the word "the" cannot be a tenseless verb, so the first pattern does not match. In (6), the second buffer cell does not have the feature "ngstart," so the rule doesn't match.

However, the above patterns will accept ungrammatical sentences. To reject ungrammatical sentences, we can use verb subcategorisation as a supplement to the above rules. One cannot say:

(8) *I want to the school with you.

(9) *I will hit to wash you.

In English, only certain verbs can take infinitive complements. "To" can only be used as an auxiliary verb starting a VP when the verb can take an infinitive complement. Hence, by activating the rules to handle the VP usage only when the infinitive is allowed, the problem is partly reduced. Also by classifying the verb for PPs with the preposition "to," the problem is simplified. This is merely taking advantage of subcategorisation in verb phrases. Taking advantage of this subcategorisation greatly reduces, but does not eliminate, the possible conflict.

We have seen what to do if the verb will only accept a toPP or a VP. The final difficult situation arises whenever the following three conditions are true: (1) the verb will accept a toPP and a toVP, (2) the item in the second buffer cell has the features "tenseless" and "ngstart" and, (3) the toPP is a required modifier of the verb. Although this situation rarely arises, the above rule will make the wrong decision if the ambiguous word is being used as a noun. In this situation, ROBIE will make the wrong decision, and has no capability to better decide. By default, the principles of Right Association and Minimal Attachment apply as discussed in [Frazier and Fodor, 1978].

A free text analysis done on a cover story in *TIME* magazine (*TIME*, 1978) resulted in 55 occurrences of the word "to." The two rules mentioned above in conjunction with verb subcategorisation gave the correct interpretation of all of these. These rules were also checked on the MECHO corpus [Milne, 1983] and the ASHOK corpus [Martin, Church, and Patil, 1981]. There were no violations of these rules in either of these.

2.6 *Adjective/Noun and Noun/Noun Ambiguity*

In general, noun/noun ambiguity requires semantic information to resolve. That is, the word is known to be a noun, but its semantic definition is ambiguous. This paper only addresses ambiguities which can be resolved with syntactic information. As a result, this ambiguity is not discussed further, but is included only for completeness.

Adjective/noun ambiguity is beyond the scope of the present research and is handled in a simple-minded way. If the word following the ambiguous adjective/noun word can be a noun, then the ambiguous word is used as an adjective. In other words, all conflicts are resolved in favour of the adjective usage. This problem arises in these examples:

(10) The plane is inclined at an angle of 30 degrees above the horizontal.

(11) A block rests on a smooth horizontal table.

In (10), "horizontal" is a noun, while in (11), it is an adjective. The above algorithm handles these cases.

This approach takes advantage of the lookahead of the deterministic parser. A word should be used as an adjective if the following word can be an adjective or a noun. However, this approach would fail on examples such as:

(12) The old can get in for half price.

(13) The large student residence blocks my view.

However, most readers find these to be garden path sentences.

2.7 *Why Do These Techniques Work?*

In this section we have seen many examples of the resolution of ambiguity. To handle these examples, we merely constructed a compound lexical entry for each word, composed of the features of each part of speech the word could be and allowed the pattern matching to perform the disambiguation. This technique has been used by [Winograd, 1972]. Why does this work so well?

English has a fairly strict structural order for all the examples presented here. Because of this, in each example we have seen, the use of the word as a different part of speech would be ungrammatical. Although these techniques have been used for non-deterministic parsers, their effectiveness has not been investigated for a deterministic parser.

Most ambiguities are not recognised by people because only one of the alternatives is grammatical. In many situations, when fixed constituent structure is taken into account, other uses of an ambiguous word are not possible and probably not even recognised. Since fixed constituent structure rules out most alternatives, we have been able to handle the examples in this paper without any special mechanisms. In the introduction to this paper, it was stated that a clean and simple method of handling ambiguity was desired. I feel that this goal has been met for these examples.

3 *The Role of Agreement in Handling Ambiguity*

Using the simple techniques presented in the last sections, we can handle many cases of part-of-speech ambiguity, but there are many examples we cannot resolve. For example, the second of each pair of sentences below would be disambiguated incorrectly.

(14) I know that boy is bad.

(15) I know that boys are bad.

(16) What boy did it?

(17) What boys do is not my business.

(18) The trash can be smelly.

(19) The trash can was smelly.

Many people wonder what role person/number codes and the relatively rigid constituent structure in the verb group play in English. In this section, we will explore their role by attempting to answer the question, "What use is the fixed structure of the verb group and person/number codes."

3.1 *Ungrammatical Sentences*

Before we proceed, let us look at an assumption Marcus made in his parser, that it would be given only grammatical sentences. This assumption makes life easy for someone writing a grammar, since there is no need to worry about grammatical checking. Hence no provision was made for ungrammatical sentences and the original parser accepted such examples as:

(20) *A blocks are red.

(21) *The boy hit the girl the boy the girl.

(22) *Are the boy run?

This simplification causes no problems in most sentences, but can lead to trouble in more difficult examples. If the parser's grammar is loosely formulated because it assumes it will be given grammatical examples only, then un-grammatical sentences may be accepted. If the syntactic analysis accepts un-grammatical sentences as grammatical, then it is making an error. Using grammatical constraints actually helps parsing efficiency and disambiguation. In the next sections we will look at the consequences of this assumption as well as those of rejecting ungrammatical sentences.

3.2 Subject/Verb Agreement

We know that the verb group has a complicated but relatively fixed constituent structure. Although verbals have many forms, they must be mixed in a certain rigid order. We also know that the first finite verbal element in each sentence must agree with the subject in person and number. That is, one cannot say:

(23) *The boy are run.

(24) *The boy will had been run.

(25) *The boys had are red.

etc.

While Marcus's parser enforced these observations to some extent, he did not follow them throughout his parser. We want to enforce this agreement throughout ROBIE. Checking the finite or main verb, to be sure that it agrees in number with the subject, will lead to the rejection of the above examples. This was done by adding the agreement requirement into the pattern for each rele-vant rule as will be explained later.

Buffers 1 and 2 must agree before a rule relating the subject and verb can match. This check looks at the number code of the NP and the person/number code of the verb and checks whether they agree. The routine for subject/verb agreement is very general and is used by all the subject/verb rules. The routine can only check the grammatical features of the buffers.

3.3 Marcus's Diagnostics

Marcus [1980] did handle some part-of-speech ambiguities. The words "to," "what," "which," "that," and "have" could all be used as several parts of speech. For each of these words he also used a "Diagnostic" rule. These Diag-nostic rules matched when the word they were to diagnose arrived in the first buffer position and the appropriate packets were active. Each diagnostic would examine the features of the three buffers cells and the contents of the Active Node Stack. Once the diagnostic decided which part of speech the word was being used as, it either added the appropriate features, or explicitly ran a grammar rule. Marcus did not give each word a compound lexical entry as we have done here.

Most of the grammar rules in his parser were simple and elegant, but the diagnostics tended to be very complex and contained many conditionals. In some cases they also seemed rather *ad hoc* and did not meet the goal of a simple, elegant method of handling ambiguity.

For example, consider the THAT-DIAGNOSTIC (from [Marcus, 1980, p.291]):

```
[that][np]  ⇒  in the Packet CPOOL (Clause pool of rules)


"If     there is no determiner of second
        and there is not a qp of second
        and the nbar of 2nd is none of massn,npl
        and 2nd is not-modifiable
then    attach as det
else    if c is nbar
        then label 1st pronoun, relative pronoun
        else label 1st complementiser."
```

Notice that if the word "that" were to be used as a determiner, then it would be attached after the NP was built! This is his primary role for disambiguating the word "that." Marcus's parser also had three other rules to handle different cases.

It seems that these rules did not "elegantly capture generalisations" as did the rest of his parser. These rules are considered undesirable and should be corrected to comply with the criteria for simple and elegant techniques in resolving ambiguity. I wanted a method which used no special mechanism, or routine, other than that needed to parse grammatical sentences. These diagnostics are certainly special mechanisms and do not meet this goal. Can we cover the same examples in a more simple and principled way?

In this section, we will look at each of these diagnostics in turn and show how they have been replaced in the newer model. We will also look at a few other examples of ambiguity which Marcus did not handle, but are related to our discussion here.

3.4 *Handling the Word TO*

The handling of "to" by Marcus's diagnostic can be replaced by the method outlined in Section 2.5. This method was motivated to handle grammatical sentences and meets our criterion for a simple approach.

3.5 *Handling WHAT and WHICH*

For both "what" and "which," the ambiguity lies between a relative pronoun and a determiner. The following examples show various uses of both words:

(26)	Which boy wants a fish?	det
(27)	Which boys want fish?	det
(28)	The river which I saw has many fish.	rel. pron.
(29)	What boy wants a fish?	det
(30)	What boys want is fish.	rel. pron.

There is some debate about the part of speech to be assigned the word "which." Some linguists consider it to be a quantifier [Chomsky, 1965], while others consider it to be a determiner [Akmajian and Heny, 1975, Chapter 8]. We shall adopt the determiner analysis, making the problems for "what" and "which" similar.

To determine the correct part of speech for these two words, Marcus used the following diagnostics [Marcus, 1980, p. 286]:

```
[which]  ⇒  in the packet CPOOL
"If    the NP above Current Node is not modified
       then label 1st pronoun, relative pronoun
       else label 1st quant,ngstart,ns,wh,npl."


[what][t]  ⇒  in the packet NPOOL
"If    2nd is ngstart and 2nd is not det
       then label 1st det,ns,npl,n3p,wh;
          activate parse-det
       else label 1st pronoun,relpron,wh."
```

These diagnostics would make the word in question a relative pronoun if it occurred after a headnoun, or a determiner if the word occurred at the start of a possible noun phrase.

If we follow the approach in the last section, and give each word a compound lexical entry composed of the determiner and relative pronoun features, we find that these words are always made determiners unless they occur immediately after a headnoun. In other words, the "which" examples are all parsed correctly, but (30) is parsed incorrectly. This happens because the determiner rule will always try to match before the rule for WH questions can take effect.

This simple step gives the correct analysis if the ambiguous word is to be a determiner, but will still err on (30).

The rule to parse a relative pronoun and start a relative clause is active only after the headnoun has been found. At this time, the rule for determiners is not active. Therefore, if the word "what" or "which" is present after a headnoun, the only rule which can match is the rule to use it as a relative pronoun and it will be used as a relative pronoun. We have resolved the simple case of "what" as a relative pronoun using only the simple techniques of the last section. For these sentences:

(31) What block is red?

(32) Which boy hit her?

(33) Which is the right one?

ROBIE produces the correct analysis, but still errs on (30). This error is because "what" is being used as a relative pronoun, but it does not follow a headnoun. Without any additional changes to the parser, we get two things. Firstly, if the word occurs after the headnoun, then the NP-COMPLETE packet rules are active and it will be a relative pronoun. In fact, since relative clauses can occur only after the end of an NP, this correctly resolves the relative pronoun uses. If the word occurs at the start of an NP, then it will be made a determiner.

This approach has exactly the same effect and coverage as did Marcus' diagnostics, but we have not needed any special rules to implement it. It will now provide the correct interpretation for "which," but will make some errors for the word "what." Marcus' "what-diagnostic" will treat "what" as a determiner whenever the item in the second buffer cell could start a NP. This is usually correct, but "what" will be treated as a determiner in all of the following:

(34) What boys want is fish.

(35) What blocks the road?

(36) What climbs trees?

(37) What boys did you see?

(38) What blocks are in the road?

(39) What climbs did you do?

In this paper, we are adopting the following analysis for WH clefts such as (34). The initial WH word, "what" is a relative pronoun and attached as the WH-COMP of the subject S node. The subject is the phrase "What boys want." The main verb of the sentence is "is" and the complement "fish." The exact details are not important, only that the word "what" or "which" is a not determiner at the start of a WH cleft. In sentences (34–36), the word "what" is not used as a determiner. In the analysis we are using, it is a relative pronoun and is used as the WH-COMP for the S. In sentences (37–39), the word "what" is used as a determiner. Marcus admits that this diagnostic produces the incorrect result in this case [Marcus, 1980, p. 286] His diagnostic will make "what" a determiner in all of these examples, as will my analysis.

In [Milne, 1982], the idea of potential garden path sentences is presented. These are sentences which may or may not lead to a garden path. Each garden path sentence has a partner, which is similar, but not a garden path. It is proposed that the decision as to how to resolve the ambiguity which may lead to a garden path should be made by semantics and not by syntax. This theory is called the Semantic Checking Hypothesis. For full details see [Milne, 1983].

One can also see that each of the above pairs is a pair of potential garden path sentences. For each pair, the two buffers contain the same words. Hence our two buffer lookahead is not sufficient to choose the correct usage of the word "what." There is no way to make "what" a relative pronoun in the case where the headnoun is plural, but a determiner in the case where the headnoun is singular for all arbitrary sentences using only two or three buffers.

With regard to the Semantic Checking Hypothesis then, it is suggested that this decision is based on non-syntactic information. I believe that intonation is critical in these examples. Unfortunately there is insufficient experimental evidence to determine for certain whether this is true. Finally, the problem of "what" and "which" as sentence initials, with no noun in the second buffer seems to arise very rarely. I have found no examples of this problem in free text analysis.

The current parser (ROBIE) cannot obtain the extra information provided by intonation to help resolve this case. As a result it follows Marcus's diagnostic and makes "what" a determiner in each of the above cases. This is because "what" is defined as a determiner that can agree with either a singular noun or a plural noun, as it was in Marcus's parser.

3.6 Handling THAT

In ROBIE, "that" is defined as a singular determiner, a pronoun, a relative pronoun, and a complementiser. Marcus had four diagnostics to handle the word "that." We have seen one of these at the start of this section. In this sub-section we see how these four diagnostics can be replaced in a simple way. Let us consider how to handle the uses of "that" one at a time.

Firstly, as a determiner. The following sentences illustrate the problem in identifying this usage.

(40) I know that boy should do it.

(41) I know that boys should do it.

Marcus assumed that PARSIFAL would be given only grammatical sentences to parse. If determiner/number agreement is not given to a parser, then it will, incorrectly, make "that" a determiner in (41), producing the wrong analysis. The way to prevent this is to enforce number agreement in the rule DETERMINER by insisting that the determiner agree with the noun in number. The determiner usage will be grammatical only when the headnoun has the same number. If we make this a condition for the rule to match, then "that" will not be made a determiner in (41) and ROBIE will get the correct parse.

For this case, the agreement check would make sure that one of the following patterns match:

```
[det,ns]   [noun,ns]
[det,npl]  [noun,npl]
```

The above two cases are handled properly because number agreement blocks the interpretation of the (41) as a determiner. This approach leads to the correct preference, when there is an ambiguity and accounts for the difficulty in (42) vs. (43):

(42) That deer ate everything in my garden surprised me.

(43) That deer ate everything in my garden last night.

The second experiment in [Milne, 1982], showed that (42) is a garden path sentence, while (43) is not. In both sentences, it is believed the subject uses the word "that" as a determiner. "Deer" is both singular and plural, so it fits the above rule. In (42), "that" must be used as a complementiser to make the sentence grammatical. The approach outlined above will use "that" as a determiner in an ambiguous case such as this.

These two simple techniques, word order and agreement, are sufficient to handle all the examples we have just presented. In addition, free text analysis has shown no violations to this approach [Milne, 1983]. These techniques provide the same coverage as Marcus's diagnostic, with the added bonus that the determiner is attached before the NP is built.

"That" can only be a complementiser when a "that S-" is expected and the packet of rules to provide this analysis are active. Hence the rules using "that" to start an embedded sentence are only activated when the verb has the feature "THAT- COMP" or at the start of a sentence. The rules in "THAT- COMP" will fire when "that" is followed by something which can start an NP. This ensures that the S- will have a subject and means that "that" will be taken as a pronoun in the following sentences:

(44) I know that hit Mary.

(45) I know that will be true.

but it will be taken as a complementiser in these sentences:

(46) I know that boys are mean.

(47) I know that Tom will hit Mary.

It seems that unless the S- has a subject, the pronoun use of "that" is preferred. Otherwise one would have a complementiser followed by a trace, rather than an unmarked complementiser, followed by a pronoun. This rule provides more complete coverage than Marcus's diagnostic since it examines the second buffer cell.

The rule to handle pronouns in general is of low priority and will only fire after all other uses have failed to match. "That" is treated in the same way.

"That" will be identified as a relative pronoun only if it occurs after a headnoun and the packet NP-COMPLETE is active. This situation will be handled in the same manner as the usual relative clause rules and will then cover:

(48) I know the boy that you saw.

(49) I know the boy that hit you.

The most difficult case for "that" is when the verb is subcategorised:

V NP S-

That is, it can take an NP subject, followed by a "that" S-. For these examples, ROBIE may have to decide if the series of words following "that" is a relative clause or an embedded sentence.

In the following sentences, the lookahead would have to be more than three buffers. Parentheses indicate words in the buffers. The last word is the disambiguating word.

(50) I told the girl (that)(the)(boy) hit the story.

(51) I told the girl (that)(the)(boy) will kiss her.

It can be seen that in these sentences, the disambiguating word is outside our three buffers. How do people handle these and what should our parser do? In [Milne, 1983] it was shown that when the syntax could not resolve the ambiguity with its two buffer lookahead, the decision of which interpretation to use might be made using non-syntactic information. In [Milne, 1983], it was stated that if context can affect the interpretation of the sentence, then non-syntactic information is being used to select the interpretation. The reader can experiment for himself and see that context does affect the interpretation of these sentences. Therefore it is predicted that non-syntactic information is being used to interpret these sentences and this problem should not be resolved on a syntactic basis, but a non-syntactic one.

This explains why some of these examples cause difficulty and others do not. The psychological evidence from cases using "that" is scant and I feel no conclusions can be reached here. My theory predicts that context will strongly affect these examples and, if they are strongly biased to the incorrect reading, a garden path should result.

One well-known example in this area is (52):

(52) I told the girl that I liked the story.

(53) I told the girl whom I liked the story.

(54) I told the girl the story that I liked.

These examples were tested in the [Milne, 1982]. The results suggested that (52) was read faster than the other two examples. Many of the subjects were questioned informally after the experiment about their interpretation of the sentence. All reported only one meaning; the S- reading. None of the subjects said that they noticed the relative clause reading, hence the result. The experiment, however, was not designed formally to distinguish these.

To handle the examples we have seen in this section, Marcus had four diagnostics, one of which was very complicated. I have just shown how to handle all four cases of "that" without any special rules, merely substituting enforced agreement and rejecting ungrammatical sentences.

3.7 Handling the Word HAVE

Let us now look at the elimination of Marcus's HAVE-DIAG in relation to the use of agreement we have been discussing in this section. The problem with "have" is illustrated by the following sentences:

(55) Have the students take the exam.

(56) Have the students taken the exam?

In these, we must decide if "have" is an auxiliary verb or a main verb and whether the sentence is a yes-no-question or an imperative. The sentences have the same initial string until the final morpheme on "take." To handle this case, Marcus used this rule [Marcus, 1980, p. 211]:

```
"(RULE HAVE-DIAG PRIORITY:5 IN SS-START
[have,tenseless][np][t] ⇒
If      2nd is ns,n3p or 3rd is tenseless
Then    run imperative next else
if      3rd is not verb
        then run yes-no-question next
             else if not sure, assume it's a y/n-q
                and run yes-no-question next)."
```

This rule seems to be necessary in order to distinguish between the question and the imperative. If one tries to ascertain exactly what occurs, the apparent complexity is revealed. Note also that Marcus's rule defaults to a yes-no-question twice in this diagnostic. The following sentences illustrate the distinction this rule makes.

(57) Have the boy take the exam.

(58) Have the boy taken the exam.

(59) Have the boys take the exam.

(60) Have the boys taken the exam?

It can be seen that YES-NO-QUESTION should run only when the NP following is plural and the verb has "en" (i.e., "taken"). For example, in (60) "the boys" is plural and the verb is "taken." None of the other examples above have both "boys" and "taken." This can also be understood as: the sentence is an imperative if the item in the 2nd buffer cell is not plural and the verb is tenseless. Statements (57–59) are imperatives because either the noun (boy) is singular ((57) and (58)) or the verb is tenseless (59). The second part of the rule takes care of the fact that the third buffer cell must contain a verb for the imperative, as this would be the main verb of the embedded sentential object.

Let us look more closely at the reason that only (60) is a question. Firstly, if the sentence is a yes-no-question, then aux-inversion must occur. When this happens, "Have" will be adjacent to the verb which was in the third buffer cell. In order for ROBIE to continue, the verb must have an "en" ending, or "have" and the next verb will not agree in aspect. This is the basis for discrimination in the earlier examples (57–60).

Secondly, in (57) and (58), the noun phrases are singular and both sentences are imperatives. Had the sentence been a yes-no-question, "have" would need to agree with the subject which must then be plural.

Hence, in effect, Marcus' rule checks for number agreement between the subject and verb and checks that the fixed order of the verb group is obeyed. Let us now look at other situations where this is necessary.

PARSIFAL would accept the following ungrammatical strings:

(61) *Are the boy running?

(62) *Has the boys run?

(63) *Has the boy kissing?

(64) *Has the boy kiss?

For a yes-no-question, the inverted auxiliary must agree with the verb after it has been inverted. To stop these ungrammatical constructions we must enforce verb agreement. The pattern for the rule YES-NO-QUESTION should be:

```
[auxverb][np][verb], agree[auxverb,verb],agree[verb,np].
```

This constraint enforces agreement of the verb and auxiliary verb and the subject and verb. Again this check is based only on the linguistic features of the buffers.

Such a constraint effectively blocks the ungrammatical constructions. (The parser will fail if the auxiliary has been inverted, since the auxiliary will not be parsed.) Also the subject NP must agree with the auxiliary verb, so we can also add "agree(auxverb,np)" to the rule, as we did with the HAVE-DIAG! So, by correcting the yes-no-question rule, the HAVE-DIAG is redundant.

In this section we have seen that Marcus's HAVE-DIAG can be replaced by merely exploiting agreement. It should be pointed out that although this approach has the same coverage as Marcus's diagnostic, it is wrong in some cases. [Milne, 1983] has a full discussion.

3.8 *Plural Head Nouns*

There is a class of ambiguities which can be resolved merely by enforcing subject/verb agreement. In this section, we will see an example from the class of words with the features noun, verb, final-s (plural). If we have two words, each of which can be a plural noun or a singular verb, we can enumerate four cases. Let us look at these possibilities and see that these cases can be disambiguated by simple rules using subject/verb agreement. The following examples illustrate all the possibilities:

(65) The soup pot cover handle screw is red.

(66) The soup pot cover handles screw tightly.

(67) *The soup pot cover handles screws tightly.

(68) The soup pot cover handle screws tightly.

(69) The soup pot cover handle screws are red.

Each of the words "pot, cover, handle, screw" can be either a noun or a verb. The "end of constituent" problem is to find out which word is used as the verb and which words make up the complex headnoun. The possible distributions of the morpheme "s" among two words gives us four cases. We will deal with each of these in turn.

Case 1: In (65) each noun is singular. For this case all ambiguous words must be nouns and part of the headnoun. Due to subject/verb agreement, a singular noun must match a 3rd person singular (v3s) verb, i.e., one without the letter "s." This case excludes that possibility since none of the words have an "s" at the end. Hence they must all be nouns.

Case 2: In (66) "handles" is a plural noun and each word before it must be a noun. When a singular noun/verb word follows "handles," the word (screw) must be a verb and "handles" is the last of the headnouns. It is not possible to use "handles" in this situation as a verb, and "screw" as a noun because of subject/verb agreement.

Case 3: The examples in this case have two consecutive plural nouns as in (67), where both words have noun/verb ambiguity. (Do not confuse plural "s" with possessive "s.")
   When the first plural is a noun, then the second one can be a verb only if it is part of a different constituent. Examples of this are the following. (Sentences beginning with "?" are considered grammatical but unacceptable to most readers.) The last two are from [Martin, Church, and Patil, 1981].

(70) ?The soup pot machine handles screws easily.

(71) The soup pot machine handles screw easily.

(72) Which years do you have costs figures for?

(73) Do you have a count of the number of sales requests and the number of requests filled?

Because there is a non-plural headnoun followed by a plural headnoun, this case is really a subset of Case 4. In general, the problems and issues for Case 4 dominate the resolution of ambiguities involving plural head nouns.

Case 4: Sentences (68) and (69) both have the same word initial string until after "screws," but in (68) "screws" is a verb while in (69) "screws" is part of the headnoun. In this situation, where the final word in a series is plural, each word before it must be a noun. The word itself can be either a noun or a verb, depending on what follows. These can be recognised as a pair of potential garden path sentences, as discussed in [Milne, 1982]. Therefore, this is the case to which the Semantic Checking Hypothesis applies and the predictions of [Milne, 1982] apply.

In that paper, the idea of potential garden path sentences is presented. These are sentences which may or may not lead to a garden path. Each garden path sentence has a partner, which is similar, but not a garden path. It is proposed that the decision as to how to resolve the ambiguity which may lead to a garden path should be made by semantics and not by syntax. This theory is called the Semantic Checking Hypothesis. For full details see [Milne, 1983].

In this section, we have looked at resolving a simple case of noun/verb ambiguity. In order to resolve this ambiguity, it was necessary merely to exploit agreement between the subject and verb in number and person.

Due to number and subject verb agreement, these facts have a linguistic base. They rely on the fact that a final "s" marks a plural noun, but a singular verb. If the verb is v3s (verb agrees with a 3rd person, singular noun, as with the "s"), then the subject of the verb must be singular, or else the sentence is ungrammatical. This is why all the words before the v3s word must be nouns. If any of these words were used as a verb, then subject-verb agreement would be violated. This is why (67) is ungrammatical. If the verb is v-3s (agrees with any noun phrase except 3rd person, singular i.e., no "s"), then the subject cannot be singular. (65) has no plural subject and so cannot have a v-3s verb. In (66) "handles" provides a plural subject, so "screw," which is v-3s, can agree.

3.9 Noun/Modal Ambiguity

We will now consider noun/modal ambiguity as demonstrated by "can" and "will." Both can be either a noun or a modal (i.e., could, should, would, can, will, might, etc.):

(74) The trash can was taken out.

(75) The trash can be taken out.

(76) The paper will was destroyed.

(77) The paper will be destroyed.

Each of these words is entered in the dictionary both as a noun and a modal. Due to agreement requirements, the modal/noun word can only be grammatically used as a modal if the word following it is a tenseless verb, i.e., the pattern:

```
[modal][tenseless]  ⇒  modal usage
```

applies. Handling noun/modal ambiguity can be quite easy. When the noun modal word appears in the first buffer cell one merely has to look at the contents of the second buffer cell to see if it contains a tenseless verb. This can be complicated though, if the auxiliary is inverted or the sentence is an imperative. The following examples show how this can arise:

(78) Let the paper will be read.

(79) Will the paper can be re-used?

In sentence (78) the fragment "Let the paper" implies that "will" can only be used as a noun, as the sentence already has one tensed verb. In the parser, the noun/modal word is first encountered inside the NP packets and the parser must decide whether to use the word as part of the headnoun or to leave it in the buffer cell to be used as a modal verb. These rules do not know whether a verb has been found previously. Hence, not all information from the sentence is used. If all the information is available at the time the noun/modal ambiguity is being resolved, these sentences would be unambiguous and people would have no trouble reading them.

Subjects were asked to read the above examples in the second experiment presented in [Milne, 1982]. The results showed convincingly that they are potential garden paths. Many naive readers had considerably more difficulty with them than with their more straight-forward counterparts. This was predicted for reasons that will be explained below.

This result seems surprising. If the subjects used all information available at the time the noun/modal word was encountered, then they should have had no trouble with these sentences. The fact that these are garden paths indicates that the readers did not use all the information available to them. Notice also that the ambiguity can be reformulated as: "Do we have the end of a noun phrase, or a complex headnoun?"

We have already seen a case where people do not seem to use all the information available to them. In [Milne, 1983] several end-of-NP problems were presented which could lead to a garden path. In each of these, it was shown that the ambiguity was resolved on the basis of non-syntactic information, without regard to the following words in the sentence. In other words, we saw that the reader did not use all the information available. There is one crucial difference though. In the previous cases, non-syntactic information was used because the syntactic processor with its limited lookahead was sometimes unable to choose the correct alternative. In this case, the information necessary has already been absorbed by the parser.

This suggests that the choice of alternatives is made locally inside the NP parsing rules, without regard to information about the type of sentence being parsed. In other words, the two buffer pattern applies regardless of the rest of the sentence. This assumes that a noun/modal word followed by a tenseless verb is being used as a modal. This is similar to Fodor, Bever, and Garrett's [1974] canonical sentoid strategy: a bottom-up analysis that took every N-V combination as a new S. Let us look at why this might be true in the parser.

When the parser starts to parse a NP, it creates a new NP node and pushes it to the bottom item of the Active Node Stack. This operation makes the NP node the Current Active Node and parsing of the old Current Active Node is suspended. If the parser is parsing an S node, for example at the start of the sentence, then work on this node will be suspended until the NP node has been completed and dropped into the buffer cell.

In ROBIE, unlike PARSIFAL, the pattern matcher for the grammar rules is allowed only to inspect the grammatical features of the two buffers. This means that the parser is unable to examine the contents of the Active Node Stack and, hence, the information that a tensed verb has already been found is unavailable to the NP parsing rules. This, then, suggests that the ambiguity will be resolved on the basis of local information only.

It should be pointed out that although ROBIE does not examine the Active Node Stack, the current packet reflects its contents. For example, if the parser is parsing the major S node, the packet SS-VP will be active, but if the parser is parsing an embedded S node, the packet Embedded-S will be active. This information can be considered to provide local context to the parsing rules. This is the same as in PARSIFAL.

Noun/Modal ambiguity is an end-of-NP problem and the choice of alternatives is made on the basis of limited and local information. This suggests that non-syntactic information may be used to resolve the ambiguity. There is one further possibility. The semantic choice mechanism is attempting to find the end of an NP. So far it has asked the question, "Can this item be part of the NP?" However, the end-of-NP problem can be reformulated as, "Is it better to use this as part of the NP, or as the start of the verb group?" It is conceivable that the end of NP mechanism uses "will" as the start of the verb group in the majority of occurrences, hence leading to the apparent modal preference in these examples:

(80) The trash can hit the wall.

(81) The paper will hit the table.

Due to lack of data, it is not clear exactly what people do in this situation and this would seem to provide an interesting area for further investigation.

3.10 *What About HER*

Another problem is the word "her," which can be used as a pronoun or as a possessive pronoun. Note that we can say:

(82) Tom kissed her.

(83) Tom kissed her sister.

Clearly in (82) "her" is a pronoun and in (83) "her" is a possessive determiner. When multiple part-of-speech definitions were added to ROBIE and the simple disambiguation method used, ROBIE always made "her" a possessive determiner. This difficulty arose in Marcus's parser because the rule to start a NP was ordered before the rule to parse a pronoun. These rules were copied directly into ROBIE's grammar. Since the word "her" has both the features "ngstart" and "pronoun," it could match both rules. Unfortunately, as Marcus's rules were stated, it always matched the NP starting rule, and hence was used as a determiner by the parser. This indicates one problem that can arise in the writing of a parser grammar.

To handle possessive determiners, PARSIFAL and ROBIE have a rule with the pattern:

```
[poss-np]
```

This rule will match a possessive pronoun after it has been made into an NP. It will also match any possessive NP, such as: "the boy's" or "the boy's mother's." The rule then adds the feature "determiner" to the NP, making it eligible for the NP starting rule. By degrading the possessive NPs to determiners, both parsers easily handle examples of left branching such as:

(84) The boy's mother's brother is his uncle.

Another problem arose in (82) because the possessive NP rule was not sufficiently constrained. It is possible to use "her" as a determiner only where the next word can be part of a nounphrase with that determiner. To enforce this, the second buffer cell is checked to be certain that its contents will take the determiner. Using this approach, "her" in (82) would not be converted to a possessive determiner. The rule DETERMINER can run only if the next item will "take a determiner."

This check is made by the syntactic category of the following word, rather than by a specially marked feature. This check could be done by having a list of all the possible categories as the pattern of the second buffer cell. As an implementation detail, this is in the form of an agreement check, merely to simplify this rule and to show its generality.

The only remaining problem occurs when the verb can take one or more objects and the item after the word "her" can be either the second object, or an NP with "her" as a determiner. For example:

(85) I took her grapes.

(86) He saw her duck.

(87) I gave her food for the dog.

The examples presented above are all examples of global ambiguity, which is discussed in more detail in [Milne, 1983]. In these cases the check of "will the next word take a determiner?" may or may not lead to the wrong analysis. This problem also interacts with the top-down component of verb phrase parsing and the semantic restrictions presented by it.

The conflict between the determiner and possessive usage can be modelled as a conflict of rule priorities. If the possessive use is preferred, then this rule should match first. Conversely, if the object use is preferred, then the object rule should match first. Any error in reading these examples would be due to one rule having priority over the other, when the reverse should be the case. Finally, notice that with no help from either intonation or context, either analysis is possible. That is, there is not enough information in the sentence to determine a unique interpretation.

We have now shown how to replace all the diagnostics Marcus used. In doing this, we enforced number and verb agreement on the rules before they could run. This was motivated to reject ungrammatical items, rather than for the handling of ambiguity. While there are still a few problems due to global ambiguity, the approach reported here has the same coverage as Marcus' diagnostics, and provides a better explanation of why people have trouble on certain sentences.

4 Possible Uses for Agreement in English

In this paper, we have seen several occurrences of ambiguity, for each of which we have found a parallel situation that could lead to acceptance of ungrammatical sentences by ROBIE. We then used person/number codes or the fixed structure of the verb group to block these unacceptable readings. Most of our ambiguity problems were also handled by this method. Although this has been used before with non-determinings. Most of our ambiguity problems were also handled by this method. Although this has been used before with non-deterministic parsers, it was not obvious that it would provide enough information to enable deterministic parsing.

Once person/number codes are taken into account, the number of potential ambiguous readings is dramatically reduced. In many cases, only one of the ambiguous possibilities was grammatical. It should be noted that there are a few difficult cases which we have not had time to describe in this paper; these are discussed in detail in [Milne, 1983].

Marcus had a few rules to resolve part of speech ambiguity, but they were *ad hoc*. We have seen that we can replace these rules very simply by merely exploiting agreement.

In the introduction, it was stated that handling lexical ambiguity was a major test for deterministic parsing. In this paper we have seen that many cases of ambiguity can be resolved in a simple way. This is possible because of the constraints imposed by number agreement and word order. In fact, many cases of the seemingly difficult problem of lexical ambiguity turn out to be easily resolved in a deterministic parser, since the deterministic parser uses more information, i.e., two buffer cells instead of one, to make decisions.

References

Akmajian, A. and Heny, F. 1975. *An Introduction to the Principles of Transformational Syntax.* Cambridge: MIT Press.

Chomsky, Noam. 1965. *Aspects of the Theory of Syntax.* Cambridge: MIT Press.

Dewar, H., Bratley, P., Thorne, J. 1969. A program for the syntactic analysis of English sentences. *Communications of the ACM* 12(8).

Fodor, Jerry, Bever, T., Garrett, M. 1974. *The Psychology of Language.* New York: McGraw-Hill.

Fodor, Janet and Frazier, Lynn. 1978. The sausage machine: A new two-stage parsing model. *Cognition* 6:291–325.

Kuno, S. 1965. The predictive analyzer and a path elimination technique. *Communications of the ACM* 8(10).

Marcus, Mitchell. 1980. *A Theory of Syntactic Recognition for Natural Language.* Cambridge: MIT Press.

Martin, William, Church, K., Patil, R. 1981. *Preliminary Analysis of a Breadth-First Parsing Algorithm: Theoretical and Experimental Results.* MIT AI Lab, presented at Modeling Human Parsing Strategies Symposium, Austin, Texas.

Milne, Robert. 1982. Predicting garden path sentences. *Cognitive Science* 6:349–373.

Milne, Robert. 1983. *Resolving Lexical Ambiguity in a Deterministic Parser.* D.Phil. Dissertation, University of Edinburgh, Edinburgh, Scotland.

TIME. 9 Jan. 1978. Good ole Burt; Cool-eyed Clint.

Winograd, Terry. 1972. *Understanding Natural Language.* New York: Academic Press.

3

*Resolving Lexical Ambiguity
Computationally with
Spreading Activation and
Polaroid Words*

Graeme Hirst

Department of Computer Science
University of Toronto
Toronto, Canada

1 *Introduction*

Any computer system for understanding natural language input (even in relatively weak senses of the word *understanding*) needs to be able to resolve lexical ambiguities. In this paper, I describe the lexical ambiguity resolution component of one such system.

The basic strategy used for disambiguation is to "do it the way people do." While cognitive modeling is not the primary goal of this work, it is often a good strategy in artificial intelligence to consider cognitive modeling anyway; finding out how people do something and trying to copy them is a good way to get a program to do the same thing. In developing the system below, I was strongly influenced by psycholinguistic research on lexical access and negative priming—in particular by the results of Swinney [1979], Seidenberg, Tanenhaus, Leiman, and Bienkowski [1982], and Reder [1983]. In Section 5 below, I will discuss the degree to which the system is a model of ambiguity resolution in people.

The system adheres to the following principles:

- Disambiguation cues come from many sources: syntax, word meaning, context, and knowledge of the world. The resolution component must be able to appeal to any or all of them.

- In general, all possible meanings of a word should be considered. Earlier computational methods such as scripts [Schank and Abelson, 1977], in which the context pre-selects allowable meanings for ambiguities, are much too inflexible, and are in conflict with the experimental results mentioned above.

- Resolution happens as soon as possible. If sufficient disambiguating information precedes the word, then resolution occurs immediately; otherwise, it happens as soon as subsequent words have provided enough information, and in any case it must occur by the end of the sentence. It is clear that people work like this; they don't, for example, wait until a sentence is complete and then go back and start resolving the lexical ambiguities.

- Determining which case slot is flagged by a preposition or a particular syntactic position is a process not unlike the disambiguation of content words, and should be handled as far as possible by the same mechanism. That is, both tasks are a kind of lexical disambiguation, so if one process can deal with some or all of both, then, by Occam's Razor, we should prefer it over two independent processes.

Despite our respect for psychological reality as a design strategy (and not as an end in itself), the resolution component is part of an artificial intelligence system, and must therefore also be able to work with the other components of the system; compromises were sometimes necessary.

This work is part of a project on semantics and ambiguity in natural language understanding. Other components of the system include a syntactic parser, named Paragram [Charniak, 1983a], based on that of Marcus [1980]; a semantic interpreter named Absity [Hirst, 1983; 1987]; a structural disambiguator called the Semantic Enquiry Desk [Hirst, 1984a; 1987]; and a knowledge representation and inference system called Frail [Wong, 1981a, 1981b; Charniak, Gavin, and Hendler, 1983].

Absity is a compositional semantic interpreter that runs in tandem with the parser. Every time the parser creates a new syntactic structure from words or from smaller structures, Absity constructs a semantic object to correspond to that structure, using the semantic objects that correspond to the words or smaller parts. Thus starting from words and their meanings, parsing and semantic interpretation proceed in lockstep, and there is always a well-formed semantic representation for every partial or complete syntactic structure. If the sentence is structurally ambiguous, that is, if the parser has to make a choice between two structures, it will ask the Semantic Enquiry Desk to decide which alternative is best. The semantic objects are represented in the Frail frame language. For the purposes of the present paper, Frail may be thought of as a fairly conventional representation composed of interconnected schemas, with an associated inference and retrieval mechanism; Hirst [1987] discusses in detail the adequacy of such representations as a target for semantic interpretation.

There is an immediate catch in this interpretation scheme. Occasionally a word cannot be disambiguated until some time after its occurrence, whereas Absity wants its semantic object as soon as the word appears. But usually the meaning of a single ambiguous word does not affect the immediate processing of the next few words after it. What we do, therefore, is give Absity a *fake* semantic object, with the promise that in due course it shall be replaced by the real thing. The fake is labeled with everything else that Absity needs to know about the object (such as its syntactic category or possible categories), Absity builds its semantic structure with the fake, and when the real object is available, it is just slipped in where the fake is.

The fakes that we give Absity can be thought of as self-developing Polaroid[1] photographs of the semantic object, and the promise is that by the time the sentence is complete, the photograph will be a fully developed "picture" of the desired semantic object. Even as the picture develops, Absity is able to manipulate the photograph, build it into a structure, and indeed do everything with it that it could do with a fully developed photograph, except look at the final picture. Moreover, like real Polaroid photographs, these have the property that as development takes place, the partly developed picture will be viewable and usable in its intermediate form. That is, just as one can look at a partly developed Polaroid picture and determine whether it is a picture of a person or a mountain range, but perhaps not which person or which mountain range, so it is possible to look at *Polaroid Words* and get an idea of what the semantic object they show looks like.

I will describe the operation of Polaroid Words in Section 3. Before that, in Section 2, I discuss marker passing, a mechanism that Polaroid Words uses for finding associations between words.[2] In Section 4, I discuss some of the

---

1 *Polaroid* is a trademark of the Polaroid Corporation for its range of self-developing photographic products and other products. The word is used here to emphasize the metaphor of a self-developing semantic object, and the system described herein carries no association with, or endorsement by, the Polaroid Corporation.
2 These sections differ in some details from the description of an earlier design in Hirst and Charniak [1982].

ways in which Polaroid Words are not yet adequate, and then, in Section 5, look at the extent to which Polaroid Words are a psychological model. I assume throughout this chapter that the input sentence is not structurally ambiguous; in Hirst [1987] I show how Polaroid Words work together with the Semantic Enquiry Desk, each constraining the other, when the correct parse of the sentence cannot be determined immediately.

2 Marker Passing

It is well known that an association between one sense of an ambiguous word and other words in the sentence or context can be an important disambiguation cue. Psycholinguistic research on lexical disambiguation has shown that semantic priming—that is, the previous occurrence of an associated word—speeds up people's disambiguation, and may lead the retrieval process straight to the correct meaning.[3]

The lexical disambiguation program for Absity therefore needs a mechanism that will allow it to find semantic associations. Quillian suggested as long ago as 1962 that following connections in a semantic network is an excellent way of finding such associations. Our mechanism for this will be *marker passing* in the Frail knowledge base.

Marker passing can be thought of as passing tags or markers along the arcs of the knowledge base, from frame to frame, from slot to filler, under the rules to be discussed below. It is a discrete computational analogue of *spreading activation* in semantic memory. The network of frames or schemas corresponds to the conceptual and lexical network of semantic memory, and a connection implies a semantic relationship of some kind between its two nodes. Passing a marker from one node to another corresponds to activating the receiving node. If marker passing is breadth-first from the starting point (new markers being created if a node wishes to pass to two or more other nodes simultaneously), then marker passing will "spread" much as spreading activation does.[4]

Marker passing was first used in artificial intelligence by Quillian [1968, 1969], who used it to find connections between concepts in a semantic network. Marker passing is, of course, expensive when the net is interestingly large. Fahlman [1979], who used it for deduction in his NETL system, proposed super-parallel hardware for marker passing. Although the present scheme is much simpler than Fahlman's, I too assume that hardware of the future will,

---

3 Or perhaps straight to an incorrect meaning, if the semantic prime is misleading; see Section 5.1.

4 Note that this is a very localist system in which each node represents a concept. It is thus in contrast to distributed connectionist-style systems, in which a single concept is represented by a *collection* of nodes among which activation may pass.

like people of the present, be able to derive connections between concepts in parallel, and that the serial implementation to be described below is only an interim measure.

2.1 *Marker Passing in Frail*

The frame language Frail contains a built-in marker passer (*MP* for short) that operates upon the Frail knowledge base [Charniak, Gavin, and Hendler, 1983]. The MP is called with the name of a node (a frame, slot, or instance) as its argument to use as a starting point. From this origin, it marks all nodes in the knowledge base that participate in assertions that also contain the origin; these can include slots, slot restrictions, and IS-A relationships. For example, suppose the origin is to be the frame that describes libraries:

(1) [frame: library

    isa: institution

    slots: (function (store-books lend-books))

            (employee (librarian))

    ...]

Markers would be placed on institution, store-books, lend-books, employee, librarian, and so on. Markers take the form of a list of node names interleaved with the connection that permitted the marker to be placed, so that there is always information to retrace the path.

Once all the nodes reachable in one step from the origin are marked, each node reachable from these nodes—that is, each node two steps from the origin—is marked. For example, if a slot in the frame store-books contains book (as it surely would), then book would be marked. Thus marker passing proceeds, fanning out from the origin until all nodes whose distance is *n* or less from the origin have been marked, where *n* defaults to 5 if the programmer doesn't specify otherwise.[5]

If at any time during marker passing the MP comes upon a node already marked by a previous call, then a *path* (or *chain*) has been found between the origin node of the present call and that of a previous call. The MP uses the pre-existing mark on the node to construct the full origin-to-origin path. Suppose that in the example above, the book node had been found to be already marked, indicating a connection to it from publisher; the MP can then note

---

5 See my remarks in Section 5.3 about 'magic numbers' in marker passing and 'spending' activation.

that a path has been found between `library` and `publisher`. It is also possible that the origin itself has been marked by a previous call to the MP, resulting in an instantly discovered path. We call such paths *immediate paths* to distinguish them from *constructed paths*, such as that of the example above in which the intersection occurs at a third node.

When marking is finished, the MP returns a list of all the paths (if any) that it found. One may, at any time, clean the markers from all nodes in the knowledge base.

2.2 Lexical Disambiguation with Marker Passing

In this section, I give a very simple example of lexical disambiguation with the Frail marker passer that was discussed in the previous section. In later sections, I will refine and extend these disambiguation mechanisms considerably.

The marker passer operates independently of Absity and in parallel with it. That is, following only morphological analysis, the input sentence goes to both the Paragram parser and the MP, both of which separately grind away on each word as it comes in. Suppose the input is (2), an example chosen especially because it contains several ambiguous words that can be resolved purely by association cues:

(2) Nadia's <u>plane</u> <u>taxied</u> to the <u>terminal</u>.

The words *plane*, *taxi*, and *terminal* are all ambiguous. Note that the ambiguity of *taxi* is categorial: it can be a noun meaning **vehicle with driver for hire**, or a verb meaning (of an airplane) **to travel at low speed on the ground**. Since the MP has no access to syntactic information, it looks at all meanings for each word, regardless of part of speech; marker chains from origins that later prove to be syntactically inappropriate will simply be ignored by other processes.

As the words come in from left to right, the MP passes markers from the frames representing each known meaning of each open class word in the sentence (including unambiguous ones such as *Nadia*). In (2), short paths would be found between the frames `airplane` and `airport-building`, which were starting points for *plane* and *terminal*, because the latter would be a frame mentioned in one of the activities described in the frame for the former. Likewise, `airplane` and `aircraft-ground-travel` (*plane* and *taxi*) will be connected, because the latter is an activity attributed to the former. These connections indicate that the corresponding meanings of *plane*, *terminal*, and *taxi* should be chosen. (A path will also be found between `airport-building` and `aircraft-ground-travel`, but this gives no new information.) Markers will also be passed from the frames representing the other meanings of *plane*, *taxi*, and *terminal*, namely `wood-smoother`, `taxicab`, and `computer-ter-`

`minal`, but these paths will go off into the wilderness and never connect with any of the other paths.

2.3 *Constraining Marker Passing*

Since marker passing is a blind and mindless process, it is clear that many paths in the knowledge base will be marked besides the ones that provide useful disambiguating information. In fact, if the MP gets too carried away, it will eventually mark everything in the knowledge base, as every node in the base can be reached from any other, and one will then find paths between the wrong senses of ambiguous words as well as between the right senses. For example, a connection could be found between `airplane` and `computer-terminal` simply by passing markers up the IS-A chain from `airplane` through `vehicle` and the like to `mechanical-object`, and then down another IS-A chain from there to `computer-terminal`. Therefore, to prevent as many "uninteresting" and misleading paths as possible, we put certain constraints on the MP and prohibit it from taking certain steps.

First, as I mentioned in Section 2.1, Frail passes markers a maximum of n arcs from the origin. One would normally choose n to be small compared to the size of the knowledge base. Second, Frail permits the programmer to specify restrictions on passing markers along various types of path. For example, by default the MP will pass markers only upwards along IS-A links, not downwards—that is, markers are passed to more general concepts, but never to more particular ones (thereby prohibiting the path from `mechanical-object` to `computer-terminal` mentioned above). These restrictions are specified in the form of a predicate supplied by the programmer and attached to the name of the arc. Before attempting to pass a marker, the MP will evaluate the predicate, which has access to the origin, the present node, and the path between them; if the value of the predicate is `nil`, no marker is passed.

Determining exactly what restrictions should be placed on marker passing is a matter for experiment [see Hendler, 1986, 1987]. I postulate restrictions such as an *anti-promiscuity rule*: not allowing paths to propagate from nodes with more than c connections, for some chosen c. This is because nodes with many connections tend to be uninteresting ones near the top of the IS-A hierarchy—`mechanical-object`, for example. We must be careful, however, not to be so restrictive that we also prevent the useful paths that we are looking for from occurring. And no matter how clever we are at blocking misleading paths, we must be prepared for the fact that they will occasionally turn up. The problem of such *false positives* is discussed by Charniak [1983b, 1986], who posits a *path checker* that would filter out many paths that are uninteresting or silly.

3 *Polaroid Words*

In Section 1, I introduced the idea of the Polaroid Word mechanism (*PW* to its friends), which would be responsible for disambiguating each word. As I noted, there are many sources of information that can be used in disambiguation; it is up to the mechanism of the PW to use whatever information is available to it to make a decision for each word. Often, as in the case of example (2) of Section 2.2, all that is required is looking at the paths found by the marker passer. At other times, MP will return nothing overwhelmingly conclusive; or, in the case of a polysemous word—one whose several meanings are related—more than one meaning may be marked. It is then necessary for PWs to use other information and negotiate between possible meanings. In this section I will describe in detail this aspect of the operation of Polaroid Words.

3.1 *What Polaroid Words Look Like*

While it would be quite possible to operate Polaroid Words under the control of a single supervisory procedure that took the responsibility for the development of each "photograph," it seems more natural instead, because of the parallelism, to put the disambiguation mechanism (and the responsibility) into each individual Polaroid Word. That is, a PW will be a procedure, running in parallel with other PWs,[6] whose job it is to disambiguate a single instance of a word. At this point, however, we find we must stretch the Polaroid photograph metaphor, for unlike that of a real self-developing photograph, a PW's development cannot be completely self-contained. The PWs will have to communicate with one another and with their environment in order to get the information necessary for their disambiguation. So disambiguation is, in effect, a relaxation process. The idea of communicating procedures, one per word, brings to mind Small's word experts [Adriaens and Small, this volume]. The similarity between PWs and Small's procedures is, however, only superficial; the differences will become apparent as we describe PWs in detail.

Instead of having a completely different PW for each word, we have but one kind of PW for each syntactic category; for example, there is a noun PW and a verb PW. Each noun uses the same disambiguation procedure as all the other nouns; each verb uses the same procedure as the other verbs, and similarly for other syntactic categories.[7] The knowledge about the meaning of each individual word is kept distinct from the disambiguation procedure itself, and

---

6 In the implementation described below, only one PW is active at a time, in order to simplify the programming.

7 At present, PWs are implemented only for nouns, verbs, prepositions, and, in rudimentary form, noun modifiers. Determiners are straightforward, and PWs for them may exist later; see Section 3.5.

indeed much of the knowledge used by PWs is obtained from the Frail knowledge base when it is necessary. When a new PW is needed, an instance of the appropriate type is cloned and is given a little packet of knowledge about the word for which it will be responsible. (Sometimes I will be sloppy and call these packets Polaroid Words as well. No confusion should result.) As far as possible, the packets contain only lexical knowledge—that is, only knowledge about how the word is used, rather than world knowledge (already available through Frail) about the properties of the word's denotations.

The simplest packet of knowledge is that for a noun: it just contains a list of the semantic objects—the frames or schemas in the Frail knowledge base— that the noun could represent. Figure 3.1 shows the knowledge packet for the noun *slug*. Any information needed about properties of the senses of the noun is obtained from the Frail knowledge base.

The packet for prepositions and pseudo-prepositions[8] is a little more complicated; listed with each possible semantic object, whose semantic type is *frame slot*, is a *slot restriction predicate* for each—a predicate that specifies what is required of an instance to be allowed to fill the slot. Figure 3.2 shows the packet for the preposition *with*; it assumes that the preposition is a case flag. (PWs for prepositions of noun-modifying PPs are discussed in Hirst [1987, Section 7.2].) A simple predicate, such as physobj ("physical object"), requires that the slot-filler be under the specified node, in this case physobj, in the IS-A hierarchy. A complex predicate may specify a Boolean combination of features that the filler must satisfy; thus in Figure 3.2 the filler of instrument must be a physobj, but not an animate one.

```
[slug (noun):
    gastropod-without-shell
    bullet
    metal-stamping
    shot-of-liquor]
```

Figure 3.1 Packet of knowledge for *slug* for noun Polaroid Word; each line is the name of a frame in the Frail knowledge base.

---

8 *Pseudo-prepositions* are the case flags that occur as a syntactic position: *SUBJ*, *OBJ*, and *IN-DOBJ* for subject, object, and indirect object positions. Pseudo-prepositions are inserted by the parser, and are thereafter treated like other prepositions. See Hirst [1987, Section 3.4] for discussion of why this is a good idea.

```
[with (prep):
    instrument    (and physobj (not animate))
    manner        manner-quality
    accompanier   physobj]
```

Figure 3.2 Packet of knowledge for *with* for preposition Polaroid Word; each line is the name of a slot and a corresponding slot restriction predicate.

```
[operate (verb):
    [cause-to-function
        agent         SUBJ
        patient       SUBJ, OBJ
        instrument    SUBJ, with
        method        by
        manner        with
        accompanier   with]
    [perform-surgery
        agent         SUBJ
        patient       upon, on
        instrument    with
        method        by
        manner        with
        accompanier   with] ]
```

Figure 3.3 Packet of knowledge for *operate* for verb Polaroid Word; each entry is a frame with a set of slots and the prepositions that may flag each slot.

The predicates listed in the packet for each slot are, in effect, the most restrictive predicate compatible with the restrictions on all instances of the slot for all verbs. In English, for example, an animate entity can never be the instrument of an action. Ideally, there would be a process that would automatically compile the preposition information packets from the knowledge base and would help ensure they remain consistent with one another when words are added or changed.

Verbs have the most complex knowledge packets. Figure 3.3 shows the packet for *operate*. For each meaning, the case slots that it takes are listed, with the preposition or prepositions that may flag each slot. Slot restriction predicates for each slot need not be specified in verb packets, because they may be immediately found in the corresponding frames in the knowledge base. These predicates will, in general, be more restrictive than the predicates given in the PW for the corresponding preposition, but they must, of course, be compatible. For example, in the `perform-surgery` frame, the predicate on `instrument` may be `(property sharp)`, which particularizes the predicate shown for `instrument` in Figure 3.2; a predicate such as `hanim` ("higher animate being") would contradict that in Figure 3.2 and would indicate trouble somewhere. It should be clear that if the semantics are properly characterized, contradictions will not occur, but, again, an automatic system for maintaining consistency would be helpful.

```
[buy (verb):
    [purchase
         destination   SUBJ
         source        from
         sold-item     OBJ
         exchange      for
         beneficiary   for, INDOBJ] ]
[sell (verb):
    [purchase
         destination   to, INDOBJ
         source        SUBJ
         sold-item     OBJ
         exchange      for
         beneficiary   for] ]
```

Ross sold the lemming to Nadia.
```
(a ?x (purchase ?x (source=Ross)
                   (destination=Nadia)
                   (sold-item=lemming26)))
```
Nadia bought the lemming from Ross.
```
(a ?x (purchase ?x (source=Ross)
                   (destination=Nadia)
                   (sold-item=lemming26)))
```

Figure 3.4 Abbreviated packets of knowledge for *buy* and *sell*, using the same frame but different mappings of case flags to slots, and examples of their use in Frail.

Unlike the other PW knowledge packets, the verb packets contain information that might also be readily obtained from Frail's knowledge base, namely the slots that each verb frame has. Because the knowledge packet has to include a listing of the prepositions that flag each of the verb's slots, the slots themselves have to be listed, necessarily adding a little world knowledge to the word knowledge. The alternative, listing the flags in the Frail definition of the frame in the knowledge base, would just be the same sin at a different site. It might be more elegant if we were able to remove this information from the individual verbs altogether, and rather store generalizations about case flags as they relate to the semantic properties of verbs. That is, since verbs are classified in Frail's IS-A hierarchy under such generalizations as `transitive-action` and `transfer-action` in order to support the obvious needs of inference, and since this also provides a nice generalization of slots (for example, all `transfer-actions` have `source` and `destination` slots) we could store a small table that mapped each general verb frame category to a set of flags for its slots. Alas, English is just not quite regular enough to permit this; verbs can get quite idiosyncratic about their case flags. We have already seen in Figure 3.3 that the two senses of *operate* have different sets of case flags, although both are `transitive-actions`. Another example is the common senses of the verbs *buy* and *sell*, which are often analyzed as referring to the same frame, varying only in how the case flags are mapped to its slots; see Figure 3.4 for an example. We should not complain about the idiosyncrasy of case flags, however, for it is often a great help in verb disambiguation, especially if the verb is polysemous.

3.2 *How Polaroid Words Operate*

PWs operate in parallel with Absity and the parser. Each word comes in to the parser and its syntactic category or possible categories are assigned from the lexicon. A PW process is created for the word for each of its possible syntactic categories; those for categories that prove to be incorrect will not survive. The way the processes work is described below.

There are two easy cases. The first, obviously, is that the word is unambiguous. If this is the case, the PW process merely announces the meaning and uninterestingly hibernates—as soon as PWs have narrowed their possible meanings to just one, they always announce the fact and knock off work. The second easy case is that the marker passer, which has been looking for paths between senses of the new word and unrejected senses of those already seen, finds a nice connection that permits one alternative to be chosen. This was the case with example (2) of Section 2.2. I will discuss in Section 5.3 exactly what makes a marker passing path "nice." In general, short constructed paths are nice, and immediate paths are nicer.

If neither of these cases obtains, then the PW has to find out some more about the context in which its word occurs and see which of its alternatives fits best. To do this, it looks at certain preceding PWs to see if they can provide disambiguating information; I will describe this process in a moment. Using the information gathered, the PW will eliminate as many of its alternatives as possible. If this leaves just one possibility, it will announce this fact and stop work; if still undecided, it will announce the remaining possibilities and then sleep until a new word, possibly the bearer of helpful information, comes along.

Communication between PWs is heavily restricted. The only information that a PW may ask of another is what its remaining possibilities are; that is, each may see other partly or fully developed photographs. In addition, a PW is restricted in two ways as to the other PWs it is allowed to communicate with. First, since a sentence is processed from left to right, when a PW is initially invoked it will be the rightmost word in the sentence so far and may only look to PWs on its left. As new words come in, the PW will be able to see them, subject to the second constraint, namely that each PW may look only at its *friends*.[9] Friendships among PWs are defined as follows: Verbs are friends with the prepositions and nouns they dominate; prepositions are friends with the nouns of their prepositional phrase and with other prepositions; noun modifiers are friends with the noun they modify. In addition, if a prepositional phrase is a candidate for attachment to a noun phrase, then the preposition is a friend of the head noun of the NP to which it may be attached. The intent of the friendship constraints is to restrict the amount of searching for information that a PW has to do; the constraints reflect the intuition that a word has only a very limited sphere of influence with regard to selectional restrictions and the like, so PW communication is limited to what seems the minimum necessary for the task.

An "announcement" of its meaning possibilities by a PW takes the form of a list of the one or more alternatives from its knowledge packet (with their slot restriction predicates and so on if they are included in the packet) that the PW has not yet eliminated. An announcement is made by posting a notice in an area that all PWs can read; when one PW asks another for its possibilities, what it is actually doing is reading this notice. (PWs only read their friends' notices, of course.)

From the information that the notices provide, a PW eliminates any of its meanings that don't suit its friends. For example, each case slot may occur at most once in a sentence, so if one preposition PW has already decided that it flags, say, the *agent* slot, then a new preposition PW could cross *agent* off its own list. A preposition PW will also eliminate from its list any cases that its

---

9 Note that friendship constraints do not apply to the marker passer.

dominating verb does not allow it to flag, and any whose predicates are incompatible with its noun complement. Its friends may still be only partly developed, of course, in which case the number of eliminations it can make may be limited. However, if, say, one of its cases requires a `hanim` filler but none of the alternatives in the partly developed noun is `hanim`, then it can confidently cross that case off its list. The PW may use Frail to determine whether a particular sense has the required properties. What is happening here is, of course, very like the use of selectional restriction cues for disambiguation; see Hirst [1987, Section 5.5] for discussion of the differences.

Similarly, nouns and verbs can strike from their lists anything that doesn't fit their prepositional friends, and nouns and noun modifiers can make themselves compatible with each other by ensuring that the sense selected for the noun is a frame with which the modifier's sense will fit. (If a PW finds that this leaves it with no alternatives at all, then it is in trouble; this is discussed in Section 4.)

When a PW has done all it can for the time being, it announces the result, a fully or partly developed picture, and goes to sleep. The announcement wakes up any of its friends that have not yet made their final decision, and each sees whether the new information—both the new word's announcement and any marker passing chain between the old word and the new—helps it make up its mind. If so, it too makes an announcement of its new possibilities list, in turn awakening its own friends (which will include the first PW again, if it is as yet undecided). This continues until none can do any more and quiescence is achieved. Then the next word in the sentence comes in, its PW is created, and the sequence is repeated.

3.3 *An Example of Polaroid Words in Action*

Let's consider the following example, concentrating on the subordinate clause shown in (4):

(3) Ross found that the slug would operate the vending machine.

(4) SUBJ the slug operate OBJ the vending machine.

Notice that the parser has inserted the pseudo-prepositions *SUBJ* and *OBJ*. We want to work out that *the slug* is a metal stamping, not a gastropod, a bullet, or a shot of whiskey; that the frame that *operate* refers to is `cause-to-function`, not `perform-surgery`; and that *SUBJ* and *OBJ* indicate the slots `instrument` and `patient` respectively. *Vending machine*, we will say, is unambiguous. For simplicity, we will ignore the tense and modality of the verb. The PWs for *slug*, *with*, and *operate* were shown in Figures 3.1, 3.2, and 3.3; those for the other words are shown in Figure 3.5.

```
[SUBJ (prep):
     agent          animate
     patient        thing
     instrument     physobj
     source         physobj
     destination    physobj]

[OBJ (prep):
     patient        thing
     transferee     physobj]

[vending machine (noun):
     vending-machine]
```

Figure 3.5 Packets of knowledge for *SUBJ*, *OBJ*, and *vending machine*.

Disambiguation of the subordinate proceeds as follows. The first words are *SUBJ* and *slug*; their PWs, when created, have not yet enough information to do anything interesting, nor has marker passing from the senses of *slug* produced anything (since there are no other words with which a connection might be found yet). Then *operate* comes along, and tells the others that it could mean either cause-to-function or perform-surgery. It too has no way yet of deciding upon its meaning. However, the *SUBJ* PW notices that neither meaning of *operate* uses *SUBJ* to flag a source or destination case, so it can cross these off its list. It also sees that while both meanings can flag their agent with *SUBJ*, both require that the agent be hanim. None of the possibilities for *slug* has this property, so the *SUBJ* PW can also cross agent off its list, and announce that it means either instrument or patient.

This wakes up the *operate* PW, which notices that only one of its meanings, cause-to-function, can take either an instrument or a patient flagged by *SUBJ*, so it too announces its meaning. The *slug* PW is also woken up, but it is unable to use any of this information.

Next comes the word *OBJ*. It could be patient or transferee, but the verb *operate* doesn't permit the latter, so it announces the former. Note that if *operate* had not already been disambiguated from previous information, this would happen now, as the *operate* PW would notice that only one of its senses takes any case flagged by *OBJ*. Upon hearing that *OBJ* is going to be patient, the PW for *SUBJ* now crosses patient from its own list, since a case slot can appear but once in a sentence; this leaves it with instrument as its meaning. The PW for *slug* is not a friend of that for *OBJ*, so *OBJ's* announcement does not awaken it. (It is awakened by *SUBJ's* move, but cannot use the information.)

The noun phrase *vending machine* now arrives, and we assume that it is recognized as a canned phrase representing a single concept (see also [Becker, 1975; Wilensky and Arens, 1980a; 1980b]). It brings with it a marker passing chain that, depending on the exact organization of the frames, might be this:

(5) `vending-machine` $\Rightarrow$ `coin` $\Rightarrow$ `metal-stamping`

since a fact on the `vending-machine` frame would be that they use `coins`, and a `coin` IS-A `metal-stamping`. This is enough for the *slug* PW to favor `metal-stamping` as its meaning, and all words are now disambiguated. Now that processing is complete, all markers in the knowledge base are cleared away.

3.4 *Recovery from Doubt*

Now let's consider this example, in which marker passing is not used at all:

(6) The <u>crook</u> operated a pizza parlor.[10]

This proceeds as example (4) of the previous section did, until *operate* arrives. Since *crook* can either be something that is `hanim`, namely a `criminal`, or not, namely a `shepherd's-staff`, *SUBJ* is unable to make the move that in the previous example disambiguated both it and *operate*, though it can cross `patient` off its list. Still, when *OBJ* comes along, the *operate* PW can immediately eliminate `perform-surgery`. Let us assume that *pizza parlor* is an unambiguous canned phrase, as *vending machine* was. However, after it is processed, the PWs reach a standstill with *SUBJ* and *crook* still undisambiguated, as MP, unaware of current trends in organized crime, finds no connection between *crook* and *pizza parlor*.

If it happens that at the end of the sentence one or more words are not fully disambiguated, then there are three ways that they may yet be resolved. The first is to invoke knowledge of *preferred* or *deprecated meanings* for them—that is, meanings that are especially common or rare. Preferred and deprecated meanings are indicated as an additional part of the knowledge packet for each word; a word can have zero or more of each. For example, the meaning `female-swan` of *pen* is deprecated, and should never be chosen un-

---

10 This is exactly the same meaning of *operate* as in the previous example: `cause-to-func-tion`. In a context like this, the action is continuous, a matter I ignore here.

less there is positive evidence for it (such as strong or weak marker passing chains—see next paragraph); the meaning `writing-instrument` is preferred, and the meaning `enclosure` is neither preferred nor deprecated. The possibilities that remain are ranked accordingly, and the top one or ones are chosen. In the present example, therefore, the two unfinished PWs look for their preferred meanings. It is clear that in English, *agent* is far more common for SUBJ than the other remaining possibility, *instrument* and so the *SUBJ* PW should prefer that. This, in turn will wake up the *crook* PW, which now finds the requirement that its meaning fit *operate*'s `agent`, and therefore chooses `criminal`, completing disambiguation of the sentence. [11]

The second possibility at the end of the sentence is to use "weak" marker passing chains. It may be the case that during processing of the sentence, marker passing found a path that was considered too weak to be conclusive evidence for a choice. However, now that all the evidence available has been examined and no conclusion has been reached, the weak path is taken as being better than nothing. In particular, a weak path that runs to a deprecated meaning is used as evidence in support of that meaning. In the present implementation, the trade-off between weak chains and preferred meanings is accomplished by "magic numbers" (see Section 5.3).

If neither preferred meanings nor weak chains help to resolve all the remaining ambiguities, then inference and discourse pragmatics may be invoked. It should be clear that Polaroid Words with marker passing are not a replacement for inference and pragmatics in word sense and case disambiguation; rather, they serve to reduce substantially the number of times that these must be employed. However, there will still be cases where inference must be used. For example, the following sentences couldn't be disambiguated without inference about the relative aesthetics of factories and flora:

(7) The view from the window would be ruined by the addition of a <u>plant</u> out there.

(8) The view from the window would be improved by the addition of a <u>plant</u> out there.

Similarly, when a president tells us (9):

(9) I am not a <u>crook</u>. [12]

---

11 It is possible that the results will vary depending on which PW applies its preferred meaning first. It is unlikely that there is a single "correct" order for such situations. If a sentence is really so delicately balanced, people probably interpret it as randomly as Polaroid Words do.
12 Nixon, Richard Milhous. 11 November 1973.

neither marker passing nor Polaroid Words will help us discover that he or she is not denying being a shepherd's staff, even though we may readily determine that shepherd's staff he or she is not.[13]

Throughout this process, however, it should be kept in mind that some sentences are genuinely ambiguous to people, and it is therefore inappropriate to take extraordinary measures to resolve residual problems. If reasonable efforts fail, PWs can always ask the user what he or she really meant:

(10) **User:** I need some information on getting rid of moles.

System: What exactly is it that you wish to get rid of? Unsightly skin blemishes, some cute but destructive insectivorous garden pests, uterine debris, unwanted breakwaters, chili and chocolate sauces, or enemy secret agents that have penetrated deep into your organization?

(11) **User:** Are there any planes in stock?

System: We've got two carpentry planes and a Boeing 747.

(The system does not actually have such a natural language response component.)

One particular case of genuine ambiguity corresponds to when PWs *deadlock*. Deadlock between two (or more) PWs is possible if one says "I can be X if you are A, and I can be Y if you are B," while the other says, conversely, "I can be A if you are X, and I can be B if you are Y." In other words, the sentence has two readings, corresponding to the choices $X + A$ and $Y + B$. This can happen if two "parallel" MP paths are found:

(12) Ross was escorted from the bar to the dock. *(a courtroom scene or a harborside scene)*

(13) Each bill requires a check.[14] *(each* **invoice** *requires a* **negotiable instrument***, or each* **proposed law** *requires a* **verification of correctness***, or various other combinations)*

Deadlock cases are probably very rare—it is hard to construct good examples even out of context, let alone in a context—and PWs have no special mechanism for dealing with them.

---

13 The present implementation does not have such an inference or pragmatics system available to it.

14 Readers in countries where the spelling *cheque* is used should pretend that the example was read aloud to them.

3.5 *Cues Unused*

Many words can be disambiguated by syntactic cues; for example, many of the various senses of *keep* may be distinguished by the syntactic form of the object.[15] At present, Polaroid Words do not have this sensitivity, because of limited communication between PWs and the Paragram parser. I do not anticipate major difficulties in changing this in future versions of Polaroid Words.

Because PWs are not sensitive to syntax yet, they cannot yet handle passive sentences. Also awaiting this sensitivity are PWs for determiners. For example, the word *the* translates as either the or the-pl, depending on whether its NP is marked as singular or plural. Determiner PWs would be particularly simple, as they do not have to deal with marker passing nor provide feedback to any other PWs. A sensitivity to syntax would also assist the resolution of nouns such as *rock*, some senses of which can be pluralized and others of which cannot.

A second unused disambiguation cue is global context. Marker passing is used as a mechanism for local (intra-sentence) context cues, but the system has at present no representation of global context. It is my conjecture that it will not work simply to extend marker passing so that paths may be constructed between words of a sentence and the one before it. Rather, there should be a representation of context as an area in the knowledge base; this may include some nodes that were senses of words of previous sentences, instances created by the semantic representations of the sentences, nodes that participated in inferences made as sentences were read, and so forth. (Such representations of context are also motivated by the need to analyze reference and connections in discourse; see Hirst [1981a; 1981b].) Marker passing may then be extended to include this representation of context.

Because neither syntax nor global context are used yet, discourse focus cannot be used. Strictly speaking, Polaroid Words are wrong to even *try* to disambiguate *slug* in our example of Section 3.3, *the slug operated the vending machine*. Rather, a clever system would have first recognized that the use of the definite article *the* implies that a disambiguated referent for the NP can be found in the focus, and no other disambiguation action need be taken (unless no referent is found). Of course, this wouldn't help if the NP were *a slug*.

The last unused cue is the requirement made by some verbs that certain of their cases must be present or that certain combinations of cases are prohibited. Adding this would allow preposition PWs to rule out possibilities in which none of them translate to a required case. In English, however, required cases are only a very weak cue, for English has few compulsory cases, and syntax

---

15 For example, the word *keep* may mean **maintain** if followed by a direct object (*Nadia keeps chickens*), **continue to be** if followed by an adjectival phrase (*Nadia kept calm*), and **continue to do** if followed by a gerund (*Nadia kept dancing*).

serves to enforce most of them. A well-known example is the verb *break*, for which at least one of the cases *agent, patient*, and *instrument* must be present and be flagged by *SUBJ*. If we assume that the input is well-formed, then there will be a subject and it will be one of these three. An example of a compulsory case not enforced by syntax is the *location* case of the **place in position** sense of *put*:

(14) Ross put the luggage on the shelf.

(15) *Ross put the luggage.

This is a fact about the word *put* itself. An example of a prohibited combination of cases is the restriction for many (all?) verbs that an action in which the *patient* is flagged by the surface subject may not have an *instrument* expressed unless the verb is passive:

(16) The window broke.

(17) *The window broke with a rock.

(18) The window was broken with a rock.

4 *What Polaroid Words Can't Do*

It is possible, as I mentioned in Section 3.2, that a PW could cross all its meanings off its list and suddenly find itself embarrassed. One possible reason for such an occurrence is that the word, or one nearby, is being used metaphorically, metonymically, or synecdochically, or, more generally, in a sense that the system does not know about. It is not possible in such cases to determine which word was actually responsible for the failure. Thus, if the **female swan** sense of *pen* is unknown, and a failure therefore occurs on (19):

(19) The pen flew ...

there is no way of telling that the missing meaning is in *pen* rather than *fly*. Ideally, the system should try to look for possible metaphors, as in (20):

(20) The pen flew across the page.

Research by Gentner [1981a, 1981b] suggests that if the system is looking for a possible metaphor, it should try the verb first, because verbs are inherently more "adjustable" than nouns; Gentner found that nouns tend to refer to fixed entities, while verb meanings bend more readily to fit the context. For example, people tend to paraphrase (21) [Gentner, 1981a, p. 165]:

(21) The lizard worshipped.

as (22) rather than (23):

(22) The small grey reptile lay on a hot rock and stared unblinkingly at the sun.

(23) The nasty, despicable person participated in the church service.

Thus if a noun PW and a verb PW have irreconcilable differences, the noun should take precedence over the verb (regardless of which occurred first in the sentence—[Gentner, 1981a, p. 165]).[16] If the system is still unhappy after doing its best to interpret the input metaphorically, it should ask the user for help and try again. None of this is included in present-day Polaroid Words.

Note that these problems occur only in cases where slot restrictions are tested. In the case of conflicting unambiguous words, one or both being used in a new, metaphoric, metonymic, or synecdochic sense, the conflict will not be noticed until the final Absity output is sent to Frail, since there is no reason to have checked for consistency. This will also be the case when strong marker passing paths have caused a meaning to be chosen without checking slot restrictions, and in Section 5.1 I show that this is a desirable state of affairs.

5 *Psychological Reality*

Although cognitive modeling is a strategy for artificial intelligence system building rather than the main goal in this work, claims of psychological reality are interesting in their own right. In this section, therefore, I look at the degree of psychological reality in Polaroid Words with marker passing. I then discuss the importance of human data in the correct use of marker passing.

---

16 There are, of course, exceptions to this general strategy. In particular, some sentences cannot be interpreted metaphorically, or any way other than literally; and sometimes the verb takes precedence over the noun. This sentence (due, I believe, to George Lakoff) exemplifies both cases: *My toothbrush sings five-part madrigals.* The word *madrigal* is quite unambiguous, and fits so well with the literal meaning of *sing*, that the incompatibility of selectional restrictions on toothbrush and the agent slot of sing is resolved in favor of the latter, and the sentence gives most people an image of a toothbrush that is somehow singing. [I am grateful to Eugene Charniak for pointing this out to me.]

5.1 *Polaroid Words, Marker Passing, and Psycholinguistic Models*

Some degree of psychological reality was built into Polaroid Words from the start, in that their design was heavily influenced by the results of Swinney [1979; Swinney, this volume; Onifer and Swinney, 1981], who found that all meanings of an ambiguous word were accessed regardless of context. Similarly, PWs in all contexts start off with all their possible meanings available. This is in contrast to prior choice models such as the Schank and Abelson [1977] script approach, in which one meaning has already been selected as the right one for the context, each context having its own lexicon to evoke. As we saw in Section 1, the weight of evidence is now against these models. PWs also differ from ordered-search models in which meanings are tried one at a time, in a fixed order, until one fits.

Also, in accordance with Tanenhaus, Leiman, and Seidenberg's results [1979; Tanenhaus, this volume], all PW meanings are activated without regard for part of speech, since the marker passer has no access to syntactic information. Even though those meanings for what turns out to be the wrong syntactic category will be ignored, they will nevertheless have been used as the origin for marker passing, a fact which may affect later words (and probably adversely! See Section 5.2).

In addition, the use of marker passing as a mechanism for finding semantic associations was intended from the start to operate so as to model the effect of semantic priming. Unlike, for example, Hayes's CSAW disambiguation system [Hayes, 1977a; 1977b], which only searches its network for associations when it needs them, the MP is continually active in the background, spreading markers around and finding and reporting associations even between unambiguous words. A node from which a marker has been passed is, of course, just like one that has been semantically primed by spreading activation, in that it has been set up to permit a rapid detection of concept association. (I will, however, qualify these remarks in the next section.) The separation of world knowledge from lexical knowledge, with marker passing occurring only in the former, suffices to prevent contextually inappropriate meanings of a word from being pre-activated, in accordance with Lucas's results [1983].

However, the model is at variance with the results of Seidenberg, Tanenhaus, Leiman, and Bienkowski (STLB) [1982] published after the initial design of Polaroid Words (as described in Hirst and Charniak [1982]) was completed. STLB found that although multiple access is the norm, selective access seems to occur for semantically primed sentences such as (24):

(24) The farmer bought the <u>straw</u>.

All the same, a synthesis is possible if we make the following modification to PWs and MP. On starting, and before anything else happens, a new PW first checks whether any of its senses is already marked, that is, whether any immediate paths are available. If one is found, then that sense is chosen right away. Otherwise, things go on as before, with MP proceeding from all senses, looking for constructed paths. Since in the former case marker passing does not spread from unchosen meanings, they have not, in any real sense, been accessed. Thus, consistent with STLB's results, strong semantic priming would result in selective access but multiple access is still the norm—where strong semantic priming is, by definition, priming that results in an immediate marker passing path.

With or without this change, the model predicts speed differences in the disambiguation of semantically primed sentences such as (24), compared with non-priming biased sentences:

(25) The man walked on the <u>deck</u>.

The system will process (24) much faster than (25), because (24) should require only looking for MP chains, while (25) will look at the chains, find nothing, and then spend time dealing with slot restriction predicates in order to choose the right meaning of *deck*. The original model predicts two speed classes, the modified model predicts three. While these predictions seem plausible, there are as yet no relevant psychological data.

Polaroid Words also have the property that they can be led astray as people are by *negatively primed* sentences with *garden-path semantics* [Reder, 1983]. Thus, PWs will make the same mistakes that most people do with sentences such as (26), in which the wrong meaning of an ambiguous word receives strong semantic priming:

(26) The astronomer married the <u>star</u>.

Reder found that comprehension 'errors'—that is, inability to see the simple, literal meaning—increased markedly in such sentences. For example, in (26), people often take *star* to be **astronomical object** instead of **celebrity**, although this violates selectional restrictions on *marry*, and then become confused, or attempt to reinterpret the sentence metaphorically.[17] Similarly, MP will find the obvious chain between `astronomer` and `astronomical-object`; the PW for *star* will therefore choose the wrong meaning, and will not even notice that it violates the slot predicate for `marry`, because it doesn't even consider such matters if it is happy with the MP path. The error will be discovered only after the sentence is fully interpreted and Frail attempts to evaluate the erroneous

---

17 There seem to be wide individual differences in the processing of such sentences. This is to be expected, as people will differ in their mental organization of concepts and hence in the exact boundary effects of spreading activation.

frame statement that was built. Similarly, intuition suggests that people who have trouble with the sentence only detect the error at a late stage, and then invoke some kind of conscious error recovery mechanism, such as interpreting the sentence as a metaphor.

However, many people do seem to be able to recover from disambiguation errors in which the garden-path pull is not as strong as that of (26). Daneman and Carpenter [1983, p.566] gave subjects texts such as (27), in which subjects tended to initially choose the wrong meaning for the underlined word:

(27) The lights in the concert hall were dimmed. The audience watched intently as the famous violinist appeared on the stage. He stepped onto the podium and turned majestically to face the audience. He took a <u>bow</u> that was very gracefully propped on the music stand. The enthusiastic applause resounded throughout the hall.

They found that ability to recover from erroneous disambiguation correlated with scores on a reading span test,[18] which in turn correlated with verbal SAT scores.[19] Unfortunately, PWs presently recover from disambiguation errors like a reader with a very poor reading span—that is, they can't!

Lastly, PWs are in accord with psychological reality in that, when initially activated, they do not look at words to their right. They are thus in accord with the results of Stanovich and West [1983, p.55], who found, contrary to previous suggestions [Underwood, 1981], that there is in reading no effect from semantic characteristics of words in the right parafovea, that is, words to right of the fixation point.

In general, PWs (like the rest of the Absity system) are consistent with the trend of recent psychological results strongly suggesting that human language comprehension processes are modular, with limited interaction.

5.2 Psychological Non-Reality

In this section, I look at ways in which the system is at variance with psychological data, or for which psychological data are not yet available, but for which the predictions of PWs seem implausible [Hirst, 1984b].

One important way in which MP differs from psychological reality is in the decay of spreading activation. The data of Tanenhaus, Leiman, and

---

18 In these tests, subjects had to read a set of sentences aloud, and then recall the last word of each. A subject's reading span is the size of the set they could handle without errors in recall.

19 The Scholastic Aptitude Test (SAT) is a standardized test taken by applicants for college admission in the United States. It includes a test of verbal ability.

Seidenberg [1979] and Seidenberg, Tanenhaus, Leiman, and Bienkowski [1982] show that the facilitative effect of the activation of contextually incorrect meanings lasts less than 200 msec (at least in those cases where rejection can be immediate). This suggests that activation of unchosen meanings decays very quickly. On the other hand, in the PW system all markers remain until the end of the sentence, at which time they are all reset. This may mean that paths are found between these unchosen senses and senses of later words, a clearly misleading occurrence. While the PWs (or path checker; see Section 2.3) could check for such paths and eliminate them, it would be better if they didn't occur at all. At present, Frail does not support any form of selective removal of markers, so decay of activation from unchosen meanings could not be included in the present PW system.

The length of time that an ambiguous word may remain unresolved, with several alternatives active, probably also differs between PWs and people. In the present implementation, resolution will sometimes not take place until the very end of the sentence (see Section 3.4).[20] Most psycholinguistic studies have looked only at cases where there is sufficient information to disambiguate a word as soon as it occurs, and the data on how long people will hold off resolution, hoping that more cues will come in if there is initially insufficient information, are equivocal.

The two studies on the question of which I am aware are that of Hudson and Tanenhaus [1984] and that of Granger, Holbrook, and Eiselt (GHE) [1984]. Hudson and Tanenhaus found that when there is no disambiguating information, both possible meanings of an ambiguous word remained active 500 msec after the word, but only one was active at the next clause boundary even though there had been no disambiguating information. The implication is that a best guess is made. GHE's findings were quite different. They looked at two-sentence texts in which the second sentence might require reinterpretation of an ambiguous word that had occurred, with misleading bias, in the first. For example:

(28) The CIA called in an inspector to check for <u>bugs</u>. Some of the secretaries had reported seeing roaches.

The first sentence is intended to make the reader decide that *bugs* means **hidden-microphones**, while the second requires that it actually be **insects**. After reading such sentences, subjects had to decide quickly whether a presented word was semantically related to the text. The error rate was extremely high compared to control cases in which the word presented was related to the "in-

---

20 An earlier decision may be forced by the Semantic Enquiry Desk if the information is needed to resolve a structural ambiguity; see Hirst [1987, Sections 7.2.7 and 7.3.2].

correct" meaning of the ambiguous word of a sentence with misleading bias. GHE took this as evidence for *conditional retention*, i.e., both meanings being retained for the ambiguous word, even across the sentence boundary.

The results of GHE are suspect for several reasons. First, their test for whether a word sense was active was not a proper on-line measure of activation. Second, their probe words are suspect. Thus for (28), their probes were *ant* (related to the text) and *spy* (unrelated to the text). Subjects who said that *spy* was related to the text were deemed to have made an "error," and this was taken as support for the hypothesis that the "incorrect" meaning of *bug* was still active. But clearly the word *spy* **is** related to the text, regardless of how the subject handles the word *bug*, simply because the word *CIA* was present in the text! Indeed, it is hard to imagine how to construct a probe that is sensitive to the activity of the "incorrect" meaning of the ambiguous word and yet not sensitive to the global context that was deliberately introduced to create the misleading bias.

What, then, can we reliably say about when a final decision is made on an ambiguous word? Intuition (which is not always a reliable source) suggests that while people will delay a decision on an ambiguous word for a little while, they will, nevertheless, usually make a final decision within a few words (or constituents?) of the ambiguity.[21] That a decision may be delayed is evidenced by the fact that people are not generally garden-pathed by sentences such as these:

(29) Nadia's favorite club is the five-iron.

(30) Nadia's favorite club is The Carlton.

(31) Nadia's favorite book is *The House at Pooh Corner*. *(book =* **literary work***)*

(32) Nadia's favorite book is her signed first edition of *The House at Pooh Corner*. *(book =* **printed volume***)*

If people made an immediate "best guess" at the meaning of the ambiguous words *club* and *book*, then at least one of each of the above pairs should be inconsistent with the way a given individual is predisposed to guess, and therefore be a garden-path sentence for that individual. (Obviously, the strategy of making an immediate best guess would make language comprehension rather

---

21 Nevertheless, there is evidence [Just and Carpenter, 1980; Daneman and Carpenter, 1983] for the psychological reality of a "sentence wrap-up" process in reading, in which remaining loose ends, such as unresolved references, are treated. It is possible that some residual disambiguation occurs as part of this process.

difficult at times.) It seems, therefore, that disambiguation of the examples above is incomplete until the final NP of the sentence is understood.

On the other hand, however, it is my intuition that a word such as *crook* in sentence (6) of Section 3.4 is not resolved at the end of the sentence, as in PWs, but long before, possibly by the time the verb is processed:

(33) The crook operated ...

This choice seems to be based on probability: inanimate *instrument* subjects are a lot less frequent than animate *agents*, and, moreover, shepherd's staffs are rather unusual instruments for operating anything. The choice does not occur right after *crook* on the basis of the relative infrequency of shepherd's staffs as a topic of modern urban conversation, as most people have no trouble with (34):

(34) The crook fell from the hook on which it was hanging.

This suggests that PWs should use a *cumulating evidence* approach and jettison unlikely alternatives quickly if there is no positive evidence for them. That is, one does not make an immediate best guess, but one does make a reasonable guess as soon as there is enough information to do so, even if one cannot be definite.[22] This has the advantage of helping to prevent combinatorial explosion. However, I have been loath to consider using this approach in Polaroid Words, in view of the dearth of data on the corresponding human behavior and the fuzziness of the whole notion. Any interim solution would have to fall back on "magic numbers," and we have too many of those already (see next section). Nevertheless, PWs do use the relative frequency of the various meanings of an ambiguous word in some of their decisions (avoiding where possible tricks with magic numbers; see Section 3.4), but since we know little of how people use word frequency in lexical ambiguity resolution, I have limited its use in PWs to tidying up loose ends at the end of a sentence. Another possibility that might be considered is to retain the present timing of decision making in PWs, but add a mechanism that watches out for looming combinatorial explosion and forces PWs to make an early guess if it senses danger.

Another prediction of Polaroid Words for which there is no psychological data is that case selection is performed by a subset of essentially the same mechanisms as lexical disambiguation. It is not clear how such a prediction

---

22 Kurtzman [1984] found that, in the case of structural ambiguity, the point of resolution varies widely, sometimes coming long before the disambiguating information, and sometimes not, in a manner very consistent with the idea of accumulating evidence. However, I know of no data addressing this issue for lexical ambiguity.

could even be tested. The system also predicts the psychological reality of pseudo-prepositions, which almost certainly cannot be sustained.

Lastly, a few words should be said about marker passing. While we were happy to admit it as a discrete model of spreading activation, it should be pointed out that there are several competing theories of spreading activation. While these vary in their closeness to Frail marker passing, almost all of them differ in one important way. They assume that there is a certain limited amount of activation available to spread, and that spreading along a link 'costs' activation. Spreading stops when all activation is 'spent.' When activation arrives at each node, it is divided among the outgoing arcs and an amount of it is passed along each. The division need not be equal; some links in the network may be *stronger* than others, and more activation spreads across strong links [Collins and Loftus, 1975; Lorch 1982]. However, in Frail (and, hence, in MP) at present, all links are of equal strength, and all markers have the same status. (This is to be changed in future versions of Frail. It is also planned that the amount of activation spread from a node will be inversely proportional to the number of siblings it has [Hendler, 1986].)

5.3 *Marker Passing, Path Strength, and Magic Numbers*

One of the more vexed problems in using association cues for disambiguation, is knowing when an association is strong enough to be considered conclusive evidence. We know from the existence of semantic garden-path sentences that associations alone should sometimes cause immediate jumping to a conclusion; we also know that this isn't true of all associations, for we are not garden-pathed by sentences like (35):

(35) The <u>lawyer</u> stopped at the <u>bar</u> for a drink. *(bar is not taken in any of its legal senses)*

We therefore need some measure of the strength of an association, so that PWs will be able to jump to conclusions (rightly or wrongly) in the same situations that people do.[23] Although frequency of the use of the concepts should be a factor in determining the strength of an association (see also [Anderson, 1983]),[24] I shall limit my remarks below to a discussion of the *semantic distance* between two concepts.

---

23 We have already identified one such situation in Section 5.1, namely, whenever an immediate MP path is found.
24 Eugene Charniak (personal communication) has suggested that PWs should jump to a conclusion whenever marker passing selects a preferred meaning.

I mentioned in the previous section that most theories of spreading activation assume that different links have different strengths, though Frail does not attempt to model this. It is generally assumed that link strength is correlated with semantic distance—that a link between two concepts is strong exactly when they are very closely associated. Cases when this occurs may include one concept being a salient property of the other (**edibility, food**), or, possibly, a particularly good exemplar of the other (**robin, bird**);[25] a high frequency of use also strengthens a link [Collins and Loftus, 1975; Anderson, 1983] and hence the association between the concepts. On the other hand, de Groot [1983] has found that activation does not spread to associates of associates of a node—for example, **bull** and **cow** are linked and so are **cow** and **milk**, but activation from **bull** does not reach **milk**. Thus, PWs need a way to take an MP path and determine its strength, i.e., the semantic distance between its endpoints, by looking at the links and nodes that it includes.

The present, inadequate method of measuring path strength is a function of the length of the path, the nodes it passes through, and the links it uses. I use the following heuristics:

•   The shorter the path, the stronger it is.

•   The more arcs that leave a node, the weaker the connections through that node are (see also the anti-promiscuity rule, Section 2.3).

These methods, though I use them, are unsatisfactory because, like the marker passing constraints (Section 2.3), they rely heavily on *magic numbers*. For example, the second suggests that any node will not be vague if it has only N arcs, but $N + 1$ arcs will invariably tip the scale. This seems unlikely. And even if there were a neat threshold like that, how do we know that N is it?—it is merely a number that seems to work in the present implementation, but there is no principled reason for it. There is, of course, well-known evidence for the psychological reality of magic numbers in certain perceptual and short term memory processes [Miller, 1956], but it is hard to believe that this carries over to marker passing in long term memory, where activation seems to be a continuous, not discrete, variable.

It is hoped that future versions of MP will be able to include such features as path strength and the weakening of activation as it gets further from the origin, so that we won't have to worry about *posthoc* measurements of path

---

25 It is often reported that people are faster at making categorization judgments for typical exemplars such as **robin**—**bird** than atypical ones such as **chicken**—**bird** [Rips, Shoben, and Smith, 1973; Smith, Shoben, and Rips 1974; Collins and Loftus, 1975]. This may be taken as evidence for the existence of typicality links, though Collins and Loftus [1975] show that it may be explained by the procedures by which positive and negative evidence for such decisions is gathered and evaluated.

strength. This would be a first step in approximating the continuous nature of spreading activation.

6 *Conclusion*

I have presented a pair of cooperating mechanisms that both disambiguate word senses and determine case slots by finding connections between concepts in a network of frames and by negotiating with one another to find a set of mutually satisfactory meanings. PW processes work in parallel with a parser, Paragram, and a semantic interpreter, Absity, permitting them to deal with ambiguous words as if their semantic object were assigned immediately. (Hirst [1987, Chapter 7] shows how PWs can also help in structural disambiguation.) The same PW control structure may be used for all syntactic categories. Polaroid Words minimize the need for separate, ill-motivated, purely linguistic knowledge; they have access to system's world knowledge and use it wherever possible.

Polaroid Words are implemented as processes that interpret data structures containing purely lexical information that each word has in its dictionary entry. This is in contrast to approaches such as Small's [Adriaens and Small, this volume], where the meaning of a word is represented as a large, barely constrained procedure, different for every word, which parses and performs semantic interpretation as well as lexical disambiguation. Rather, the parser, Absity, and the marker passer do much of the work that Small requires his "word experts" to perform. We thereby capture generalizations in disambiguation, needing only one type of PW for each syntactic category and relying almost exclusively on general world knowledge.

Polaroid Words do not yet use syntactic disambiguation cues or global context, nor can they handle metaphor and metonymy. Table 1 shows some examples of sentences that the system can handle and some that it can't.

Acknowledgments

This work grew out of many discussions with Eugene Charniak. I have also received helpful comments on it from James Allen, Phil Hayes, Jim Hendler, Jennifer Holbrook, Susan Hudson, Margery Lucas, Susan McRoy, Amy Rakowsky, Anonymous Referee, and Nadia Talent. Jean-Pierre Corriveau and Diane Horton commented helpfully on earlier drafts of the paper. Parts of this paper are based on a chapter of Hirst [1987], and are used with the kind permission of Cambridge University Press. At Brown University, financial support for this work was provided in part by the U.S. Office of Naval Research under

Table 1   What Polaroid Words can and can't do

Sentences that can be disambiguated

SUBJ the slug operated OBJ the vending machine.

SUBJ the crook operated OBJ the pizza parlor.

SUBJ the crook wanted to kidnap OBJ Ross.

SUBJ Nadia's plane taxied to the terminal.

SUBJ the man walked on the deck.

SUBJ the deep philosopher threw OBJ the peach pit into the deep pit.

Sentences that can't be disambiguated

The astronomer married the star. *Marker passing is misled.*

The view from the window would be improved by a plant. *Requires inference.*

I want to eliminate some moles. *No disambiguating information.*

Ross was escorted from the bar to the dock. *Two parallel MP paths.*

SUBJ the vending machine was operated by the slug. *No passives yet.*

---

contract number N00014-79-C-0592 (Eugene Charniak, Principal Investigator). Preparation of this paper at the University of Toronto was supported by the Natural Sciences and Engineering Research Council of Canada.

References

Adriaens, G. and Small, Steven. This volume.

Anderson, John Robert. 1983. A spreading activation theory of memory. *Journal of Verbal Learning and Verbal Behavior* 22(3):261–295.

Becker, Joseph D. 1975. The phrasal lexicon. In *Proceedings, [Interdisciplinary Workshop on] Theoretical Issues in Natural Language Processing*, pp. 70–73. Cambridge, Massachusetts.

Charniak, Eugene. 1983a. A parser with something for everyone. In King, Margaret (ed.), *Parsing Natural Language*, pp. 117–149. London: Academic Press.

Charniak, Eugene. 1983b. Passing markers: A theory of contextual influence in language comprehension. *Cognitive Science* 7(3):171–190.

Charniak, Eugene. 1986. A neat theory of marker passing. *Proceedings, Fifth National Conference on Artificial Intelligence (AAAI-86)*, pp. 584-588. Philadelphia, August 1986. Los Altos: Morgan Kaufmann Publishers..

Charniak, Eugene; Gavin, Michael Kevin; and Hendler, James Alexander. 1983. The FRAIL/NASL reference manual. Technical Report No. CS–83–06, Department of Computer Science, Brown University, February 1983.

Collins, Allan M. and Loftus, Elizabeth F. 1975. A spreading-activation theory of semantic processing. *Psychological Review* 82(6):407–428.

Daneman, Meredyth and Carpenter, Patricia A. 1983. Individual differences in integrating information between and within sentences. *Journal of Experimental Psychology: Learning, Memory and Cognition* 9(4):561–581.

DeGroot, Annette M. B. 1983. The range of automatic spreading activation in word priming. *Journal of Verbal Learning and Verbal Behavior* 22(4):417–436.

Fahlman, Scott Elliot. 1979. *NETL: A System for Representing and Using Real-World Knowledge.* (MIT Press series in artificial intelligence). Cambridge: MIT Press.

Gentner, Dedre. 1981a. Some interesting differences between nouns and verbs. *Cognition and Brain Theory* 4(2):161–178.

Gentner, Dedre. 1981b. Integrating verb meanings into context. *Discourse Processes* 4(4):349–375.

Granger, Richard H, Jr; Holbrook, Jennifer K., and Eiselt, Kurt P. 1984. Interaction effects between word-level and text-level inferences: On-line processing of ambiguous words in context. In *Proceedings, Sixth Annual Conference of the Cognitive Science Society*, pp. 172–178.

Hayes, Philip J. 1977a. *Some Association-based Techniques for Lexical Disambiguation by Machine.* Doctoral dissertation, Département de Mathématiques, École polytechnique fédérale de Lausanne. Published as Technical Report No. 25, Department of Computer Science, University of Rochester, June 1977.

Hayes, Philip J. 1977b. On semantic nets, frames and associations. In *Proceedings, 5th International Joint Conference on Artificial Intelligence*, Cambridge, Massachusetts, pp. 99–107. Los Altos: Morgan Kaufmann.

Hendler, James Alexander. 1986. *Integrating Marker-Passing and Problem Solving: A Spreading-Activation Approach to Improved Choice in Planning.* Doctoral dissertation [available as Technical Report No. CS–86–01], Department of Computer Science, Brown University, January 1986.

Hendler, James Alexander. 1987. Issues in the design of marker-passing systems. In Boudeaux, J. C. Hamill, Bruce W. and Jernigan, Robert (eds.), *The Role of Language in Problem Solving 2*. Amsterdam: North-Holland.

Hirst, Graeme. 1981a. *Anaphora in Natural Language Understanding: A Survey* (Lecture notes in computer science 119). New York: Springer-Verlag.

Hirst, Graeme. 1981b. Discourse-oriented anaphora resolution in natural language understanding: A review. *American Journal of Computational Linguistics* 7(2):85–98.

Hirst, Graeme. 1983. A foundation for semantic interpretation. In *Proceedings, 21st Annual Meeting of the Association for Computational Linguistics*, pp. 64–73. Cambridge, Massachusetts.

Hirst, Graeme. 1984a. A semantic process for syntactic disambiguation. In *Proceedings, Fourth National Conference on Artificial Intelligence (AAAI-84)*, pp. 148–152. Austin, August 1984. Los Altos: Morgan Kaufmann.

Hirst, Graeme. 1984b. Jumping to conclusions: Psychological reality and unreality in a word disambiguation program. In *Proceedings, Sixth Annual Conference of the Cognitive Science Society*, pp. 179–182. Boulder, June 1984.

Hirst, Graeme. 1987. *Semantic Interpretation and the Resolution of Ambiguity.* (Studies in natural language processing). Cambridge: Cambridge University Press.

Hirst, Graeme and Charniak, Eugene. 1982. Word sense and case slot disambiguation. In *Proceedings, National Conference on Artificial Intelligence*, pp. 95–98. Pittsburgh, August 1982. Los Altos: Morgan Kaufmann.

Hudson, Susan B. and Tanenhaus, Michael K. 1984. Ambiguity resolution in the absence of contextual bias. In *Proceedings, Sixth Annual Conference of the Cognitive Science Society*, pp. 188–192. Boulder, June 1984.

Just, Marcel Adam and Carpenter, Patricia A. 1980. Inference processes during reading: From eye fixations to comprehension. *Psychological Review* 87(4):329–354.

Kurtzman, Howard Steven. 1984. *Studies in Syntactic Ambiguity Resolution.* Doctoral dissertation, Department of Psychology, Massachusetts Institute of Technology, 13 September 1984. Indiana University Linguistics Club.

Lorch, Robert F, Jr. 1982. Priming and search processes in semantic memory: A test of three models of spreading activation. *Journal of Verbal Learning and Verbal Behavior* 21(4):468–492.

Lucas, Margery M. 1983. Lexical access during sentence comprehension: Frequency and context effects. In *Proceedings, Fifth Annual Conference of the Cognitive Science Society*, Rochester, New York, May 1983.

Marcus, Mitchell P. 1980. *A Theory of Syntactic Recognition for Natural Language.* Cambridge: MIT Press.

Miller, George Armitage. (1956). The magical number seven, plus or minus two: Some limits on our capacity for processing information. *Psychological Review* 63(2):81–97.

Onifer, William. and Swinney, David A. 1981. Accessing lexical ambiguities during sentence comprehension: Effects of frequency of meaning and contextual bias. *Memory and Cognition* 9(3):225–236.

Quillian, M Ross. 1962. A revised design for an understanding machine. *Mechanical Translation* 7(1):17–29.

Quillian, M Ross. 1968. Semantic memory. In Minsky, Marvin Lee (ed.), *Semantic Information Processing*. Cambridge: MIT Press.

Quillian, M Ross. 1969. The teachable language comprehender: A simulation program and theory of language. *Communications of the ACM* 12(8):459–476.

Reder, Lynne M. 1983. What kind of pitcher can a catcher fill? Effects of priming in sentence comprehension. *Journal of Verbal Learning and Verbal Behavior* 22(2):189–202.

Rips, Lance J., Shoben, Edward J., and Smith, Edward E. 1973. Semantic distance and the verification of semantic relations. *Journal of Verbal Learning and Verbal Behavior* 12(1):1–20.

Schank, Roger Carl and Abelson, Robert Paul. 1977. *Scripts, Plans, Goals and Understanding: An Enquiry into Human Knowledge Structures*. Hillsdale: Erlbaum.

Seidenberg, Mark S., Tanenhaus, Michael K., Leiman, James Mehner, and Bienkowski, Marie A. 1982. Automatic access of the meanings of ambiguous words in context: Some limitations of knowledge-based processing. *Cognitive Psychology* 14(4):489–537.

Smith, Edward E., Shoben, Edward J., and Rips, Lance J. 1974. Structure and process in semantic memory: A featural model for semantic decisions. *Psychological Review* 81(3):214–241.

Stanovich, Keith E. and West, Richard F. 1983. The generalizability of context effects on word recognition: A reconsideration of the roles of parafoveal priming and sentence context. *Memory and Cognition* 11(1):49–58.

Swinney, David A. 1979. Lexical access during sentence comprehension: (Re)Consideration of context effects. *Journal of Verbal Learning and Verbal Behavior* 18(6):645–659.

Swinney, David A. This volume.

Tanenhaus, Michael K. This volume.

Tanenhaus, Michael K., Leiman, James Mehner, and Seidenberg, Mark S. 1979. Evidence for multiple stages in the processing of ambiguous words in syntactic contexts. *Journal of Verbal Learning and Verbal Behavior* 18(4):427–440.

Underwood, Geoffrey. 1981. Lexical recognition of embedded unattended words: Some implications for reading processes. *Acta Psychologica* 47:267–283.

Wilensky, Robert and Arens, Yigal. 1980a. PHRAN: A knowledge-based approach to natural language analysis. Memo UCB/ERL M80/34, Electronics Research Laboratory, University of California, Berkeley.

Wilensky, Robert and Arens, Yigal. 1980b. PHRAN: A knowledge-based natural language understander. In *Proceedings, 18th Annual Meeting of the As-*

sociation for Computational Linguistics, pp. 117–121. Philadelphia, June 1980.

Wong, Douglas. 1981a. Language comprehension in a problem solver. In *Proceedings, 7th International Joint Conference on Artificial Intelligence*, pp. 7–12. Vancouver, August. Los Altos: Morgan Kaufmann.

Wong, Douglas. 1981b. *On the Unification of Language Comprehension with Problem Solving*. Doctoral dissertation [available as Technical Report No. CS-78], Department of Computer Science, Brown University.

4

Are Vague Words Ambiguous?

Steven L. Lytinen

Department of Electrical Engineering and Computer Science

The University of Michigan

1 *Introduction*

A difficult problem facing natural language understanding systems which use a frame-based [Minsky, 1975] representation scheme is the *frame selection* problem [Charniak, 1982], the task of selecting the appropriate frame(s) to represent the meaning of a given input. There are instances in which this is a relatively straightforward task. For example, a natural language system which processed stories about crime might very easily have an ARREST frame, which would capture the system's knowledge about what happens when a criminal is arrested by the police. If such a frame existed, it would be easy to select this frame to represent a sentence like "The police arrested a criminal," since the word "arrested" refers quite directly to the ARREST frame. More often, however, frame selection is much less straightforward. For instance, the ARREST frame would also be appropriate to represent "The police took a suspect into their custody," although no single word in this sentence unambiguously refers to ARREST.

In many previous natural language understanding systems, frame selection has been viewed as a *lexical ambiguity* problem. In this approach, words which can refer to more than one possible frame are treated as ambiguous, in that part of the system's knowledge about these words is a list of the possible frames to which they could refer. Frame selection rules take on the form of disambiguation rules, in that they are responsible for choosing which sense of an ambiguous word is being used in a given context (i.e., which frame should be chosen from the list).

In this paper, it will be argued that treating frame selection as lexical disambiguation is a mistake for a large class of words, which I will call *vague*. As an alternative, I will propose an approach in which frame selection for these words is performed by a *concept refinement* process. In this approach, the representation of a vague word is also vague initially. As more about the context is filled in by the parser, the initially vague representation is refined, or further specified.

The concept refinement approach to frame selection is driven by a knowledge base which is not lexically based, in direct contrast to disambiguation approaches. Instead, a hierarchically organized knowledge base of frames is used, in conjunction with a set of concept refinement rules which encode the system's knowledge about when contextual information should cause further refinement of the system's representations. The same hierarchy and same set of concept refinement rules is used to select frames for all vague words.

The concept refinement approach to frame selection has been implemented in a natural language understander which was part of the MOPTRANS system [Lytinen, 1984], a machine translation system which translated short (1–3 sentence) newspaper articles about terrorism and crime between several different languages. The system parsed stories in English, Spanish, French, German, and Chinese. The generator for this system produced translations in English or German. Twenty-five to 50 example stories were successfully translated for each input language.

The MOPTRANS parser used the same knowledge base of frames and frame selection rules to parse stories in all five input languages. This indicates that not only is frame selection knowledge for vague words not lexically-based, this knowledge is not even specific to the processing of a particular language.

2 What is a Vague Word?

Many words in English and other languages have different meanings in different contexts. In this paper, I will make a distinction between two types of words for which this is the case: *vague* words and *genuinely ambiguous* words. This distinction roughly corresponds to the distinction between *polysemous* words (words whose different meanings are related) and *homonomous* words (words whose meanings are unrelated). To explain this distinction, consider the following sentences:

John the went to the store.

John went to Australia in a plane.

John went to California to start a new job.

Chances are that in a rich enough representational system, each of these three uses of "went" would result in the selection of a different frame. This is because the different situations that "went" refers to cause us to expect different things. These expectations should be reflected by different representational structures. In the first example, we would expect that John would not stay at the store long, and would probably buy something there. So a frame like SHOPPING-TRIP would be appropriate. In the second sentence, since we know that John used an airplane to go to Australia, AIRPLANE-TRIP would be a better frame to use. Finally, in the third sentence, a frame like CHANGE-RESIDENCE would capture the meaning of "went" best.

Although "went" is ambiguous in that the same frame would not be used to represent all uses of the word, the possible frames all have something nontrivial in common. Namely, they all refer to a change in location. Moreover, "went" *completely covers* all actions which fit this description; in other words, any action which could be described as "a change in location" could be expressed using the word "went." Because of this, "went" is an example of a *vague* word.

In contrast, the possible meanings of other ambiguous words do not share commonalities in meaning. For example, consider the following uses of the word "draws":

John draws impressionistic paintings.

A winning team draws a lot of fans.

It is true that the meanings of "draws" illustrated by these examples have something in common, in that they both refer to some sort of action. However, "draws" does not completely cover this description, because there are many actions which cannot be expressed using this word. Because of this, "draws" is *genuinely ambiguous.* As is the case for vague words, more than one frame could be used to represent "draws," but there is no abstract description of these frames for which "draws" could be used to express any coloration of the abstract description.

Putting this distinction another way, here is a test designed to determine whether a word is vague or genuinely ambiguous:

1. If a word always refers unambiguously to the same frame, then it is neither vague nor ambiguous.

2. Otherwise, come up with the most specific description possible of the word which encompasses all of its possible meanings. This description should not use disjunctions (i.e., it cannot simply be a list of the word's meanings, which would be the most specific such description).

3. Try to think of an action or object, of any level of specificity, which fits the abstract description. If there is any such action or object which could not be expressed using the word in question, then the word is genuinely ambiguous. If not, the word is vague.

Obviously this is not a formal test, but it captures the intuitive difference between vague and genuinely ambiguous words. This distinction, I will claim, is important with regards to frame selection.

3 *Frame Selection as Word Disambiguation*

Frame selection in many previous parsers has been treated as a word disambiguation problem. For example, consider the ELI parser [Riesbeck and Schank, 1976]. Parsing knowledge in ELI was encoded largely in the form of *requests*, which were test-action pairs stored mainly in the parser's lexicon. A request could be in one of two states: active or inactive. A request was activated when the parser encountered a word whose dictionary entry contained it. Once active, a request stayed active until it *fired*, or was executed; or until it was explicitly deactivated by another request. A request fired if it was in the active state and the conditions of active memory satisfied the test portion of its test-action pair.

Requests were responsible for making most of the decisions that took place during parsing, including frame selection. Requests performed frame selection, by means of word disambiguation, in one of two ways, which more or less corresponded to *bottom-up* and *top-down*. In the bottom-up method, the dictionary entry of a word which could refer to more than one frame (which in ELI were Conceptual Dependency primitives [Schank, 1975]) contained pointers (in the form of requests) to all the possible primitives to which it could refer. Thus, selecting a frame for a word was a matter of disambiguating the word to one of its meanings. A word was disambiguated when one of the requests in the dictionary definition of the ambiguous word fired, thereby choosing the word sense that it pointed to as the meaning of the word.

The bottom-up method performed the disambiguation of the word "wants" in the following two examples:

John wants Mary.

John wants the book.

The Conceptual Dependency parses for these two sentences are quite complicated, and the details of how "wants" is represented are not relevant here, since it is represented the same way for both sentences. What is represented differently in these two examples is the object of John's wanting:

$$\text{JOHN} \leftrightarrow \text{wants} \leftarrow \text{MARY} \leftrightarrow \text{PTRANS} \leftarrow \text{Mary} \leftarrow \begin{array}{l} \rightarrow \text{John} \\ \\ \leftarrow \text{?} \end{array}$$

$$\text{JOHN} \leftrightarrow \text{wants} \leftarrow \text{?} \leftrightarrow \text{ATRANS} \leftarrow \text{book} \leftarrow \begin{array}{l} \rightarrow \text{John} \\ \\ \leftarrow \text{?} \end{array}$$

The difference between the representations reflects the fact that the first sentence means, more or less, the same as "John wants Mary to be near him," while the second sentence is closer to "John wants possession of the book to be passed to him." Thus, in the first representation, the CD primitive PTRANS (transfer of physical location) is used, while ATRANS (transfer of control of an object) is the appropriate primitive in the second example.

In order to produce two different parses for these two sentences, Riesbeck's dictionary definition of the word "wants" contained two requests (among others), each of which would produce one of the two conceptual dependency configurations above. These requests, in prose form, were as follows:

> If "wants" is followed by a word which refers to an inanimate object, then its OBJECT is an ATRANS of the inanimate object to the ACTOR of "wants."

> If "wants" is followed by a word which refers to a person, then its OBJECT is a PTRANS of the person to the ACTOR of "wants."

At times, frame selection was also performed in a top-down fashion. This method was similar to the bottom-up method, in that frame selection was still treated as a disambiguation problem. In this method, however, the dictionary definition of the ambiguous word consisted simply of a list of word senses. A request from some previous word in the text was then responsible for selecting a word sense, and thus selecting a frame to represent the ambiguous word.

The top-down method was used to disambiguate the word "beat" in the following example:

> John and Mary were racing. John beat Mary.

The dictionary definition of "beat" consisted of two senses, BEAT1 and BEAT2. BEAT1 corresponded to the "physical beating" sense of "beat," while BEAT2 corresponded to the "victory" sense of the word, as in the example above. BEAT1, the sense corresponding to a physical beating, was the default sense of the word. Thus, if no requests fired when the parser encountered the word "beat," it was taken to mean BEAT1. In the example above, however, the context of "racing" activated a request, which activated a "contextual cluster of conceptualizations." This cluster contained information about other conceptualizations which were likely to appear in a racing story, as well as information about which senses of ambiguous words would be used in a racing context. One piece of information in the cluster pointed to by "racing" was that the sense BEAT2, the sense meaning "victory," is the sense of "beat" used in racing stories. Thus, when the contextual cluster of conceptualizations was activated by the word "racing," a request was activated which expected the sense BEAT2 of "beat." When the parser encountered the word "beat," this request fired, and BEAT2 was activated instead of BEAT1.

The frame selection problem was somewhat limited in the ELI system, in that representations consisted of the 12 or so Conceptual Dependency primitives. Thus, there was a relatively small number of frames from which to choose. However, this approach to frame selection has been used in other systems as well, in which frame selection was a larger problem. For example, in the Integrated Partial Parser (IPP) [Lebowitz, 1980], which parsed stories in the domain of terrorism, much more specific frames, or S-MOPS, were used to represent texts. Thus, the number of frames which a word could refer to was potentially much larger.

IPP's frame selection process was very similar to ELI's top-down disambiguation. For instance, the word "seized" could refer to several different frames, including HIJACK, TAKE-OVER (a building), and KIDNAP. Part of the dictionary definition of "seized" included a list of possible frames from which to choose. Then, expectations (in the form of requests) from already active frames were responsible for deciding which sense of the word was appropriate; i.e., which frame to choose. Thus, if the frame EXTORT was already active, then "seized" was disambiguated to the sense meaning HIJACK, since hijackings are often part of extortions.

Another system which used a similar approach was the Word Expert Parser [Small, 1980]. In this system, request-like test-action pairs called *demons* were used in a similar fashion to disambiguate words. The dictionary definition of each ambiguous word in the system contained a discrimination net of possible frames to which the word could refer, as well as a group of demons which were used to find the word's slot-fillers and to determine under what conditions a particular frame should be chosen. For example, Small's parser was capable of selecting any of several frames to represent the word "throw," corresponding to meanings such as "to throw out garbage," "to throw a party," "to throw in the towel," and "to throw a ball." Frames such as PERSON-THROW, THROW-OBJECT-TO-LOCATION, THROW-OUT-GARBAGE, etc., organized into a discrimination net, were contained in the word's dictionary entry. Also included in the dictionary entry were demons to fill the slots of whatever concept "throw" referred to, and then determine which concept "throw" referred to based on the slot-fillings. Some of these demons were the following, in prose form:

Look for an active concept in memory and assign it as the agent of "throw."

If the agent of "throw" is a PERSON, then refine "throw" to PERSON-THROW.

Wait for a concept after "throw" which is a MEAL, GARBAGE, a SMALL-PHYSOBJ, and PERSON, a CONTEST, or a PARTY, and assign it as the object of PERSON-THROW.

If the object of PERSON-THROW is GARBAGE, then refine PERSON-THROW to THROW-OUT-GARBAGE.

If the object of PERSON-THROW is a SMALL-PHYSOBJ, then refine PERSON-THROW to THROW-OBJECT-TO-LOCATION.

These rules are very much in the spirit of Riesbeck's requests for bottom-up disambiguation.

A somewhat different approach to frame selection as word disambiguation was presented in in [Hirst, 1983]. Hirst used what he called *Polaroid Words* to disambiguate semantically ambiguous words, provided all the possible uses of a word were of the same syntactic class. In his approach, the dictionary entry of an ambiguous word contained a list of all of its different possible meanings. At parse time, a Polaroid Word was built for each ambiguous word in a sentence. Each Polaroid Word was responsible for eliminating all but one of its word's possible senses, by means of testing each sense's compatibility with the surrounding context. To enable this, Polaroid Words communicated with each other in limited ways. When one possible meaning of a word was eliminated, the Polaroid Word responsible for the word communicated this to other Polaroid Words, which in turn used this information to try to eliminate possible meanings of their ambiguous words. Thus, possibilities were gradually eliminated, until the disambiguation process was complete.

An example which Hirst presented was the sentence "The slug operated the vending machine," in which both "slug" and "operated" were ambiguous words. Their dictionary definitions were the following:[1]

```
[slug (noun):                [operate (verb):
   gastropod-without-shell      [cause-to-function
   bullet                          agent        SUBJ
   metal-stamping                  patient      SUBJ, OBJ
   shot-of-liquor]                 instrument   SUBJ, with]
```

---

1 The dictionary definitions shown here are slightly simplified, with some portions that are irrelevant to this example left out.

```
[perform-surgery
    agent        SUBJ
    patient      upon,  on
    instrument   with]
```

The dictionary definition of "operate," in addition to providing a list of its possible meanings, also provided information as to where the semantic cases of the frames that it could refer to could be found. Thus, if "operate" meant PERFORM-SURGERY, then its subject would fill the AGENT case, its PATIENT would follow the preposition "upon" or "on," etc.

Hirst's parser used pseudo-prepositions, SUBJ and OBJ, inserted before the subject and object of the sentence. These pseudo-prepositions were treated as regular words, and were defined in the dictionary according to the semantic cases that they could mark. Since they could mark more than one case, they too were ambiguous. Here are their dictionary definitions:

```
[SUBJ (prep):              [OBJ (prep):
    agent      animate         patient     thing
    instrument physobj         transferee  physobj]
    patient    physobj]
```

The disambiguation process worked as follows. First, "operated" provided the information to SUBJ that if SUBJ marked the AGENT case, the noun phrase that followed would have to be HANIM (higher animate). Since "slug" could not refer to a HANIM, SUBJ used this information to conclude that it did not refer to AGENT, leaving INSTRUMENT and PATIENT as possibilities. Next, since the definition of "operate" specified that SUBJ would flag the AGENT case if "operate" meant PERFORM-SURGERY, this meaning of "operated" could be eliminated, since SUBJ had already eliminated AGENT as a possible meaning. Thus, "operated" meant CAUSE-TO-FUNCTION.

Once "operated" was disambiguated, OBJ knew that it must mark the case PATIENT, due to case information from the CAUSE-TO-FUNCTION definition of "operate." Since cases could only be marked once in a sentence, this provided SUBJ with enough information to conclude that it must refer to INSTRUMENT. Finally, "slug" was disambiguated by a different mechanism, called *marker passing*, which found a path between the METAL-STAMPING sense of "slug" and "vending machine."

Hirst's approach is different from Riesbeck's and Small's in that his system's slot-filling rules, which relied more heavily on an explicit syntactic analysis of the input text, were separated from the system's disambiguation rules. However, all three approaches have in common the fact that associated with every ambiguous word is knowledge about all possible frames which could be used to represent the word. Also, each system used an approach in which one or more decision-making structures (i.e., requests, demons, or Polaroid Words) were built for each possible meaning of an ambiguous word. Each one of these structures was responsible for determining whether or not a particular frame should be selected.

The implication of this approach is that frame selection knowledge is organized around particular words. In other words, there is little or no frame selection knowledge that is more general, that can apply to the selecting of a frame for a class of words, or for the process in general. Associated with every word is an exhaustive list of the possible frames which could represent the word, along with knowledge about when it is appropriate to select which frame. This knowledge is encoded in terms of rules about specific meanings of particular words, not in terms of broader rules that apply to the problem in general.

4 Frame Selection as Concept Refinement

The word disambiguation approaches of previous systems may or may not be appropriate for frame selection in the case of genuinely ambiguous words.[2] However, it is definitely a mistake to use this approach in frame selection of vague words. One problem with this approach is that it requires that a word be associated with a list of all the possible frames which could be used to represent the word. For very vague words, we would need a very long list.

Another problem with the disambiguation approach to frame selection is its implication that knowledge about frame selection is specific to individual words. According to this approach, for example, the knowledge that "John went to California to start a new job" refers to the frame CHANGE-RESIDENCE is part of our knowledge about the word "went." Clearly this is not the case. We would conclude the same thing if another verb was used, such as "John moved to California to start a new job," or "John traveled to California to start a new job." It seems clear that the same knowledge is responsible for frame selection in each of these examples. This knowledge has nothing to do with the particular lexical items used in these sentences, but rather has to do with our understanding of what employment entails, such as the fact that one usually lives near where one works; and the knowledge that one can change where one lives by performing the action CHANGE-RESIDENCE, which is a type of changing one's location. If one accepts that it is this sort of knowledge

---

2 For a criticism of this approach to word disambiguation in general, see [Birnbaum, 1985].

that is used in frame selection for this sort of example, then clearly a different approach to frame selection is needed for vague words.

I will now discuss the approach used by the MOPTRANS system, in which frame selection for vague words is treated as a *concept refinement* problem. In this approach, knowledge used to refine the representations of vague words is encoded in a small number of general inference rules, which are used in conjunction with a hierarchically arranged set of frames. The frames range from very general to very specific, depending on their position in the hierarchy.

To explain this approach, let us consider frame selection for a very general Spanish phrase, "hacer diligencias," which was encountered by the MOP-TRANS program. Literally, this phrase means "to do diligent actions." Often, it is equivalent to the English "to run errands," as in the following example:

> Spanish: Maria no puede ir a la reunion porque tiene que HACER MU-CHAS DILIGENCIAS.
>
> English: Mary cannot go to the gathering because she HAS TO RUN A LOT OF ERRANDS.

However, it can mean many other things, depending on the context in which it appears. This is because often the context provides enough information to allow the reader to infer quite specifically what action the phrase refers to. Here are some examples:[3]

> Spanish: Juanita salio a HACER UNAS DILIGENCIAS AL MER-CADO.
>
> English: Juanita went TO SHOP FOR GROCERIES.
>
> Spanish: Va a pintar su apartamento? — Si, pero antes tengo que HACER UNAS DILIGENCIAS PARA VER si consigo la pintura que quiero.
>
> English: Are you going to paint your apartment? — Yes, but first I have TO GO SEE if I can find the paint that I want.
>
> Spanish: La policia REALIZA INTENSAS DILIGENCIAS PARA CAP-TURAR a un reo que dio muerte a una mujer.
>
> English: The police ARE UNDERTAKING AN INTENSE INVESTIGA-TION in order to capture a criminal who killed a woman.

From these examples, we see that many, many actions can be expressed in Spanish using "hacer diligencias," and thus many different frames could be used to represent the phrase in different contexts.

---

3 Sometimes, the verb "realizar" (to realize or achieve) is used in place of "hacer."

How can we devise frame selection rules for a vague phrase like "realizar diligencias"? At first glance, one might think that we could devise features which would discriminate between at least some of the different frames which the phrase can refer to. For instance, in the police investigation story above, the fact that POLICE is the ACTOR of "realizar diligencias" might be enough to discriminate this sense of the phrase. However, this is not the case, as the following example illustrates:

> Spanish: La reina Isabela va a visitar a la ciudad de Nueva York el lunes. La policia realiza diligencias para insurar su seguridad durante la visita.
>
> English: Queen Elizabeth will visit New York city on Monday. The police are taking precautions to insure her safety during her visit.

Let us continue to look at this particular use of "realizar diligencias." What parts of the context of the police investigation example are relevant to determining that "realizar diligencias" means POLICE-INVESTIGATION in this example? To answer this, consider the line of reasoning that a human reader might follow in order to infer that "realizar diligencias" means POLICE-IN-VESTIGATION in the earlier example. First, since the prepositional phrase "para capturar" (in order to capture) follows "realizar diligencias," a human reader knows that the action expressed by "realizar diligencias" somehow will lead to a capture, or that the capture is the goal of the "diligencias." Capturing something involves getting control of it, and we know that before we can get control of an object, we have to know where it is and we have to find it. This indicates that perhaps "realizar diligencias" refers to some sort of finding. But when police are trying to find something in order to get control of it, they usually do a formal type of search, or an investigation. Therefore, we know that in this case, the phrase refers to a police investigation.

What we would like, then, is to devise frame selection rules which parallel this line of reasoning. In essence, this line of reasoning is a refinement process. Each inference limits further the type of action to which "realizar diligencias" could refer. At first, we know nothing more than that the phrase is referring to some action. Then, it is limited to be a type of FIND. Ultimately, we can infer that it is an INVESTIGATION.

The frame selection method used in the MOPTRANS system follows a similar refinement process. The frames in MOPTRANS are arranged hierarchically, from most vague to most specific. The dictionary definitions of words consist of pointers into this hierarchy. The level of specificity at which the definition of a word points to the hierarchy depends on how vague it is.

To make this more clear, consider the process which MOPTRANS goes through to select the frame POLICE-INVESTIGATION in the example above. Several frames are used during this process. Their organization is as follows:

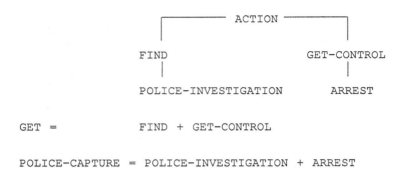

In this diagram, GET and POLICE-CAPTURE are script-like structures [Schank and Abelson, 1977] which provide information about stereotypical sequences of events. In addition to this event-sequential information, the dotted lines connecting the concepts ACTION, FIND, etc., represent IS-A links. All of the concepts in this IS-A hierarchy have case frames, specifying the prototypical fillers for various slots, such as ACTOR, OBJECT, etc. For example, the case frame for FIND indicates that its ACTOR should be a PERSON, its object should be a PHYSICAL OBJECT, and its RESULT should be a GET-CONTROL. The case frame for POLICE-INVESTIGATION indicates that its ACTOR should be an AUTHORITY, its OBJECT should be a CRIMINAL, and its RESULT is an ARREST.

With this hierarchical memory organization and scriptal knowledge, very general rules can be used to select the right frame for "realizar diligencias," along the same lines that a human reader would follow to infer the phrase's meaning. First, the dictionary definition of the word "capturar" points to the concept GET-CONTROL in the hierarchy above. From the event sequence GET above, we know that GET-CONTROL is often preceded by the event FIND. Since the story says that some action, "diligencias," precedes the GET-CONTROL, we can infer that the action is probably a FIND. This suggests the following general inference rule: If a scene of a script is mentioned in a story, then other scenes of the same script can be expected to be mentioned. Thus, if an abstraction of another scene of the script is mentioned, we can infer that the abstraction actually is the other scene. In more concrete terms, in this example GET-CONTROL is a scene of the script GET. Another scene of GET is the scene FIND. "Realizar diligencias" refers to an abstraction of the concept FIND, namely ACTION. Since GET-CONTROL was mentioned, indicating that other scenes of the script GET are likely to be encountered, we can infer that the ACTION is actually a FIND, since ACTION is an abstraction of FIND.

Put more precisely, this line of influencing can be expressed in the following rules:

Script Activation Rule: If an action which is part of a stereotypical event sequence is activated, then activate the stereotypical event sequence, and expect to find the other actions in that sequence.

Expected Event Specialization Rule: If a word refers to an action which is an abstraction of an expected action, and the slot-fillers of the action meet the prototypes of the slot-fillers of the more specific action, then change the representation of the word to the more specific expected action.

Next, consider how we can infer that the FIND is a POLICE-INVESTIGATION. First, in the story the ACTOR of the FIND is the POLICE. One piece of knowledge that we have about POLICE is that often they are the ACTORs of POLICE-INVESTIGATIONs, since that is part of their job. Then, since the IS-A hierarchy tells us that POLICE-INVESTIGATION is a refinement of the concept FIND, we can infer that in this story, the FIND is most likely a POLICE-INVESTIGATION.

This suggests the following inference rule:

Slot-Filler Specialization Rule: If a slot of concept A is filled by concept B, and B is the prototypical filler for that slot of concept C, and concept C IS-A concept A, then change the representation of concept A to concept C.

In this case, concept A is FIND, and concept B is the POLICE. The POLICE are the prototypical ACTORs of concept C, a POLICE-INVESTIGATION. Since FIND is above POLICE-INVESTIGATION in the IS-A hierarchy, then we can conclude that FIND in this case refers to POLICE-INVESTIGATION.

Thus, three general inference rules, the script activation rule, the expected event specialization rule, and the slot-filler specialization rule, can perform the disambiguation of "realizar diligencias" in the examples above. These rules require the organization of knowledge structures in a hierarchical fashion, so that they can use this hierarchy to guide the refinement of concepts. They also require the existence of event sequences (scripts) in memory, to provide expectations as to what actions are likely to occur together in stories.

Given these rules, frame selection in the police investigation example would proceed as follows. First, a general representation would be built for "realizar diligencias", simply, the concept ACTION. Then, the ACTOR of ACTION would be filled in by an appropriate slot-filling rule (such as one which equated the subject of "realizar diligencias" with its ACTOR) with the concept AUTHORITY (the representation of "policia"). Next, the concept GET-CONTROL would be built from the word "capturar." This would also cause the event sequence GET to be activated, because of the script activation rule above. This, in turn, would cause the concept ACTION to be changed to the concept FIND, due to the expected event specialization rule above. Now, since the ACTOR slot of FIND is filled by AUTHORITY, and since the prototype of the ACTOR slot of POLICE-SEARCH is AUTHORITY, the concept FIND would be changed to be POLICE-INVESTIGATION because of the slot-filler specialization rule.

These same concept refinement rules can perform frame selection for other examples of vague words. For example, consider the following uses of the word "seized":

Iranian students seized control of the American Embassy in Tehran.

A gunman seized control of a Boeing 727 and diverted it to Cuba.

A gunman seized three people as hostages and demanded a $5 million ransom.

As we saw earlier, "seized" is a sufficiently vague word in the domain of terrorism and crime to refer to several possible frames. In the examples above, it refers to the frames TAKE-OVER-BUILDING, HIJACK, and TAKE-HOSTAGES. Thus, in the disambiguation approach, "seized" would be defined as having three separate meanings, one for each frame. However, in MOP-TRANS, "seized" is simply defined as having only one sense, meaning GET-CONTROL. All of the more specific frames to which "seized" could refer are under GET-CONTROL in the hierarchy. Thus, the slot-fillings of the ACTOR and OBJECT slots of GET-CONTROL cause the appropriate frame to be selected by the concept refinement rules. If the OBJECT of the GET-CONTROL is a BUILDING, then the frame TAKE-OVER-BUILDING is chosen, because the slot-filler BUILDING matches the prototype for the OBJECT slot of TAKE-OVER-BUILDING, which IS-A GET-CONTROL.[4] Similarly, if the

---

4 It could be that there are other frames in the system that are GET-CONTROLs whose OBJECT is a BUILDING. For instance, if the system contained a structure like FORECLOSURE, this action would have a prototype of BUILDING for its OBJECT slot, too. However, the additional information that the ACTOR of this action is "Iranian students" would still cause the frame TAKE-OVER-BUILDING to be selected, because the ACTOR slot-filler would violate the prototype for the ACTOR of a FORECLOSURE.

OBJECT is filled with a VEHICLE, then the system would choose the frame HIJACK, because the prototypical OBJECT for a HIJACK is a VEHICLE. The same is true of "hostages," which matches the prototype for the OBJECT of TAKE-HOSTAGES.

5 Comparison to Other Work

Although I have presented several systems which use a lexical disambiguation approach to frame selection, it is not the case that all previous work on frame selection has used this approach. Thus, it is worth noting some similarities between the MOPTRANS parser's frame selection techniques and some other previous systems. First, a similar observation about lexically-based disambiguation rules was made in [Schank, Birnbaum, and Mey, 1981]. Schank et al. noted that vague words like "take," "use," etc., would require an explosively large number of distinct word senses. They asserted that this problem arises because the word sense disambiguation approach to frame selection "remains, at root, based on the old notion that the meaning of an utterance is a simple, additive function of the meanings of the words it contains." Schank et al. did not propose a solution to the problem of large numbers of word senses, except to say that the definitions of vague words should consist of "crude descriptions" of what they might mean in a given context. Then, this crude description would be used as a "search key" for indexing inside of more specific frames, to try and find a match between the crude description and a more specific frame.

The FRUMP system [DeJong, 1979], which produced summaries of newspaper articles from many domains, used an approach to frame selection that was similar in some ways to that of MOPTRANS. DeJong used discrimination nets called sketchy script initiator discrimination trees (SSIDTs) to guide frame selection. One SSIDT existed for each conceptual dependency primitive. An SSIDT, when given a conceptual dependency representation, selected a frame, or "sketchy script," on the basis of the roles and role fillers contained in the CD representation. Thus, a text was first decomposed into its CD representation, then parsing rules would fill in various roles in the representation, and finally an SSIDT selected a sketchy script on the basis of what roles were filled in, and how they were filled.

SSIDT's selected the sketchy script $EARTHQUAKE for the word "trembled," as in "The ground trembled." First, the word "trembled" was represented by PTRANS, the CD primitive for physical motion. In addition, "trembled" provided the information that the motion was cyclical in manner. Then, parsing rules assigned "ground" to be the OBJECT of this PTRANS. Finally, the SSIDT consisted of the following:

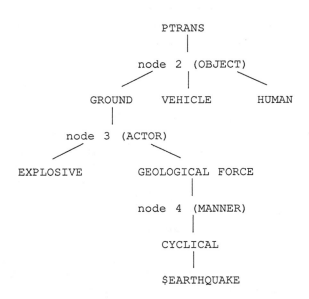

Thus, the role-fillers of PTRANS, in this case the fact that the OBJECT was the ground and the MANNER of the motion was cyclical, guided the SSIDT to the sketchy script $EARTHQUAKE.

This approach to frame selection does not suffer from the same rule explosion as the lexically based approach. Also, it can select an initial frame for a story, unlike the frame-based approach. However, it has the disadvantage of requiring large, ad hoc discrimination trees, whose only purpose is to disambiguate words. Also, it depends on the ability to represent initially a text in terms of conceptual dependency primitives. While this works well for words such as "trembled," which refer very clearly to physical actions, it is not as easy to represent the meanings of all words in terms of conceptual dependency primitives.

MOPTRANS' frame selection process is also similar in some respects to the Incremental Description Refinement process used in RUS [Bobrow and Webber, 1980]. In this system, a taxonomic lattice [Woods, 1978] is used to refine the semantic interpretation of a sentence as it is being parsed. The refinement process is similar to the frame selection method I have described here in that it relies on a hierarchical structure to provide the information needed to discriminate to more specific concepts in the hierarchy. For example, the sentence "John ran the drill press" was parsed in this system using a taxonomic lattice containing nodes RUN-CLAUSE, PERSON-RUN-CLAUSE, RUN-MA-CHINE-CLAUSE. The parser refined its semantic interpretation of the sentence from RUN-CLAUSE to the more specific PERSON-RUN-CLAUSE and finally RUN-MACHINE-CLAUSE as more information was provided by the parse of the sentence.

There are many differences between the RUS system and the frame selection system which I have described here. Although the refinement process itself and the structure of the hierarchies used in the two systems are similar, the content of the nodes in these hierarchies is completely different. First, the nodes in the taxonomic lattice of RUS are not at all independent of lexical items. Thus, the node RUN-MACHINE-CLAUSE would be distinct from OPERATE-MACHINE-CLAUSE, and from nodes corresponding to other verbs which can refer to the operation of a machine. This is in contrast to the nodes in the hierarchy which I have discussed here, which are meant to be elements in a conceptual representational system. Second, since the nodes in RUS's taxonomic lattice are not meant to be conceptual representations, RUS contains no script-like knowledge about likely sequences of nodes. In contrast, the frame selection system which I have presented here also makes use of script-like sequences of events, which are meant to represent conceptual facts about the world. The information provided by this scriptal knowledge is an important part of the frame selection process which I have described here.

Finally, frame selection in MOPTRANS shares many common features with the approach used in the Word Expert Parser, discussed earlier. The two systems, as well as FRUMP, have in common the fact that frame selection is driven by a discrimination net which organizes the possible frames that could be chosen. However, a major difference between WEP's approach and the approach used in MOPTRANS is that each ambiguous word in WEP had its own discrimination net, as well as its own set of rules for using the discrimination net. In MOPTRANS, only one discrimination net is used for all vague words, as well as a single set of concept refinement rules.

6 *Conclusion*

I have presented a set of general inference rules, including the Script Activation Rule, the Expected Event Specialization Rule, and the Slot-Filler Specialization Rule, which can be used to select frames for vague words. These rules draw on information from a hierarchically organized conceptual memory which provides knowledge about abstractions of events and sequences of events. This frame selection method is in sharp contrast to the lexically based disambiguation methods which I discussed earlier, in which an exhaustive list of the possible frames to which a vague word could refer is needed. This list can be very long in the case of very vague words. MOPTRANS' approach is also in sharp contrast to the disambiguation approach in that frame selection knowledge in MOPTRANS is not specific to particular words. Instead of having a separate list of frames for every ambiguous word as well as a separate body of knowledge about how to select a frame from each list, MOPTRANS has a general set of concept refinement rules, and a single hierarchy of frames which is used to refine the representation of all vague words.

Although the concept refinement approach does not suffer from the difficulties that I have discussed with regard to disambiguation methods, there are unresolved issues in this approach also. First, it is possible to mislead MOPTRANS so that it refines its representation when in fact it should not. For example:

John got a TV at Macy's.

John got a TV at Macy's as a prize for being their millionth customer.

Given the appropriate frames in MOPTRANS' conceptual hierarchy, MOPTRANS would select the frame BUY for the first sentence. The initial representation of "got" would be the frame ATRANS, representing a transfer of control of an object (in this case the TV). Then, since a TV is an object which is likely to be purchased, and since BUY is a refinement of ATRANS, the representation would be refined to BUY. However, in the second sentence, this inference would be in error. In this case, information later in the sentence indicates that the frame WIN is more appropriate. Thus, in this example, MOPTRANS would not choose the correct frame.

To overcome this problem, we could design frame selection rules which are more conservative. In other words, we could delay the choosing of a more specific frame until we are sure that all other frames have been eliminated as possibilities. However, this approach does not seem feasible. There are examples in which the choice of a frame would have to be delayed for a long time:

John got a TV at Macy's. He had been wanting one for a long time, but he had no money. He took his gun to the store and pointed it at the salesman's head.

Here we see that the cue that BUY is not the correct frame does not appear until two sentences later in the story. In general, is is difficult to put a limit on how long we would have to wait to be sure that no other frame could apply. Thus, it is not practical to wait to choose a frame until all other frames are eliminated. Instead, it seems more plausible that some sort of backup mechanism is needed, to undo cases in which concept refinement has been applied erroneously.

Another difficulty for the concept refinement approach is that, in reality, very few words are strictly vague, as I have defined the term. First, words are often some combination of genuinely ambiguous and vague. That is, words often have distinct word senses, each of which is vague. Clearly it is necessary for this approach to frame selection to interact with an approach for genuinely ambiguous words. Second, many words which do not have distinct, genuinely ambiguous senses still are not vague as I have defined the term. Often, although many or all of the frames which could represent a word do indeed have some non-trivial abstract description in common, it is not the case that absolutely every action or object which fits this description could be expressed using the word. For example:

The coyote ran off the end of the cliff and went to the valley below.

One can understand that "went" in this sentence means "fell," but it is not a very natural-sounding sentence. This presents a problem for the concept refinement approach to frame selection, as this approach would predict that this use of "went" should be perfectly acceptable.

There are two possible explanations for this problem. First, it might be that our abstract description of "went," namely "to change one's physical location," is incomplete. Perhaps we need to add more to it, to exclude such actions as falling off a cliff. It might be that if "went" is used to describe a change in location of an animate agent, then that change in location is one that is normally an intentional one. Thus, since one does not normally want to fall off a cliff, "went" is not an appropriate word to describe this action. However, even if we can find a description such as this which excludes changes in location which cannot be expressed using "went," it is non-trivial to add these restrictions to the hierarchical information in the system. Certainly we do not want to add the frame IF-ANIMATE-AGENT-THEN-INTENTIONAL-PTRANS to our hierarchy, as this is rather ad hoc.

Another possible explanation for why some vague words cannot be used to describe certain actions is that there may simply be no good reason to use vague words in some contexts. Why would a speaker want to use the word "went" in the above example, when there is available to him a perfectly good English word, "fell," which describes the action that he wants to convey quite accurately? At other times, it might be advantageous to use a vague word, so as to convey uncertainty, or not to definitely commit oneself. Thus, reasoning about the speaker's goals and intentions might play a role in the frame selection process, and at times limit the application of concept refinement rules.

Acknowledgments

This research was conducted at Yale University, Department of Computer Science, and was supported in part by the Advanced Research Projects Agency of the Department of Defense, monitored by the Office of Naval Research under contract No. N00014-82K-0149.

References

Birnbaum, L. 1985. Lexical ambiguity as a touchstone for theories of language analysis. In *Proceedings of the Ninth International Joint Conference on Artificial Intelligence*, UCLA, pp. 815–819. Los Altos: Morgan Kaufmann.

Bobrow, R., and Webber, B. 1980. Knowledge representation for syntactic/semantic processing. In *Proceedings of the First National Conference on Artificial Intelligence*, Stanford University, pp. 316–323. Los Altos: Morgan Kaufmann.

Charniak, E. 1982. Context recognition in language comprehension. In Lehnert, W., and Ringle, M. (eds.), *Context Recognition in Language Comprehension*, pp. 435–454. Hillsdale: Lawrence Erlbaum Associates.

DeJong, G. 1979. *Skimming Stories in Real Time: An Experiment in Integrated Understanding*. PhD Thesis, Yale University, May 1979, Research Report No. 158.

Hirst, G. 1983. *Semantic Interpretation Against Ambiguity*. PhD Thesis, Brown University, Department of Computer Science, Providence, RI, Research Report No. CD-83-25.

Lebowitz, M. 1980. Generalization and memory in an integrated understanding system. Research Report No. 186, Yale University Department of Computer Science, New Haven, CT.

Lytinen, S. 1984. *The Organization of Knowledge in a Multi-Lingual, Integrated Parser*. PhD Thesis, Yale University, Department of Computer Science, New Haven, CT, Research Report No. 340.

Minsky, M. 1975. A framework for representing knowledge. In Winston, P. (ed.), *The Psychology of Computer Vision*. New York: McGraw-Hill.

Riesbeck, C., and Schank, R. 1976. Comprehension by computer: Expectation-based analysis of sentences in context. Research Report #78, Yale University Department of Computer Science, New Haven, CT.

Schank, R. 1975. *Conceptual Information Processing*. Hillsdale: Lawrence Erlbaum Associates.

Schank, R., and Abelson, R. 1977. *Scripts, Plans, Goals, and Understanding*. Hillsdale: Lawrence Erlbaum Associates.

Schank, R., Birnbaum, L., and Mey, J. 1981. Integrating semantics and pragmatics. In *Proceedings of the XIIIth International Congress of Linguists*, Tokyo, Japan, September.

Small, S. 1980. *Word Expert Parsing: A Theory of Distributed Word-based Natural Language Understanding*. PhD Thesis, University of Maryland, Department of Computer Science, College Park, MD.

Woods, W. 1978. Taxonomic lattice structures for situation recognition. In *Theoretical Issues in Natural Language Processing – 2*, July.

5

Disambiguation in a Lexically Based Sentence Understanding System

Domenico Parisi
Cristiano Castelfranchi
Istituto di Psicologia
C.N.R., Rome

Ambiguity, defined as the existence of potential alternative choices at particular points in the processing of a sentence, is perhaps the most serious problem in constructing a sentence understanding system. A sentence understanding system is inevitably a very complex system, made up of a large number of complexly interacting components, and ambiguity choice points can show up in the functioning of each of these components. In the present paper we will examine the problem of ambiguity and disambiguation from the point of view of a lexically based model of the sentence understanding system. In Section 1 we briefly describe the model. In Section 2 a classification of different types of ambiguity is presented. In Section 3 we discuss in general terms how the model deals with disambiguation. In Sections 4 and 5 the syntactic and encyclopedic disambiguation mechanisms are described. Finally, in Section 6 we present some extensions of the encyclopedic mechanism to solve other problems of sentence understanding.

1 *A Lexically Based Sentence Understanding System*

Sentence understanding is made up of two basic components: surface and deep understanding. Surface understanding is whatever information is extracted from the input sentence using the system's linguistic knowledge: knowledge of the lexicon and syntax of a particular language. Deep understanding consists of changes that this information produces in the system's knowledge of the world. These changes are a joint product of the input sentence, linguistic knowledge and pre-existing world knowledge.

A sentence's surface meaning is represented as a network of nodes connected by directed binary arcs. The basic unit in such a network is a propositional unit, which is made up of: (a) a predicate (predicate node), (b) the predicate's argument(s) (X or C nodes), (c) the unit's identifying label (C node). The C node which is the label of the unit has pointers (arcs) to the predicate node (written as a word in capital letters) and to the X or C argument node(s). X nodes represent objects or persons, C nodes represent facts or events described by the propositional unit of which the C node is the label. If a predicate has more than a single argument, the different arguments are identified by numbers on arcs. Propositional units are connected together by sharing arguments or when the label of one unit becomes an argument of another unit. For example, the surface meaning of the sentence

(1) The dog chases the cat in the garden

is represented by the following network

(2)

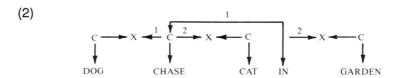

Our model constructs this surface meaning solely through the use of a lexicon; all syntactic and semantic knowledge is stored with each lexical entry. Lexical entries have their meaning represented by the same type of network as sentences. Hence, the basic operation in the construction of a sentence's surface meaning is assembling the partial networks corresponding to the various words in the input sentence so that the sentence's correct total network is generated. This is brought about by executing "assembly instructions" carried by words in the lexicon as part of their lexical meaning. For example, the word *chases* carries two assembly instructions on each of the two arguments of the predicate CHASE. When the sentence (1) is processed, the instruction on the "chaser" argument of CHASE assembles this argument with the argument of the word *dog*, and the instruction on the "chased" argument of CHASE assembles it with the argument of the word *cat*.

There are a dozen different kinds of assembly instructions which differ in the constraints they must obey. These constraints are basically of two types. The first type of constraint is related to the existence of "control" predicates. In addition to "semantic" propositional units, the meaning of lexical entries includes "control" propositional units, i.e., units that have the function of controlling the assembly process. Assembly instructions differ in the kind of control predicates that their assembly argument must possess, or not possess, in order for the instruction to be executed. For example, the lexical meaning of verbs and adjectives includes a control propositional unit with TEMP (= temporal) as predicate and their C label as argument. Adverbs and adverbial prepositions, like *in* in sentence (1), carry an assembly instruction (CARG) on their C label requiring that the C assembly argument the instruction is looking for be marked with the control predicate TEMP. This insures that the adverb is assembled with the correct C argument yielding a network like (2). By contrast, the assembly instruction (SATARG) carried by *chases* on each of its two arguments requires that the assembly argument not be marked by the control predicate SAT (= saturate), i.e., it requires an unfilled assembly argument. Since this kind of assembly instruction marks its assembly argument with SAT when executed, this insures that the two identical assembly instruction of *chases* do not take the same assembly argument twice.

A second type of constraint concerns "where" an assembly instruction must look for its assembly argument. The total search space of a sentence is divided up into sub-spaces and each particular type of assembly instruction is restricted as to which sub-space it can inspect for an assembly argument. There are two basic types of spaces: sentential spaces (S-spaces) and nominal spaces (N-spaces). For example, the total search space of the sentence:

(3) (S(N The dog) chases (N the cat) in (N the garden))

is divided up into sub-spaces as shown. Notice that in this notation, parentheses do not segment a sentence's words into phrases, as it is customary in linguistics, but they represent a hierarchical structure of search spaces which contain the propositional units carried by the sentence's words. The CARG assembly instruction carried by the word *in* must look for its assembly argument inside the same S-space the word ends up in. On the other hand, the two SATARG instructions on the two arguments of *chases* must find their assembly argument in a N- space one level down.

Each space in a sentence has two working memories associated with it. One memory is Expectation (E), the other is Not Executed Instructions (NEI).

E stores expectations that must be satisfied by the words occurring in the space. When an expectation is satisfied it is canceled from E. A space can only be closed if E is empty, i.e., all the space's expectations must be satisfied. S-spaces have an expectation of a word carrying a TEMP control predicate. As already noted, verbs and adjectives carry this predicate. N-spaces expect a word carrying a HEAD control predicate. Nouns and pronouns carry this predicate.

The NEI memory associated with each space stores assembly instructions carried by the words occurring in the space that it has been impossible to execute using the arguments or labels of the preceding words and hence must be executed on the successive words. For example, when processing the word *chases* in sentence (1), the assembly instruction on the "chaser" argument of *chases* is executed on the preceding word *dog*, but the assembly instruction on the "chased" argument of *chases* cannot be executed since *dog* is already "saturated." This instruction is therefore stored in NEI and it will be executed on the following word *cat*. NEI also must be empty when the space is closed.

Sub-spaces are opened and closed by "space management procedures" (SMPs) that are carried by words as part of their lexical meaning. Different categories of words carry different types of SMPs. The SMP carried by a word decides to (a) open a new space, (b) close the current space, or (c) maintain the current space, as a function of the current situation. Basically, the "current situation" means (a) whether the current space is an S-space or a N-space, and (b) whether the current space can be closed or not, i.e., whether the E and NEI memories of the space are empty or not.

2 Some Types of Ambiguity

As already observed, ambiguity choice points may exist at all points along the processing route of a sentence. Consider a sentence like:

(5) A girl was fishing on the bank.

A can refer to a specific entity or to a class of entities (e.g., *A girl can make a man happy*). *Girl* can be a head noun or a noun modifier (e.g., *girl friend*). *Was* can be an auxiliary verb or a main verb (e.g., *Bill was a lawyer*). *Fishing* can be a progressive verb form or a noun (e.g., *Fishing is boring*). *On* can be an adverbial predicate or a main predicate (e.g., *The girl was on the bank*). *Bank* can mean "river bank" or "savings bank."

Here is an incomplete list of types of ambiguity from the point of view of our model.

2.1 *Ambiguity due to Optional Assembly Instructions*

Some assembly instructions are obligatory but other instructions are optional, i.e., they may remain unexecuted. The two instructions carried by the verb *to take* are obligatory (compare **He took*). To eat has an obligatory instruction on its "eater" argument (compare **Ate an apple*) but an optional instruction on its "eaten" argument (compare *John ate an apple* but also *John ate*).

Optional instructions can lead to ambiguity points. Consider a sentence like *John gave the girl who was eating a slice of pizza...* . When it arrives at *a slice of pizza* the system can either assemble the argument of *slice* with the "eaten" argument of *was eating* or assemble it with the "receiver" argument of *gave*. The first choice would be appropriate in this case: *John gave the girl who was eating a piece of pizza an apple*. The second in this case: *John gave the girl who was eating a slice of pizza*.

2.2 *Ambiguity due to the Order of Execution of Assembly Instructions*

In some languages like Italian, but not English, a sentence like *The dog is chasing the cat* is ambiguous between an interpretation in which the dog is the chaser and the cat the chased one, and an interpretation in which the roles are interchanged. The verb *to chase* comes from the lexicon with two assembly instructions on the verb's "chaser" and "chased" arguments. If the "chaser" instruction is executed first, the dog is interpreted as the chaser in the above sentence—since the word *dog* has already arrived when *is chasing* is processed—and the cat as the chased. However, if the two assembly instructions of *to chase* are executed in the reverse order, the dog becomes the chased and the cat the chaser. In English only the first order of execution is allowed, in Italian both (even if the first is the preferred one).

2.3 *Ambiguity due to Space Management Procedures*

Some SMPs carried by words contain ambiguity points within themselves. For example, the SMP carried by an adverb, e.g., *yesterday*, includes one such ambiguity point: if the adverbial occurs inside a space which can be closed and it is not the sentence's total space, the procedure can either close the current space or do nothing (i.e., neither close nor open a space). Consider the sentence

(6) Bill said that Mary left yesterday.

This sentence has two interpretations. In one interpretation *yesterday* is assembled with *left*, in the other with *said*. The reason is that the word *yesterday* arrives at a point in the processing of the sentence where the word's SMP can either close the current space or do nothing. If the first alternative is adopted, i.e., we have (S(N Bill) said that (S(N Mary) left) yesterday), *yesterday* is assembled with the verb of its space, i.e., *said*. If the second alternative is followed, we have (S(N Bill) said that (S(N Mary) left yesterday)), and *yesterday* is assembled with left. Notice that in the sentence *Bill said yesterday that Mary left* the word *yesterday* arrives at a different point in the processing of the sentence, where the current space cannot be closed and therefore there is no ambiguity point: the SMP must do nothing.

2.4 Lexical Ambiguity: Mostly Syntactic

The various types of ambiguity we have reviewed so far are not lexical ones in that, even if they occur when executing a lexical entry's meaning, they are not due to a given lexical entry having multiple readings. Since the meaning of a lexical entry has a semantic component (one or more predicate-argument units) and a syntactic component (control propositional units, assembly instructions and space management procedures), lexical ambiguities can be usefully divided up into two subtypes. The multiple readings differ (mostly) in their syntactic component or (mostly) in their semantic component. (We say "mostly" because differences often occur in both components.)

An example of a mostly syntactic lexical ambiguity is the word *stop* as a verb and as a noun: the SMPs of the two readings are different. Another example is a preposition like *in* which has three readings (with three different SMPs) exemplified in the three sentences: *The wine is contained in the bottle, John is in the kitchen, John is sleeping in the kitchen*. A third example is the word *raced* which has at least two readings (with different SMPs and different assembly instructions) exemplified in the two sentences *The horse raced past the barn* and *The horse raced past the barn fell*.

2.5 Lexical Ambiguity: Mostly Semantic

Semantic lexical ambiguity is due to lexical entries with multiple readings that differ mostly in their semantic component. This is the classic case of *bank* which has two readings that are both nouns (same SMP) but carry different propositional units (river bank and savings bank).

3 How to Traverse an Ambiguity Choice Tree

In contrast with the existence of multiple ambiguity choice points of so many different types during the processing of a sentence, ambiguity is seldom noticed by the human understanding system—with the exception of garden path sentences. This requires that a sentence understanding system must be equipped with a powerful disambiguation mechanism or mechanisms. A disambiguation mechanism is some device that uses information of various kinds in order to identify the appropriate alternative at an ambiguity point and to spot wrong paths. The various ambiguity points in a sentence make up a hypothetical tree and the disambiguation mechanism must identify the correct path through the tree—the path corresponding to the appropriate reading of the sentence. If the selection of a particular alternative were made on a random basis one would expect a high proportion of failures, many more than the observed occurrences of garden path sentences. However, if the selection of alternatives is based on preferences, then these preferences might succeed in guiding the system on the right track through the tree most of the times. The small number of failures are the garden path sentences.

What is expected from a preference mechanism which simulates human performance is the following:

1. It generally does not lead to failures but gives the correct alternative at each point as the preferred one.

2. In the case of sentences with multiple interpretations it yields only one interpretation, i.e., the one that human beings would spontaneously impose on the sentence.

3. In the case of garden path sentences it leads to a failure.

Four basic types of preferences can be identified.

3.1 *Language Preferences*

One route at an ambiguity point can be the preferred one in the language itself. This preference can be based on frequency or familiarity. For example, *bank* has two semantic readings, but the reading "savings bank" might be preferred to the reading "river bank" because the first reading is more frequently used in the language.

3.2 *Text Preferences*

A particular reading can be the preferred one in a particular text. For example, in a text about rivers, flood, and waters, the "river bank" readings of *bank* might be preferred to the "savings bank" reading, reversing the language preferences. More specifically, if one reading of an ambiguous word has been successfully selected in the preceding text the same reading is selected for other occurrences of the word in the same text.

3.3 *Syntactic Preferences*

A particular reading of a syntactically ambiguous word can be preferred to its alternative readings if the system is able to take in consideration the syntactic context. For example, the progressive reading of *fishing* is preferred to the noun reading in the syntactic context of sentence (5).

3.4 *Encyclopedic Preferences*

If the words in a sentence activate entities in the system's encyclopedia of world knowledge, a semantically ambiguous word would activate two such entities instead of just one. If we represent the system's encyclopedia as a semantic network, the preferred reading would be the reading which activates the encyclopedic node connected by the shortest path to the nodes activated by the other words in the sentence. For example, in the sentence *John took the money to the bank* the "savings bank" reading of *bank* is the preferred one because the path connecting the "savings bank" node activated by the word *bank* with the node activated by the word *money* is shorter than the path connecting the "river bank" node with the "money" node.

All these preference sources are combined together to yield *the* preferred alternative at a choice point. The likelihood that a disambiguating mechanism based on all four types of preferences will identify the correct processing path through the tree can be further increased if the system can delay the decision at a choice point until one or more successive words have been at least partly processed. One might assume that delaying a decision at an ambiguity point is a structural, fixed feature of the sentence understanding system, as in parsers with "windows" of a fixed number of constituents (e.g., [Marcus, 1980]). Alternatively, the model might assume that delaying is strategic, i.e., a decision is delayed only if, and until, it is considered too risky to be adopted We prefer the second alternative but will not discuss the pro and cons of the two possibilities here.

Another possibility is that of "partial processing" [Small, 1980]. If the system judges a decision at a choice point too risky to be adopted it can do some of the processing at once—the part that is compatible with all the alternatives—and delay the remaining processing until the moment that additional information from the successive context is available. For example, in processing the word *that*, the system can open a finite tense S-space—which is compatible with both the subordinating conjunction and the relative pronoun reading of *that*—and delay the decision as to how to further process the word.

Language and text preferences can be conceived of as permanent and temporary rankings of preferences, respectively, based on frequency of usage or some other mechanism. (For a mechanism involving text-sensitive syntactic preferences within an augmented transition network parser, see [Ferrari and

Stock, 1980]). In any case we won't say anything further about them and will dedicate the rest of this paper to a closer examination of the other two types of preferences: syntactic and encyclopedic preferences. These preferences are based on two fundamental types of knowledge used by the sentence understanding system: syntactic and real world, or encyclopedic knowledge. Syntactic knowledge is what allows the system to select the subordinate reading of the ambiguous word *that* in the sentence *Bill thinks that Mary left* as against the relative pronoun reading of the same word. On the other hand, encyclopedic knowledge is used to select the "savings bank" reading of *bank* in the sentence *Bill took the money to the bank,* as against the "river bank" reading.

Syntactic knowledge and encyclopedic knowledge are used by the system as preference mechanisms and for identifying failures (garden path sentences). In the classical garden path sentence *The horse raced past the barn fell* syntactic knowledge signals a failure when the word fell comes in. Encyclopedic knowledge signals a failure at the end of the semantic garden path sentence *The astronomer married a star* [Charniak, 1983].

In the next two sections we will look more closely at the structure and functioning of the syntactic and encyclopedic disambiguation mechanisms.

4 *The Syntactic Disambiguation Mechanism*

As already noted, disambiguation is a sentence understanding system has two tasks: selecting the preferred route at an ambiguity choice point, i.e., the route that is most likely to lead to the correct interpretation of the sentence, and determining that an incorrect route has been taken so that the system is forced to abandon that route and go back and re-process the sentence. We will consider the role of syntactic information in each task.

To make a decision at an ambiguity point sensitive to the preceding syntactic context, we assume that a syntactically ambiguous word has a disambiguation procedure associated with it. Consider a word like *that* which has two readings: as a subordinating conjunction and as a relative pronoun. (We are omitting the third demonstrative reading.) Consider these five preceding contexts in which the word may occur:

(7) That ...   (1, 2)

(8) Bill said that ...   (1, 2)

(9) The man that ...   (1, 3, 7)

(10) Bill met the man that ...   (1, 3, 4, 6)

(11) Bill told the man that ...   (1, 3, 4, 5)

What we want is that in contexts (7) and (8) the subordinating conjunction reading be selected, in contexts (9) and (10) the relative pronoun reading, while in context (11) no syntactic preference be expressed. (In this last case a strategic decision to wait until more words are processed would be appropriate.) These syntactic preferences can be generated by the following disambiguation procedure carried by the word *that* itself (remember that there are only two types of spaces: S-spaces and N-spaces).

(12)

1	Is the current space an S-Space?			
2	Yes:	Select the subordinating conjunction reading		
3	No:	Has the TEMP expectation of the S-space above been satisfied?		
4		Yes:	Does the NEI memory of the S-space above contain a SATCARG assembly instruction?	
5			Yes:	No preference
6			No	Select the relative pronoun reading
7		No:	Select the relative pronoun reading	

The steps through the procedure for each of the contexts (7)–(11) are listed in the right column of (7)–(11).

Turning to the second disambiguation task, i.e., ascertaining that a wrong processing route at a preceding choice point has been taken (garden path sentences), syntactic information plays a role in this task by providing four "well-formedness principles." If one or more of these principles are violated by a processing route, that route must be discarded. The principles refer to the well-formedness of search spaces for assembly instructions. In order to close a space:

1. The space's expectation must be satisfied.

2. The space's NEI memory cannot contain obligatory assembly instructions.

3. The units contained in the space must form a connected network (i.e., no units can be isolated from the other units).

4. The space cannot be the sentence's total space.

Consider the sentence *The horse raced past the barn fell.* We assume that when *raced* is processed the system selects the past reading of *raced* as the preferred reading as against the passive reading using both the language preferences and the syntactic context preferences. This leads to the following space structuring of the sentence's total space when the system arrives at the word *fell*:

(13) (S(N The horse) raced past (N the barn

When the system processes the word *fell* the space management procedure carried by *fell*—the same procedure of the past reading of *raced*—closes the N-space of *barn* and then it is forced to close the sentence's total space since the space's TEMP expectation has already been satisfied by *raced*. But this violates well-formedness principle D and the sentence is recognized as a garden path sentence. The system goes back to the beginning of the sentence and reprocesses it selecting this time the passive reading of *raced*. This reading has a different SMP than the past reading of *raced*. The new SMP opens a lower S-space:

(14) (S(N The horse (S raced

The new choice is along the path leading to the final correct result:

(15) (S(N The horse (S raced past (N the barn)) fell)

5 *Encyclopedic Disambiguation Mechanism*

Encyclopedic knowledge is represented in our system as a very large network of nodes and arcs of the same general type that represents a sentence's surface meaning. However, both X and C nodes are now differentiated into three subtypes representing individuals, sets of individuals, and classes.

Encyclopedic nodes are initially activated by the words in the input sentence. There are five types of activation mechanisms: (a) Predicate nodes are activated by predicates of lexical entries. (b) Class nodes are activated by the corresponding lexical entries (lexical activation of class nodes). (c) Class nodes are activated by assembled fragments of the surface network (syntactic activation of class nodes). (d) Pre-existing individual or set nodes are activated by definite noun phrases. (e) New nodes created by the sentence (e.g., by undefined noun phrases) are also activated.

For example, given the sentence *A ferocious dog was chasing the cats*, the following encyclopedic nodes are activated:

- The predicate nodes of DOG, FEROCIOUS, CHASE, and CAT.

- The class nodes of dogs, ferocious dogs, cats, and chasings, if such nodes are present in the encyclopedia.

- A pre-existing set node of cats.
- The newly created individual nodes of a dog and of a specific chasing event.

As soon as nodes are activated by the input sentence, a parallel search for the shortest path between pairs of activated nodes begins. (For related views see [Charniak, 1983; Fahlman, 1979; Cottrell and Small, 1984; Waltz and Pollack, 1985].) Consider, however, that this search for the shortest path between pairs of activated nodes is modulated by the sentence network which is progressively constructed by the surface understanding component using syntactic and lexical knowledge. In other words, it is not the case that for each pair of nodes that are activated in the encyclopedia, the system looks for the shortest path connecting them independently of the other activated nodes and of the network which is being constructed at the surface level.

Consider the sentence

(16) The dog chases the cat.

When the system arrives at the word *chases* two encyclopedic nodes among others are activated, the node of the dog and the node of the particular chasing event. From the point of view of encyclopedic knowledge alone there are two equivalent paths connecting them: "the dog is the chaser in the chasing event" and "the dog is the chased one in the chasing event." It is the surface network that is being constructed using the first two words of sentence (16) that selects the correct path between the two. In fact, the assembly instruction on the "chaser" argument of *chases* is executed on *dog*, hence of the two shortest paths the first is the correct one.

Consider now the sentence:

(17) Picasso's paintings were bought by him in 1923

After the system has processed the word *paintings*, at the surface level an unspecified REL predicate (the lexical meaning of genitive -s) connects the argument of *Picasso* and the argument of *paintings*. In the encyclopedia two nodes among others are activated by the sentence's initial words: the individual node of Picasso and a set node of paintings. The shortest path connecting these two nodes is likely to be the path "paintings painted by Picasso." However, when the following words *were bought by him* are processed the system must change the previously identified path to a different one: "paintings owned by Picasso."

We can conclude that the surface sentence network puts constraints on the search for the shortest paths connecting sentence activated encyclopedic nodes in at least two ways:

1. The path connecting some pairs of sentence activated nodes is just a generalized replica of the path connecting the corresponding nodes in the sentence network. For example, given a sentence like (16), the path connecting the class of dogs and the class of chasings must be "the dogs are the chasers" and not "the dogs are the chased ones."

2. The path connecting other pairs of sentence activated nodes must be compatible with paths in the sentence network, even if the encyclopedic path is not the shortest path between the two nodes. This produces semantic garden path sentences. For example, in a sentence like (17), the shortest path between Picasso and the paintings (through PAINT) is later changed to a longer path (through PERSON and OWN), because only the second path is compatible with the sentence network (*were bought by him*). The same is true for a sentence like *The astronomer married a star* in which the shorter path connecting the class of astronomers with the class of celestial bodies is canceled in favor of a longer path connecting astronomers and celebrities because only the latter path is compatible with the sentence network (*married a star*).

The search of the shortest path between activated nodes is a parallel search. The basic operation consists of an already activated node activating its neighbor nodes, i.e., nodes separated from the activated node by just one single arc. The search is assumed to start simultaneously from both of a pair of nodes initially activated by the sentence. When the search starting from node A reaches a node already activated by the search starting from node B, the shortest path connecting the two nodes has been found. Parallelism means that all just activated nodes activate all their neighbors simultaneously. Hence, search time is a function of length of path only, not of network density (average number of neighbors per node).

The network that represents the system's knowledge of the world can be assumed to be a network with high density but short paths between pairs of sentence activated nodes. Hence, in principle, parallelism appears to be an appropriate choice for a model of the encyclopedic disambiguation mechanism. However, the total number of activated nodes is high in such a network. If one assumes there is a cost for each activated node one may want to find a way to reduce the number of activated nodes per search. Furthermore, even if connecting paths between sentence activated nodes are generally short, it would be nice to be able to reduce their length thereby obtaining a reduction both of total search time and of the total number of activated nodes per search. This points to the need for some heuristics.

One type of heuristic that might produce the desired results while remaining consistent with the logic of parallel search in a simple network is the following. A network of nodes and unlabelled undirected arcs can be conceptualized as a pile of "cards," one card for each node in the network. The card of node N lists the names of all the neighbors of node N. "Node N activating its neighbors" means that the cards of all the nodes listed on the card of node N are extracted from the pile of cards. Let us now define the notion of a "pseudoneighbor of node N" as a node which (a) is not a neighbor of N, and (b) nonetheless, has its name listed on the card of node N. This implies that when N activates its neighbors, the pseudoneighbors of N are simultaneously activated. If the pseudoneighbors are selected in a manner that maximizes the likelihood of a pseudoneighbor being either a node activated by the search process started from the other node, or at least a node lying on the shortest path leading to that other node, a general reduction of the size of the network is obtained which affects both search time and the total number of activated nodes per search.

That pseudoneighbors must be chosen selectively is underlined by the fact that pseudoneighbors can be "close" or "distant." A "close" pseudoneighbor of node N is a pseudoneighbor of N which is a neighbor of a neighbor of N. A "distant" pseudoneighbor of node N is a pseudoneighbor of N which is not a neighbor of a neighbor of N. While close pseudoneighbors are a well-defined and relatively restricted set of nodes, distant pseudoneighbors are potentially all the nodes in the network. Therefore, if one wants to include distant pseudoneighbors on the card of node N, one must choose them carefully so as to minimize their number (and not overcrowd the card of node N) and at the same time maximize the advantages in search time and total number of activated nodes. Learning in such a system can be thought of as the intelligent addition of pseudoneighbors to a node's card.

The structural characteristics of our network indicate a number of pseudoneighbor candidates along the following lines:

- A predicate node has only the C label nodes of propositional units containing the predicate as its neighbors. Pseudoneighbors of the predicate node are the argument nodes of each of these propositional units.

- A C label node of a propositional unit has as its neighbors (a) the unit's predicate node, (b) the unit's argument node(s), and possibly (c) the C label nodes of units having the C node as their argument. If (c) is true, pseudoneighbors of the C label node are the predicate node and possibly the other argument node(s) of these units.

- An X node has only the C label nodes of units having the X node as their argument as its neighbors. Pseudoneighbors of the X node are the predicate node and the other argument node(s), if any, of each of these units.

In addition to these structural pseudoneighbors—all of them close pseudoneighbors—other pseudoneighbor candidates can be found by looking at a number of properties of knowledge representation schemas that have been repeatedly discussed in the literature: ISA hierarchies, PART OF hierarchies, defining properties of class nodes, frames, prototypical knowledge, causal chains, temporal chains, and so on. For example, an ISA hierarchy can include a large number of sub-classes, but for most uses, what the system must know is that an individual node (say, a particular dog) is a member of one or two classes high in the hierarchy (say, "animals" or "living things"). These especially useful nodes can be pseudoneighbors of the class node of "dogs" while other classes (say, "spaniels" or "mammalians") also in the hierarchy are not. Another example concerns frame-like knowledge. For instance, one thing that we know about "maids" is that they work in "homes." If the class node of "maids" and the class node of "homes" are sentence activated nodes and the system must find the shortest path connecting them, it can find that path in a single step if "homes" is a pseudoneighbor of "maids" and/or vice versa.

We thus propose that the basic mechanism of encyclopedic disambiguation consists of finding the shortest path between sentence activated nodes. Semantic lexical ambiguity is typically solved by finding which of the two alternative encyclopedic nodes activated by an ambiguous word is connected by the shortest path with the other sentence activated nodes. Consider the two sentences:

(18) John took the money to the bank.

(19) The girl was fishing on the bank.

We assume the following fragment of the system's encyclopedia:

(20)

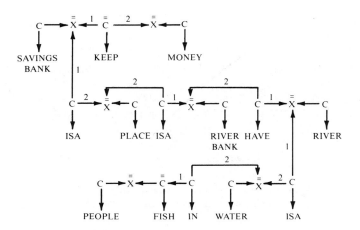

There is a class node of savings banks (class nodes are indicated by double bars) which keep money and are a sub-class (ISA) of places. There is a class node of river banks that rivers have and that is also a sub-class of places. Furthermore, rivers are a sub-class of waters where people fish. When sentence (18) is processed the class node of money is activated and then the two readings of *bank* activate the alternative nodes of "savings banks" and of "river banks." Since the money node is closer to the "savings bank" node than to the "river bank" node the former alternative is selected. When sentence (19) is processed, the node of fishing is closer to the "river bank" node and the second alternative is selected.

SMP-internal ambiguity can be solved by the same mechanism. Consider the following sentence (said with a very special emphasis if spoken):

(21) Bill said that Mary left aloud.

Here, "saying" belongs to a sub-class of activities that can be executed "aloud," which is not true for "leaving":

(22)

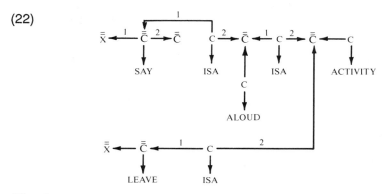

The shorter path between "saying" and "aloud" selects the alternative of assembling *aloud* with *said* and not with *left*—which would be the syntactic preference.

Finally, ambiguity due to optional assembly instructions can also be solved by finding the shortest path between sentence activated nodes. Consider this sentence:

(23) John gave the girl who was eating a book.

When the system is processing *a book* the alternative of not executing the optional instruction on the "eaten" argument of *eat* is selected and *book* is assembled as the "object of giving" argument of *give* since "books" are a sub-class of "things that are given" but not a sub-class of "things that are eaten":

(24)

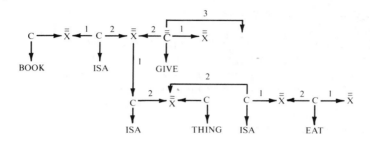

6 *Solving Additional Deep Understanding Problems*

In addition to solving ambiguity problems finding the shortest path between sentence activated nodes can also solve a number of additional problems of deep understanding. We will briefly mention five of these problems: (a) identification of pronoun referents; (b) metonymy resolution; (c) specification of relationships; (d) specification of the meaning of generic terms; (e) salience of particular aspects of a word's meaning.

6.1 *Identification of Pronoun Referents*

Consider the following text:

(25) Bill left the newspaper on the table. It was a nice piece of furniture.

The pronoun *it* must be assembled with *table* and not with *newspaper*. We assume that the following is a fragment of the system's encyclopedia:

(26)

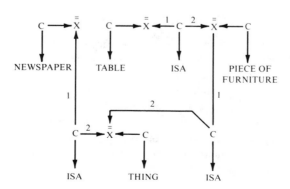

There is a class of newspapers and a class of tables, which is a sub-class of the class of things that are pieces of furniture. On the basis of the sentence network extracted from (25), the argument of *it* is identified as a "piece of furniture." Of the two candidates to be the reference of *it, table and newspaper*, the first is selected because there is a short path connecting "piece of furniture" and "table" while there is a longer path connecting "piece of furniture" and "newspaper" (through the class of "things" in general).

6.2 *Metonymy Resolution*

Consider the sentence:

(27) The pot is boiling.

To deeply understand this sentence, the system must understand that what is boiling is not the pot itself but some liquid contained in the pot. This is achieved by finding the shortest path connecting the node of pots and the node of "things that boil" in an encyclopedic fragment like the following:

(28)

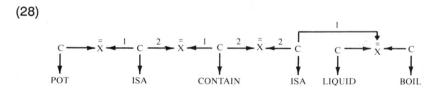

where pots are a sub-class of containers and liquid things are a sub-class of things that can be contained and can boil. Hence, sentence (27) is interpreted as "the liquid which is contained in the pot is boiling."

6.3 *Specification of Relationship*

Relationships between entities are left unspecified in surface understanding in genitive constructions (e.g., *Picasso's paintings*), noun-noun modification (e.g., *bus station*), and derived adjectives (e.g., *national policies*). Deep understanding requires that these relationships be specified by using the knowledge which lies on the shortest path connecting the corresponding encyclopedic nodes. (On the interpretation of noun-noun modification see also [Finin, 1980]). For example, *bus station* is interpreted as "station where buses stop" and *national policies* is interpreted as "policies adopted by a nation" on the basis of the following encyclopedic fragments:

(29)

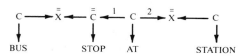

(30)

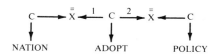

The expression *Picasso's paintings* is interpreted at surface level as "painting having some relationship to Picasso." At a deep level, however, the relationship between Picasso and the paintings is specified as "paintings painted by Picasso."

6.4 Specification of the Meaning of Generic Terms

A *container of apples* can be a basket or a bag but not a bottle or a glass while the opposite is true for a *container of wine* ([Anderson et al., 1976]). *To begin a book* means (for ordinary people, not for writers or book binders) "to begin reading a book" while *to begin a meal* means "to begin eating a meal." The verb *to begin* means generically "to begin some activity" and this meaning is specified by finding the shortest path between the sentence activated encyclopedic nodes:

(31)

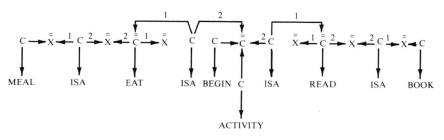

"Meals" are a sub-class of "things that are eaten" and "eating" is a sub-class of activities. "Books" are a sub-class of "things that are read" and "reading" is another sub-class of activities. "Activities" are "things that begin." The shortest path between "beginning" and "meals" passes through "eating" while the shortest path between "beginning" and "books" passes through "reading."

6.5 *Salience of Particular Aspects of a Word's Meaning*

The encyclopedic meaning of a word like *diamond* may contain both the property of "being hard" and the property of "being shiny." However, in the sentence *The man cut the diamond* the first property of diamonds is made salient while in the sentence *The diamond reflected the light* the second property becomes salient [Barsalou, 1982; Tabossi, 1982]. This is obtained by finding the shortest path between diamonds and "things that are cut" in the first sentence, and between diamonds and "things that reflect light" in the second sentence, in the following encyclopedia:

(32)

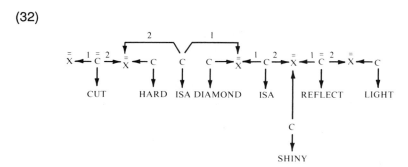

7 *Conclusions*

We have discussed a number of problems of disambiguation within a lexically distributed sentence understanding system. Syntactic knowledge contributes to disambiguation through the disambiguation procedures carried by the lexical entries and applied to the preceding context and through the four well- formedness principles that signal failures in syntactic garden path sentences. Encyclopedic knowledge operates through spreading activation and shortest path finding to select contextually appropriate readings of ambiguous words and to solve a number of additional problems of deep understanding.

Our system has been partially implemented (with Giovanni Toffoli and Stefano Nolfi) in Common LISP on the IBM AT (with 3 MB of central memory) and on the MicroVAX II. The version for the Italian language has very good syntactic coverage (surface understanding) while the English version only covers the most basic syntactic types of English. Fragments of encyclopedic knowledge have also been implemented to deal with examples of the various types of deep understanding problems previously discussed. Currently the system is being revised to generate a more connectionist implementation with syntactic and encyclopedic knowledge represented in a more uniform way, and in which understanding is obtained by an interaction of the two types of knowledge in a shared network. In the new implementation, disambiguation is brought about by following alternative paths in a parallel way, and waiting for the context, both preceding and subsequent, to send additional activation to one alternative and eliminate the others.

Acknowledgments

Many ideas discussed in this paper have emerged from work done with Oliviero Stock. We thank him.

References

Anderson, R.C., Pichert, J.W., Goetz, E.T., Schallert, D.L., Stevens, K.V., Trollip, S.R. 1976. Instantiation of general terms. *Journal of Verbal Learning and Verbal Behavior* 15:667–679.

Barsalou, L.W. 1982. Context-independent and context-dependent information in concepts. *Memory and Cognition* 10:82–93.

Charniak, E. 1983. Passing markers: A theory of contextual influence in language comprehension. *Cognitive Science* 7:171–190.

Cottrell, G.W., Small, S.L. 1984. Viewing parsing as word sense discrimination: A connectionist approach. In B.G. Bara and G. Guida (eds.), *Computational Models of Natural Language Processing*. Amsterdam: North-Holland.

Fahlman, S. 1979. *NETL: A System for Representing and Using Real-World Knowledge*. Cambridge: MIT Press.

Ferrari, G., Stock, O. 1980. Strategy selection for an ATN syntactic parser. *Proceedings of the Eighteenth Meeting of the Association for Computational Linguistics*. Philadelphia, PA.

Finin, T.W. 1980. The semantic interpretation of compound nominals. Technical Report No. T-96, Champaign-Urbana: University of Illinois, Coordinated Science Laboratory.

Marcus, M.P. 1980. *A Theory of Syntactic Recognition for Natural Language*. Cambridge: MIT Press.

Small, S.L. 1980. Word expert parsing: A theory of distributed word-based natural language understanding. Technical Report No. 954, Dept. of Computer Science, University of Maryland.

Tabossi, P. 1982. Sentential context and the interpretation of unambiguous words. *Quarterly Journal of Experimental Psychology* 34A:79–90.

Waltz, D.L., Pollack, J.B. 1985. Massively parallel parsing: A strongly interactive model of natural language interpretation. *Cognitive Science* 9:51–74.

6

An Account of Coherence, Semantic Relations, Metonymy, and Lexical Ambiguity Resolution

Dan Fass

Rio Grande Research Corridor
Computing Research Laboratory
New Mexico State University

1 Introduction

This chapter attempts to clarify the relationship between the resolution of lexical ambiguity, semantic relations, and metonymy within an account of coherence. We define coherence as the synergism of knowledge, where synergism is the interaction of two or more discrete agencies to achieve an effect of which none is individually capable. In our account, semantic relations and metonymy are instances of coherence and coherence is also used in resolving lexical ambiguity. This account of coherence, semantic relations, metonymy and lexical ambiguity resolution is embodied in Collative Semantics, hereafter CS. CS is a semantics for natural language processing which extends the ideas of Preference Semantics [Wilks, 1973; 1975a; 1975b; 1978; Fass and Wilks, 1983].

To explain the account of coherence, we establish two sets of relationships that involve coherence and then unify those relationships. Section 2 establishes the first relationship which is between coherence, semantic relations, and metonymy. We take the general conception of coherence used in theories of discourse and extend that conception downward from the discourse level to the sentence level to argue that semantic relations and metonymies in sentences are instances of coherence.

Section 3 establishes a second relationship which is between coherence and the resolution of lexical ambiguity. We develop a conception of coherence that is grounded in properties of semantic networks that are a common kind of knowledge representation scheme. Two basic kinds of coherence relation, termed "inclusion" and "distance," are distinguished. We then extend this conception of coherence upward and argue that inclusion and distance underlie two of the main approaches to lexical ambiguity resolution.

The last part of Section 3 combines the two sets of relationships to produce the skeleton of our account of coherence: [1] Basic notions of coherence are founded on principles of knowledge representation. [2] Semantic relations and metonymy within sentences are instances of coherence. [3] Coherence is used for lexical ambiguity resolution. [4] Discourse phenomena are instances of coherence.

Section 4 fills out the skeleton by connecting [1] to [2] and [2] to [3]. It establishes these connections by describing the four components of CS and their interrelationships. The four components are *sense-frames*, *collation*, *semantic vectors*, and *screening*. Sense-frames are the knowledge representation scheme and represent individual word-senses. Collation matches the sense-frames of two word-senses, finds any metonymies between the sense-frames of the word-senses, and also discriminates the semantic relations between the word-senses as a complex system of mappings between their sense-frames. Semantic vectors represent such systems of mappings produced by collation and hence the semantic relations encoded in those mappings. Screening chooses between two semantic vectors by applying rank orderings among semantic relations, and a measure of conceptual similarity, thereby resolving lexical ambiguity. Sense-frames and collation supply the connection between [1] and [2]. Semantic vectors and screening provide the link from [2] to [3]. What unifies our account of coherence is the treatment of semantic relations that collation discriminates ([1] to [2]) and semantic vectors represent ([2] to [3]).

CS is embodied in a natural language program called *meta5*. Section 5 gives an example sentence that contains lexical ambiguity. *Meta5* discriminates the semantic relations between pairs of word-senses in the sentence, finds an instance of metonymy between one pair, and resolves the lexical ambiguity. Section 6 provides a brief summary.

2 *Coherence, Semantic Relations, and Metonymy*

This section selectively surveys the literatures on coherence, semantic relations, and metonymy, and argues that semantic relations and metonymy are cases of coherence.

Coherence is a central notion in theories of discourse (see, e.g., [Van Dijk, 1977; de Beaugrande and Dressler, 1981; Van Dijk and Kintsch, 1983; Myers et al., 1986, pp.6–8]). In discourse theories, coherence refers to how a discourse "hangs together," "makes sense," or is "meaningful." Discourse theories view the coherence of a discourse as amalgamated from the coherence relations between sentences in that discourse (e.g., [Van Dijk, 1977]). Little attention is paid by discourse theories to coherence relations that exist within parts of sentences. The coherence relations within a sentence determine the coherence of that sentence. These coherence relations include semantic relations and metonymy.

In our view, semantic relations between terms are complex systems of mappings or structural relationships between linguistic descriptions of those terms. This view of semantic relations draws from definitions of metaphor as systems of relationships or "implicative complexes" [Black, 1979], mappings [Carbonell, 1981], correspondences between domains [Tourangeau and Sternberg, 1982], and selective inferences [Hobbs, 1983a].

Next, we develop some terminology for describing semantic relations. The two terms in a semantic relation are called the *source* and the *target* [Martin, 1985]. The *source* initiates and directs the mapping process, the *target* has mappings laid upon it. A semantic relation also implies direction from the source towards the target.

Six types of semantic relations are distinguished. These relations are termed *literal, metaphorical, anomalous, redundant, inconsistent,* and *novel.* Brief definitions of the six semantic relations are now given, together with an example sentence for each relation. These sentences assume a null context, in which there are no complicating effects from prior sentences or the pre-existing beliefs of producers or understanders. The *meta5* program analyzes all six sentences.

The definitions of literal, metaphorical, and anomalous semantic relations begin with the observation by Katz [1972], Wilks [1973] and others that a satisfied selection restriction or preference indicates a literal semantic relation, whereas a violated restriction indicates a metaphorical or anomalous semantic relation.

Metaphorical and anomalous semantic relations are distinguished by the presence or absence of a relevant analogy. The importance of relevance in recognising metaphors has been argued (e.g., [Tversky, 1977; Hobbs, 1983a]). Frequently, it has been claimed that the critical match in a metaphorical relation is some correspondence or analogy between two properties (e.g., [Wilks, 1978; Ortony, 1979, p. 167; Tourangeau and Sternberg 1982, pp. 218–221; Gentner, 1983]).

This description of redundant, inconsistent, and novel semantic relations is an expansion of Katz and Fodor's ideas on "attribution" [1964, pp. 508–509], which were a development of some ideas by Lees [1960].

(1) "The man drank beer."

There is a literal relation between "man" and "drink" in (1) because "drink" prefers an animal as its agent (i.e., it is animals that drink) and a man is a type of animal, so the preference is satisfied.

(2) "The car drank gasoline." (adapted from [Wilks, 1978])

By contrast, the semantic relation between "car" and "drink" in (2) is metaphorical because "drink" prefers an animal as its agent but a car is not a type of animal so the preference is violated. However, there is an analogy between animals and cars that is relevant in the context of a sentence about drinking, such as (2). The relevant analogy is that animals drink potable liquids as cars use gasoline, hence the metaphorical relation between "car" and "drink."

(3) "The idea drank the heart."

In (3), the semantic relation between "idea" and "drink" is anomalous. This is because "idea" is not a preferred agent of "drink" and no relevant analogy can be found between animals (the preferred agent) and ideas.

(4) "His wife is married."

The semantic relation between "wife" and "married" is semantically redundant in (4) because the information asserted by the source ("married") is the same as pre-existing information in the target ("wife") because, by definition, a wife is a married woman.[1]

(5) "His wife is unmarried."

---

1 Another, less common kind of redundant relation occurs when the information asserted by the source is more general than pre-existing information in the target.

In (5), the semantic relation between "wife" and "married" is inconsistent because the information added by "unmarried" is incompatible with "married" in the definition of a wife as a married woman. In our terminology, inconsistent semantic relations include contradictory and contrary ones.[2]

(6) "His wife is young."

Finally, (6) contains a novel semantic relation between "wife" and "young" because the information asserted by the source ("young") does not match with any pre-existing information in the target ("wife"); in other words, the asserted information is unknown.[3]

A distinction is made between semantic relations and semantic "properties." Semantic properties include metaphor, anomaly, redundancy, and inconsistency. Semantic relations are *relations between* two or more linguistic structures, such as words or senses of words; semantic properties are the same relations expressed as *properties of* linguistic structures, such as constituents or sentences, or even whole texts. In the simplest cases, such as a constituent of only two terms, a semantic property is due to the single semantic relation found between the two terms. In more complex instances, a semantic property is ascribed to a linked group of semantic relations, such as the semantic relations that occur between the terms of a sentence.

(7) "The ship ploughed the waves."

Sentence (7) contains simple and complex forms of metaphor as a semantic property. In "the ship ploughed" the single metaphorical relation between "ship" and "ploughed" comprises a metaphor for the constituent. Also, the whole sentence comprises a metaphor due to the triangle of semantic relations between "ship," "ploughed," and "waves."

Another form of coherence apart from semantic relations is metonymy. Metonymy is a nonliteral figure of speech in which the name of one thing is substituted for that of another related to it [Lakoff and Johnson, 1980, pp. 35–40]. The technical term for a nonliteral figure of speech is a *trope*. Other tropes apart from metonymy include metaphor, simile, irony, understatement (litotes), and overstatement (hyperbole). Metonymy is a widespread semantic phenomenon, yet it has received little attention in linguistics [Jakobsen and Halle, 1956;

---

2 Contrary relations exist between terms gradable on some scale, e.g., hot/cold and big/small whereas contradictory relations exist between ungradable terms, e.g., female/male, single/married [Lyons, 1963, pp. 460–469; Lehrer, 1974, p. 26]. This difference is compatible with the standard philosophical distinction between contraries and contradictories [Lyons, 1977, p. 272].
3 Another kind of novel relation is where the information asserted by the source is more specific than pre-existing information in the target.

Levin, 1977; Sapir, 1977; Reddy, 1979; Sadock, 1979; Lakoff and Johnson, 1980; Searle, 1981; Van Eynde, 1982; Hobbs, 1983b; 1986] and even less in natural language processing [Martin, 1986]. Most of these references only mention metonymy very briefly.

A common example of metonymy is synechdoche, where the part stands for the whole, as in (8) [Reddy, 1979, p. 309].

(8) "You'll find better ideas than that in the library."

As Reddy observes, there is a chain of metonymies between "ideas" and "library": The ideas are expressed in words, words are printed on pages, pages are in books, and books are found in a library.

Lakoff and Johnson group individual cases of metonymy into seven general "metonymic concepts" [1980, pp. 38–39]. Three of those metonymic concepts, with example sentences, are:

PRODUCER FOR PRODUCT

"He bought a *Ford.*"

"I hate to read *Heidegger.*"

CONTROLLER FOR CONTROLLED

"*Nixon* bombed Hanoi."

"*Napoleon* lost at Waterloo."

OBJECT USED FOR USER

"The *sax* has the flu today."

"The *buses* are on strike."

Metonymy and metaphor are often difficult to separate, as a simple sentence illustrates:

(9) "Denise drank the bottle."

A potable liquid is drunk, not a bottle, but in (9) how can it be determined that "bottle" is being used metonymically rather than metaphorically?

There is much confusion in the literature about the relationship between metaphor and metonymy. One view is that metonymy is a type of metaphor, a view which Genette [1970] has traced, according to Levin [1977, p. 80]. Searle [1981, p. 280] claims to hold this view, though he claims, not strongly. A second and antithetical view is that metaphor is a type of metonymy. Dubois et al.

[1970] reduce metaphor to synechdoche and Jakobson and Halle [1956] reduce synechdoche to metonymy. This observation is also from Levin [Jakobson and Halle, 1956]. Finally, a third view is that metonymy and metaphor are entirely different, for example Lakoff and Johnson's [1980, pp. 36–37] view.

In our view, metonymy is a different type of conceptual relatedness from semantic relations generally, not just metaphorical ones. The main differences, as we see them, are explained in Section 4. However, what metonymy shares with semantic relations and other tropes is that all of them are manifestations of general conceptual relatedness or coherence. The reason is that tropes and semantic relations are the synergism of knowledge. To see this, consider as an example the metaphorical relation observed in sentence (2) and the relevant analogy that is central to its recognition. Synergism is the interaction of two or more discrete agencies to achieve an effect of which none is individually capable. The analogy in (2) arises from the interaction of three agencies that are "car" (the surface subject), "animal" (the expected agent), and "drink" (the relevant context; also the main sentence verb). The analogy is an effect achieved of which none of the three agencies is individually capable. The analogy is a synergism of knowledge and hence the metaphorical relation as a whole is a more complex synergism of knowledge.

In this section, a conception of coherence has been developed that includes semantic relations and metonymy. In the next section, another conception of coherence is developed in which coherence is used to resolve lexical ambiguity. The two conceptions of coherence share the same definition, that coherence is the synergism of knowledge, but the difference between the conceptions is in their derivation. The conception of coherence in this section is derived downward from theories of discourse and truth, whereas the conception of coherence in the next section is derived upward from properties of knowledge representation, specifically semantic networks.

3 Coherence and Lexical Ambiguity Resolution

This section discusses two well known approaches to the resolution of lexical ambiguity and attempts to show how they utilize coherence. We call these approaches the *inclusion-based* and *distance-based* approaches. Inclusion-based approaches include Preference Semantics, message passing, and CS. Distance-based approaches include spreading activation and marker passing schemes.[4] Our contention is that each approach is founded on two different basic notions

4 A third approach to lexical ambiguity resolution is the "activation-based" approach used in connectionist schemes (e.g., [Cottrell and Small, 1983; Waltz and Pollack, 1985]) but that approach is not considered here.

of coherence that exist in semantic networks, that we call *inclusion* and *distance*.

We begin with a definition of a semantic network, but as the definition uses the terms "genus," "species," and "differentia" from classification theory, they are defined first. The genus is the name of a class that includes subordinates called the species. The differentia is that set of properties by which a species is distinguished from other species of the same genus. Take for example

Car: A vehicle that carries passengers.

The word "vehicle" serves as the genus term while "that carries passengers" differentiates cars from other species such as buses and motorbikes. Now "semantic network" can be defined. A semantic network is a taxonomy of genus and species terms in which the network nodes are the terms and the network arcs that link the nodes have labels that denote class inclusion between the terms.

In a semantic network, a path between any pair of nodes has two intrinsic properties that are the two basic notions of coherence. One intrinsic property is the semantic distance, or number of arcs traversed, between the two nodes. For example, "vehicle" and "car" have a small distance between them whereas "animal" and "car" have a much greater distance between them. The other intrinsic property is the inclusion relation between the individuals that the names of the two nodes refer to. For example, the path between network nodes for "vehicle" and "car" denotes inclusion because a car is a type of vehicle; on the other hand, the path between "animal" and "car" denotes exclusion because a car is not a type of animal.

So, the two basic notions of coherence are distance and inclusion. Both distance and inclusion describe kinds of conceptual relatedness. A short distance indicates close conceptual relatedness (i.e., "vehicle" and "car") whereas a long distance indicates remote conceptual relatedness (i.e., "animal" and "car"). Inclusion signifies conceptual relatedness (i.e., a "vehicle" is a "car") whereas exclusion signifies conceptual unrelatedness (i.e., a "car" is not an "animal").

Note that these basic notions of coherence are not explicit in a semantic network. Instead, distance and inclusion are a by-product of path building between nodes in that network. In other words, this new concept of coherence is the synergism of knowledge, just as it was in Section 2. Synergism, once again, is the interaction of two or more discrete agencies to achieve an effect of which none is individually capable. The agencies here are network nodes, the interaction is path building, and the effect achieved is the basic kinds of coherence, i.e., distance and inclusion. Next, it is shown how these two basic kinds of coherence underlie inclusion-based and distance-based approaches to lexical ambiguity resolution.

Inclusion-based approaches include Katz's semantic theory [Katz and Postal, 1964; Katz, 1972], Preference Semantics, message passing [Rieger and Small, 1979; Small and Rieger, 1982], and CS. All of these are based on the satisfaction and violation of selection restrictions, which are called expectations in message passing, and preferences in Preference Semantics and CS.[5] The notions of *satisfaction* and *violation* are based on inclusion, which is one of the two basic kinds of coherence. All these inclusion-based approaches use a semantic network as their knowledge representation. Satisfied selection restrictions, preferences and expectations are all paths denoting inclusion through such a network. Conversely, violated selection restrictions, preferences and expectations are all paths denoting exclusion. For example, if a selection restriction were for "vehicle" then "car" would satisfy the restriction because a car is a type of vehicle; but if the restriction were for "animal" then "car" would cause a violation because a car is not a type of animal.

Those in the inclusion-based approach differ among themselves in their use of satisfied and violated selection restrictions, preferences, or expectations to achieve lexical disambiguation. In Katz's theory, the sentence reading chosen must contain only satisfied selection restrictions. In Preference Semantics, the sentence reading chosen is the best available where the best is the reading with the greatest number of satisfied preferences, even if it also contains violated preferences. See Fass and Wilks [1983] for further discussion.

Distance-based approaches include schemes for spreading activation [Quillian, 1968] and marker passing [Charniak, 1983; Hirst, 1983]. All of these approaches seek the path with the shortest distance between two nodes in a semantic network, i.e., the second basic kind of coherence. Search is unconstrained except for the ruling out of certain path sequences [Charniak, 1983, 1986] and the use of mathematical functions for limiting the length of network paths [Hirst, 1983; Charniak, 1986].

The conception of coherence developed in this section is grounded in properties of semantic networks, which are a common kind of knowledge representation. The properties of distance and inclusion are basic kinds of coherence that emerge from network paths and underpin two of the main approaches to lexical ambiguity resolution. If this conception of coherence is integrated with the conception of coherence from Section 2 then our account of coherence is that: [1] Basic notions of coherence are founded on principles of knowledge representation (from Section 3). [2] Semantic relations and metonymy in sentences are instances of coherence (from Section 2). [3] Coherence is used for

---

5 The terms "preference" [Wilks, 1975a] and "expectation" [Schank, 1975] highlight different aspects of the use of selection restrictions. Wilks emphasises that selection restrictions may or may not be satisfied, hence the word "preference." Schank stresses that selection restrictions are used for top-down prediction, hence the term "expectation."

lexical ambiguity resolution (Section 3). [4] Discourse phenomena are instances of coherence (Section 2).

Still missing from this account are the links between [1], [2], [3], and [4]. Section 4, which is on CS, attempts to supply some of the missing detail. The link sought between [1] and [2] must answer to questions of how the basic kinds of coherence are used in the recognition of semantic relations and metonymy. CS establishes a connection from [1] to [2] for inclusion only. The link sought between [2] and [3] shows how semantic relations and metonymy are put to use in resolving lexical ambiguity. Again, CS provides only a connection for an inclusion-based approach. We do not attempt to connect [4] to the others.

4 *Collative Semantics*

CS has four components, which are *sense-frames, collation, semantic vectors*, and *screening*. Sense-frames are dictionary entries for individual word-senses. In CS, word-senses perform the function of semantic primitives. Sense-frames are composed of other word-senses that have their own sense-frames, much like Quillian's [1968] planes. This ultimately leads to circular definitions (as in a real dictionary) but the circularity is not a problem. There are no semantic primitives in the sense of Schank's [1975] Conceptual Dependency or Wilks's Preference Semantics.[6]

Each sense-frame consists of two parts, an *arcs* section and a *node* section, that correspond to the genus and differentia commonly found in a real dictionary definition. The arcs part of a sense-frame contains a labelled arc to its genus term (a word-sense with its own sense-frame). The most common arc labels describe types of class inclusion such as "supertype" that denote membership in a class of individuals by a class of individuals and "superinstance" that denotes membership of an individual within a class of individuals.

Together, the arcs of all the sense-frames comprise a densely structured semantic network of word-senses called the *sense-network*. This general architecture of a semantic network with frame-like structures as nodes is similar to many frame-based and semantic network-based systems, such as Quillian's [1968] memory model, schema theory [Norman and Rumelhart, 1975], KRL [Bobrow and Winograd, 1977], FRL [Roberts and Goldstein, 1977], KLONE [Brachman, 1979], and Frail [Wong, 1981].

The node part of a sense-frame is the differentia that provides a "definition" of the word-sense represented by the sense-frame that differentiates it

---

6 One of the main claims of CS to be a semantics is its treatment of semantic primitives (see Fass [1986]).

from other word-senses. There are three types of sense-frame node. Sense-frame nodes for nouns (node-type 0) resemble Wilks's [1978] pseudo-texts. The nodes contain lists of two-element and three-element lists called *cells*. Cells contain word-senses and have a syntax modelled on English. Each cell expresses a piece of functional or structural information and can be thought of as a complex semantic feature or property of a noun. Figure 6.1 shows sense-frames for two senses of the noun "crook." Crook1 is the sense meaning "thief" and crook2 is the shepherd's tool.

All the terms the reader sees are word-senses with their own sense-frames.[7] It1 is a *meta-pronoun* that refers to the word-sense being defined by the sense-frame. So, for example, crook1 can be substituted for it1 in [it1, steal1, valuables1]. Common dictionary practice is followed: word senses are listed separately for each part of speech and numbered by frequency of occurrence. Hence in crook2, the cell [shepherd1, use1, it1] contains the noun sense shepherd1 while the cell [it1, shepherd1, sheep1] contains the verb sense shepherd1.

Sense-frame nodes for adjectives and adverbs (node-type 1) contain a *preference* and an *assertion*. Preferences and assertions are distinctions among kinds of conceptual information. A preference contains information expressing a restriction on the local context (see [Fass and Wilks, 1983] for further discussion of the notion of preference). An assertion contains information to be imposed on the local context. The preference-assertion distinction provides the basis for distinguishing two classes of semantic relation. One class (literal, metaphorical and anomalous relations) is derived from the information contained in preferences; the other class (novel, redundant, and inconsistent relations) uses assertion information.

```
sf(crook1,                          sf(crook2,
   [[arcs,                             [[arcs,
     [[supertype, criminal1]]],          [[supertype, stick1]]],
   [node0,                             [node0,
     [[it1, steal1, valuables1]]]]).     [[shepherd1, use1, it1],
                                         [it1, shepherd1, sheep1]]]]]).
```

Figure 6.1 Sense-frames for crook1 and crook2.

---

7 The terms used as labels for sense-frame parts ("arcs," "node0," "node1," "node2," "preference" and "assertion"), arc labels ("supertype," "superinstance," etc), and case labels (e.g., "agent," "object" and "instrument") are not word-senses but words used in a particular sense that could be replaced by word-senses. Sense-frames for them could be defined and added to the lexicon and *meta5* would run just as it does now, once minor changes were made to a few of its functions. However, using word-senses as labels mars the appearance of sense-frames which is why the words used for labels have not been replaced.

```
sf(male1,
    [[arcs,
        [[superproperty, sex1],
        [property, male1]]],
    [node1,
        [[preference, organism1],
        [assertion,
            [[sex1, male1]]]]]]).
```

Figure 6.2 Sense-frame for male1 (adjective).

```
sf(eat1,
    [[arcs,
        [[supertype, [ingest1, expend1]]]],
    [node2,
        [[agent,
            [preference, animal1]],
        [object,
            [preference, drink1]]]]]]).
```

Figure 6.3 Sense-frame for eat1 (verb).

Figure 6.2 shows the sense-frame for the adjective sense male1. The cell [superproperty, sex1] indicates membership of the property class sex. The cell [property, male1] signifies that being male is a property of males. The preference is for an organism because this is what "male" predicates over. The assertion is that any entity to which "male" is applied is of the male sex.

Sense-frame nodes for verbs and prepositions (node-type 2) are case frames containing case subparts filled by case roles such as "agent," "object" and "instrument." Case subparts contain preferences, and assertions if the verb describes a state change.

Figure 6.3 shows the sense-frame for the verb sense eat1. The agent preference is for an animal and the object preference is for food, an edible solid.

The second component of CS is the process of collation. Collation matches the sense-frames of two word-senses and finds a system of multiple mappings between those sense-frames, thereby discriminating the semantic relations between the word-senses. The basic mappings are paths found by a graph search algorithm that operates over the sense-network. Five types of path are distinguished. Two path-types denote inclusion; three denote exclusion. These paths are used to build more complex mappings found by a frame-matching algorithm. The frame-matching algorithm matches the sets of cells from two sense-frames. Seven types of cell match are distinguished. The sets of cells, which need not be ordered, are inherited down the sense-network. A series of structural constraints isolate pairs of cells that are matched using the graph search algorithm. Paths denoting inclusion are sought between terms occupying identical positions in those cells.

A notion of relevance is computed dynamically from the sentence context. Relevance divides the set of cells from the source sense-frame into two subsets. One cell is selected as *relevant* given the context; the remaining cells are termed *non-relevant*. Collation matches both the relevant and non-relevant cells against the cells from the target sense-frame.

Semantic relations are discriminated as different systems of mappings. Space does not permit a thorough explanation of these different systems, but we briefly explain how they encode and differentiate the definitions of literal, metaphorical, and anomalous relations given in Section 2.

A first subsystem of mappings consists of a single sense-network path found between source and target. A literal semantic relation has an inclusive sense-network path, whereas both metaphorical and anomalous relations have an exclusive path. In other words, a literal semantic relation has a satisfied selection restriction or preference, as in sentence (1), whereas a metaphorical or anomalous semantic relation has a violated selection restriction or preference, as in (2) and (3).

A second subsystem distinguishes metaphorical from anomalous semantic relations. It records the match of the relevant cell from the source sense-frame with one of the cells from the target sense-frame. For a metaphorical relation the match of cells is analogical whereas for an anomalous semantic relation the match of cells is not analogical. In other words, a metaphorical relation contains a relevant analogy, as in (2), while an anomalous relation does not, as in (3).

In collation, metonymy is treated as a type of inference and metonymic concepts are encoded as *metonymic inference rules*. Below are the four types of metonymic concepts currently represented, ordered from most common (synechdoche) to least, together with example sentences in which they occur. All of the sentences are analysed by *meta5*:

Part for Whole
"Arthur Ashe is *black*." (= skin colored black)

Container for Contents
"Mary drank the *glasses*." (= the potable liquid in the glasses)

Artist for Artform

"Anne reads *Steinbeck*." (= the writings of Steinbeck)

"Ted played *Bach*." (= the music of Bach)

Co-Agent for Activity

"Ashe played *McEnroe*." (= tennis with McEnroe)

Container for Contents is not a metonymic concept distinguished by Lakoff and Johnson [1980]; it is the opposite of **Part for the Whole**, in other words, it is a type of **Whole for the Part**. **Artist for Artform** is a type of PRODUCER FOR PRODUCT. **Co-Agent for Activity** is another metonymic concept that is not distinguished by Lakoff and Johnson.

The application of metonymic inference rules is called metonymic inferencing. Metonymic inferencing is part of the general process of discriminating the preference-based class of semantic relations (literal, metaphorical and anomalous relations) that is best described in a flow chart (see Figure 6.4). Figure 6.4 shows that metonymic inferencing is a special strategy tried after failure to discover a literal semantic relation, hence metonymy is non-literal, i.e., a trope. A successful rule establishes the relationship between the original source or the target ("the name of one thing") and a term ("another related to it") that substitutes for one of them. The substitute source or target is used to compute a semantic relation which can be literal, metaphorical or anomalous. Metonymy therefore helps to establish a semantic relation.

The third component of CS is the semantic vector which is a form of representation, along with sense-frames; but sense-frames represent knowledge, whereas semantic vectors represent coherence. Semantic vectors are therefore a kind of *coherence representation*. A semantic vector is a data structure that contains nested labels and ordered arrays structured by a simple dependency syntax. The labels form into sets. Each label set signifies a different source of knowledge. One set is "preference" and "assertion." Preferences and assertions are from sense-frame nodes. Another set is "relevant" and "non-relevant." Relevance is knowledge from the context. The third set is "path-type" and "cell matches." Path-types, and hence cell matches, are sought over the sense-network. The nesting of labels shows the order in which sources of knowledge are introduced. The ordered arrays represent the mappings. Five-column arrays are for the five path types; seven-column arrays are for the seven types of cell match. Each column contains a positive number which shows the number of occurrences of a particular path-type or cell match.

Together, the labels and arrays of a semantic vector specify the synergistic interaction of sources of knowledge in a semantic relation. In other words, the labels and arrays represent coherence. To see this, recall once again that coherence is defined as the synergism of knowledge, and that synergism is the inter-

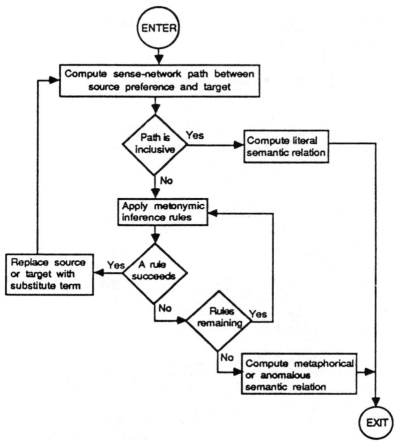

Figure 6.4 Metonymic inferencing.

action of two or more discrete agencies to achieve an effect of which none is individually capable. In a semantic vector, the discrete agencies are the three knowledge sources, their interaction is the systems of mappings, and the effect achieved is the six types of semantic relation. Examples of semantic vectors for literal and anomalous semantic relations are given in the next section.

The fourth component of CS is the process of screening. During analysis of a sentence constituent, *meta5* computes a semantic vector for pairwise combinations of word-senses. These word-sense combinations are called *semantic readings* or simply *readings*. Each reading has an associated semantic vector. Screening chooses between two semantic vectors and hence their attached semantic readings. Rank orderings among semantic relations are applied. In the event of a tie, a measure of conceptual similarity is applied.

The ranking of semantic relations aims to achieve the most coherent possible interpretation of a reading. The rank order among preference-based semantic relations is

literal $\Rightarrow$ metaphorical $\Rightarrow$ anomalous.

The class of preference-based semantic relations takes precedence over the class of assertion-based semantic relations for lexical disambiguation. Precedence among assertion-based semantic relations follows Grice's [1975] Maxim of Quantity which is to try and make your contribution as informative as possible

novel M $\Rightarrow$ (inconsistent or redundant).

If the semantic vectors are still tied, then the measure of conceptual similarity is employed. The match of two sense-frames is interpretable as the conceptual distance between their domains. We have developed a measure of conceptual distance called the *distance number*.[8] A large distance number indicates strong conceptual similarity or relatedness (i.e., close domains) whereas a small or negative distance number indicates weak conceptual similarity (i.e., distant domains).

Each semantic vector has a distance number. Two distance numbers, and hence two semantic vectors, are compared using heuristics called *scoring metrics*. The scoring metrics compare relative strength of conceptual relatedness. Strong conceptual relatedness (a large distance number) is chosen over weak conceptual relatedness (a small distance number). The *relative strength number* is one distance number less the other. As a general rule, the larger the distance numbers are, the bigger the relative strength number must be to choose between them. In other words, if two distance numbers both indicate strong conceptual relatedness then one distance number must be considerably larger—and therefore much more strong relatively—than the other number, to choose between those numbers. The scoring metrics specify ranges for the relative strength number and distance number that introduce a degree of fuzziness into the choices that are made.

---

8 The distance number is derived as follows. The conceptual distance between the domains of two sense-frames is defined as the proportion of *similarities* to *differences* between their matches of cells. Similarities are cell matches that denote inclusion, and the number of occurrences of those matches is the *similarity number*. Likewise, differences are those cell matches denoting exclusion, and the number of those matches is the *difference number*. The similarity number less the difference number is the distance number.

Detail can now be supplied for the missing links between [1], [2], and [3] in the skeleton account of coherence outlined in Section 3. The first missing link from [1] to [2] is a description of how inclusion is employed in the recognition of semantic relations and metonymy (distance is not used in CS). Our explanation is that collation uses sense-network paths to discriminate semantic relations and perform metonymic inferencing. The semantic relations are systems of mappings built from sense-network paths denoting inclusion and exclusion, and metonymies are inference chains whose links are the same sense-network paths.

The second missing link from [2] to [3] is an account of how semantic relations and metonymy are used in the resolution of lexical ambiguity. Our explanation first notes that metonymy establishes semantic relations and that only semantic relations figure directly in lexical ambiguity resolution. The connection between semantic relations and lexical ambiguity resolution is then explained using semantic vectors. Semantic relations are represented in semantic vectors as systems of mappings; and screening uses those mappings to resolve lexical ambiguity by applying rank orderings of semantic relations and, if necessary, a measure of conceptual similarity (the relative strength number).

All four components play roles in filling the missing links between [1] and [3]. The fillers of the first missing link ([1] to [2]) are sense-frames and collation, and the fillers of the second missing link ([2] to [3]) are semantic vectors and screening. Note that it is the treatment of semantic relations by collation and semantic vectors that binds the two conceptions of coherence as derived upward from semantic networks (in Section 2) and downward from discourse theory (in Section 3) because collation discriminates semantic relations ([1] to [2]) that semantic vectors represent ([2] to [3]).

5 *Example*

This section gives a relatively simple demonstration of sentence analysis by *meta5*. The *meta5* program is written in Quintus Prolog and consists of a lexicon containing the sense-frames of 460 word-senses, a small grammar, and semantic routines that embody collation and screening, the two processes of CS.[9] *Meta5*'s analysis of (10) illustrates the connection between semantic relations, metonymy, and lexical ambiguity resolution in CS.

---

9 *Meta5*'s grammar is adapted from the grammar of *XTRA* [Huang, 1985], an English-Chinese machine translation program also written in Prolog. *XTRA* is the latest in a succession of programs that originate from Boguraev's [1979] natural language analyser that was written in LISP. Huang's and Boguraev's programs use versions of Preference Semantics.

(10) "Mary drank the glasses."

Sentence (10) contains lexical ambiguity because there are three senses of "glasses" in *meta5*'s lexicon. The first sense of "glass" (glass1) is the material; the second sense (glass2) is the drinking vessel; and the third sense (glasses3) is spectacles. The metonymy in (10) is between "drink" and the second sense of "glass." "Drink" prefers a potable liquid as its object (it is potable liquids that are drunk) and a metonymic inference (**Container for Contents**) is found between potable liquid and glasses as drinking vessels because drinking vessels contain potable liquids.

Meta5 is syntax-driven. The semantic routines that embody CS are called after syntactic recognition of a noun phrase or the main sentence verb. The first call to the semantic routines is after the grammar recognises a noun phrase in subject position. In sentence (10) the subject noun phrase is "Mary." The noun phrase semantic routine matches all pairwise combinations of adjective and noun senses and outputs semantic readings for the best (or equal best) combinations. In (10) there is only one semantic reading because *meta5*'s lexicon contains only one sense of "Mary." Control is returned to the grammar that then recognises the main sentence verb, which in (10) is "drank." Another semantic routine is called that matches all readings of the subject noun phrase ("Mary") against all senses of the main sentence verb ("drank"). In (10) there is only one verb sense of "drink" so only mary and drink1 are matched and a semantic reading of them both is output by the semantic routine. Control passes back to the grammar that recognises the object noun phrase. The noun phrase semantic routine is called; it outputs three semantic readings, each containing a sense of "glasses." Another semantic routine is called that matches those three readings against the single reading for the sentence subject and verb. We will now investigate those matches.

The first match is between the verb sense drink1 and glass1, the material. In the sense-frame for the verb sense drink1 (Figure 6.5) note that the object preference is the noun sense drink1, the potable liquid. Collation matches the source, the noun sense drink1, against the target, which is glass1 (see Figure 6.5). Collation uses its graph search algorithm to seek the sense-network path between the noun sense drink1 and glass1. The path between them is exclusive, i.e., the material glass1 is not a type of drink1. A literal relation has an inclusive path so the semantic relation between the verb sense drink1 and glass1 is not a literal relation—it must therefore be metaphorical or anomalous.

Collation then seeks a metonymic inference between the noun sense drink1 and glass1 but fails to find one.

Finally, collation employs its frame-matching algorithm to match the cells of the noun sense drink1 and glass1. The list of cells for the noun sense drink1 is inherited down the sense-network, as Figure 6.6 shows. For ease of reading, it1 has been replaced by drink1.

```
sf(drink1,
    [[arcs,
        [[supertype, [ ingest1, expend1]]]],
      [node2,
        [[agent,
          [preference, animal1]],
        [object,
          [preference, drink1 ]]]]]).
```

```
sf(drink1,                          sf(glass1,
    [[arcs,                             [[arcs,
        [[supertype,                       [[supertype, substance1]]],
          [[energy_source1, liquid1]]]],    [node0,
      [node0,                               [[composition1, silicate1],
        [[behaviour1, liquid1],             [behaviour1, brittle1]]]]]).
        [animal1, drink1, it1]]]]).
```

Figure 6.5 Sense-frames for drink1 (verb and noun) and glass1 (noun).

Cells of drink1

```
[[bounds1,  distinct1],
 [composition1,  organic1],
 [extent1,  three_dimensional1],
 [animacy1,  nonliving1],
 [behaviour1,  liquid1]
 [animal1,  drink1,  drink1]]
```

Figure 6.6 Cells of drink1 (noun).

Next, the relevant cell of the noun sense drink1 is isolated. A simple, dynamic notion of relevance is used: What is relevant is the sense of the main sentence verb. This is dynamic because what is relevant changes as the sense of the main sentence verb changes. In the present example, the verb sense drink1 is relevant. The list of cells for the noun sense drink1 is searched for one referring to drinking. The relevant cell in the list is [animal1, drink1, drink1], which is compared against the inherited cells of glass1, but no match is found (see Figure 6.7). As no analogy was found, the semantic relation between the verb sense drink1 and glass1 is an anomalous one.

Relevant cell of drink1   Cells of glass1

[animal1, drink1, drink1]   [[bounds1, unbounded1],
                               [animacy1, nonliving1],
                               [extent1, three_dimensional1],
                               [composition1, silicate1],
                               [behaviour1, brittle1]]

Figure 6.7 Match of relevant cell.

Non-relevant cells of drink1	Non-relevant cells of glass1	Cell matches
[[extent1, three_dimensional1], [animacy1, living1],	[[extent1, three_dimensional1], [animacy1, living1],	2 identical cell matches
[bounds1, bounded1],	[bounds1, unbounded1],	1 sister cell match
[composition1, organic1], [behaviour1, liquid1]]	[composition1, silicate1], [behaviour1, brittle1]]	2 estranged cell matches

Figure 6.8 Matches of non-relevant cells.

Figure 6.8 shows the final set of cell matches, which is between the non-relevant cells of the noun sense drink1 and the cells of glass1. The two sets of cells have been ordered for ease of reading. Two of the cells of drink1 and glass1 are identical: Liquids and materials are both three-dimensional and inanimate. Three of the sets of cells have incompatibilities. One set of cells are in a *sister* match and are direct contrasts. A drink is bounded whereas glass is unbounded.[10] The other sets of cells are *estranged* matches that are less direct contrasts. All of these matches are recorded in a semantic vector (see Figure 6.9).

In Figure 6.9, the "preference" label indicates that a preference has been matched (rather than an assertion). "Path_type" stands for types of sense-network path. Each column in the first array signifies a different path type. The 1 in the fifth column of the first array is the exclusive path found between the noun sense drink1 and glass1 that is termed an *estranged* path type.

---

10 Humans conceive of entities like a drink as a finite amount enclosed in something whereas types of matter such as glass or water are conceived of as continuous and unlimited in extent. See Talmy [1978, pp. 17–18] and Lakoff and Johnson [1980].

```
[preference,
    [[path_type,              | First array :
        [0, 0, 0, 0, 1]],     | exclusive sense-network path
    [cell_matches,
        [[relevant,           | Second array :
            [0, 0, 0, 0, 0, 1, 5]],  | no match of relevant cell
        [non_relevant,        | Third array :
            [0, 2, 1, 0, 2, 0, 0]]]]]]  | matches of non-relevant cells
```

Figure 6.9 An anomalous semantic relation.

The columns in the second and third arrays signify cell matches. "Cell_matches" stands for matches of cells. "Relevant" signifies the match of the relevant cell. The 1 in the sixth column of the second array is the unmatched relevant cell [animal1, drink1, drink1]. The 5 is the five distinctive cells of glass1 that did not match [animal1, drink1, drink1]. This is the match of 6 cells, 1 from the source and 5 from the target (see Figure 6.7). The sum of array columns is

$$((0 + 0 + 0 + 0 + 0) \times 2) + ((1 + 5) \times 1) = (0 \times 2) + (6 \times 1) = 6.$$

"Non_relevant" signifies the matches of the non-relevant cells. In the final array, the 2 in the second column is the two identical cell matches shown in Figure 6.8. The 1 and 2 in the third and fifth columns are the 3 incompatibilities. There were no unmatched cells (indicated by the zeroes in the last two columns). Ten cells are matched, 5 from the source and 5 from the target (see Figure 6.9). The sum of the columns in the array is

$$((0 + 2 + 1 + 0 + 2) \times 2) + ((0 + 0) \times 1) = (5 \times 2) + (0 \times 1) = 10.$$

The second match tried by *meta5*'s semantic routines is between the verb sense drink1 and glass2, the drinking vessels. Collation matches the noun sense drink1 (the source) against glass2 (the target), which is the object preference of the verb sense drink1 (see Figure 6.10). Collation seeks the sense-network path between the object preference, the noun sense drink1, and glass2. The sense-network path between them is exclusive, so glass2 is not a type of drink1. The metonymic inference rules are applied and the **Container for Contents** rule succeeds. The metonymic inference is that a glass2 contains drink1. To put this another way, glasses are drinking vessels (containers) that contain potable liquids (contents), i.e., drinks.

A successful metonymy establishes the relationship between a source or target ("the name of one thing") and a term ("another related to it") that substitutes for one of them. In the successful **Container for Contents** metonymy, the target (glass2) is replaced by the metonym (drink1). Collation now matches the original preference (drink1) against the new target (drink1). They are identical, which is an inclusive relationship, so a literal semantic relation is discriminated.

The cells of the source noun sense drink1 and the target noun sense drink1 are matched together. The cells of drink1 are inherited down the sense-network and the same relevant cell as for the first reading is isolated (see Figure 6.7) and matched against the target. Not surprisingly, the relevant cell [animal1, drink1, drink1] is identical to a cell in the target. The cell [animal1, drink1,

```
sf(drink1,
    [[arcs,
        [[supertype, [ ingest1, expend1]]]],
    [node2,
        [[agent,
            [preference, animal1]],
        [object,
            [preference, drink1]]]]]).
```

```
sf(drink1,                          sf(glass2,
    [[arcs,                             [[arcs,
        [[supertype,                        [[supertype, vessel1]]],
            [[energy_source1, liquid1]]]],  [node0,
    [node0,                                     [[composition1, glass1],
        [[behaviour1, liquid1],                 [behaviour1, brittle1],
        [animal1, drink1, it1]]]]).             [it1, contain1, drink1],
                                                [human_being1,
                                                    drink1, [from1, it1]]]]]).
```

Figure 6.10 Sense-frames of drink1 (verb and noun), and glass2.

```
[preference,
    [[path_type,                        First array :
        [0, 1, 0, 0, 0]],               inclusive sense-network path
    [cell_matches,
        [[relevant,                     Second array :
            [0, 1, 0, 0, 0, 0, 5]],     identical match of relevant cell
        [non_relevant,                  Third array :
            [0, 5, 0, 0, 0, 0, 0]]]]]]  matches of non-relevant cells
```

Figure 6.11 A literal semantic relation.

```
sf(glasses3,
  [[arcs,
    [[supertype, optical_device1]]],
  [node0,
    [[composition1, [metal1, plastic1]],
    [it1, contain1, [2, lens1]]]]]]).
```

Figure 6.12 Sense-frame for glasses3.

drink1] is removed from the list of cells in the target to prevent it from being used a second time and then the non-relevant cells are matched. The cells are all identical. Figure 6.11 shows the resultant semantic vector.

In Figure 6.11, the 1 in the second column of the first array is the identical "path" found between source and target (both are the noun sense drink1). The second array records the match of the relevant cell. The 1 in the second column indicates the "identical" cell match that was discovered; the 5 in the seventh column are those cells in drink1 that remain unmatched. Those five cells are matched in the comparison of non-relevant cells, which the third array records in its second column (i.e., the matches were all identical).

The screening process of CS applies the rank ordering *literal* $\Rightarrow$ *metaphorical* $\Rightarrow$ *anomalous* to the two readings of sentence (10). The literal semantic relation between the verb sense drink1 and glass2 is chosen over the anomalous semantic relation between drink1 and glass1.

The final match tried by *meta5*'s semantic routines is between the verb sense drink1 and glasses3, the spectacles. Figure 6.12 shows the sense-frame for glasses3.

The object preference of the verb sense drink1 is once more the noun sense drink1. Collation seeks the sense-network path between the noun sense drink1 and glasses3. The path found is one of exclusion, i.e., spectacles are not a type of potable liquid. Metonymic inferencing is tried but fails. Consequently, the semantic relation between the verb sense drink1 and glasses3 must be either metaphorical or anomalous. The rank ordering of semantic relations in the screening process states that a literal relation is preferred over metaphorical or anomalous ones, and a literal relation already exists for an earlier sentence reading, so processing of the semantic relation between drink1 and glasses3 is halted. There are no more pairs of word senses to compare so the reading returned for sentence (10) is between "drink" and the second sense of "glass" that included the **Container for Contents** metonymy.

6 *Summary*

This chapter has attempted to describe the relationship between semantic relations, metonymy, and lexical ambiguity resolution. Coherence was used as an explanatory concept that organised that relationship. CS was introduced as a theoretical framework in which the role of coherence in the relationship between semantic relations, metonymy, and lexical disambiguation was made more concrete. Finally, an example from *meta5* was used to make the description of CS and the relationship between all four phenomena (coherence, semantic relations, metonymy, and lexical disambiguation) yet more concrete.

Coherence is the main theoretical focus of CS, together with semantic primitives. Collation produces coherence, semantic vectors represent coherence, and screening uses coherence. In CS, the representation and processing of knowledge (sense-frames and collation) are distinguished from the representation and processing of coherence (semantic vectors and screening).

There are many phenomena that a coherence-based approach such as CS can explore. We have argued that semantic relations and tropes such as metonymy are manifestations of coherence. Other tropes include simile, irony, overstatement (hyperbole), and understatement (litotes). Coherence exists between linguistic structures of all sizes. We have argued that coherence exists within sentences and is prominent in approaches to lexical ambiguity resolution. Coherence also exists between sentences—it is basic to theories of discourse. Coherence merits thorough investigation as it appears to play a substantial role in cognition, not just semantic relations, metonymy and lexical ambiguity resolution.

Acknowledgments

The work reported here is funded by the New Mexico State Legislature, administered by its Scientific Technical Commission as part of the Rio Grande Research Corridor.

References

Beaugrande, R. de and R. Dressler. 1981. *Introduction to Text Linguistics*. New York: Longman.

Black, M. 1979. More about metaphor. In Andrew Ortony (ed.), *Metaphor and Thought*, pp. 19–43. London: Cambridge University Press.

Bobrow, D.G. and T. Winograd. 1977. An overview of KRL, a knowledge representation language. *Cognitive Science* 1:3–46.

Boguraev, B.K. 1979. Automatic resolution of linguistic ambiguities. Technical Report No. 11, University of Cambridge Computer Laboratory, Cambridge.

Brachman, R.J. 1979. On the epistemological status of semantic networks. In N.V. Findler (ed.), *Associative Networks: Representation and Use of Knowledge By Computers,* pp. 3–50. New York: Academic Press.

Carbonell, J.G. 1981. Metaphor: An inescapable phenomenon in natural language comprehension. Research Report CMU-CS-81-115, Dept. of Computer Science, Carnegie-Mellon University.

Charniak, E. 1983. Passing markers: A theory of contextual influence in language comprehension. *Cognitive Science* 7:171–190.

Charniak, E. 1986. A neat theory of marker passing. In *Proceedings of the 5th National Conference on Artificial Intelligence (AAAI-86),* pp. 584–588. Philadelphia, PA. Los Altos: Morgan Kaufmann.

Cottrell, G.W. and S.L. Small. 1983. A connectionist scheme for modelling word-sense disambiguation. *Cognition and Brain Theory* 6:89–120.

Dubois, J. et al. 1970. *Rhetorique Generale.* Paris: Larousse.

Van Dijk, T.A. 1977. *Text and Context: Explorations in the Semantics and Pragmatics of Discourse.* London: Longman.

Van Dijk, T.A. and W. Kintsch. 1983. *Strategies of Discourse Comprehension.* New York: Academic Press.

Van Eynde, F. 1982. Ambiguity. In J. Erlandsen, F. Van Eynde, J. McNaught, H. Somers and L. Destombes, Dictionary and semantics in eurotra. Eurotra Contract Report ET-10-SEM, European Communities, Luxembourg.

Fass, D.C. 1986. Collative semantics: An approach to coherence. Memorandum MCCS-86-56, Computing Research Laboratory, New Mexico State University, New Mexico.

Fass, D.C. and Y.A. Wilks. 1983. Preference semantics, ill-formedness and metaphor. *American Journal of Computational Linguistics* 9:178–187.

Genette, G. 1970. La rhetorique restreinte. *Communications* 16:158–171.

Gentner, D. 1983. Structure mapping: A theoretical framework for analogy. *Cognitive Science* 7:155–170.

Grice, H.P. 1975. Logic and conversation. In P. Cole and J. Morgan (eds.), *Syntax and Semantics 3: Speech Acts,* pp. 41–58. London: Academic Press.

Hirst, G.J. 1983. Semantic interpretation against ambiguity. Technical Report No. CS-83-25, Dept. of Computer Science, Brown University.

Hobbs, J.R. 1983a. Metaphor interpretation as selective inferencing: Cognitive processes in understanding metaphor (part 1). *Empirical Studies of the Arts* 1:17–33.

Hobbs, J.R. 1983b. Metaphor interpretation as selective inferencing: Cognitive processes in understanding metaphor (part 2). *Empirical Studies of the Arts* 1:125–141.

Hobbs, J.R. 1986. Sublanguage and knowledge. In R. Grishman and R. Kittredge (eds.), *Analyzing Language in Restricted Domains: Sublanguage Description and Processing*, pp. 53–68. Hillsdale: Erlbaum.

Huang, X-M. 1985. Machine translation in the SDCG (semantic definite clause grammars) formalism. In *Proceedings of the Conference on Theoretical and Methodological Issues in Machine Translation of Natural Languages*, pp. 135–144. Colgate University, New York.

Jakobson, R. and M. Halle. 1956. *Fundamentals of Language*. The Hague: Mouton.

Katz, J.J. 1972. *Semantic Theory*. New York: Harper International Edition.

Katz, J.J. and J.A. Fodor. 1964. The structure of a semantic theory. In J.A. Fodor and J.J. Katz (eds.), *The Structure of Language: Readings in the Philosophy of Language*, pp. 479–518. Englewood Cliffs: Prentice-Hall.

Katz, J.J. and P. Postal. 1964. *An Integrated Theory of Linguistic Description*. Cambridge: MIT Press.

Lakoff, G. and M. Johnson. 1980. *Metaphors We Live By*. London: Chicago University Press.

Lees, R.B. 1960. The grammar of english nominalizations. *International Journal of American Linguistics* 26:3.

Lehrer, A. 1974. *Semantic Fields and Lexical Structure*. Amsterdam: North Holland.

Levin, S.R. 1977. *The Semantics of Metaphor*. Baltimore: John Hopkins University Press.

Lyons, J. 1963. *Structural Semantics*. Oxford: Blackwell.

Lyons, J. 1977. *Semantics, Volumes 1 and 2*. Cambridge: Cambridge University Press.

Martin, J.H. 1985. Knowledge acquisition though natural language dialogue. In *Proceedings of the 2nd Annual Conference on Artificial Intelligence Applications*. Miami, Florida.

Martin, J.H. 1986. Learning by understanding metaphors. In *Proceedings of the 8th Annual Conference of the Cognitive Science Society*, Amherst, Massachusetts.

Myers, T., K. Brown and B. McGonigle. 1986. Introduction: Representation and inference in reasoning and discourse. In T. Myers, K. Brown and B. McGonigle (eds.), *Reasoning and Discourse Processes,* pp. 1–12. London: Academic Press.

Norman, D.A., D.E. Rumelhart and the LNR Research Group. 1975. *Explorations in Cognition*. San Francisco: Freeman.

Ortony, A. 1979. Beyond literal similarity. *Psychological Review* 86:161–180.

Quillian, M.R. 1968. Semantic memory. In M. Minsky (ed.), *Semantic Information Processing*, pp. 216–270. Cambridge: MIT Press.

Reddy, M.J. 1979. The conduit metaphor—a case of frame conflict in our language about language. In A. Ortony (ed.), *Metaphor and Thought*, pp. 284–324. London: Cambridge University Press.

Richards, I.A. 1936. *The Philosophy of Rhetoric*. London: Oxford University Press.

Rieger, C.J. and S. Small. 1979. Word expert parsing. Technical Report No. TR-734, Dept. of Computer Science, Univ. of Maryland.

Roberts, R.B. and I.P. Goldstein. 1977. The FRL manual. MIT AI Memo No. 409, Massachustts Institute of Technology, Cambridge Mass.

Sadock, J.M. 1979. Figurative speech and linguistics. In A. Ortony (ed.), *Metaphor and Thought*, pp. 46–63. London: Cambridge University Press.

Sapir, J.D. 1977. The social uses of metaphor. In J.D. Sapir and J.C. Crocker (eds.), *The Social Use of Metaphor: Essays on the Anthropology of Rhetoric*. Philadelphia: University of Philadelphia Press.

Schank, R.C. 1975. The structure of episodes in memory. In D.G. Bobrow and A. Collins (eds.), *Representation and Understanding*, pp. 237–272. New York: Academic Press.

Searle, J. 1981. Metaphor. In M. Johnson (ed.), *Philosophical Perspectives on Metaphor*, pp. 248–285. Minneapolis: University of Minnesota Press.

Small, S. and C.J. Rieger. 1982. Parsing and comprehending with word experts (a theory and its realization). In W.G. Lehnert and M.H. Ringle (eds.), *Strategies for Natural Language Processing*, pp. 89–147. Hillsdale: Erlbaum.

Tourangeau, R. and R.J. Sternberg. 1982. Understanding and appreciating metaphors. *Cognition* 11:203–244.

Waltz, D.L. and J.B. Pollack. 1985. Massively parallel parsing: A strongly interactive model of natural language interpretation. *Cognitive Science* 9:51–74.

Wilks, Y.A. 1973. An artificial intelligence approach to machine translation. In R.C. Schank and K.M. Colby (eds.), *Computer Models of Thought and Language*, pp. 114–151. San Francisco: Freeman.

Wilks, Y.A. 1975a. A preferential pattern-seeking semantics for natural language inference. *Artificial Intelligence* 6:53–74.

Wilks, Y.A. 1975b. An intelligent analyser and understander for English. *Communications of the ACM* 18:264–274.

Wilks, Y.A. 1978. Making preferences more active. *Artificial Intelligence* 10:1–11.

Wong, D. 1981. On the unification of language comprehension with problem solving. Technical Report No. CS-78, Department of Computer Science, Brown University.

7

A Model of Lexical Access of Ambiguous Words

Garrison W. Cottrell

Institute for Cognitive Science
Department of Computer Science and Engineering
University of California, San Diego

1 *Introduction*

The most frequently used words in English are highly ambiguous. For example, "go" has 63 meanings listed in the Merriam Webster Pocket Dictionary [Hirst, 1983]. One problem facing a parser (human or not) is selecting the proper meaning of a word from the large number of possibilities. This is an instance of the standard search problem in Artificial Intelligence. Introspectively, this does not seem like a problem for humans—we seem to effortlessly choose the correct meaning of a word. It is thus an interesting problem both for psycholinguists and computer scientists to know how the search for word meanings is carried out. Perhaps it can help the parsers we write.

Within the domain of Artificial Intelligence there is considerable interest in parallel architectures for both machines and computational models (see also [Lesser and Erman, 1977; Fahlman, 1980; Hillis, 1981; Fahlman, Hinton, and Sejnowski, 1983]). One such computational paradigm which has met with considerable enthusiasm, as well as skepticism, is the connectionist approach developed by Feldman and Ballard [1982; Feldman, 1982]. This theory was developed to reflect the current understanding of the information processing capabilities of neurons. Consequently, the type of processing it supports is characterized by spreading activation and mutual inhibition. While it is still at an early stage, the paradigm has been successfully applied in models of visual recognition of noisy inputs [Sabbah, 1982], motor control [Addanki, 1983], limited inference in semantic networks [Shastri and Feldman, 1984] and word sense disambiguation [Cottrell and Small, 1983]. I believe it can be a useful cognitive modeling tool as well. My intention here is to demonstrate how a simple connectionist model of a low level process in sentence comprehension can be effective in explaining psychological results.

There are usually two goals in building a cognitive model: to explain the existing data, and to make empirically verifiable predictions. In order to explain the data, it must be possible to form a clear correspondence between the elements of the model and the elements of the world that the model attempts to explain. While many would argue, and have argued [Feigenbaum and Feldman, 1963], that the neuronal level is the wrong place to start such an enterprise, I claim that in order to explain the wealth of psycholinguistic data on low level language processing,[1] the correspondence must be at a level below the functional. That is, that the *mechanisms* involved in carrying out these functions must be considered if we are to attain real explanatory power. Functional level models are effective in demonstrating what functions must be carried out; however, mechanism level models are better at explaining data from processing tasks. Second, cognitive models should make predictions that render them falsifiable. The model given here of lexical access makes several predictions which may be refuted or substantiated by subsequent research.

Within the domain of sentence processing, various levels of analysis have been identified and generally agreed upon (eg. phonological, lexical, syntactic, semantic and pragmatic). However, the characteristics of the interaction between these levels have been the focus of much study and debate [Forster, 1979; Marslen-Wilson and Tyler, 1980]. One question is whether these systems can be regarded as independent modules or whether processing at one level influences processing at another. The process of lexical access (defined below) presents a unique opportunity for modeling. The lexical level of processing has been studied in recent years by psycholinguists who have focused intensively on the modularity question. What has emerged is a fairly well understood set of results which appears to favor the modular view. As noted above, apart from the obvious consequences of the modularity issue for AI, researchers should also be interested in this process because obtaining the correct meaning of a word from the lexicon represents a search problem. The following section reviews the psycholinguistic research. This is followed by a description of a simple model of lexical access which explains apparent anomalies in the psycholinguistic results and makes empirically verifiable predictions.

---

1 By "low level" I do not mean to imply the functional level/mechanism level distinction. I simply mean early stages of processing, such as phonological and lexical.

2 *Lexical Access*

The process of accessing all of the information about a word, (i.e., phonological codes, orthographic codes, meaning and syntactic features) is called *lexical access*. Here, we will mainly be concerned with the access of meaning and syntactic class, and will use the term "lexical access" to refer to this process. It is useful to distinguish three stages in the processing of lexical items, of which access is the second: (1) decoding the input and matching it with a lexical item, (2) accessing the information about the item, and (3) integrating the information with the preceding context. These are termed prelexical, lexical and postlexical processing, respectively. An important research question has been to discover whether, to what degree, and through what channels these levels interact. Does each level receive only the completed output of the previous level (the "modular" view)? Or, can processing at one level affect processing at adjacent or even more distant levels (the "interactive" view)? Is the answer somewhere between these extremes?

Recent studies of lexical access have borne directly on the question of whether preceding context only influences integration (post access), or whether it affects lexical access directly. A common approach in this research is to study the effects of context on the processing of ambiguous words. The empirical question is whether or not the intra-sentential context constrains the search in the lexicon for the appropriate meaning of an ambiguous word. The interactive view holds that context affects lexical access, so that only a single meaning is accessed (the Prior Decision Hypothesis). The modular view holds that all meanings of the word are accessed initially, since the lexical access mechanism can't "know" what the context requires; then all meanings are passed to the integration level, where context selects the proper one (the Post Decision Hypothesis). Early research produced mixed results, with some studies supporting one hypothesis, and some the other [Conrad, 1974; Foss and Jenkins, 1973; Holmes, 1977; Lackner and Garret, 1972; Swinney and Hakes, 1976]. However, most of these studies only looked at one time point of the process, which as later results show, explains the discrepancy.

Later work by Swinney [1979] and others [Tanenhaus, Leiman, and Seidenberg, 1979; Seidenberg, Tanenhaus, Leiman, and Bienkowski, 1982] has shown that the *time course* of lexical access is important. In these studies, the *semantic priming effect* is used to measure the activation of word meanings. Subjects are presented with two words in sequence, a *prime* and *target*. They have to perform some task on the second (target) word. If the prime is associatively or semantically related to the target (e.g., DOCTOR followed by NURSE) subjects are faster and more accurate at processing the target than if the prime is an unrelated word (e.g., BREAD followed by NURSE) [Meyer and Schvaneveldt, 1971]. Semantic priming has been shown to operate crossmodally, i.e., a spoken word can prime a visually presented word [Swinney et al., 1979].

In the Swinney [1979] experiment, subjects listen to a sentence containing an ambiguous priming word (e.g., BUG) while performing a lexical decision task (is this a word or not?) to the target flashed on a screen. The targets are semantically related to both meanings of the priming word (e.g., SPY and ANT for BUG). If subjects are faster at one or both of these compared to a control target (e.g., SEW) it is inferred that the corresponding meaning of BUG was accessed. This approach is superior to phoneme monitoring experiments, in that relatively normal sentence processing is possible, and definite evidence of the activation of a particular meaning is obtained (rather than just an indication of increased processing load).

When the target immediately follows an ambiguous word, Swinney found priming for both meanings, but when the target is three syllables later, (approximately 1000–1500 msecs) only priming for the appropriate meaning is found. This occurred even when there was strong biasing context for one meaning. An example sentence is: *Rumor had it that, for years, the government building had been plagued with problems. The man was not surprised when he found several spiders, roaches, and other* **bugs** *in the corner of his room.* Swinney's initial experiments concerned noun-noun ambiguities with equibiased readings (i.e., either of two meanings was presumed to occur equally often). These results were also shown to hold for noun-verb ambiguities (Prather and Swinney, reported in [Swinney, 1982]) and strongly biased noun-noun ambiguous words (with one frequent and one infrequent meaning) [Onifer and Swinney, 1981]. In the latter study, there was no significant difference in the priming obtained for the dominant and subordinate meanings at the end of the word. This suggests that lexical access may be independent of frequency effects. Further support for this hypothesis may be found in a study by Yates [1978], but his experiment did not employ an on-line measure.

An interesting variation on these experiments by William Onifer, reported in Swinney [1982], was done on schizophrenics. The results for healthy subjects were replicated with schizophrenics except with respect to which meaning remained activated. That is, they accessed both frequent and infrequent meanings initially, but by three syllables later priming was obtained for only the most frequent meaning of the word, regardless of the sentential bias. Swinney notes that this is support for the view that lexical access is independent of and prior to the decision process that chooses the pertinent meaning of the word, since this decision process appears to be selectively impaired in schizophrenics.

These results have been confirmed in concurrent research by Tanenhaus, Leiman and Seidenberg [1979] and Seidenberg, Tanenhaus, Leiman and Bienkowski [1982]. Their experiments used a similar cross-modal priming paradigm, but the task was to name the word visually presented, rather than make a lexical decision. Also, the ambiguous word was the last word in the sentence.

They studied the time course of priming as well, but in a much narrower time interval: the test word was presented at 0 and 200 msecs after the end of the ambiguous word. They found the same pattern of results as Swinney (with one exception, discussed below), but they were able to show that selection happened within 200 msecs. Subsequent experiments by Lucas [1984] at more time points have further narrowed the decision time to between 125 and 150 msecs after the end of the word (but see the discussion below).

In addition to narrowing the decision window, Seidenberg et al. discussed two types of context which may differ in their effects on lexical decision. They contrasted *pragmatic* context, resulting from world knowledge, with what they termed a *semantic* priming context, resulting from associative and semantic relationships between word meanings, as in the following sentences.

1. The man walked on the *deck*. (pragmatic)

2. The man inspected the ship's *deck*. (semantic: ship $\Rightarrow$ deck)

3. The man walked on the ship's *deck*. (semantic and pragmatic)

The first sentence contains a pragmatic bias towards the "ship" related meaning of deck; one is more likely to walk on that kind. The second sentence contains a word highly semantically related to one meaning. The third contains both types of information. The experiments of Seidenberg et al. examined lexical access in a neutral context, a pragmatic context, and a semantic context. They found multiple access with neutral and pragmatic context, but selective access (only one reading active at the end of the word) with the semantic priming context. This result held for noun-noun ambiguities, but not noun-verb ambiguities, where multiple access occurred in all conditions (including syntactic context, such as *they all began to _____* or *the carpenter picked up the _____*). These results are summarized in Table 1.

Table 1   Summary of Seidenberg et al. [1982] Experimental results

Context Type	Ambiguity Type	Outcome
Neutral	Noun-Noun	Multiple Access
Syntactic	Noun-Verb	Multiple Access
Pragmatic	Noun-Noun	Multiple Access
Semantic	Noun-Verb	Multiple Access
Semantic	Noun-Noun	Selective Access

The discussion of these results follows the account given in Seidenberg et al. [1982]. The finding of selective access in the noun-noun condition is contrary to the findings of Swinney [1979], where multiple access for noun-noun ambiguities was obtained in a strongly biasing context. However, there are several differences between the two experiments which may explain the discrepancy. First, Swinney's experiments used the lexical decision task rather than naming, which may be subject to "backwards priming"[2] from the target to the ambiguous word (see [Koriat, 1981]). These effects seem to arise in lexical decision but not naming tasks [Seidenberg, Waters, Sanders and Langer, 1984]. Second, Swinney's ambiguous words appeared in the middle of a sentence, rather than at the end, as in the Seidenberg et al. [1982] experiments. The fact of a word being sentence-final may make a difference to lexical access. If so, this effect would have to apply differentially to noun-noun ambiguities, and only in a semantic context. The most probable explanation, however, according to Seidenberg et al., is that Swinney did not differentiate and control for the two types of context distinguished in the Seidenberg experiments. It appears that many of his materials did not contain strongly associated lexical items, and when they did, the associate was often more than four words away from the ambiguous word. If the priming effect decays rapidly, then the priming words may have been too far away to affect lexical access.

It remains to discuss why the selective access result was obtained in the first place. Seidenberg et al. [1982] attribute the result to intralexical priming by the strong associate preceding the ambiguous word. It should be noted that the only meaning of "intralexical" in this context that makes sense is actually "intrasemantic": A single *meaning* of the word, and not the lexical representation of the word itself, is primed. Also, as pointed out by Hirst [1983], priming must not spread from the meaning to the lexical item itself, or priming of all meanings would eventually result. This is also in accord with results that semantic priming is not transitive [DeGroot, 1983]. So, the appropriate meaning of the word is primed by the associated word's meaning and blocks or inhibits the alternate reading.

Based on the results of the Seidenberg et al. study, then, we can conclude that there is a differential effect of types of context on lexical access of ambiguous words. A particularly strong context, consisting of a lexical item strongly related to one meaning of the ambiguous word, leads to selective access. This effect appears to be modulated by the type of ambiguity involved. If it is a between-class ambiguity (noun-verb), multiple access is obtained regardless of context, but if it is a within-class ambiguity (noun-noun), then the effect holds. The next section describes the Seidenberg et al. model of the lexi-

---

2 Backwards priming refers to the phenomenon of the *target* word activating the corresponding meaning of the *prime*, somehow facilitating a positive response.

cal access process in order to provide a foil for the model presented in the following section.

3 *The Seidenberg et al. Model of Lexical Access*

Seidenberg et al. [1982] present a model to account for their results. It is based on four implications they draw from their research. First, that the results support a modular, autonomous account of the lexical access process. The only contextual effect, selective access of noun-noun ambiguities, was due to intralexical priming, which in their view is local to the lexicon. Second, the results indicate that there are at least two classes of context which interact with word recognition in different ways. Third, the differential results for noun-noun and noun-verb ambiguities suggest that syntactic information is encoded in the mental lexicon. This point is obvious, but the question is *how* syntactic information is encoded. Seidenberg et al. suggest that a word's syntactic class is encoded with the lexical representation. However, it is also possible that it is encoded with a word's meaning representation. As will be seen, the model suggests an intermediate position. Finally, the results suggest that studies which illuminate the time course of comprehension are essential to decoding the structure of the processor(s).

The Seidenberg et al. model is a combination of Morton's [1969] logogen model and Collins and Loftus's [1975] spreading activation model. A lexical logogen governs recognition, and is connected to semantic memory where it activates its meaning(s) via spreading activation (see Figure 7.1). The meaning nodes are accessed along pathways from the lexical nodes in the order of relative activation levels. The meaning nodes may be primed by the access of words highly related to one meaning, which is the only exception to the automaticity and autonomy of lexical access. They posit that if there are large differences in activation due to frequency or priming, then selective access obtains.

Figure 7.1 The Seidenberg et al. model of lexical access.

To account for the differential effect of the semantic context on noun-noun vs. noun-verb ambiguities, they posit that nouns and verbs have different nodes with identical recognition procedures in the lexical network (as in the right half of Figure 7.1). Now, the story goes, for noun-verb ambiguities with one meaning primed, both nodes get recognized because they share all the same features, and both meanings are accessed. In the noun-noun case (left side of Figure 7.1), if one meaning is primed, that *pathway* is followed first. Note that this explanation implies serial evaluation of the possibilities in the noun-noun priming case.

4 *A Connectionist Model of Lexical Access*

We turn now to my model, beginning with a short introduction to the connectionist paradigm. Connectionist models consist of simple processing units connected by weighted links. The units have a bounded *activation* (the following model uses the range 0 to 1), which is a function of their *input* and an *output,* which in the following model is just the activation threshold. The input is a vector of weighted outputs from other units or from sources external to the model. The activation function computes the activation based on the current activation and the inputs. In the kind of models suggested by Feldman and Ballard [1982] there are no constraints on the functions that can be used, though they are usually kept simple, so as not to exceed the suspected computational ability of a neuron. The basic idea is that a unit stands for a value of some parameter and receives inputs from other units which represent evidence for that value, positive or negative. The links between the units are weighted to represent *constraints* between parameter values. Thus, much of the information is contained in the connections between units (hence the name "connectionism"). A unit's output represents a confidence in the hypothesis that its value is represented by its input. The typical way to go about building connectionist models is to decide which elements of the domain we want to model, choose a way to encode those elements as units, and then wire the units together so as to encode constraints between the elements. Finally, we must choose an appropriate activation function.

This approach is useful when one is programming a network to do a task—that is, determining the wiring and setting the weights by hand. It lends itself to *localist* representations—that is, a unit represents one concept at a relatively large granularity, allowing the modeler to determine the appropriate constraints. This is to be contrasted with *distributed* connectionist models, in which a concept is represented by a pattern of activation across a set of units, rather than the activation of a single unit. At present there are reasons to prefer the latter approach (exemplified by Kawamoto's chapter in this volume) as being more neurologically plausible, and, when coupled with learning algorithms that set the weights, more elegant. However, there are still interesting lessons to be learned from the localist, programmed approach, and the following model can be considered a macro-level description of how a distributed connectionist network might parse language.

In order to place the lexical access model in context, I briefly describe the overall model of sentence processing of which it is a part [Cottrell and Small, 1983; Cottrell, 1985]. The model consists of a four component, three level network shown in Figure 7.2. The lexical level consists of units representing the words in the language, presumably activated by phoneme or letter recognition networks at a lower level such as those developed by McClelland and Rumelhart [1981]. These units in turn, activate units at the word sense level, buffering the syntactic and semantic features of their definitions. This is the process of lexical access. If a word is ambiguous, features corresponding to all of its definitions are activated and compete with one another. From here, the semantic features activate relational nodes in the semantic network, which uses a case-based representation of the conceptual structure of a clause [Fillmore, 1968; Cook, 1979]. Based on the "best fit" among the (possibly several) case relations, feedback is generated to the word sense level, causing the meanings which participate in those case relations to win over competing meanings. Similarly, the syntax network feeds back on the lexical entries at the word sense level that fit best with a surface structure parse of the sentence. These systems operate in parallel and mutually constrain the word senses and each other.

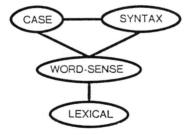

Figure 7.2 Overview of the system.

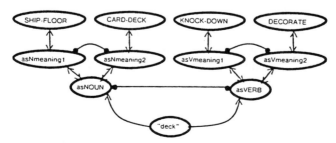

Figure 7.3 Connectionist lexical access model.

The model of how the words activate their senses is shown in Figure 7.3. The network shown is for the word "deck," since it is ambiguous in at least four ways, with two noun meanings and two verb meanings. For the purposes of this discussion, this network is assumed to be dedicated to "deck"—no other word uses this network. The network for a noun-noun ambiguous word would just consist of the left half of this network, (right half for verb-verb), and a noun-verb ambiguous word would just have the outer "V" of seven nodes. The lowest node is a unit at the lexical level. This is assumed to be activated by a phoneme or letter recognition network. The top row of nodes represent the various meanings of the lexical item at the word sense level. These are connected to the case-fitting component. The lexical node activates its meaning nodes through a discrimination network, starting with the grossest distinctions possible, then progressing to the finer ones. Note that the most efficient way to do this is to make two-way splits between large classes of alternatives (divide and conquer), if possible, since the inhibitory connections are minimized this way.[3] It is assumed that syntactic information is more discriminatory than semantic information, i.e., that the distinction into "noun" and "verb" divides up the possibilities more than divisions based on meaning.

The alternatives at any discrimination inhibit one another, so that one path through the network eventually "wins" and the meaning nodes that the other paths support fade away. This is the decision process, which is driven by feedback to the meaning nodes from the semantic and syntactic levels of the network. In the case of a biasing sentence, this feedback is from nodes representing the role that meaning could play in the sentence as described above. In the case of semantic priming, the meaning node is directly primed by a node representing the relation of the prime's meaning to this meaning, as in the Collins and Loftus [1975] model of semantic priming. The unfortunate meaning node that does not get top down feedback (or does not get as much) will not be able to provide as much feedback to the pathway nodes which activated it, and its pathway will be inhibited by the pathway nodes that do get more feedback.

In order to account for the modular nature of lexical access, two simple assumptions were necessary. First, the units are thresholded (i.e., they can collect activation but they will not fire until they cross threshold, as in Morton's [1969] "logogen" model) and second, top down links have lower weights than bottom up links. A unit may thus be activated above threshold by bottom up evidence, but not by top down evidence. This combination of threshold and weighting acts as a barrier to top down information affecting lower level processes such as recognition. It may come in to play, however, *after* recognition of the lexical item has begun, in the decision process. This assumption is

---

3 For n nodes to be mutually inhibitory, we need $(n-1)*(n)$ inhibitory connections. If we arrange them in a binary tree, we need $n-1$ inhibitory connections, but $2*n-1$ units, so we are making a connection/unit tradeoff.

independently motivated at all levels of these networks by the need to prevent top down activation from hallucinating inputs.

An interesting feature of this network is that the meanings themselves are not mutually inhibitory. When one considers constraints between units, there is no functional reason to assume that a particular *meaning* in isolation from its source (a particular lexical item) is not compatible with another meaning. However, it *is* reasonable to assume that the *assignments* of different meanings to the same use of a word is inconsistent. Indeed, if the meanings themselves were mutually inhibitory, then one would expect that a word with the same meaning as an inappropriate reading of a previous word in the sentence (assuming the meaning node is shared) would be harder to process than a control word. For example, this would imply that it should be hard to understand *I had a* **ball** *at the* **formal dance**. The model would predict, however, that people would be slower at processing sentences such as *I had a* **ball** *at the* **ball**.

5 An Example Run

The results of running the model using the ISCON simulator [Small et al., 1982] are presented in Figure 7.4. It will be helpful to refer to Figure 7.3 to understand the trace. To simulate priming, a driver node, m1 (not shown), provides constant feedback to SHIP-FLOOR throughout the simulation. (In a complete model this would be a node representing one of the types of SHIP-FLOOR. For example, m1 could be PART-OF-SHIP, activated by the context prime "ship's.") The units average their input from three sites, bottom up, top down, and inhibitory. The first two sites take the maximum of their inputs, and the inhibitory site uses a sigmoid function to enhance the difference in inhibition between two units that are close to each other in activation level. This helps avoid the problem of two units getting into equilibrium without one suppressing the other below threshold. Bottom up weights are 1.0, top down are 0.5, and inhibitory weights are –0.5. The threshold is set at 0.3. The potential function is similar to the one used by McClelland and Rumelhart [1981].

At step 5, SHIP-FLOOR has been primed by the context prime m1. Now "deck" is given external input for 30 steps. At step 13, the semantic discrimination nodes (the "as Xmeaning" nodes) have just fired (not visible at Figure 7.4's resolution), but their activation has not spread to the meaning nodes yet. Notice that SHIP-FLOOR has been primed now to near threshold. Thus the bottom up activation from "as Nmeaning1" causes it to fire in step 14, while the other meaning nodes have to accumulate more activation for several steps before they will fire. This gives SHIP-FLOOR a chance to increase the relative activation of nodes that are on its feedback path, before the other meaning nodes fire. This allows the nodes on that path to begin to win over their competition so that by step 24, "as Nmeaning2" has been suppressed. This results in CARD-DECK fading from lack of support. Also, "as Nmeaning1" is no longer inhibited by "as Nmeaning2," so it rises, giving more support to "as-NOUN," which then suppresses "asVERB." Later, KNOCK-DOWN and DEC-ORATE fade due to lack of support from "asVERB."

Thus, this model claims that there is always multiple access followed by fast decision for within-class ambiguities. Between-class ambiguities take longer to resolve because the decision is made farther away in the network from the disambiguating feedback.

However, the model can be something of a chameleon. The results of Seidenberg et al. suggest that different contexts may have different strengths. A second simulation was run, in which the input from the context prime m1 was increased to the point where it caused SHIP-FLOOR to cross threshold and fire without bottom up input, breaking the "barrier" to top down activation. In this case, the barrier holds one level down; it is "as Nmeaning1" that becomes primed to just below threshold. When activation reaches that level of the network, this node fires first and suppresses "as Nmeaning2" before it can activate CARD-DECK. Thus, the model can exhibit selective access of within-class ambiguities, depending on the strength of priming.

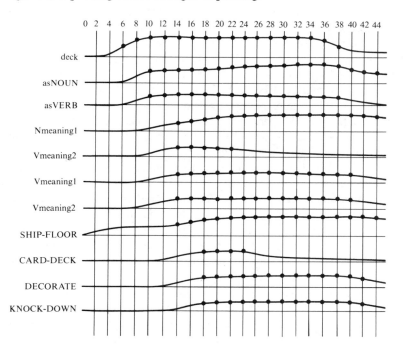

Figure 7.4 Activation levels of the units of Figure 7.3 over time. Numbers across the top are steps of the simulation, a "•" in the activation curve means the unit has crossed threshold and is firing.

6 *Discussion*

This model makes several claims about lexical access. First, decisions within a syntactic class happen "nearer" the meaning nodes than decisions between classes, so an incorrect meaning node fades faster when within the same class as its competitors than when its competitors are in different classes. Thus noun-noun decisions are faster than noun-verb decisions, as was seen in the sample run. Thus it predicts that verb-verb ambiguities, which have not been tested (to my knowledge) in the psycholinguistic literature, will act like noun-noun ambiguities. However, the Seidenberg et al. study used homonyms (words with unrelated meanings). Verbs tend to polysemy (related meanings). Because this may affect the results, I will restrict the claim to verb-verb homonyms.

In order to explain different context effects I have to mention some claims about context. We saw that in the model, feedback does not flow freely downward from the priming node (m1) through the meaning node (SHIP-FLOOR) because it is blocked by SHIP-FLOOR's threshold. However, when activation comes up from "deck" through the other nodes, the barrier is broken, and feedback flows down. If we assume that higher levels of processing act the same way, then in the case of pragmatic context, no feedback to meaning nodes would occur before the meaning node actually fires because it is too far away in the network. By this time, multiple access has occurred, and a target word to be named (say, "spade") can take advantage of the priming from all meanings of "deck."

The case illustrated in the sample run was one of priming context with a noun-noun ambiguity (ship's ⇒ deck). Here, the contextual priming word is so closely related to one of the ambiguous word's meanings that they are not far away in the semantic network, and direct priming of the meaning occurs (eg., "ship's" ⇒ SHIP-PART ⇒ SHIP-FLOOR). A decision will be reached much more quickly than in the case of pragmatic context, where the feedback has to come from farther away, semantically (and thus actually, in terms of nodes and links), in the network. Therefore, the model claims that there will be faster decisions in strongly priming contexts. Yet, contrary to Seidenberg et al., multiple access did occur in this version of a semantic context. I will rely on the prediction of the relative speed of ambiguity resolution in different contexts to resolve this. Naming presumably requires at least two stages, recognition and production. The word to be named is presented at the end of the contextually primed ambiguous word. If the decision for the ambiguous word is over before the recognition stage of naming completes, the naming process could not make any use of priming from the alternate meaning of the ambiguous word. Thus the model claims multiple access always occurs, and if the word to be named were presented slightly *before* the end of the ambiguous word, we would see multiple access.

A second and not incompatible explanation for the results is that priming can have variable strength. In the second simulation, very strong priming caused selective access. The explanation is that, depending on the strength of priming, either we have multiple access followed by fast decision, or in the case of very strong priming, selective access obtains. Finally, in the case of four way ambiguous words such as "deck," the model claims that we would see the pattern of results seen in the sample run: In a semantic context, the alternate meaning within the same class would be deactivated first, then the meanings in the other class.

7 Conclusion

A connectionist model of lexical access was presented that accounts for the data and makes empirically verifiable claims. This model has several advantages over that of Seidenberg et al. in that:

1. The model doesn't need to posit nodes with identical recognition procedures.

2. The decision process is motivated by the discrimination network and the difference between nouns and verbs "falls out" of that representation.

3. It is a computational model.

With respect to Artificial Intelligence, it is a parallel model which tackles the problem of the decision process between the possibly many meanings of a word in a parallel processing framework.

Acknowledgments

I would like to thank Michael Tanenhaus and James Allen for helpful comments on this paper. Any errors that remain are mine. This work was supported by NSF grants MCS-8209971 and IST-8208571.

References

Addanki, S. 1983. *A Connectionist Approach to Motor Control*. Ph.D. thesis, Computer Science Dept., Univ. of Rochester.

Collins, A. M. and E.F. Loftus. 1975. A spreading activation theory of semantic processing. *Psychological Review* 82:407–428.

Conrad, C. 1974. Context effects in sentence comprehension: A study of the subjective lexicon. *Memory and Cognition* 2:130–138.

Cottrell, G. W. and S. Small. 1983. A connectionist scheme for modeling word sense disambiguation. *Cognition and Brain Theory* 6:89–120.

Fahlman, S.A. 1980. The Hashnet interconnection scheme. Technical Report, Computer Science Department, Carnegie-Mellon University.

Fahlman, S.A., G. E. Hinton, and T.J. Sejnowski. 1983. Massively parallel architectures for AI: NETL, Thistle, and Boltzmann machines. In *Proceedings of the National Conference on Artificial Intelligence*, Washington, D.C. Los Altos: Morgan Kaufmann.

Feigenbaum, E.A. and J. Feldman (eds.). 1963. *Computers and Thought*. New York: McGraw Hill.

Feldman, J.A. 1982. Dynamic connections in neural networks. *Biological Cybernetics* 46:27–39.

Feldman, J.A. and D. Ballard. 1982. Connectionist models and their properties. *Cognitive Science* 6: 205–254.

Forster, K.I. 1979. Levels of processing and the structure of the language processor. In W.E. Cooper and E.C.T. Walker (eds.), *Sentence Processing*. Hillsdale: Erlbaum.

Foss, D. and C. Jenkins. 1973. Some effects of context on the comprehension of ambiguous sentences. *Journal of Verbal Learning and Verbal Behavior* 12:577–589.

Hirst, G. 1983. *Semantic Interpretation Against Ambiguity*. Soon to be published Ph.D. dissertation, Brown University.

Holmes, V.M. 1977. Prior context and the perception of lexically ambiguous sentences. *Memory and Cognition* 5:103–110.

Lackner and Garret. 1972. Resolving ambiguity: Effects of biasing context in the unattended ear. *Cognition* 1:359–372.

Lesser, V.R. and L. Erman. 1977. A retrospective view of the Hearsay-II architecture. In *Proceedings of the Fifth International Joint Conference on Artificial Intelligence*, Cambridge, MA. Los Altos: Morgan Kaufmann.

Marslen-Wilson, W.D. and L.K. Tyler. 1980. The temporal structure of spoken language understanding. *Cognition* 8:1–71.

McClelland, J.L. and D.E. Rumelhart. 1981. An interactive activation model of the effect of context in perception: Part I, An account of basic findings. *Psych. Review* 88:375–407.

Meyer, E. and R.W. Schvaneveldt. 1971. Facilitation in recognizing pairs of words: Evidence of a dependence between retrieval operations. *Journal of Experimental Psychology* 90:227–234.

Morton, J. 1969. Interaction of information in word recognition. *Psychological Review* 76:163–178.

Sabbah, D. 1982. A connectionist approach to visual recognition. Technical Report No. 107 and Ph.D. thesis, Computer Science Dept., Univ. of Rochester.

Seidenberg, M.S., M. Tanenhaus, J. Leiman, and M. Bienkowski. 1982. Automatic access of the meanings of ambiguous words in context: Some limitations of knowledge-based processing. *Cognitive Psychology* 14:489–537.

Shastri, L. and J.A. Feldman. 1984. Semantic networks and neural nets. Technical Report No. 131, Dept. of Computer Science, Univ. of Rochester.

Small, S.L., L. Shastri, M. Brucks, S. Kaufman, G. Cottrell, and S. Addanki. 1982. ISCON: An interactive simulator for connectionist networks. Technical Report No. 109, Department of Computer Science, Univ. of Rochester.

Swinney, D.A. 1979. Lexical access during sentence comprehension: (Re)consideration of context effects. *Journal of Verbal Learning and Verbal Behavior* 18:645–660.

Swinney, A. and T. Hakes. 1976. Effects of prior context upon lexical access during sentence comprehension. *Journal of Verbal Learning and Verbal Behavior* 15:681–689.

Swinney, D.A., W. Onifer, P. Prather, and M. Hirshkowitz. 1979. Semantic facilitation across sensory modalities in the processing of individual words and sentences. *Memory and Cognition* 7:159–165.

Tanenhaus, M., J. Leiman, and M.S. Seidenberg. 1979. Evidence for multiple stages in the processing of ambiguous words in syntactic contexts. *Journal of Verbal Learning and Verbal Behavior* 18: 427–440.

8

Distributed Representations of Ambiguous Words and Their Resolution in a Connectionist Network

Alan H. Kawamoto

Program in Experimental Psychology
University of California, Santa Cruz

1 *Introduction*

During the past few years, there has been a renewed interest in distributed memory models and distributed representations. These models have been implemented as networks of simple processing elements that represent feature-like information whose activation levels are propagated to other elements in the network. This propagation of activation levels through the network constitutes processing of the input by the network.

One important aspect of processing by these networks is the ability to reconstruct a complete pattern that had been previously learned by providing just a fragment of the pattern. This fragment can be specified by any of a number of different sources of information. In fact, one appealing aspect of distributed models is that the inherent parallelism of these networks allows constraints from multiple sources to be considered simultaneously.

One domain in which the properties of networks described above, content-addressability and consideration of multiple simultaneous constraints, play a fundamental role is lexical access. Accessing the meaning of a word is not a trivial process, as most words have a number of different meanings and the appropriate meaning must be accessed. Although no one disputes the importance of context in resolving an ambiguity, *how* context plays a role in this process has been widely debated. According to those who believe that language comprehension is an autonomous process, *all* meanings of an ambiguous word are activated and the contextually appropriate meaning is selected from among those activated. On the other hand, according to those who believe that language comprehension is an interactive process, only the contextually appropriate meaning should be activated.

Evidence for the interactive position has been reported by Schvaneveldt, Meyer, and Becker [1976] using a lexical priming paradigm. To study ambiguity, Schvaneveldt et al. [1976] used word triplets in which the second word in the sequence was ambiguous and the first and third words were related to one of two different senses of the ambiguous word. In cases where the first and third words were related to the *same* sense (e.g., SAVE-BANK-MONEY), recognition of the third word was facilitated relative to a control. However, when they were related to *different* senses, (e.g., RIVER-BANK-MONEY), comparable facilitation was not found. Schvaneveldt, et al. [1976] thus concluded that the semantic context lead to access of only the contextually appropriate meaning of the ambiguous word.

However, on-line studies using a different variant of the lexical priming task gave opposite results [Seidenberg et al., 1982; Swinney, 1979; Tanenhaus et al., 1979]. In these studies, the test string was presented visually at some point during an auditory presentation of a sentence containing the prime (an ambiguous word). Using a lexical decision task, Swinney [1979] showed that a test word related to *any* meaning of the ambiguous word was primed despite the semantic context provided by the preceding words in the sentence. However, activation of all meanings was found only if the test word was presented immediately following the ambiguous prime word. When the test was presented two to three syllables later, only the contextually appropriate meaning was activated [Swinney, 1979]. This finding thus calls into question the results of Schvaneveldt et al. [1976]. In addition, Swinney [1982] found that all meanings of categorial ambiguities, those ambiguities having different parts of speech as well as different meanings, were also activated despite syntactic cues in the sentences (e.g., *to* preceding a verb and *the* preceding a noun). Similar results were obtained by Tanenhaus et al. [1979] using a naming task for sentence final ambiguous words.[1]

While the debate between those investigators advocating an interactive processing position and those advocating an autonomous one has focussed on

---

1 In contrast to the results of Swinney [1979], Seidenberg et al. [1982] found no evidence of multiple activation for non-categorial ambiguities given a semantic context. Seidenberg et al. propose that these contradictions may be a result of the degree to which the preceding context constrained one interpretation.

the role of context in resolving ambiguity, others have argued that relative frequencies of the different senses of an ambiguous word are of primary importance [Forster and Bednall, 1976; Hogaboam and Perfetti, 1975]. According to this view, the different meanings of an ambiguous word are accessed in order of their frequencies, independent of context. If the initial meaning accessed is inconsistent with the context, the next most frequent meaning is accessed and tested against the context. This continues until a meaning consistent with the context is accessed.

Some attempt has been made to correlate subjective dominance with an objective measure such as frequency of occurrence. One such study was conducted by Galbraith and Taschman [1969]. In this study, subjects were required to give a spelling of a homophone (two words that have the same pronunciation but different spellings) or to free-associate a word to it. There was a fairly good correlation between the relative number of times a particular response was made and the relative dominance norms from Thorndike and Lorge [1938]. Similar results were found by Warren, Bresnick, and Green [1977] when subjects were required to note the first meaning that came to their minds when presented with a homograph (two words that have the same spelling). Although subjects in the two studies described above appeared to have accessed only one meaning, there is evidence that all meanings of polarized as well as equi-probable ambiguous words are activated immediately after presentation of an ambiguous word [Onifer and Swinney, 1981]. However, the subordinate meaning appears to be activated more slowly [Simpson and Burgess, 1985].

Rather than arguing for the primacy of either context or relative dominance, some investigators [Carpenter and Daneman, 1981; Simpson, 1981] argue that both must be considered. In his review of the literature, Simpson [1984] points out that studies to date have consistently shown that more than one meaning will be activated, but the degree or rate of activation is sensitive to both relative dominance and context.

Up to this point, the discussion has concentrated on the factors influencing resolution of an ambiguity. Let us now consider what happens once one of the meanings has been accessed. For example, given an ambiguous word, people can easily access a number of different meanings just as they can perceive different configurations of an ambiguous visual stimulus, such as the Necker cube. In fact, as discussed earlier, some believe that these meanings are accessed in order of relative frequency. In one experiment along these lines, Hogaboam and Perfetti [1975] generated sentences where context biased one sense of an ambiguous word. The subject's task was to determine whether the test word, always the last word of the sentence, had an alternative meaning. Hogaboam and Perfetti found that subjects were quicker to respond positively that the word had an alternative meaning if the subordinate sense rather than the dominant sense was primed. The differences in response times were larger for polarized ambiguous words compared to nearly equi-probable ones. In addition, these investigators found that the ambiguity was missed more often if the dominant sense was consistent with the context.

Another example of effects subsequent to access of one sense of an ambiguous word, is illustrated by sentences with successive categorially ambiguous words. As Lashley [1951, p. 112] has noted:

> ...The input is never into a quiescent or static system, but always into a system which is already actively excited and organized. In the intact organism, behavior is the result of interaction of this background of excitation with input from any designated stimulus. Only when we can state the general characteristics of this background of excitation, can we understand the effects of a given input.

Consider this sentence:

(1) The old dog the footsteps of the young.[2]

Most people have problems with this sentence because the categorially ambiguous word *old* is used in its less frequent noun sense rather than its more frequent adjectival sense. However, in the sentence above, the more frequent adjectival sense of *old* is accessed upon initial reading of this sentence. Since an adjective is almost always followed by a noun or an adjective, the noun sense rather than the verb sense of *dog* would be accessed. This choice, however, leaves the sentence without a predicate. On the other hand, if a noun or a categorially ambiguous word whose dominant sense is a noun precedes *dog (dogs* in this example) as in

(2) The rash dogs the animals of the forest.

fewer people should be "garden-pathed." In this example, the *noun* sense of rash (skin irritation) rather than the adjectival sense (hasty) is more likely to be accessed. Consequently, the verb sense of *dogs* will be accessed and no difficulty in interpreting the sentence should be encountered.

In this study, a network of simple processing elements that *learns* a set of ambiguous lexical items simulates the results described above. This network operates as a content-addressable memory. In contrast to conventional computer memories in which the contents are accessed by specifying the physical addresses of the desired data, content-addressable memories are accessed by specifying some portion of the desired information. This information specified initially corresponds to activation of certain elements in the network. The ini-

---

2 This example is taken from Hirst [1983] and is attributed to Yorick Wilks.

tial activation leads to subsequent activation of the remaining elements in the network through the connections between pairs of elements.

2 The Model

2.1 Goals

The goal of the first part of this paper is to demonstrate that a network consisting of simple processing elements can learn, by modifying the strengths of the connections between pairs of elements in the network, a lexicon consisting of ambiguous entries. Once the network has been trained, the effects of context and relative dominance on the resolution of ambiguity as well as the time course of the resolution process will be simulated. Although this model bears superficial resemblance to earlier models of semantic memory [Collins and Loftus, 1975] and word recognition [McClelland and Rumelhart, 1981] in which nodes are connected to other nodes in a network, this approach differs in its emphasis on learning, and in the information represented by a node. Unlike earlier interactive activation models [e.g., Cottrell, 1984; McClelland and Rumelhart, 1981], this model uses a distributed rather than a local representation scheme to encode a word. Although an important motivation for a distributed representation scheme arises from considerations of learning, this study demonstrates that a distributed model does allow multiple activation and competition among alternatives typically found in interactive activation models.

In the second part of this paper, sequential effects occurring after one meaning has been accessed will be considered. To simulate these effects, the connections between elements in the network will undergo habituation, a transient modification of the connection strengths, once a word has been accessed to allow access of the alternative meaning. This scheme has been previously explored in simulating properties of a different form of ambiguity, multistable perception [Kawamoto and Anderson, 1985]. Next, a second set of elements will be added to the existing network in order to model word transition effects. This set of elements stores the most recently accessed word. Connections from certain elements in the second set of elements to corresponding elements in the first allow word transition regularities of sentences generated by a simple context-free grammar to be captured. These constraints will be used to resolve categorial ambiguities.

2.2 Representation

The lexicon learned by the network consists of the 12 pairs of ambiguous 4-letter words listed in Table 1.

Table 1 Lexical entries and their frequencies defined for the simulations

	lexical entry				frequency
	spelling	pronunc.	p.s.	meaning	

A C I D	a s @ d	no un	[c][h][e][m][i][c][a][l]	4
A C I D	a s @ d	no un	[c][h][e][m][l][s][d][r]	3
F I N E	f i_ n $	ad jc	[a][d][e][q][u][a][t][e]	4
F I N E	f i_ n $	no un	[p][a][y][m][o][n][e][y]	3
F L A T	f l a t	ad jc	[p][l][a][n][e][s][r][f]	4
F L A T	f l a t	no un	[a][p][t][m][b][l][d][g]	3
L E A D	l e $ d	no un	[h][v][y][m][e][t][a][l]	4
L E A D	l e_ $ d	ve rb	[g][f][o][r][w][a][r][d]	3
R O S E	r o_ z $	no un	[s][p][f][l][o][w][e][r]	4
R O S E	r o_ z $	ve rb	[h][u][e][w][h][t][r][d]	3
W I N D	w i n d	no un	[b][l][o][w][n][a][i][r]	4
W I N D	w i_ n d	ve rb	[e][n][c][i][r][c][l][e]	3
B L U E	b l u: $	ad jc	[h][u][e][c][b][l][a][u]	6
B L U E	b l u: $	ad jc	[e][m][o][t][n][s][a][d]	1
C O L D	k o_ l d	ad jc	[f][r][i][g][d][t][m][p]	6
C O L D	k o_ l d	no un	[c][h][i][l][w][t][m][p]	1
D O V E	d @ v $	no un	[w][i][l][d][b][i][r][d]	6
D O V E	d o_ v $	ve rb	[h][e][d][f][i][r][s][t]	1
K N O B	$ n o. b	no un	[r][n][d][h][a][n][d][l]	6
K N O B	$ n o. b	no un	[r][n][d][m][o][u][n][t]	1
L O N G	l o. ng $	ad jc	[d][i][m][n][l][o][n][g]	6
L O N G	l o. ng $	ve rb	[y][e][a][r][n][d][s][r]	1
R I N G	r i ng $	no un	[f][i][n][g][e][r][j][w]	6
R I N G	r i ng $	ve rb	[b][e][l][s][o][u][n][d]	1

The relative frequency of each entry, defined arbitrarily for the simulation, is also indicated. Each entry consists of its spelling, pronunciation, part of speech, and meaning. The spelling will be represented by 48 graphemic features, the pronunciation by 48 phonemic features, the part of speech by 24 syntactic features, and the meaning by 96 semantic features. Thus, each entry is represented by a total of 216 binary features. Details of this mapping are given below. To facilitate initial coding and interpretation of simulation results presented in later sections, the values of twelve features will be grouped together and encoded as a unique 3-character sequence (including spaces) as presented in Table 1.[3] The representation of one of the entries, the dominant sense of *WIND* is shown in detail in Table 2.

Table 2   Example of the explicit representation for one entry (the dominant entry of WIND) showing each 3-character sequence and the corresponding feature values.

sequence	values
' W '	--++-----+--
' I '	-+--------++-
' N '	-+-+------+-
' D '	-+--+----+--
' w '	--------++--
' i '	+---+++++---
' n '	-++-+---+---
' d '	-+-+-+-+----
' no '	--+---+-+--+
' un '	+---++-----+
' [b]'	-++-+--+-+++
' [l]'	-+-+---+-+--
' [o]'	-------+++-+
' [w]'	+-+--+---+-++
' [n]'	-+-+++----+-
' [a]'	-+-+-+++--++
' [i]'	-++-+----++-
' [r]'	+++++----+++

3 These 3-character sequences are used instead of single characters to avoid ambiguity in the interpretation of the patterns. Thus, the pattern represented by 'e ' is different from the pattern represented by '[e] '.

Graphemic field: Each of the four letters in a word is represented by the twelve features devised by Eleanor Gibson [1969].[4] The twelve features of each of the four letters are simply concatenated to generate the 48 features that comprise the graphemic field. A graphemic feature thus represents one feature of one of the four letters.

Phonemic field: The representation of the pronunciation of a word parallels the representation of the spelling. In this case, the different symbols used in a pronunciation key represent the values of twelve phonetic features.[5] Therefore, one of the 48 phonemic features represents a phonetic feature of one of the four symbols representing the pronunciation. Note that this coding scheme still captures a fair amount of similarity between two different different pronunciations. For example, the two phonemic representations of the homograph *WIND,* /w i n d / and /w i_ n d /, differ in only 6 (corresponding to the difference between the representations of 'i ' and 'i_ ') of the 48 phonemic features.

Syntactic field: 24 features are used to represent the part of speech. Unlike the graphemic and phonemic representation, the values of all 24 features are defined randomly. To be consistent with the rest of the representation, the values of the first set of twelve and second set of twelve syntactic features are represented by the 3-character sequences 'ad jc ' (adjective), 'no un ' (noun), and 've rb ' (verb).

Semantic field: The meaning of each entry is represented by 96 unique semantic features.[6] As in the case of the phonemic and syntactic representations, the features are not based on any previously defined feature set. Again, the values of a group of twelve features will be encoded as a 3-character sequence. For example, the values for the first twelve semantic features for the verb sense of *WIND* are '+-++----+++-' and encoded as the 3-character sequence '[e] '. For this word the values of the last twelve semantic features are also '+-++----+++-' since they too are encoded as '[e] '. However, the first set of twelve and the last set of twelve features represent completely different semantic features.

---

4 Although it has been argued that the neural representation may be quite different [Anderson and Mozer, 1981], this representation has been adopted here because feature sets such as these capture the property that perceptually similar characters have similar representations.

5 The number of features used in the representation was based on implementation considerations. Unlike the coding scheme for letters, a feature in this representation cannot be mapped onto any conventional phonetic feature set.

6 There has recently been a great deal of interest in the representation of concepts [for review, see Smith and Medin, 1981]. While it is true that a number of attempts have been made to enumerate feature lists, the representation used here merely attempts to capture overall subjective similarity without precisely defining individual features. Thus, semantically similar (as judged by the author) entries have identical values for a large number of semantic features. This is manifested as identical 3-character sequences in one or more corresponding positions as in [h][u][e][c][b][l][a][u] and [h][u][e][w][h][t][r][d].

2.3 *Network Architecture*

The architecture of the network used here is illustrated in Figure 8.1. It is based on the work of Anderson and his colleagues [Anderson et al., 1977; Anderson, 1983] and is similar to the work of a number of others [Kohonen, 1977; McClelland and Rumelhart, 1985]. The entire network consists of 2 sets of 216 elements, where each of the 216 elements corresponds to one of the 216 features that comprise a lexical entry. This gives rise to a distributed representation in which each word is represented by all 216 elements in a set of elements and each element participates in the representation of every word.

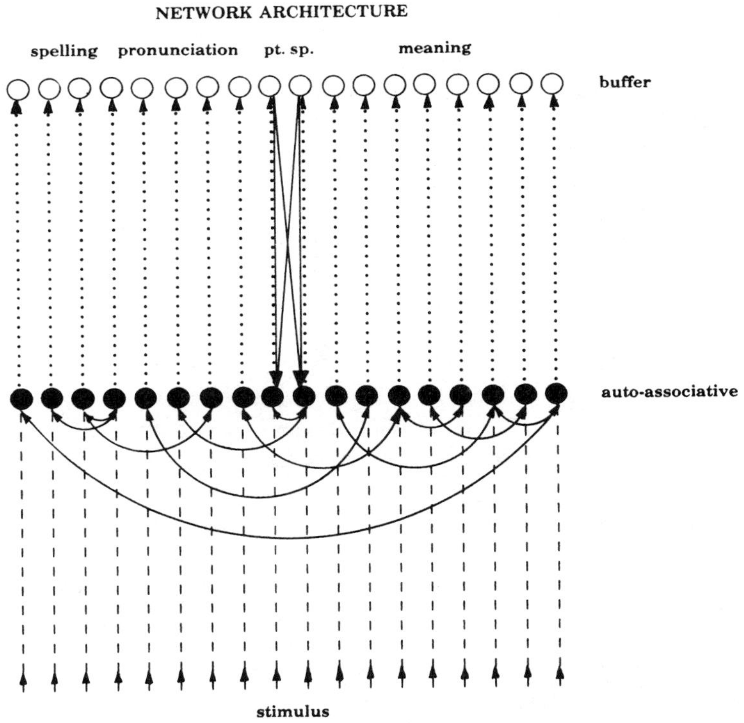

NETWORK ARCHITECTURE

Figure 8.1 A schematic showing the architecture of the network used in this study. There are two sets of 216 elements (only some of which are shown) representing the spelling, pronunciation, part of speech, and meaning of a lexical entry. The first set, the auto-associative elements, receives input from the environment as well as from every element in that set. The second set, the buffer elements, acts as a memory buffer that stores the most recently accessed word. There are connections from some of the elements in the buffer set back to corresponding elements in the auto-associative elements.

The input provided from the environment can activate elements in the first set of elements. This first set of 216 elements will be referred to as the auto-associative network because each element forms modifiable connections with every other element in the set to form the auto-associative connections, **A**. These auto-associative connections allow the pronunciation, part of speech, and meaning of a word to be accessed given only its spelling. Once this information has been accessed, it is transmitted to the second set of 216 elements via connections from elements in the auto-associative set of elements to corresponding elements in the second set. This second set of elements will be referred to as the buffer elements because it acts as a memory buffer that stores the most recently accessed word. There are also modifiable connections, **T**, from the buffer elements back to the auto-associative elements. In the current implementation, only connections between elements representing the part of speech are allowed. These connections are used to capture word transition constraints allowed by a grammar.

The activity of an element in the auto-associative network is represented as a real value ranging between −1.0 and +1.0. This activity changes with time (where time changes in discrete steps) such that the activity of an element, a_i, at time t is simply the sum of some fraction, δ, of its activity at the previous time step and the activity of all the other elements, a_j, weighted by the connection strength, A_{ij}. That is,

$$a_i(t) = LIMIT \left[\delta a_i(t-1) + [\sum_j A_{ij} a_j(t-1)] \right], \tag{3}$$

where *LIMIT* constrains the activity to the range from −1.0 to +1.0. If a stimulus is presented over a period of time, there is an additional term

$$a_i(t) = LIMIT \left[\delta a_i(t-1) + [\sum_j A_{ij} a_j(t-1)] + s_i \right], \tag{4}$$

where **s** represents the input. In the final set of simulations where the stimulus consists of sequences of words, the constraint on word transitions is incorporated as

$$a_i(t) = LIMIT \left[\delta a_i(t-1) + [\sum_j A_{ij} a_j(t-1)] + s_i + [\sum_j T_{ij} b_j] \right], \tag{5}$$

where **T** captures the syntactic constraints and **b** is the pattern of activity corresponding to the most recently accessed word stored in the buffer.

2.4 Learning

An important aspect of modeling efforts of this type is the training involved in producing a network that successfully regenerates the complete pattern learned given only part of the pattern. This is achieved by modifying the connection strengths between pairs of elements to capture the correlations in their activities. One approach introduced by the early investigators of learning in networks [Rosenblatt, 1962; Widrow and Hoff, 1960] is *error-correction*. Modification of the connection strengths proceeds by minimizing (i.e., correcting) the error between the desired output and the actual output. For example, if the pattern **g** representing a complete lexical entry is to be learned, that pattern is provided as the input from the environment to the auto-associative network. Once a pattern is instantiated in these elements, each element receives input from all the other elements in the auto-associative network weighted by the strength of the connections from those elements. The difference between the correct value of the i*th* element of **g**, g_i (the input from the environment), and the sum of the weighted input from the other elements, g_i', is used to determine the extent of the modification. Here, g_i' is simply

$$g_i' = LIMIT \left[\sum_j A_{ij}g_j\right].$$ (6)

After a learning trial, each connection strength A_{ij} is modified by

$$\Delta A_{ij} = \eta(g_i - g_i')g_j,$$ (7)

where η is a scalar learning constant.

2.5 Habituation

Because the auto-associative connections form a positive feedback loop, once all the elements in the first set reach their minimal or maximal activation, the pattern of activity no longer changes. One solution to this problem, habituation of the connections A_{ij}, corresponds to a transient modification of the connection strengths while the network is in this state.[7] This modification takes the following form: temporarily decrease those connection strengths between pairs of elements whose activities are positively correlated, and increase those connection strengths between pairs of elements whose activities are negatively correlated once all the elements become maximally or minimally activated. The effect of habituation decays exponentially, however, and so the contribution of habituation is given by

$$H_{ij}(0) = \beta b_i b_j$$ (8a)

$$H_{ij}(t + 1) = H_{ij}(0) + \gamma H_{ij}(t),$$ (8b)

---

7 Habituation does not have to be restricted to the stable state. This simplification has been adopted to simplify the computation and is not expected to cause any significant difference in the results.

where β is a negatively valued constant, **b** is the pattern of activity corresponding to the most recently accessed word, γ is a decay constant, and t is the number of iterations following the start of habituation. Thus, the effect of habituation on the connection strengths is

$$A_{ij}(\tau + t) = A_{ij}(\tau) + H_{ij}(t), \qquad (9)$$

where τ is the number of iterations for all the auto-associative elements to reach their minimal or maximal activation levels, $A_{ij}(\tau + t)$ is the current strength of a connection, and $H(t)$ is the cumulative effect of habituation.

3 Resolution

3.1 Example

Before analyzing the effects of relative dominance and context on resolution, a description of the learning procedure and an example of how the network accesses a lexical entry will be given. Learning begins with the connection strengths all set to 0, and modification of the weights is carried out on each learning trial according to the error-correction scheme outlined above. A total of 800 learning trials were used, with each pair of ambiguous words presented an average of slightly less than 67 times. The ratios of presentation of the two senses were 6:1 for the polarized homographs and 4:3 for the nearly equi-probable homographs. During learning, the number of times a particular entry is presented varies probabilistically as a function of its relative frequency. With each learning trial, the only modifications in the network are the changes in the strengths of connections. There is no counter associated with a given lexical entry that is explicitly incremented each time that entry is presented.

Once training is completed, the network's ability to access lexical information is tested by presenting only the spelling of a word. This is implemented by activating just the elements in the network corresponding to the graphemic field with the appropriate pattern of activation. Consider, for example, the pattern of activity that arises after presentation of the stimulus 'WIND' shown below:

W I N D _ _ _ _ _ _ _ _ _ _ _ _ _ .

The activity, present only in the graphemic field, corresponds to values of the features for the letters *W, I, N,* and *D* in the first, second, third, and fourth letter positions, respectively. The level of activity is +0.25 for features that are present, and −0.25 for features that are absent. The activities of the remaining elements are set to 0.

After the stimulus is presented to the network, activation spreads through the network via the connections, and subsequent patterns of activity are analyzed. Selected patterns of activation from this sequence are shown in Figure 8.2. In this figure, the activity of each of the 216 elements in the auto-associative network is indicated by the height above or below the null activity level. Initially, there is activity only in the graphemic field. After one time step, other elements in the network are activated by the graphemic elements (weighted by the connection strengths). After a few time steps, some elements become saturated (i.e., reach their maximal or minimal levels of activation). Finally, after a number of time steps, all elements become saturated.

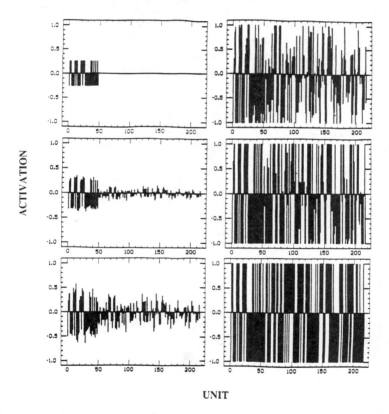

Figure 8.2 Activation of element following the presentation of a stimulus. The panels show the activity of all 216 auto-associative elements at various points from onset of the stimulus (upper left panel) to access of the entry (lower right panel). Initially, there is activity only in the graphemic field represented by elements 1–48. With time, every element becomes activated (panels on the left). More elements become saturated, until finally all are saturated (panels on the right).

As an aid in interpreting the state of the network, the activities of sets of 12 elements are interpreted based on the encoding scheme described earlier. If all twelve elements are at their maximal or minimal activity level, the 3-character sequence corresponding to that exact pattern of activity is displayed. If the pattern of activity does not exactly correspond to one of the previously defined patterns, the activity for that set of 12 elements is interpreted as '* '. In those cases in which one or more elements in a set of twelve are not at their minimal or maximal levels, that set is interpreted as '_ '. Using this interpretation scheme, the successive states of the network for the example illustrated in Figure 8.2 are shown in Table 3. In this example, the dominant sense of *WIND* is accessed. Note that the unambiguous elements are the first to saturate, as evidenced by saturation of the phonemic elements representing 'w ', 'n ', and 'd ' before those representing the pronunciation of the letter *I*. This is consistent with the longer naming times found for homographs with more than one pronunciation [Seidenberg et al., 1984].

Table 3   Interpretation of the successive patterns of activation that arise in the auto-associative network following presentation of 'WIND'. The numbers at the left indicate number of iterations through the network.

	spelling				pronunc.				p.s.					meaning				
input:	W	I	N	D	_	_	_	_	_	_	_	_	_	_	_	_	_	_
0	_	_	_	_	_	_	_	_	_	_	_	_	_	_	_	_	_	_
1	_	_	_	_	_	_	_	_	_	_	_	_	_	_	_	_	_	_
2	_	_	_	_	_	_	_	_	_	_	_	_	_	_	_	_	_	_
3	_	_	_	_	_	_	_	_	_	_	_	_	_	_	_	_	_	_
4	_	_	_	_	_	_	_	_	_	_	_	_	_	_	_	_	_	_
5	_	_	_	D	_	_	_	d	_	_	_	_	_	_	_	_	_	_
6	_	I	N	D	_	_	n	d	_	_	_	_	_	_	_	_	_	_
7	W	I	N	D	w	_	n	d	_	_	_	_	_	_	_	_	_	_
8	W	I	N	D	w	_	n	d	_	_	_	_	_	_	_	_	_	_
9	W	I	N	D	w	_	n	d	_	_	_	_	_	_	_	_	_	_
10	W	I	N	D	w	_	n	d	_	_	_	_	_	_	_	_	_	_
11	W	I	N	D	w	_	n	d	_	_	_	_	_	_	_	_	_	_
12	W	I	N	D	w	_	n	d	_	_	_	_	[o]	_	_	[a]	_	_
13	W	I	N	D	w	_	n	d	no	un	_	_	[o]	_	[n]	[a]	[i]	[r]
14	W	I	N	D	w	i	n	d	no	un	_	_	[o]	_	[n]	[a]	[i]	[r]
15	W	I	N	D	w	i	n	d	no	un	_	_	[o]	_	[n]	[a]	[i]	[r]
16	W	I	N	D	w	i	n	d	no	un	[b]	[l]	[o]	[w]	[n]	[a]	[i]	[r]

3.2 Relative Dominance

In this section, the effect of relative dominance in determining the meaning accessed is explored. Twelve simulation "subjects" were used, with each "subject" corresponding to a network trained using a unique learning sequence which was generated probabilistically. Thus, the total number of times a word is presented, as well as the actual sequence of words presented during training, vary for each network.

3.2.1 Results and Discussion

The first analysis, shown in Table 4, illustrates the effect of relative dominance in determining the meaning accessed. For polarized ambiguous words (relative frequency of 6:1), the dominant meaning was accessed in all cases. However, in 14 of the trials (approximately 25%) for words that were nearly equi-probable, the *subordinate* meaning was accessed initially. These results are consistent with the empirical evidence relating the degree of dominance and the percentage of times the dominant meaning is initially accessed [Galbraith and Taschman, 1969; Warren et al., 1977].

Table 4   Summary comparing equi-probable and polarized ambiguous words in the number of "subjects" (out of twelve) for which the subordinate rather than the dominant meaning was fully activated.

word	# of times subordinate accessed
equi-probable (4:3)	
ACID	7
FINE	1
FLAT	2
LEAD	2
ROSE	0
WIND	0
polarized (6:1)	
BLUE	0
COLD	0
DOVE	0
KNOB	0
LONG	0
RING	0

These results can be understood by considering how consistent the pattern of activity is with respect to the connection strengths. This measure of consistency is analogous to the amount of energy (in a thermodynamic sense) and has been defined explicitly as

$$E = - (1/2) \sum_i \sum_j A_{ij} a_i \, a_j. \tag{10}$$

where A_{ij} is the connection strength from element i to element j, and a_i and a_j are the activations of the auto-associative elements i and j, respectively [Hopfield, 1982]. Given a particular set of connection strengths (determined by learning in this case), different activity patterns have different energies. The more consistent a particular pattern of activity is with respect to the connection strengths, the lower the energy of that pattern of activity. When the energy values for all possible activity patterns are plotted, an "energy landscape" is obtained. These energy landscapes are characterized by ridges (regions that have larger energy values relative to surrounding regions) and valleys (regions that have smaller energy values relative to the surrounding regions). It has been shown [Hopfield, 1982; Golden, 1986] that the activity of these networks evolves to a state corresponding to a local energy minimum.

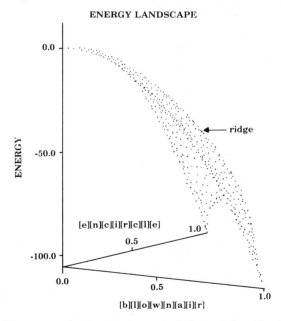

Figure 8.3 The energy landscape for part of plane defined by the subordinate and dominant senses of *WIND*. There is a ridge separating the space into two valleys. The lowest points in these valleys correspond to the dominant and subordinate senses of *WIND*.

Figure 8.3 shows the energy landscape for part of the plane within the space defined by the two senses of *WIND*. The axes are two rays that begin at the origin (the point corresponding to an activity of 0.0 for all the elements in the network) and pass through the points in the 216-dimensional space that correspond to the the dominant and subordinate senses of *WIND*. Two features of these landscapes should be noted: (1) There are two points of local energy minima that correspond to the two senses of an ambiguous word. (2) There is a ridge between each pair of points. These features of the landscapes are formed as a result of the learning.

Although the general features are the same for all pairs of words, the precise values of the energy minima and the locations of the ridge differ. Table 5 shows the energies corresponding to the subordinate and dominant senses of each ambiguous word, the location of the ridge separating the points corresponding to the different senses, and the sense accessed for one of the twelve networks.

Table 5 Summary of various features of the energy landscape for one of the twelve networks and their relation to the sense that is accessed. The features being compared are the energies of the subordinate and dominant senses of each ambiguous word, and the location of the ridge separating the two minima. Values less than 0.50 for the location of ridge mean that the ridge is closer to the point corresponding to the subordinate sense.

word	sense accessed	E(subordinate)	E(dominant)	ridge location
equi-probable (4:3)				
ACID	subordinate	−102.7	−102.1	0.51
FINE	dominant	−101.6	−104.3	0.49
FLAT	dominant	−100.1	−105.7	0.47
LEAD	dominant	−102.5	−105.0	0.49
ROSE	subordinate	−104.6	−102.0	0.51
WIND	dominant	−104.4	−105.3	0.50
polarized (6:1)				
BLUE	dominant	−86.7	−106.8	0.31
COLD	dominant	−81.7	−107.0	0.22
DOVE	dominant	−79.5	−107.2	0.34
KNOB	dominant	−77.5	−107.1	0.00
LONG	dominant	−81.1	−106.8	0.35
RING	dominant	−76.0	−107.3	0.30

We will look at the values for one network rather than the average values of all the networks because we can see how the energy landscape that arises with one particular learning sequence influences the meaning accessed by that network.

The energies corresponding to the different senses of a word vary with relative frequency. The mean energy values for those entries with relative frequencies of 6, 4, 3, and 1, are −107.0, −104.1, −102.6, and −80.4, respectively. For polarized ambiguous words, the energy corresponding to the dominant entry is always lower because of the the huge imbalance in the number of times the dominant sense is presented during learning relative to the subordinate one. For the nearly equi-probable ambiguous words, the energy corresponding to the dominant entry, while usually lower than that of the subordinate one, need not be as is the case for *ACID* and *ROSE*. This can arise for a number of reasons. First, the actual learning sequence may contain more examples of the "subordinate" entry, a situation more likely with the equi-probable homographs. (Recall that the learning sequence is determined probabilistically.) Furthermore, since the learning is affected by recency, on those occasions when the subordinate entry of an ambiguous word is more prevalent among the last entries learned compared with the corresponding dominant entry, the lower energy may again correspond to the "subordinate" entry. Also, since the representation is a distributed one, the similarity of the subordinate sense to the other words learned may also have an effect. For example, one possible reason for the deeper minimum of the subordinate sense of *ROSE*, [h][u][e][w][h][t][r][d], is its similarity to the dominant sense of *BLUE*, [h][u][e][c][b][l][a][u].

The relative values of the energy minima corresponding to the two senses of an ambiguous word are correlated with the location of the ridge relative to these two senses. The index for the location of the ridge given in Table 5 ranges from 0.0 to 1.0, with a value of 0.50 indicating that the ridge is midway between the points corresponding to the two senses. Values less than 0.5 indicate that the ridge is closer to the subordinate sense. The location of the ridge is important because it determines which sense is accessed when an ambiguous word is presented in isolation. A word presented in isolation corresponds to the system beginning at a point equi-distant from each of the two senses. Since these systems move downhill in energy, the system will eventually reach the local minimum on the same side of the ridge as the starting point. That minimum always corresponds to the dominant sense if the ambiguous word is polarized and usually corresponds to the dominant sense if the word is nearly equi-probable. However, in two cases, *ACID* and *ROSE,* the subordinate sense is accessed. For these two words, the relative depth of the two energy minima and the location of the ridge is opposite that of all the other words in which the dominant sense is accessed.

Other models such as the logogen model [Morton, 1969], the interactive activation model [McClelland and Rumelhart, 1981] and the READER model

[Thibadeau et al., 1982] can account for these effects of relative frequency. Unlike these models, however, there is no explicit local representation of the frequency in terms of either a lower threshold or higher base level of activation for frequent words. Since the representation of a word is distributed, word frequency must be captured solely through the strengths of the entire set of connections. Despite the fact that frequency information is not represented locally, the model can simulate the effects of relative dominance.

3.3 *Context and Time-Course*

In this set of simulations context effects and the time-course of resolution will be explored. Context is provided by activating elements comprising either the syntactic or semantic fields with a pattern of activation appropriate for one sense of an ambiguous word. Consider *WIND,* for example. The dominant sense of *WIND* is a noun with the meaning [b][l][o][w][n][a][i][r], and the subordinate sense is a verb with the meaning [e][n][c][i][r][c][l][e]. In the example, the inputs for *WIND* with the appropriate syntactic contexts are

W I N D _ _ _ _ no un _ _ _ _ _ _ _ _ , and

W I N D _ _ _ _ ve rb _ _ _ _ _ _ _ _ .

Analogously, the inputs for *WIND* with the appropriate semantic contexts are

W I N D _ _ _ _ _ _ [b] [l] _ _ _ _ _ _ , and

W I N D _ _ _ _ _ _ [e] [n] _ _ _ _ _ _ .

Such a representation for context is a natural one for systems using distributed representation schemes. Since semantically similar items have similar semantic representations, presentation of a priming stimulus will result in activity in the semantic field that is similar to the representation of the subsequent word. For example, the sense of *BLUE* meaning [h][u][e][c][b][l][a][u] would prime the sense of *ROSE* meaning [h][u][e][w][h][t][r][d].[8] This is quite different from previous examples of networks demonstrating spreading activation in which words are represented as single nodes and connections (perhaps weighted) between nodes are used to link semantically similar items [Collins and Loftus, 1975].

---

8 When just the words *BLUE ROSE* are presented, people will probably interpret *ROSE* as a noun rather than as an adjective. This probably arises because *ROSE* is used as a noun more frequently than as an adjective and because a sequence consisting of an adjective followed by a noun is very common in English. This can be overcome by a stronger bias as seen in *PINK GREY BLUE ROSE.*

Although one might argue that context introduced in this fashion is unrealistic, this simplification has been used because it provides a clearer theoretical account of empirical observations. A more plausible scheme for context will be presented in the second half of this paper.

3.3.1 *Results and Discussion*   Table 6 shows the successive states of the network given a syntactic context and a semantic context for the subordinate and dominant senses of *WIND*. In all cases, the contextually appropriate meaning is accessed.

Table 6   Interpretation of successive patterns of activation that arise with the presence of a context. The number at the left of each line indicates the number of iterations through the network. In all cases, the contextually appropriate sense becomes fully fully activated. (Note: some of the patterns have been removed for brevity.)

```
input:  W  I  N  D  _  _  _  _  no un _  _  _  _  _  _  _  _

   0    _  _  _  _  _  _  _  _  _  _  _  _  _  _  _  _  _  _
   .
   4    _  _  _  _  _  _  _  _  no un _  _  _  _  _  _  _  _
   5    _  I  _  D  _  _  _  d  no un _  _  _  _  _  _  _  _
   6    _  I  N  D  _  _  n  d  no un _  _  _  _  _  _  _  _
   7    _  I  N  D  w  _  n  d  no un _  _  _  _  _  _  _  _
   8    W  I  N  D  w  _  n  d  no un _  _  _  _  _  _  _  _
   9    W  I  N  D  w  _  n  d  no un _  _  _  _  _  [a]_    [r]
  10    W  I  N  D  w  i  n  d  no un _  _  _  _  _  [a]_    [r]
  11    W  I  N  D  w  i  n  d  no un [b]_    [o]_    [n][a]_    [r]
  12    W  I  N  D  w  i  n  d  no un [b][l][o][w][n][a][i][r]


input:  W  I  N  D  _  _  _  _  ve rb _  _  _  _  _  _  _  _

   0    _  _  _  _  _  _  _  _  _  _  _  _  _  _  _  _  _  _
   .
   5    _  I  N  D  _  _  _  d  ve rb _  _  _  _  _  _  _  _
   6    W  I  N  D  _  _  n  d  ve rb _  _  _  _  _  _  _  _
   7    W  I  N  D  w  _  n  d  ve rb _  _  _  _  _  _  _  _
   8    W  I  N  D  w  _  n  d  ve rb _  _  _  _  _  _  _  _
   9    W  I  N  D  w  i_ n  d  ve rb _  [n]_    [i]_    _  [l][e]
  10    W  I  N  D  w  i_ n  d  ve rb [e][n][c][i][r]_    [l][e]
  11    W  I  N  D  w  i_ n  d  ve rb [e][n][c][i][r][c][l][e]


input:  W  I  N  D  _  _  _  _  _  [b][l]_  _  _  _  _  _

   0    _  _  _  _  _  _  _  _  _  _  _  _  _  _  _  _  _  _
   .
   5    _  I  N  D  _  _  _  d  _  _  _  _  _  _  _  _  _  _
   6    W  I  N  D  w  i  _  d  _  _  _  _  _  _  _  _  _  _
   7    W  I  N  D  w  i  n  d  _  _  [b]_    [o]_    _  [a][i][r]
   8    W  I  N  D  w  i  n  d  no un [b][l][o][w][n][a][i][r]


input:  W  I  N  D  _  _  _  _  _  [e][n]_  _  _  _  _  _

   0    _  _  _  _  _  _  _  _  _  _  _  _  _  _  _  _  _  _
   .
   5    _  I  _  D  _  _  _  _  _  _  _  _  _  _  _  _  _  _
   6    W  I  N  D  _  _  _  d  _  _  _  _  _  _  _  _  _  _
   7    W  I  N  D  w  _  n  d  _  _  _  _  _  _  _  _  _  _
   8    W  I  N  D  w  i_ n  d  _  _  _  [e][n]_    _  _  [c]_    [e]
   9    W  I  N  D  w  i_ n  d  ve rb [e][n][c]_    [r][c][l][e]
  10    W  I  N  D  w  i_ n  d  ve rb [e][n][c][i][r][c][l][e]
```

Time Course of Activation

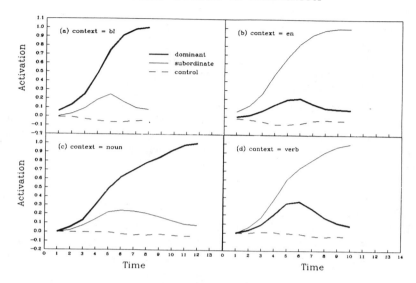

Figure 8.4 Time-course of resolution. The activation of two meanings of WIND, [b][l][o][w][n][a][i][r] and [e][n][c][i][r][c][l][e], as well as the meaning of a control word, [h][u][e][c][b][l][a][u], are plotted as a function of time. The time-course of resolution is given for cases where (a) a semantic context biases the dominant meaning, (b) a semantic context biases the subordinate meaning, (c) a syntactic context biases the dominant meaning, and (d) a syntactic context biases the subordinate meaning. In all cases, *both* meanings are initially activated, but only the contextually appropriate meaning is eventually fully activated.

Although the effects of *both* frequency and context have, with a few exceptions [Simpson, 1981; Carpenter and Daneman, 1981], been largely ignored in considering how an ambiguity is resolved, these factors are important in this model. As discussed in the previous section, the relative frequencies of the two senses of an ambiguous word determine the energies corresponding to the two senses and the location of the ridge in that landscape. Context, on the other hand, determines where in this landscape the system begins. Without any context, the initial state is equi-distant to the two senses of an ambiguous word. With a disambiguating context, the initial state is closer to the stable state corresponding to the context. If the initial state and sense corresponding to the context are on the same side of the ridge, the contextually appropriate sense will be accessed.

Although only the contextually appropriate sense is eventually accessed, there is evidence that *both* senses are initially activated [Swinney, 1979; Tanenhaus et al., 1979]. To analyze the time-course of resolution in this system, the degree to which the different senses of an ambiguous word are activated after each iteration was found. The measure of activation used was the normalized dot product (the sum of products of corresponding elements divided by the number of elements) of the activity in the semantic field with each of the two meanings of the ambiguous test word as well as with one meaning of the *BLUE*, [h][u][e][c][b][l][a][u], as a control. In Figure 8.4, the activations of the dominant and subordinate meanings of *WIND* and the meaning of the control are shown as a function of time. The results of a semantic context biasing the dominant and subordinate senses are shown in Figures 8.4a and 8.4b, respectively. The effects of a syntactic context are shown in Figures 8.4c and 8.4d. With either a syntactic or semantic context, only the contextually appropriate meaning becomes completely activated.

However, despite the context provided, *both* meanings of the test word are partially activated initially. Initially, the activities of all of the elements are within the limits of the maximal and minimal activation levels. At this point, the system is in a linear range of the network and the subsequent activity of an element is simply the weighted sum of its input. Since the connections from elements in the graphemic field to elements in the semantic field reflect the pair-wise associations of both the dominant and subordinate meanings with the corresponding spelling, activation corresponding to *both* meanings will be elicited simultaneously while the system is in the linear range. Once a unit reaches its minimal or maximal activation level, however, the system becomes non-linear. Essentially, this non-linearity initiates a competition between the two senses that continues until one meaning becomes maximally activated and the other minimally activated. Without this non-linearity, *both* senses would continue to increase (albeit at different rates). The competition observed here is thus quite different from that found in systems using local representations: there are no explicit inhibitory connections between single units representing different senses that are in competition.

4 Successive Stable States

4.1 Alternative Meaning

In the previous simulations, we have seen how frequency and context influence which state the network settles into (i.e., which is sense accessed). After settling into a stable state, the network can be forced out of that state by habituation, a transient modification of the connection strengths based on the current activation of the network elements. These changes have been defined earlier in equations (8) and (9). For these simulations, the initial activity of the auto-associative elements will be set to a pattern of activation corresponding to one of the two senses of an ambiguous word. Unlike the previous simulations, the spelling of the word will be provided as an input to the network until the second sense is retrieved. By presenting this input at a large gain, the graphemic field will remain fixed.

4.1.1 Results and Discussion Table 7 shows an example of the successive states of the network from an initial stable state to a new stable state that arise under habituation. In this particular case, the initial state is the dominant sense of *WIND*. With habituation, the network is driven out of this stable state to another stable state, the subordinate sense of *WIND*.

Table 7   Interpretation of successive patterns of activation that arise after one sense has been accessed and habituation (a transient modification of the connection strengths) has been initiated. The numbers at the left correspond to the number of iterations through the network. (Note: some of the patterns have been removed for brevity.)

```
input:  W  I  N  D  _  _  _  _  _  _  _  _  _  _  _  _  _  _  _

   0    W  I  N  D  w  i  n  d  no un [b][l][o][w][n][a][i][r]
   .    W  I  N  D  w  i  n  d  no un [b][l][o][w][n][a][i][r]
  18    W  I  N  D  w  i  n  d  no un [b]_   [o][w][n][a][i][r]
  19    W  I  N  D  _  i  n  d  no un [b]_   [o][w][n][a]_  _
  20    W  I  N  D  _  i  n  d  no un [b]_   [o]_  _ [a]_  _
  21    W  I  N  D  _  _  n  d  no un _   _ [o]_  _ [a]_  _
  22    W  I  N  D  _  _  n  d
  23    W  I  N  D  _  _  n  d
  24    W  I  N  D  _  _  _  d
   .    W  I  N  D
  29    W  I  N  D  _  _  _  d  ve rb
   .    W  I  N  D  _  _  _  d  ve rb
  34    W  I  N  D  _  _  n  d  ve rb
   .    W  I  N  D  _  _  n  d  ve rb
  38    W  I  N  D  _  _  n  d  ve rb  _  _ [c][i]_  _ [l]_
  39    W  I  N  D  _  _  n  d  ve rb  _  _ [c][i]_  _ [l]_
  40    W  I  N  D  _  _  n  d  ve rb  _  _ [c][i]_ [c][l]_
  41    W  I  N  D  _  _  n  d  ve rb  _ [n][c][i]_ [c][l]_
  42    W  I  N  D  _  _  n  d  ve rb  _ [n][c][i]_ [c][l]_
  43    W  I  N  D  _  _  n  d  ve rb  _ [n][c][i]_ [c][l]_
  44    W  I  N  D  w  i_ n  d  ve rb  _ [n][c][i]_ [c][l]_
  45    W  I  N  D  w  i_ n  d  ve rb [e][n][c][i]_ [c][l]_
  46    W  I  N  D  w  i_ n  d  ve rb [e][n][c][i]_ [c][l]_
  47    W  I  N  D  w  i_ n  d  ve rb [e][n][c][i]_ [c][l][e]
  48    W  I  N  D  w  i_ n  d  ve rb [e][n][c][i][r][c][l][e]
```

Table 8   Summary of the maximal activation of the subordinate, A(subordinate), and the dominant, A(dominant), meaning after initial access of the dominant and subordinate meanings, respectively.

word	A(subordinate)	A(dominant)
equi-probable (4:3)		
ACID	1.00	1.00
FINE	0.64	1.00
FLAT	0.57	1.00
LEAD	0.78	1.00
ROSE	0.86	1.00
WIND	1.00	1.00
polarized (6:1)		
BLUE	0.77	1.00
COLD	0.56	1.00
DOVE	0.58	1.00
KNOB	0.50	1.00
LONG	0.28	0.81
RING	0.37	1.00

Access of the alternative sense depends on the values chosen for the parameters β and γ from equation (8). The values of β and γ used in these simulations are −0.0003 and 0.95, respectively. For these values, the alternative is accessed successfully in the majority of cases.[9] Since the alternative sense is not always accessed, the maximal level of activation of the alternative meaning will be used as an index. These maximal levels of the alternative sense for one "subject" (i.e., one of the twelve networks) are shown in Table 8.

There are two points to note. First, with one exception *(LONG)*, the dominant sense did become fully activated when the initial state of the system corresponded to the subordinate sense (see the column labeled A(dominant) in Table 8). On the other hand, the subordinate sense was fully activated when the ini-

---

9   If the magnitude of the values chosen for β and γ are not large enough, the network will tend to remain in the initial stable state. On the other hand, if the magnitude of β is much larger than that used here, the network would be forced into a state in which the polarity of every element's initial activation level becomes reversed (i.e., the network would be forced into the opposite corner).

tial state of the system corresponded to the dominant sense only for *ACID* and *WIND*. These results are consistent with psycholinguistic data showing that human subjects are more likely to produce an alternative meaning when the preceding context primes the subordinate sense [Hogaboam and Perfetti, 1975]. However, the results of the simulation do not necessarily support an ordered search model. As Onifer and Swinney (1981) have pointed out, the task used by Hogaboam and Perfetti may be examining a process that occurs long after lexical access. Second, subsequent access of the subordinate sense depends on the relative dominance of the two senses. Both *ACID* and *WIND*, the only two words for which the subordinate meanings were accessed, have senses that are nearly equi-probable. This is also reflected in the larger maximal activation levels of the subordinate meanings of the equi-probable words compared to the polarized words. These results seem to capture one's intuition that the subordinate sense of a highly polarized word (e.g., *LONG)* is harder to access than one that is equi-probable (e.g., *LEAD)*.

These effects of habituation can be described in terms of changes in the energy landscape. Since habituation modifies the connection strengths, the energy landscape also changes. Specifically, habituation raises the energy corresponding to the state the network initially settled into until that state no longer corresponds to a local energy minimum. The system then moves from that state down to a more energetically favorable state. The state that the network will tend to settle into is the state corresponding to the alternative sense because it is usually local energy minimum closest to the first stable state. This tendency is enhanced by providing the spelling of the word as an input to the network.[10]

Other connectionist models also manifest similar behavior. In the Boltzmann machine [Ackley et al., 1985], for example, the probability that the system is in a particular state corresponds to the energy of that state relative to others according to the Boltzmann distribution. Similar observations have been made by Selman [1985] who found two different syntactic interpretations flipping from one interpretation to another in a Boltzmann network.

4.2 *Word Transitions*

The last set of simulations deals with how the current word affects processing of the subsequent word in a sentence. In particular, the way in which the part of speech of the current word determines the sense of a categorially ambiguous

---

10 If the spelling of the word is not fixed by providing that stimulus as an input to the network at a large amplitude, the activity of the network might move into a nearby local minimum that does not correspond to the alternative sense. For example, it may move toward a state that corresponds to a synonym of the original word since the two words, by virtue of their shared semantic features, would be close to each other in the state space.

word that follows it will be explored. Although this effect was discussed earlier, it is being reexamined here to demonstrate how such a context can arise in a more natural fashion.

Syntactic context arises because only certain classes of words can follow certain others in a grammatical sentence. Rather than considering all possible transitions in the English language, only those found in sentences generated by a simple context-free grammar will be included. The transitions considered are determiner $\Rightarrow$ {adjective, noun}, adjective $\Rightarrow$ {adjective, noun}, and noun $\Rightarrow$ {preposition, verb}. Although quite simple, the process is not trivial because of the non-determinism involved in all cases. As a further simplification, differences in the relative frequencies of these transitions will be ignored.

To simulate this effect of word transitions, a second set of elements that buffers the most recently accessed word is needed. As illustrated earlier in Figure 8.1, there are connections from the elements comprising the syntactic field of these buffer elements to the syntactic field of the auto-associative elements. These connections are modified to capture the allowable syntactic transitions defined above.

In addition to the additional network structure, control mechanisms are required to process sequences of words. As introduced in the previous section, the connections in the auto-associative network undergo habituation once a word is accessed. The stable pattern of activation (corresponding to access of a word) is transmitted to the buffer elements and displaces the pattern of activation currently instantiated there. The part of speech of this word will then provide a constraint on the part of speech of the subsequent word. Finally, the current word of the sentence will be replaced with the subsequent one as the input to the auto-associative network.[11]

4.2.1 Results and Discussion

Table 9 shows selected states obtained when the sequence, *"COLD DOVE WIND"* is presented to the network. As expected from the frequency bias, the dominant sense of *COLD* is accessed. Since the part of speech of the dominant sense of *COLD* is an adjective, the next word must be an adjective or a noun if the input string is to be grammatical. Since *DOVE* can be either a noun or a verb, the word transition regularities constrain the choice to the dominant noun

---

11 This corresponds to the change in eye fixation of a reader. There is good evidence [Carpenter and Daneman, 1981] that a reader continues to fixate a word until processing of that word is completed. While the control mechanism used here is appropriate for reading, a different mechanism would be required to process speech.

sense as obtained in the simulation. In this case, both syntactic context and relative dominance are biased toward the noun sense. However, in other cases, syntactic context must override a relative dominance bias. This, in fact, is the situation that arises with *WIND*. Since the noun sense of *DOVE* is accessed, the subordinate verb sense rather than the dominant noun sense of *WIND* should be accessed, as indeed it is. Note that if the word preceding *WIND* is an adjective, the noun reading should be accessed instead.

Table 9   Interpretation of patterns of activation generated by the sequence COLD DOVE WIND. After all the elements reach their maximal or minimal activation levels, the next word in the sequence becomes the input.

COLD	0	—	—	—	—	—	—	—	—	—	—	—	—	—	—	—	—	—	—
	1	—	—	—	—	—	—	—	—	—	—	—	—	—	—	—	—	—	—
	2	—	—	—	—	—	—	—	—	—	—	—	—	—	—	—	—	—	—
	3	—	—	—	D	—	—	—	—	—	—	—	—	—	—	—	—	—	—
	4	C	O	—	D	—	—	—	—	—	—	—	—	—	—	—	—	—	—
	5	C	O	L	D	—	—	—	d	—	—	—	—	—	—	—	—	—	—
	6	C	O	L	D	—	o_	—	d	—	—	—	—	—	—	—	[t]	—	[p]
	7	C	O	L	D	k	o_	l	d	—	—	—	—	[i]	—	—	[t]	—	[p]
	8	C	O	L	D	k	o_	l	d	ad	jc	[f]	[r]	[i]	—	[d]	[t]	—	[p]
	9	C	O	L	D	k	o_	l	d	ad	jc	[f]	[r]	[i]	[g]	[d]	[t]	[m]	[p]
DOVE	10	C	O	L	D	k	o_	l	d	ad	jc	[f]	[r]	[i]	[g]	[d]	[t]	[m]	[p]
	.	C	O	L	D	k	o_	l	d	ad	jc	[f]	[r]	[i]	[g]	[d]	[t]	[m]	[p]
	20	C	O	L	D	k	o_	l	d	ad	jc	[f]	[r]	[i]	[g]	[d]	[t]	[m]	[p]
	30	—	O	—	—	—	o_	l	—	—	—	—	—	—	—	—	[t]	—	—
	40	D	O	V	E	—	—	v	$	no	un	—	—	—	—	[b]	—	—	—
	41	D	O	V	E	d	—	v	$	no	un	—	—	—	—	[b]	—	—	—
	42	D	O	V	E	d	—	v	$	no	un	—	—	—	—	[b]	—	—	—
	43	D	O	V	E	d	@	v	$	no	un	—	[i]	—	[d]	[b]	[i]	—	—
	44	D	O	V	E	d	@	v	$	no	un	[w]	[i]	[l]	[d]	[b]	[i]	[r]	[d]
WIND	45	D	O	V	E	d	@	v	$	no	un	[w]	[i]	[l]	[d]	[b]	[i]	[r]	[d]
	.	D	O	V	E	d	@	v	$	no	un	[w]	[i]	[l]	[d]	[b]	[i]	[r]	[d]
	50	D	O	V	E	d	@	v	$	no	un	[w]	[i]	[l]	[d]	[b]	[i]	[r]	[d]
	60	—	—	—	—	d	—	v	$	—	—	—	—	—	—	[b]	—	—	[d]
	70	—	—	*	D	—	—	—	d	ve	rb	—	—	—	—	—	—	—	—
	80	W	I	N	D	w	i_	n	d	ve	rb	—	—	—	—	[r]	[c]	[l]	[e]
	81	W	I	N	D	w	i_	n	d	ve	rb	—	—	—	—	[r]	[c]	[l]	[e]
	82	W	I	N	D	w	i_	n	d	ve	rb	—	—	[c]	[i]	[r]	[c]	[l]	[e]
	83	W	I	N	D	w	i_	n	d	ve	rb	—	—	[c]	[i]	[r]	[c]	[l]	[e]
	84	W	I	N	D	w	i_	n	d	ve	rb	—	—	[c]	[i]	[r]	[c]	[l]	[e]
	85	W	I	N	D	w	i_	n	d	ve	rb	—	[n]	[c]	[i]	[r]	[c]	[l]	[e]
	86	W	I	N	D	w	i_	n	d	ve	rb	[e]	[n]	[c]	[i]	[r]	[c]	[l]	[e]

Although the relative frequencies of syntactic transitions were not considered here, they could easily have been. In such a case, these biases, like the relative dominance biases of ambiguous words, can also influence resolution of the ambiguity. Consider the sentence fragment:

(11)   The cats fish like ....

How *like* is interpreted depends on how *fish* is interpreted, as the following sentences illustrate.

(12a) The cats fish like experts.

(12b) The cats fish like died.

In sentence 12a, *fish* must be interpreted as a verb, whereas in sentence 12b, it must be interpreted as a noun (the subject of the subordinate clause). Of these two sentences, people are likely to be "garden-pathed" with the latter because a noun is more likely to be followed by a verb rather than another noun. This is true despite the fact that the noun reading of *fish* is more common than the verb reading.

As seen above, the relative frequencies of particular part of speech transitions are important in resolving categorial ambiguities. Infrequent transitions exert less influence than more frequent ones. It is for this reason that errors during learning (if not excessive) can be tolerated by this model.

The current model is far too simplistic to allow consideration of other aspects of sentence comprehension. As it currently stands, only constraints imposed by the part of speech of the preceding word are considered. However, the meaning of that word must also be considered. More importantly, other words beside the immediate predecessor, both preceding and following the current word, must be considered as Waltz and Pollack [1985] have done.

Up to this point, it has been assumed that the meaning accessed by the network should be identical to one of the two meanings of a word contained in the lexicon. This assumption, however, is too rigid and surely does not reflect what occurs when people access the meaning of a word. The meaning of a word is very context dependent, with different shades of meaning expressed with different words in the sentence. Consider, for example,

(13a) The boys fish for trout in the lake.

(13b) The boys fish for keys in their pockets.

(13c) The boys fish for compliments.

Context effects along these lines have recently been illustrated in a model based on many of the principles used here [McClelland and Kawamoto, 1986].

The use of distributed representations provides a natural account of polysemy. Because distributed representation schemes represent a word as a pattern of features, no decision has to be made whether or not a meaning is sufficiently distinct to warrant creation of a new node for that word as required in a local representation. If a particular meaning is used with sufficient frequency, that combination of features would become a stable pattern. This issue is related to the distinction between prototype and exemplar models of concepts discussed in more detail elsewhere [Knapp and Anderson, 1984; McClelland and Rumelhart, 1985].

Along related lines, a distributed representation allows enough flexibility to imagine how neologisms might be generated. For example, the following sentence from Clark and Clark [1979] illustrates a common situation in which a noun is used as a verb:

(14) He wristed the ball over the net.

In contrast to the examples earlier in this section where syntactic transitions influenced which of two possible senses is chosen, these word transition constraints can *alter* how a word is used, while retaining the semantic features of that word [Kawamoto, 1985].

5 Conclusion

A network of simple processing elements learns 12 pairs of ambiguous words. Each word consists of a graphemic, a phonemic, a syntactic, and a semantic field represented as 216 features. Each of the 216 features corresponds to an element in the network. The network learns the lexical entries by instantiating a word in the network and then modifying the connections strengths between all pairs of elements to capture the correlation in their activation levels. Each entry is presented to the network during the learning with a probability based on its relative frequency of occurrence.

Once the network has been trained, the dynamics of the resolution process is explored. When just the spelling of a word is presented to the network, the dominant sense is always accessed for words whose two senses occur with very different frequencies, and most of the time for words whose two senses occur with almost equal frequency. To simulate the effect of context, parts of the syntactic or semantic fields are presented together with the spelling. With either a syntactic or a semantic context, the contextually appropriate sense is accessed.

The resolution of the ambiguity is not a discrete process completed in a single step, but rather it is one that follows a time-course. Initially, both senses of the ambiguous word are activated. However, only one of the two senses becomes fully activated. The activation of the alternative sense diminishes as a result of competition. In this model, the same temporal pattern of resolution is observed with both syntactic and semantic priming.

The pattern that emerges is one in which relative dominance and context *both* influence, from the outset, which meaning of an ambiguous word is accessed. In this model, meanings are neither accessed serially in order of relative frequency and compared with the context, nor does context and relative frequency exert an influence only after all meanings are initially activated. Simpson [1984] reaches similar conclusions in his review.

The major difference between this model and previous models based on activation levels [Carpenter and Daneman, 1981; Cottrell, 1984] is how different words are represented. In previous work, each lexical entry is considered to be a single node in a network. Here, a distributed representation is used in which each entry is represented as a *pattern* of activation over all the units in a network. The same set of units is used to represent *all* entries.

The choice of a distributed representation has important consequences in determining how context and relative frequency are implemented. Using a local representation, priming arises from activity that spreads from one node to other nodes representing semantically related items. Semantic distance is measured by the number of nodes between the prime and the target. With a distributed representation, priming arises from similar semantic features of the prime and target. The greater the similarity (compare NURSE-DOCTOR with NURSE-BUTTER), the greater the amount of priming.

A second important difference is how frequency information is stored. With a local representation, one can simply increment a counter each time that word is encountered. This information can then be used to determine a base-level of activity (that is higher for more frequent words) or a threshold (that is lower for more frequent words). With a distributed representation, however, frequency information is stored throughout the set of connections. The same set of connections must be used to store the frequency information for *all* entries. Thus, frequency information is distributed over the entire set of connections just as the representation of a word is distributed over the entire set of elements. Although frequency information is not stored locally, the energy measure defined in equation 10 can be used to show that such a bias is indeed stored by the network.

Another difference between this model and others previously mentioned is whether there is competition between the different senses and if there is, how that competition is implemented. In the READER model [Thibadeau et al., 1982], for example, the alternative readings of an ambiguous word is suppressed only after one of the readings reaches threshold. The use of a distributed representation leads to a difference in how this competition is implemented. With a local representation, competition is implemented by inhibitory links between different senses [Cottrell, 1984; this volume]. In the model presented here, competition is initiated only when the system becomes non-linear (i.e., some elements in the network become maximally or minimally activated). Without this non-linearity, there would be no competition and the activation of all senses would continue to increase, albeit at different rates.

Effects following the resolution of the ambiguity have also been explored. For example, people are able to generate more than one meaning of an ambiguous word when asked to. By habituating the connections, the alternative meaning of an ambiguous word can be accessed. Consistent with empirical findings, access of the alternative meaning is more likely when the subordinate meaning is given initially.

Habituation is one solution to the criticism that connectionist networks are unable to find sequences of stable states. Another way to generate sequential behavior is to provide a continually changing input as in the study by Rumelhart et al. [1986]. Both of these proposals are used to simulate processing of a sequences of words generated by a simple grammar. Here, legal word transitions provide a syntactic context in a more natural fashion. Although these constraints don't allow the part of speech of the following word to be predicted with certainty, they are sufficient to resolve a number of categorial ambiguities.

Clearly, however, syntactic and semantic contexts must be provided by other words in the sentence in addition to the previous one. Such effects have recently been explored in a model similar to the one presented here [McClelland and Kawamoto, 1986]. In their study, co-occurrence information was used to select the appropriate meaning of an ambiguous word.

In the study presented here, we have seen how a distributed representation captures the effects of frequency and contextual biases quite naturally. Moreover, the flexibility of this type of representation allows both polysemy and ambiguity to be treated identically, and suggests how neologisms might be handled. Although the use of distributed representations in psychology is not very widespread, demonstrations of their utility in a variety of different domains encourages continued exploration of these ideas.

Acknowledgments

Preparation of this manuscript was supported by a Sloan Postdoctoral Research Fellowship and by grant NSF–BNS–8214728 to James Anderson. This work is based on a thesis that was submitted to the Department of Psychology, Brown University. I would like to thank my advisor, James Anderson, as well as Gregory Murphy and Peter Eimas for serving on my committee. I would also like to thank Geoffrey Hinton who pointed out how energy landscapes can be considered in the habituation process, and James McClelland along with four anonymous reviewers for providing useful comments. Finally, I would like to thank Mardy Geyer for drafting some of the figures.

References

Ackley, D. H., Hinton, G. E., and Sejnowski, T. J. 1985. A learning algorithm for Boltzmann machines. *Cognitive Science* 9:147–169.

Anderson, J. A. 1983. Cognitive and psychological computation with neural models. *IEEE Transactions on Systems, Man, and Cybernetics* SMC-13: 799–815.

Anderson, J. A., and Mozer, M. 1981. Categorization and selective neurons. In G. Hinton and J. Anderson (eds.), *Parallel Models of Associative Memory*. Hillsdale: Erlbaum.

Anderson, J. A., Silverstein, J. W., Ritz, S. A., and Jones, R. S. 1977. Distinctive features, categorical perception, and probability learning: Some applications of a neural model. *Psychological Review* 84:413–451.

Carpenter, P. A., and Daneman, M. 1981. Lexical retrieval and error recovery in reading: A model based on eye fixations. *Journal of Verbal Learning and Verbal Behavior* 20:137–160.

Clark, E. V., and Clark, H. H. 1979. When nouns surface as verbs. *Language* 4:767–811.

Collins, A. M., and Loftus, E. F. 1975. *Psychological Review* 82: 407–428.

Cottrell, G. W. 1984. A model of lexical access of ambiguous words. In *Proceedings of the Fourth National Conference on Artificial Intelligence,* pp. 61–67. Austin, Texas. Los Altos: Morgan Kaufmann.

Forster, K. I., and Bednall, E. S. 1976. Terminating and exhaustive search in lexical access. *Memory and Cognition* 4:53–61.

Galbraith, G. G., and Taschman, C. S. 1969. Homophone units: A normative and methodological investigation of the strength of component elements. *Journal of Verbal Learning and Verbal Behavior* 8:737–744.

Gibson, E. 1969. *Principles of Perceptual Learning and Development.* Englewood Cliffs: Prentice-Hall.

Golden, R. M. 1986. The "Brain-State-in-a-Box" neural model is a gradient descent algorithm. *Journal of Mathematical Psychology* 30:73–80.

Hirst, G. 1983. *Semantic Interpretation Against Ambiguity.* Ph.D. Thesis, Department of Computer Science, Brown University.

Hogaboam, T. W. and Perfetti, C. A. 1975. Lexical ambiguity and sentence comprehension. *Journal of Verbal Learning and Verbal Behavior* 14:265–274.

Hopfield, J. J. 1982. Neural networks and physical systems with emergent collective computational abilities. In *Proceedings of the National Academy of Sciences USA* 79:2554–2558.

Kawamoto, A. H. 1985. *Dynamic Processes in the (Re)Solution of Lexical Ambiguity.* Ph. D. Thesis, Department of Psychology, Brown University.

Kawamoto, A. H., and Anderson, J. A. A neural network model of multistable perception. *Acta Psychologica* 59:35–65.

Knapp, A., and Anderson, J. A. 1984. A signal averaging model for concept formation. *Journal of Experimental Psychology: Learning, Memory, and Cognition* 10:616–637.

Kohonen, T. 1977. *Associative Memory.* Berlin: Springer.

Lashley, K. S. 1967. The problem of serial order in behavior. In Jeffress, L. A. (ed.), *Cerebral Mechanisms in Behavior.* New York: Hafner.

McClelland, J. L., and Kawamoto, A. H. 1986. Mechanisms of sentence processing: Assigning roles to constituents of sentences. In McClelland, J. L. and Rumelhart, D. E. (eds.), *Parallel Distributed Processing: Explorations in the Microstructure of Cognition, vol. 2.* Cambridge: MIT Press.

McClelland, J. L., and Rumelhart, D. E. 1981. An interactive activation model of context effects in letter perception: Part 1. An account of basic findings. *Psychological Review* 88:375–407.

McClelland, J. L. and Rumelhart, D. E. 1985. Distributed memory and the representation of general and specific information. *Journal of Experimental Psychology: General* 114:375–407.

Morton, J. 1969. Interaction of information in word recognition. *Psychological Review* 76:165–178.

Onifer, W., and Swinney, D. A. 1981. Accessing lexical ambiguities during sentence comprehension: Effects of frequency of meaning and contextual bias. *Memory and Cognition* 9:225–236.

Rosenblatt, F. 1962. *Principles of Neurodynamics: Perceptrons and the Theory of Brain Mechanisms.* Washington: Spartan Press,

Rumelhart, D. E., Smolensky, P., McClelland, J. L., and Hinton, G. E. 1986. Schemata and sequential thought processes in PDP models. In McClelland, J. L. and Rumelhart, D. E. (eds.), *Parallel Distributed Processing: Explorations in the Microstructure of Cognition, vol. 2.* Cambridge: MIT Press.

Schvaneveldt, R. W., Meyer, D. E., and Becker, C. A. 1976. Lexical ambiguity, semantic context, and visual word recognition. *Journal of Experimental Psychology: Human Perception and Performance* 2:243–256.

Seidenberg, M. S., Tanenhaus, M. K., Leiman, J. M., and Bienkowski, M. 1982. Automatic access of the meanings of ambiguous words in context: Some limitations of knowledge-based processing. *Cognitive Psychology* 14:489–537.

Seidenberg, M. S., Waters, G. S., Barnes, M. A., and Tanenhaus, M. K. 1984. *Journal of Verbal Learning and Verbal Behavior* 23:383–404.

Selman, B. 1985. Rule-based processing in a connectionist system for natural language understanding. Technical Report No. CSRI–168, Computer Systems Research Institute, University of Toronto.

Simpson, G. B. 1981. Meaning dominance and semantic context in the processing of lexical ambiguity. *Journal of Verbal Learning and Verbal Behavior* 20:120–136.

Simpson, G. B. 1984. Lexical ambiguity and its role in models of word recognition. *Psychological Bulletin* 96:316–340.

Simpson, G. B., and Burgess, C. 1985. Activation and selection processes in the recognition of ambiguous words. *Journal of Experimental Psychology: Human Perception and Performance* 11:28–39.

Smith, E. E., and Medin, D. L. 1981. *Categories and Concepts.* Cambridge: Harvard University Press.

Swinney, D. A. 1979. Lexical access during sentence comprehension: (Re)consideration of context effects. *Journal of Verbal Learning and Verbal Behavior* 18:645–659.

Swinney, D. A. 1982. The structure and time-course of information interaction during speech comprehension: Lexical segmentation, access, and interpretation. In J. Mehler, E. C. T. Walker, and M. Garrett (eds.), *Perspectives on Mental Representation.* Hillsdale: Erlbaum,

Tanenhaus, M. K., Leiman, J. M., and Seidenberg, M. S. 1979. Evidence for multiple stages in the processing of ambiguous words on syntactic contexts. *Journal of Verbal Learning and Verbal Behavior* 18:427–440.

Thibadeau, R., Just, M. A., and Carpenter, P. A. 1982. A model of the time course and content of reading. *Cognitive Science* 6:157–203.

Thorndike, E. L., and Lorge, I. 1938. *The Teacher's Book of 30,000 Words.* New York: Teacher's College, Columbia University.

Waltz, D. L., and Pollack, J. B. 1985. Massively parallel parsing: A strongly interactive model of natural language interpretation. *Cognitive Science* 9: 51–74.

Warren, R. E., Bresnick, J. H., and Green, J. P. 1977. Definitional dominance distributions for 20 English homographs. *Bulletin of the Psychonomic Society* 10:229–231.

Widrow, G., and Hoff, M. E. 1960. Adaptive switching circuits. *Institute of Radio Engineers, Western Electronic Show and Convention, Convention Record Part 4,* pp. 96–104.

9

Process Synchronization, Lexical Ambiguity Resolution, and Aphasia

Helen Gigley
Department of Computer Science
University of New Hampshire

1 *Introduction*

From the title of this chapter, one might think that the focus will be to elaborate at length on the role of lexical ambiguity in studies of aphasia. However, given the current state of evidence, this cannot be done. Instead, a processing based theory of sentence understanding in a model called HOPE,[1] provides the vehicle for elaborating a viewpoint of the following:

1. How lexical ambiguity can be effectively processed in a neural-like connectionist architecture;

2. How lesions that are not rule-based affect the disambiguation process; and

3. How these lesion results can provide hypotheses of performance problems to define unique aphasic patient profiles.

---

1 The name is adopted from the legend of Pandora and her wedding gifts from Zeus. HOPE was the only gift that did not escape when Pandora opened her wedding gifts out of curiosity and accidentally released all of human affliction on the world.

The successful development of a model of sentence understanding that deals with these issues requires consideration of a different set of constraints than those used in the study of natural language performance and theory. The process of lexical ambiguity resolution is a critical part of the overall process of sentence understanding. Two linguistically defined types of lexical ambiguity resolution usually comprise the focus of studies of sentence processing, syntactic disambiguation and semantic disambiguation. Syntactic disambiguation refers to resolving ambiguity across syntactic categories of the senses of a word. Semantic disambiguation, in contrast, refers to resolving which meaning sense within a syntactic category is appropriate for the sentence sense. Other constraints on sentence understanding can be derived from linguistic theory and psycholinguistic behavior.

In order to develop an understanding of the relationship of the human brain to language, one can expand the constraint set to include evidence from neurolinguistic studies. Here, these constraints are described in the context of aphasia. Furthermore, understanding brain function and language also requires attention to architectural and processing constraints of the brain. HOPE [Gigley, 1982; 1983; 1984; 1985b; 1986] is an example of a model which has been developed to demonstrate how these constraints can be successfully integrated to study language performance under impaired (lesioned) conditions.

Processing simulations of sentence understanding in HOPE demonstrate aspects of syntactic ambiguity resolution that provide insights into performance problems known to exist for aphasic patients. The critical aspect of the simulations under aphasic (lesioned) conditions is the selective impairment of signal propagation synchronization, rather than rule manipulation (the usual focus of neurolinguistic studies). The remainder of this introduction provides background on the design decisions underlying the stated constraints.

1.1 *Relating Sentence Understanding to the Brain*

Sentence understanding results from processes within a special architecture, the human brain. The processes are dynamic and are achieved within a connected architecture composed of homogeneous processing units. The computations of this architecture are achieved by asynchronous signal propagations. Within such a system of dynamic signal propagation, time synchronization of signals becomes a critical factor of the computations. One synchronization technique employs time windows (intervals) to permit effective signal propagation. A window of time consists of a time-bounded interval during which the activity level of information remains sufficient to affect processing.

In addition to architecturally defined processing constraints, behavioral constraints are also necessary to relate brain and sentence understanding. Normal language processing study based on linguistic theory is the focus of psycholinguists. Neurolinguists relate issues of sentence processing to the brain by studying people with language problems and known brain lesions (aphasics). It has been claimed since the mid-1800s [Broca, 1861; Wernicke, 1874; Lichtheim, 1885] that the study of language dissolution following certain brain lesions provides a useful window on the normal brain processes subserving language.

1.2 *Aphasia in Brief*

Aphasia is the degraded language performance that results following certain brain damage, usually involving areas of the left hemisphere. The resulting language manifestations include language production difficulties such as the inability to name objects; inability to produce the closed class words, including morphological endings; inability to repeat; and production of fluent, yet contentless, sentences. These impairments occur alone or in combination, and to differing degrees in individual people. Classification of aphasia depends on language production ability—only recently has there been significant study in language comprehension deficits apart from those of production.

1.3 *HOPE's Role as a Model of Aphasic Processing*

HOPE was developed within the noted constraints to be a processing model of single sentence comprehension where processing is defined within a connectionist architecture composed of thresholded processing units, spreading activation across distributed AI representations, and automatic decay and state-change mechanisms reported at the single-cell level (see also [Thompson, 1967]).

Sentence comprehension in HOPE consists of determination of the speaker intended agent/object referents and bindings at the end of the processing computation. The bindings are dynamic and depend on the temporal context of processing represented by a state of activity across all information known to the model.

Of critical importance to understanding the design is the fact that HOPE does not model a particular type of aphasia. It models natural language processing in *normal* conditions as activity propagation among connected units. Furthermore, the parameterized nature of the model necessitates tuning, so that a syntactically well-formed sentence leads to a correct state of activity at the end of processing. Once tuned, HOPE can model process degradation, and importantly, it does so as process de-synchronization affecting rates of activity decay, spreading activation across different aspects of the process, and firing affectiveness.

Thus HOPE defines a processing view of sentence comprehension that includes constraints introduced by the architecture. Simultaneously, it permits degradations of the normal process producing results that can be compared to aphasic performance to develop new insights and hypotheses regarding causes of degraded language performance. Computer modelling thus enables a process motivated analysis. A task situation related to one of the time-induced simulations of HOPE occurs when manipulations of the rate of speech are used in clinical study [Blumstein et al., 1985; Brookshire, 1971; Laskey et al., 1976; Liles and Brookshire, 1975]. Some of these studies have shown that the role of time may be more critical to processing than has been thought.

2 HOPE Models Normal Sentence Processing

HOPE, a connectionist model of single sentence comprehension, has been developed to provide a basis for the study of how a brain-like architecture can "compute" a meaning from a serially introduced input [Gigley, 1982; 1983; 1985a; 1985b]. The focus of the process is syntactic disambiguation. HOPE has been developed within the constraints of human performance evidence. All of its representations are based upon evidence reported in psycholinguistic and neurolinguistic studies or supported within linguistic theory. It relates psycholinguistic studies of performance under normal conditions to neurolinguistic studies of impaired performance to infer how brain function may subserve a given behavior.

Studies of aphasia provide the basis for the neurolinguistic performance data. Brain lesions in aphasia are experiments of nature, and are often large, involving diverse parts of the brain, and affecting several aspects of performance in addition to language. However, they provide the most extensive evidence currently available relating the study of language to specific areas of the brain.

HOPE was developed to integrate viewpoints of brain processing with behavioral evidence of language performance in an attempt to bring together different levels of investigation of natural language processing. The development was motivated by two factors: (a) that developing computational models sharpens understanding of the problem being studied because of the necessary explication of many assumptions during design; and (b) that understanding of language processing requires consideration of the nature of the process, in the context of a very particular computational architecture (the brain).

HOPE differs from a number of other connectionist models in its use of time, where synchronization issues can be directly addressed. Unfortunately, synchronization problems cannot be studied under experimental conditions at this time. One interesting timing experiment (de-synchronization experiment) would be to slow down selectively the propagation of certain types of information. The impossibility of achieving this slow-down under experimental conditions with human subjects gives models such as HOPE an enormous potential usefulness.

By hypothesizing timing problems as an underlying cause of aphasic comprehension deficits, HOPE produces simulated results including (a) misinterpretation of word sense (incorrect disambiguation) for recognized lexical items; and (b) incorrect agent/object discrimination. Furthermore, it suggests a view on performance problems of aphasics as representation loss, while showing that the explicit loss or omission can be produced by a timing de-synchronization problem.

3 Viewing Ambiguity in Processing

There are many notions of ambiguity, involving multiple viewpoints of the same object. Many computational natural language processing approaches attempt to eliminate all or most ambiguity in their implementations. Recently, more attempts have been made to include ambiguity and to develop ways of addressing problems that occur when processing it. Several of these are described in other chapters of this book. In addition, recent advances in neurophysiology have demonstrated that neural processing itself is quite ambiguous. While omitting details of the neurophysiological evidence, we shall describe aspects of it that are relevant to the model.

4 An Interpretation of Neural Ambiguity—Neural Evidence of Multiple Representation and Multiple Effect

Is neural activity ambiguous? If so, how can it be represented within a computational processing paradigm? There are at least two aspects of neural ambiguity to be addressed, involving (a) the interpretation of the thresholding mechanism of a cell and the effects of firing; and (b) the representation of information at a cellular level. The effects of firing relate both to the connectivity of the network and the states of the individual cells.

4.1 Multiple effects of firing

Recent studies of cortical organization [Kaas et al., 1979; Merzenich et al., 1983] demonstrate that somatosensory input from one surface area maps onto at least two distinct cortical areas. Multiple representations are suggested as functionally distinct based on the recovery of structure in these distinct cortical areas following nerve transection.

These latter studies demonstrate that different degrees of reorganization occur in different recepto-topic mappings in cortex following resection. This suggests that while the representations contain certain organizational features that are the same, i.e., correlated relationships of the surface inputs to positionally related and organized structures in cortex, they may encode different *functional* relationships. Support for this interpretation of the data comes from the fact that the areas are not of the same size and exhibit different interconnectivity patterns.

Abstracting from this evidence to language processing, a similar mapping correspondence can be postulated. For a given phonetic input pattern, chunking may be possible in two different ways, with functionality corresponding to suitability for the context.

A specific example of this is found in the response to the question: What do mice and grass have in common?[2]

/th-uh-k-ae-t-ih-l-ee-t-th-eh-m/

which can be understood as either of the following:

1.   The cattle eat them.

2.   The cat'll eat them.

While we cannot ascribe a given function to the multiple effect of firing, multiple output must be considered. The next section examines some of the data regarding cellular processes to show that they also exhibit ambiguity.

4.2 Meaning within a Single Cell

Different combinations of pre-synaptic activity can lead to the same intracellular state, implying that the cell state represents one or more possible *interpretations* simultaneously. (See the discussion of hidden units by Hinton [Hinton 1986; Hinton et al., 1986].) The question thus arises whether the cell has computed a single function. Since the cause of firing may be ambiguous, the result of cellular activity can only be interpreted in the context of the states of those cells affected by this activity. These states are also influenced by external priming, in the sense that they may have prior existing activities which could be related to the inputs of the firing cell.

Figure 9.1 illustrates multiple input conditions producing the same internal state for a cell. The example shows the internal state reaching threshold, but the point is equally applicable to subthreshold activity states.

---

2 Example courtesy of John Limber.

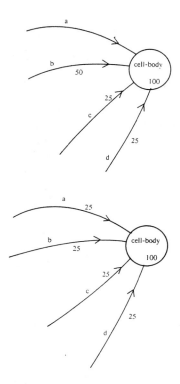

Figure 9.1 Information state is ambiguous. The threshold state can arise due to different combinations and amounts of input. There are no explicit interconnections which prohibit multiple instances of input to produce the same internal "cellular" state. Whether the inputs are from only three paths or four as shown, the information will fire. At the same time, these same inputs can affect the states of the information which will be affected by the firing state.

Another example of ambiguity important for models incorporating distributed control can be seen in considering a global network of cells to represent a unit. The firing pattern and the internal state of the global network over time characterize the network (its *meaning* to the external world). Thus it may be important to note not only which cells are firing, but also the activation of cells that are not firing, as they form part of the context of the network, a part that remains hidden if one considers only the firing patterns. A discussion along these lines, attempting to define a concept as an activity pattern over a network, can be found in Hinton et al. [1986].

Analyzing the overall performance characteristics of a system designed to simulate behavioral processing interactions over time depends heavily on the adjustment of firing cell patterns (tuning). Tuning parameters determine the time properties of signal propagation and thus the overall synchronization of signals. Recall that we also need to observe subthreshold changes in state oc-curring during processing in order to form hypotheses about the types of infor-mation affected during the time-course of processing as a consequence of a le-sion. Analyzing the subthreshold states with respect to how they arise, and how they differ in occurrence and degree from the normal tuned process over time provides the processing based explanation that underlies the hypothesized per-formance deficits in the overt observed behavior of the system. This will be de-scribed within an example from lesioned simulation contexts in Sections 13.2 and 13.3.

HOPE relies on activity propagation within neural networks to address the neurophysiological ambiguity issues just described. The system makes deci-sions by the propagation of activity levels, driving the representation units to a global stabilized state. Unit activity levels are initialized and subsequently rein-forced or inhibited by interactions with (a) external stimuli and (b) other units connected and representing meaning in the network. Activity levels interact via explicit propagation pathways to converge to a final state.

HOPE uses distributed representations of knowledge. Depending on the connections among the representations, the control can be shown to support both serial and parallel computation (see also [Lashley, 1951]). The ordered processing of phonetic information must be accomplished serially, while phonetic and semantic processing are carried out in parallel (for example). Note also that the system simultaneously updates computations to the entire network in parallel. The model of aphasic sentence comprehension benefits sig-nificantly from this dual control representation. HOPE uses parallelism to cap-ture a syntactically disambiguated meaning representation from a serially processed input of phonetically represented words. The convergence of net-work activity within constrained temporal windows leads to representation of the proper meaning of each word within the context of the sentence.

5 *Representation of Ambiguity in HOPE*

The multiple meaning/multiple effect evidence (discussed above) regarding the organization of the cerebral cortex leads to two model constraints:

1. Information must be represented ambiguously to express multiple viewpoints simultaneously; and

2. Active units must have multiple effects due to their interconnected structure.

The remainder of this section provides examples from HOPE showing the application of the constraints to model architecture.

5.1 *HOPE Representations Have Multiple Simultaneous Interpretations*

HOPE representations are defined within an hierarchical graph processing extension to LISP called GRASPER-UNH [Arcidiacono, 1985]. (This is a version of the GRASPER system from the University of Massachusetts [Lowrance, 1978].) The representations within an hierarchical graph allow multiple viewpoints for each represented unit. In GRASPER, graphs are defined as collections of nodes and arcs (directed edges). Hypergraphs or spaces are defined as collections of nodes and arcs or subgraphs (see also [Berge, 1970]). HOPE representations are collections of node and arc-node pairs (arcs with end nodes) and are interpreted as units of information used by the simulation system. Information has an ambiguous meaning by membership in more than one graph space (hypergraph) or subgraph, where a subgraph represents a different context of the single node or arc-node pair.

Multiple effects are defined as processes across different spaces of information. Each such space represents information of a particular type and has a regular structure. Figure 9.2 shows the interconnections across the spaces traced during HOPE simulations.

The same unit simultaneously exists in multiple spaces in order to represent multiple viewpoints and potentially diverse functional roles. Figure 9.3 (Section 7.1) illustrates this through the model representation of the open class word "barks." Note that the architecture of different spaces (and concomitant functional roles of units) comes from the constraints imposed by evidence from neurophysiology.

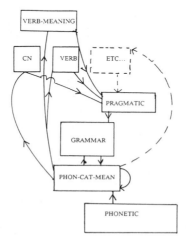

Figure 9.2 Space names represent types of information. Arrows indicate directions of activation paths. All paths may be active simultaneously during a compute-time update.

5.2 HOPE Space Representations are Behaviorally Motivated

Behavioral and linguistic constraints dictate the level of representation of the conceptual knowledge spaces in the model. The spaces represent different interpretations of the information, as determined from (a) available data (primarily neurolinguistic); and (b) computational constraints. The grammar representation in the GRAMMAR space was chosen for its power to achieve particular computational requirements.

The major linguistically defined aspects of performance based on independently observable degradation in aphasia include representations (a) at a PHONETIC level, used as a word percept level; (b) at a meaning aspect level, represented as the multiple possible meaning interpretations for each lexical item in the PHON-CAT-MEAN space; (c) in a GRAMMAR space of grammatical information; and (d) in a PRAGMATIC space of contextually appropriate meanings for utterances. Other aspects of linguistic information affected include morphological endings, agreement, and case constraints. Each of these types of linguistic information is also included in the HOPE model. Table 1 lists the knowledge spaces used in HOPE with a brief explanation of their contents.

Table 1   Graph spaces used in HOPE to define the types of information included in the architecture. Each is behaviorally motivated within evidence from neurolinguistics, psycholinguistics or linguistic theory.

SPACE NAME	CONTENTS
CATEGORY	Names of all lexical categories, ie, defined by word category types.
GRAMMAR	The categorial grammar specification.
PHONETIC	The phonetic encoding of all known words.
PHON-CAT-MEAN	A network representation of all category-meaning arc-node pairs associated with each phonetic word.
PRAGMATIC	Contains context of final interpretation. (Initially empty in the current version.) Contains network representation of the meaning on termination.
VERB-MEANING	Case-control-information for base form of all defined verbs.
INTERPRETATION	Contains interpretation functions for all category types included in a model.
CN	All noun meanings and their morphological relationships, if specified.
VERB	All verb meanings and their morphological relationships, if specified.
ETC.	A space exists for each category type and contains all lexical items of each type.

6 *Aphasic Evidence and HOPE Representations*

A detailed overview of clinical research and neurolinguistic studies which have provided the basis of HOPE can be found in Gigley [1982]. Here, a summary of the evidence will be presented to demonstrate ways of inferring aspects of interacting functional processes from the behavioral data in the literature.

Types of aphasia produce different characteristic types of performance breakdown. Many books describe the generally agreed upon characteristics of these degraded behaviors [Davis, 1983; Lecours, Lhermitte, and Bryans, 1983; Jenkins, Jiménez-Pabón, Shaw, Sefer, 1975]. Several different standardized testing procedures concur with the classification descriptions and provide ways to measure the performance abilities among certain agreed upon dimensions of aphasic performance [Goodglass and Kaplan, 1983/1972; Kertesz, 1980; Lecours et al., 1983]. The classification rests chiefly on evaluation of language production. It includes evaluations of factors such as free conversation and picture description motivated speech, noting the following:

- paraphasias (semantic and/or phonetic);
- average length of utterance;
- syntactic form of utterance;
- word-finding difficulty; and
- intonation contour.

Tests aiding in the assessment of auditory comprehension include pointing to body parts, color selection, and following commands. Evaluation of other aspects of performance related to language would include assessment of some of the following:

- writing skills and reading skills;
- arithmetic computations;
- number reading and writing;
- singing; and
- reciting nursery rhymes or familiar song lyrics.

For an introduction to the neural strata or brain regions which are affected in diagnosed aphasic persons, see Lecours et al. [1983] and Kertesz [1979]. A neural connectionist perspective is given in Geschwind [1965].

In general, neurolinguistic and clinical studies involving aphasic patients use the patient classification criteria to group the subjects for analysis. A concern in performing any study with aphasic patients is whether or not they differ in a statistically significant way on the task at hand. Each statistically substantiated difference is used to infer the possible role of different areas of the brain in language behavior.

While the focus of studies of brain and language has been chiefly on language production ability, recently there has been a shift toward analyzing the associated comprehension abilities. When Paul Broca first evaluated his patients in 1861, he thought there was little if any involvement of the ability to understand. On the other hand, Wernicke described in 1874 a group of patients who produce inappropriate speech and have difficulty comprehending. Subsequent researchers found on careful analysis that the class of patients described by Broca did indeed have some problems in comprehension ability, although significantly less noticeable than for the aphasics described by Wernicke.

Aspects of language affected to different degrees include the phonetic ability, evidenced by phonetic paraphasias in speech, and the ability to repeat (to reactivate a stored phonetic string). For a spoken word, picture selection across different categories determines the ability of a patient to understand. Through the use of carefully designed tests, the role of determiners has been noted to be affected in certain patients. Many Broca's patients do not use the closed class words in speech. It was discovered that they also do not process them uniformly in understanding [Caplan et al., 1981; Goodenough et al., 1977; Zurif et al., 1976]. The logical content conveyed by the use of "the" versus "one" can be specifically affected. An overview of the details of several of these studies can be found in Zurif and Blumstein [1978]. These observations, focusing on the closed class words, suggest a problem with grammatical competence.

Other processing problems related to grammatical competence have been demonstrated, specifically for Broca's aphasics, or more recently, for agrammatic aphasics (a subset of Broca's aphasics who have a problem with grammatical morphemes). These include an inability to determine the agent and object consistently when they occur in semantically reversible sentences, sentences in which it makes sense for either the agent or the object to perform the action designated by the main verb (e.g., "The boy hit the girl" is reversible, while "The boy ate the apple" is not). At one time it was thought that both normals and aphasics used word order constraints to understand these sentences. However, recent evidence has shown this assumption is not adequate for all individuals [Schwartz, Saffron and Marin, 1980].

Recent work by [Blumstein et al., 1982] has shown that even though Wernicke's patients cannot consistently verbalize a response to demonstrate what they have understood, the access path to meanings is available and that priming occurs in an auditory task. Broca's aphasics, on the other hand, had difficulty demonstrating the same automatic access ability. Importantly, in the study with Broca's patients, no attempt was made to provide different intertime prime-presentation stimulus effects to determine the presence of a time effect of the task.

It is known that time affects performance in aphasia, sometimes positively and sometimes negatively [Blumstein et al., 1985; Brookshire, 1971; Laskey et al., 1976; Liles and Brookshire, 1975]. Furthermore, in normals, the critical nature of time as a factor is substantiated in the findings of Swinney [1979] and Seidenberg et al. [1982] which demonstrate that differences in onset times can affect the observed results of a study.

This neuropsychological data has been used to constrain (a) the processing strategies of HOPE, and (b) the types of lesions that could arise under processing. The model design needed to include ways to lesion that would not require one to recode rules, or to redesign the process to accommodate the lesion; the brain does not stop processing until it is reprogrammed in the recovery phase. It continues to process even though the results may be less than optimal and often include errors.

In addition, aspects of the representation have been abstracted from linguistic concepts that have received support from related psycholinguistic study. These include an independent phonetic representation at some level. It is still not firmly decided whether the basis of this representation is at the level of morphemes, syllables, or words [Marslen-Wilson and Tyler, 1980; Marslen-Wilson and Welsh, 1978]. HOPE uses representations of word symbols. Word meaning and automatic access have been supported in the works of Seidenberg et al. [1982] and Swinney [1979]; HOPE employs simultaneous access of multiple meaning connections for each phonetic word representation (in the PHON-CAT-MEAN space).

The role of pragmatics in capturing the contextually appropriate relations conveyed within a sentence has been studied in linguistics and in artificial intelligence. As a representation for the result of the interactive process, a pragmatic representation includes case bindings which have been interactively determined in the time course of processing (e.g., agent and object). There is no claim in the present system beyond the functional role of such a representation, with work on this topic planned for the future.

Many studies note that grammar exists independent of lexical items and their associated meanings, and that it can be characterized independent of any particular language. By this we mean that there is a grammar for each language, but do not claim that all grammars are the same. Furthermore, the effect of lesions specifically on grammatical structure and grammatical functions suggests that the grammar should be separately represented, yet linked to the lexical items, and to the interpretation of each lexeme. Linguistic categories are syntactic/semantic category types and have two roles: (1) they make predictions of the form class of individual lexical items or composed semantic types; and (2) they map the lexeme and category type into a meaning representation type in the pragmatic space, representing its interpreted semantic representation.

After specification, the model is tuned for normal performance and then can be used to study the effects of lesions. The role of tuning and redefining parameter values to define lesions is described in Section 12 within the context of model generated hypotheses. Having provided the motivation for the space representations, we shall give specific examples of HOPE graphs.

7 The HOPE Lexicon—A Distributed Representation of a Word

A word definition consists of a collection of units distributed across the model spaces. A word unit in a particular space represents one perspective within a multidimensional word representation. Certain descriptions and constraints on word definition must be satisfied during experimental specification of a model:

1. All words must have a phonetic representation, stored in the PHONETIC space;

2. Each phonetic representation must have at least one category meaning pair associated with it in the PHON-CAT-MEAN space (including the category type of the meaning and an orthographic representation);

3. Grammatical (lexical) categories are defined via word membership specification (e.g., a common noun (CN) meaning of a word indicates the inclusion of common noun as a category type in the GRAMMAR space and inclusion of the word in the separate CN space containing all common noun meanings);

4. Structural morphological relations are contained within appropriate syntactic category spaces (e.g., common noun (CN) relations such as singular-plural are within the CN space, morphological relations among verb forms such as past or third-singular are in the VERB space);

5. Meaning control information for verbs is present in the VERB-MEANING space; presently, the units depicting linguistic control information represent a case description for each verb; and

6. Each defined linguistic category type must have an associated category interpretation procedure, specifying its categorial representation in the PRAGMATIC space and initial unit values.

The system insures that all aspects of the distributed representation for a word are specified before allowing termination of model definition and initialization of the system. Note that all linguistic categories described in this chapter concern a particular model specification within the HOPE architecture. A wide variety of different models can be specified, using the basic representation and control mechanisms of HOPE.

7.1 *An Open Class Word Representation*

Open class and closed class words differ in representational complexity, particularly in their effects during interpretation on the PRAGMATIC representation. The open class words produce instances of information within the PRAGMATIC representation, while the closed class words perform functional compositions, such as semantic or case constraint checks, and produce relational representations in the PRAGMATIC space. Figure 9.3 illustrates the spatial representation for the syntactically ambiguous open class word "barks" (common noun and intransitive verb).

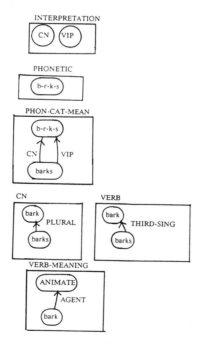

Figure 9.3 Graph space representation for the word [b-r-k-s]. A word is represented as a distributed collection of information encoded as nodes and arcs. Morphological information is shown as it is stored separately for noun relations and for verb relations. The VERB-MEANING space contains all user specified case control information for every verb included in the model. Each node or arc with the same name represents the same information. The different spaces or hypergraphs provide different contexts of interpretation for the information.

7.2 *Interpretation Functions of Linguistic Types*

Each linguistic category type (a syntactic/semantic category type) has an associated interpretation function represented by the nodes in the INTERPRETA-TION space of word representations. The lexical representations embody a theory of distributed meaning representation, including declarative and context dependent dynamic aspects. As a whole, the word representations incorporate linguistic assumptions about form and meaning decomposition and activation that constitute an integral part of HOPE's processing paradigm.

8 *Linguistic Performance Assumptions Inherent in the HOPE System Design*

During processing, all aspects of word meaning are activated over time. Interesting questions exist regarding the actual time course of spreading activation, and we have thus made decisions on temporal issues that have no particular performance support. HOPE spreads activity to the category part of a word meaning before accessing its morphological aspects. No evidence from studies of human processing currently supports morphological pre-processing, simultaneous processing, or post-processing.

Rather than serving as a rule-based process, HOPE assumes that the grammar reflects an association of co-occurring linguistic types over time. Categorial grammar [Ajdukiewicz, 1935; Lewis, 1972; Montague, 1974] provides a formalism that can be expressed as an association grammar for this purpose. A simple categorial grammar for English is represented in the GRAMMAR space of each graph and is used in a feedback/feedforward sense for syntactic priming of the input string processing [Gigley, 1985a]. In addition, every information type defined in the graph has an associated process to compute its firing effect. The actual time course of these processes in people is not known.

Linguistic category types have an associated interpretation process triggered upon activation of their lexical or composed meaning and dependent on this meaning for their exact effect. Each such syntactic/semantic type is assumed to have a specific effect on the process of sentence understanding or interpretation. The names of the category types, whether syntactically or semantically triggered are the same.

Nodes in the PRAGMATIC space denote the referents for objects or verbs and agent/object bindings. Since HOPE currently does not incorporate sufficient sophistication in meaning activation and coordination, pragmatic knowledge processing currently involves construction of symbol structures. In the future, pragmatic units will instead become active at a threshold level due to actual spreading activation.

Current model processing leads to interpretation of direct objects before the binding of agents. This ordering is based on the fact that the transitive property of the verb must be established to know that the first constituent is the agent. Consideration of passive and active sentences adds further support for this assumption. One cannot assume that the first constituent, although the subject, is the agent until the verb for the sentence is understood and until either the passive nature of the sentence is established, or a represented object structure for the sentence exists. When during sentence processing are such bindings actually determined? Performance studies to determine such factors must still be done.

9 *The Internal Control of Disambiguation in HOPE*

HOPE uses two types of spreading activation (see also [Anderson, 1976; Collins and Loftus, 1975; Quillian, 1980]), (1) automatic activation of aspects of the meanings of words; and (2) context-dependent activation with variable effects. Activation can result in execution of a process, a change in the state of information, or an activation of some aspect of a word meaning representation. The paradigm uses feedforward and feedback interconnections to define activity value (or firing frequency) propagations among knowledge representations (units in spaces). The results of these propagations over time produce convergent states that can be behaviorally interpreted.[3]

Modification of activity values during processing achieves a dynamic control structure for parsing and interpretation, which varies with the global context of the model. This control structure fits the behaviors reported in the aphasiology literature, and observable in work with patients. Use of this control strategy allows definition of appropriate knowledge representations and modification of timing synchrony to provide a suitable environment to study normal aspects of processing as well as the effects of simulated lesions.

9.1 *Spreading Activation during Processing*

Automatic spreading activation to different aspects of meaning is a basic premise of the HOPE model. Memory activation can be thought of as the activation over time of the information representing the meaning of a given node or arc, and is only excitatory. Decision activation occurs as the result of firing activity

---

3 See [Ackley, et al. 1985; Anderson, et al., 1977; Barto and Sutton, 1981; Barto, et al., 1984; Cottrell, 1983; Cottrell and Small, 1983; Dean, 1980; Gordon, 1982; McClelland and Rumelhart, 1981; 1986; Reiss, 1962; Rumelhart and McClelland, 1986; Waltz and Pollack, 1985; Wood, 1978; 1980; 1982] for related discussions of connected models.

propagation, which can be excitatory or inhibitory or both (to different spaces), and occurs in the context of combined inputs.

First the automatic spread, memory activation, will be described. Then the effects of firing, decision activation, and their interpretation as activity spread will be explained. At the end of the section, the role of time in the effectiveness of the spreading activation paradigm which HOPE exemplifies will be discussed.

9.1.1 *Automatic Spreading Activation*

9.1.1 *Automatic Spreading Activation* Automatic spreading activation occurs during the activity spread from the category part of a word meaning to its meaning in the GRAMMAR space. No other aspects of meaning are activated in the current model, so this is the only occurrence in HOPE of this type of spread.

Figure 9.4 contains a simplified graphical viewpoint of the grammatical aspects of each word meaning in PHON-CAT-MEAN (as part of the overall word meaning) and in GRAMMAR (with its own meaning). Multiple instances of meaning for the word "saw" are shown (labelled (a)) with the syntactic aspects of each sense denoted by an arc name in PHON-CAT-MEAN. These are underlined (b1-3) to denote that they are arc names in the PHON-CAT-MEAN space as well as nodes in the GRAMMAR space. The nodes connected by the PREDICT arc to the category nodes in the GRAMMAR space and the nodes connected by the TO-FORM arc represent grammatical aspects of the meaning of the category (c).

The GRAMMAR space contains only the meanings of the linguistic categories. Each category defined within a given model has a meaning used in temporal coordination of firing activity propagation, achieved through the use of (1) prediction in grammar meanings (PREDICT connections) and (2) interpretation and composition of meaning (feedback with TO-FORM connections). Not all category types incorporate both aspects in their meanings. Some category types do not make predictions, but are only predicted, (e.g., node CN in Figure 9.4(b1)).

The meaning of VTP (transitive verb) illustrates the role of meanings in the grammar. VTP predicts the occurrence of a TERM type (d), and after the TERM is successfully interpreted, the interpretation of the VTP that primed the TERM meaning occurs. Execution of the interpretation function for VTP composes semantically with the TERM, checking for object constraint satisfaction and activating a semantic type VIP as indicated in the TO-FORM part of the VTP meaning representation in the GRAMMAR (e). Currently, the computation of the composition leads to activation of the meaning representation of corresponding units and semantic types in the PRAGMATIC space.

Given this brief description of the grammar and how it is used, the process of spreading activation from the category part of a word meaning following

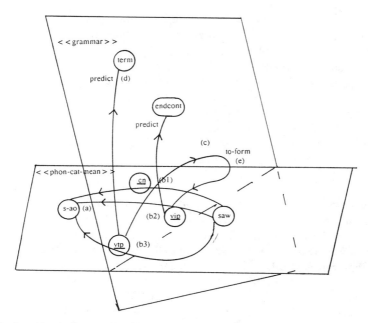

Figure 9.4 Examples of multiple viewpoints of the same information as seen in different spaces. CN, VIP, and VTP in PHON-CAT-MEAN are the arc names defining part of the "meaning" for each sense of the homophone, s-ao. The underline is to note their arc representation. Each has a meaning in GRAMMAR, shown as nodes. The grammatical "meaning" for each syntactic type is only partially shown as the figure is designed to convey the notion of "space" ambiguity. Connections can therefore be seen as having meaning in another perspective that is an elaboration of their appearance in a different one.

lexical access will now be described. For a discussion of the role of grammar in feedback control, see [Gigley, 1985a].

Lexical access proceeds from the PHONETIC representation in an automatic way to all possible meanings in parallel, all with the same initial level of activation. The tuning process led to multiple meanings of the same category type having different initial values than meanings of different types. The normal spread of category information to the category meaning representation in the GRAMMAR space occurs during the time interval following word meaning activation. For example, if a word such as "saw" (/s-ao/) is heard then all of its defined meanings are activated immediately.

1. CN—saw (tool)

2. VIP—saw (intransitive verb)

3. VTP—saw (transitive verb)

At the subsequent time interval update, each meaning whose category type has a predict aspect (defined in the GRAMMAR) automatically sends activity to the meaning of those categories in the GRAMMAR.

The meanings of VIP and VTP predict an ENDCONTour and a TERM respectively. ENDCONTour represents an input feature interpreted here as a category type based on the suprasegmental aspect of the speech signal occurring at the end of a phrase or sentence in ordinary speech. Both category nodes become active in the subsequent time display of the figure (characterizing fixed time spreading activation). A similar set of events is assumed to occur for the other (unimplemented) aspects of meaning.

9.1.2 *Threshold Firing—Asynchronous Spreading Activation* Threshold firing results when a sufficient amount of activity accrues at a unit of information in the model. Activity propagation arising in this way is referred to as decision activation. In the simulations of unimpaired processing, decision activation propagation has effects in the subsequent time update.[4] This propagation often has multiple effects, including excitation and inhibition.

As an example of excitation, imagine a VTP meaning in the PHON-CAT-MEAN space firing and semantically composing with an already interpreted TERM meaning in the PRAGMATIC space to produce, at the subsequent time interval, a direct object determination. Simultaneously, two different kinds of inhibitory effects occur, inhibiting (1) all the meanings attached to the same homophone; and (2) all active meanings of the same linguistic category type as the firing meaning.

The effects of firing information have multiple effects because of the interconnections across representation types. Firing information propagation is computed differently for each linguistic category type. The syntactic/semantic type determines the nature the computation. However, the effect of the firing depends on the state of all the receiving information.

Examine the following sentence:

The boy saw the building.

The meaning of the VTP is semantically composed with with the most recently understood TERM in PRAGMATIC (representing the building). However, if the most recently interpreted TERM is in a decayed state, it may not be recognized as the most recently heard TERM and the wrong TERM may be attached to the verb as the object of the sentence. In particular, the attachment of THE

---

4 An expansion to HOPE permitting modification of the effectiveness of both types of spreading activation has recently been implemented [Gigley, and Haarmann, 1987; Haarmann,1987]. This provides a finer control over the study of the time driven processing interactions.

BOY as direct object in the example sentence can occur, and HOPE contains no built in constraints to stop such mis-interpretation from occurring. As a matter of fact, such misinterpretations along with their observable causes are the focus for designing and building the model in the first place.

The next section will explain the nature of parallelism in HOPE's design. It simultaneously encompasses two views of parallelism and thus differs in design from the other computer models described in this book. Furthermore, using the time dimension as one of the factors in parallelism is critical to defining lesionability within the model.

10 *Parallelism in HOPE*

This section discusses the computational and representational parallelism of the HOPE model. The computations are described and the role of tuning is elaborated. Once the nature of the internal control is clarified, the next section illustrates syntactic disambiguation in the simulation of sentence comprehension in the model. It demonstrates the importance of time to the simulation by demonstrating that the model performance after an artificial lesion occurs because of process de-synchronization and can explain aphasic performance degradation. It furthermore shows specific ways to observe this in people, suggesting several factors of task definition in clinical study which have previously received little attention. Lastly, we discuss behaviors thought to be due to knowledge specific lesions, which can be explained by de-synchronization of processes [Gigley, 1982; 1983; 1986; Gigley and Haarmann, 1987; Haarmann, 1987].

10.1 *Neural-like Computations Define Two Views of Parallelism*

There are two different perspectives of parallelism in the HOPE model, (1) the concurrent application of the update computations applied in parallel to all defined information in the HOPE graph; and (2) the separate simultaneous processing of information at different levels, such as phonetic information, meaning access, and interpretation. This is observed in a HOPE simulation by tracing the time course of events within one space over the entire simulation run.

10.1.1 *Parallelism in Computation* The exact nature of the computations is the manipulation of activity values. At the start of a simulation, all units of information are in the resting state, with no activity value or state description.

The processing of words introduces activity to the units over time, which spreads automatically to associated meaning units, and asynchronously (by threshold firing) throughout the graph over time. The spread of the activity is computed during an update computation and is affected by subsequent introduction of new words as they occur in the sentence input. The model does not incorporate a facility to include semantic priming contexts external to the sentence in the representation.

As previously described, each unit of information in HOPE is a threshold unit. It collects activity as a passive receiver until the activity reaches a parameter defined value and then it sends the activity to its connections. Each connected node or arc-node pair maintains its own state description and can be thought of as a separate processor. A state description includes an activity value, rate of decay (and an on/off decay switch), and a state of readiness (or refractoriness). The absence of any state information represents the resting state.

The update computations for all information units in the graph (the PHONETIC, PHON-CAT-MEAN, GRAMMAR, and PRAGMATIC spaces) include: DECAY, THRESHOLD-FIRING, CHANGE-OF-STATE, and MEANING-PROPAGATION. The duration for each state and the threshold are parameter controlled. There is a separately defined NEWWORD introduction process which requires a time parameter to define the number of computed updates between word inputs. DECAY is presently represented as a percentage decrease in activity if there is no new input; it is exponential. Two different decay rates reflect two different states of information, one before threshold firing, called the SHORT-TERM state, and the other after both threshold firing and the subsequent REFRACTORY state of the firing information, called the POST-REFRACTORY state.

Update computations are applied in lock step fashion to all information in one state of the graph representation, producing the subsequent state representation of the entire graph network. Since all computations are based on the same state space of information units, they occur in parallel. There are no specific computations directly computing changes within a single space. The changes affected are made by these general computations that constitute the HOPE architecture.

Thus the changes occurring within each space over time comprise a different kind of parallelism than that which is directly computed. One can analyze the PHONETIC processes, the MEANING or syntactic disambiguation processes, and the PRAGMATIC interpretation processes over time, independently, and as they co-occur in parallel. These processes as observed independently are the parallel processes which many systems discuss in their processing paradigms.

11 *A Summary of the HOPE Architecture*

This section provides a brief overview of the neural-like computations, which are homogeneous across spaces. Details can be found in [Gigley, 1982].

Information interacts asynchronously due to threshold firing. The order of firing and its magnitude are indirectly controlled using timing parameters that affect the applicability of the update computations. The exact computations that occur at any time slice of the process depend on the global state of the model and are context dependent. The update computations are as follows:

1. *NEW-WORD-RECOGNITION*: Introduction of the next phonetically recognized word in the sentence.

2. *DECAY*: Automatic memory decay exponentially reduces the activity of all active units that do not receive additional input. It is an important part of the neural processes that occur during memory processing.

3. *REFRACTORY-STATE-ACTIVATION*: An automatic change of state that occurs after active information has reached threshold and fired. In this state, the information can not affect or be affected by other information in the system.

4. *POST-REFRACTORY-STATE-ACTIVATION*: An automatic change of state which all units enter after existing in the *REFRACTORY-STATE*. The decay rate is different than before firing, although still exponential.

5. *MEANING-PROPAGATION*: Automatic spreading activation to the distributed parts of recognized words' meanings.

6. *FIRING-INFORMATION-PROPAGATION*: Asynchronous activation propagation that occurs when information reaches threshold and fires. It can be *INHIBITORY* and *EXCITATORY* in its effect. *INTERPRETATION* results in activation of a pragmatic representation of a disambiguated word meaning. These computations are independent and use the activity and state information distributed at each unit of the representation to determine when to apply to the unit and update its information.

During simulations, both the change of state over time and the cause of the change can be observed. Analyzing both aspects of the process provides the information that is useful in comparing the "normal" and "lesioned" simulations of the model. In this way, the effects of a given lesion can suggest hypotheses in a well defined linguistic context. Furthermore, each simulation must be run on a complete cover set of sentences (for any specific model), thus hypothesizing a unique clinically verifiable patient profile [Gigley, 1982; 1983; 1986; Gigley and Duffy, 1982].

In HOPE, activity propagation depends on the state of the system at any moment in time. Simulation of sentence comprehension occurs through the interactions of multiple asynchronous processes. The context dependent nature of the processing effects provides a potential variability in performance that cannot be accounted for in other neurally motivated approaches to language behavior. As a result, the model processes in a normal state and continues to process even in an impaired state (a lesion experiment) without redesign or reprogramming. The brain in a language impaired patient does not stop functioning, but performs in a degraded manner.

The ability to lesion the model and continue to process arises from parameterizations that can be clinically interpreted to characterize the process degradation. Lesions, characterized by parameter changes, affect processing independently of competence issues. These lesions are distinct from those usually claimed to produce the behavior difficulties, those that reduce explicit knowledge or eliminate rules. Change to a parameter value produces modifications in the overt behavior of the model over time and in its final result. The analysis of these resultant changes gives value to the model. Interpreting the time course of the process suggests clinical behavioral patterns that are plausible, although not necessarily previously noted in aphasic patients.

12 *The Role of Time in HOPE Processing*

This section describes the overall computation of HOPE as an integration of all the processes already described.

12.1 *The Role of Parameters*

The system computes results by spreading activation. Time-dependent processes, whose actions depend on the values of certain parameters, cause this spreading activation. Table 2 illustrates the current set of system parameters, and thus the adjustable processing characteristics of the system. The parameter values define a temporal coordination enabling activity values to remain at sufficient levels for long enough periods of time for unit firing activity to produce normally expected results (i.e., sentence comprehension).

Parameter adjustment represents the only available control over the actual process. Temporal coordination depends on the following: (1) the duration of the DECAY interval; (2) the duration of the POST-REFRACTORY state in different spaces; (3) the amount of DECAY; (4) the interval between introduction of new words; (5) the amount of propagation occurring when something fires; and (6) the initial activity values for new information and for POST-RE-FRACTORY-STATE activity. These values coordinate how long activity re-

Table 2   Modifiable Parameters which are tuned to achieve normal results in the final state of simulation over a grammatical cover set of sentences. The affect of each parameter on the processes of the system is given in the parentheses along with the value that has been used during the normal simulations. The lesioned simulations were achieved by modifying the word-decay-time-interval parameter from two to one in the slowed propagation lesion, and by changing the short-term-decay-time-interval from 2 to 1 for the short term lesion.

compete-inhibit-constant (homophone competition)	72
end-cont-predict	59
feed-constant (propagation %)	33
threshold value	100
memory-constant (initial activity)	98
memory-decay-rate	98
memory-decay-time-interval	1
multi-mean-init	75
pragmatic-rest-interval	1
rest-state-activity level	0
rest-state-decay	98
semantic-type-inhibition-constant	85
short-term-decay-interval	2
short-term-decay-rate	91
single-cat-init	95
single-mean-init	95
termination-count	6
word-decay-rate	91
word-introduction-interval	2
phonetic-firing-time length	1
phon-cat-mean-firing-time length	1
pragmatic-firing-time length	1

mains at a sufficient level to be effective during the processing, and are set by tuning the model using sentences of all valid syntactic types (i.e., the cover set of the current grammar).

12.2 Tuning a Model

Tuning involves running and re-running the model, changing the parameters each time until the correct final activity and sentence representation states are achieved. The parameters are changed on each execution, usually one at a time, until the expected *normal* representation occurs as the final state of the process for each of the entire cover set of sentences.

In the current system, a final state consists of the contextually correct meaning of the input representation in the PRAGMATIC space. This includes appropriate linguistic types and correct labelling of case relationships. The PHONETIC space contains active information at a subthreshold level representing the word sequence of the input. The PHON-CAT-MEAN space, because of the way interpretation proceeds during processing, contains a trace of what was interpreted and in what order. This consists of a right to left trace of interpretation within constituents and can be interpreted by analyzing units at subthreshold levels in the POST-REFRACTORY state.

Tuning enables the FIRING STATE to occur for the correct syntactic/semantic combinations within suitable time bounds, i.e., before activity has a chance to DECAY back to the REST state. The system has no direct way to program the co-occurrence of high activity values in several units simultaneously except by altering the system parameters discussed above. Tuning can be a difficult problem, and in fact, may not always be possible. However, maximum variability in processing and lesionability require such an architecture.

13 *Syntactic Disambiguation over Time*

This section provides examples of normal and degraded processing. Two different lesion conditions illustrate simulated artificial aphasia, slowing propagation, and increasing the decay rate of information. Both lesions produce effects because of their disruption of tuned synchronization of activity propagations within the process. Each lesion produces different global patient performance characteristics.

13.1 *"Normal" Simulations of Sentence Processing*

Let us return to the example sentence mentioned earlier:

The boy saw the building.

Actual model input is in the form of a phonetic transcription of words as follows:

[th-uh b-oy s-ao th-uh b-ih-l-d-ih-ng]

Introduction of the third word of the sentence, "saw" (s-ao), occurs as the previously heard words, "the" and "boy" are composed (referentially interpreted) as a TERM in the PRAGMATIC space. The TERM meaning of "the boy" will fire in the next time interval. The GRAMMAR reflects a previous CN (common noun) prediction that has been satisfied. When s-ao enters the process affecting the PHONETIC and PHON-CAT-MEAN spaces, no predictions from previously processed inputs are active. During the next update, all meanings of s-ao (in the PHON-CAT-MEAN space) affect the GRAMMAR space (by spreading activation). All meanings of s-ao are activated at an equal level when the word is recognized.

Several updates later, the TERM referent for THE BUILDING has been introduced and an interpretation composed, and it is ready to fire. A state of competing meaning representations exists in the PHON-CAT-MEAN space, with most meanings of b-ih-l-d-ih-ng inhibited relative to the CN meaning. The CN meaning of s-ao is also inhibited when compared to the activity of the other s-ao meanings, since they remain in the same state and have undergone the same decay. Both differences are the result of firing of the CN meaning for b-ih-l-d-ih-ng and show the effects of disambiguation among all competing meanings for the one that is firing. Firing of the TERM meaning will provide feedback to all active VTP meanings in PHON-CAT-MEAN resulting in a firing state, VTP-SAW.

The next important event is the meaning disambiguation for the VTP (transitive verb meaning) of s-ao. This is due to the feedback effect from THE BUILDING term which just fired (as described). When the VTP meaning fires (as the disambiguated meaning), in addition to its inhibitory affect on all competing meanings, it triggers constraint satisfaction processes to determine the case roles of the previously "understood" terms (i.e., agent and object).

The final state of the simulation is shown in Figure 9.5. The order of interpretation can be seen in PHON-CAT-MEAN, where the subthreshold activity values of the state description vectors having "*" as their POST-RE-FRACTORY state represent the first to last order of interpretation in increasing value. For instance, the meaning of BUILDING (b) was interpreted before the meaning of THE (c). In the PHONETIC space, observing the increasing order of subthreshold activity level of all information in the POST-REFRACTORY state provides a trace of the phonetic input.

Note that no tree representation explicitly forms part of the process or the interpretation. All aspects of grammar usually manifest in creating a tree structure are used here to coordinate the processing in a time dependent way. However, with the information in the PHON-CAT-MEAN space in this final state, a tree representation of the structure which has been processed can be reconstructed from the final states of the information activated during the process (if this is desired).

Process-Interval 15

pragmatic

boy = (78 *)   term
                                 ←belongs-to—boy = (88 *)
      ←agent—saw   ←belongs-to—building = (0 #)

building = (90 *)   vip
                                 ←belongs-to—saw = (98 *)
      ←dir-obj—saw

sentence
      ←belongs-to—saw = (0 #)

grammar

cn = (0 $)   term = (0 $)
endcont = (0 $)

phon-cat-mean

                                             (a)
    b-ih-l-d-ih-ng   s-ao
      ←cn—building = (92 *) (b)   ←cn—saw = (30)
      ←vip—building = (78)   ←vip—saw = (60)
      ←vtp—building = (72)   ←vtp—saw = (98 *)

    b-oy   th-uh
      ←cn—boy = (68 *)   ←det—the = (94 *)
                                             (c)
    end
      ←endcont—stop** = (96 *)

phonetic

    b-ih-l-d-ih-ng = (92 *)   s-ao = (84 *)
    b-oy = (80 *)   th-uh = (88 *)
    end = (96 *)

Figure 9.5 (opposite) Final state representation of the understood relationships conveyed by the sentence is shown in PRAGMATIC. Within PHON-CAT-MEAN one can trace the order of interpretation or disambiguation of sense which has occurred. All information in PHON-CAT-MEAN in the POST-REFRACTORY state (*) has been interpreted. The order of interpretation is found in the increasing activity levels for this information. The lower the activity, the earlier the interpretation (a). Similarly, in PHONETIC, there is a trace of the input process for information in the * state (c). The order of introduction, from earliest to latest, is also increasing order, excepting repeated words.

13.2 *A "Slowed Propagation" Lesion Simulation*

This section will show the effects of slowing down the spreading activation to the GRAMMAR predictions relative to the rate of propagation of all other processes. As a result, predictions do not occur in time for the normal input speed, the model misses the intended meaning of a given word, and substitutes for it the incorrect meaning of another word (later in the input).

Examine the effects of this "slowed-propagation" lesion on the same example sentence as above. The critical time in the simulation is when the incorrect interpretation fires as a result of slowed prediction. When the third word of the sentence, s-ao, is heard, all of its meanings are activated simultaneously. The CN meaning-SAW of s-ao reaches threshold. Contrasting this with the normal processing example, the GRAMMAR is in a different state; whereas previously the CN sense of the word "boy" was understood, slowed propagation prevents the CN prediction from being ready when the "boy" is heard, remaining active for the subsequent input. This leads to a threshold value for the CN meaning of "saw."

The final state of understanding as represented for this degraded (lesioned) simulation is shown in Figure 9.6, and can be compared with Figure 9.5. The misinterpretations of words intended to have different functions in the sentence cause the verb meaning for s-ao to be omitted, leading instead to an interpretation as a CN in the PRAGMATIC space. Furthermore, instead of the CN meaning for b-ih-l-d-ih-ng, it becomes the verb of the sentence (as shown in the PRAGMATIC space). This provides a plausible interpretation for the sequence of homophones of the sentence, but it is not the intended one. The plausible meaning is that there is some idea of a saw related to the act of building. Another difference is that an adequate referent for the agent relationship of the verb cannot be determined.

By comparing the results of simulation under this *lesion* condition for each of a cover set of sentences, one can develop an hypothesized patient profile of the performance under certain computationally well-defined lesions. Determining the relation of these hypotheses with actual performance by aphasic patients is the goal of the clinical validation studies which must be undertaken.

```
Process-Interval 9
```

pragmatic
======

```
    CONSTRAINT-ERROR*
        ←agent—  building (c)
    agent
        ←FOR— MISSING-TERM*
    saw = (86 *)      (a)
    sentence
        ←belongs-to— building = (109 )  (b)
```

grammar
======

```
    cn = (78)              term = (68)
    endcont = (0 $)
```

phon-cat-mean
======

```
    b-ih-l-d-ih-ng                   s-ao
        ←cn— building = (48)      ←cn— saw = (88 *)
        ←vip— building = (0 #)    ←vip— saw = (68 )
        ←vtp— building = (48)     ←vtp— saw = (75 )
    b-oy                             th-uh
        ←cn— boy = (54 )                 ←det— the = (70 )
    end
        ←endcont— stop** = (0 #)
```

phonetic
======

```
    b-ih-l-d-ih-ng = (96 *)   s-ao = (88 *)
    b-oy = (84 *)             th-uh = (92 *)
    end = (0 #)
```

Figure 9.6 The final state of processing for the Slowed Propagation Lesion is shown and should be compared with Figure 9.5. Note the number of misinterpretations which have occurred. Instead of the intended verb meaning for SAW, it is interpreted as a CN (a). In addition, the disambiguated meaning for BUILDING is seen to be the verb for the sentence (b). While this is not the intended "meaning" of the sentence, it has some plausibility for the lexical combinations of the sentence. The noted missing referent for an agent (c) occurs because a complete TERM has not been interpreted due to repetition of the word, THE.

13.3 *An "Increased Memory Decay Lesion" Simulation*

Another sort of impairment in normal processing involves the speed with which automatic decay occurs in all active information. By analyzing the final states over a complete cover set of sentences, this lesion can be shown to produce a qualitatively different hypothesized patient profile than in the previous case.[5]

Figure 9.7 shows the final state representation for the example sentence under the faster decay lesion condition. As can be seen by comparing this final state with the two others, the effect is of a different nature. The model does not understand a verb, although all words of the sentence are recognized and accessed. Only complete noun phrases are determined as specific referents (a) and (b). It is as if the hypothesized patient can only process noun phrases.

This result is only partially verified when the entire cover set of sentences is simulated. Some contexts allow interpretation of the verb. These contexts seem to relate to the location and complexity of the noun phrases regardless of the ambiguity of the verb. This is mentioned to provide a richer idea of what can actually be interpreted from a simulation, but the details are beyond the scope of this paper. The next section briefly discusses some of these aspects to demonstrate how one can use such a model as a basis for forming performance hypotheses. Models such as HOPE attain additional value in providing a tool for sharpening our skills in developing adequate theories on which to base our investigations.

14 *Developing Hypothesized Patient Profiles—The Role of Disambiguation*

The previous sections have provided examples of disambiguation based on linguistic (syntactic/semantic) knowledge during processing within the HOPE architecture. They have been illustrated with the results from a single example sentence, although a true lesion experiment requires more than one sentence simulation (as mentioned). Factors such as sentence length, the meaning competitor set for each homophone, and the state of the grammar can all affect different sentences in different ways.

One way to analyze the full implications of any given defined model within the normal and impaired conditions is by validating the simulations with all possible linguistically correct sentence types over which a given model is defined (the cover set). When analyzing the cover set, one can evaluate the overall performance pattern to develop hypotheses about what types of infor-

---

5 This has been described in detail in [Gigley 1982; 1986].

Process-Interval 17

<u>pragmatic</u>

```
boy = (74 *)                 term
                     (a)     ←belongs-to— boy = (78 *)
building = (86 *)    (b)     ←belongs-to— building = (90 *)
```

<u>grammar</u>

```
cn = (0 $)                   term = (0 $)
endcont = (0 $)
```

<u>phon-cat-mean</u>

```
b-ih-l-d-ih-ng               s-ao
   ←cn— building = (86 *)     ←cn— saw = (19 )
   ←vip— building = (52 )     ←vip— saw = (47 )
   ←vtp— building = (51 )     ←vtp— saw = (46 )
b-oy                         th-uh
   ←cn— boy = (62 *)          ←det— the = (88 *)
end
   ←endcont— stop** = (90 *)
```

<u>phonetic</u>

```
b-ih-l-d-ih-ng = (86 *)     s-ao  = (78 *)
b-oy = (74 *)               th-uh = (82 *)
end = (90 *)
```

Figure 9.7 The final state of processing under the Faster Decay Lesion condition. Comparing Figure 9.7 with Figure 9.5, the normal final state, one sees that there are no verb meanings interpreted. Only complete noun referents have been determined (a) and (b). Based on this single sentence, it seems that verbs are ignored during processing. On comparing the figure with Figure 9.6, one finds a very different state of comprehension. It has been found that the overall synopsis of final states for the entire cover set of sentences under the two different "lesion" conditions is distinct.

mation are critical during processing and when they take effect. The set of sentences used to tune the model and used to analyze the degraded performance results is based on a minimal set of sentences which includes one instance of each linguistically valid sentence type. An example set is shown in Table 9.3, including ambiguous and unambiguous sentences. The degree of ambiguity for the ambiguous sentences was not considered in this selection.

As an additional test, one can control the number of meanings for each word of the sentence and their combinations in correct sentences. This set of simulations provide more refined hypotheses and are useful in the design of studies to validate the results of HOPE performance, and constitutes the focus of our current work (see also [Gigley and Haarmann, 1987]). For instance, when running a simulation with slowed propagation but without any syntactic or semantic ambiguity, such as "The boy slapped the girl," interpretation problems remain. Deficiencies in disambiguation do not cause problems but the model experiences difficulty in interpreting the beginning parts of sentences. However, if the subject is a proper name, then it is the only correctly interpreted part of the sentence.

Interpretation of the degraded performance focuses on the time course of processing and the window in which composition occurs (or must occur for normal comprehension). Issues of disambiguation and process can be raised that relate to the number of meanings possible for each of the words in each location of the sentence and how these meaning sets interact syntactically (no meaning representations yet exist). The interactions depend on time and linear ordering. For instance, a sentence such as "The boy slapped the girl" contains no ambiguities for any of the words. However, a sentence falling within the same syntactic specification, "The boys took a shovel" may cause some problems, due to multiple meanings for the last word, including a verb meaning. Of interest is whether competing verb meanings are fired for SHOVEL as well as TOOK under the slowed-propagation lesion. The results found during simulation for the second sentence indicate that this does not occur. Instead, the first determiner of the sentence triggers the noun meaning for shovel and only the end of the sentence is interpreted as "took the shovel." Distinctions such as this can be tested within suitably defined studies.

By carefully analyzing the states of the different levels of representation in different process-time intervals, and at subthreshold levels of activity in the output over time as well as in the final states, one can develop hypothesized patient profiles. These are performance characteristics which are suggested from the results of the simulation. The activity present in the different spaces leads to profiles which specify (1) the ability to repeat sentences; (2) the ability to note the end of utterances; (3) how much of the sentence was understood; and (4) whether and how much was misunderstood and in what way. The interested reader can refer to Gigley [1986], where the development and use of hypothesized patient profiles is described.

Developing a model like HOPE enables the study of system dynamics and observation of the explicit changes in process results occurring as a result of systematic modification of timing parameters and degradations of information available to the process. Since each specific lesion is carefully defined relative to a normally working model, one can manipulate factors considered relevant to the degraded human condition (i.e., the particular brain lesion) to gain some processing motivated insights as to the cause of the related degraded performance. Due to the complexity of the interactions, computational models provide the only tool to enhance our abilities in this direction.

15 *Conclusions*

This chapter has introduced concepts of ambiguity within a processing control paradigm based on current understanding of neural processes. The HOPE model includes representation of ambiguity on many levels, in the representations as well as in the actual computations which are applied to the representations. HOPE demonstrates how context in a time-course process can effectively be used to disambiguate meanings. It furthermore illustrates how possible misinterpretations can occur due to de-synchronization of activity signal affects within a naturally constrained processing model. These misinterpretations fall within the global characterization of difficulties in understanding reported for aphasic patients in the literature.

There is a tremendous volume of research awaited on all levels. At the neural process level, research is needed to determine whether distance or length of axon can be related to time course of processing or to determine the functional role of multiple connections. At the performance level, the time-course of decisions during processing must be determined, reflecting that agent and/or object determination have been made. Within aphasiology, it must be determined whether any of the numerous assumptions explicitly as well as implicitly encoded in HOPE are valid, and whether any of the performance predictions for aphasic patients hold.

Finally, it is hoped that by providing an initial attempt to deal with ambiguity along the dimensions as described throughout this chapter, others will see new and additional relationships that can be further expanded in other contexts. Instead of programming by eliminating ambiguity, HOPE focuses on controlling ambiguity within the time course of processing.

Throughout this chapter, ambiguity has been studied as an integral part of a functioning system. Only by directly confronting the problem of ambiguity in such a way can we really gain an understanding of its complexity. Finally, the fact that neural ambiguity pervades in the wetware computational facility, suggests that it could provide a clue to the complexity of cognitive function in general. At least, HOPE's computational paradigm provides an explicit example of what can be gained by focusing on it.

Acknowledgments

The preparation of this paper was supported through a Faculty Research Initiation Grant and a Biomedical Research Support Grant at the University of New Hampshire.

The author wishes to thank Mr. Henk Haarmann for asking the right kinds of questions to make the explanations more appropriate, and the reviewers for their helpful comments on earlier drafts, especially Steve Small for his expert editing of the final revision.

References

Ackley, D. H., Hinton, G. E., and Sejnowski, T. J. 1985. A learning algorithm for Boltzmann machines. *Cognitive Science* 9(1):147–169.

Ajdukiewicz, K. 1967. Die Syntaktische Konnexität, 1935, translated as Syntactic connexion. In S. McCall (ed.), *Polish Logic*, pp. 207–231. Oxford.

Anderson, J. 1976. *Language, Memory and Thought*. Hillsdale: Erlbaum.

Anderson, J., Silverstein, J., Ritz, S. and Jones, R. 1977. Distinctive features, categorical perception, and probability learning: Some applications of a neural model. *Psychological Review* 84(5):413–451.

Arcidiacono, T. 1985. *GRASPER-UNH: A Tool for Constructing and Processing Directed Graphs with Lisp*. MS Thesis, Department of Computer Science, University of New Hampshire.

Barto, A. G. and Sutton, R. S. 1981. Landmark learning: An illustration of associative search. *Biological Cybernetics* 42:1–8,

Barto, A. G., Sutton, R.S. and Anderson, C. W. 1983. Neuronlike elements that can solve difficult learning control problems. *IEEE Transaction on Systems, Man and Cybernetics* 13:835–846.

Berge, C. 1970. *Graphes et Hypergraphes*. Paris: DONOD.

Blumstein, S. E., Milberg, W., and Shrier, R. 1982. Semantic processing in aphasia: Evidence from an auditory lexical decision task. *Brain and Language* 17:301–315.

Blumstein, S., Katz, B. Goodglass, H., Shrier, R. and Dworetsky, B. 1985. The effects of slowed speech on auditory comprehension in aphasia. *Brain and Language* 24:246–265.

Broca, M. P. 1861. Remarques sur le Siège de la Faculté du Langage Articulé, Suivies d'une Observation d'Aphémie (Perte de la Parole). Extracted from *Bulletin de la Société d'Anthropologie,* 2 série, t. VI:330–357.

Brookshire, R. H. 1971. Effects of trial time and inter-trial interval on naming by aphasic subjects. *Journal of Communication Disorders* 3:289–301.

Caplan, D., Matthei, E. and Gigley, H. 1981. Comprehension of gerundive constructions by Broca's aphasics. *Brain and Language* 13:145–160.

Collins, A. M., and Loftus, E. A. 1975. A spreading activation theory of semantic processing. *Psychological Review* 82(6):407–428.

Cottrell, G. W. 1985. *A Connectionist Approach to Word Sense Disambiguation.* Ph.D. Dissertation, Computer Science Department, University of Rochester, Rochester, NY.

Cottrell, G. W., and Small, S. L. 1983. A connectionist scheme for modelling word sense disambiguation. *Cognition and Brain Theory VI* 1:89–120.

Davis, G.A. 1983. *A Survey of Adult Aphasia.* Englewood Cliffs: Prentice-Hall.

Dean, P. 1980. Recapitulation on a theme by Lashley? Comment on Wood's simulation lesion experiment. *Psychological Review* 87(5):470–473.

Geschwind, N. 1965. Disconnection syndromes in animals and man, Part I and Part II, LXXXVIII:237–294;585–644.

Gigley, H. M. 1982. *Neurolinguistically Constrained Simulation of Sentence Comprehension: Integrating Artificial Intelligence and Brain Theory.* Ph.D. Dissertation, University of Massachusetts, Amherst. Available, University Microfilms, Ann Arbor, Michigan.

Gigley, H. M. 1983. HOPE—AI and the dynamic process of language behavior. *Cognition and Brain Theory* 6(1):39–88.

Gigley, H. M. 1984. From HOPE en l'ESPERANCE—On the role of computational neurolinguistics in cross-language studies. In *Proceedings of COLING-84,* Stanford University, California.

Gigley, H. M. 1985a. Grammar viewed as a functioning part of a cognitive system. In *ACL Proceedings—23rd Annual Meeting,* Chicago, Illinois.

Gigley, H. M. 1985b. Computational Neurolinguistics—what is it all about? In *IJCAI-85 Proceedings,* Los Angeles, CA. Los Altos: Morgan Kaufmann.

Gigley, H. M. 1986. Studies in artificial aphasia—experiments in processing change. In *Proceedings of the Ninth Annual Symposium on Computer Applications in Medical Care* Baltimore, Maryland, November, 1985c. Selected to appear in *Journal of Computer Methods and Programs in Biomedicine* 22(1):43–50.

Gigley, H. M., and Duffy, J. R. 1982. The contribution of clinical intelligence and artificial aphasiology to clinical aphasiology and artificial intelligence. In R. H. Brookshire (ed.), *CLINICAL APHASIOLOGY, Proceedings of the Conference,* Minneapolis, MN.

Gigley, H. M. and Haarmann, H. J. 1987. Can synchronization deficits explain aphasic comprehension errors? In *Proceedings Conference of the Cognitive Science Society*, Seattle, WA.

Goodenough, C., Zurif, E., Weintraub, S. 1977. Aphasics' attention to grammatical morphemes. *Language and Speech* 11–19.

Goodglass, H. and Kaplan, E. 1983. 1972. *The Assessment of Aphasia and Related Disorders*. Philadelphia: Lea and Febiger.

Gordon, B. 1982. Confrontation naming: Computational model and disconnection simulation. In M. A. Arbib, D. Caplan, and J. Marshall (eds.), *Neural Models of Language Processes*. New York: Academic Press.

Haarmann H. J. 1987. *A Computer Simulation of Syntactic Understanding in Normals and Aphasics: Slowed Activity Propagation*. MS Thesis, Cognitive Science, Psychological Laboratory, Katholieke Universiteit, Nijmegen, The Netherlands.

Hendrix, G. 1978. The representation of semantic knowledge. In D. E. Walker (ed.), *Understanding Spoken Language*, pp. 121–181. Amsterdam: Elsevier North-Holland.

Hinton, G. E. 1986. Learning distributed representations of concepts. In *Proceedings the Cognitive Science Society*, Amherst, MA.

Hinton, G. E., McClelland, J. L., and Rumelhart, D. E. 1986. Distributed representations. In D. E. Rumelhart and J. L. McClelland (eds.), *Parallel Distributed Processing*. Cambridge: MIT Press.

Jenkins, J.J., Jiménez-Pabón, E., Shaw, R.E., and Sefer, J.W. 1975. *Schuell's Aphasia in Adults: Diagnosis, Prognosis and Treatment.*. New York: Harper and Row.

Kaas, J., Nelson, R., Sur, M. Lin, C-S., and Merzenich, M. 1979. Multiple representations of the body within the primary somatosensory cortex of primates. *Science* 204:521–523.

Kertesz, A. 1979. *Aphasia and Associated Disorders: Taxonomy, Localization, and Recovery*. New York: Grune and Stratton.

Lashley, K. S. 1967/1951. The problem of serial order in behavior. In L. A. Jeffress (ed.), *Cerebral Mechanisms in Behavior*. New York: Hafner.

Laskey, E. Z., Weidner, W. E., and Johnson, J. P. 1976. Influence of linguistic complexity, rate of presentation, and interphrase pause time on auditory verbal comprehension of adult aphasic patients. *Brain and Language* 3:386–396.

Lecours, A. R., Lhermitte, F. and Bryans, B. 1983. *Aphasiology*. London: Baillière Tindall.

Lewis, D. 1972. General semantics. In Davidson and Harman (eds.), *Semantics of Natural Language,* pp. 169–218.

Lichtheim, L. 1885. On aphasia. *BRAIN* VII: January, 433–484.

Liles, B. Z. and Brookshire, R. H. 1975. The effects of pause time on auditory comprehension of aphasic subjects. *Journal of Communication Disorders* 8:221–235.

Limber, J. Example ambiguous question and phonetic response. Psychology Department, University of New Hampshire, Durham, NH 03824, personal communication.

Lowrance, J. 1978. GRASPER 1.0 reference manual. COINS Technical Report No. 78–20, University of Massachusetts, Amherst.

Marslen-Wilson, W. and Tyler, L. 1980. The temporal structure of spoken language understanding. *Cognition* 8:1–71.

Marslen-Wilson, W. and Welsh, A. 1978. Processing interactions and lexical access during word recognition in continuous speech. *Cognitive Psychology* 10:29–63.

McClelland, J. L. and Rumelhart, D. E. 1981. An interactive activation model of context effects in letter perception: Part I, an account of basic findings. *Psychological Review* 88(5):375–407.

McClelland, J. L. and Rumelhart, D. E. 1986. *Parallel Distributed Processing, Volume 2, Psychological and Biological Models.* Cambridge: MIT Press.

Merzenich, M., Kaas, J., Wall, J., Nelson, R., Sur, M. and Felleman, D. 1983. Topographic reorganization of somatosensory cortical areas 3b and 1 in adult monkeys following restricted deafferentation. *Neuroscience* 8:33–55.

Montague, R. 1979/1974. English as a formal language. In R. H. Thomason (ed.), *Formal Philosophy.* New Haven: Yale University Press.

Quillian, M. R. 1980/1968. Semantic memory. In M. Minsky (ed.), *Semantic Information Processing.* Cambridge: MIT Press.

Reiss, R. 1962. A theory and simulation of rhythmic behavior due to reciprocal inhibition in small nerve nets. In *Proceedings AFIPS Spring Joint Computer Conference*, pp. 171–194.

Rumelhart, D. E. and McClelland, J. L. 1986. *Parallel Distributed Processing, Volume 1: Foundations.* Cambridge: MIT Press.

Schwartz, M. Saffran, M. and Marin, O. 1980. The word order problem in agrammatism: I. comprehension. *Brain and Language* 10(2):249–262.

Seidenberg, M. Tanenhaus, M. Leiman, J. and Bienkowski, M. 1982. Automatic access of the meanings of ambiguous words in context: Some limitations of knowledge-based processing. *Cognitive Psychology* 14(4):489–537.

Swinney, D. A. 1979. Lexical access during sentence comprehension: (Re)consideration of context effects. *Journal of Verbal Learning and Behavior* 18:645–659.

Thompson, R. F. 1967. *Foundations of Physiological Psychology.* New York: Harper and Row.

Waltz D. L. and Pollack, J. B. 1985. Massively parallel parsing: A strongly interactive model of natural language interpretation. *Cognitive Science* 9(1):51–74.

Wernicke, C. 1969/1874. The symptom complex of aphasia. *Boston Studies in the Philosophy of Science* IV:34–97. Dordrecht: D. Reidel Publishing Co.

Wood, C. C. 1978. Variations on a theme by Lashley: Lesion experiments on the neural model of Anderson, Silverstein, Ritz, and Jones. *Psychological Review* 85(6):582–591.

Wood, C. C. 1980. Interpretation of real and simulated lesion experiments. *Psychological Review* 87(5):474–476.

Wood, C. C. 1982. Implications of simulated lesion experiments for the interpretation of lesions in real nervous systems. In M.A. Arbib, D. Caplan, and J. Marshall (eds.), *Neural Models of Language Processes*. New York: Academic Press.

Zurif, E. B. and Blumstein, S. E. 1978. Language and the brain. In M. Halle, J. Bresnan, and G. A. Miller (eds.), *Linguistic Theory and Psychological Reality*. Cambridge: MIT Press.

Zurif, E. B., Green, E., Caramazza, A., and Goodenough, C. 1976. Note on grammatical intuitions of aphasic patients: Sensitivity to functors. *Cortex* 12:183–186.

II

EMPIRICAL STUDIES

10

Implications of Lexical Ambiguity Resolution for Word Recognition and Comprehension

Greg B. Simpson
University of Nebraska at Omaha

Curt Burgess
University of Rochester

Any complete explanation of the comprehension of language, by human or machine, must account for the processes by which a single interpretation is given to any indeterminate linguistic message. Much of the interest in this interpretation problem has been focussed at the level of the individual word. The implications of the lexical ambiguity problem go far beyond words with multiple dictionary entries, however. We believe that the issues involved in lexical ambiguity research are applicable to a wide range of comprehension phenomena. First, as all words will normally have more information associated with them than is required in any particular context, the selection processes that typify ambiguous words are, to some extent, relevant to all lexical access. We have argued further that word-level ambiguity only exemplifies in an obvious way, characteristics that exist at virtually all levels of language comprehension. We have suggested, for example, that such phenomena as metaphor, idiom, and indirect requests present a comprehender with essentially the same interpretive dilemma occasioned by words with more than one possible meaning [Simpson, Burgess, and Peterson, 1986]. Therefore, although most ambiguity research to date has been aimed at understanding the ability of context to select word meaning, we believe that the area has implications that extend far beyond this primary concern. In the present chapter, we will first review briefly some of the recent research in lexical ambiguity. More detailed and comprehensive reviews are available elsewhere [Seidenberg, Tanenhaus, Leiman, and Bienkowski, 1982; Simpson, 1984], so this one will not be extensive. We will then discuss extensions of lexical ambiguity research to other issues of word recognition. In particular, we will discuss the implications of our research for general word recognition models. Finally, we describe a series of studies using lexical ambiguity to explore qualitative changes that occur with development of the ability to use context in facilitating word recognition, a problem to which the methodology of ambiguity seems very well suited.

1 *An Overview of Research in Lexical Ambiguity*

As researchers concerned with an apparently narrow range of phenomena within language processing, we have occasionally been forced to defend ourselves against charges, first, that ambiguous words represent only an anomalous minority of all words, and second, that context is so strong in normal language processing that, functionally, ambiguity does not even exist. As one colleague once remarked, "The only ambiguous sentences I've ever seen are in psycholinguistics textbooks." We believe that these arguments are faulty for two reasons. First, as stated above and as we will discuss again later, we believe that vagueness of meaning is not restricted to words with multiple dictionary entries. Second, we would argue that it is only the textbook examples of ambiguity that are anomalous. Such common examples of lexical ambiguity as

1. I was startled by the strength of the punch.

or of syntactic ambiguity as

2. Visiting relatives can be a nuisance.

are unusual in that they represent rather rare cases in which both interpretations become available to the reader simultaneously, or very nearly so. This characteristic, of course, makes them excellent as examples for textbooks, but very poor representatives of typical language use. Nevertheless, the fact that most potentially ambiguous sentences (even such obvious examples as those above) are rendered unambiguous by the context in which they appear does not dismiss the ambiguity problem. Rather, it defines it. It is by some process or set of processes that context has the effect that it has, and it has been the goal of the research in lexical ambiguity to elucidate those processes.

1.1 *Models of Ambiguity Processing*

Three general models of ambiguity processing have been proposed. A context-dependent model takes the view that access is restricted to the meaning of an ambiguous word that is appropriate in context. Whenever a context biases a particular meaning (which, of course, is most of the time), that meaning alone becomes activated [Glucksberg, Kreuz, and Rho, 1986; Schvaneveldt, Meyer, and Becker, 1976; Simpson, 1981].

An ordered-access model [Forster and Bednall, 1976; Hogaboam and Perfetti, 1975; Simpson and Burgess, 1985] relies upon the fact that the various meanings of ambiguous words are not equally frequent, except in rare cases, and that this meaning frequency is considered by a comprehender when an ambiguous word is encountered. The model holds that whenever an ambiguous word is presented, its dominant, or most frequent, meaning becomes active first. In its strong form [Hogaboam and Perfetti, 1975], it contends that this frequency bias is unaffected by context. That is, even if a sentence were to be strongly biased toward a subordinate meaning, the dominant would still be retrieved first. Only if a subsequent test of that meaning indicates incompatibility with the context is another meaning retrieved, in this case the second most frequent. This serial, self-terminating search continues until the proper meaning is found. Of course, such a search process is not the only way in which meaning frequency information may be implicated in recognition of ambiguous words. It is possible, for example, that meanings undergo activation in parallel, but that the more frequent meanings reach recognition threshold more rapidly than do less frequent meanings. In fact, our own research [Simpson and Burgess, 1985], to be discussed below, supports exactly such a view.

The third model contends that all meanings of an ambiguous word are retrieved whenever it occurs, and that this process is not sensitive to context [Onifer and Swinney, 1981; Seidenberg et al., 1982; Swinney, 1979; Tanenhaus, Leiman, and Seidenberg, 1979]. In its purest form [e.g., Onifer and Swinney, 1981], the initial activation of a word's memory representation is driven by the form (phonological or graphemic) of a stimulus, and therefore simultaneously yields all of the information that is associated with that form. Context plays a role only after all meanings have been retrieved, to select the one that is appropriate to it. Once again, however, a multiple-access model does not necessarily require that all meanings become available at the same rate [e.g., Seidenberg et al., 1982]. Again, some of our research discussed below speaks to the idea that all meanings are activated, but reach threshold at different times.

It is the third, multiple-access, view that has in some form become predominant in the minds of most word recognition researchers. Much of the model's support derives from experiments investigating the time course of the activation of contextually appropriate and inappropriate meanings [Lucas, 1984; Onifer and Swinney, 1981; Seidenberg et al., 1982; Swinney, 1979; Tanenhaus et al., 1979]. In these studies, subjects listen to sentences ending in ambiguous words. The sentences may be biased toward one of the homograph's meanings. Following the offset of the ambiguous word, a stimulus is presented visually, to which the subject responds, either by naming or by making a lexical decision. The visual target may be a word related to the same meaning of the ambiguous word as that indicated by the context, to the other meaning, or may be a completely unrelated word. These studies have found that if the interval between the ambiguous word and the target is very brief, responses to words related to either the contextually appropriate or inappropriate meanings are facilitated in comparison to those for unrelated words. If the target is delayed, however, then only appropriate associates are facilitated. The interpretation of these results is that both of the meanings are activated on the ambiguous word's presentation, and that the sentence context acts only in a post-access selection stage. Once the correct meaning is selected, the other is discarded. The speed of the selection process, and the fact that only the meaning finally selected comes to awareness, has led to the conclusion that the initial access and selection processes are automatic [Posner and Snyder, 1975] or, at least, veiled controlled processes [Shiffrin and Schneider, 1977].

Many of the studies in this area have attempted to select ambiguous words whose meanings are approximately equally common. One version of the multiple-access view, however, holds that exhaustive access is the rule even for words whose meanings are less balanced. Onifer and Swinney [1981] conducted a study in which they presented sentences auditorily that contained ambiguous words. While listening to the sentences, subjects were also required to make lexical decisions to visually presented targets. If a target was presented immediately after the occurrence in the sentence of an ambiguous word, a response to it was facilitated if it was an associate of the ambiguous word. This effect obtained regardless of whether the target was related to the same meaning of the ambiguous word as that biased by the sentence, or another meaning, again supporting an exhaustive access view. Furthermore, this pattern of results was found regardless of the frequency of the homograph's meaning represented either by the context or the target. Onifer and Swinney concluded that meaning frequency also was not represented in the initial access process, but was considered only in a subsequent stage (see also [Kinoshita, 1985]).

We have found, however, that at least in some circumstances, meaning frequency influences very early stages of ambiguous word processing [Simpson and Burgess, 1985]. We presented subjects visually with ambiguous word primes, which were followed by targets for lexical decisions. Targets were words related to the ambiguous prime through its more frequent (dominant) meaning, or through its less frequent (subordinate) meaning. In the rest of the word pairs, the prime and target were unrelated. Furthermore, we varied the stimulus onset asynchrony (SOA), allowing as little as 16 msec to elapse between prime and target onset. At this very brief SOA, there was a very clear advantage for the dominant meaning. Responses to dominant associates showed 32 msec facilitation compared to the unrelated condition, while responses to subordinate associates were 1 msec slower than those to unrelated words. As the SOA was increased, the subordinate meaning began to show facilitation as well, until, at a 300 msec SOA, it was equal to that shown be dominant targets. At still longer SOAs, however, the dominant meaning maintained its high degree of activation, while the facilitation for the subordinate meaning declined. By 750 msec, there was again only facilitation for the dominant. A subsequent experiment confirmed that the decrease of activation of the less frequent meaning at long SOAs could be traced to processes that allocated limited-capacity resources to the dominant meaning, leading to interference in the recognition of words related to the subordinate (this aspect of the experiment will be discussed further in a later section). We concluded on the basis of that study that a simple distinction between between the strongest forms of ordered- and exhaustive-access models was unreasonable. Both meanings were activated, but at a rate commensurate with their relative frequencies. We believe that this pattern of results clearly shows the importance of studying a wide range of SOA values. It is clear that selection of a single SOA (as was typical of early ambiguity research) could lead erroneously to conclusions suggesting that either exhaustive or ordered access occurred in all cases. Taken together, the recent studies manipulating SOA have shown that support for any of the three models may be obtained, depending on the context-target interval that is selected.

As Simpson and Burgess [1985] used ambiguous primes in isolation (i.e., not embedded in biasing context), the results must be attributable to processes occurring completely within a lexical level of processing. This suggests that the representation of an ambiguous word contains information relevant to the frequencies of its various meanings. It is not immediately clear why such information should not have an influence even when the word is contained in a sentence that biases its interpretation. Simpson [1981] did show effects of meaning frequency in sentence contexts that were either strongly or weakly biased toward one meaning. The results of this study showed that both meaning frequency and context influenced the word recognition sequence, but that a very strong context was required to overcome the dominance effect. The difficulty in overcoming dominance is logical, as in normal comprehension, dominance and context usually support one another, as the most frequent meaning is, by definition, the one most commonly appropriate to the context.

In conclusion, it is clear to us that a simple view of these models as mutually exclusive is not ideal. In our own research with ambiguous words in isolation, we have found a pattern of results that contains elements of exhaustive and ordered access. Meaning frequency was clearly implicated in the recognition process, in contradiction of one very strong version of an exhaustive access model in which the initial retrieval is based only on the perceptual form of the stimulus (e.g., [Onifer and Swinney, 1981]). On the other hand, the results were equally incompatible with the strongest form of ordered access, that is, one characterized by a serial self-terminating search process (e.g., [Hogaboam and Perfetti, 1975]). One of us has also argued previously [Simpson, 1984] that there is a very consistent pattern among sentence context studies for the contextually appropriate meaning to enjoy at least a slight advantage over the inappropriate (though this advantage is often small and nonsignificant), across a wide variety of experimental environments. Just as we showed that activation of all meanings does not preclude an effect of meaning frequency [Simpson and Burgess, 1985], so may it allow some effect of context.

Obviously, these issues can only be resolved with further data. Regardless of the outcome of such research, however, lexical ambiguity will continue to have implications beyond the question of autonomy of language comprehension processes. Some of these implications are discussed in the next section. We will first discuss briefly the relevance of ambiguity research to the recognition of "unambiguous" words, and even for comprehension processes occurring far above the lexical level. Finally, we will review some of our attempts to use ambiguity as a model for understanding the development of word recognition abilities, and to try to distinguish between two general word recognition models.

2 Applications of Lexical Ambiguity

2.1 The Indeterminacy of Meaning

We have argued [Simpson et al., 1986] that ambiguity arising from the fact that some lexical items have two or more distinct dictionary entries, is simply an extreme and obvious example of a general vagueness or indeterminacy that is pervasive in language. Certainly, at the lexical level, all words will be subject to varying interpretations in different contexts (e.g., [Caramazza and Grober, 1976]). Research on the instantiations of general terms [Anderson, Pichert, Goetz, Schallert, Stevens, and Trollip, 1976; Whitney and Kellas, 1984], semantic flexibility [Barclay, Bransford, Franks, McCarrell, and Nitsch, 1974], and on context-dependent and independent attributes of words [Barsalou, 1982; Whitney, McKay, Kellas, and Emerson, 1985] suggest that all words carry with them more information than a person requires for comprehension of any particular message. The processes by which some of this information is selected for use in context are no less important for single-meaning words than they are for ambiguous ones. Even proper nouns exhibit this type of indeterminacy. Clark [1983; Clark and Gerrig, 1983] has argued that the appropriate sense of a word or name is not always retrieved at all, but occasionally generated spontaneously. In other words, not even names, which might seem reasonable candidates for words having a specific and consistent meaning across contexts, are free of the kind of vagueness that only shows itself more clearly in lexical ambiguity.

This indeterminacy of meaning by no means stops at the lexical level. Ambiguity at the syntactic level has generated considerable research as well [Bever, Garrett, and Hurtig, 1973; Ferreira and Clifton, 1984; Tyler and Marslen-Wilson, 1977]. Even beyond syntax is the consideration of such types of figurative language as metaphor, idiom, and indirect speech acts. These linguistic devices, in a manner similar to lexical ambiguity, present a comprehender with the necessity of selecting from among a set of possible interpretations. Presumably, a person uses context to help this selection process, as one does with ambiguous word meanings. We have also suggested [Simpson et al., 1986] that the frequency of meanings of ambiguous words may also have parallels in figurative speech, such as the syntactic frozenness of idiomatic expressions [Gibbs and Gonzales, 1985] or conventionality of indirect speech acts [Gibbs, 1981]. It is beyond the scope of the present chapter to discuss these possible extensions of lexical ambiguity, and they are dealt with elsewhere in this volume. It has simply been our intent, in this brief section, to argue that far from being unusual in language, ambiguity is widespread. It is only more prominent in the case of multiple-meaning words. It appears that much less is given explicitly in a linguistic message than we need for full understanding; the comprehender is constantly in a position of selecting among possible interpretations. Therefore, the issues studied in lexical ambiguity are important at virtually every level of language understanding.

In the remainder of this section, we discuss ways in which lexical ambiguity research may be used to shed light on questions beyond those regarding the autonomous or interactive nature of word recognition processes. Ambiguity allows for the separate assessment of retrieval of distinct meanings of a single word. It is therefore very well suited to the study of cases in which we suspect that different kinds of lexical access operations may obtain, either between different populations, or in different presentation environments. We have used ambiguity research in attempts to examine differences in word recognition processes carried out by the two cerebral hemispheres, and to look at developmental changes in word processing skills. The latter research is reviewed below, while the former is discussed elsewhere in this volume [Burgess and Simpson, Chapter 16, this volume]. We have also argued [Simpson, 1984] that lexical ambiguity may be used to examine general word recognition models, as different m appear to imply different patterns of access of the meanings of ambiguous words. We believe that some aspects of our research [Simpson and Burgess, 1985] speak to this issue, and these are also reviewed later in this chapter.

2.2 Ambiguity and Development of Word Recognition

Research in the developmental aspects of lexical access has shown consistently that children show the same kinds of benefits from context that adults show. In fact, a large number of studies have shown that contextual effects are *greater* in younger children and/or poorer readers [Schvaneveldt, Ackerman, and Semlear, 1977; Schwantes, 1981; Schwantes, Boesl, and Ritz, 1980; Simpson and Lorsbach, 1983; Simpson, Lorsbach, and Whitehouse, 1983; Stanovich, West, and Feeman, 1981; West and Stanovich, 1978]. Intuitively, such a result may seem surprising, as we would perhaps expect that readers should become more efficient as they grow older, not less so. The result is expected, however, if one views visual word recognition in terms of the use of phonological and orthographic, as well as contextual, information. If younger or poorer readers are less adept than older or better readers at stimulus encoding [Perfetti and Roth, 1981; Simpson et al., 1983], then there is a greater opportunity for context to have an influence [Stanovich, 1980]. Therefore, the decreasing context effects can be seen as the result of an increase in efficiency in another component of visual word recognition. We wondered, however, if there was another way in which children may still show improvement in context use with age. As younger children use context more, there might also be a tendency for them to use it more diffusely, while older children might restrict lexical activation to a narrower range of information. Based on our earlier arguments that a message typically requires less information for its comprehension than is available, such narrower processing would indeed be more efficient.

No literature exists to tell us whether there might be such an age-related increase in the specificity of context. A study by Merrill, Sperber, and McCauley [1981] did show that better readers encoded only those features of a noun that were consistent with the context. In that study, children made color-naming responses to words (printed in colored ink) that were features of a noun contained in a sentence. For example, subjects might hear, "The girl touched the cat," and then respond to "fur" or "claw," presented visually. For good readers, only the former feature led to color-naming interference, while for poor readers, both features interfered with the response. Lexical ambiguity is a phenomenon that we believed is ideal for studying qualitative differences in the amount of information activated during word recognition. If younger children are less restrictive in their context use, then they should be most likely to show exhaustive access of the meanings of ambiguous words. Older children, however, may be more likely to narrow processing to a single meaning.

We conducted two experiments [Simpson and Foster, 1986] to test whether older children might be more sensitive than younger ones to the frequency of meanings of homographs, as we had found adults to be [Simpson and Burgess, 1985]. Performing such research with second-graders presented several problems of stimulus selection. Although it was clear upon questioning, that children this young understood that words could have multiple meanings, and that they knew many such words, they did not know both meanings for all of the words that we had used in our research with adults. Furthermore, for some words, both meanings were present for the children, but not in the same order of dominance as for adults. For example, second-graders think first of a playground apparatus when presented with "bar," while college students think of something else. After we identified a set of ambiguous words for which children knew two meanings, and in the same order of dominance as adults [Nelson, McEvoy, Walling, and Wheeler, 1980], we presented them in a priming experiment. Second, fourth, and sixth graders named word targets that were primed by ambiguous words. Targets were related to the prime through its dominant or subordinate meaning, or were unrelated. Second and fourth graders both showed a pattern of exhaustive access, with both meanings displaying facilitation compared to the unrelated condition. Sixth graders, however, showed facilitation only for dominant associates, indicating a narrower processing of the ambiguous prime. The largest change in the amount of facilitation occurred between grades two and four. The largest qualitative change, however (i.e., change in the distribution of facilitation between the meanings), occurred between fourth and sixth grades. In fact, although sixth graders showed less facilitation overall than did fourth graders, the older children's facilitation for the dominant meaning was greater. This is the only case we know of in which contextual influence in word recognition increases with age, and it arises because the oldest children were able to restrict that influence to a single meaning.

Our research with adults [Simpson and Burgess, 1985] had led us to the conclusion that the restriction of activation to the most frequent meaning was the result of the second of two stages, the first of which was the activation of all meanings (with rate of activation dependent upon dominance), and the second the result of allocation of processing resources to information related to that dominant meaning. To examine whether the age differences in our first developmental investigation were traceable to differential reliance on these two stages, we performed a second experiment.

In this experiment, children again named targets that were primed by ambiguous words. In this case, however, we included a neutral prime condition (a row of dashes) on some trials, in order to separate the contextual influence into facilitation effects of a related context and inhibitory effects of an unrelated context (the usual indicator of deliberate allocation of attention). We also varied the SOA (as we had in our adult research), using values of 150, 300, and 750 msec, to examine possible developmental changes in the time course of ambiguous word processing. In our research with adults, only facilitation for the dominant meaning was found at very short SOAs, with subordinate associates and unrelated words not differing from each other. We reasoned that if younger children only engaged in the first stage of automatic activation of both meanings, then they should show no change in their pattern of responses as a function of SOA. Older children, on the other hand, might be expected to show a pattern tending toward inhibition of unrelated words and those related to the less frequent meaning of the ambiguous prime. This is essentially the pattern that was obtained. Second and fourth graders again showed facilitation for both meanings, and no inhibition for unrelated targets. There was a tendency for dominant associates to begin showing facilitation at earlier SOAs, but only the sixth graders showed any inhibition for subordinate associates at the longest SOA, indicating that only they engaged in the second stage of allocating resources to the dominant meaning. Our conclusion from this research was that children become more selective in their context use with age. They do so by deliberately directing attention to some of the information automatically activated on presentation of context. Younger children show the same initial activation, but not the subsequent selection process. It is the second process that is under greater subject control, which we have previously found to increase in children's word recognition [Simpson and Lorsbach, 1983]. In both studies, we have found that such deliberate processes become prominent (in word recognition) between grades four and six, well after children have begun to show the decline in magnitude of contextual facilitation typically found with increasing age. The word recognition processes of children, in other words, undergo qualitative as well as quantitative change, and we would argue that lexical ambiguity provides an ideal paradigm by which to study such qualitative changes.

2.3 *Ambiguity and Word Recognition Models*

Questions regarding the effects of context on word recognition have been among the most active in cognitive psychology in recent years. Generally, most of this work (both that with single-word and sentence contexts) has revolved around two models of context effects: one derived from the work of Posner and Snyder [1975], and the other, the verification model of Becker [1980; Becker and Killion, 1977]. According to the former view [Neely, 1976, 1977; Stanovich and West, 1979, 1981], there are two ways in which context may affect subsequent word recognition. The first is through a rapid and automatic spread of activation among closely related words [Collins and Loftus, 1975]. The second is via a slower, conscious allocation of processing resources to some of these activated words. If one of these words is then presented, its recognition is quite fast. If, however, unrelated information occurs, attention must be redirected, and a response based on this unrelated information is delayed, relative to a condition in which no context has occurred. Complete discussion of the application of such a model to ambiguous words is available elsewhere [Simpson, 1984]. For the time being, we will say only that this model fits quite comfortably with the lexical ambiguity literature dealing with ambiguous words in isolation, as well as that concerned with the effects of biasing context. In the latter case, it is held that the first, automatic stage leads to the simultaneous activation of all meanings. The second, more conscious stage involves the selection of a single contextually appropriate meaning and its integration with the building representation of the discourse. Ambiguity researchers [e.g., Yates, 1978] as well as more general word recognition theorists [e.g., Stanovich and West, 1983] have argued in favor of such an interpretation of context effects on ambiguity. In the absence of context, our research [Simpson and Burgess, 1985] has supported such a model, showing that, initially, activation builds for both meanings (at rates commensurate with their frequencies) until both are activated to approximately the same degree. Subsequently, the advantage for the dominant meaning is reestablished, and associates of the less frequent meaning are treated as unrelated words, resulting in inhibition of responses based on them. Such inhibition is typically taken as strong evidence that a controlled process is operating.

The verification model [Becker, 1979, 1980; Becker and Killion, 1977; Eisenberg and Becker, 1982] provides a substantially different explanation for the effects of context. When a word is presented, a set of candidates is generated on the basis of features extracted from the word. A second stage, verification, consists of a comparison of these candidates with the visual representation of the stimulus until a match is found. Prior context, however, leads to the creation of a set of candidates even before the stimulus is presented. When it then occurs, the verification can begin without awaiting the creation of the set based on visual features. According to Becker [1980], furthermore, facilitation and inhibition effects arise from the adoption of two processing strategies that yield semantically generated sets of different sizes. If the semantic set is made up of a small number of candidates, the comparison is performed very quickly. This will result in facilitation for a word in the set, but an unrelated word will not show much inhibition, as verification based on feature extraction may begin as soon as the comparison of the short semantically based list is complete. If the semantic set is long, however, this will have the effect, on the average, of reducing facilitation for items in the set. In addition, there will be considerable inhibition for words not in the set, as their verification must await completion of the first comparison. In short, stimuli that lead to the generation of large semantic sets show an inhibition-dominant pattern of responding, while those that result in smaller lists will yield a picture of facilitation dominance.

Becker [1980] discussed the relevance of his model to the processing of ambiguous words in context. He suggested, based on a comparison of research that had shown context-dependent access [Swinney and Hakes, 1976] and research showing exhaustive access [Conrad, 1974] that different kinds of contexts would lead to the adoption of different strategies. Strongly biasing context should lead to selective access, as the semantic set of candidates would be related to the biased meaning. Weaker context, on the other hand, would allow the semantic set to be formed from candidates related to either meaning, and more equal facilitation for each would be seen. Becker also predicted that a pattern of selective access should be seen in an environment of facilitation dominance, as it arises from a small semantic set. Nonselective access, on the other hand, should be accompanied by an overall pattern of inhibition dominance.

Although we did not include biasing context in our earlier research [Simpson and Burgess, 1985], we nevertheless had some opportunity to test some predictions from the verification model, as it makes general predictions about the distribution of facilitation and inhibition effects for any case in which the the selectivity of processing is a concern. Becker [1980] indicates that selective processing of homographs should lead to facilitation dominance, while multiple activation results in inhibition dominance. We had found a pattern of selective access at a long SOA, so we conducted a subsequent experiment, which included a neutral condition, to separate facilitation and inhibition effects. Furthermore, we varied the proportion of trials on which dominant and subordinate targets were presented. For one group of subjects, dominant and subordinate targets occurred with equal frequency. For another, 80% of the targets were related to the dominant meaning; for a third, only 20% of the trials used dominant targets, while 80% were related to the subordinate meaning. According to a two-process approach to ambiguous word recognition, we would expect subjects to focus attention on one meaning, showing facilitation for words related to it, and inhibition both for unrelated words and associates of the other meaning, relative to the neutral prime condition. In both the 50%- and the 80%-dominant conditions, we would expect the selected meaning to be the dominant one. We reasoned, however, that if subjects are able to control the retrieval process, then in the 20%-dominant condition, facilitation should be seen only for that meaning, whereas dominant associates, along with unrelated words, would show inhibition. On the other hand, the verification model predicts that selective access should be seen in an overall environment of facilitation dominance, because selective retrieval should result in a smaller semantic set. We also thought it possible, however, that even in the 20%-dominant group, subjects could not eliminate dominant associates from the semantic set. If this were the case, we would expect the 20% condition to lead to equivalent response times for associates of either meaning, within an overall pattern of inhibition dominance.

The results were clearly more supportive of the two-process approach. The 50%- and 80%-dominant groups showed facilitation for the more frequent meaning only, and inhibition for all other targets (unrelated and those related to the subordinate meaning). In other words, we obtained selective access within a pattern of both facilitation and inhibition. Indeed, even the results of the 20%-dominant group did not deviate from this pattern. However, in this latter group, the inhibition of subordinate associates was much smaller than in the other conditions. This, coupled with the fact that nearly half of the subjects in this group showed facilitation for subordinate targets, led us to entertain the possibility that the data for the 20% group represented the combined data from two subgroups of subjects, one showing a pattern similar to that of the 80% subjects, and a second that was able to focus instead on the subordinate meaning. In order to examine this possibility, we performed a median split of the 20% group, based on the amount of facilitation for subordinate-related targets. The results of that split are shown in Figure 10.1.

The right panel of Figure 10.1 shows the subgroup that displayed the greatest amount of inhibition for subordinate meanings. This group shows a pattern that is similar to that obtained for the 80% group. The left panel represents the group that showed facilitation for subordinate associates. This group shows facilitation for both meanings, but not inhibition for unrelated targets.

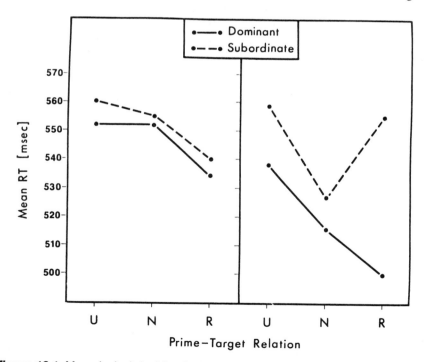

Figure 10.1 Mean lexical decision latency as a function of prime-target relatedness and meaning dominance for two subgroups of subjects receiving 20% dominant targets.

This pattern of facilitation without inhibition suggests that this subgroup of subjects did not engage in the kind of post-access process that characterized the other subgroup or those in the 80%-dominant group. It does not appear that subjects are able to control access to ambiguous word meanings to the extent of reversing the usual trend, and select only subordinate meanings at the expense of the more frequent.

This conclusion was further confirmed by a group of subjects that again received only 20% dominant targets, but this time were informed of the prevalence of subordinate trials, and specifically instructed to attempt to focus on the less frequent meanings. This group nevertheless showed strong facilitation only for the dominant meaning, and inhibition for the subordinate. Taken together, the results of this study led us to conclude that the frequency of an ambiguous word's meaning is a powerful determinant of the speed with which it can be retrieved, and a factor that is not easy to overcome [Lucas, 1984; Simpson, 1981].

The results of our research, then, have generally been more in line with an ambiguity model that is based on a two-process word recognition view than with the verification model. Although Becker [1980] made his predictions for ambiguous words on the basis of the effects of context, the model does predict that any selective access should appear in a facilitation-dominant pattern. That clearly was not the case, as we repeatedly found both facilitation and inhibition accompanied by selection of the dominant meaning only. The one case in which we did find a facilitation-dominant pattern was also the only one in which we found nonselective access. In no case, then, did the picture of results favor the verification view.

3 *Concluding Remarks*

Although we did not initially intend for our research to consist primarily of tests of general models of word recognition or of developmental aspects of lexical processing, we do believe that the work in ambiguity has implications for these areas. In light of our earlier arguments regarding the tendency for all words (and, indeed, higher levels of linguistic processing) to exhibit an indeterminacy of meaning, it is clear that any model of word recognition requires an explanation of processes by which such indeterminacy may be resolved. Likewise, the developmental research is of interest not only because of what it might tell us of the development of ambiguity processing *per se*, but also because of what it may tell us more generally about qualitative, strategic changes in linguistic processes with increasing age. We believe, in short, that ambiguity is of intrinsic interest because of its prevalence in language, and of interest also as a tool for exploring other facets of human language use.

Acknowledgments

Preparation of this manuscript was supported in part by a U.S. Department of Education Grant G008630072 to the Kansas Bureau of Child Research and the Learning Disabilities Institute of the University of Kansas, and was completed while the first author was a fellow in the Child Language Program of the University of Kansas.

References

Anderson, R.C., Pichert, J.W., Goetz, E.T., Schallert, D.L., Stevens, K.V., and Trollip, S.R. 1976. Instantiation of general terms. *Journal of Verbal Learning and Verbal Behavior* 15:667–679.

Barclay, J.R., Bransford, J.D., Franks, J.J., McCarrell, N.S., and Nitsch, K. 1974. Comprehension and semantic flexibility. *Journal of Verbal Learning and Verbal Behavior* 13:471–488.

Barsalou, L.W. 1982. Context-independent and context-dependent information in concepts. *Memory and Cognition* 10:82–93.

Becker, C.A. 1979. Semantic context and word frequency effects in visual word recognition. *Journal of Experimental Psychology: Human Perception and Performance* 5:252–259.

Becker, C.A. 1980. Semantic context effects in visual word recognition: An analysis of semantic strategies. *Memory and Cognition* 8:493–512.

Becker, C.A., and Killion, T.H. 1977. Interaction of visual and cognitive effects in word recognition. *Journal of Experimental Psychology: Human Perception and Performance* 3:389–401.

Bever, T.G., Garrett, M.F., and Hurtig, R. 1973. The interaction of perceptual processes and ambiguous sentences. *Memory and Cognition* 1:277–286.

Burgess, C., and Simpson, G.B. This volume.

Caramazza, A., and Grober, E. 1976. Polysemy and the structure of the subjective lexicon. In C. Rameh (ed.), *Georgetown University Round Table on Languages and Linguistics*, pp. 181–206. Washington, DC: Georgetown University Press.

Clark, H.H. 1983. Making sense of nonce sense. In G.B. Flores d'Arcais and R. Jarvella (eds.), *The Process of Understanding Language*, pp. 297–331. New York: Wiley.

Clark, H.H., and Gerrig, R.J. 1983. Understanding old words with new meanings. *Journal of Verbal Learning and Verbal Behavior* 22:591–608.

Collins, A.M., and Loftus, E.F. 1975. A spreading-activation theory of semantic memory. *Psychological Review* 82:407–428.

Conrad, C. 1974. Context effects in sentence comprehension: A study of the subjective lexicon. *Memory and Cognition* 2:130–138.

Eisenberg, P., and Becker, C.A. 1982. Semantic context effects in visual word recognition, sentence processing, and reading: Evidence for semantic strategies. *Journal of Experimental Psychology: Human Perception and Performance* 8:739–756.

Ferreira, F., and Clifton, C., Jr. 1984. The role of discourse context in resolving syntactic ambiguity. Paper presented at the annual meeting of the Psychonomic Society, San Antonio, Texas.

Forster, K.I., and Bednall, E.S. 1976. Terminating and exhaustive search in lexical access. *Memory and Cognition* 4:53–61.

Gibbs, R.W., Jr. 1981. Your wish is my command: Convention and context in interpreting indirect requests. *Journal of Verbal Learning and Verbal Behavior* 20:435–444.

Gibbs, R.W., Jr., and Gonzales, G.P. 1985. Syntactic frozenness in processing and remembering idioms. *Cognition* 20:243–259.

Glucksberg, S., Kreuz, R.J., and Rho, S. 1986. Context can constrain lexical access: Implications for interactive models of language comprehension. *Journal of Experimental Psychology: Learning, Memory, and Cognition* 12: 323–335.

Hogaboam, T.W., and Perfetti, C.A. 1975. Lexical ambiguity and sentence comprehension. *Journal of Verbal Learning and Verbal Behavior* 14:265–274.

Kinoshita, S. 1985. Sentence context effects on lexically ambiguous words: Evidence for a postaccess inhibition process. *Memory and Cognition* 13: 579–595.

Lucas, M. 1984. Frequency and context effects in lexical ambiguity resolution Technical Report No. 14. University of Rochester, Cognitive Science, Rochester, NY.

Merrill, E.C., Sperber, R.D., and McCauley, C. 1981. Differences in semantic encoding as a function of reading comprehension skill. *Memory and Cognition* 9:618–624.

Neely, J.H. 1976. Semantic priming and retrieval from lexical memory: Evidence for facilitatory and inhibitory processes. *Memory and Cognition* 4: 648–654.

Neely, J.H. 1977. Semantic priming and retrieval from lexical memory: Roles of inhibitionless spreading activation and limited capacity attention. *Journal of Experimental Psychology: General* 106:226–254.

Nelson, D.L., McEvoy, C.L., Walling, J.R., and Wheeler, J.W., Jr. 1980. The University of South Florida homograph norms. *Behavior Research Methods and Instrumentation* 12:16–37.

Onifer, W., and Swinney, D.A. 1981. Accessing lexical ambiguities during sentence comprehension: Effects of frequency of meaning and contextual bias. *Memory and Cognition* 9:225–236.

Perfetti, C.A., and Roth, S. 1981. Some of the interactive processes in reading and their role in reading skill. In A.M. Lesgold and C.A. Perfetti (eds.), *Interactive Processes in Reading*, pp. 269–297. Hillsdale: Erlbaum.

Posner, M.I., and Snyder, C.R.R. 1975. Attention and cognitive control. In R.L. Solso (ed.), *Information processing and cognition: The Loyola Symposium*, pp. 55–85. Hillsdale: Erlbaum.

Schvaneveldt, R.W., Ackerman, B.P., and Semlear, T. 1977. The effects of semantic context on children's word recognition. *Child Development* 48: 612–616.

Schvaneveldt, R.W., Meyer, D.E., and Becker, C.A. 1976. Lexical ambiguity, semantic context, and visual word recognition. *Journal of Experimental Psychology: Human Perception and Performance* 2:243–256.

Schwantes, F.M. 1981. Locus of the context effect in children's word recognition. *Child Development* 52:895–903.

Schwantes, F.M., Boesl, S.L., and Ritz, E.G. 1980. Children's use of context in word recognition: A psycholinguistic guessing game. *Child Development* 51: 730–736.

Seidenberg, M.S., Tanenhaus, M.K., Leiman, J.M., and Bienkowski, M. 1982. Automatic access of the meanings of ambiguous words in context: Some limitations of knowledge-based processing. *Cognitive Psychology* 14:489–537.

Shiffrin, R.M., and Schneider, W. 1977. Controlled and automatic human information processing: II. Perceptual learning, automatic attending, and a general theory. *Psychological Review* 84:127–190.

Simpson, G.B. 1981. Meaning dominance and semantic context in the processing of lexical ambiguity. *Journal of Verbal Learning and Verbal Behavior* 20:120–136.

Simpson, G.B. 1984. Lexical ambiguity and its role in models of word recognition. *Psychological Bulletin* 96:316–340.

Simpson, G.B., and Burgess, C. 1985. Activation and selection processes in the recognition of ambiguous words. *Journal of Experimental Psychology: Human Perception and Performance* 11:28–39.

Simpson, G.B., Burgess, C., and Peterson, R.R. 1986. *Comprehension Processes and the Indeterminacy Of Meaning*. Manuscript submitted for publication.

Simpson, G.B., and Foster, M.R. 1986. Lexical ambiguity and children's word recognition. *Developmental Psychology* 22:147–154.

Simpson, G.B., and Lorsbach, T.C. 1983. The development of automatic and conscious components of contextual facilitation. *Child Development* 54: 760–772.

Simpson, G.B., Lorsbach, T.C., and Whitehouse, D. 1983. Encoding and contextual components of word recognition in good and poor readers. *Journal of Experimental Child Psychology* 35:161–171.

Stanovich, K.E. 1980. Toward an interactive-compensatory model of individual differences in the development of reading fluency. *Reading Research Quarterly* 16:32–71.

Stanovich, K.E., and West, R.F. 1979. Mechanisms of sentence context effects in reading: Automatic activation and conscious attention. *Memory and Cognition* 7:77–85.

Stanovich, K.E., and West, R.F. 1981. The effect of sentence context on ongoing word recognition: Tests of a two-process theory. *Journal of Experimental Psychology: Human Perception and Performance* 7:658–672.

Stanovich, K.E., and West, R.F. 1983. On priming by a sentence context. *Journal of Experimental Psychology: General* 112:1–36.

Stanovich, K.E., West, R.F., and Feeman, D.J. 1981. A longitudinal study of sentence context effects in second-grade children: Tests of an interactive-compensatory model. *Journal of Experimental Child Psychology* 32:185–199.

Swinney, D.A. 1979. Lexical access during sentence comprehension: (Re)consideration of context effects. *Journal of Verbal Learning and Verbal Behavior* 18:645–659.

Swinney, D.A., and Hakes, D.T. 1976. Effects of prior context upon lexical access during sentence comprehension. *Journal of Verbal Learning and Verbal Behavior* 15:681–689.

Tanenhaus, M.K., and Lucas, M.M. In press. Context effects in lexical processing. *Cognition*.

Tanenhaus, M.K., Leiman, J.M., and Seidenberg, M.K. 1979. Evidence for multiple stages in the processing of ambiguous words in syntactic contexts. *Journal of Verbal Learning and Verbal Behavior* 18:427–440.

Tyler, L.K., and Marslen-Wilson, W.D. 1977. The on-line effects of semantic context on syntactic processing. *Journal of Verbal Learning and Verbal Behavior* 16:683–692.

West, R.F., and Stanovich, K.E. 1978. Automatic contextual facilitation in readers of three ages. *Child Development* 49:717–727.

Whitney, P., and Kellas, G. 1984. Processing category terms in context: Instantiation and the structure of semantic categories. *Journal of Experimental Psychology: Learning, Memory, and Cognition* 10:95–103.

Whitney, P., McKay, T., Kellas, G., and Emerson, W.A., Jr. 1985. Semantic activation of noun concepts in context. *Journal of Experimental Psychology: Learning, Memory, and Cognition* 11:126–135.

Yates, J. 1978. Priming dominant and unusual senses of ambiguous words. *Memory and Cognition* 6:636–643.

Lexical Processing and Ambiguity Resolution: An Autonomous Process in an Interactive Box

P. A. Prather
University of Illinois, Chicago

David A. Swinney
The Graduate Center
City University of New York

1 *Introduction*

Examinations of the nature of lexical ambiguity resolution have formed the major arena for study of a number of the basic questions concerning natural language understanding. Chief among these, and one which has been most clearly elaborated and detailed by Fodor [1983], is that concerning mental modularity. This issue, which revolves around the question of whether human cognition is, in general, comprised of a set of informationally encapsulated, autonomous sybsystems, or whether it is a totally interactive system, lies at the heart of our basic conception of the nature of cognitive activity. There appears to be undeniable support for the modularity thesis at some level of processing (see e.g., [Fodor, 1983; Garrett, 1985]). However, that portion of the argument specific to the modularity of *lexical* processing has proven extraordinarily vexatious. Examinations of lexical autonomy/modularity represent a field of endeavor that has produced seemingly conflicting evidence and a myriad of counterclaims throughout the short history of psycholinguistics.

In what follows, we organize old and present new evidence that bears on the issue of whether or not initial word perception is accomplished by an autonomous lexical processing subroutine—in short, a module. In the course of this analysis, we examine critical issues and relevant evidence concerning lexical ambiguity resolution.

Ambiguity is ubiquitous in language; it exists at every level of processing (from acoustic/phonetic to semantic to structural, etc.). An obvious, but important, point about this observation is that there is no reason to believe (nor has anyone seriously proposed) that these disparate types of ambiguity are each resolved in the same manner during language processing. We argue here that this same general point holds true for lexical ambiguity: there is no uniform, invariant solution to lexical ambiguity resolution (although such solutions may be monogenic). Rather, lexical ambiguity resolution is a complex function of at least four general types of issues: (1) The nature of the temporal processing requirements during perception (e.g., speed of utterance, speed of required response, etc.). (2) The nature of the available "contextual" information in which the ambiguity occurs (e.g., type of constraints, level of information, relationship to ambiguity). (3) The nature of the processing strategies recruited for analysis (e.g., automatized routines, intentional strategies, linguistic/perceptual vs. problem solving routines, etc.). (4) The nature of the response required of the processing system or, in experiments, of the experimental situation (e.g., passive comprehension, rapid recognition, use of the ambiguity in novel manner, etc.). The complexity and interactivity of these issues cannot be overrated.

This chapter will elaborate on certain aspects of each of these issues in ambiguity resolution, with a focus on the underlying question concerning mental modularity. In what follows, we detail evidence which we feel strongly supports the view that there is a brief period of time in the perception of a word during which the lexical processing routine cannot be interrupted or influenced by prior information or by other ongoing, non-lexical processes. We conceptualize this as a narrow temporal "window" of autonomous lexical processing, a "window of contextual impenetrability," if you will. However, the "window" accounts for only a small part of what traditionally is considered to be lexical processing, and the temporal parameters of this window are not fixed. Whether or not the lexicon is considered to be an autonomous module will be based in large part, we argue, on how the boundaries (temporal and otherwise) of the lexicon are defined. We will also examine lexical ambiguity resolution evidence which has been argued to support the non-modularity view of lexical processing, and we provide an alternative explanation of these data, one focussed on issues of specialized processing strategies and erroneous initial assumptions underlying these experiments. In addition, we present some data to substantiate our arguments.

We begin with a brief consideration of the parameters of lexical processing, following which we present evidence supporting the view that there is a brief "window" of contextual invulnerability in lexical processing that meets the criteria for autonomy. We then consider the implications of this evidence for characterization of the lexicon as a truly modular component in language processing in the light of certain counterclaims. Finally, we briefly consider the merits of recent claims about what has been called backward priming, claims that have been argued to undermine the autonomy view.

2 Parameters of Lexical Processing

Current models of cognitive organization typically allow that there are several separable domains of cognitive processing, among them the language domain. Within the language domain, it is generally held that acoustic/phonetic, lexical, and semantic and syntactic processes are at least potentially separable information sources. Garrett [1984], Forster [1979], Fodor [1983], and Morton [1982], among others, have argued that in fact these are separate and autonomous subroutines or sub-modules within the language domain, each potentially operating at least somewhat in parallel with the others, in cases where interactions among these information sources are limited to the outputs of these autonomous modules. (Note, however, that there is much disagreement among those cited above concerning the degree of parallelism in the system.)

Within this conceptualization, the lexicon is generally characterized as that module within which either the acoustic/phonetic or orthographic code (depending on input modality) is connected with an informational data base for that code, a data base which contains information that allows assignment of word meaning, recognition that the code constitutes a word, or whatever else is required of the processor. Word understanding thus involves perception of the speech/orthographic code which provides access to this data base; word production involves the reverse of this process of assigning a code from a given meaning/data base (see e.g., [Garrett, 1984; Bowles and Poon, 1985]). One of the major areas of controversy in characterizing the lexicon is the question of whether or not the assignment of meaning in comprehension (the process typically labeled lexical access) is influenced by non-lexical knowledge. Simply put, can a prior context direct access in the lexicon? The implications with respect to claims of modularity are obvious: if lexical access is penetrated by prior context, then it is not an autonomous process. If, alternatively, access operates independent of contextual effects, then it is autonomous (at least with respect to semantic information). This question has been examined empirically primarily by studying the assignment of meaning to ambiguous words—the resolution of lexical ambiguity. If a prior, disambiguating context serves to restrict access to just one meaning of an ambiguous word, the autonomy view of lexical access is undermined.

Results from studies examining effects of a prior context on disambiguation have appeared to sometimes support and sometimes contradict autonomy claims. Before examining this evidence, however, a brief consideration of the temporal characteristics of the lexical processing is in order. As is undoubtedly clear, our decision about whether or not to characterize lexical processing as autonomous will hinge on careful assessment of precisely what is to be considered as purely lexical processing and what is categorizable as being outside of (either pre- or post-) lexical processing.

2.1 *The Time Course of Automatic and Intentional Lexical Processes*

Inferences about the nature and time course of lexical processing have been derived primarily from various types of "on- line" studies, the most influential of which to date have been those using semantic priming effects. In initial demonstrations of the priming effect, it was shown that prior processing of a word facilitates subsequent (repeat) processing of both that word and words highly associated with it [Meyer and Schvaneveldt, 1971]. Since then, evidence has been accumulating to support an inference that priming is an obligatory, fast-acting and autonomous process—in short, an automatic one (e.g., [Neely, 1977; Seidenberg et al., 1984]).

In one of the clearest demonstrations that priming is automatic and obligatory, Neely [1977] told subjects to expect words from a particular category (building parts) following words from another category (body parts). Subjects were presented word pairs sequentially, and asked to make lexical decisions on the second word. On most trials, when a body part was the prime, the target was in fact a building part (e.g., "heart - door"); however, on some trials, unexpected but associatively related targets were presented (e.g., "heart - chest"). Neely examined these expectancy and associative relationships at several different SOAs, and found that facilitation was determined by associative relationships alone at short SOAs (less than 450 msec), but that as SOA increased, facilitation was increasingly determined by expectancy relationships. By 2000 msec, *only* expectancy relationships were facilitated, and unexpected targets, even when associatively related, were *inhibited.*

These data suggested that lexical access involves an initial process of activation of the node associated with a particular phonological code and its associates, independently of "top down," intentional processes. Only subsequently are intention or context observed to have an effect on lexical processes. Results from a number of studies are consistent with this inference that "early" priming effects (those existing immediately after presentation of the prime) are automatic and are based only on associative relationships. In a careful study of different types of "association" between words, Seidenberg, Waters, Sanders and Langer [1984] found that certain types of association did, but others did *not*, facilitate performance on a naming task. With an SOA (Stimulus Onset Asynchrony) of 500 or 600 msec, and an ISI (Interstimulus Interval, that is, time between offset of first and onset of second stimulus) of 0 msec, syntactic priming (e.g., "men-swear," "whose-planet"), proportion of related pairs (inducing a relatedness set), and backward associations (e.g., "paper-fly," "toy-tinker") were all found to be non-facilitators. By contrast, forward associative primes (e.g., "fly-paper," "tinker-toy," "dog-bark") *did* facilitate performance on the naming task within the range that Neely found to be "pre-intentional." Consistent with the results of Seidenberg et al., den Heyer, Briand, and Dannenbring [1983] report that manipulating the proportion of related pairs (a manipulation reasonably argued to affect intentional processing) affected performance on a lexical decision task at a 1000 msec SOA but not at a 75 msec SOA.

In all, these and other data suggest an important distinction between associative and intentional effects of a prime on a target with respect to time course of processing. (See [Posner and Snyder, 1975; Shiffrin and Schneider, 1977], for discussion of the more general basis for this distinction.) In the remainder of this paper, we will distinguish between these two types of facilitation effects by referring to them as "associative priming" and "intentional context effects" respectively.

Initiation of associative priming effects seems to occur relatively quickly; a number of studies have demonstrated associative priming with as short as a 40 to 50 msec SOA (e.g., [Fischler and Goodman, 1978; Warren, 1972, 1977]). Less well established is duration of associative priming, as most research has focussed on determining whether and how soon priming effects obtain. In one of the few studies directed towards examining the time course of decay of automatic priming effects, Warren [1972] suggested that "activation" persists for about 40 sec post-stimulus presentation (see also [Loess and Waugh, 1967]). However, while facilitation effects do (or can) seem to persist for a relatively long period of time, it is not clear if those effects are due to associative priming or rather to intentional maintenance of that initially automatic effect. As noted above, Neely [1977] found that associative priming occurs at least as early as 250 msec, while intentional context effects initiate considerably later (at about 750 msec, in his study). It is at least possible, then, that priming effects measured after about 750 msec reflect intentional (though not necessarily conscious) rather than automatic processing. Note, however, that the temporal demarcation dividing automatic associative priming from intentional effects is more likely a function of the *type* of processing going on than an *absolute* temporal parameter.

2.2 *Paradigm-based Issues in the Examination of Lexical Processing*

Most priming studies have used a paradigm in which subjects are presented with isolated pairs or triplets of words, some subset of which are related associatively. It seems quite likely that, whether or not they are told to look for relationships between words in a pair, subjects would adopt such an approach as a strategy on the assumption that there must be some reason the experimenter isolated these two words together (see [de Groot, Thomassen, and Hudson, 1982; Swinney, 1981], for similar arguments). Also, since stimulus inputs stop after the target item in these paradigms, there is no external stimulus to disrupt or inhibit processing of the target word as there is in normal conversational speech. Thus, the pair or triplet paradigms provide a perfect setting for controlled or intentional effects to take place. Thus, the "pair" paradigm does not seem particularly well suited to studying the time course of automatic associative priming effects in normal, fluent language; while it may accurately reflect initiation of priming, it cannot guarantee separation of intentional from automatic effects.

In a recent study designed to examine this issue, Prather, Pasquotto, Seimen, and Lawson [1986] used a "continuous list" rather than a "pair" paradigm to study the time course of automatic priming. A long list (216) of words was presented one at a time on a video monitor; SOA between words varied from 500 to 2250 msec, and the ratio of associatively related to unrelated words occurring sequentially in the list was 14 to 166 (8.4%). The subjects' task was to read each word as quickly as possible (a "naming" task). As soon as the subject began to say the word, it was removed from the screen and the SOA initiated. The assumption in using this paradigm was that reading lists rather than isolated pairs of words would minimize using a strategy of looking for relationships between words, particularly when very few of the words were related. Also, because words were presented continuously, subjects could not choose (consciously or unconsciously) to delay their response to a target. In all, it is a task that may give a better look at automatic processing effects than does the pair paradigm.

Using this paradigm, Prather et al. found a small (non-significant) facilitation for forward-associated items at 500 msec. That effect increased and was largest (and significant) at 700 msec, then gradually decreased to the point where there was no significant effect by 2250 msec (see Figure 11.1). These data are taken as evidence that automatic effects diminish passively over time and, at least in this continuous processing task, are gone within approximately 2 seconds. It is important to note that Prather et al. did not find immediate "early" priming using the continuous list paradigm. Given that immediate priming is virtually always found when using the pair paradigm on these materials, it seems reasonable to assume that lack of an immediate effect in this study has to do with the paradigm used. One possible explanation of the difference is that continuous processing may encompass both the automatic facilitation seen in the pair paradigm *and* an inhibition effect. Processing of a lexical code may yield activation of associates and inhibition of non-associates of words in the list. Together, these might well produce a narrowing of the "window" (change in onset of both the beginning and end points) during which automatic associative priming takes place.

With respect to the general temporal course of processing, however, the basic conclusion is similar whether using continuous or pair presentations: there seems to be a short period of time during which lexical priming is automatic, in the sense of being passive and unintentional, followed rapidly by availability of lexical processes of intentional or controlled processes. When processing is rapid and continuous (a situation that discourages specific intentional strategies between words), automatic associative priming effects are largest roughly 700 msec after occurrence of the word and are virtually gone within 2 sec. When intentional processes are allowed or encouraged, both the initial rise time and the decay of associate priming appears to be somewhat earlier (see, e.g., [Neely, 1977; Simpson, 1984]).

To summarize the evidence from studies of temporal and paradigmatic issues in examinations of lexical processing, it can be seen that data from lexical priming studies suggest that there exists a temporal "window" of autonomous lexical processing during which the data base connected to a phonological/orthographic code and its close associates are activated. This temporal window seems to be relatively narrow, where the specific beginning and end points of the window vary with specific task and materials conditions. However, the important point is that processing of information in that window appears to be immune from intentional effects.

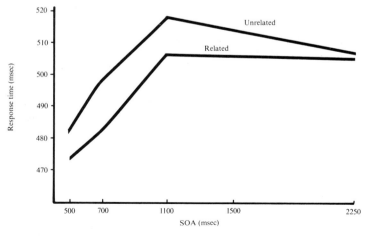

Figure 11.1 Mean reaction time for primed words (Related) and their unprimed controls (Unrelated) when presented in continuous list format at variable SOAs.

3 Accessing Ambiguous Words in the Lexicon: Ambiguity Resolution

Having discussed some aspects of the temporal and paradigmatic boundaries on lexical processing, we now turn to empirical studies examining the question of whether or not prior contexts (particularly semantic and syntactic contexts) can *restrict* lexical access for an ambiguous word. In particular, we consider whether or not the early "automatic" period in lexical processing is truly autonomous. It is important in this regard to briefly consider the issue of precisely what *types* of effects can be taken as support for and against a modularist position. The lexical modularist position holds that *non-lexical* processes will not directly influence *lexical* access. It is important to note that associative priming (priming between associated lexical items) is actually a within-lexical effect. Consequently, a "context" that is associatively related and (temporally near) an ambiguous word could act on processing of that ambiguous word *within* the lexical module. This type of effect cannot be taken as evidence for interaction *between* modules (see [Fodor, 1983; Seidenberg et al., 1982; Tanenhaus, Carlson and Seidenberg, 1984]). Consequently, to claim strong evidence against a lexical modularist position and in favor of some alternative type of interactive model, either a distant context greater than 200 or so msecs) or a non-associative context would have to be shown to restrict access. With that in mind, we review studies that examine the effects of context on ambiguity processing.

3.1 Context Effects and Ambiguous Words

A number of different paradigms have been used to examine the effects of context on ambiguous words, notably: phoneme monitoring, word monitoring, sentence decision, Rapid Serial Visual Presentation (RSVP), modified Stroop (interference) tasks, and various priming paradigms, both within modality (e.g., [Schvaneveldt et al., 1976]) and across modalities (e.g., [Swinney, 1979; Tanenhaus, Leiman, and Seidenberg, 1979]). Only certain of these tasks, however, are of relevance in examining the issue of restricted access. Studies demonstrating that ambiguous words place an increased load on processing based on tasks such as phoneme or word monitoring (e.g., [Foss and Jenkins, 1973]) offer only indirect evidence for multiple access of meanings. If context restricts access, the prediction is not just that there will be a decrease in processing load, but more specifically, that the contextually inappropriate meaning will not be present. It could, for example, be the case that context will reduce processing load in such studies by allowing faster access to one or both meanings, but will *not* restrict access to just one meaning (see, e.g., [Onifer and Swinney, 1981]). In short, processing load offers suggestive evidence, but only tasks sensitive to which meanings have been accessed offer convincing evidence for or against *restricted* access. Paradigms using priming and interference effects *do* allow for examination of which meanings have been accessed. Consequently, in the following review, we will restrict consideration to studies that have used priming or interference paradigms.

Studies are also differentiated with respect to whether the ambiguous target word is presented in the context of a pair or triplet of isolated words or rather in the context of a sentence. This difference is an important one. As noted earlier, a paradigm in which words are presented as isolated pairs allows and even encourages looking for relationships between words, which seems likely to increase the effects of a context over those effects normally available in discourse processing. Sentence contexts, on the other hand, are more likely to disallow such intentional processing. While all paradigms allow examination of some type of context effects, they cannot be compared directly, nor will results using one type of context necessarily predict effects observed when using the other. Consequently, data from pair and sentence studies is considered separately, even though this paper is intended to focus primarily on ambiguity resolution in normal language comprehension.

3.2 *Word Studies*

As elaborated earlier, there have been a large number of studies that use word pairs to examine priming effects. However, only a few have systematically examined the effects of a prior associative prime on access of *ambiguous* words. When evaluated in terms of the time course of lexical processing, evidence from those studies is consistent with claims that a prior priming context does not restrict access. This evidence therefore supports claims for autonomy of the lexical access routine.

Simpson [1981] presented ambiguous words in pairs with an ambiguous word as the prime and one of its two meanings as the target (e.g., "bank-money," "bank-river"); the control condition was an unrelated ambiguity-target pair (e.g., "calf-money"). While there was no semantic context in this experiment, Simpson elected non-equibias ambiguous words, that is, words that had an inherent bias towards one meaning (for example, the "money" meaning of bank is much more frequent than the "river" meaning). The prime word was presented until the subject made a lexical decision, and then the target immediately followed (0 msec ISI). The results showed significant facilitation on a lexical decision task for the target word related to the dominant meaning of the ambiguity ("bank-money"), but no facilitation for the subordinate meaning ("bank-river"), relative to the relevant control pair. Simpson argued from these data that meanings of ambiguous words are retrieved in order, and that the dominant meaning is retrieved first and exclusively if there is no contradictory context. In a more recent study, however, Simpson and Burgess [1985] varied the delay between prime and target, and found that while the dominant meaning is facilitated at shorter SOAs (16 msec), both meanings are facilitated at a slightly longer SOA (100 msec); subsequently, activation of the subordinate meaning diminished while that of the dominant meaning increased. It seems, then, that the rise time for the dominant meaning is more rapid and that that meaning is selected for continued attention, while the subordinate meaning is accessed but somewhat more slowly, at least when there is no prior semantic bias.

With respect to the effects of a semantic bias, Schvaneveldt, Meyer, and Becker [1976] offer a very comprehensive examination of the effects of context on ambiguity resolution. In their study, Schvaneveldt et al. presented subjects with sequential word triplets. The subjects made a lexical decision on each word, and as soon as the decision was made for one, the next word in the triplet was presented. Experimental triplets included an ambiguous word as the first or second word in the triplet; contexts included a concordant bias, that is, a word that biased the ambiguity towards the target word (e.g., "save-bank-*money*"), a bias discordant with that word (e.g., "river-bank-*money*") and a "null" bias (e.g., "river-date-*money*"). Basically, the results showed that when there was a concordant context, lexical decision on the target word (here, "money") was facilitated relative to the null-context condition; when the context was discordant, the target word was not facilitated.

These data are taken as consistent with an inference that when there is a strong prior biasing context, only one meaning of an ambiguous word, the contextually appropriate meaning, is accessed. However, given Simpson's results with longer SOAs, the conclusion in favor of restricted *access* must be viewed with some caution. It could as well be argued that the amount of time between words in each triplet was of sufficient duration to allow intentional processing, and therefore selection from rather than restriction of accessed meanings. While the procedure in Schvaneveldt et al. included presenting each word as soon as a decision had been made on the prior word, average decision time was 500–600 msec. SOA, then, would be in that range, which clearly is long enough to allow intentional suppression of the non-biased meaning of the ambiguous word (as demonstrated in [Neely, 1977; Simpson and Burgess, 1985]) and therefore to argue against a claim that the biasing context acted to restrict access.

In contrast to the Schvaneveldt et al. results, Oden and Spira [1983] offer evidence consistent with an inference of full elaboration of ambiguous words presented in triplets, regardless of context condition—but again at an ISI sufficient to allow intentional processing. In one condition of their study, subjects heard two biasing words and then an ambiguous word, each presented at "about" a rate of one every 3/4 second; there was a subsequent 500 msec ISI, and the visual presentation of a colored word related to one meaning of the ambiguity. The subjects' task, a variation of the Stroop interference task, was to name the color of the word.

Using this paradigm, Oden and Spira found that *both* meanings of the ambiguous word showed an interference effect, suggesting that both are accessed but that the meaning consonant with the contextual bias consistently showed a larger effect than the other meaning. In short, context affected *degree* of activation but did not restrict activation to just one meaning. As with Schvaneveldt et al., the length of the delay between context and ambiguous words, and between ambiguous words and the colored word to be read, raises problems with respect to inferences about automatic access processes. It is at least possible (if not plausible) that within that 500 msec ISI, subjects intentionally initiated a full elaboration process; subjects might, for example, have noticed that the colored word was sometimes related to the "unexpected" meaning of a word, and subsequently started to elaborate both meanings. It should also be noted that direct comparisons, particularly with respect to time course comparisons, cannot be made between priming tasks and interference tasks. These tasks are quite different, their time courses have not been directly compared, and it cannot be assumed that they would be similar either in rate or direction of changes over time.

Overall, while data from studies using isolated words are consistent with a claim that all meanings of ambiguous words are elaborated at least briefly, they are far from definitive. A particular problem with these studies is failure to examine a broad range of inter-word delays in order to characterize the time course of lexical access in the presence of a context (as Simpson has done for ambiguous words in the absence of context).

3.3 *Sentence Studies*

The majority of studies using priming to examine the effects of sentence context on the processing of ambiguous words are, as with the word studies, consistent with an exhaustive access position. These include the study of Tanenhaus et al. [1979] using syntactic contexts, and Swinney's studies using semantic contexts with equibias and non-equibias ambiguities ([Onifer and Swinney, 1981; Swinney, 1979; Swinney, Onifer, Prather, and Hirshkowitz, 1979]). While these studies differed in types of ambiguity (noun-verb vs. noun-noun), dominance of meanings, and task (naming vs. lexical decision, during-sentence vs. end-of-sentence), they were consistent in finding that regardless of direction of prior biasing context, priming was demonstrated for words related to *both* meanings of the target ambiguity. As with the word studies, examination of the time course showed that both meanings were available only for a delimited period. Unlike the word studies (where both meanings seemed to become available only after a short delay), both meanings were facilitated when examined *immediately* following the target word.

Tanenhaus et al. [1979] presented subjects with sentences biased towards one meaning of ambiguities that had independent noun-verb meanings (e.g., "watch"). The ambiguity was always the last word in the sentence, and was followed at a 0, 200, or 600 msec ISI by a visually-presented word related to one meaning of the sentence (e.g., "look"). Regardless of contextual bias, words related to both meanings were facilitated on the naming task at the 0 msec delay; by 200 msec, however, only the word related to the contextually appropriate meaning was facilitated. Swinney [1979] similarly presented subjects with sentences biased towards one meaning of an ambiguous word. In this study, however, the ambiguous words were selected to have 2 noun meanings of equal strength, and the task involved lexical decision on a visually-presented word that was presented while the auditory sentence was ongoing. Again, the visual word was presented with either a 0 msec ISI or 3 syllable (approximately 800 msec) ISI following the ambiguous word. And again, words related to both meanings were facilitated downstream.

While supportive of a claim that all meanings of an ambiguous word are accessed regardless of prior bias, one criticism raised about these studies has been that the apparent facilitation of words related to both meanings may be an artifact of using equibias ambiguities (see [Hogaboam and Perfetti, 1975]). It may be that about half the subjects access one meaning first, and half the other meaning first, resulting in both meanings being facilitated *on average* but not by *all* subjects. To test for that possibility, Onifer and Swinney [1981] essentially replicated Swinney [1979] using ambiguous words that showed a strong bias towards one meaning. The original results replicated; words related to both the dominant and subordinate meaning were facilitated, even in the case where the context was biased toward the dominant meaning. Recently, this study itself was replicated by Gildea [1984].

More recently, Oden and Spira [1983] have questioned the claim that context has *no* effect on the lexical access process. They argue that, while there is convincing evidence that context does *not* restrict access, their research suggests that context does affect *degree* of activation of an ambiguity's multiple meanings. In that sense, context can affect the access process. In the study they offer as support for this position, subjects listened to sentences that included a bias towards one meaning of equibias ambiguities, with the ambiguous word as the last one in the sentence; 500 msec after the end of that sentence, a Stroop color naming task was performed on a word that was related to one meaning of the sentence. Interference effects were obtained for both meanings, but were significantly greater for the contextually appropriate meaning, i.e., context affected the *degree* of activation of the multiple "word senses" of an ambiguity. Oden and Spira acknowledge, however, a clear problem with their interpretation: because they test 500 msec after the ambiguity, they may be examining a post-lexical *decision* process rather than lexical access. In short, their data are consistent with the preceding studies in suggesting that context has an effect on relative activation of meanings of an ambiguity shortly after access. However, their data do not speak to the issue of whether or not that effect is taking place within the "window" of automatic lexical processing.

To summarize briefly, those studies which have examined the time course of lexical processing within what we have called the "window" of automaticity support an inference that all meanings of an ambiguous word are made available in this access process, and that one meaning is selected relatively quickly thereafter. The selected meaning is the one consistent with prior bias or, if none is present, with the preference/frequency bias for that word. These data are taken as support for a claim that there is at least a brief period of autonomy, that is, of modularity, during lexical processing.

There is, however, one sentence study in which a prior context *does* seem to restrict access to just one meaning of an ambiguous word. However, for reasons cited earlier, the results of this study also do not contradict claims for autonomy of lexical processing. Rather, they are consistent with the prediction that the one condition under which a context could restrict access would be when the "context" is a lexical associate that, through automatic priming effects, facilitates one meaning of the ambiguity automatically. The effect was obtained by Seidenberg et al. [1982]. Across four studies, they presented subjects with an auditory phrase or sentence that ended with an ambiguous word; then at either a 0 or 200 msec ISI, subjects were presented with a word to read aloud. In one study, a general semantic context was selected (disambiguation with no words or phrases associatively related to the target, e.g., "You should have played the *spade*"). As with other studies reported above, words related to both meanings of ambiguous words were facilitated at 0 msec.

In two other Seidenberg et al. studies, however, the context was selected to be lexical, that is, the context was a strong lexical associate presented within the same phrase as (and therefore temporally near) the target ambiguity (e.g., "Although the *farmer* bought the *straw*"). In that condition, only the contextually-appropriate meaning was facilitated for the noun-noun ambiguities. This result is consistent with the prediction that a temporally close associative context could restrict access to just one meaning as an automatic (within-lexicon) process (see also discussion in [Seidenberg et al., 1982]). This is one of a few studies to use naming rather than lexical decision, and it presents the target word at the end of the sentence which may allow some strategic processing (similar to the argument for "pair" vs. "list" processing presented earlier). Still, the finding is an important one, it is consistent with theoretical predictions, and it warrants further empirical attention.

To summarize, across a number of studies using a variety of paradigms, the data have consistently supported two inferences. (1) Both meanings of an ambiguous word are accessed even in the presence of a biasing context *except* when the context is lexical and temporally near to the target ambiguity. (2) The automatic access routine is temporally delimited to about 200 msec post-ambiguity. In short, the evidence favors a model in which access is brief but exhaustive except (perhaps) in the case where the context acts within the lexical module. This conclusion is based on the weight of the evidence rather than on any definitive study; as Simpson [1984] points out, the results of most studies are open to question based on methodological issues, and there has been little consistency in materials, tasks, or temporal range explored across studies that would allow the systematic building of a model of the lexicon and its internal processes.

The one remaining serious challenge to this general conclusion comes from a recent set of studies reported by Glucksberg, Kreuz and Rho [1986]. They argue that evidence supporting contextually independent lexical access derived from priming studies (again, arguably the strongest evidence supporting the lexical modularity hypothesis) is confounded due to the possibility of backward priming, and they provide a study that uses a non-word interference paradigm that, so it is claim, demonstrates contextually directed lexical access. Because this claim is so critical to the issues we have raised above, we will now consider the Glucksberg et al. arguments in some detail.

4 *On Backward Priming: Why It Isn't*

In what follows, we will first briefly describe the claims made about backward priming and evaluate these claims on logical and empirical grounds. Following that, we will briefly evaluate the Glucksberg et al. evidence and provide some new evidence that bears on their study.

The possibility of something called backward priming has been raised by Glucksberg et al. as an alternative explanation to that typically given to findings of exhaustive access using a cross-modal priming task (CMLP). Glucksberg et al. argue that only the contextually constrained interpretations of an ambiguity are ever accessed when a lexical ambiguity is heard, but that the acoustic *form* of the ambiguous word remains in "echoic" memory for a period following access of the appropriate interpretation. According to this view, what happens in a CMLP task is that if (when) the contextually *in*appropriate probe (visual target word) is presented at the end of the ambiguity, that word, too, enters some form of memory. It is here that "backward priming" is argued to take place; the relationship of the (contextually inappropriate) probe word in memory to the *unchosen* meaning of the acoustic form of the ambiguity in echoic memory is somehow noticed and serves to activate this (previously unaccessed) interpretation. This, in turn, serves to make lexical decisions to the contextually inappropriate probe word faster than those to an unrelated control word. In short, the presentation of the inappropriate probe word as a lexical decision target has an effect on the acoustic form of an ambiguous word that occurred temporally earlier, causing reprocessing of that ambiguity, which results in "access" of the contextually inappropriate meaning of that ambiguity which, in turn, "primes" the decision to the target/probe word itself.

While conceivably true, this seems to be a tortuous explanation of how priming obtains for contextually inappropriate meanings of words in the CMLP task. Consider, for example, that if the contextually inappropriate probe word has to be accessed to begin with for the relationship between itself and the *un*-accessed meaning of the ambiguous word to be noticed, why is there facilitation in making a lexical decision to the probe at all? Surely a lexical decision could have been made in response to the *initial* access of the probe? All of this later processing seems superfluous with regard to actually making a lexical decision to the target. Despite this and other such questions, however, the claim does represent a scenario worth considering and evaluating carefully. In what follows, we deal with a few of what we take to be the major points in the Glucksberg argument, beginning with the concept of backward priming itself.

Backward priming is a concept that has derived from sources independent of the Glucksberg claims, thus strengthening the potential plausibility of their arguments. Most notably, Kiger and Glass [1983] (see also [Koriat, 1981]) demonstrated a relative savings for lexical decisions made in response to visually presented words (stimulus duration of 30 msecs) when they were followed immediately (35 msecs later) by an associatively related word, as compared to when they were followed by a non-word. The basic question is, is this priming at all?

There is every reason to believe that rather than priming, these researchers have demonstrated a diminution-of-interference effect. After all, asking subjects to make a lexical decision in response to a very briefly reported word, and requiring them to immediately process another word following *that* word (all within 65 msecs) is most likely to cause a great deal of interference in lexical decision to that initial word. In fact, the average reaction time to make lexical decisions in experiments 2 and 3 of Kiger and Glass (the only one of their experiments in which a significant experimental-control difference was found) was on the order of 700 msecs. This is considerably longer than normal isolated (or "pair") lexical decision RTs (which typically average in the 400–500 msec range). Such long RTs certainly suggest a great deal of interference might be taking place in making the initial decision. The savings discovered for priming associates in this task suggests that the interference lessened somewhat when the following word was associatively related.

The single way in which one might determine if these effects were essentially driven by priming or by inhibition would be to employ a "neutral" prime. Unfortunately, in the one experiment in which a form of "neutral" prime was used by Kiger and Glass (Experiment 1), no significant effects of "backward priming" were obtained. It is probably not accidental that reaction times in this study (their Experiment 1) averaged about 475 msecs. Here the "backward" context followed the target word by a far longer delay than in the other studies, and provided a condition where one might hope to obtain somewhat interference-free reaction times. Thus, it seems to be far from clear that there is any evidence for something that can reasonably be called *backward* priming. It seems much more likely that what we have here is unrelated to priming, backward or forward. What, then, is the basis for believing that backward priming can in fact occur?

In an attempt to determine whether or not we could obtain evidence for backward priming between auditorily and visually presented items, we recently conducted a study involving 48 word-pair associates. In this experiment, the first member of the word pair (or a non-word filler) was heard auditorily and the subject was required to make a lexical decision to that item. The second member of the associate pair or a control word was presented at an ISI of 0, 300, or 600 msecs. This was run, with appropriate counterbalancing, on 36 subjects. While null results are normally problematic things to report, here they have interpretive value. As can be seen in Table 1, no priming or interference was found for this cross-modal variation of the Kiger and Glass experiments at any of the SOAs.

Regardless of whether or not one believes that the visual domain effects that Kiger and Glass report represent "backward" priming or lessening of interference effects, it is necessary for the Glucksberg et al. argument that these effects obtain in the cross-modal paradigm. In this attempt to obtain such results (a good faith attempt that we believe was a strong one), we failed to find any evidence that cross-modal processing produces either effect. It might be noted that the lack of an effect in the cross-modal paradigm reinforces the notion that the within-mode paradigm of Kiger and Glass produced interference effects. In the CMLP, visual information cannot physically (peripherally) interfere with the initially presented, auditory item.

Table 1   Lexical decisions in response to the first item of an associated or "control" pair, presented in cross-modal format with variable SOAs.

Pair Type	SOA (msec)		
	0	300	600
Associated	598	609	607
Nonassociated	602	604	601

Hence, at one level, it is not clear that the argument for backward priming made by Glucksberg et al. is an independently motivated one; there appears to be only very suspect evidence to support the notion that backward priming obtains at all, although backward interference effects may indeed occur within a modality.

However, even if there is no independent evidence for backward priming, one must also consider the Glucksberg et al. evidence on its own merits. In their paper, these researchers present clever and interesting experimental work that they take to support the non-modularist position. However, as we attempt to show below, all of their work hangs on slender threads of assumptions that we believe to be incorrect, a belief for which we present some direct empirical support.

Briefly, Glucksberg et al. make the argument that if backward priming exists in the CMLP paradigm, and if they can come up with a form of this paradigm which *prevents* backward priming itself but uses the same general cross-modal approach to studying access of meanings for lexical ambiguities in restricted contexts, then they could determine if the Onifer and Swinney [1981] results were caused by this hypothesized backward priming effect. What they devised was an experiment using the Onifer and Swinney auditory materials (lexical ambiguities in biasing sentential contexts), but with non-word probes rather than word probes. These non-word probes were misspellings of words that, were they not misspelled, would have formed good associate probes for the various interpretations of the lexical ambiguities. For example, CONDRY and CONBISHUN were non-word probes for the ambiguity STATE; here, CONDRY is similar to COUNTRY and CONBISHUN is similar to CONDITION, the two interpretations of the ambiguous word STATE.

It was argued that because these were non-words, they could not be accessed lexically and therefore could not provide lexical priming—either forward or backward. Thus, it was argued that if the same type of effect was found for CONDRY but not for CONBISHUN when they were presented immediately following occurrence of the ambiguity STATE in a sentence that was contextually biased toward the "country" interpretation, then this would be evidence that *only* the contextually relevant interpretation of a lexical ambiguity is accessed, that lexical access is neither modular nor contextually independent, and that the effects obtained by Onifer and Swinney were due to backward priming (while these new effects *couldn't* be due to priming). They argue that their data support such an interpretation. However, it appears to us that this is a premature conclusion, and to substantiate our claim, we will briefly present some data that bear directly on the major underlying assumption of Glucksberg's research.

The entire premise of the Glucksberg et al. experiment hinges on the notion that non-words such as CONBISHUN cannot or will not prime (facilitate) the processing of related words. If they do, then whatever results Glucksberg et al. obtain with their task, they *cannot* be results that are impervious to "backward priming" effects (if such exist at all). And, of course, that was the point of their experiment—to run something that couldn't be subject to priming. In their paper, they mention that a pilot study was run examining the effects of the non-word probes on lexical decision to the lexical ambiguities used in the sentence study, and no facilitory effects for the related items were found, relative to the control non-words. This is an absolutely critical finding to the entire premise of the experiment, and it was important to run it as they did. However, we have been examining the effects of phonetic and orthographic priming and interference in our lab for some time as have many others (see, e.g., [Seidenberg and Tanenhaus, 1979]), and have had pilot words which indicated to us that non-words were at times sufficiently close to "real" words, either phonetically or orthographically, to prime decisions to other "real" words.

It certainly seems quite possible that, for example, anyone reading CON-BISHUN might well make a word of it (i.e., might access possible words it could be), regardless of the fact that it was, in a formal sense, a non-word. In fact that is, by and large, the task that we all have as listeners and readers. We make sense of something even if it is misspelled or mispronounced—and such processing appears to be very automatized in adults. Hence, we were exceptionally curious about the lack of an effect of related non-words on the ambiguities. Consequently we ran an experiment using the Glucksberg et al. material in a straightforward priming task.

In this experiment, each of Glucksberg's experimental non-words and their respective control non-words were presented visually immediately prior to and also at an ISI of 300 msecs prior to the ambiguous word, which also appeared visually. The material set comprised exactly the material set used in the Glucksberg experiment, along with an equal number of non-word target items (48) also preceded by non-words. The design constituted a 4 (between) × 2 (within) subjects design, and was run on 46 subjects. As can be seen in Table 2, significant effects of "related" non-word facilitation were obtained, compared to the appropriate Glucksberg "control" non-words. In short, these non-words do prime. Given that non-words prime in this condition, the results of Glucksberg et al. are not explainable in terms of their non-words preventing backwards priming, and thus their experiment neither demonstrates that the Onifer and Swinney results were likely due to backward priming nor that only a single contextually relevant meaning of the ambiguity was accessed in their study.

What, then, do the Glucksberg et al. results indicate? While it is difficult to know precisely without further work, it seems reasonable to focus on the fact that we know little about the nature and time course of interference effects that Glucksberg relies on (RTs to the Glucksberg non-words were interference RTs). It may well be that the processing of the Glucksberg non-words was sufficiently slow that the interference effects were a result of processing that

Table 2. Lexical decision reaction times in response to ambiguous words following presentation of the Glucksberg et al. non-word stimuli.

Non-word Type	ISI(msec)	
	0	**300**
Related non-words	568	592
Control non-words	548	558

occurred entirely outside of the "window" of lexical access. Or perhaps they reflect nothing of the ambiguity at all, and only reflect processing of the prior biasing context. Whatever the answer, their data do not appear to be problematic for claims of autonomous lexical access.

5 The Lexicon: An Interactive Box with an Autonomous Component Process

In our introductory remarks, we suggested that the test of whether or not lexical priming is modular involves a determination of whether or not non-lexical information affects processing *within* the lexicon. If so, then the process is not encapsulated, that is, is not independent and therefore not an autonomous module. Available evidence suggests that there is a narrow temporal window during lexical processing within which prior semantic and syntactic contexts cannot affect the access routine. Based on studies of lexical ambiguities, the only prior context that has been shown to affect access of an ambiguity within the first few hundred milliseconds after its auditory or visual presentation has been a prior lexical associate presented temporally close to the ambiguity; all other contexts seem to affect selection of the appropriate meaning only after context-independent processing.

Is the lexicon an autonomous module? It certainly appears to be, although it may be that the definitive work in the area is yet to be done. Certainly, as we better understand the nature of automatic and interactive processing routines, we will be better able to address the basic question. It seems sufficient at present to say that, given what we know now, aspects of lexical processing are autonomous, and lexical ambiguity resolution involves a process of exhaustive retrieval of information stored in the data base for a word, followed by post-access, context-determined processing which normally results in a single conscious meaning for an ambiguous word in the normal course of sentence comprehension.

Acknowledgments

Preparation of this manuscript was supported in part by an NIMH grant and by a fellowship from the FIDIA Corporation to the first author, and by NIH Grant NS21806 to the second author. We would like to thank an anonymous reviewer for comments helpful to our revision of this manuscript, particularly with respect to an interpretation of work by Schvaneveldt et al. consistent with our model of the lexicon.

References

Bowles, N., and L. Poon. 1985. Effects of priming in word retrieval. *Journal of Experimental Psychology: Learning, Memory and Cognition* 11:272–285.

den Heyer, K., K. Briand, and G. Dannenbring. 1983. Strategic factors in a lexical-decision task: Evidence for automatic and attention-driven processes. *Memory and Cognition* 11:374–381.

Fodor, J. 1983. *Modularity of Mind.* Cambridge: Bradford-MIT Press.

Fischler, I. and G. Goodman. 1978. Latency of associative activation in memory. *Journal of Experimental Psychology: Human Perception and Performance* 4:455–470.

Foss, D. and C. Jenkins. 1973. Some effects of context on the comprehension of ambiguous sentences. *Journal of Verbal Learning and Verbal Behavior* 12:577–589.

Gildea, P. 1984. Unpublished dissertation, Princeton University.

Glucksberg, S., R. Kreuz and S. Rho. 1986. Context can restrain lexical access: Implications for models of language comprehension. *Journal of Experimental Psychology: Learning, Memory and Cognition* 12:323–335.

Hogaboam, T. and C. Perfetti. 1975. Lexical ambiguity and sentence comprehension. *Journal of Verbal Learning and Verbal Behavior* 14:265–274.

Kiger, J. and A. Glass. 1983. The facilitation of lexical decisions by a prime occurring after the target. *Memory and Cognition* 11:356–365.

Koriat, A. 1981. Semantic facilitation in lexical decisions as a function of prime-target association. *Memory and Cognition* 9:587–598.

Meyer, D. and R. Schvaneveldt. 1971. Facilitation in recognizing pairs of words: Evidence of a dependence between retrieval operations. *Journal of Experimental Psychology* 90:227–234.

Morton, J. 1982. Disintegrating the lexicon: An information processing approach. In J. Mehler, E. Walker and M. Garrett (eds.), *Perspectives on Mental Representation.* Hillsdale: Erlbaum.

Neely, J. 1977. Semantic priming and retrieval from lexical memory: Roles of inhibitionless spreading activation and limited capacity attention. *Journal of Experimental Psychology: General* 106:226–254.

Onifer, W., and D. Swinney. 1981. Accessing lexical ambiguities during sentence comprehension: Effects of frequency of meaning and contextual bias. *Memory and Cognition* 9:225–236.

Oden, G. and J. Spira. 1983. Influence of context on the activation and selection of ambiguous word senses. *Quarterly Journal of Experimental Psychology* 35a:51–64.

Prather, P., J. Pasquotto, A. Seimen and D. Lawson. 1986. *The Time Course of Lexical De-activation.* Manuscript, University of Illinois at Chicago.

Posner, M. and C. Snyder. 1975. Facilitation and inhibition in the processing of signals. In P. Rabbit and E. Dornic (eds.), *Attention and Performance V.* London: Academic Press.

Schvaneveldt, R., D. Meyer and C. Becker. 1976. Lexical ambiguity, semantic context, and visual word recognition. *Journal of Experimental Psychology: Human Perception and Performance* 2:243–250.

Shiffrin, R., and W. Schneider. 1977. Controlled and automatic human information processing II: Perceptual learning, automatic attending, and a general theory. *Psychological Review* 84:127–180.

Simpson, G. 1981. Meaning, dominance, and semantic context in the processing of lexical ambiguity. *Journal of Verbal Learning and Verbal Behavior* 20:120–136.

Simpson, G. and C. Burgess. 1985. Activation and selection processes in the recognition of ambiguous words. *Journal of Experimental Psychology: Human Perception and Performance* 11(1):28–39.

Seidenberg, M., M. Tanenhaus, J. Leiman, and M. Bienkowski. 1982. Automatic access of the meanings of ambiguous words in context: Some limitations of knowledge-based processing. *Cognitive Psychology* 14:489–537.

Seidenberg, M., G. Waters, M. Sanders, and P. Langer. 1984. Pre- and post-lexical loci of contextual effects on word recognition. *Memory and Cognition* 12:315–328.

Seidenberg, M. and M. Tanenhaus. 1979. Orthographic effects in rhyme and monitoring. *Journal of Experimental Psychology: Human Learning and Memory* 5:546–554.

Swinney, D. 1979. Lexical access during sentence comprehension: (Re)consideration of context effects. *Journal of Verbal Learning and Verbal Behavior* 18:645–660.

Swinney, D., W. Onifer, P. Prather and M. Hirshkowitz. 1979. Semantic facilitation across sensory modalities in the processing of individual words and sentences. *Memory and Cognition* 7:159–165.

Swinney, D. 1981. Lexical processing during sentence comprehension: Effects of higher order constraints and implications for representation. In Meyers,

Laver, and Anderson (eds.), *The Cognitive Representation of Speech.* Amsterdam: North-Holland.

Tanenhaus, M., G. Carlson and M. Seidenberg. 1984. Do listeners compute linguistic representations? In Zwicky, Kartuunen, and Dauty (eds.), *Natural Language Parsing: Psycholinguistic, Theoretical, and Computational Perspectives.* Cambridge: Cambridge University Press.

Tanenhaus, M., J. Leiman, and M. Seidenberg. 1979. Evidence for multiple stages in the processing of ambiguous words in syntactic contexts. *Journal of Verbal Learning and Verbal Behavior* 18:427–441.

Warren, R. 1972. Stimulus encoding and memory. *Journal of Experimental Psychology* 94:90–100.

Warren, R. 1977. Time and the spread of activation in memory. *Journal of Experimental Psychology: Human Learning and Memory* 3:458–466.

Chapter

12

Is Multiple Access an Artifact of Backward Priming? [1]

Michael K. Tanenhaus
Curt Burgess

Mark Seidenberg
McGill University

Studies of words with multiple senses (lexical ambiguity) have played a prominent role in addressing questions about how lexical access is affected by context [Simpson, 1984]. Three questions have been of primary interest: (1) Does lexical access make available one or more than one sense of an ambiguous word? (2) Does prior context constrain lexical access such that only the contextually biased sense is initially accessed? (3) Does the relative frequency (dominance) of the different senses affect access and mediate the effects of biasing context? In order to answer these questions, it is necessary to make use of methodologies that track rapid and often unconscious changes in representation over time. Task specific artifacts are of considerable concern with these methodologies. As a result, the study of lexical ambiguity cannot be divorced from methodological questions about how to interpret results obtained with these 'on-line' methodologies.

During the last decade cross-modal lexical priming techniques have been the most widely used methodology for studying lexical ambiguity resolution in

1 This research was supported by NICHD grant HD 18944, NSF grant BNS-8217378 and grant A7924 from the Natural Science and Engineering Research Council of Canada.

context. In these experiments, an auditorially presented sentence or fragment is interrupted or followed by a visual target word that is related to an ambiguous word in the sentence. A speeded response to the target word is used to infer what information was accessed when the word was processed. One of the most robust results emerging from this literature is that both contextually biased and unbiased sense of ambiguous words are typically activated. Recently, however, it has been suggested that 'multiple access' is an artifact of backward effects of the target on the prior ambiguous word. In this chapter we briefly review the results of the cross-modal literature and evaluate the extent to which multiple access is an artifact of backward priming. Although we cannot offer a definitive answer, we conclude that it is unlikely.

1 *Some Background*

Most early on-line studies of lexical ambiguity used a dual-task logic with the phoneme monitoring task [Foss, 1970]. Phoneme detection times to target phonemes following an ambiguous word were compared with phoneme detection times following an unambiguous control word. The assumption was that access of more than one meaning of an ambiguous word should make processing more difficult and thus increase phoneme detection times. This result obtained in a number of studies, even when the context biased one sense of the ambiguous word, leading to the conclusion that multiple senses of ambiguous words are typically accessed ([Foss, 1970; Foss and Jenkins, 1973; Cairns and Kamerman, 1975]; but see also [Swinney and Hakes, 1976]). However, these results were called into question by Mehler, Segui, and Carey [1978] and Newman and Dell [1978], who pointed out a number of uncontrolled variables in prior phoneme monitoring studies and did not find an ambiguity effect when appropriate controls were used. The issue of whether or not ambiguity increases phoneme monitoring times has never been completely resolved [Swinney, 1979; Cairns and Hsu, 1980], in large part because researchers have begun to question the assumption that multiple access need necessarily result in increased processing load.

2 *Lexical Priming*

A number of studies in the early 1970s, beginning with Meyer and Schvaneveldt [1971], found that recognition of a target word is facilitated when the target is preceded by a semantically related 'prime' word. This facilitation, or 'priming' is indexed by faster lexical decisions and naming times to 'primed' target words, and slower color naming times when the target word is printed in one of several colors [Warren, 1972; 1974].

Lexical priming was generally taken to provide a measure of automatic lexical access under conditions where only a small proportion of the prime and target trials were related. Tweedy, Lapinski, and Schvaneveldt [1977] showed that the magnitude of priming with the lexical decision task increases with the proportion of related prime and target trials. However, Fischler [1977] demonstrated that priming obtains even when subjects have no reason to expect a relationship between the prime and target. In his study, only the last target word in the experiment was preceded by a semantically related prime word. In an important and influential study, Neely [1977] showed that whether or not expectancies influence lexical priming depends crucially on time, with expectancy effects taking several hundred milliseconds to develop. In addition to demonstrating that there was a time window in which priming was not influenced by conscious expectancies, Neely's studies demonstrated that lexical priming could be used to trace the time course of lexical processing.

3 Cross-Modal Lexical Priming

The phenomenon of lexical priming provided psycholinguists with a methodology for separating access of lexical information from increases in processing load. Priming to a target which is related to a particular sense of an ambiguous word could provide direct evidence for that sense having been activated.

Conrad [1974] first applied the lexical priming methodology to ambiguity resolution in sentences using a cross-modal procedure, in which subjects listened to a sentence presented auditorially and then named the color of target word presented visually. She reasoned that interference exhibited in naming the color of a target word related to a sense of an ambiguous word, would provide evidence for that sense having been activated. Conrad found that sentence-final ambiguous words interfered with related targets, regardless of whether or not the target was related to the sense of the ambiguous word that was biased by the sentence. Swinney [1979] and Tanenhaus, Leiman, and Seidenberg [1979] directly examined the time course of ambiguity resolution. Tanenhaus et al. [1979], using biasing syntactic contexts and a naming task, found priming to targets related to the biased and unbiased sense when a target word immediately followed a sentence-final ambiguous word, but facilitation only to contextually biased senses with a 200 msec delay. Swinney [1979], using semantically biased contexts with a lexical decision task in which the target word was presented and the sentence continued, found no effects of context when the target immediately followed an ambiguous word, but context effects three syllables later. This procedure, which was originally developed by Swinney, Onifer,

Prather and Hershkovits [1979], is the most flexible and widely used cross-modal procedure.

There is now an extensive literature of cross-model lexical priming studies of ambiguity resolution in different types of biasing contexts [Hudson and Tanenhaus, 1984; Lucas, in press; Oden and Spira, 1982; Onifer and Swinney, 1981; Seidenberg, Tanenhaus, Leiman, and Bienkowski, 1982; Simpson, 1981; Tabossi, Columbo, and Job, in press; Tanenhaus and Donnenwerth-Nolan, 1984]. Studies examining the effects of biasing syntactic context on ambiguous words drawn from different syntactic classes (e.g., 'rose') have found priming to targets related to appropriate and inappropriate senses, when the visual probes are presented immediately after the ambiguous word. Thus, syntactic context does not appear to constrain lexical access. When a short delay (e.g., 200 msec) is introduced between the ambiguous word and the target, only contextually appropriate targets are primed.

The story is more complex for semantically biasing contexts, in part because whether or not targets related to contextually inappropriate senses are primed at short delay intervals depends both upon the relative frequencies of the component senses and the nature of the contextual bias. A number of studies have found priming to targets related to both contextually biased and unbiased senses when targets are presented immediately after the ambiguous word, with only contextually biased targets being primed shortly thereafter. For example, Onifer and Swinney [1981] and Lucas [in press] found initial access both to dominant and subordinate readings at short delay intervals. However, selective access has been obtained under certain special circumstances. In two experiments, Seidenberg et al. found that only targets related to biased senses were facilitated when the context contained a word that was strongly related to one sense of the ambiguous word. Tabossi [this volume] discusses a series of experiments in which she found priming only to the contextually biased sense when the context primed lexical features of the dominant sense of an ambiguous word. Targets related to both biased and unbiased senses were primed when the context biased the subordinate sense. With a 120 msec delay between the ambiguous word and a target word, Simpson [1981] found priming to subordinate readings only when they were contextually biased. All studies that have probed at delay intervals of 200 msec or more have found priming only for targets related to the contextually biased sense, except for Oden and Spira [1983], who found priming for targets related to the semantically unbiased sense with a 500 msec delay, although there was significantly more priming for targets related to the biased sense.

In sum, the dominant sense of an ambiguous word always seems to be accessed, regardless of contextual bias. Subordinate senses may or may not be accessed depending upon the nature of the context, although it is important to note, that priming to a target related to a sense of an ambiguous word provides clear evidence for that sense having been accessed, whereas the absence of priming does not rule out the possibility that that sense was activated at an earlier point in time. Thus it is difficult to distinguish between selective access and rapid ambiguity resolution without examining a range of prime-target stimulus onset asynchronies (SOAs).

There have also been a number of studies that have traced the time course of lexical access for visually presented ambiguous words using lexical priming. Simpson and Burgess [1985] examined priming to targets related to the dominant and subordinate readings of an ambiguous word at a range of SOAs. At 16 msec, only targets related to dominant readings were facilitated. At 100 and 300 msec both dominant and subordinate related targets were facilitated, whereas at 500 and 750 msec dominant related targets were facilitated, and subordinate related targets were inhibited. Holley-Wilcox and Blank [1980] used ambiguous words with equiprobable senses. With a 500 msec SOA, they found an equivalent level of priming to target words related to ambiguous prime words and to targets related to unambiguous prime words compared to unrelated control primes. This pattern of results provides the strongest support for multiple access. If only one meaning were being accessed on each trial, then less priming should have obtained to targets when they were preceded by ambiguous related primes than unambiguous related primes. Seidenberg et al. [1982] found the same pattern of results as Holley-Wilcox and Blank using neutral sentence contexts and a cross-modal naming task. Senytka, Tanenhaus, and Seidenberg [1982] used equiprobable and biased ambiguous words with three SOAs: 50 msec, 150 msec, and 450 msec. They found multiple access at the 150 and 450 msec SOAs, although there was a trend towards less priming (relative to unambiguous related primes) for equiprobable and subordinate related targets compared to dominant related targets, suggesting that the 450 msec SOA was sampling an intermediate point during sense selection.

Taken together, these results converge on a picture of lexical ambiguity resolution in which initial recognition makes available in parallel all of the common senses of an ambiguous word, with the senses becoming available in order of frequency. In general, the information made available during lexical access is unaffected by the nature of the biasing context.

4 Backward Priming

Recently, however, the interpretation of the cross-modal lexical priming literature has been called into question by studies that have demonstrated so-called "backward priming." Backward priming refers to facilitation in the recognition of a word by another word that is presented at a later point in time. The possibility that backward priming might contribute to lexical priming was first considered by Warren [1974]. Warren conducted a study in which subjects named the color of a visually presented target word that was preceded by an auditory prime word. The prime-target pairs were either "forward" associates in which the target word was an associate of the prime (e.g., stork-baby) or "backward" associates in which the primes were associates of the targets (e.g., baby-stork). Warren found priming effects, reflected in increased color naming latencies, only for the forward associates. Thus, he concluded that priming was due to faster recognition times to the target as a result of prior processing of the prime. However, Koriat [1981] later found backward priming using the same stimuli as Warren. Koriat's experiment used visual presentation of both the prime and target and the lexical decision task. Kiger and Glass [1982] also found backward effects using a different procedure. They found that lexical decisions in response to a target word were facilitated when the word was followed by an associatively related word. Seidenberg, Waters, Sanders, and Langer [1984] compared forward and backward associates using the naming and lexical decision tasks. Backward priming obtained only with the lexical decision task. Seidenberg et al. concluded that backward priming is primarily due to post-lexical strategic processes to which the naming task appears to be relatively immune.

As Koriat argued, backward priming could compromise the conclusions drawn from lexical priming studies of ambiguity. It is possible, for instance, that only the contextually appropriate sense of an ambiguous word is initially activated. When a target word is presented that is related to the alternative sense, (i.e., the contextually unbiased sense), that sense is then activated through backward priming, perhaps because processing of the ambiguous word and the target overlaps [Glucksberg et al., 1986]. Alternatively, all priming obtained at short delay intervals in cross-modal tasks could be due to backward priming from the target.

It is important to note that backward priming has never been demonstrated under cross-modal conditions similar to those that obtain in most cross-modal ambiguity studies. Nonetheless, the fact that it has been observed under any conditions introduces uncertainty about the interpretation of the ambiguity literature. The uncertainty will remain until the range of conditions under which backward priming obtains are understood or until a methodology is developed that can eliminate possible backward effects.

Gildea and Glucksberg [1984] proposed such a methodology. They developed a version of the cross-modal lexical decision paradigm in which interference in response to a nonword target related to either the primary or secondary sense of an ambiguous word was used to diagnose access of that sense. Thus accessing the *fish* sense of the ambiguous word SCALE would interfere with a decision to reject FISCH as a word in a lexical decision task. Gildea and Glucksberg developed a set of nonwords modeled on the targets used by Onifer and Swinney [1981] and demonstrated that the nonword did not facilitate making a lexical decision to the word it was modeled on (i.e., FISCH did not prime FISH). Thus the stimuli are not subject to possible backward effects. In a replication of Onifer and Swinney [1981], Glucksberg, Kreuz and Rho [1986] found that nonword targets showed interference relative to controls only when they were related to the context. These results obtained regardless of whether the context biased the dominant or the subordinate sense of the ambiguous word. Glucksberg et al. concluded that context can constrain lexical access and that previous demonstrations of multiple access were in fact due to backward priming.

Glucksberg et al.'s results do not, however, provide unequivocal evidence for selective access. An alternative explanation of their results is that the nonword interference task is sensitive to contextual relatedness, but insensitive to lexical priming. If this were the case, the nonword interference results would not bear on the critical question of whether or not contextual information can determine what information is initially activated during lexical access. Given the important implications of the Glucksberg et al. results for the interpretation of cross-modal priming experiments, we decided to further investigate the nonword decision task.

5 Some Experimental Studies

In a recent series of experiments we have examined the effects of a prime word on lexical decisions to nonword targets that were modeled on a word related to the prime. With the exception of some additional control conditions, the prime words and targets were those used by Glucksberg et al. [1986].

5.1 EXPERIMENT 1

In the first experiment, the nonwords that Glucksberg et al. used in their related condition, and the words that they were modeled on, were rotated through three prime conditions: (1) An ambiguous related condition where the prime was an ambiguous word, with one sense related to the nonword target, (2) An unambiguous-related condition in which the prime was an unambiguous word related to the nonword, (3) An unambiguous-unrelated condition in which the prime was unrelated to the target. The nonword targets were related to either the dominant or the subordinate sense of the ambiguous word. We also repeated the experiment using the words that the nonwords were modeled on as targets. The prime words were displayed for 750 msec on a CRT, and then replaced by a target string to which the subject made a lexical decision. The results are presented in Table 1.

Table 1   Single-word priming experiments with a 750 msec SOA. Mean lexical decision latencies to targets (in msec).

Related Nonword Target Experiment		
	Dominant	**Subordinate**
Ambiguous-Related	742	753
Unambiguous-Related	754	744
Unambiguous-Unrelated	741	755

Replication with Word Targets		
	Dominant	**Subordinate**
Ambiguous-Related	706	737
Unambiguous-Related	696	686
Unambiguous-Unrelated	735	698

The data for the word targets show the same pattern as Simpson and Burgess [1985]: target words related to dominate readings were facilitated, whereas target words related to subordinate readings were inhibited. For the nonwords, however, no interference obtained for either ambiguous primes or related unambiguous primes. The failure to obtain interference to nonword targets related to ambiguous word primes is consistent with the hypothesis that the nonword interference task is insensitive to lexical priming. However, before drawing this conclusion we conducted two further studies using the Glucksberg et al. stimuli.

5.2 EXPERIMENTS 2 and 3

Word-nonword pairs were selected to form three conditions. In the first condition the ambiguous prime was followed by a related nonword (i.e., SCALE-WEIGN). The first control condition consisted of the control nonwords used by Glucksberg et al. In this control condition the ambiguous prime is followed by a nonword formed from rearranging the letters of a related nonword (i.e., WEIGN produces WINGE). The third condition used the same control as in the previous experiment. The wordlike nonwords (i.e., WEIGN) were rotated such that the nonword targets were paired with unrelated primes (i.e., BUG-WEIGN). Targets in these three conditions corresponded to the dominant associates from the Glucksberg et al. stimuli. If the rearranged controls are easier

Table 2   Single-word priming experiments with nonword controls and rotated nonword controls.

	Visual Prime/Visual Target	Auditory Prime/Visual Target
Ambiguous-Related	668	651
Nonword Control	647	624
Rotated Control	674	642

to reject as words, then interference should be eliminated when the ambiguous word is compared to an unrelated, but not rearranged, nonword.

An experimental trial consisted of a 500 msec fixation point, followed by an ambiguous word (or filler word), followed by the target. These two experiments differ only in the mode of presentation of the prime. In one experiment the prime was presented for 500 msec on the CRT and was then (flash) masked. In the other experiment, the prime was presented auditorially and the fixation point and target were presented on the CRT. The target word was presented immediately at the offset of the prime word.

The results for Experiments 2 and 3 are presented in Table 2.

As in Experiment 1, lexical decisions to nonwords were not significantly slower when they were preceded by related prime words compared to unrelated prime words, regardless of whether the prime was presented visually or auditorially. However, lexical decisions to related nonwords were slower than lexical decisions to the rotated nonwords used by Glucksberg et al. Thus it appears that the control nonwords use by Glucksberg et al. are easier to reject in the lexical decision task than the related nonwords, probably because they are orthographically less word-like.

5.3 EXPERIMENT 4

The results of the three experiments discussed above demonstrate that the nonword interference task is not well suited to studying ambiguity resolution. The task is not sensitive to lexical priming which is the diagnostic used to determine whether or not a sense of an ambiguous word has been accessed. Why then did Gluckberg et al. find robust interference effects when nonwords were related to the contextually biased sense of an ambiguous word? The most likely possibility is that the task is sensitive to general contextual relatedness. We tested this hypothesis by repeating Glucksberg et al.'s critical experiment with two important changes. First, we presented nonword targets one word earlier than they did, that is before the ambiguous word. Second, to avoid any back-

Table 3   Representative sentences, target presentation points, and nonword targets. Note: The up-arrow (⇑) in each sentence indicates the point at which the target was presented. Targets following each sentence are the related nonword and nonword control, respectively.

- Before he started his diet he had been afraid to get on a ⇑ LADDER (replaces SCALE) but now he was pleased to see that dieting had been worth it and he was thinner.
  Targets: WEIGN - WINGE

- The congress has imposed a new gas ⇑ LAW (replaces TAX) which will make the cost of gasoline climb by at least ten per cent.
  Targets: INCUMM - CUMMIN

- She formed the clay using a ⇑ TOOL (replaces MOLD) because she wanted the bowl she was making to be perfectly round.
  Targets: SHAYP - PAYSH

ward effects of the ambiguous word on the target word, we replaced the ambiguous word with a word that was unrelated to the target, but that was still congruous with the preceding context. Any interference in making a lexical decision to the target word could thus be attributed to the preceding context. The unrelated target words were the nonword variants used by Glucksberg et al. Table 3 presents several representative trials, selected from our stimuli. The table illustrates the sentences, targets, and interruption points used by Glucksberg et al. [1986] and the modifications we introduced.

Subjects listened to the sentences through headphones and made a lexical decision to a letter string that occurred during the sentence. Lexical decisions to nonword targets were significantly slower when the word that they were modeled on was related to the preceding context (993 msec) than when it was unrelated (955 msec). Similar results obtained in a second experiment in which we compared related nonword targets to the nonword controls used by Glucksberg et al.

5.4 *EXPERIMENT 5*

Taken together then, the results of our experiments demonstrate why Glucksberg et al. obtained a data pattern consistent with selective access. The task that they were using was sensitive to contextual relatedness but not to lexical access. One puzzle remains, however. If the nonword interference task is sensitive to contextual relatedness, then why didn't the lexical primes act as a context in our first three experiments? One possibility is that the post-lexical use of lexical primes is strategic, whereas contextual integration with sentential contexts is highly automated. If this speculation is correct, then we should observe nonword interference with lexical primes when subjects are encouraged to make use of the the prime-target relationship.

One way of encouraging subjects to make strategic use of prime-target relationship is to use a high proportion of related prime-target pairs. As we discussed earlier, the magnitude of priming effects observed with lexical decision increases as a function of the proportion of related primes and targets, although some priming remains, even when subjects have no basis for expecting a relationship between the prime and the target [Fischler, 1977]. These results are generally taken as evidence for both an automatic and a strategic component to lexical priming [Tweedy, Lapinski, and Schvaneveldt, 1978; Seidenberg et al., 1984]. In a last experiment, we manipulated the proportion of related primes and targets in order to see if nonword interference would obtain when a high proportion of primes and targets were related.

The trials were presented on a CRT. Targets were related only to the dominant meaning. Three target relatedness proportions were used in this experiment: 1/5, 1/3, or 1/2. The relatedness proportion was manipulated by varying

Table 4   Proportion manipulation. Mean lexical decision latencies to targets (in msec).

Related Nonword Target Experiment			
	Related	**Unrelated**	**Difference**
1/5 Related	823	818	+5
1/3 Related	688	697	−9
1/2 Related	751	728	+23

Replication with Word Targets			
	Related	**Unrelated**	**Difference**
1/5 Related	658	705	−47
1/3 Related	596	615	−19
1/2 Related	646	665	−19

the number of unrelated filler trials in a list. Thus, all subjects saw the same ambiguous words. We also repeated the experiment using the words that the nonwords were modeled on as targets. The results are presented in Table 4.

The results clearly support the hypothesis that nonword interference effects are strategic. Nonword interference obtained only when half of the trials contained primes related to the nonword. No interference obtained when a lower proportion of related prime-target trials were used. When the nonwords were replaced by the words they were modeled on, significant facilitation obtained regardless of the proportion of prime-target pairs. The absence of a proportionality effect with word targets is somewhat surprising, however.

We now have a straightforward explanation why Glucksberg et al. found nonword interference only to targets related to the contextually biased sense of a preceding ambiguous word. The nonword interference task, as used by Glucksberg and colleagues, is sensitive only to contextual integration. Thus, the context effects obtained by Glucksberg et al. reflect the fact that only the contextually appropriate sense of an ambiguous word is integrated with the preceding context, whereas the inappropriate sense is rapidly discarded.

Why should lexical decisions to nonwords should reflect primarily contextual integration processes? It is now well established that lexical priming paradigms, especially lexical decision, are sensitive both to variables that influence lexical access and variables that influence post-lexical and strategic processes [Balota and Chumbley, 1984; Forster, 1979; Seidenberg et al., 1984]. It is also becoming clear that experimental tasks differ in the degree to which they are sensitive to lexical and post-lexical processes. For instance, the lexical decision task is more sensitive to strategic processes than the naming task. In general, tasks that require subjects to make explicit decisions are more likely to be influenced by strategic factors than tasks that do not require explicit decisions. It seems clear why the lexical decision task might be sensitive to general contextual relatedness. A letter string that can be easily integrated with the preceding context is more likely to be a word, or conversely less likely to be a nonword. It is less obvious why lexically related words should facilitate lexical decisions. The most widely accepted explanation is that lexical representations are primed by associatively or semantically related words through a rapid spreading activation process (but see also [Norris, 1986]). Glucksberg et al. assumed that the activation of a lexical representation should make it more difficult to reject an orthographically similar nonword. However, whether or not this is true may depend upon a range of factors including the similarity of the word and the nonword. In fact White [1986] has recently reported *faster* lexical decisions to nonword targets that were highly associated with a preceding prime word. It seems likely that there are circumstances in which the priming of a lexical representation will interfere with lexical decisions to related nonwords, however, this clearly was not the case for the stimuli used by Glucksberg, Rho, and Kreuz [1986].

6 *General Discussion*

Although our results challenge the conclusion by Glucksberg et al. that they have demonstrated that context can constrain lexical access, these results do not directly address the issue of whether or not the multiple access of word senses obtained in most cross-modal lexical priming studies is an artifact of backward priming. This issue is likely to remain unresolved until the temporal conditions under which backward effects occur in cross-modal studies have been carefully examined. However, there are a number of recent results that suggest that multiple access is unlikely to be an artifact of backward priming.

As we have seen, several cross-modal studies have found evidence for selective access when targets immediately followed the ambiguous word. Seidenberg et al. [1982] found that selective access occurred when a context contained a word semantically related to or associated with one sense of an ambiguous word. Tabossi [in press] has demonstrated selective access when a context emphasizes salient features of the dominant sense of an ambiguous word. In both of these studies, multiple access was observed at the same target delay interval as is seen using other types of contexts. Tabossi's studies are the most convincing because the contexts with which she found multiple access were modeled on those used by Onifer and Swinney [1981]. At the very least, these studies demonstrate that certain types of contexts—essentially those that activate some of the features of the lexical representation of a word—are effective either in blocking contextually inappropriate senses, or at least in rapidly inhibiting them (see [Tanenhaus, Dell, and Carlson, 1987; and Tanenhaus and Lucas, 1986] for discussion).

The fact that both multiple and selective access obtain at the same time delay is problematic for the backward priming account of multiple access. These data rule out a simple temporal overlap story for backward priming, in which backward priming obtains whenever a word is rapidly followed by a related word. Alternatively, one can argue that backward priming obtains only when a word has not yet been integrated into its context. If this is the case, however, most contexts do not constrain lexical access enough to block backward priming. Thus, information that is compatible with the bottom-up input but not with the context is briefly available for most types of contexts. In other words, context typically does not constrain lexical access.

However, some recent empirical evidence suggests that backward priming may not play a role in most cross-modal experiments. Peterson and Simpson [1987] directly examined backward priming in a cross-modal lexical priming experiment. They constructed prime-target pairs in which the direction of association was either forward, i.e., the target was an associate of the prime, or backward, i.e., the prime was an associate of the target. At a 0 msec delay using auditorially presented targets and visual targets, they found both forward and backward priming with both the naming task and lexical decision tasks. At a 200 msec delay, they found forward and backward priming with lexical decision, and only forward priming with naming. When the same prime and targets were used in contexts that biased the prime word, only forward priming obtained with both tasks. The Peterson and Simpson contexts were similar to those used by Onifer and Swinney [1981]. Thus it seems likely that multiple access would have been obtained with their contexts had the primes been ambiguous words, although this remains to be demonstrated. A study that compares backward priming and ambiguity resolution in biasing sentential contexts would help clarify whether or not multiple access is a result of backward priming.

There is, however, a recent study by Van Petten and Kutas [1987] that would seem to support a backward priming explanation for the standard multiple-access data pattern obtained with naming and lexical decision. Van Petten and Kutas measured event-related brain potentials to targets following ambiguous words in sentential contexts. The sentences were presented one word at a time and the target was presented at either 200 or 700 msec after the onset of the target. At the short SOA, unrelated targets, as well as targets related to the contextually unbiased sense of the ambiguous word, showed a larger N400 than the targets related to the contextually biased sense. However, the waveform to the targets related to the contextually unbiased sense began to converge with the waveform to the contextually related targets approximately 300 msec later. They argue for a backward priming interpretation of their results.

The line of research initiated by Van Petten and Kutas is important and innovative because ERPs can provide a continuous on-line measure of processing without requiring subjects to make a conscious decision [Kutas and Van Petten, in press]. However, the interpretation of their results is far from clear. It is possible, for example, that N400 may index the perceived congruity of a word in context, but not automatic priming effects. If so, the Van Petten and Kutas results would be equally consistent with either multiple access or selective access for the same reasons that the Glucksberg et al. results do not distinguish between these positions.

Van Petten and Kutas [1987] may well be correct in attributing the late convergence of the waveforms to the contextually biased and unbiased targets to a backward effect. However, the backward effect that is being monitored by N400 may be a late conscious effect that is not related to initial lexical access. For instance, it could occur when subjects become aware of the relationship between the target and the prime much in the same way that one often becomes aware of a pun after a short lag. It is also possible that the early portion of the waveform to the target is reflecting general contextual congruity, whereas the later portion is reflecting the effects of the preceding ambiguous word. If this interpretation turns out to be correct, then the Van Petten and Kutas study would actually be demonstrating multiple access. In any case, the final interpretation of the Van Petten and Kutas results will have to await further research investigating the relationship between N400 and forward and backward priming, and further research that investigates the relationship between N400 and automatic and strategic priming.

7 Conclusion

We began this chapter by noting that there are empirical studies of ambiguity resolution that are closely tied to methodological issues concerning on-line measures. In order to use lexical ambiguity as a window on the interface between context and lexical access, one needs experimental techniques that can be used to trace the availability of the information which becomes available during the word recognition process. Cross-modal lexical priming is one of the few candidates for such a methodology and during the last decade it has been used extensively to study the effects of context on lexical processing. One of the most robust findings that emerges from this literature is that under a wide range of conditions, both the contextually biased and unbiased senses of an ambiguous word are briefly activated. Recently, it has been suggested that multiple access might be an artifact of backward effects of the visually presented target word used in these studies. The possibility of task-specific artifacts is one that plagues all attempts to study on-line language comprehension, and the backward priming issue is far from resolved. However a careful consideration of the pattern of data obtained in cross-modal experiments, as well as a critical evaluation of the experimental evidence marshalled in support of the backward priming hypothesis, suggests it is unlikely that the results of the cross-modal literature are seriously compromised by backward priming. The best prognosis is that cross-modal priming will continue to be an important tool in research investigating the resolution of lexical ambiguity.

8 Coda: Modularity and Lexical Ambiguity

Much of the impact of the lexical ambiguity studies of the late 1970s and early 1980s was due to the fact that multiple access was counterintuitive, especially given the top-down flavor of the interactive models that were then preferred. The ambiguity results, in conjunction with studies of context effects in visual word recognition (e.g., [Stanovich and West, 1983], for a review), seemed to provide strong evidence against hypothesis testing style models of reading and language processing. In the light of recent empirical and theoretical developments, multiple access seems less counterintuitive and its theoretical implications for the modularity debate less clear.

Multiple sense activation now appears to be one of a class of multiple activation phenomena in lexical processing. Multiple pronunciations of non-homophonic homographs, such as *wind* are activated in visual word recognition. Phonological and orthographic representations of words are activated in both auditory and visual word recognition. There is also some evidence both from gating studies as well as cross-modal studies that semantic information related to competing lexical candidates is activated prior to auditory word recognition (see [Marlsen-Wilson, 1987] for a recent review).

Both autonomous and interactive models now embrace the notion of multiple access and the general principle of bottom-up priority. The parallel activation of multiple sources of information is characteristic of connectionist interactive models. Indeed, multiple access is a feature of several implemented connectionist models of lexical ambiguity [Cottrell, this volume; Kawamoto, this volume]. The debate between modular and interactive models comes down to whether or not top-down feedback occurs between message-levels contexts and early lexical processing [Dell, 1985]. Autonomous models do not allow for such feedback, whereas interactive models make use of it to enable contextual information to constrain lower-level processes. Autonomous models predict that conceptual expectations based on context should not be able to influence the initial lexical access, whereas interactive models predict that it may or may not, depending on the strength of the context. At this point in time the lexical ambiguity literature can be used—and has been used—to support the claims of both interactive and noninteractive models. Whether or not there are contexts that block access to contextually inappropriate senses via feedback, and whether or not the type of feedback that obtains violates modularity assumptions, is an issue that remains to be decided.

References

Balota, J. I., and Chumbley, D. A. 1984. Are lexical decisions a good measure of lexical access? The role of word frequency in the neglected decision stage. *Journal of Experimental Psychology: Human Perception and Performance* 10:340–357.

Cairns, H. S., and Hsu, J. R. 1980. Effects of prior context on lexical access during sentence comprehension: A replication and reinterpretation. *Journal of Psycholinguistic Research* 9:319–326.

Cairns, H. S., and Kamerman, J. 1975. Lexical information processing during sentence comprehension. *Journal of Verbal Learning and Verbal Behavior* 14:170–179.

Conrad, C. 1974. Context effects in sentence comprehension: A study of the subjective lexicon. *Memory and Cognition* 2:130–138.

Cottrell, G.W. This volume.

Dell, G. 1985. Positive feedback in hierarchical connectionist models: Applications to language production. *Cognitive Science* 9:3–23.

Fischler, I. 1977. Semantic facilitation without association in a lexical decision task. *Memory and Cognition* 5:335–339.

Fischler, I. 1977. Associative facilitation without expectancy in a lexical decision task. *Journal of Experimental Psychology: Human Perception and Performance* 3:18–26.

Foss, D. J. 1970. Some effects of ambiguity upon sentence comprehension. *Journal of Verbal Learning and Verbal Behavior* 9:699–706.

Foss, D. J., and Jenkins, C. M. 1973. Some effects of context on the comprehension of ambiguous sentences. *Journal of Verbal Learning and Verbal Behavior* 12:577–589.

Gildea, P., and Glucksberg, S. 1984. *Does Context Constrain Lexical Access For Ambiguous Words?* Paper presented at the meeting of the Psychonomic Society, San Antonio, TX.

Glucksberg, S., Kreuz, R. J., and Rho, S. 1986. Context can constrain lexical access: Implications for models of language comprehension. *Journal of Experimental Psychology: Learning, Memory, and Cognition* 12:323–335.

Greenspan, S. L. 1986. Semantic flexibility and referential specificity of concrete nouns. *Journal of Memory and Language* 25:539–557.

Hogaboam, T. W., and Perfetti, C. A. 1975. Lexical ambiguity and sentence comprehension. *Journal of Verbal Learning and Verbal Behavior* 14:265–274.

Holley-Wilcox, P., and Blank, M. A. 1980. Evidence for multiple access in the processing of isolated words. *Journal of Experimental Psychology: Human Perception and Performance* 6:75–84.

Hudson, S.B., and Tanenhaus, M.K. 1984. Ambiguity resolution in the absence of contextual bias. In *Proceedings of Cognitive Science 6*.

Kawamoto, A. H. This volume.

Kiger, J. I., and Glass, A. L. 1983. The facilitation of lexical decisions by a prime occurring after the target. *Memory and Cognition* 11:356–365.

Koriat, A. 1981. Semantic facilitation in lexical decision as a function of prime-target association. *Memory and Cognition* 9:587–598.

Kutas, M., and Van Petten, C. In press. Event-related brain potential studies of language. In P. K. Ackles, J. R. Jennings, and M. G. Coles (eds.), *Advances in Psychophysiology (Vol. 3)*. Greenwich: JAI Press.

Lucas, M. 1984. Frequency and context effects in lexical ambiguity resolution. Technical Report No. URCS-14, University of Rochester, Department of Psychology.

Lucas, M. In press. Frequency and context effects in lexical ambiguity resolution. *Language and Speech*.

Marslen-Wilson, W. D. 1987. Functional parallelism in spoken word-recognition. *Cognition* 71–102.

Mehler, J., Segui, J., and Carey, P. 1978. Tails of words: Monitoring ambiguity. *Journal of Verbal Learning and Verbal Behavior* 17:29–35.

Merrill, E., Sperber, R. D., and McCauley, C. 1981. Differences in semantic coding as a function of reading comprehension skill. *Memory and Cognition* 9:618–624.

Meyer, D. E., and Schvaneveldt, R. W. 1971. Facilitation in recognizing pairs of words: Evidence of a dependence between retrieval operations. *Journal of Experimental Psychology* 90:227–234.

Neely, J. H. 1977. Semantic priming and retrieval from lexical memory: Roles of inhibitionless spreading activation and limited-capacity attention. *Journal of Experimental Psychology: General* 106:226–254.

Newman, J.E., and Dell, G.S. 1978. The phonological nature of phoneme monitoring: A critique of some ambiguity studies. *Journal of Verbal Learning and Verbal Behavior* 17:359–374.

Norris, D. 1986. Word recognition: Context effects without priming. *Cognition* 22:1–44.

Oden, G. C., and Spira, J. L. 1982. Influence of context on the activation and selection of ambiguous word senses. *Quarterly Journal of Experimental Psychology* 35A:51–64.

Onifer, W., and Swinney, D. A. 1981. Accessing lexical ambiguities during sentence comprehension: Effects of frequency of meaning and contextual bias. *Memory and Cognition* 9:225–236.

Peterson, R. R., and Simpson, G. B. 1987. *The Effect of Backward Priming on Word Recognition in Single-Word and Sentence Contexts.* Paper presented at the meeting of the Eastern Psychological Association, Washington, D.C.

Seidenberg, M. S., Tanenhaus, M. K., Leiman, J. M., and Bienkowski, M. 1982. Automatic access of the meanings of ambiguous words in context: Some limitations of knowledge-based processing. *Cognitive Psychology* 14:489–537.

Seidenberg, M. S., Waters, G. S., Sanders, M., and Langer, P. 1984. Pre- and post-lexical loci of contextual effects on word recognition. *Memory and Cognition* 12:315–328.

Simpson, G. B. 1981. Meaning dominance and semantic context in the processing of lexical ambiguity. *Journal of Verbal Learning and Verbal Behavior* 20:120–136.

Simpson, G. B. 1984. Lexical ambiguity and its role in models of word recognition. *Psychological Bulletin* 96:316–340.

Simpson, G. B., and Burgess, C. 1985. Activation and selection processes in the recognition of ambiguous words. *Journal of Experimental Psychology: Human Perception and Performance* 11:28–39.

Smith, F. 1971. *Understanding Reading.* New York: Holt.

Stanovich, K. E., and West, R. F. 1983. On priming by a sentence context. *Journal of Experimental Psychology: General* 112:1–36.

Swinney, D. A. 1979. Lexical access during sentence comprehension: (Re)Consideration of context effects. *Journal of Verbal Learning and Verbal Behavior* 18:645–659.

Swinney, D. A., and Hakes, D. T. 1976. Effects of prior context upon lexical access during sentence comprehension. *Journal of Verbal Learning and Verbal Behavior* 15:681–689.

Swinney, D., Onifer, W., Prather, P., and Hershkovits, M. 1979. Semantic facilitation across sensory modalities in the processing of individual words and sentences. *Memory and Cognition* 7:159–165.

Synetka, D. A., Tanenhaus, M. K., and Seidenberg, M. S. 1982. *Accessing the Component Readings of Ambiguous Words. A Chronometric Analysis*. Paper presented at the meeting of the American Psychological Association, Washington, D. C.

Tabossi, P. This volume.

Tabossi, P., Columbo, L., and Job, R. In press. Accessing lexical ambiguity: Effects of context and dominance. *Psychological Research*.

Tanenhaus, M. K., and Lucas, M. M. 1987. Context effects in lexical processing. *Cognition* 25:213–234.

Tanenhaus, M. K., and Donnenwerth-Nolan, S. 1984. Syntactic context and lexical access. *Quarterly Journal of Experimental Psychology* 36A:649–661.

Tanenhaus, M. K., Dell, G. S., and Carlson, G. 1987. Context effects in lexical processing: A connectionist perspective on modularity. In J. Garfield (ed.), *Modularity in Knowledge Representation and Natural Language Understanding*. Cambridge: MIT Press.

Tanenhaus, M. K., Leiman, J. M., and Seidenberg, M. S. 1979. Evidence for multiple stages in the processing of ambiguous words in syntactic contexts. *Journal of Verbal Learning and Verbal Behavior* 18:427–440.

Tweedy, J. R., Lapinski, R. H., and Schvaneveldt, R. W. 1977. Semantic-context effects on word recognition: Influence of varying the proportion of items presented in an appropriate context. *Memory and Cognition* 5:84–89.

Van Petten, C., and Kutas, M. 1987. Ambiguous words in context: An event-related potential analysis of the time course of meaning activation. *Journal of Memory and Language* 26:188–208.

Warren, R. E. 1972. Stimulus encoding and memory. *Journal of Experimental Psychology* 94:90–100.

Warren, R. E. 1974. Association, directionality, and stimulus encoding. *Journal of Experimental Psychology* 102:151–158.

White, H. 1986. Semantic priming of nonwords in lexical decision. *American Journal of Psychology* 99:479–485.

Sentential Context and Lexical Access

Patrizia Tabossi

Dipartimento di Psicologia
Università di Bologna
Italy

An important question in recent psycholinguistic research has been whether lexical access—the initial activation of semantic information attached to a lexical representation—can be affected by the context in which the word occurs. Clearly context does ultimately influence lexical processing. The issue is whether context has its effect at an early stage in lexical processing, or post-lexically, that is, after initial lexical activation has taken place.

Most research on context effects in lexical processing has focused on one class of lexical items: ambiguous words (but see also [Potter and Faulconer, 1979; Tabossi, in press; and Whitney, McKay, Kellas, and Emerson, 1985]). Since the initial demonstrations that ambiguous words in sentences take longer to process than unambiguous words [Foss, 1969; 1970] a great deal of work has been devoted to the development of experimental procedures to measure on-line processing and to the assessment of their reliability for studying ambiguity resolution.

Probably the best-known and most influential work on ambiguity resolution is the research done by Swinney and colleagues using a cross-modal lexical decision paradigm [Swinney, Prather, and Hirshkovitz, 1978]. In this task, subjects perform a lexical decision on a visually presented string of letters, while listening to a sentence containing an ambiguous word. The visual word appears at the offset of the ambiguous item and either is related to one of its meanings or else is a control, unrelated word. If the sentence which biases one interpretation of the ambiguous word, has an effect on its access, then the ambiguous word will be an effective prime only for the visual word related to that meaning. If, however, there is a point in time at which all meanings of the ambiguous word are activated, then the ambiguous word will prime a visual target word related to any of its meanings, regardless of contextual bias. According to Swinney and his associates, one of the major advantages of this paradigm is that the visual target is presented simultaneously with the offset of the ambiguity, thus ensuring that the lexical decision reflects access rather than post-access phenomena. Moreover, "the task reflects the access of the auditory (priming) words through the relative facilitation of lexical decision made to visual words, without drawing attention to the relationship involved" [Swinney, 1979, p. 648].

This paradigm was used by Swinney [1979] in a study in which the subjects listened to sentences such as the following:

The man was surprised when he found several spiders, roaches, and other bugs in the corner of his room.

Precisely at the offset of the ambiguity (bug), a target word was presented visually for lexical decision. The target was either related to one meaning of the ambiguity (e.g., ANT or SPY) or was an unrelated control (e.g., SEW). Lexical decisions to targets related to either meaning of the ambiguity were faster than responses to the control word, regardless of the sentential bias.

These and other similar results (e.g., [Conrad, 1974]) have led to a view in which access to an ambiguous word, or more generally lexical access, is an exhaustive, context-insensitive sub-process of the process of language comprehension. Context becomes operative only at a post-access stage, guiding the selection of the contextually relevant meaning of the ambiguous word (but see also [Hogoboam and Perjetti, 1975; Schvaneveldt, Meyer, and Becker, 1976; and Glucksberg, Kreuz, and Rho, 1986]).

Although there has been a great deal of discussion about the theoretical relevance of context independent lexical access for Fodor's modularity theory of cognition [Fodor, 1983] and the methodological difficulties associated with on-line procedures, relatively little attention has been paid to the central issue of how different types of context might influence lexical access.

One exception is a study by Seidenberg, Tanenhaus, Leiman, and Bienkowski [1982], in which subjects performed a naming task after listening to a sentence containing an ambiguous word. They used two classes of ambiguous words: ambiguous words with two noun senses (e.g., *straw*, *spade*), and ambiguous words with at least one noun sense and one verb sense (e.g., *rose*, *tire*). Sentential contexts were also of two types: priming and non-priming. Priming contexts biased one meaning of the ambiguous word by means of a lexical item highly semantically related or associated to that meaning (e.g.,

"Although the farmer bought the straw"; "The gardener cut the ”), whereas non-priming contexts biased the ambiguous word by providing either syntactic or pragmatic information (e.g., "John began to tire," "You should have played the spade"), depending on the type of ambiguous word. In non-priming contexts access was always exhaustive, whereas in priming contexts noun-verb ambiguities were still exhaustively accessed, but noun-noun ambiguities were accessed selectively. Seidenberg et al. [1982] concluded that lexical access does not seem to be sensitive to context effects, but appears to be affected by the structure of the ambiguous word.

Although studies examining the effect of semantic context on ambiguity resolution have failed to provide evidence for semantic context effects, some studies using unambiguous words have found clear context effects. Schwanen-flugel and Shoben [1985], for example, investigated the effects of sentential constraints on the recognition of expected and unexpected words. They found that highly constraining sentences, i.e., sentences which specify strongly the semantic features that must be included in the to-be-recognized word, facilitated recognition only of the expected words, whereas less constraining sentences had weaker, but broader effects. In addition, when highly constraining sentences were frequently completed by expected words, these sentences inhibited the recognition of unexpected words.

The constraints established by the sentential contexts in Schwanenflugel and Shoben [1985] are very similar to those used in a recent study on the access of unambiguous words [Tabossi, in press]. Here the subjects performed a lexical decision task on a visual target (e.g., YELLOW) after listening to a sentence that either primed one aspect of the meaning of an unambiguous word in the sentence (priming condition), or primed no specific aspect of the noun's meaning (neutral condition), or primed another aspect of its meaning (inhibiting condition), as in the following example:

Priming: In the light, the blond hair of the little girl had the lustre of gold (gold is yellow).

Neutral: At the lecture, the clever teacher spoke at length about gold (no specific aspect of gold).

Inhibiting: In the shop, the artisan shaped with ease the bar of gold (gold is malleable).

The results showed that lexical decision to the word YELLOW, presented at the offset of *gold*, was fastest after the priming context, next faster after the neutral context, and slowest after the inhibiting context. Since in the same study a further experiment ruled out the possibility that the observed facilitative effects reflected the facilitation produced on YELLOW by previous words in the sentence (e.g., *blonde*, *lustre*), the findings were interpreted as evidence that a sentential context which imposes sufficient constraints on what semantic features are to be found in a following word can affect the access to that word, facilitating the activation of the contextually pertinent aspects of its meaning, and inhibiting the activation of the non-pertinent ones.

The semantic contexts used in studies of lexical ambiguity resolution seem to differ from the feature priming contexts used by Tabossi et al. and by Schwanenflugel and Shoben. Consider for example, an influential study by Onifer and Swinney [1981]. They constructed sentences which biased either the dominant or subordinant meaning of an ambiguous word as in examples (1) and (2):

(1) The housewife's face literally lit up as a plumber extracted her lost wedding ring from the sink.

(2) The office walls were so thin that they could hear the ring of their neighbor's phone whenever a call came in.

Sentence (1) biases the dominant meaning of "ring," whereas sentence (2) biases its subordinate meaning. Onifer and Swinney found that lexical decisions to visual targets related to either the biased or unbiased meaning were facilitated when the targets were presented immediately after the ambiguous word, regardless of whether they were related to the dominant or subordinant meaning. However, unlike the contexts used by Tabossi et al. and Schwanenflugel and Shoben, the Onifer and Swinney sentences do not make salient any specific aspect of the meaning of either sense of "ring" (e.g., "precious," "round" or "noisy").

In a recent study [Tabossi, Columbo, and Job, 1987], my colleagues and I examined lexical ambiguity resolution using feature priming contexts. The subjects listened to a sentence which contained an ambiguous word and biased its dominant or its secondary meaning by priming a very characteristic aspect of either of them, as in the following examples:

(3) The violent hurricane did not damage the ships which were in the port, one of the best equipped along the coast.

(4) Deceived by the identical colour, the host took a bottle of barolo, instead of one of port, and offered it to his guests.

Sentence (3) biases the dominant meaning of *port* by priming its being safe, whereas sentence (4) biases the secondary meaning of the ambiguity and primes the fact that *port* is a red wine. Precisely at the offset of *port*, the subjects performed a lexical decision task on a visual word which either denoted the aspect of the meaning of the ambiguity primed by one of the two sentences or was a control (e.g., SAFE, RED, SHORT).

Table 1   Mean reaction times (msec) for lexical decision to target words in the context biasing the dominant meaning and in the context biasing the secondary meaning of an ambiguity.

Type of Target	Type of Context	
	Dominant Bias	**Secondary Bias**
Dominant	653	736
Secondary	692	732
Control	704	798

The results (see Table 1) showed that following sentence (3), SAFE was responded to faster than either RED or SHORT, which did not differ significantly from each other, whereas following sentence (4), SAFE and RED did not differ reliably from each other and both were faster than SHORT.

According to these findings, lexical access appears to be sensitive to context as well as dominance effects. When context primes a very characteristic aspect of the dominant meaning of an ambiguity, both context and dominance converge on the same piece of information which is accessed, whereas information about the secondary meaning need not be activated at all. However, when the sentence primes a relevant aspect of the secondary meaning of the ambiguity, the information activated by the context and that activated as a result of dominance effects differ, yielding the exhaustive access observed in the data.

While showing that there may be selective effects of context on lexical access, Tabossi et al. [1987] provides no conclusive evidence on whether the nature of the contextual information is entirely responsible for the effects. In addition to the way in which the sentences biased the ambiguous items, the materials used in this work also differed from those employed by Onifer and Swinney [1981] in another important respect. In Tabossi et al. the related visual words denoted characteristic aspects of one meaning of the ambiguity but did not have a strong associative link to it, whereas in Onifer and Swinney [1981] the visual words which were not controls were mostly either associates or synonyms of one meaning of the ambiguous word. Therefore, they are more likely to be sensitive to, and hence to reflect, intra-lexical relations of the ambiguities rather than their contextual interpretation [Barclay, Bransford, Franks, McCarrell, and Nitsch, 1974].

However, the hypothesis that the different relation holding between ambiguities and visual words in the two studies might play some part in the explanation of their discrepancy, has been ruled out by a series of three recent cross-modal studies.

The rationale of the first experiment in Tabossi [submitted for publication] was as follows: If either the nature of context or the type of link between an ambiguity and a related visual word or both can affect the way in which lexical information is accessed, then the same ambiguous words that in Tabossi et al. [1987] were found to be selectively accessed in the dominant biasing context, should be shown to be accessed exhaustively if both the above factors are varied. More specifically, if the ambiguous word (e.g., port) occurs in a sentence that biases its dominant meaning, but primes no specific aspect of it (e.g., "The man had to be at five o'clock at the port, for a very important meeting"), and, in addition, its related visual words are associated to either of its meanings, but denote no specific aspect of it (e.g., SEA, LIQUEUR), then as in Onifer and Swinney [1981] no selective effects should be observed.

The prediction was confirmed by the results which showed that the subjects were faster at deciding that both SEA and LIQUEUR, presented at the offset of *port*, were words than at deciding that the control HAND was a word. Here, unlike what had been observed in Tabossi et al. [1987], SEA and LIQUEUR did not differ from each other and both were facilitated with respect to the control.

Two further experiments provided support for the claim that the nature of context is the only factor responsible for the selective effects obtained in Tabossi et al. [1987]. In fact, lexical decisions on the same targets which the ambiguity exerted selective effects of priming on in that study (e.g., SAFE and RED) were found to be equally facilitated with respect to the control (e.g., SHORT) when they were presented following a biasing, non-priming context (e.g., "The man had to be at five o'clock at the port for a very important meeting"). By contrast, SEA and LIQUEUR, which were previously found not to differ from each other, were indeed reliably different when presented after a constraining context (e.g., "The violent hurricane did not damage the ships which were in the port, one of the best equipped along the coast"). Under this context, in fact, deciding that SEA is a word was faster than deciding than either LIQUEUR or HAND were words (see Table 2).

Taken together, the studies described here support the hypothesis that lexical activation can be selective, provided that prior context supplies the necessary information. These results call for a reconsideration of the context insensitive model of lexical access. But this conclusion, that I believe to be correct, is unlikely to convince the skeptics, or at least not before some of the methodological questions often raised in connection with the paradigm and the task used in the reported studies have been discussed.

Table 2   Mean reaction times (msec) for lexical decision to target words in the three experimental conditions (contextually congruent, contextually incongruent, and control) as a function of the type of contextual bias (constraining vs. non-constraining) and of the ambiguity-target link (associate vs. feature denoting).

Type of Context and Ambiguity-Target Link	Experimental Conditions		
	Congruent	Incongruent	Control
Non-constraining Context Associate Visual Words (Exp 1)	592	600	643
Non-constraining Context Feature Denoting Visual Words (Exp 2)	605	619	648
Constraining Context Associate Visual Words (Exp 3)	643	688	682

1 *Methodological Considerations*

In the current literature on lexical access, methodological arguments are usually put forward to explain contradictory results. These arguments vary depending on whether they are proposed to discount evidence which appears to be in favour of the non-autonomous model of lexical activation or *vice versa*. These discussions, together with the ever increasing attention to what processes are really tapped by the most widely used experimental techniques [Warren, 1972; Posner, 1968; Cutler and Norris, 1979; Lupker, 1984] indicate the great difficulty of setting up paradigms which on the one hand reflect lexical activation when it occurs during the very fast processing of language, and on the other hand do not alter and interfere with the specific phenomena under investigation.

One point which is often made by those supporting the context-insensitive model is that selective effects observed in several studies are likely to reflect post-access, rather than immediate access phenomena. A similar explanation probably applies to results such as those obtained by Simpson [1981]. Using the cross-modal paradigm he found that when an ambiguity (e.g., *count*) with a dominant and a secondary meaning (e.g., related to numbers and nobility, respectively) occurred in a non-biasing sentential context, its dominant meaning was accessed first, whereas when the sentence weakly biased one meaning, access was selective if the bias was towards the dominant meaning and was exhaustive otherwise. When the ambiguity occurred in a strongly biasing context, however, only its contextually pertinent meaning was accessed.

While supporting a model in which both dominance and context seem to affect lexical access, these results are hardly compelling. In fact they have been obtained using a lexical decision task on visual words that, instead of being presented exactly at the offset of the ambiguity, appears 120 msec after the ambiguity had occurred, and this is a long enough delay to justify the suspicion that the results reflect later phenomena rather than the initial activation of the ambiguity. But even if one used the cross-modal paradigm presenting the visual targets precisely at the offset of an ambiguity, the results obtained may still be considered to reflect post-access phenomena if the task performed by the subjects is the lexical decision [Seidenberg, Waters, Sanders, and Langer, 1984].

Not all lexical decision studies, however, are open to these criticisms. In particular, when the data support the context insensitive model, the results themselves indicate that post-access phenomena have not occurred. Unfortunately, findings of this sort may be vulnerable to other arguments. In Onifer and Swinney [1981], for instance, lexical decision was performed on very short, usually monosyllabic visual targets following equally short ambiguous words, and there is evidence that facilitation may be exerted not only by a preceding word on a subsequent one, but also *vice versa* [Kiger and Glass, 1983]. In order for these backward effects of priming to take place, processing on the first occurring word must not have been completed by the time the second word is presented, and this is more likely to be the case with short words such as those employed in Onifer and Swinney [1981]. Thus, selective effects of access may not have been obtained in that study, simply because backward priming prevented them from being detected.

To what extent are these various methodological issues going to affect the interpretation of the results illustrated above? In my view, very little. In fact, they all rely on the fact that either specific sets of ambiguity-target pairs or the task performed on the targets affect, in one way or the other, the results obtained in a given study. But the way in which these factors operate, supposedly reflecting processes other than the intended ones, must remain constant if materials and task are kept fixed. Instead, in these studies, different results were obtained using the same task (lexical decision) and the same sets of materials, which therefore cannot account for the findings.

Perhaps there is still one objection to which these results are open and which, if correct, may reconcile them with the context insensitive model. It is possible that in the experiments in which selective effects were observed, the faster decisions obtained on the targets related to the contextually pertinent meaning of the ambiguities were not the result of facilitation produced by the selective access to the ambiguous items. Rather, other words in the preceding contexts may have primed the targets, speeding up lexical decision on them, while access to the ambiguities was still exhaustive. "The violent hurricane did not damage the ships which were in the port, one of the best equipped along the coast," for example, was found to facilitate SAFE with respect to RED and SHORT, and SEA with respect to LIQUEUR and HAND. According to this hypothesis, words such as *damage* or *ships* might have primed SAFE and SEA, thus facilitating lexical decision on them. But if *port* had been accessed exhaustively, lexical decision on RED and LIQUEUR related to the contextually incongruent meaning of the ambiguity, though slower than SAFE and SEA, should still have been faster than the controls. In neither experiment, however, was there evidence that a similar facilitation had occurred and there are grounds to believe that lexical decision in cross-modal studies may not be sensitive to such long distance effects [Tabossi, in press].

2 *Conclusions*

There are two major conclusions that can be drawn from this discussion. The first is methodological. As we have seen, experimental procedures for the investigation of the real time phenomena involved in language comprehension are necessarily complex and their interpretation is not straightforward. Indeed, a better comprehension of what processes are reflected by different techniques is one of the major goals in current research, and without its clarification, genuine progress in the area will hardly be achieved. But, given the relevance of methodological questions, restricting the discussion on lexical access to such problems is both misleading and unwarranted. In fact, as the different results obtained in the above studies indicate, the available techniques may be fruitfully employed to clarify issues that are of theoretical interest.

The second point is empirical. Contrary to what is currently claimed, lexical activation during comprehension is not always exhaustive and insensitive to prior contextual information. Whether lexical access can be directed by a preceding sentential context depends upon the nature of the contextual constraint. While sentences providing syntactic or pragmatic information or including a word semantically related to one meaning of an ambiguous word do not seem to be able to direct access to that meaning, selective effects can be yielded in contexts which operate by imposing constraints on what information is to be found in an incoming word.

Although, as has already been pointed out, these feature priming mechanisms have been shown to be effective in several tasks involving lexical processing, how they actually function in contexts other than the very simple experimental ones is still unclear. For example, what exactly are the features on which a constraining context imposes its restrictions? According to Schwanenflugel and Shoben [1985], "'featural restrictions' is meant to refer to more than the traditional sense of the term 'features' and includes constraints based on general knowledge as well" (p. 248). In the work reported here, aspects of either meaning of an ambiguity were collected empirically, asking a number of people to characterize, for instance, a port. The features actually primed by the sentences and referred to by one set of visual words had two characteristics: A) They were the features most frequently produced by the people—"central" features, according to Barsalou's [1982] terminology. B) They were features that were never produced as associates to the ambiguous words by a different group of judges. But if sentential contexts can affect the activation of "central" features of a word's meaning, how effective are they in the activation of less "central" pieces of lexical information? Also, given a feature, what information should be included in a sentence to prime it? Even if for experimental purposes one can construct simplified priming contexts using well-known constraints, such as verbal selectional restrictions, or the intuition of independent judges, the general issue of what information is available to a listener at a given time during comprehension as a result of his understanding of a fragment of the on-going discourse remains open. Clarification of these contextual mechanisms is required—as I have hopefully been able to demonstrate. In order to build an adequate theory of lexical access, investigation of how sentential context operates upon the activation of lexical information might, in addition, provide us with a useful perspective on those processes involved in real-time language comprehension, processes which are as yet little understood.

Acknowledgments

This research was supported by C.N.R., grants CT 84.1659 and CT 85.2567.

References

Barclay, J. R., Bransford, J. D., Franks, J. J., McCarrell, N. S., and Nitsch, K. 1974. Comprehension and semantic flexibility. *Journal of Verbal Learning and Verbal Behavior* 13:471–481.

Barsalou, L. W. 1982. Context-independent and context-dependent information in concepts. *Memory and Cognition* 1:82–93.

Conrad, C. 1974. Context effects in sentence comprehension: A study of the subjective lexicon. *Memory and Cognition* 2:130–138.

Cutler, A., and Norris, D. G. 1979. Monitoring sentence comprehension. In W. E. Cooper, and E. C. T. Walker (eds.), *Sentence Processing: Psycholinguistic Studies Presented to Merrill Garrett*. Hillsdale: Erlbaum.

Doolings, D. J. 1972. Some context effects in the speeded comprehension of sentences. *Journal of Experimental Psychology* 93:56–62.

Fodor, J. A. 1983. *The Modularity of Mind: An Essay on Faculty Psychology.* Cambridge: Bradford.

Foss, D. J. 1969. Decision processes during sentence comprehension: Effects of lexical item difficulty and position upon decision times. *Journal of Verbal Learning and Verbal Behavior* 8:457–462.

Foss, D. J. 1970. Some effects of ambiguity upon sentence completion. *Journal of Verbal Learning and Verbal Behavior* 9:699–706.

Glucksberg, S., Kreuz, R. J., and Rho, S. 1986. Context can constrain lexical access: Implications for models of language comprehension. *Journal of Experimental Psychology: Learning, Memory, and Cognition* 3:323–333.

Hogaboam, T. W., and Perfetti, C. A. 1975. Lexical ambiguity and sentence comprehension. *Journal of Verbal Learning and Verbal Behavior* 14:265–274.

Kiger, J. I., and Glass, A. L. 1983. The facilitation of lexical decisions by a prime occurring after the target. *Memory and Cognition* 11:356–365.

Lupker, S. J. 1984. Semantic priming without association: A second look. *Journal of Verbal Learning and Verbal Behavior* 23:709–733.

Onifer, W., and Swinney, D. A. 1981. Accessing lexical ambiguity during sentence comprehension: Effects of frequency of meaning and contextual bias. *Memory and Cognition* 9:225–236.

Posner, M. I. 1978. *Chronometric Explorations of Mind.* Hillsdale: Erlbaum.

Potter, M. C. and Faulconer, B. A. 1979. Understanding noun phrases. *Journal of Verbal Learning and Verbal Behavior* 18:509–521.

Schwanenflugel, P. J. and Shoben, E. J. 1975. The influence of sentence constraint on the scope of facilitation for upcoming words. *Journal of Memory and Language* 24:232–252.

Seidenberg, M. S., Tanenhaus, M. K., Leiman, J. M., and Bienkowski, M. 1982. Automatic access of the meanings of ambiguous words in context: Some limitations of knowledge-based processing. *Cognitive Psychology* 14:489–537.

Seidenberg, M. S., Waters, G. S., Sanders, M., and Langer, P. 1984. Pre- and post-lexical loci of contextual effects on word recognition. *Memory and Cognition* 12:315–328.

Simpson, G. B. 1981. Meaning, dominance, and semantic context in the processing of lexical ambiguity. *Journal of Verbal Learning and Verbal Behavior* 20:120–136.

Swinney, D. A. 1979. Lexical access during sentence comprehension: (Re) consideration of context effects. *Journal of Verbal Learning and Verbal Behavior* 6:645–659.

Swinney, D. A. , Onifer, W., Prather, P., and Hirshkowitz, M. 1979. Individual words and sentences. *Memory and Cognition* 7:159–165.

Tabossi, P. In press. Effects of context on the immediate interpretation of unambiguous nouns. *Journal of Experimental Psychology: Learning, Memory, and Cognition.*

Tabossi, P. Submitted for publication. Accessing lexical ambiguity in different types of sentential context.

Tabossi, P., Colombo, L., and Job, R. 1987. Accessing lexical ambiguity: Effects of context and dominance. *Psychological Research* 49:161–167.

Warren, R. E. 1972. Stimulus encoding and memory. *Journal of Experimental Psychology* 94:90–100.

Whitney, P., McKay, T., Kellas, G., and Emerson, W. A. Jr. 1985. Semantic activation of noun concepts in context. *Journal of Experimental Psychology: Learning, Memory, and Cognition* 11:126–135.

The Verb Mutability Effect: Studies of the Combinatorial Semantics of Nouns and Verbs

Dedre Gentner
University of Illinois

Ilene M. France
Carnegie-Mellon University

This paper investigates the combinatorial semantics of nouns and verbs in sentences: specifically, the phenomenon of meaning adjustment under semantic strain. The first issue in semantic adjustment is the locus of change. Gentner [1981b] proposed the verb mutability hypothesis: that the semantic structures conveyed by verbs and other predicate terms are more likely to be altered to fit the context than are the semantic structures conveyed by object-reference terms. To test this claim, in Experiments 1 and 2 subjects paraphrased simple sentences in which verbs and nouns were combined with varying degrees of semantic strain: e.g., "The daughters weakened," or "The lizard worshipped." The resulting paraphrases were analyzed for change of meaning in three different ways. The results confirmed that verbs alter meaning more than nouns do.

The second question is how this meaning adjustment takes place. In particular, is meaning adjustment governed by orderly semantic processes, or is it primarily pragmatic and context-driven? This question was investigated in Experiments 3a and 3b. The results indicate that, although meaning adjustment is initiated in response to a mismatch with context, it is nevertheless characterized by orderly semantic processes. This paper concerns combination of meaning:

specifically, how the meanings of nouns and verbs combine to make new sentence meanings. We focus on cases where the noun and verb are semantically ill-matched. Understanding such cases is useful not only in explaining metaphorical extension but also in constraining the set of explanations that can apply in normal sentence processing. When simple straightforward combinations such as

The professor pondered.

are considered, it is difficult to know how much of the processing is new and how much is invoking of prestored structures. But now consider a semantically strained combination, such as "The butterfly pondered." For sentences like this, in which the noun and verb are semantically ill-matched, we can be fairly sure that the meaning is not prestored: some kind of active combinatorial processing must take place during interpretation.

How are such sentences interpreted? It could be that such sentences are simply uninterpretable anomalies, as some construals of Chomsky's [1965] selectional restriction would suggest. Assuming that interpretation is possible, this presumably requires some kind of meaning adjustment. Therefore the first question is where this adjustment typically takes place. One linguistically attractive view is that the verb will dominate the sentence meaning, and the noun will be reinterpreted to fit the semantic restrictions imposed by the verb. For example, given "The butterfly pondered." a hearer would resolve the conflict between noun and verb by altering the noun: e.g., by deciding that 'butterfly" referred to a person wearing bright-colored clothes, or perhaps to a particularly insouciant person. This view was put forth by Chafe [1970] and other linguists as part of a general verb-centered model of sentence meaning. It arose from the intuitively plausible view that the verb provides the organizing framework for the representation of a sentence. The conception of verb centrality has been an important part of theories of sentence meaning since the advent of case grammar [Fillmore, 1966; 1968]. The psychological interpretation of case grammar was that the verb is the central relational element in a sentence, around which the nouns cluster, each related to the central event by its own thematic relation—who did it, with what, to whom, and so on. [Fillmore, 1966; 1968]. Verb-centered sentence representations have been used in all areas of cognitive science: psychology [Kintsch, 1974; Norman and Rumelhart, 1975], computer science [Schank, 1973; 1974], and linguistics [Chafe, 1970; Fillmore, 1966; 1968]. In addition to being an important theoretical notion, verb centrality has received empirical support in tasks involving judgment of sentence meaning [Gollob, 1968; Healy and Miller, 1970; Heise, 1969; 1970], and in tasks requiring performance under disruption [Gladney and Krulee, 1967].

The verb, in this view, provides the relational framework for the sentence. Therefore it seems reasonable that the verb should determine which classes of nouns can fill its argument slots. Chafe [1970, p. 97–98] makes this prediction. He compares the verb to the sun, in that "anything which happens to the sun affects the entire solar system," whereas "a noun is like a planet whose internal modifications affect it alone, and not the solar system as a whole." Similarly, Healy and Miller [1970] compare the verb to the plot of a play and the nouns to the actors who merely act out the plot. Thus, considerations of verb central-ity suggest that the verb semantic structure should govern the semantics of the nouns in a sentence.

Yet informal observation suggests that the opposite pattern often occurs: the verb meaning often adapts to the noun meaning in cases of strain. The first author informally presented many people with the sentence

The flower kissed the rock.

and asked them to report what they pictured in response to the sentence. If fixed verb meaning was the rule, people might have reported a picture of a flower-like person and a rock-like person engaged in a literal act of kissing. In-stead, they reported something like "a daisy drooping over a rock, with its petals pressed against the rock," or "a daffodil blown gently across the rock and brushing it lightly." They preserved noun meaning and altered the verb.[1]

This brings us to the central hypothesis of this paper, the *verb mutability* hypothesis [Gentner, 1981b]: When the noun and verb of a sentence are semantically mismatched, the normal recourse is to make an adjustment to the verb's meaning in interpreting the sentence. Briefly put, in case of mismatch, the verb gives in. Such a claim is, of course, contrary to the verb-centralist pre-diction that the meaning of the verb should dominate that of the noun. Later in this paper, we will consider whether verb-central theories need necessarily imply verb-dominant interpretation strategies.

Plan of the Paper   The first requirement in this research is to determine where change of meaning occurs. A major difficulty in carrying out this kind of research is to devise objective tests of change of meaning. Since beginning this research with Albert Stevens in 1973, I and my colleagues have come up with three different methods for measuring change of meaning. Indeed, from a psychological point of view, one of the contributions of this paper is these methodological innovations. However, since readers from other disciplines may wish to skim over the experimental techniques, we have organized the paper

---

1 Talmy [personal communication, 1980] mentions a similar phenomenon. He asked people to de-scribe what they imagined for the sentence "She wafted through the crowd." People tended to de-scribe a woman strolling gracefully through a crowd, changing direction frequently in response to local interactions. Again, people altered the notion of *wafting* to be some motion a person could do; they did not reinterpret the subject *she* to be something that could *waft*.

into three parts. Part I describes experiments designed to test where change of meaning occurs. Part II presents experiments on the nature of the adjustment process. Part III is a summary and theoretical discussion. Readers who wish to touch lightly on the experimental methodology may want to read the Rationale at the beginning of Part I, possibly the experiments in Part II, and the theoretical discussion in Part III.

Part I: *Experiments on Where Change of Meaning Occurs*

Rationale In two experiments, subjects were asked to paraphrase simple sentences of the form "The noun verbed." The sentences were composed using all 64 possible pairs in a matrix of eight nouns and eight verbs. (See Figure 14.1.) Of the eight nouns, two were human, two animate non-human, two concrete, and two abstract, according to the hierarchy discussed by Clark and Begun [1971]. (It should be noted that not every step in their hierarchy is used here.) Correspondingly, the eight verbs were divided into two each of verbs preferring for their subject nouns either human, animate non-human, concrete or abstract nouns.

When the noun and the verb agreed, the sentences were normal-sounding. For example, the verb "limp" prefers an animate subject and "mule" is a animate noun; thus "The mule limped." should be an acceptable sentence. The sentence "The daughter limped." is also acceptable, because "daughter" is animate (and human as well). However, when the nouns violated the verbs' subject preferences, the sentences were strained. For example, if "limp" is paired with a nonanimate noun such as "lantern," then the resulting sentence "The lantern limped." is semantically strained.

The verb mutability hypothesis predicts that under semantic strain, subjects will alter the meaning of the verb more than that of the noun in paraphrasing the sentences. To test this, three different measures of change of meaning were applied to the paraphrases:

1. **Divide-and-rate method** (pilot experiment): judges divided the paraphrases into the part that came from the original noun and the part that came from the original verb; then ratings were collected between the original words and the paraphrase segments that came from them.

2. **Double-paraphrase method** (Experiment 1): A new group of subjects paraphrased the paraphrases. Then we simply counted the occurrences of any original noun or verb in the reparaphrases. The number of original words that resurfaced in these reparaphrases was taken as a measure of

meaning preservation. The reasoning is that the more a word's meaning was distorted in the initial paraphrase, the less likely it is that the original word will return in the second paraphrase. For example, the noun *lizard* is more likely than the verb worship to return in a reparaphrase of "The small gray reptile lay on a hot rock and stared unblinkingly at the sun."

3. **Retrace method** (Experiments 1 and 2): A new group of subjects was given the eight original nouns (or the eight original verbs). Then they were read the 64 paraphrases. Their job was to guess for each paraphrase which word had occurred in the original sentence. Their accuracy was taken as a measure of the degree of meaning preservation. The reasoning is that the more a word's meaning had been altered in the paraphrase, the harder it should be to retrace that original word.

The results bore out the verb mutability hypothesis. By all three measures, verbs changed meaning more than nouns. Further, this differential was greatest in the semantically strained sentences, indicating that the verb adjustment was a response to the strain, rather than, say, a reflection of some general vagueness in verb meanings.

1 PILOT STUDY

1.1 Paraphrase Task

1.1.1 Method

Subjects Sixteen subjects, all undergraduates at the University of California at San Diego, participated in the original paraphrase task, receiving class credit in psychology courses.

Materials Sentences were constructed using nouns and verbs that varied in compatibility with each other. The basic design was the 8 × 8 matrix shown in Figure 14.1, which led to 64 sentences of the form "The noun verbed."

Each subject paraphrased a set of eight sentences, selected so that no subject received the same noun or verb more than once. There were eight such sentence sets, to make a total of 64 sentences distributed across eight groups of two subjects each. The order in which sentences were paraphrased was randomized for each subject.

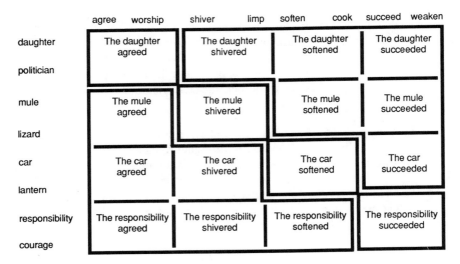

Figure 14.1 Matrix of noun-verb combinations used in Experiments 1 and 2, showing the diagonal, above-diagonal and below-diagonal sectors.

Procedure   Subjects were asked to paraphrase the sentences in a natural manner: they were asked to imagine that they had overheard the sentence in passing and were trying to decide the most natural interpretation possible. They were also told not to repeat any content words from the original sentences. Subjects were eliminated if (1) they failed to complete all 8 paraphrases; or (2) they used the original words in the paraphrase in two or more instances; or (3) if they gave two or more patently silly responses, such as "Humpty Dumpty meets King Kong." In fact, most subjects were able to perform the task.

1.1.2 Results

Qualitative examination of the paraphrases suggested that, as predicted, verb adjustment was the dominant strategy of interpretation. When meaning adjustment took place, the meaning of the verb was generally adjusted to fit the meaning of the noun. Other response types also occurred, although infrequently. One was noun adjustment, in which the meaning of the noun was adjusted to fit the verb. A third strategy was to adjust both the noun and the verb. The remaining strategies were even less frequent. The fourth was simple repetition of one word or the other. For example, "The daughter worshipped" was paraphrased as "The daughter prayed to God." Subjects had been instructed not to repeat any content words, so these repetitions were errors, possibly due to carelessness. Repetition errors occurred more often for nouns than for verbs. The fifth response type was pronoun substitution, in which the noun was replaced by a pronoun. For example, the sentence "The mule weakened" was paraphrased as "He became less stubborn." Finally, the sixth response type, which occurred infrequently, was a word-by-word paraphrase that preserved the independent meanings of both words. In sentences with low strain, this led to a reasonable paraphrase; for example, "The lizard limped" was paraphrased as "The small amphibian [sic] had an injured leg." On the other hand, for sentences with high semantic strain, the rote strategy led to an unsatisfactory paraphrase; for example, "The lizard worshipped" was paraphrased as "The reptile adored" by one subject. Only a small percentage of the responses fell into the fourth, fifth and sixth categories and we will have little to say about them.

The main question from our point of view is whether, when subjects did perform semantic adjustment, the locus of change was the noun or the verb. To obtain objective judgments of relative degree of meaning adjustment, we used a *divide-and-rate* task, as follows.

1.2 Divide-and-Rate Task

1.2.1 Division Task

Three upper-division, linguistically sophisticated psychology students at the University of California at San Diego, who did not know the hypothesis of the study, read the 128 paraphrases as well as the original sentences. They were asked to indicate for each paraphrase which part came from the original noun and which from the verb. In the cases on which the three judges agreed, their segmentations were then used in a similarity-rating task. Unfortunately, rater agreement was low, so we used only one paraphrase of each sentence in the subsequent rating task. These 64 segmented paraphrases generated 128 similarity judgments, as described below. In seven cases, individual sentence paraphrases that were impossible to score were replaced, using new paraphrase subjects.

1.2.2 Ratings Task

Subjects   A new group of 10 undergraduates from the University of California at San Diego students served as raters. They received class credit for their participation.

Procedure   Subjects were read each original noun, along with the corresponding part of the paraphrase (i.e., the part of the paraphrase judged to have come from the noun, and similarly for the verbs). There were 64 noun comparisons and 64 verb comparisons. They were asked to rate the similarity, on a 1–10 scale, for each pair of phrases they were read. For example, they would rate how similar *lizard* was to *small reptile*, or how similar *worshipped* was to *lay on a hot rock and stared unblinkingly at the sun*. Verbs and nouns were randomly mixed in order of presentation. The comparisons were read in a semi-random order, so that pairs involving the same original word were interspersed with other pairs.

1.2.3 *Results*

The average similarity rating for nouns was 7.6 and the average rating for the verbs was 6.8 (t = 3.73; p < .005). Thus, the noun paraphrases were judged more similar to the original nouns than the verb paraphrases were to the verbs. These results suggest that the verbs changed meaning to a greater extent than the nouns.

1.3 *Discussion*

Although the results of this study were promising, the divide-and-rate methodology had serious drawbacks. First, it was exceedingly time-consuming and irritating to the judges. Second, it had the disadvantage that many of the paraphrases had to be discarded because the judges could not agree on which part came from which of the original words. Finally, the judgment was based implicitly on a debatable assumption: that the noun and the verb of the original sentence have separable manifestations in a paraphrase, rather than interacting to produce one unified interpretation. Therefore, for the next study two further methods for judging change of meaning were adopted. These were the *double-paraphrase* measure and the *retrace measure*.

In the *double paraphrase* method, after the initial paraphrases were collected, a second group of naive subjects was asked to paraphrase the paraphrases. Then these reparaphrases were scored for any occurrence of the *original* noun or verb. The relative number of nouns and verbs from the original sentences that resurfaced in these reparaphrases was taken as the measure of meaning preservation. The reasoning is that the better a word's meaning is preserved in the original paraphrase, the more likely the word itself is to return in the second paraphrase.

In the *retrace* measure, new groups of subjects were given the paraphrases and told to figure out which words had occurred in the original sentence. They were given, say, the original eight possible nouns. Then they were read the paraphrases, and for each paraphrase they were asked to circle which noun they thought had occurred in the original sentence from which the paraphrase had been generated. Another group of judges performed the same retrace task for the verbs. The relative accuracy of their choices provided a measure of the relative degree of meaning change in nouns versus verbs. The reasoning here was that the more a word's meaning had been altered in the paraphrase, the harder it should be to trace back to that original word.

The double-paraphrase and retrace measures of meaning change were utilized in Experiment 1. In other respects, this study was a larger-scale replication of the pilot study. The basic paraphrase task was identical; the chief difference was in the methodology for judging change of meaning. One important feature of this experiment was that the new methodology, particularly the retrace method, allowed a finer-grained analysis of the conditions under which meaning change occurred.

2 Experiment 1

2.1 Initial Paraphrase Task

2.1.1 Method

Subjects   There were 54 subjects, all undergraduate psychology students at the University of Washington, Seattle. They received credit in psychology classes for their participation. Six of these were eliminated for failure to comply with the instructions (see Pilot Study), leaving 48 subjects.

Procedure   The stimulus materials and method of collecting the original paraphrases were identical to those in the pilot study. Each subject paraphrased eight sentences, chosen so that the same subject never saw a given noun or verb more than once. Thus, eight groups of subjects were required to cover the matrix of 64 sentences. There were six subjects in each of these eight groups. This meant that there were six paraphrases of each of the original sentences.

2.1.2 Results

Table 1 shows sample paraphrases for normal and strained sentences. Qualitatively, it can be seen that the strained sentences lead to considerable semantic adjustment, particularly for the verb.   To verify these patterns objectively, two further tasks were performed. After the original paraphrase had been generated, two new sets of subjects were run on the double-paraphrase task and the retrace task.

Table 1 Results of Experiment 1: Sample responses to matched and under-matched (semantically strained) sentences

Matched

The politician worshipped

The public servant praised God.

The man in charge of public affairs gave praise.

The candidate looked to his campaign manager for advice on every detail.

Undermatched

The lizard worshipped

The hypocritical person went to church.

The pet is thankful for the hand that feeds it.

The chameleon stared at the sun in a daze.

The car worshipped

The vehicle only responded to him.

The automobile loved a good driver.

Someone's vehicle was given a rest on a Sunday.

The responsibility worshipped

He never minded having a heavy work load.

They fulfilled their social obligations by going to church.

The commitment prayed.

2.2 Double-paraphrase task

2.2.1 Method

Subjects An additional 48 subjects yoked to the original 48 subjects participated. All were undergraduates from the University of Washington, who received class credit for their participation.

Procedure Each new subject was given the eight original paraphrases written by one of the original subjects, and was told to paraphrase these eight sentences as naturally as possible. These double-paraphrase subjects were given no information as to the original source of the sentences.

2.2.2 *Results*

The dependent variable was the number of nouns and verbs from the original matrix that reappeared in the reparaphrases. As predicted, nouns outnumbered verbs: 74 nouns (19% of a possible 384) reappeared, as contrasted with 16 verbs (or 4%) (t = 7.03; p < .01). Thus, by the reparaphrase measure, the degree of change of meaning is greater in verbs than in nouns.

2.3 *Retrace task*

2.3.1 *Method*

Subjects The subjects were 84 college students from the Cambridge, Massachusetts area, who were paid for their participation.

Procedure Half the subjects traced nouns; the other half traced verbs. The noun groups were given a list of the eight nouns that had appeared in the original sentences. They were told that they would hear paraphrases generated by other subjects from a set of original sentences, and that each of the original sentences had contained one of the nouns on their sheet. They were not given any information about the verbs in these original sentences. Then they were read each of the 64 paraphrases in one covering set, as defined below. For each paraphrase they were to circle the noun that they thought had occurred in the original sentence on which the paraphrase was based. Parallel procedures were followed with the verb group.

For this task, the original 384 paraphrases were grouped into six covering sets, where a *covering set* is defined to be a set of 64 paraphrases that entirely covers the matrix of combinations. To make one covering set requires pooling responses from eight of the original subjects, since each original subject paraphrased eight of the 64 sentences in the matrix. Thus, the original 48 subjects yielded six covering sets. Each of these covering sets was read to a group of seven noun subjects. This meant that there were six groups of seven noun-retrace subjects, or 42 noun-retrace subjects, and similarly 42 verb-retrace subjects.

2.3.2 *Combinatorial Patterns*

One advantage of the retrace task is that it allows us to go beyond the overall comparison of nouns and verbs and examine more detailed combinatorial patterns. The matrix of combinations can be divided into three distinct sectors, as shown in Figure 14.1. First is the diagonal, the matched sector, in which the noun matches the argument specification of the verb.[2] On the diagonal, a verb like *limp*, which calls for an animate subject, is paired with the animate noun *mule* or *lizard*. These sentences (e.g., "The lizard limped") are low in semantic strain. The second sector is the over-matched sector above the diagonal. Here the noun exceeds the argument specification of the verb. The verb *limp*, for example, receives as its subject the nouns *daughter* and *politician*, which are not merely animate, but also human. Sentences in the above-diagonal, over-matched sector should be at least as low in semantic strain as the diagonal sentences.[3] The third sector, below the diagonal, is under-matched. Here the noun fails to meet the subject specifications of the verb. So, for example, the verb *limp*, which calls for an animate subject, is instead combined with a nonanimate concrete noun like *lantern*, or with an abstract noun like *responsibility* to make a sentence like "The lantern limped." This below-diagonal, undermatched sector is the area of greatest semantic strain. Change of meaning should be greatest here, and retrace accuracy lowest.

2.3.3 *Results*

As Figure 14.2 shows, the results fit the predictions of the verb mutability hypothesis.

The retrace judgments were considerably more accurate for nouns than for verbs, bearing out the claim that the verb meanings had been more altered in paraphrase than the noun meanings. Further, retrace accuracy is lower for the under-matched (below-diagonal) sector than for the other two sectors. Finally, the interactions, discussed below, indicate that verb change of meaning is greatest where semantic strain is highest.

A mixed-measure analysis of variance[4] was performed over the responses of the 84 retrace subjects. The variables were Form-class (noun versus verb,

---

2   The term "argument specification" is used here to preserve neutrality as to whether to invoke selectional restrictions or some other account of semantic compatibility.

3   In fact, because the stimuli were taken randomly from standard word lists, the diagonal and above-diagonal matches vary somewhat in their naturalness. In particular, the diagonal entry "The car softened." seems a rather awkward match.

4   In analyzing these results proportions were used throughout, because of unequal cell numbers. The above- and below-diagonal sectors each have 24 cells, while the diagonal sector has only 16 cells.

between subjects), Matching (matched, over-matched and under-matched, within subjects), and Covering-set (the six complete sets of paraphrases, each generated by a group of eight original subjects, a between-subject factor).[5] The design was thus Form-class(2) × Covering-set(6) × Matching(3).The results were quite strong. There are main effects for Form-class, confirming that nouns were better retraced than were verbs [$F(1,72) = 220.28$, $p < .0001$], and Matching, confirming that retrace accuracy was lowest in the under-matched sectors [$F(2,144) = 103.43$, $p < .0001$]. The interaction between Form-class and Matching was also significant [$F(2,144)] = 23.8664$, $p < .0001$]. This interaction is important, for it reflects the fact that the retraceability difference between nouns and verbs was greatest in the undermatched sector. That is, verbs change meaning most when semantic strain is greatest.

There was also a main effect of Covering-set [$F(5,72) = 8.30$, $p < .0001$], and all interactions with Covering-set were significant. We take this to mean either that there were differences among the specific original paraphrases or the specific groups of retrace subjects or both. Such differences are not surprising in complex psycholinguistic tasks, and they do not alter the main findings.

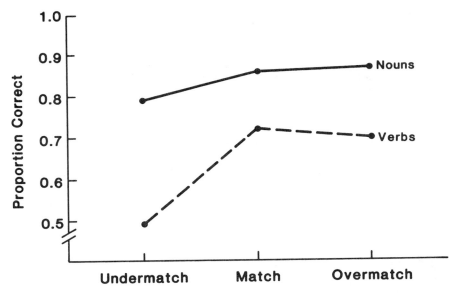

Figure 14.2 Results of Experiment 1, using the retrace measure.

---

5 In these analyses, the term "subject" refers to the retrace subjects.

2.4 *Discussion*

One useful feature of the experiment so far is the opportunity to compare three measures of change of meaning. Our initial method, the divide-and-rate method, was straightforward in its logic: the idea was simply to find the part that came from the noun and the part that came from the verb and ask which differed more from the original word meaning. But this method turned out not to be straightforward in practice, since the raters could not agree on "the part that came from the noun (or verb)." Therefore two new methods were devised. Though more indirect in their logic, the retrace and double-paraphrase methods actually turned out to be far less problematical than the divide-and-rate method. Like the divide-and-rate method, these new methods still require running two sets of subjects for every result. The key difference is that all the tasks involved are intuitive for subjects. This means that they do not require the discarding of large amounts of data and that we can have more confidence in the data we collect. A key point here is that all three methods led to the same conclusions. Therefore we now have converging methods of assessing change of meaning.

The three measures of change of meaning used in the pilot study and in Experiment 1 all produced the same results: that under semantic strain the primary locus of change is the verb. They also indicate that the adjustment in verb meaning is orderly. The patterns of change indicate that the verb preserved its meaning insofar as possible. Given a compatible noun, the verb was paraphrased in a way that preserved its meaning; but given an incompatible noun, the verb meaning was adjusted to fit. Our subjects appeared to treat the nouns as referring to fixed prior entities, and the verbs as conveying mutable relational concepts to be extended metaphorically if necessary to agree with the nouns. However, before drawing conclusions, we must consider another possible interpretation. It could be that the patterns of mutability stemmed simply from word-order conventions, rather than from form-class differences. In the sentences used, the noun preceded the verb and served as topic. Perhaps the differences between nouns and verbs can be attributed to given-new strategies based on the order of information [Clark and Haviland, 1977]. Thus, in the sentence "The lizard worshipped," lizard, being first, was the given, and hence more likely to be taken as fixed. To check this possibility, in Experiment 2 the word order was changed so that the verb occurred first. All sentences were of the form "Worshipped was what the lizard did." Otherwise, the procedure, including the set of nouns and verbs used, was as in Experiment 1. Again paraphrases were collected, and again these paraphrases were subjected to further manipulations in order to gain a measure of change of meaning. Because the retrace task allows investigation of where the greatest change of meaning occurred, we used the retrace task to gauge change of meaning.

3 Experiment 2

3.1 Paraphrase Task

3.1.1 Method

Subjects   There were 53 subjects, all undergraduate psychology students at the University of Washington who received class credit for their participation. Five of these were eliminated for failure to comply with the instructions (see Pilot study), leaving 48 subjects.

Materials   As in Experiment 1, there were 64 sentences corresponding to the 64 noun-verb combinations. These were divided into eight sets of eight such that each subject paraphrased eight sentences, with no noun or verb repeated. Sentences had the form "Verbed was what the noun did" (e.g., "Worshipped was what the lizard did").

Procedure   The procedure for the original paraphrase task was identical to that used in Experiment 1.

3.2 Retrace Task

3.2.1 Method

Subjects   The subjects were 84 college students from the Cambridge, Massachusetts area, who were paid for their participation.

Procedure   The procedure was as in Experiment 1. The noun-retrace subjects heard the paraphrases and circled which of the original nouns they thought had been in the sentence, and similarly for the verb-retrace subjects.

3.3 Results

Again, the results were as predicted by the verb mutability hypothesis. Figure 14.3 shows that the proportion correct in the retrace task was considerably higher for noun-retrace than for verb-retrace subjects.

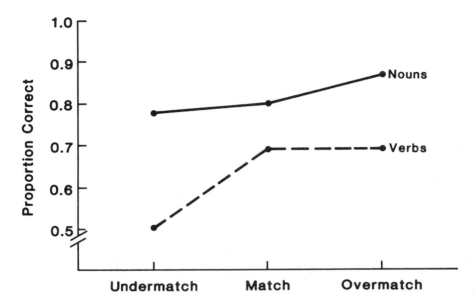

Figure 14.3 Results of Experiment 2, using the retrace measure.

Moreover, the retrace disadvantage for verbs is greatest in the undermatched sector.

A mixed-measure analysis of variance was performed over the responses of the retrace subjects. As in Experiment 1, the variables and design were Form-class(2) × Covering-set(6) × Matching(3). There was a main effect of Form-class [$F(1,72) = 254.72$, $p < .0001$], confirming that verbs were less accurately retraced than nouns. There was also a main effect of Matching [$F(2,144) = 82.27$, $p < .0001$], confirming that the greatest distortion was in the undermatched sectors. The key interaction between Form-class and Matching was again significant [$F(2,144) = 28.16$, $p < .0001$], confirming that the mutability difference between nouns and verbs is greatest in the undermatched sector, the area of greatest semantic strain. As in Experiment 1, the main effect of Covering-set was significant [$F(5,72) = 4.50$, $p < .001$] and all interactions with Covering set were significant, again indicating differences in the original paraphrases and/or the retrace groups.

Part II: *Experiments on What Kinds of Meaning Change Occur*

Experiments 1 and 2, and the pilot study, produce a clear convergent pattern of results. First, when a semantic adjustment is effected, the verb is the primary locus of change. These results support Gentner's [1981b] verb mutability hypothesis: in case of conflict, the verb gives in to the noun. A second important finding is that in Experiments 1 and 2 we obtained a gradient of verb adjustment from sentences of low semantic strain to sentences of high semantic strain. The verb disadvantage in retraceability is greatest in sentences with high semantic strain. That is, the greatest changes in verb meaning occur in the sentences of greatest strain: i.e., in the undermatched sector. This suggests that verb meaning adjustment is selective and systematic.

Overall, the results of Experiments 1 and 2 indicate that the verb is the locus of change in a sentence when semantic strain forces meaning adjustment, and that the greater the strain, the greater the adjustment. Now we ask how these adjustments occur. Experiments 3a and 3b were designed to examine more closely the mechanisms of change of meaning. In order to permit a closer analysis of the mechanisms, we limit the verbs to a subset of the verbs of possession. By comparing verbs that share the same stative, that of *possession* [Rumelhart and Norman, 1975], we can more closely examine which components are preserved and which are altered when subjects interpret the sentences. The verbs of possession were chosen because they have been studied previously [Bendix, 1966; Fillmore, 1968; Gentner, 1975; Schank, 1972].

Experiment 3a was conducted with several goals in mind. First, it was intended to extend the locus-of-change results of Experiments 1 and 2 to *object* nouns as described below. Second, it provided an initial examination of the processes by which change of meaning occurs. Third, it yielded initial stimuli for a planned choice task (Experiment 3b). As in Experiments 1 and 2, we gave subjects sentences to paraphrase as naturally as possible. To allow us to generalize the verb mutability phenomenon, there were some changes from the materials of the first two experiments. First, the verbs used were a set of eight possession verbs, such as *borrowed* and *bought*. Second, the sentences were of the form "Sam borrowed a vase," or "Sam bought a doctor," so that the key noun was the *object* noun instead of the subject/agent noun. This allowed a check on whether the verb mutability results in Experiments 1 and 2 reflect general verb-noun interactions, or are specific to interactions with subject or agent nouns. (Recall that in Experiment 2, even though the sentences used verb-first word order (e.g., "Worshipped was what the lizard did."), the noun (e.g., *lizard*), retained its role as the agent or experiencer.)

In Experiment 3a, all the subject nouns were proper names; the experimental manipulation concerned only the object slot. Thus, subjects paraphrased sentences like "George bought doom," where the question was whether *bought* would be altered more than *doom*. The nouns used as objects were either concrete nouns (e.g., *vase*), nouns denoting human occupations (e.g., *doctor*), or abstract nouns, either positive (e.g., *luck*) or negative (e.g., *doom*). We predicted that the concrete nouns would produce low-strain phenomena, and that the human and abstract nouns used as objects of possession verbs would produce high-strain phenomena. That is, verbs would alter meaning more when paired with human and abstract objects than when paired with concrete objects. We further predicted that, as before, subjects would attempt to preserve as much of the verb's meaning as possible. Beyond this, we wished to investigate whether there would be any pattern as to *how* the verb meaning would be adjusted.

4 *Experiment 3a*

4.1 *Method*

Subjects Subjects were sixteen University of Illinois undergraduates who were paid for their participation.

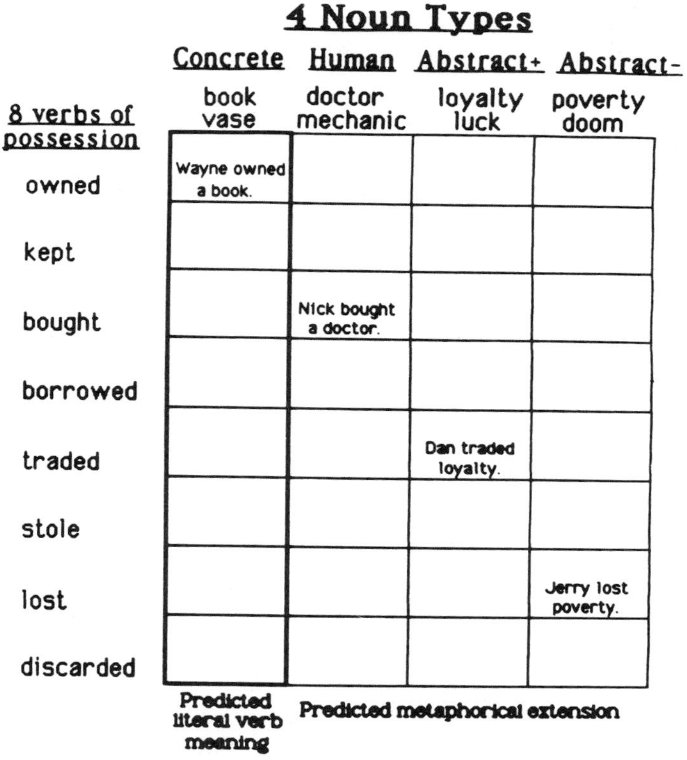

8 verbs of possession	Concrete book vase	Human doctor mechanic	Abstract+ loyalty luck	Abstract− poverty doom
owned	Wayne owned a book.			
kept				
bought		Nick bought a doctor.		
borrowed				
traded			Dan traded loyalty.	
stole				
lost				Jerry lost poverty.
discarded				

Predicted literal verb meaning   Predicted metaphorical extension

Figure 14.4 Matrix of verb-object combinations used in Experiment 3a.

Materials Sentences were constructed from a set of eight verbs of possession and eight nouns which served as direct objects. The matrix from which the sentences were generated is shown in Figure 14.4.

All sentences were of the form "X verbed the object." Sentence subjects were masculine proper names (e.g., "Arnold stole a book."). There were eight such names, counterbalanced across the verb and object combinations. The eight object nouns consisted of two concrete nouns (*book* and *vase*), two human nouns (*doctor* and *mechanic*), and four abstract nouns; two abstract+ nouns with positive connotations (*luck* and *loyalty*) and two abstract– nouns with negative connotations (*poverty* and *doom*). All nouns except the concrete nouns resulted in nonliteral sentences, which were predicted to be relatively high in semantic strain.

Sentences were constructed from this matrix in the same manner as in the previous experiments, making 64 sentences. Sixteen filler sentences were also included. The filler sentences were syntactically similar to the test sentences. They consisted of a masculine proper first name, a verb and a direct object. Of the filler sentences, six contained verbs of possession not used in the study (e.g., "Paul received a clock.") and ten contained other randomly chosen verbs (e.g., "Patrick spilled paint."). None of the filler sentences containing verbs of possession violated a selectional restriction of the verb. The filler sentences were included chiefly to keep subjects from falling into a pattern of expecting odd sentences.

Procedure The procedure was the same as that used in Experiments 1 and 2. Each subject paraphrased eight stimulus sentences interspersed with 16 filler sentences for a total of 24 paraphrases.

Qualitative Scoring One rater judged the sentences and scored the type of adjustment strategy used.[6]

4.2 Results

Results again showed that verbs exhibited more change of meaning than did nouns. Figure 14.5 shows the adjustment strategies used by paraphrase subjects.

---

6 The second author served as rater. (At this point in the project, the second author was unaware of any specific hypotheses as to the results. However, because only one rater was used, these results should be taken as suggestive.)

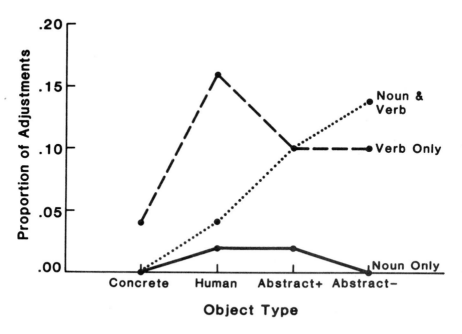

Figure 14.5 Results of Experiment 3a: Proportions of adjustment strategies

Verb adjustment occurred much more frequently than did noun adjustment. Further, although it often happened that verb meanings were changed while noun meanings were left intact, nouns seldom changed meaning without a concomitant change in verb meaning. The same range of alternate paraphrase strategies was seen as in Experiments 1 and 2; the only exception was rote word-by-word paraphrase, which was a frequent strategy for literal sentences. The proportion of rote responses was .16 for concrete object nouns, and .02 for each of the nonliteral cases—human, abstract+ and abstract−. As in the previous experiments, pronoun substitution and repetition of original words were very rare.

Examination of the paraphrases suggests that subjects treated the strained sentences as requiring metaphorical extensions of normal verb use. The pattern of verb adjustments suggests systematic processes underlying these metaphorical extensions. When interpreting the semantically strained sentences, it seems that subjects tended to retain some of the structure of the verb. What changed was the domain of discourse of the verb. For example, a verb that normally conveys a causal change of possession (e.g., *discard*) would be interpreted as a causal change in some other dimension. The sentence "Marvin discarded a doctor" was paraphrased as "Marvin consulted a different practitioner of medicine." Note that in this paraphrase there is no loss of *possession*, but rather a loss of the *services* of Marvin's current doctor. The causal change of state remains, and with it the fact that it was Marvin who initiated the change of state, but the notion of ownership is lost. Similarly, "Bill owned luck." was paraphrased as "Bill always has good things happen to him." Again, the state of possession is not retained in the paraphrase, although the notion of an enduring state of events is. Bill does not continue to *possess* luck, but he continues to *experience* lucky events. These responses appear to reflect an orderly, rule-governed process, rather than an *ad hoc* attempt to make sense from nonsense.

4.3 *Discussion*

One purpose of Experiment 3a was to generate stimulus materials to use in a choice task. Experiment 3b used a forced-choice task in order to establish tighter experimental control, and to eliminate the problem of the subjective interpretation of paraphrase data. It sought more closely to examine the process of verb metaphorical extension. With this task we hoped to obtain objective data on the kinds of semantic adjustments that occur. Before proceeding to Experiment 3b, let us review our findings so far.

Initially, it seemed that four possible views might exist as to what happens under semantic strain. First is the *normative view*, which holds that sentences that violate matching restrictions are seen as nonsensical and will either be rejected as uninterpretable or, at best, will show no systematic interpretation patterns. Although this view may seem a straw man, it is important to rule it out. So far the evidence from Experiments 1–3a argues against this position. Subjects did not reject the strained sentences, instead showing a dominant strategy of altering the verbs' meaning. However, the forced-choice task will provide a clearer test. If, as in the normative rules view, the stimulus sentence is wholly meaningless, no one response will be preferred. There should then be a random response pattern in the forced-choice task.

Views 2–4 are all versions of semantic adjustment processes. View 2 is the *radical subtraction* view: that when faced with a violation of selectional restrictions, people discard the meaning of the verb, retaining only a general sense of what verbs tend to mean. Thus a given verb, such as a verb of possession, would be distilled to a general change of state, but would lose all other aspects of its meaning. View 3, related to the previous view, is the *pragmatic amplification* view. Once it is clear that the literal meaning of the verb will not work, people might make sense of the nonliteral sentences by first suspending all or most of the usual meaning of the verb and then constructing a plausible scenario. This view emphasizes the role of pragmatics in metaphorical extension (e.g., [Searle, 1979]). In practice, this account is a combination of radical subtraction plus pragmatic amplification. First, the verb is reduced to a general change of state, and then context determines the amplification.

Views 1–3 have in common a kind of simplicity in the adjustment processes they postulate. Sentences that violate the verb's semantic restrictions are rejected outright in the strong normative view. In the radical subtraction view, such sentences will have their verbs reduced to simple changes of state—effectively, to dummy verbs that convey little specific information except that something happened. Finally, in the pragmatic amplification view, after a radical subtraction step, context may be used to fill in the intended verb.

View 4, the *minimal subtraction* view, differs from the other three in postulating greater semantic specificity in the mechanisms of adjustment. In this view subjects interpret the sentences by making minimal semantic adjustments to the verb. According to this minimal subtraction view, people interpret the sentences by performing the minimal necessary adjustments in verb meaning, rather than by postulating a general change of state and/or substituting contextual information.

The response choices for Experiment 3b were designed to reflect these four strategies. These responses were based in part on subjects' paraphrases in Experiment 3a, with the constraint that each sentence have four response choices as follows.

1. **Minimal Subtraction.** The Minimal Subtraction choice preserved the verb's meaning as closely as possible. In the literal sentences, it was simply a rote paraphrase. Thus, for the sentence "Randy stole a vase." the Minimal Subtraction response was, "Randy illegally took a flower holder that didn't belong to him." In the nonliteral sentences, a minimal change was made in the verb's meaning to produce a plausible metaphorical meaning. For example, the Minimal Subtraction response for the sentence, "Chuck stole a plumber," was "Chuck hired a plumbing specialist away from another employer."

2. **Radical Subtraction.** In the Radical Subtraction choice, all components of the verb meaning, except for the change of state, were subtracted. This interpretation was correct, but extremely underspecified. For the example sentence, "Chuck stole a plumber." the Radical Subtraction response was "Chuck had a plumbing specialist do some work for him." Here, the verb borrowed is reduced to a simple change of state.

3. **Pragmatic Amplification.** The Pragmatic Amplification choice assumed some significant suspension of the verb's usual meaning, but also added additional contextual information designed to make the sentence plausible. For example, for "Chuck stole a plumber." the Pragmatic Amplification response was "Chuck paid a very high salary and hired away his rival's best plumbing specialist."

4. **Control.** The Control choice was irrelevant to the meaning of the original sentence; however, it contained concepts associated with some of the original concepts. The Control response for "Chuck stole a plumber." was "Chuck lived by the beach and had a tool box." This choice was included as a test of the strong normative claim that nonliteral sentences are completely uninterpretable. If this were true, all four responses would be viewed as equally anomalous, and in particular the Control response would be chosen equally as frequently as the other responses. In addition, this choice served to check whether subjects were indeed interpreting the sentences.

5 Experiment 3b

5.1 Method

Subjects   Subjects were 48 University of Illinois undergraduates, who participated in the experiment as part of a course requirement.

Materials and Design   Sentences for this experiment were similar to that used in Experiment 3a, with a few exceptions. First, the verbs owned and traded were eliminated to reduce the number of stimuli. This left the verbs kept, bought, *borrowed, stole, lost,* and *discarded.* The objects were of the same basic types as in Experiment 3a. However, because no differences were found between abstract+ and abstract− nouns, this distinction was eliminated. Thus, three types of object nouns remained: concrete objects which resulted in literal sentences, and human and abstract nouns which resulted in nonliteral sentences. Six object nouns of each type were selected. The subject nouns were men's first names; a unique name was chosen for each sentence. The matrices from which the sentences were constructed are shown in Figure 14.6.

Note that the matrices for concrete and abstract objects were analogous. For concrete objects, the top row was *book, vase, lamp, chair, hammer,* and *coat.* For abstract objects, the top row was *luck, loyalty, poverty, doom, freedom* and *despair.* Note that these matrices are slightly different from those of Experiments 1 and 2. First, they are 6 × 6 instead of 8 × 8; second, *three* matrices were used here instead of one (although all three involved the same verbs). Third, each matrix contains six nouns of the same type—concrete, human or abstract. This study tests each kind of verb-noun combination more thoroughly than in previous studies.

Stimuli constructed with Human Objects

		doctor	mechanic	accountant	teacher	plumber	mailman
	kept	Steve kept a doctor.					
	bought		Jim bought a mechanic.				
	borrowed			Bob borrowed an accountant.			
6 Verbs of Possession	stole				William stole a teacher.		
	lost					Ivan lost a plumber.	
	discarded						Herbert discarded a mailman.

Figure 14.6 Sample matrix of verb-object combinations used in Experiment 3b.

Every sentence was followed by the four response choices: the Minimal Subtraction response, the Radical Subtraction response, the Pragmatic Amplification response, and the Control response. Sample stimuli are shown in Table 2. The order of the choices was varied randomly. There were also 12 filler sentences, each with four response choices.

As in Experiment 3a, sentences were generated by combining the verbs and object nouns from each matrix, with proper names as subject nouns. Each subject saw all six verbs three times, once each with a noun of each of the three object types, for a total of 18 stimulus sentences per subject. In addition, each subject saw 12 filler sentences, making a total of 30 sentences. To counterbalance any specific association of verbs with objects, a Latin Square was used. Two orders of presentation were used, one the reverse of the other. In each order, we imposed the constraint that a verb could not appear within two items of itself. Six subjects were required to cover the three matrices fully. Since we had 48 subjects, the matrices were covered eight times—four times in each of the two orders of presentation.

Table 2   Sample stimulus materials from Experiment 3b

Concrete Object: *Ernie lost a book.*

M.S.:   Ernie misplaced a volume, and now he could not find it.

R.S.:   Ernie did not have a volume.

P.A.:   Ernie ripped a volume.

CON.:   Ernie was not a good badminton player, but he liked to read.

Human Object: *Keith lost a teacher.*

M.S.:   Keith's instructor stopped working for him, despite Keith's wishes.

R.S.:   Keith no longer has the same instructor.

P.A.:   Keith's instructor got mad and stopped working for him, which was very inconvenient.

CON.:   Keith boiled some potatoes before class.

Abstract Object: *Joe lost doom.*

M.S.:   Joe was once very unhappy, but no longer is.

R.S.:   Joe does not have ill fortune.

P.A.:   Something very good happened to Joe, and he is no longer unhappy.

CON.:   Joe lived in a brick house which he liked.

M.S. = Minimal Subtraction, R.S. = Radical Subtraction
P.A. = Pragmatic Amplification, CON. = Control

Procedure   Subjects were given booklets containing two sentences per page. Each sentence was followed by four possible interpretations. Test sentences were interspersed with filler sentences. Subjects were told to imagine that while walking through a cafeteria, they overheard someone saying the stimulus sentence. They were to choose the response that they thought best reflected the meaning a speaker might have intended by the sentence.

5.2 Results

The proportion of responses of each type across all sentences is shown in Figure 14.7. It can be seen that the Minimal Subtraction response was chosen substantially more often than the others. After the Minimal Subtraction, the next most frequent response was the Radical Subtraction response in which only the change of state is preserved. Subjects rarely chose the Pragmatic Amplification response, and almost never chose the Control response.

These differences were confirmed with t-tests. All differences between adjacent pairs of responses were significant. For the frequencies of the Minimal Subtraction and Radical Subtraction, $t(47) = 11.36$, $p < .001$. For the Radical Subtraction and Pragmatic Amplification responses, $t(47) = -.32$, $p < .001$. Lastly, for the Pragmatic Amplification response and the Control Response, $t(47) = 6.39$, $p < .001$.

So far we have discussed results across all sentences. Figure 14.8 shows the results for the semantically strained sentences (i.e., sentences with human or abstract objects instead of concrete objects). Again, the Minimal Subtraction response was by far the most frequently chosen response. T-tests for the frequency of response choices confirmed that Minimal Subtraction was chosen significantly more often than its nearest competitor, Radical Subtraction for both human and abstract objects [$t(47) = 6.32$, $p < .0001$; $t(47) = 4.07$, $p < .0001$, respectively]. All other adjacent pairs were significantly different, with the exception of Pragmatic Amplification versus Radical Subtraction for human objects.

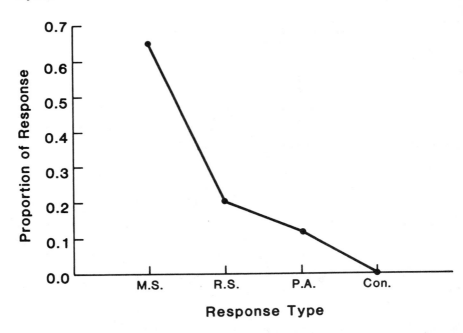

Figure 14.7 Results of Experiment 3b: Proportion of each response type. Note that the following abbreviations are used in the graph: M.S. for Minimal Subtraction, P.A. for Pragmatic Amplification, R.S. for Radical Subtraction, and CON. for Control.

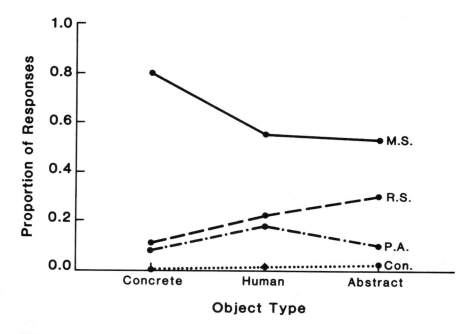

Figure 14.8 Results of Experiment 3b: Proportions of responses for each object type.

In order to test the differences between different types of objects, four one-way analyses of variance were calculated across the four types of objects, one for each response type. The Minimal Subtraction response, the Radical Subtraction response, and the Pragmatic Amplification response all varied significantly across object type.[7] [$F(2,141)$ = 20.590, p < .001], and [$F(2,141)$ = 11.488, (p) < .001] and [$F(2,141)$ = 5.666, p < .01 respectively]. This was not true for the Control response. There was no significant difference in frequency across object types for control responses.

To sum up, the Minimal Subtraction response was preferred overwhelmingly by subjects both on the literal and the nonliteral sentences. This response retains as much of the literal meaning as possible, removing only the components necessary to make sense of the sentence. After Minimal Subtraction, the next most frequent response was the Radical Subtraction response. This strategy reflects a kind of "starting up from the ground" strategy in which only the change of state is preserved. The other two responses were rarely chosen.

---

7 Note that the rate of Minimal Subtraction responses is elevated for concrete objects, due to the fact that the Minimal Subtraction choice was a literal paraphrase for the concrete objects.

The fact that subjects almost never chose the Control response corroborates other evidence in ruling out the *normative* view, which predicts that since the nonliteral sentences are nonsensical, subjects should choose randomly among the available responses. Finally, subjects rarely chose the Pragmatic Amplification response.[8]

Part III: *General Discussion*

Summary of Research This research concerns the combinatorial rules for verbs and nouns. Experiments 1 and 2 investigated the locus of change of meaning. Subjects paraphrased sentences in which the noun and the verb were either semantically matched or semantically mismatched. Using three different tests of change-of-meaning, we found that the verb changed meaning more than the noun. This was true whether the verb occurred in its normal position (e.g., "The lizard limped.") or in initial position (e.g., "Limped was what the lizard did.") The results were orderly: The degree of meaning change reflected the degree of semantic strain.

Experiments 3a and 3b extended the verb mutability results to verb + object sentences and investigated how this meaning adjustment occurs. We considered a range of interpretation strategies, varying in the specificity and complexity of the processes. The least complex was the Radical Subtraction view. In this view, in case of strain, people should preserve only the most general information about the verb—that it conveys, say, a change of possession, or possibly simply a change of state. A related possibility is that after such subtraction, people make sentences interpretable by amplifying the event with pragmatic information not specified by the verb's literal meaning. Finally, the most complex and semantically specific possibility considered is that people effect a minimal semantic adjustment in the verb's meaning: They subtract and replace the minimum number of aspects of the verb's meaning necessary to produce a coherent interpretation. The results support this Minimal Subtraction position.

The finding that people make a minimal semantic adjustment rather than the radical subtraction adjustment is in some ways surprising, since the minimal semantic subtraction strategy requires the person to use considerably more information in effecting the semantic adjustment. Since these metaphorical extensions often appear to occur without much effort, one might have expected the simpler radical subtraction strategy to have been adopted. It appears that a

---

8 It should be noted, however, that it is possible that we simply guessed wrong in constructing the pragmatic interpretations. It is impossible to rule out the possibility that subjects would have opted for the pragmatic choice given a different set of pragmatic amplifications.

rather fine-tuned semantic adjustment provides the best account of the comprehension of novel noun-verb combinations. Change of meaning does occur to accommodate contextual constraints, but our findings suggest that the change involves computations over the internal structure of the verb. Using the language of componential representation, we conjecture that people try to preserve as many components of verb meaning as possible.

Why Verb Adjustment   Why should the verb adjust more than the noun? Several mechanisms suggest themselves.

1. **The verb is outnumbered by nouns.** As discussed above, in interpreting the sentence "The flower kissed the rock." subjects normally preserve noun reference and alter the verb's meaning to fit the noun meanings. But here there are two concrete nouns as against one verb. Perhaps the verb's normal meaning, with its preference for animate arguments, is simply overridden by sheer numbers. Cottrell and Small [1983] discuss such a 'voting' mechanism in a connectionist framework. For example, the verb "throw" in "Bob threw a ball." would be interpreted as meaning *propel*, largely because this sense of "throw" is compatible with the most frequent meaning of the noun "ball" (a *spherical toy*). But in "Bob threw a ball for charity." the noun "charity" joins with the secondary sense of "ball" (a *dance*) and this coalition of two nouns shifts the meaning of "throw" from its *propel* sense to its *give-an-event* sense. Of course, with such a summation-of-activation mechanism, the verbs can vote too. In a sentence like "Bob kicked and threw the ball for charity." the *propel* sense of the verb would presumably again be dominant. But since multiple-noun sentences are more common than multiple-verb sentences, this voting mechanism will in general act to favor verb mutability.

This mechanism seems highly plausible and must surely account for some of the verb mutability effect. But it is not sufficient to explain the whole phenomenon, as our experiments indicate. In Experiments 1 and 2 we pitted one subject noun against one verb, and in Experiment 3ab we pitted one object noun against the verb (leaving the subject noun an inert proper noun). In all cases there was a substantial verb mutability effect. Therefore outnumbering cannot be the only explanation.

2. **Polysemy is greater for verbs than nouns.** Verb mutability may be related to another interesting characteristic of verbs: their relatively high degree of polysemy. Verb polysemy is easy to observe for frequent verbs; verbs like have, move or make can have dozens of meaning senses. We can have ten dollars, but also a bad dream, a lame leg, a cold, a pleasing

personality, and so on. Gentner [1981b] compared the number of dictionary meaning senses for words of different form classes across four different levels of word frequency. Across all classes, more frequent words have greater numbers of meaning senses (Zipf's Law). However, at all frequency levels, verbs have substantially more meaning senses than nouns. Indeed by this measure, verbs have greater breadth of meaning than any other form-class (with the single exception of prepositions in the highest frequency sample). Perhaps it is the greater degree of verb polysemy that accounts for the verb mutability effect. The fact that a given verb has several associated meanings means that the hearer has more options to choose from for verbs than for nouns in selecting the meaning sense that best fits a context. There is a considerable body of research showing effects of context in selecting among multiple word senses of a given word (e.g., [Anderson and Ortony, 1975; Swinney, 1979; Tanenhaus, Leiman, and Seidenberg, 1979]). Moreover, in parallel systems such as that of Cottrell and Small, the proliferation of meaning senses will tend to mean that any one sense will have rather low initial activation and thus can easily be overcome by a dissenting noun.

Verb polysemy almost surely provides one route to contextual adaptability. However, we do not believe that it can account for the whole phenomena of verb mutability. In particular, it cannot account for the results presented here. By design, many of our sentences elicited interpretations that could not plausibly have been included in the verb's existing list of senses. For example, in "The lizard worshipped." it is unlikely that the verb "worship" included *stared at the sun* among its prior word senses. People's ability to deal with novel combinations seems to go beyond simply selecting from a range of pres-tored verb meanings.

The more interesting issue, in our view, is the reverse causality between mutability and polysemy. If we ask how polysemy comes about historically, one plausible way in which a word could accrue meaning senses over time is by being relatively mutable. As its meaning is reinterpreted in different sentence contexts, some of these reinterpretations occur often enough to be remembered. The end result of the gradual accretion of contextually adapted meaning-variants would be a high degree of polysemy. In this way, verb mutability could provide a mechanism for the greater degree of verb polysemy.[9]

---

9 An interesting prediction that follows from this is that 'old' verbs that have been in the language for a long time should be more polysemous than 'new' verbs that have recently been added.

3. **Operators versus referential terms.** Verbs function as predicates over objects, while nouns serve to establish reference to individual objects (including conceptual objects). That is, verbs have the job of conveying relations or events that apply to the referents established by the nouns. The conjecture is that part of the mutability effect stems from carrying out the role of operator. One line of evidence for this claim is that in noun-noun sentences, the predicate noun (which functions as operator) typically adapts its meaning to the subject noun (which functions to establish object-reference) [Gentner, unpublished data, 1985].[10] Thus "The acrobat is a hippopotamus." conveys a clumsy acrobat, while "The hippopotamus is an acrobat." conveys an agile hippopotamus.[11] However, the degree of change of meaning for predicate nouns is not as great as we see for verbs, indicating that functional differences are not the sole explanation for the verb mutability effect.

4. **Relative semantic cohesion.** Outnumbering and greater verb polysemy can account for some of the phenomena. But we must invoke internal semantic interactions to account for the full range of verb mutability phenomena. Gentner [1981b] speculated that part of the explanation for verb semantic mutability might be that the representations of many noun concepts (in particular, object concepts) are more internally cohesive, or dense, than comparable verb representations:[12]

> Representations of object-concepts are more internally dense than representations of relational concepts: That is, the ratio between the number of internal links and the number of components linked is greater for object concepts than for relational terms. . . . Because external links allow context to push towards new interpretations, whereas internal links make for a stable interpretation of the conceptual component, verbs should be more adjustable than nouns. [Gentner, 1981b, pp. 171–175)

This suggestion has much in common with prior proposals by Langacker [1987] and Wilks [1977, 1978] as well as with some of the proposals currently under investigation in parallel architectures. We do not attempt

---

10 This work was begun in collaboration with Albert Stevens, who suggested the noun-noun issue.

11 This effect of head noun vs. predicate noun is also present in Hampton's [in press] results with sentences like "The noun which is also a noun." In fact the asymmetry between the two nouns poses a problem for his theoretical approach, which is simply to combine features of the two separate concepts.

12 To evaluate this claim the notion of *comparable* nouns and verbs must, of course, be specified. At a minimum, the factors to be equated include word frequency and morphological complexity; concreteness, imagery, and hierarchical abstractness (i.e., whether basic level, superordinate or subordinate) might also be important.

here to flesh out this proposal computationally. Instead we consider the psychological question of which aspects of the verb's meaning are most likely to be altered.

Modeling Verb Adjustment Our findings suggest that change of meaning may be a process of graded compromise in which some parts of the verb's meaning are more resistant than others. More specifically, we conjecture that verb adjustment is structurally ordered such that domain-specific components are the first to give way under semantic strain. We will model these processes using a componential representation of verb meaning. We use the representational format of the LNR notation [Abrahamson, 1975; Gentner, 1975; Norman and Rumelhart, 1975; Rumelhart and Norman, 1975]. Related models of verb semantics have been proposed in the format of generative semantics [e.g., Chafe, 1970; Jackendoff, 1976; Lakoff, 1970; McCawley, 1968; Talmy, 1976; 1980], procedural semantics [Miller and Johnson-Laird, 1976], preferential semantics [Wilks, 1977] and conceptual dependency [Cater, 1987; Schank, 1972]. (See Munro [1975] for a comparison.] However, the LNR model has the advantage that the stative is explicitly represented. For example, in representing a possession verb such as "give," CD would represent the change-of-possession as one notion: ATRANS (Agent, Object, Recipient). The LNR notation is more analytical and uses change from an initial state of possession to a final state of possession: CHANGE [POSS (Agent, Object), POSS (Recipient, Object)]. As discussed below, this is helpful in modeling verb metaphorical extension.

Figure 14.9 shows a structural representation of the meaning of the verb *give.* In a literal sentence, such as

Ida gave Sam a vase.

all the normal semantic relations specified by the verb *give* are maintained. We know that Ida once had possession of a vase, that she volitionally caused Sam to gain possession of it, and that as a result Ida no longer has the vase, but Sam does. What happens in a nonliteral sentence? For example, consider the sentence

Ida gave Sam a cold.

If we replace *vase* with the object noun *cold*, it is clear that some adjustments are necessary. Ida has not lost *possession* of the cold by transferring it to Sam. Instead, there has been a change in Sam's state of *health*. Although the possession component must be altered, some of the higher order aspects of the verb *give* are maintained. Ida has still caused a change of state for Sam, although now the dimension of change is not ownership, but a state of health.

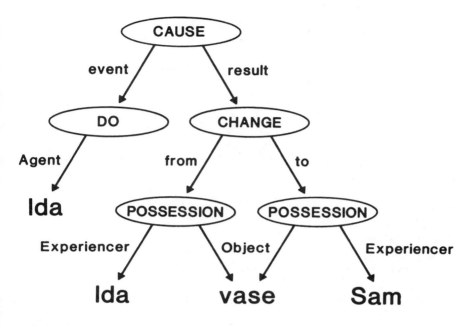

Figure 14.9 Representation of the verb semantic frame for "Ida gives Sam a vase."

To extend this idea further—that what is altered in a verb metaphorical extension is the dimension along which a change of state occurs, let us consider another example:

The moon gave the lake a silvery sheen.

Again, there has been no transfer of possession. The moon did not own the silvery sheen, nor did it transfer that ownership to the lake. Yet we clearly understand what is intended: The moon has caused a change in the color of the lake. What seems to be retained here from the ordinary meaning of give is a causal change of state. Only the nature of the dimension or state has to alter to accommodate the context. The rest of the verb's structure, particularly the higher order **DO-CAUSE-CHANGE** structure, is retained. Thus, it is the domain-specific components—the bottom-level components in our diagram— that have changed. We believe this is a rather general strategy in verb metaphorical extension. The components that specify the particular change of state are easily overridden by the surrounding nouns, but the verb retains as much of its higher order structure as possible.

If these kinds of semantic adjustment processes occur, we might expect to find greater comprehension times for sentences with semantic strain (though the exact predictions would of course depend on which aspects of the process were modeled as parallel). Ongoing research by Brown, Marslen-Wilson and Tyler, using an on-line word monitoring task, provides some support for this prediction [Brown, personal communication, July, 1986, Nijmegen, The Netherlands]. They find that subjects take longer to process anomalous verb-noun combinations than normal combinations. Purely pragmatic violations (e.g., "The man buried the guitar") take slightly longer to process than normal sentences (e.g., "The man carried the guitar."). However, it is noteworthy that semantic violations lead to still longer processing times than pragmatic viola-tions. Semantic anomalies—violations of selectional restrictions, similar to those used here (e.g., "The man drank the guitar.")—require more processing time than pragmatic violations. There is a further increase in processing time for violations of subcategorization rules, a more severe grammatical violation than the ones used here (e.g., "The man meditated the guitar."). Thus there is some promising evidence for processing-time correlates of the kinds of seman-tic adjustment processes proposed here.

Lakoff and Johnson [1980] document many examples of metaphorical ex-tension of verbs and other relational terms. Spatial relations are particularly productive [Nagy, 1979; Reddy, 1979]. For example, to say that someone is *going to perdition* or *getting into trouble* does not convey any change in physi-cal location, but rather a change of fortune or state of well-being. In this way, verb metaphorical extension has much in common with analogy [Kittay and Lehrer, 1981]. In both cases, it is the lower order concrete information that is suspended [Gentner, 1981b, 1983]. Indeed, in a sense verbs are institutional-ized analogies.[13] They are devices for conveying relational structures inde-pendently of the concrete objects to which the structures are applied.

Verb Centrality   The results of Experiments 1–3a supported the verb muta-bility hypothesis: When a sentence exhibits semantic strain, the primary locus of change of meaning is the verb. Further, although there is little prior research on this direct question, our findings are consistent with a developmental find-ing by Reyna [1980]: Children given semantically strained sentences tended to prefer interpretations in which the verb's meaning was altered to fit the noun rather than the reverse.

These findings seem to run counter to the predictions of a verb-central position. Verbs have often been regarded as providing the relational framework

---

13   Interestingly enough, noun extension is less likely to be analogy-based and more likely to con-sist of a chain of different kinds of assocations, as Lakoff [1987] documents. As Nagy [personal communication, May 1986] put it, "Verbs are analogous, nouns metonymous."

for the event [e.g., Chafe, 1970] (see also Figure 14.9). In case grammar, it is the verb which specifies the case relations that relate the nouns to the central event [Fillmore, 1966; 1968; 1970; Healy and Miller, 1970]. Many grammars have successfully used verb-centered representations [Bresnan and Kaplan, 1975; Chafe, 1970; Fillmore, 1966; 1968; Kintsch, 1974; Norman and Rumelhart, 1975; Schank, 1973; 1974]. A natural conclusion is that if the verb provides the central frame for sentence meaning, it should be the most important and stable element. Our data indicate that verbs may, on the contrary be among the more mutable elements of the sentence.

On deeper consideration, we believe that it is possible to reconcile the valuable insights of the verb centralist approach with the phenomenon of verb mutability. That verbs function as central organizers of a sentence need not imply that they are semantically more stable than nouns. Indeed, Gentner [1981b] suggested that the mutability of verbs may arise in part from their function as a central organizer. In this view, nouns normally act to fix reference and the verb acts as an operator over the noun meaning(s). The verb's function is to link the nominal concepts into one coherent assertion, and this may mean suspending one or more of its own normal components in case of conflict between a noun argument and the verb's usual semantic structure. In particular, one relatively economical way to achieve coherence is for the lower order, domain-specific components of the verb to be suspended or replaced. Thus, verb mutability may in part result from verb centrality.

Conceptual Combination In addition to its connections with psycholinguistic models of semantic processing, this research bears on the issue of conceptual combination [Hampton, in press; Osherson and Smith 1981; 1982; Shoben and Medin, in preparation; Smith and Osherson, 1984; Smith, Osherson, Rips, Albert, and Keane, 1986]. This work is done from a cognitive rather than linguistic point of view. The major issue is how the intension and extension of a combination of two concepts relate to the intensions and extensions of the two separate concepts. Among the most detailed of these models is that of Osherson and Smith and their colleagues on noun-adjective semantic combination [Osherson and Smith 1981, 1982; Smith and Osherson, 1984; Smith, Osherson, Rips, Albert and Keane, 1986]. They demonstrate that the typicality of an item as a member of a combination cannot in general be predicted from its typicality as a member of the two separate concepts. For example, a guppy is highly typical as a *pet fish*, even though it is low in typicality as a *pet* and as a *fish*. It appears that something more is required than a simple additive or averaging operation on the external dimension of typicality. Rather, this research suggests that the internal featural representations of the concepts must be used in the combinatorial calculations.

Briefly, Osherson and Smith model nouns (e.g., *apple*) as having a list of independent attributes. An adjective (e.g., *brown*) selects a dimension (e.g., *color*), specifies a value (*brown*) on that dimension and increases the diagnosticity of its dimension, so that color is more important in a *brown apple* than in an ordinary unmodified *apple*. Conjunctions may be either positively diagnostic (e.g., *red apple*), nondiagnostic (e.g., *unsliced apple*), or negatively diagnostic (e.g., *brown apple*). Interestingly, it is on the negatively diagnostic conjunctions, like *brown apple*, that the simple combination-of-typicality model fails most severely. That is, the more a conjunction violates normal expectations, the more the typicality of the conjunction diverges from a simple combination of the typicalities of its constituents.

There are important parallels between our work and that of Osherson and Smith. The first parallel is in the diagnosticity effect: The greater the departure from normal usage, the more the meaning of the combination differs from a simple combination of the meanings of its parts. Second, and more importantly, both views agree on modeling combinatorial semantics as interactions between intensional representations. However, although the Osherson and Smith work provides a detailed model of semantic combination for adjectives and nouns, it does not provide a solution to the problem of noun-verb semantic combination. Verb meanings convey relational frames, rather than single featural dimensions, so that we will need to go beyond the kinds of dimension-plus-value representations that may suffice for simple adjectives. Moreover, a feature-list model of noun meaning is inadequate to capture the kinds of representational density arguments made above.

Indeed, recent research by Shoben and Medin [1987] suggests that simple feature-list models may be inadequate to model even some adjective-noun combinations. They point out a disadvantage of the Osherson and Smith model: It predicts that a given adjective affects only one dimension of a noun's meaning; therefore the model cannot capture interactions among different dimensions. Shoben and Medin have demonstrated such dimensional interactions in judged typicality. For example, when rated as a *large spoon*, a wooden spoon is more typical than a metal spoon; when judged as a *small spoon*, the typicality order reverses. Results of this kind lend support to the notion that, in general, modeling conceptual combination may require modeling complex structural interactions among different dimensions.

Concluding Remarks   We have studied comprehension processes by using sentences in which the noun and the verb are sufficiently mismatched that subjects must engage in active processing to interpret the sentence. These results indicate that under such conditions it is verbs that adjust to nouns rather than the other way around. We considered various explanations for the verb mutablity effect and concluded that neither outnumbering of the verb by nouns nor differential polysemy can be the sole explanation. We therefore conjecture two further factors that contribute to the verb mutability effect. The first difference is functional: Verbs function as predicates over objects, while nouns serve to establish reference to individual objects (including conceptual objects). The second difference is representational: At least for concrete terms, we conjecture that noun representations may be typically more internally cohesive than verb representations and therefore less easily altered.

The pattern of verb adjustment suggests a middle course between an extreme contextual negotiation position, in which words have no inherent meaning, and meaning is entirely contextually bound, and a fixed-meaning approach, in which rigid word meanings are simply concatenated. Change of meaning does occur to accommodate contextual constraints, but that change involves computations over the internal structure of the word meanings, particularly that of the verb. It appears that a rather fine-tuned semantic adjustment strategy may provide the best account of the comprehension of novel noun-verb combinations. Finally, we conjecture that it is typically the domain-specific components of a verb—the specific dimensional statives, such as possession or location—that are the first to go.

Acknowledgments

This research was conducted at the University of California at San Diego, at the University of Washington, Seattle, at Bolt Beranek and Newman in Cambridge, Massachusetts, and at the University of Illinois at Urbana-Champaign, and was sponsored in part by the Center for the Study of Reading, under National Institute of Education Contract No. 400-81-0030. Albert Stevens collaborated in the original development of these ideas and has greatly influenced this research. We thank Melissa Bowerman, Doug Medin, Ed Smith and Len Talmy for many insightful discussions of these issues and Gary Cottrell and Michael Jeziorski for their helpful comments on earlier versions of this paper. We also thank Monica Olmstead for her help in the research.

References

Abrahamson, A. A. 1975. Experimental analysis of the semantics of movement. In D. A. Norman and D. E. Rumelhart (eds.), *Explorations in Cognition*. San Francisco: Freeman.

Anderson, R. C. and McGaw, B. S. 1973. On the representation of meanings in general terms. *Journal of Experimental Psychology* 10:301–306.

Anderson, R. C. and Ortony, A. 1975. On putting apples into bottles: A problem of polysemy. *Cognitive Psychology* 7:167–180.

Anderson, R. C. and Shifrin, Z. 1977. The meaning of words in context. (Contract No. MS-NIE-C-400-76-016.) Champaign: National Institute of Education.

Bendix, E. H. 1966. *Componential Analysis of General Vocabulary: The Semantic Structure of a Set of Verbs in English, Hindi, and Japanese*. The Hague: Mouton.

Cater, A. W. S. 1987. Conceptual primitives and their metaphorical relationships. In R. G. Reilly (ed.), *Communication Failure in Dialogue and Discourse*. Amsterdam: Elsevier Science Publishers.

Chafe, W. L. 1970. *Meaning and the Structure of Language*. Chicago: University of Chicago Press.

Chomsky, N. 1965. *Aspects of the Theory of Syntax*. Cambridge: MIT Press.

Clark, H. H., and Begun, J. S. 1971. The semantics of sentence subjects. *Language and Speech* 14:34–46.

Clark, H. H. and Haviland, S. E. 1977. Comprehension and the given-new contract. In R. O. Freedle (ed.), *Discourse Production and Comprehension*, pp. 91–124. Norwood: Ablex Publishing.

Cottrell, G. W., and Small, S. L. 1983. A connectionist scheme for modelling word sense disambiguation. *Cognition and Brain Theory* 6:89–120.

Fillmore, C. J. 1966. Review of Bendix's componential analysis of general vocabulary: The semantic structure of a set of verbs in English, Hindi, and Japanese. *International Journal of American Linguistics* 32:Part II (2), Publication 41.

Fillmore, C. J. 1968. The case for case. In E. Bach and R. T. Harms (eds.), *Universals in Linguistic Theory*. New York: Holt, Rinehart and Winston.

Gentner, D. 1975. Evidence for the psychological reality of components: The verbs of possession. In D. A. and D. E. Rumelhart (eds.), *Explorations in Cognition*. San Francisco: Freeman.

Gentner, D. 1981a. Integrating verb meanings into context. *Discourse Processes* 4:349–375.

Gentner, D. 1981b. Some interesting differences between verbs and nouns. *Cognition and Brain Theory* 4(2):161–178.

Gentner, D. 1983. Structure mapping: A theoretical framework for analogy. *Cognitive Science* 7:2.

Gentner, D., and Loftus, E. G. 1979. Integration of verbal and visual information as evidenced by distortions in picture memory. *American Journal of Psychology* 92(2):363–375.

Gladney, T. K., and Krulee, G. K. 1967. The influence of syntactic errors on sentence recognition. *Journal of Verbal Learning and Verbal Behavior* 6 (5):692–698.

Gollob, H. F. 1968. Impression formation and word combination in sentences. *Journal of Personality and Social Psychology* 10:341–353.

Halff, H. M., Ortony, A. and Anderson, R. C. 1976. A context-sensitive representation of word meanings. *Memory and Cognition* 4:378–383.

Healy, A. I. and Miller, G. A. 1970. The verb as determinant of sentence meaning. *Psychonomic Science* 20:372.

Heise, D. R. 1969. Affectual dynamics in simple sentences. *Journal of Personality and Social Psychology* 11(3):204–213.

Heise, D. R. 1970. Potency dynamics in simple sentences. *Journal of Personality and Social Psychology* 16(1):48–54.

Jackendoff, R. 1976. Toward an explanatory semantic representation. *Linguistic Inquiry* 71:89–150.

Katz, J. J. and Fodor, J. A. 1963. The structure of a semantic theory. *Language* 39:170–210.

Kintsch, W. 1974. *The Representation of Meaning in Memory* Hillsdale: Erlbaum.

Kittay, E., and Lehrer, A. 1981. Semantic fields and the acquisition of metaphor. *Studies in Language* 5:31–63.

Lakoff, G. 1970. *Irregularity and syntax.* New York: Holt, Rinehart and Winston.

Lakoff, G. 1987. *Women, Fire and Dangerous Things.* Chicago: University of Chicago Press.

Lakoff, G. and Johnson, M. 1980. *Metaphors We Live By.* Chicago: University of Chicago Press.

McCawley, J. D. 1968. The role of semantics in a grammar. In E. Bach and R. T. Harms (eds.), *Universals in Linguistic Theory.* New York: Holt, Rinehart and Winston.

Miller, G. A. 1972. English verbs of motion: A case study in semantic and lexical memory. In A. W. Melton and E. Martin (eds.), *Coding Processes in Human Memory.* Washington, DC: Winston.

Miller, G. A. and Johnson-Laird, P. N. 1976. *Language and Perception.* Cambridge: The Belknap Press of Harvard University Press.

Munro, A. 1975. Linguistic theory and the LNR structural representation. In D. A. Norman and D. E. Rumelhart (eds.), *Explorations in Cognition.* San Francisco: Freeman.

Norman, D. A. and Rumelhart, D. E. 1975. Memory and knowledge. In D. A. Norman and D. E. Rumelhart (eds.), *Explorations in Cognition.* San Francisco: Freeman.

Osherson, D. N. and Smith, E. E. 1981. On the adequacy of prototype theory as a theory of concepts. *Cognition* 9:35–58.

Osherson, D. N. and Smith, E. E. 1982. Gradedness and conceptual combination. *Cognition* 12:299–318.

Reyna, V. 1980. When words collide: Interpretation of selectionally opposed nouns and verbs. Presented at the Sloan Symposium on Metaphor and Thought, University of Chicago, Chicago, IL, November.

Rumelhart, D. E. and Norman, D. A. 1975. The active structural network. In D. A. Norman and D. E. Rumelhart (eds.), *Explorations in Cognition.* San Francisco: Freeman.

Schank, R. C. 1972. Conceptual dependency: A theory of natural language understanding. *Cognitive Psychology* 3:552–631.

Schank, R. C. 1973. Identification of conceptualizations underlying natural language. In R. C. Schank and K. M. Colby (eds.), *Computer Models of Thought and Language.* San Francisco: Freeman.

Searle, J.R. 1979. Metaphor. In A. Ortony (ed.), *Metaphor and Thought*, pp. 92–123. Cambridge: Cambridge University Press.

Shoben, E., and Medin, D. M. 1987. *Context and Structure in Conceptual Combination.* Manuscript submitted for publication.

Shopen, T. 1973.. Main verb arguments vs. adverbs and adjuncts—a problem in defining the meaning of the sentence as the sum of its parts. Paper presented at the annual meeting of the Linguistics Society of America, San Diego, CA.

Smith, E. E. and Osherson, D. N. 1984. Conceptual combination with prototype concepts. *Cognitive Science* 8:357–361.

Smith, E.E., Osherson D.N., Rips, L.J., and Keane, M. 1986. Combining prototypes: A modification model. University of Michigan Technical Report.

Swinney, D. A. 1979. Lexical access during sentence comprehension: (Re) consideration of context effects. *Journal of Verbal Learning and Verbal Behavior* 18:645–660.

Talmy, L. 1976. Semantic causative types. In M. Shibatani (ed.), *Syntax and Semantics*, Vol. 6. New York: Academic Press.

Talmy, L. 1980. Lexicalization patterns: Semantic structure in lexical forms. In T. Shopen et al. (eds.), *Language Typology and Syntactic Descriptions.* New York: Cambridge University Press.

Tanenhaus, M., Leiman, J. and Seidenberg, M. S. 1979. Evidence for multiple stages in the processing of ambiguous words in syntactic contexts. *Journal of Verbal Learning and Verbal Behavior* 18:427–440.

Wilks, Y. A. 1977. Knowledge structures and language boundaries. In *Proceedings of the Fifth International Joint Conference on Artificial Intelligence*, Menlo Park, CA. Los Altos: Morgan Kaufmann.

Wilks, Y. A. 1978. Making preferences more active. *Artificial Intelligence* 11:197–223.

15

(Almost) Never Letting Go: Inference Retention during Text Understanding

Jennifer K. Holbrook

Department of Cognitive Sciences
School of Social Sciences
University of California, Irvine

Kurt P. Eiselt
Richard H. Granger, Jr.

Irvine Computational Intelligence Project
Department of Information and Computer Science
University of California, Irvine

Edward H. Matthei

Department of Cognitive Sciences
School of Social Sciences
University of California, Irvine

1 *Introduction*

Recent experimental investigations into the process of lexical disambiguation have resulted in the theory that all meanings of an ambiguous word are recalled simultaneously, after which the correct meaning is chosen and the incorrect meanings are suppressed (for example, Seidenberg, Tanenhaus, Leiman, and

Bienkowski [1982], Swinney [1979], and Tanenhaus, Leiman, and Seidenberg [1979]). This two-stage, multiple access/active suppression theory has influenced several artificial intelligence (AI) models of language understanding (for example, Charniak [1983], Cottrell and Small [1983], Gigley [1983], Hirst [1984], and Waltz and Pollack [1985]). These efforts have provided explanations of how the correct meaning of an ambiguous word is chosen in the milliseconds following the presentation of the ambiguous word when the syntactic or semantic information needed for disambiguation is immediately at hand. However, they fail to address the question of how lexical disambiguation is performed when the necessary cues are not readily available.

We propose that the answer to this question rests in a refinement of the active suppression theory which we call *conditional retention*. Briefly, in the conditional retention theory, no meanings are suppressed when an ambiguous word is encountered and no disambiguating information is available. Instead, the competing meanings are retained so that higher-level processes and their associated knowledge sources can be applied to the disambiguation task.

This chapter describes the conditional retention theory and its implications in detail, and shows how conditional retention in a framework of modular processing accounts for a wide range of recent experimental data on lexical disambiguation. In particular, we argue that the theory provides a coherent account of the various ways in which different contextual conditions influence facilitation of word meanings throughout the time course of lexical access. We also argue that conditional retention provides a mechanism for supplanting incorrect decisions. Finally, we discuss the relationship between these two disambiguation processes, which leads to a more unified theory of language understanding.

2 Background

As the reader of this volume will no doubt discover, the results of recent experiments investigating lexical disambiguation strongly support the theory of initial *multiple access*—that is, when human readers or listeners encounter an ambiguous word, they recall all meanings of that word, not just the appropriate one. In determining the contextually appropriate meaning of the word, it appears that context (i.e., the linguistic information processed prior to the ambiguous word) is considered only after multiple access has occurred. The relatively short time required to choose one meaning and discard the others has led researchers to propose a process called *active suppression* [Tanenhaus et al., 1979].

Besides the multiple access/active suppression theory, there have been other theories of lexical disambiguation; the most popular alternative embraced by both psycholinguistic and AI researchers has been a selective access process. For example, Swinney [1984] points out that many models of lexical access used a terminating ordered search in which the list of possible meanings for a word was examined serially in an order determined by their frequencies of use until the contextually appropriate meaning was found (see, for example, Forster [1976] and Hogaboam and Perfetti [1975]). Another approach is described by Charniak [1981]. According to his "scriptal lexicon" theory, scripts in memory (which many researchers argue are used for understanding language) are each associated with a unique lexicon. Each lexicon contains only the contextually appropriate meaning for ambiguous words that might be encountered while processing language with that script. When a word is encountered by an understander, the lexica associated with the active scripts are examined for the word and its appropriate meaning. If an appropriate meaning is not found in the scriptal lexicon, the search proceeds to a default lexicon which contains only standard definitions. Still other models of selective access rely on conditions or restrictions attached to the representations for the individual word (for example, see Riesbeck [1975] or Small and Rieger [1982]). When an ambiguous word is processed, these restrictions are compared to the existing context and the most appropriate meaning is selected.

As Birnbaum [1985] and others have noted, however, selective access solutions to the lexical disambiguation problem suffer from serious limitations. The terminating ordered search hypothesis incorrectly assumes that the most frequently used context-appropriate meaning will always be the correct meaning. The scriptal lexicon hypothesis incorrectly assumes that an ambiguous word used within a script will always refer to the predetermined script-specific sense of the word. Specific restrictions attached to individual words select the appropriate meaning in some cases, but they inevitably lead to the selection of inappropriate meanings in other cases.

Given the problems with such theories, the multiple access/active suppression theory seemed most plausible to us, and it appeared to satisfy both psycholinguists and AI researchers more than the selective access theories did. However, coming from the pragmatic-inference-processing perspective, we asked questions which many psycholinguists tend not to be interested in and which many AI researchers had not addressed: How does disambiguation at the lexical level affect disambiguation at the pragmatic level (and vice versa)? How exactly does active suppression work? If inappropriate meanings are actively suppressed, how, without reprocessing the input text, is an understander able to find a correct meaning when later text shows that the initial choice of word meaning is incorrect? (This last question is a problem of error recovery, and is referred to by some as garden path recovery. We do not use the term "garden path recovery" because of its associations with syntactic problems; we are concerned here only with lexical and pragmatic problems.)

We would expect that some lexical-level mechanism is required to allow location and re-evaluation of initially discarded inferences when an incorrect lexical inference is discovered, as is the case with supplanting pragmatic inferences [Rumelhart, 1981; Seifert, Robertson, and Black, 1982]. The active suppression theory suggests that no information about previously recalled meanings is preserved once those word meanings have been suppressed. Without some means to remember that these meanings were once potential candidates, the active suppression theory appears to preclude any explanation other than that all meanings of the original ambiguous word from the text must be reactivated. One way to reactivate these meanings is to reprocess the word. We hypothesize that human understanders ordinarily do not do this; instead, the conditional retention theory proposes that understanders have some way of recalling those meanings which were initially determined to be inappropriate [Granger, Holbrook, and Eiselt, 1984]. (The issue of whether this recall does or does not require reprocessing of input is discussed in Section 3.5.)

3 Conditional Retention

3.1 The Theory

In the conditional retention theory, all meanings of an ambiguous word are retained as long as further text is available; when there is no further text, a meaning is chosen based on previous context and the other meanings are actively suppressed. Thus, the theory of conditional retention does not contradict active suppression; conditional retention incorporates active suppression. The inadequacy of the active suppression theory by itself is illustrated in the following example:

> He made the medical students examine the tiny cell so that they would be aware of the consequences of malpractice.

In this example, the ambiguous word, "cell," is embedded in a text in which the previous text biases for one meaning, "biology," and the later context biases for another, "prison." The active suppression account of this text would have all but the "biology" reading of "cell" suppressed well before the end of the text. However, at the end of the text, we see that the "prison" reading is more appropriate. If the "prison" meaning is no longer active, there is no way to make this interpretation, yet it is obvious that the interpretation is possible. Conditional retention permits this interpretation: after "cell" is encountered, the "biology" meaning is active, but the other meanings are retained until the end of the text. In this case, the final word requires a reinterpretation of the early text and the word meaning as well, so the retained meaning ("prison") supplants the initially selected meaning ("biology") and the reinterpretation is completed. Because no text follows the disambiguating word, the other meanings are actively suppressed.

The key assumption of conditional retention is that there is a simple binary mechanism for temporarily remembering if a meaning was activated, even if activation has since ceased, and that this memory can be erased when necessary. Combining this two-state memory for a given meaning with two levels of activation for that meaning (i.e., "active" and "inactive") theoretically gives four possible states in which any meaning can exist: (1) The meaning is inactive and there is no memory of its having been recently active. (2) The meaning is inactive but there is memory of its having been recently active. (3) The meaning is active and there is memory of its having been active. (4) The meaning is active but there is no memory of its having been active.

While it is conceivable that a meaning could be active with no record of recent activation, this notion serves no useful purpose in our theory. Thus, in conditional retention theory, there are three states in which word meanings exist:

- **Active:** The meaning is active and there is some memory of its having been active. The meaning shows facilitation (i.e., shorter response times and lower error rates on experimental tasks).

- **Inactive:** The meaning is not active and there is no memory of its having been active. This could be the initial state of the meaning, or could result from either active suppression or gradual loss of activation. In this state, the meaning shows no facilitation.

- **Retained:** The meaning is *not* active but there is some memory of its having been active. The meaning does not show facilitation.

The idea that the lexical disambiguation process requires a memory of the recent history of activation stands in contrast to the assumption of the active suppression theory that disambiguation does not involve such a memory.

The various processes involved in lexical disambiguation can be defined easily in terms of transitions between the three states (see Figure 15.1). These processes are:

- **Spreading Activation:** The process of changing inactive or retained meanings to active meanings.

- **Active Suppression:** The process of changing active or retained meanings to inactive meanings.

- **Conditional Retention:** The process of changing active meanings to retained meanings. Note that inactive meanings cannot be directly changed to retained meanings.

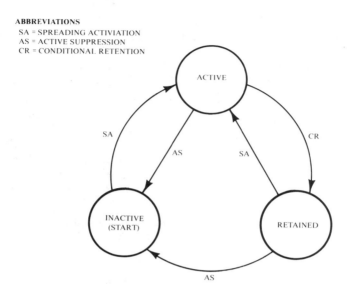

ABBREVIATIONS
SA = SPREADING ACTIVIATION
AS = ACTIVE SUPPRESSION
CR = CONDITIONAL RETENTION

Figure 15.1 State transition diagram for word meanings during lexical access and disambiguation.

Thus, in conditional retention theory, terms such as "retained" or "retention" have very specific meanings with respect to word meanings, lexical disambiguation, and related higher level memory structures and processes.

The conditional retention theory extends the active suppression theory by offering an explanation of how early, misleading text can be reinterpreted without conscious reprocessing. Neither active suppression nor any other theory of lexical disambiguation accounts for this phenomenon. However, two significant and difficult questions remain: What precisely are the conditions under which meanings are retained? For how long are the meanings retained? We address these questions in the following sections. First we examine the results of several studies of the lexical disambiguation process. Then we show that current theories do not account for the experimental data, and we offer an alternative theory which is consistent with these results. Finally we explain how this theory issues from an existing theory of the modularity of processes in language understanding.

3.2 *Wading through the Methodological Quagmire*

The past ten years of experimental research on lexical disambiguation have provided numerous insights into the disambiguation process. Though these experiments may appear to be similar, methodology has in fact varied greatly from experiment to experiment. For example, while most experiments have used the latency of the subject's response as the dependent variable, the subject's task has not been the same across experiments. Some experiments use a lexical naming task while others use a lexical decision task. The points at which probe words are presented varies as well: immediately before the ambiguous word, immediately after the ambiguous word, at selected points from 100 to 1500 msec after the word, and at the end of the clause containing the word. Seldom have any two experiments used the same set of probe points. Most experiments have employed homographic homophones as ambiguous words, but some of these studies have used noun-noun homophones and others noun-verb ambiguities. The position of the ambiguous target word also varies: in some experiments the ambiguous word is the last word in the text, but in others the ambiguous word is embedded in the text. Finally, the nature of the biasing context varies among experiments: some contexts are syntactically biased, some contexts are lexically biased (i.e., a particular word in the context strongly suggests one meaning of the ambiguous word), some are pragmatically biased (i.e., the situation, but no particular word or syntactic interpretation, strongly suggests one meaning of the ambiguous word), some contexts do not provide any bias until after the ambiguous word, and some experiments present the ambiguous word without any context at all.

Despite this lack of consistency, these experiments have provided a great deal of information about many different conditions and probe points. Yet, because of the lack of consistent methodology, constructing a clear picture of the entire lexical disambiguation process requires a certain amount of extrapolation from the various data and methodologies. This information is summarized in the following section.

3.3 *The Data*

As far as lexical disambiguation is concerned, most researchers appear to be in agreement on two important findings. The first is that lexical access itself is an automatic and autonomous process, in which all meanings of an ambiguous word are activated above resting levels of activation. The second is that with no supporting context these meanings gradually lose their activation. If previous context exists, it is used to select the preferred meaning after initial multiple access. This selection process is called post-lexical access by Seidenberg et al. [1982].

If we ignore the lack of consistent methodology across the various experiments and focus instead on their results, a picture of the post-lexical access disambiguation process emerges. What follows is a description of the time course of activation of the various meanings of an ambiguous word during the post-access period. There are two caveats we wish the reader to keep in mind: first, we describe only the relative amount of facilitation for the meanings of an ambiguous word, not the exact amount. We do this because we are attempting to answer questions about the *causes* of the different types of facilitation. Also, as few studies have used the same methods, it would be misleading to compare the actual numbers. Our second caution is that the account we give is deductive in nature. We assume that all the experimental results are valid; in doing so, we treat all data equally. While our deductive approach may strike some as somewhat lacking in empirical rigor, we argue that although no single study addresses all of our questions, each question is addressed in one or more studies.

Here is a brief account of what the experimental evidence tells us about the time course of activation at a number of probe points:

Immediately after presentation of the ambiguous word (0 msec): Multiple access occurs; all meanings of the ambiguous word are facilitated, relative to the baseline of facilitation of an unrelated or nonsense word [Hudson and Tanenhaus, 1984; Onifer and Swinney, 1981; Seidenberg et al., 1982; Swinney, 1979; Tanenhaus et al., 1979].

100 msec: There is an apparent preference for the dominant meaning, but the effects of contextual bias can be seen [Lucas, 1983].

200 msec: If the previous context biases for one meaning and there is no text following the ambiguous word, only the meaning which is appropriate to the previous context is facilitated. Thus, active suppression takes place between the 100 and 200 msec probe points [Lucas, 1983; Seidenberg et al., 1982; Simpson, 1981; Tanenhaus et al., 1979].

400 msec: If the ambiguous word is presented in isolation (i.e., the ambiguous word is part of a list of words, each presented individually), all meanings are facilitated, but the dominant meaning shows more facilitation than subordinate meanings [Warren, 1977]. If the ambiguous word is instead presented with previously biasing context, the contextually appropriate meaning is still the only one showing facilitation, as it was at 200 msec [Seidenberg et al., 1982].

500 msec: If the ambiguous word is presented within a nonbiasing context, all meanings are still facilitated [Hudson and Tanenhaus, 1984].

600 msec: If the ambiguous word is presented in isolation, only the dominant meaning is facilitated. Thus, with no context, the dominant meaning is chosen [Warren, 1977]. If the ambiguous word is instead presented with a previous biasing context, the contextually appropriate meaning is still the only one showing facilitation, as at 200 and 400 msec [Tanenhaus et al., 1979].

Three syllables after presentation (750 to 1000 msec): If the ambiguous word is presented with a previous biasing context, the contextually appropriate meaning is still the only one showing facilitation, as at 200, 400, and 600 msec [Swinney, 1979].

1500 msec: If the ambiguous word is presented with a previously-biasing context, and more text follows the word, only the contextually appropriate meaning is facilitated [Onifer and Swinney, 1981].

At the clause boundary: If the text prior to the ambiguous word did not bias for one meaning, a small but significant facilitation is evident for the dominant meaning; other meanings show no facilitation [Hudson and Tanenhaus, 1984].

3.4 *Data Meets Theory*

The information summarized in the previous section can be used to plot the amount of facilitation of the different word meanings against the time since presentation of the word for various conditions. Most studies have focused on the 0 to 200 msec range, and there is little disagreement about the time course of facilitation during this period. The latter part of the time course has not been studied as often, and a number of different curves can be projected past the 200 msec point. Obviously, each curve represents a different hypothesis about the time course of facilitation under various conditions, so we must choose a set of curves which does not contradict what is already known about the processes involved.

One hypothesis, which represents our interpretation of data presented by Hudson and Tanenhaus [1984], is given in Figure 15.2.

We will focus on this study because it gives data for the condition in which an ambiguous word is embedded in a text that contains no preceding biasing context. This condition is not otherwise described in the literature and, as we will show, the results cannot be readily explained by existing theories. The data show that both meanings of an ambiguous word are strongly facilitated at the 0 and 500 msec probe points. However, at a clause boundary the subordinate meaning shows no facilitation, and the dominant meaning is only moderately facilitated. Thus it appears that both meanings of the ambiguous word remain active until just before the end of the clause which contains the ambiguous word, at which time they both rapidly decay.

There are other possible interpretations of this data. For example, Figure 15.3 represents an interpretation in which a choice of meaning is made after the 500 msec probe point, the subordinate meaning is actively suppressed, and the dominant meaning gradually loses facilitation. In the discussion that follows, we argue that any interpretation of the Hudson and Tanenhaus data which invokes active suppression is erroneous. We also show that an interpretation that relies solely on conditional retention is incorrect as well. Finally, we propose a theory of conditional retention *and* modular processing which accounts for the Hudson and Tanenhaus data.

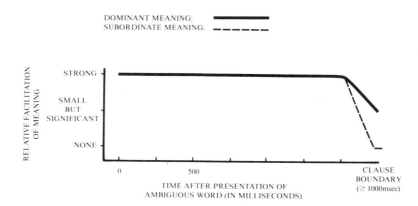

Figure 15.2 Time course of facilitation of the meanings of an ambiguous word presented in a non-biasing context—our interpretation of the data.

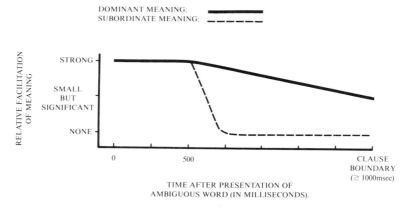

Figure 15.3 Time Course facilitation of the meanings of an ambiguous word presented in a non-biasing context—an alternative interpretation of the data.

Our argument against an active suppression explanation for the Hudson and Tanenhaus data is based on the nature of active suppression itself, as described by Tanenhaus et al. [1979]. The central idea in the active suppression theory is that when one meaning is chosen other candidate meanings are made unavailable much more quickly than they might be otherwise. (As noted above, active suppression might occur within a period of 100 msec.) Assuming for the moment that the time course in Figure 15.3 is correct, the decline of facilitation for subordinate meanings which appears immediately after the 500 msec probe point would be due to active suppression. If active suppression actually occurred there, though, it would indicate that a particular meaning had been chosen. If a particular meaning had been chosen, we would expect to see high facilitation of this meaning at the clause boundary; after all, we see it in every other condition where a meaning is chosen. The two conditions which illustrate this are: (1) The word-in-isolation condition itself [Warren, 1977]. (2) The biasing-context conditions at the 400 and 600 msec probe points [Seidenberg et al., 1982], at the three-syllable probe point [Swinney, 1979], and at 1500 msec [Onifer and Swinney, 1981]. However, the data of Hudson and Tanenhaus indicate that *no* meanings are highly facilitated at the clause boundary (though there is small but significant facilitation of the dominant meaning). Working backwards, then, it appears that no meaning has been chosen in the nonbiasing context condition. Therefore, active suppression could not have occurred, and the alternative hypothesis is incorrect.

Another possible time course is given in Figure 15.4, in which both meanings have been actively suppressed (this would require a redefinition of active suppression to include the possibility that no meanings at all need maintain facilitation). The clause boundary probe point is again the crucial test: if active suppression of all meanings occurred shortly after the 500 msec probe point, there should be no facilitation of any meaning at the clause boundary (unless meanings once suppressed somehow recover facilitation). Once again, the data of Hudson and Tanenhaus contradict this theory; though no meanings are strongly facilitated at the clause boundary, there is, as we noted above, a small but significant facilitation of the dominant meaning. Thus, the assumption that any sort of active suppression occurs is unwarranted, and the active suppression explanations must be abandoned. Other attempts we made at fitting curves to the existing data points did not seem to provide better explanations than the ones we have presented and rejected here.

Unfortunately, the conditional retention theory fares no better with the Hudson and Tanenhaus data. Conditional retention theory predicts that both meanings should maintain strong facilitation at the clause boundary when no choice is made. Yet, the data show that neither meaning is strongly facilitated.

At this point, one might argue that there may be an explanation for the data which involves neither active suppression nor conditional retention. For example, Figure 15.5 shows the approximate time course for the facilitation of the meanings of an ambiguous word presented in isolation [Warren, 1977].

Note that the time course in Figure 15.5 is very similar to that presented in Figure 15.3; perhaps the unnamed process which explains Figure 15.5 also accounts for Figure 15.3.

This interpretation of the data suggests that when there is no context, whether the word is in text or in isolation, processing will occur the same way: all meanings will retain facilitation for some time, with all but one meaning gradually losing facilitation. This, however, does not comport well with the data.

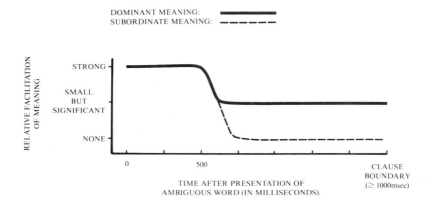

Figure 15.4 Time course of facilitation of the meanings of an ambiguous word presented in a non-biasing context—another alternative interpretation.

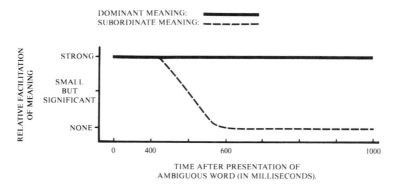

Figure 15.5 Time course of facilitation of the meanings of an ambiguous word presented in isolation—our interpretation of the data.

Inspection of the final probe points in Figures 15.3 and 15.5 reveals that the dominant meaning in the isolation condition (Figure 15.5) maintains strong facilitation while the dominant meaning in the previous nonbiasing context condition (Figure 15.3) shows only mild facilitation. If we accept the data at face value, there is a significant difference between the time courses of Figures 15.3 and 15.5. Thus, it is unlikely that the same process can account for both conditions.

Finally, one might argue that we have played both ends against the middle with the Hudson and Tanenhaus data; we first argued that there was not enough activation of the dominant meaning to support one theory, then we argued that there was too much activation of the dominant meaning to support the second. We offer two arguments in our defense. The first addresses the issue of why we say there is not enough facilitation for the first alternative explanation of the data: Hudson and Tanenhaus specifically stated that the dominant meaning's facilitation, while significant, was small; in fact, the facilitation was only discovered in a *posthoc* analysis which separated dominant and subordinate meanings [Hudson and Tanenhaus, 1984, p. 191]. Note, though, that the facilitation was significant, which is why we say there is too much facilitation to accept the other alternative theory.

As a foundation for our second argument, we propose that dominant meanings lose facilitation more slowly than subordinate meanings; further, we propose that dominant meanings have a higher resting activation. The first proposal is based on a sympathetic interpretation of the results of Warren [1977] and Lucas [1983]. These studies can be taken to show that during meaning selection dominant meanings remain active longer than subordinate meanings regardless of contextual bias. The second proposal can be defended with an equally favorable interpretation of results from Onifer and Swinney [1981]. As will be explained in more detail below, we theorize that the clause boundary causes all meanings to lose facilitation. Because the probe in the Hudson and Tanenhaus study occurred at the clause boundary, some amount of facilitation might still be evident near the end of the process. If this were so, it would most likely be seen with dominant meanings. This account specifically argues against the first alternative interpretation of the data (Figure 15.3) which would have early active suppression of all but the dominant meaning because this alternative would predict that the dominant meaning would retain facilitation beyond the clause boundary. Our account predicts that the dominant meaning will not retain facilitation beyond the clause boundary. Our account also argues against the second alternative interpretation (Figure 15.4) that would have all meanings actively suppressed around 500 msec because the mild facilitation of the dominant meaning is itself an indication of suppression at the clause boundary.

3.5 *Data Meets Theory—The Rematch*

As we have seen, both active suppression and conditional retention theories fail to explain the data completely. However, if we view this data from a slightly different perspective, a solution emerges. Let us assume, as many theorists have, that the components of language processing are *modular* [Forster, 1979; Frazier and Clifton, 1984; Frazier and Fodor, 1978]. Under this assumption, lexical disambiguation must be accomplished quickly so that other modules can use those decisions to perform higher level processing. When one module relinquishes responsibility for a certain part of the input text (a clause, for example) and another module takes over the processing of that part, the operations performed by the earlier module on that piece of text are not accessible. Thus, in the case of lexical disambiguation, meanings of ambiguous words lose facilitation at the clause boundary as the lower level processes such as simple lexical access begin work on the next clause. Though the meanings have lost facilitation, they are *retained* so that higher level processes can continue with the process of disambiguation.

There is evidence which indeed suggests that such modularity exists. For example, Sachs [1967] found that once semantic processing of text takes place, access to the syntactic information of the text is blocked. More evidence comes from research in syntactic processing which suggests that a lexical ambiguity must be reprocessed if it leads to problems at the syntactic level [Clifton, Frazier, and Connine, 1984]; in this case, the input to the lexical level is not available as input to the syntactic level of processing. In both cases, the input to a lower level and the processing done at that level are opaque to the higher level. In other words, only the *output* of a lower level of processing is available to higher levels. This argument parallels that of Fodor [1983], in which he argues that lexical access itself is a very stupid process which does no more than spread activation throughout a network. Later processes are responsible for making decisions about that activation. The particular points at which Fodor suggests these other processes come into play are essentially the same as those which we propose. The difference is that Fodor uses this apparent division of the lexical decision process to argue for modularity, while we are using modularity to argue for a division of the lexical decision process.

With respect to our theory, there are effectively three possibilities for what happens at the clause boundary when an ambiguous word is presented in a nonbiasing context. One possibility is that no meanings will be facilitated at the clause boundary; that is, there is no decision from the lexical level, and therefore no output upon which a higher level can work. The input to the lower level does not disappear, it is simply opaque to the higher level, and thus difficult to detect experimentally. Another possibility is that a choice is made; this could be a choice based on early context in the previous biasing context condition, or it could be a default choice in the previous nonbiasing context condition. In either case, the choice is made at the lexical level. It is this output which would be integrated into the representation of the text so far and processed by the higher level. The third possibility is that, rather than no meaning or one meaning being passed on to the next level, all meanings are incorporated into separate representations which are then processed by the next level. The data support only one of the possibilities offered above: that no meanings are facilitated at the clause boundary. In other words, the only hypothesis of these three which is supported by the data is the hypothesis that in the previous nonbiasing context condition, no default meaning is chosen until there is no possible resolution via later context.

This interpretation finds further support in unpublished pilot studies by Hudson and Tanenhaus [Susan Hudson D'Zmura, personal communication, October 22, 1986] which used the same procedure as the published study. In these studies, disambiguating information was presented in the clause following presentation of the ambiguous word; the information was presented both word-by-word and clause-by-clause. No reprocessing effect obtained with either presentation method. (It is important to note, however, that there was some question in these pilot studies about whether the subjects were following directions, and this may confound the results.)

It is worthwhile to speculate as to why neither of the other two possibilities occurs. There is a plausible reason for rejecting the selection of a default meaning. If the ambiguous word comes in the middle of the text (as in the Hudson and Tanenhaus [1984] study), later text may disambiguate the word; a default selection may bias towards the wrong meaning. It is safer to send all meanings or send no meaning than to send one which may lead to incorrect processing of later text.

The data also show, however, that not all meanings maintain facilitation at the clause boundary. If deactivating and retaining all meanings at the clause boundary carries essentially the same information as does keeping all meanings active—namely, that no decision was made—why deactivate the meanings? Perhaps there is some limit on how many meanings the lexical access process can keep active at any given time, or perhaps there is some other restriction which is invoked by cues such as clause boundaries. In either case, it would appear that conditional retention prevents the lexical access process from becoming overloaded by too many active meanings. These speculations deserve further investigation.

Related to this question is the issue of input reprocessing. At first glance, it might seem possible to account for the same data without conditional retention, if it is assumed that instead of retaining information derived from the input, the input is instead completely reprocessed upon discovery of a meaning selection error. There are two arguments against this alternative, though. The first is that it is a representation of input, not an exact record of the input, that is maintained. This is easily shown if the input is auditory because the signal is no longer available. But even with visual input, the evidence suggests that retention of some sort takes place. Eye-movement studies have shown that when an ambiguous word [Carpenter and Daneman, 1981] or syntactic structure [Rayner, Carlson, and Frazier, 1983] precedes disambiguating information, there is a retrograde eye movement to the locus of the ambiguity. The precision of the fixation on the ambiguous word or region, without search or random fixations, suggests that the ambiguity was recognized at the earlier point and that its location was retained.

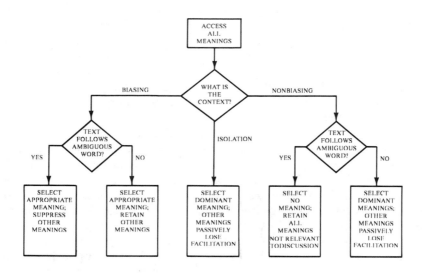

Figure 15.6 Flowchart of the lexical disambiguation process according to the conditional retention theory.

3.6 *Consequences of the Theory*

There are three important consequences of theorizing that meanings are retained but not facilitated at certain points. One result is that we gain some insight into the problem of supplanting incorrect lexical inferences: conditional retention makes it easy to find and re-evaluate word meanings that were initially rejected. How the proposed mechanism of conditional retention works in a computational model of text understanding is described in Section 4.

Another, more specific consequence has to do with the previous nonbiasing context condition. If later text selects a meaning, it does so via a different process from the post-lexical access process discussed earlier. This kind of decision is made by a higher-level process which uses syntactic or pragmatic information, and it is made *after* the lexical access process is completed. Thus, we are proposing that there are two types of post-lexical decisions: a decision that is part of the process of accessing the lexicon (i.e., what is commonly referred to as a "post-lexical decision"), and a decision that builds, confirms, or modifies the meaning of the word in the representation of the text.

The third consequence involves the previous biasing condition. For the same reasons that we expect meanings to be retained when the word is embedded in a text with a previous nonbiasing context, we expect that all meanings are retained rather than suppressed if the text goes on after the am-

biguous word. That is, because there is later text which might require the reinterpretation of earlier text, we theorize that all meanings are retained until the
end of the text (assuming the text is short; see Section 3.8 for further discussion). The difference between the previous nonbiasing context condition and
the previous biasing context condition is that in the latter, a meaning consistent
with the biasing context is selected; however, the other meanings are not
suppressed and discarded, as active suppression would suggest, but rather deactivated and retained.

   We are now ready to describe in detail the ways in which different conditions affect facilitation of meanings throughout the time course of lexical
access. (Also see the accompanying flowchart in Figure 15.6.) As an ambiguous word is encountered, multiple access occurs in an automatic, autonomous
process, regardless of whether the word appears in isolation, with previously
biasing context, or with nonbiasing context. After multiple access occurs, the
word meaning is chosen by different processes depending on the various contextual conditions. In the isolation condition, the dominant meaning is chosen;
this decision takes significantly more time than does a choice in the previous
biasing context condition. In the previous biasing context condition where the
ambiguous word comes at the end of the text, the biased-for meaning will remain facilitated while others are actively suppressed. When the word is
embedded in a previous biasing context condition a meaning will be selected,
and other meanings will be deactivated but retained in case later text requires a
reinterpretation of early text. If the later text does not require reinterpretation,
the meaning which was originally chosen remains facilitated, and the retained
meanings are suppressed. In the previous nonbiasing context condition, in
which a word is embedded in text, no meaning will be selected; at the clause
boundary, all meanings are deactivated, but the meanings will be retained so
that later text can select the correct one via a later decision process. If the later
text does not disambiguate, the dominant meaning is chosen as default at the
end of the text.

3.7 *How to Test for Conditional Retention*

We have shown how the theory of conditional retention unifies the results of
recent experimental studies of lexical access and disambiguation, although the
only evidence we have given in support of conditional retention is a *posthoc*
explanation for existing data. In order to strengthen the case for conditional retention, it remains for us to show that the theory makes correct predictions
about previously unexplained phenomena.

   Conditional retention specifically predicts that when an ambiguous word is
embedded in context and no clause boundaries occur, all meanings will maintain facilitation until the end of the text. If the pre-word and post-word con-

texts bias in opposite directions (a condition we have referred to as "conflicting context" [Granger et al., 1984]), conditional retention predicts three things:

1. All meanings will be retained until the end of the text.

2. There will be no reprocessing of the post-word text. The meaning will be chosen after the post-word text is originally processed, and the meaning will be appropriate to the contextual bias provided by the post-word text. This might mean that reinterpretation or revision of the representation for the pre-word text is necessary.

3. When the meaning appropriate to the post-word context is chosen, the other meanings will be actively suppressed.

These predictions are similar to those made by Granger et al. [1984], but reflect the changes in conditional retention theory, as summarized in Section 3.1. We are currently in the final stages of designing an experiment which will test the modified predictions and correct problems in the earlier work. If all goes well, this experiment will not only confirm the conditional retention theory and answer questions about how conflicting contexts influence lexical ambiguity resolution, but will also begin to explain how choices made in the resolution of lexical ambiguity affect higher level inference decisions.

3.8 *Summary of the Case for Conditional Retention*

A summary of the major points of the preceding section will be beneficial. We began with a description of our theory of conditional retention. In support of this theory, we presented data from several experiments which described the levels of facilitation of different meanings of ambiguous words at different times and in different conditions. The separate data points from the different studies were then distilled into a single description of the time course of lexical and post-lexical decisions in different conditions. This distillation was the result of the few data points we had and a large amount of deduction on our part. This step is the weak link in our argument for conditional retention—it is the weak link in the literature, too—not only because of the scant data available, but also because the data were the product of many different experimental methodologies. We therefore took great pains to argue for the plausibility of this time course as the best unified description of the individual data points. We showed that by incorporating conditional retention into a framework of modular processes, we were able to account for this time course. We then discussed the implications of this new theory. One implication is that there are two post-lexical decision processes: one at the lexical processing level, and the other at a higher processing level. Finally, we made explicit predictions that described the results we hope to find by testing for conditional retention in conflicting context conditions.

In the introduction, we asked two questions about conditional retention. The first was, "Conditional on what?" The account we have given of the conditions under which retention occurs has addressed this question in detail. We have also attempted to answer, or at least to begin to answer, the question, "Retained for how long?" by suggesting that retained meanings are usually not suppressed until the end of the text. Unfortunately, this is not a particularly satisfying answer, as we have offered no account of how long the text can be before retained meanings are released. This is still an open question. The remainder of this article discusses our view of the role of conditional retention in the larger picture of text understanding.

4 *The Big Picture*

Much of the work in text understanding has focused on inference processing— the use of various forms of knowledge to generate, evaluate, and incorporate information which is not explicitly represented in a written text but which is nevertheless essential to understanding the text. These inferences take place on a number of different levels, and the understander is not necessarily aware of their occurrence. For example, inference processes come into play at the lexical level in disambiguating word senses, at the syntactic level in determining pronominal referents, at the pragmatic level in connecting story events, and at all three levels in understanding any text.

Our research in language understanding has been concerned primarily with the construction of computational models of inference processes at the pragmatic level of the understanding mechanism (for example, see Granger [1980], Granger [1981], and Granger, Eiselt, and Holbrook [1983]). These processes rely on the application of semantic and episodic memory structures to input text in order to "fill in the gaps." For example, while reading the text, "John had not worked in months. He grabbed his gun and went to the bank," it is the pragmatic inference process that allows the understander to conclude that John intended to rob the bank.

At any point in the text where an inference could be generated, there is usually more than one inference possible. However, in explaining the events related explicitly in the text, some inferences may serve better than others. In the case of John's armed visit to the bank, John might well have been a bank guard who had just recovered from a lengthy illness and was preparing for his first day back on the job. This interpretation explains the explicit text events, yet somehow does not seem as plausible as the original explanation. Thus, as is the case with processing at the lexical level, the primary problem in pragmatic inference processing is disambiguation: the evaluation of competing inferences and subsequent selection of the one which best explains the events portrayed in the text.

An understander does not always choose the correct inference when faced with an ambiguous text and competing inferences. Often, an understander will make a faulty inference and then revise or supplant it later. Therefore, our research has not been limited to the processes of selecting from competing inferences, but includes the processes involved in supplanting an inference when the original choice is later found to be inappropriate.

Models of text understanding that had addressed the inference decision problem either had chosen a default inference, postponed a decision in hope that later text would provide enough information to resolve the ambiguity, or employed heuristics to increase the likelihood of making a correct initial decision. With few exceptions, these models were unable to supplant an incorrect initial inference. One of these exceptions [Granger, 1980] was able to supplant incorrect inferences by maintaining a map of pointers to all potential inferences. This map, which was separate from the representation that was eventually constructed for the input text, kept track of all the inferences generated during the processing of a text, whether or not they appeared in the final representation. Another exception [Norvig, 1983] temporarily stored rejected inferences in a separate data base in case later text showed that a rejected inference actually belonged in the final representation. These mechanisms provided solutions to the problem of supplanting inferences by making it possible to keep track of both accepted and rejected inferences. From a cognitive-modeling viewpoint, however, it seemed that a better solution must exist. The multiple access/conditional retention theory of lexical disambiguation provided just that.

Recall that in the conditional retention theory all meanings of an ambiguous word are recalled at once, after which the individual meanings are evaluated, possibly at the same time, in light of the existing context. If a choice is indicated by previous context, and no text follows, the inappropriate meanings are discarded (i.e., actively suppressed). If a choice is not indicated by previous context, or if text follows the ambiguous word, the different meanings are retained for further processing. By assuming that the meanings of individual words are in some way connected to the higher-level memory structures which generate the pragmatic inferences related to those word meanings, it seems very likely that the process of selecting a correct pragmatic inference is much the same as choosing a correct meaning at the lexical level. In fact, we simply consider lexical disambiguation to be another inference decision process. The assumption of a close relationship between word meanings and higher level memory structures is not unreasonable; in fact, it is difficult to imagine a viable theory of text understanding which does not make this assumption.

In brief, the close relationship between word meanings and pragmatic memory structures implies that the pragmatic inference decision process follows essentially the same steps as the lexical disambiguation process that we described earlier:

1. Potential pragmatic inferences which explain the same input text are generated and evaluated in parallel.

2. If one inference explains the text better than the others do, and there are no textual cues to indicate that a decision may be premature (e.g., there is still more text to process), then the other less-explanatory inferences are suppressed.

3. If no inference proves to be more explanatory than the others, all inferences are retained until later text provides the information necessary to make a decision. In the case that later text does not disambiguate, a default decision can be made, possibly on the basis of recency or frequency.

As is the case with the lexical inference decision process, retaining competing inferences at the pragmatic level makes supplanting incorrect initial inferences quite simple. If a tentative initial inference later proves to be incorrect, that inference can be deactivated while a more explanatory competing inference which had been retained is activated. However, if for some reason contradictory information appears after an inference decision has been made and the competing inferences have been suppressed, supplanting the incorrect inference will most likely require rereading of the original text and some conscious problem solving. These aspects of language understanding are well beyond the scope of this theory.

The close relationship between memory structures and inference processes at the lexical and pragmatic levels of language understanding also implies that the disambiguation processes at the lexical and pragmatic levels are highly interdependent. For example, if local syntactic and semantic information is used to select the appropriate meaning of a word, the impact will be felt at the pragmatic level. Higher level memory structures (and their accompanying inferences) which are associated with inappropriate word meanings will be ignored; those associated with the appropriate word meaning will be incorporated into the internal representation. On the other hand, when local context is not enough to disambiguate a word, pragmatic information will be used to select the appropriate meaning. These inference decisions will shape the context which in turn will influence any later inference decisions. This newly revised context might also resolve earlier inference decisions which have been postponed.

We have presented a unified theory of text understanding which explains how understanders can recover from misinterpretation at either the lexical or pragmatic levels without extensive reprocessing of the text. This theory also describes an architecture for language understanding in which the inference processes at the different levels are automatic and autonomous. Though the processes are modular and do not communicate directly, they are interdependent because they update, and are influenced by, a common memory representation. Thus, the inference decisions made at either level are reflected in changes to the memory representation, which in turn serves as the context for making later decisions at both levels.

We have built a computational model, called ATLAST, which incorporates some of the theory we have discussed here. ATLAST uses marker-passing to search a relational network for paths which connect meanings of open-class words from the input text. A single path is a chain of nodes, representing objects or events, connected by links, corresponding to relationships between the nodes. Any nodes in a path which are not explicitly mentioned in the text are events or objects which are inferred; therefore, these paths are called *inference paths*. A set of inference paths which joins all the words in the text into a connected graph represents one possible interpretation of the text. In this respect ATLAST resembles a number of other models of text understanding that utilize marker-passing or spreading activation (e.g., [Charniak, 1983; Cottrell and Small, 1983; Hirst, 1984; Quillian, 1969; Riesbeck and Martin, 1986; Waltz and Pollack, 1985]). The paths which form the current interpretation are called *active paths*.

For any given text, however, there may be a great number of possible interpretations, many of which are nonsensical. The problem then is determining which of the possible interpretations provides the best explanation of the text. ATLAST deals with this problem by applying inference evaluation metrics. These metrics are used to compare two competing inference paths and select the more appropriate one. Two inference paths compete when they connect the same two nodes in the relational network via different combinations of links and nodes. The path that fits better with the current interpretation is activated (i.e., it becomes part of the interpretation). The other path is de-activated but not discarded. Instead, that path is *retained* in order to facilitate error recovery as described below. Thus, inference paths exist in one of three conditions: the path has never been explored (or it has been explored, evaluated, and suppressed), the path is currently active and is either being used as part of the explanation for the text (or is currently being evaluated by the filter), or the path has been explored and evaluated, but no decision could be made so this path has been deactivated and retained. The choice of one inference path over another is made as soon as ATLAST discovers that the two paths compete; ATLAST does not postpone inference decisions. As the marker-passing search mechanism finds more paths, ATLAST constructs an interpretation consisting of those paths which survive the evaluation process. When the marker-passing and evaluation processes end, the surviving active paths make up the final interpretation of the text.

In theory, the search for inference paths and their evaluation take place simultaneously. In practice, though, ATLAST simulates this concurrency by alternating between marker-passing and path evaluation. During each of these cycles, a new word is read from the input, its meanings are recalled and marked, and all markers in the network are passed a fixed distance. Any path discovered in this way is then examined to see if it competes with an active path in the interpretation as it stands at that time. If so, the evaluation metrics are applied and a choice between the two competing paths is made.

The two keys to supplanting incorrect inferences in ATLAST are the retention of previously rejected inference paths and the ability to re-evaluate possibly relevant retained paths at the appropriate times. Without a mechanism for knowing when and how to re-evaluate the retained paths, the retention feature alone provides no benefit.

There are two ways in which the re-evaluation of a retained path can be initiated. The first is through direct rediscovery of the retained path by the search process. Because the passing of markers begins in different places at different times during the processing of text, the same inference path may be discovered (or more appropriately, rediscovered) more than once. If a rediscovered path is not currently part of ATLAST's interpretation of the text (i.e., the path has been discovered earlier, rejected by the evaluation metrics, but retained), that path is re-evaluated against the competing path which is part of the interpretation. This rediscovery process initiates reconsideration of some of the retained paths, but it is not dependent upon retention because these paths would be reconsidered even if they had not been retained.

Some retained paths, though, will not be rediscovered, but the inferences made from later text may change the interpretation in such a way that these paths now should be included. ATLAST uses a method of "piggy-backing" the re-evaluation of these paths onto the evaluation of paths which are directly discovered or rediscovered by the search process. If a (re)discovered path is evaluated against a competing path in the current interpretation, any subpaths or superpaths of the (re)discovered path are also evaluated against the current interpretation. In this way, ATLAST attempts to limit re-evaluation to those paths that are currently relevant. Without the ability to force re-evaluation of paths rejected early in processing but not rediscovered later, ATLAST's final interpretation probably will be incorrect. Indirectly initiating the re-evaluation of previously rejected inference paths is essential to ATLAST's error recovery capability and is dependent upon inference retention.

The principle of retention is not unique to ATLAST. As we briefly mentioned earlier, Norvig [1983] developed a mechanism which accomplished a similar end but through different means. His text understanding system, which focused strictly on pragmatic inference decisions, also used a marker-passing system to locate relevant memory structures, called frames, to explain an input text. A frame could be either inactive, active and currently used as an explanation for the text, or previously active and not currently used as an explanation. These previously-active frames were temporarily stored in a separate data base in case a currently-active frame proved to be a poor explanation. In this event, a competing, previously-active frame could be reactivated to supplant the incorrect initial choice. If a previously-active frame was not reactivated, it quickly reverted back to an inactive state. To our knowledge, no other language understanding models have used the notion of retained inference paths, though it would seem that this idea could be easily incorporated into some of them. (One might also argue that the connectionist models of Cottrell and Small [1983] and Waltz and Pollack [1985] allow for more than two levels of activation: Rejected paths could settle into a moderate level of activation or weighting, giving such paths a "head start" as later text initiates more iterative weight balancing.)

Though much remains to be done with the model, our work on ATLAST has been instrumental in refining our theory of inference decision processes in language understanding. A more detailed explanation of ATLAST is given by Granger, Eiselt, and Holbrook [1986] and Eiselt [1987].

5 *Conclusion*

The most appealing feature of conditional retention theory is that it answers questions which the other theories do not. For example, conditional retention provides a mechanism by which incorrect lexical decisions can be corrected, thus providing an explanation of supplanting. Conditional retention also explains the different time courses for facilitation of meanings in a variety of conditions: dominant and subordinate meanings, contextually appropriate and contextually inappropriate meanings, and words in isolation, words in biasing contexts, and words in nonbiasing contexts. The principle of conditional retention also provides a new perspective from which to view the pragmatic inference decision process. The ability to explain inference decision phenomena at two different levels of the language understanding process with one principle offers not only computational efficiency but also a simpler and more powerful cognitive theory.

To progress as far as we have, we were forced to reinterpret existing data using an entirely new set of assumptions. One such assumption is that unselected meanings of an ambiguous word are retained. Another assumption is that language processing is modular, which implies that the effects of lower level processing on any input are unobservable once higher levels begin processing that input. A third assumption is that the lexical decision process is carried out at higher levels of processing as well as the lexical level. These are just preliminary effects of this perspective—if the theory is correct, we have a new, productive framework in which to examine lexical disambiguation in particular and language understanding in general.

Acknowledgments

This research was supported in part by the National Science Foundation under grants IST-81-20685 and IST-85-12419 and by the Naval Ocean Systems Center under contracts N00123-81-C-1078 and N66001-83-C-0255.

References

Birnbaum, L. 1985. Lexical ambiguity as a touchstone for theories of language analysis. In *Proceedings of the Ninth International Joint Conference on Artificial Intelligence*, Los Angeles, California. Los Altos: Morgan Kaufmann Publishers.

Carpenter, P.A., and Daneman, N. 1981. Lexical retrieval and error recovery in reading: A model based on eye fixations. *Journal of Verbal Learning and Verbal Behavior* 20:137–160.

Charniak, E. 1981. Six topics in search of a parser: An overview of AI language research. In *Proceedings of the Seventh International Joint Conference on Artificial Intelligence*, Vancouver, B.C., Canada. Los Altos: Morgan Kaufmann Publishers.

Charniak, E. 1983. Passing markers: A theory of contextual influence in language comprehension. *Cognitive Science* 7:171–190.

Clifton, C., Frazier, L., and Connine, C. 1984. Lexical expectations in sentence comprehension. *Journal of Verbal Learning and Verbal Behavior* 23:696–708.

Cottrell, G.W. and Small, S.L. 1983. A connectionist scheme for modelling word sense disambiguation. *Cognition and Brain Theory* 6:89–120.

Eiselt, K.P. 1987. Recovering from erroneous inferences. Technical Report No. 87–06, Department of Information and Computer Science, University of California, Irvine.

Fodor, J.A. 1983. *The Modularity of Mind*. Cambridge: MIT Press.

Forster, K.I. 1976. Accessing the mental lexicon. In R.J. Wales and E. Walker (eds.), *New Approaches to Language Mechanisms*. Amsterdam: North-Holland.

Forster, K.I. 1979. Levels of processing and the structure of the language processor. In W.E. Cooper and E.C.T. Walker (eds.), *Sentence Processing: Psycholinguistic Studies Presented to Merrill Garrett*. Hillsdale: Erlbaum.

Frazier, L. and Clifton, C. 1984. Thematic relations in parsing. Unpublished manuscript, University of Massachusetts, Amherst.

Frazier, L. and Fodor, J.D. 1978. The sausage machine: A new two-stage parsing model. *Cognition* 6:291–325.

Gigley, H.M. 1983. HOPE—AI and the dynamic process of language behavior. *Cognition and Brain Theory* 6:39–88.

Granger, R.H. 1980. When expectation fails: Towards a self-correcting inference system. In *Proceedings of the First Annual National Conference on Artificial Intelligence*, Stanford, California. Los Altos: Morgan Kaufmann Publishers.

Granger, R.H. 1981. Directing and re-directing inference pursuit: Extra-textual influences on text interpretation. In *Proceedings of the Seventh International Joint Conference on Artificial Intelligence*, Vancouver, B.C., Canada. Los Altos: Morgan Kaufmann Publishers.

Granger, R.H., Eiselt, K.P., and Holbrook, J.K. 1983. STRATEGIST: A program that models strategy-driven and content-driven inference behavior. In *Proceedings of the National Conference on Artificial Intelligence*, Washington, D.C. Los Altos: Morgan Kaufmann Publishers.

Granger, R.H., Eiselt, K.P., and Holbrook, J.K. 1986. Parsing with parallelism: A spreading-activation model of inference processing during text understanding. In J.L. Kolodner and C.K. Riesbeck (eds.), *Experience, Memory, and Reasoning*. Hillsdale: Erlbaum.

Granger, R.H., Holbrook, J.K., and Eiselt, K.P. 1984. Interaction effects between word-level and text-level inferences: On-line processing of ambiguous words in context. In *Proceedings of the Sixth Annual Conference of the Cognitive Science Society*, Boulder, Colorado.

Hirst, G. 1984. Jumping to conclusions: Psychological reality and unreality in a word disambiguation program. In *Proceedings of the Sixth Annual Conference of the Cognitive Science Society*, Boulder, Colorado.

Hogaboam, T.W., and Perfetti, C.A. 1975. Lexical ambiguity and sentence comprehension. *Journal of Verbal Learning and Verbal Behavior* 14:265–274.

Hudson, S.B., and Tanenhaus, M.K. 1984. Ambiguity resolution in the absence of contextual bias. In *Proceedings of the Sixth Annual Conference of the Cognitive Science Society*, Boulder, Colorado.

Lucas, M. 1983. Lexical access during sentence comprehension: Frequency and context effects. In *Proceedings of the Fifth Annual Conference of the Cognitive Science Society*, Rochester, New York.

Norvig, P. 1983. Six problems for story understanders. In *Proceedings of the National Conference on Artificial Intelligence*, Washington, D.C. Los Altos: Morgan Kaufmann Publishers.

Onifer, W., and Swinney, D.A. 1981. Accessing lexical ambiguities during sentence comprehension: Effects of frequency of meaning and contextual bias. *Memory and Cognition* 9:225–236.

Quillian, M.R. 1969. The teachable language comprehender: A simulation program and theory of language. *Communications of the ACM* 12:459–476.

Rayner, K., Carlson, M., and Frazier, L. 1983. The interaction of syntax and semantics during sentence processing: Eye movements in the analysis of semantically biased sentences. *Journal of Verbal Learning and Verbal Behavior* 22:358–374.

Riesbeck, C.K. 1975. Conceptual analysis. In R.C. Schank (ed.), *Conceptual Information Processing*. Amsterdam: North-Holland.

Riesbeck, C.K., and Martin, C.E. 1986. Direct memory access parsing. In J.L. Kolodner and C.K. Riesbeck (eds.), *Experience, Memory, and Reasoning*. Hillsdale: Erlbaum.

Rumelhart, D.E. 1981. Understanding understanding. CHIP 100, Center for Human Information Processing, University of California, San Diego.

Sachs, J. 1967. Recognition memory for syntactic and semantic aspects of connected discourse. *Perception and Psychophysics* 2:437–442.

Seidenberg, M.S., Tanenhaus, M.K., Leiman, J.M., and Bienkowski, M. 1982. Automatic access of the meanings of ambiguous words in context: Some limitations of knowledge-based processing, *Cognitive Psychology* 14:489–537.

Seifert, C.M., Robertson, S.P., and Black, J.B. 1982. On-line processing of pragmatic inferences. Cognitive Science Technical Report 15, Cognitive Science Program, Yale University, New Haven, Connecticut.

Simpson, G. 1981. Meaning dominance and semantic context in the processing of lexical ambiguity. *Journal of Verbal Learning and Verbal Behavior* 20:120–136.

Small, S., and Rieger, C. 1982. Parsing and comprehending with word experts (a theory and its realization). In W.G. Lehnert and M.H. Ringle (eds.), *Strategies for Natural Language Processing*. Hillsdale: Erlbaum.

Swinney, D.A. 1979. Lexical access during sentence comprehension: (Re)consideration of context effects. *Journal of Verbal Learning and Verbal Behavior* 18:645–660.

Swinney, D. 1984. Theoretical and methodological issues in cognitive science: A psychological perspective. In W. Kintsch, J.R. Miller, and P.G. Polson (eds.), *Method and Tactics in Cognitive Science*. Hillsdale: Erlbaum.

Tanenhaus, M., Leiman, J., and Seidenberg, M. 1979. Evidence for multiple stages in processing of ambiguous words in syntactic contexts. *Journal of Verbal Learning and Verbal Behavior* 18:427–440.

Waltz, D.L., and Pollack, J.B. 1985. Massively parallel parsing: A strongly interactive model of natural language interpretation. *Cognitive Science* 9:51–74.

Warren, R.E. 1977. Time and the spread of activation in memory. *Journal of Experimental Psychology: Human Learning and Memory* 3:458–466.

16

Neuropsychology of Lexical Ambiguity Resolution: The Contribution of Divided Visual Field Studies

Curt Burgess
University of Rochester

Greg B. Simpson
University of Nebraska at Omaha

There have been many attempts to determine the relative contributions of the cerebral hemispheres to normal cognitive and language function. While it is well accepted that the left hemisphere plays a major role in language function, it is becoming less controversial to recognize certain language capabilities in the right hemisphere [Krashen, 1976; Searleman, 1977; Zaidel, 1978]. It has been suggested that research into the neuropsychological underpinnings of word recognition could potentially tell us much about comprehension processes in general[1] [Posner, 1981]. In this chapter we propose a tentative model of lexical ambiguity resolution that integrates the different lexical access patterns of the two cerebral hemispheres, and we discuss this model in the context of our current understanding of lexical access and contextual constraints.

---

1 On the other hand, investigating the neuropsychological underpinnings of cognitive processes may be a fruitless effort if one is to believe Peterson's claim that "What's going on in the brain doesn't make any sense" [R. Peterson, personal communication, March, 1985].

We will describe the divided visual field method and then briefly review our earlier experiment suggesting a frequency-coded multiple access model of lexical retrieval [Simpson and Burgess, 1985]. This experiment provided the groundwork for the divided visual field experiment upon which our model of the roles of the cerebral hemispheres in lexical ambiguity processing is based [Burgess and Simpson, in press. The model makes explicit predictions concerning the role of the left and right cerebral hemispheres in the access of ambiguous word meanings which will be discussed at the end of the chapter.

1 *The Divided Visual Field Methodology*

The divided visual field method of stimulus presentation is a widely used method that allows for input to a single hemisphere using a tachistoscope or the CRT of a computer. The logic behind the technique exploits the structure of the visual pathways. These pathways are organized such that the left visual field projects to the right hemisphere whereas the right visual field projects to the left hemisphere. Stimuli are usually projected 2 to 5 degrees to the left or right of central visual fixation, assuring that the stimuli are in the temporal visual field and thus will be projected to the contralateral hemisphere. A stimulus duration of less than 200 milliseconds allows the stimulus to be presented without allowing the subject time for an eye movement in the direction of the stimulus, which would defeat the intent of the technique (see [Sergent, 1986; Young, 1982]).

Whereas it is relatively simple to control the hemisphere of input, the hemispheres are connected by various commissures that allow for interhemispheric communication. A potential problem with the divided visual field methodology, then, is determining whether or not the stimulus was processed in the hemisphere of input or if information relevant to the stimulus was transferred to the other hemisphere for processing (see [Zaidel, 1983]). Chiarello [1985] has demonstrated that semantic priming occurs when targets are presented to either the left or right visual field. This is consistent with Zaidel's report that split brain patients were able to make lexical decisions to stimuli presented to either hemisphere. Cohen [1982] has suggested that interhemispheric transmission time is too brief to account for the large differences in reaction time that are reported in the literature and that a more reasonable explanation is that the hemisphere of input first attempts to process the information which it receives. In a series of lexical decision experiments, Hardyck, Chiarello, Dronkers, and Simpson [1985] have presented evidence that suggests that the processes involved in lexical access (sensory analysis, semantic pathway activation and the lexical decision) occur in the hemisphere of input, rather than requiring shared hemispheric resources. Their results also suggest that it is the actual lexical decision that is transmitted to the other hemisphere, not the information required to make the decision. It seems clear, then, that both the left and right hemisphere are able to access the lexicon and make a lexical decision. An additional concern in divided visual field experiments is the ability to generalize to normal cognitive or language function. For example, presenting a word in the left visual field may demand that the right hemisphere process information to an extent that would not normally occur. If the point of the VF experiment is to generalize to normal language function, then it is important at some point to be able to present convergent evidence, either using other methodologies, or by inference from the clinical neuropsychological literature. Later, we will discuss research involving brain-damaged patients that will bear on ambiguity resolution. We turn now to the discussion of the lexical access patterns of ambiguous word meanings.

2 Lexical Access of Ambiguous Word Meanings

Simpson [1984] recently reviewed the literature on the effect of lexical ambiguity on word recognition, and concluded that three models of ambiguity processing have emerged. The context-dependent model states that the meanings of ambiguous words are activated by the context of the sentences in which they occur, so that only the contextually appropriate meaning of the ambiguous word is activated [Glucksberg, 1984; Glucksberg, Kreuz, and Rho, 1986; Schvaneveldt, Meyer, and Becker, 1976; Simpson, 1981].

The single access model proposes that the meanings of an ambiguous word are retrieved serially, according to their frequency [Forster and Bednall, 1976; Hogaboam and Perfetti, 1975]. The most frequent meaning is retrieved first, and the search stops if that meaning is appropriate in context. If it is not, the next most frequent meaning is selected. This serial self-terminating search continues until a fit is made with the context. In the absence of context, retrieval favors the dominant (most frequent) meaning [Simpson, 1981].

Finally, the multiple access model states that all word meanings are retrieved upon the presentation of an ambiguous word, after which context influences the selection of the appropriate meaning. Context affects the selection process, but lexical activation occurs automatically for all meanings [Holley-Wilcox and Blank, 1980; Onifer and Swinney, 1981; Seidenberg et al., 1982; Swinney, 1979; Tanenhaus et al., 1979]. The multiple access model differs from the single access view in that the multiple access model claims that all meanings are activated in parallel. In contrast, the single access model claims that only the most frequent meaning is retrieved and if a fit with context is not made then retrieval for the next most frequent meaning occurs. Onifer and Swinney [1981] interpret their results in favor of a multiple access model in

which all word meanings are accessed regardless of the frequency of association between the ambiguous word and its meaning. Seidenberg et al. [1982]
have suggested that the speed of activation of ambiguous word meanings is a
function of their frequency. Thus, there are two possible accounts of multiple
access models which are distinguished by their frequency constraints:
frequency independent multiple access and frequency-coded multiple access.[2]

2.1 A Frequency-coded Multiple Access Process

Pertinent to the discussion here is our work describing access of ambiguous
word meanings as a frequency-coded, multiple access process [Simpson and
Burgess, 1985]. We used a lexical decision task in a semantic priming paradigm with ambiguous words and either their more dominant (i.e., frequent) associates (*BANK—MONEY*) or their subordinate (i.e., less frequent) associates
(*BANK—RIVER*). We used five SOAs[3] (16, 100, 300, 500, and 750 msec) in
which the prime was presented for the duration of the SOA. We found that
facilitation occurred for the dominant associates very early in the recognition
process (16 msec SOA) and was present at all SOAs. The pattern for the subordinate meanings was different. There was no facilitation for the subordinate
meanings at the earliest SOA (16 msec), but by our intermediate SOA (300
msec) facilitation for the subordinate meanings was equivalent to that for the
dominant meanings. The equivalent facilitation by 300 msec for the dominant
and subordinate meanings suggests that multiple access has occurred. However,
the facilitation for the subordinate meaning increased slowly relative to the
dominant meaning, indicating that this retrieval is frequency-coded. At longer
SOAs, facilitation for the dominant meaning was maintained, while facilitation
for the subordinate meaning declined. By the 750 msec SOA, we found no
facilitation for the subordinate condition. In another experiment in the series,
we determined that there was inhibition for the subordinate meanings at the
750 msec SOA.[4] These results suggest that multiple meanings of ambiguous
words are activated automatically, in a frequency-coded order. Attentional processing, then, allocates resources to the dominant meaning, resulting in the inhibition of responses to the subordinate meaning.

---

2 A more complete account of the general processes involved in ambiguous word recognition can
be found in Simpson and Burgess [this volume].

3 Stimulus onset asynchrony (SOA) is the time interval between the onset of the prime and the
onset of the target.

4 Inhibitory effects are demonstrated by slower responses to unrelated targets than targets
preceded by neutral stimuli. The redirection of resources to a memory location unrelated to the target necessitates a time-consuming reallocation of those resources [Neely, 1977; Stanovich and
West, 1979].

2.2 Lexical Access of Ambiguous Word Meanings in the Cerebral Hemispheres

As we discuss lexical access patterns in the cerebral hemispheres, recall that our results at the briefer SOAs suggest a frequency-coded multiple access process. These early SOAs are usually thought to reflect the automatic passive spread of activation in memory [Neely, 1976, 1977; Stanovich and West, 1979, 1981, 1983]. Yet, at the long SOA, inhibition of the subordinate meaning had occurred, presumably reflecting attentional or controlled processing. The distinction between automatic and controlled processing has also been shown to be crucial in studies distinguishing hemispheric processing capabilities as well.

2.2.1 Automatic and Controlled Processing Chiarello [1985] compared automatic and controlled processing by varying the proportion of related trials in a semantic priming experiment using a lexical decision task. The logic of a proportion manipulation is similar to our use of SOAs of different durations. The low proportion of related trials provides a subject with less opportunity (or reason) to develop any strategies or attentional biases, and therefore any semantic priming that occurs in this condition is held to be due to an automatic spread of activation throughout the memory network [Seidenberg et al., 1982]. On the other hand, with a high proportion of related trials, subjects presumably are able to restrict attention to a smaller set of words that are likely to be related. Anticipating a related trial leads the subject to focus attention on prime-related information resulting in quicker recognition on those trials. This manipulation should allow subjects to use controlled processes when the proportion of related trials was high, but when the proportion of related trials was low, subjects should be using only automatic processes. Related trials occurred only 25% of the time in one experiment, while in the other, they occurred 75% of the time. Chiarello found that semantic priming occurred in both hemispheres in her automatic condition, with the priming being greater in the right hemisphere. The pattern was different, however, in the controlled condition. Whereas priming still occurred in both hemispheres, it was now greater in the left hemisphere. Chiarello concluded that the left hemisphere is primarily responsible for controlled processing of semantic relationships.

2.2.2 Hypotheses Concerning Lexical Access in the Hemispheres
These experiments led us to explore the availability of dominant and subordinate meanings of ambiguous words in the left and right hemispheres and the speed with which they are retrieved. Generalizing from our experiments [Simpson and Burgess, 1985] and from Chiarello's [1985] studies, we hypothesized that using a brief SOA (35 msec) and a longer SOA (750 msec) would allow us to separate automatic and controlled processing. The short SOA should tap automatic processes because of the rapid onset of spreading activation [Hasher

and Zacks, 1979; Posner and Snyder, 1975]. Automatic processing should occur in both hemispheres [Chiarello, 1985], but should be restricted to the dominant associate [Simpson and Burgess, 1985]. Controlled processing should only occur in the left hemisphere and the longer SOA should be long enough for this type of processing to occur. We would expect inhibition of the subordinate associates at the 750 msec SOA, but only in the left hemisphere. The role of right hemisphere processing of the subordinate associates was more difficult to predict. Since controlled processing was not anticipated, any activation for the subordinate associates would be left to decay. However, if the right hemisphere lexicon consists of only a subset of the entries found in the left hemisphere [Zaidel, 1978] and these entries are dominant associates, then facilitation for subordinate associates might not occur.

2.2.3 *Experimental Methodology*

We conducted an experiment similar to our earlier study, but using the divided visual field methodology. Ambiguous primes were presented foveally and 48 right-handed subjects made lexical decisions to targets that were presented in the left or right visual field.[5] All subjects responded with their right hand. Stimuli were vertically presented to avoid a directional scanning bias (see [Bradshaw, Nettleton, and Taylor, 1981]). Words subtended a maximum visual angle of 5.2 degrees with a 2.0 degree foveal eccentricity to the left or right.

A trial consisted of a fixation point followed by an ambiguous word followed by the target. A fixation point appeared in the center of the CRT. The prime was presented two seconds later in the same location for 35 msec, and was then masked for the remainder of the SOA (0 or 715 msec).[6] The target followed, and was randomly presented 2 degrees to the left or right of the fixation point for 185 msec, and was then masked for 50 msec. The screen was blanked after the mask. Presentation of the target initiated timing of the subject's response. The intertrial interval was five seconds. Subjects were given three blocks of practice trials (20 trials per block). Word targets were related to the ambiguous prime through the dominant or subordinate meaning. Ambiguous primes were also used for the nonword trials. Nonwords were formed by replacing letters of words, while maintaining pronounceability.

---

5 The experiment also included a neutral trial condition but this condition did not provide a reliable baseline against which to measure facilitation and inhibition (see [Burgess and Simpson, in press]; also [Chiarello, 1985]). Visual field presentation and the vertical orientation of the stimuli may have contributed to the development of specific attentional strategies to the neutral trial (see [Jonides and Mack, 1984]).

6 It was important to know that our (flash) mask did not compromise the ability of the first word to prime a related target. We feel confident that this was not the case since priming occurred at the 35 msec SOA in the RVF (40 msec for the dominant associate, 22 msec for the subordinate associate). Priming also occurred in the LVF. In addition, after practice trials subjects were usually able to report the prime.

2.2.4 *Experimental Results* It is important to distinguish between automatic and controlled processing in studies examining hemispheric processing capabilities [Chiarello, 1985]. As mentioned earlier, we used two SOAs in order to separate automatic and controlled processing. It was expected that the 35 msec SOA would be brief enough to reflect the passive and automatic spread of activation in memory, whereas the 750 msec SOA would provide enough time for inhibition of responses to subordinate associates to occur. Inhibition such as this, is thought to be caused by the redirection of resources to a memory location unrelated to the target, necessitating a time-consuming reallocation of those resources.

The results for targets presented to the left hemisphere and our earlier findings with central presentation are quite similar. Facilitation for the dominant meaning occurred at both SOAs. Less facilitation occurred for the subordinate associates at the brief SOA, and what appears to be a strong inhibitory effect (i.e., responses to related subordinate trials are *slower* than responses to unrelated trials) has occurred by 750 msec (see Figure 16.1). The results with right hemisphere presentation are in marked contrast to those with left hemisphere presentation. Facilitation for the dominant meaning is present at the 35 msec SOA, but is less at the 750 msec SOA. Thus, activation is not being maintained for the dominant meaning as it was in the left hemisphere. There was no effect of visual field in the error rate. Fewer errors were made on related than on unrelated, and on dominant than on subordinate related trials. Error proportions suggested no speed-accuracy trade-off that would qualify the reaction time findings. The most striking difference between the hemispheres is for the subordinate meaning. In the right hemisphere, little facilitation is present at the 35 msec SOA, but activation builds and by the 750 msec SOA strong facilitation is present. The absence of inhibition for the subordinate meaning in the right hemisphere is consistent with Chiarello's [1985] finding. We can speculate that if the right hemisphere is not capable of controlled processing for semantic retrieval, the decline in facilitation for the dominant meaning in the right hemisphere is a decay process.

The impression we are left with is that left hemisphere processing of the meanings of ambiguous words parallels the findings we obtain with centrally projected stimuli. That is, facilitation for the dominant meaning at both SOAs, less facilitation for the subordinate meaning at the brief SOA, and a strong inhibitory effect that has occurred by 750 msec. Our interpretation of the strong inhibitory effect for the subordinate meaning at the 750 msec SOA is that the inhibition is an active suppression, not just response inhibition that one might expect from redirecting attentional resources to a memory location unrelated to the target. Subject response latencies were *longer* to subordinately related trials than to unrelated trials.

Clearly the processing in the right hemisphere is different. Facilitation declines for the dominant meaning while the subordinate meaning shows an in-

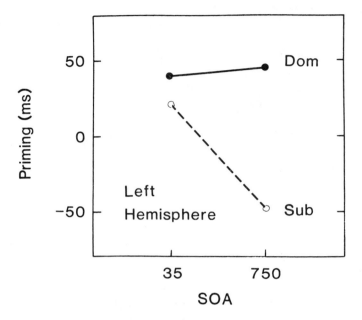

Figure 16.1 Mean priming of dominant (Dom) and subordinate (Sub) associates at 35 msec and 750 msec SOAs for the left and right hemispheres

crease, suggesting no inhibitory processes in the right hemisphere for these semantic relationships. It is as though the subordinate meanings remain available for retrieval longer than would be expected based on research using central projection. We now turn to a discussion of the role of these differing patterns of processing.

3 Specific Considerations

3.1 Implications for Normal Language Understanding

Most simply, the present data suggest a mechanism in which the left hemisphere calls upon the right hemisphere to access memory information when it is needed.[7] This leaves several questions that need to be answered. First, at what point in language processing would the left hemisphere need to call upon the right hemisphere for this information? Second, what is the specific nature

---

7 We assume at the outset that most of our subjects, being right handed, were left hemisphere dominant for language function.

of the information that the left hemisphere requires from the right? And third, what is the nature of the mechanism that allows the transfer of this information?

For the purpose of discussing the first two questions consider the following sentence and two of its possible completions.

1.   The man stood by the *bank* for the better part of an hour before

    a.   going in to deposit his money.

    b.   catching a fish worth taking home.

The first portion of the sentence, *The man stood by the*, is not biased toward any particular meaning of *BANK*. In fact, not until nine words after *BANK* does context begin to disambiguate *BANK*. Let's look at what probably happens when *BANK* is encountered. With no constraining context, it is relatively safe to assume that a frequency-coded multiple access would occur with the meanings of *BANK* (as in [Simpson and Burgess, 1985]; also see [Hudson and Tanenhaus, 1984]). Until the sentence is disambiguated by context, it would seem to be more efficient to maintain both meanings of *BANK*, rather than to reactivate a meaning if the initial interpretation turned out to be wrong. We saw in Simpson and Burgess [1985] that the dominant meaning is maintained over a long range of SOAs. So in case (1a) the appropriate meaning has maintained activation and can be selected for integration in the sentence representation. What about case (1b), however?

We saw in Simpson and Burgess [1985] that subordinate meanings lose activation after about 300 msec. When the less frequent meaning, *RIVER*, is needed, as it is in (1b), it would require reactivation. Reactivation at this point would be very costly since the less frequent meaning is now less available in the left hemisphere. However, this would not be necessary if activation for the appropriate meaning were maintained and therefore still available in the right hemisphere. At the point of the disambiguating context, then, the reader would still have the appropriate meaning available in the right hemisphere. In the present model, the subordinate meaning would be accessed from the right hemisphere roughly 400–500 msec (sufficiently long for inhibition to occur in the left hemisphere, see [Simpson and Burgess, 1985]) after presentation of the ambiguous word. Of course, if the disambiguating information preceded the ambiguous word, selection of either meaning could occur from the left hemisphere before the subordinate meaning was inhibited.[8]

---

8 Inhibition of subordinate meanings occurs both when targets are centrally presented and when they are presented to the left hemisphere. If the right hemisphere maintains activation for the subordinate meaning, why then is that subordinate meaning not available with central presentation? We believe that recourse to meanings maintained in the right hemisphere occurs only when a sentential context calls for them. We thank Susan Garnsey for raising this question.

An interesting situation exists when the sense ambiguity is a verb. This is a context in which the right hemisphere may play a role in the recovery from a garden-path. Multiple access would occur for all meanings of a verb, such as *pass*, but only the contextually appropriate sense would remain active, while the other senses would be inhibited (see [Carlson and Tanenhaus, 1987; Cottrell, 1985]). In the absence of context, the most frequent sense would remain active. Consider the following example:

2a. Ralph *passed* the test to his complete surprise.

2b. Ralph *failed* the test to his complete surprise.

2c. Ralph *passed* the test to the person behind him.

2d. Ralph *handed* the test to the person behind him.

In examples (2a) and (2c), different senses of the verb *pass* are selected by the disambiguating context. Note that disambiguation does not occur until well after the ambiguous verb. Examples (2b) and (2d) are control sentences using unambiguous verbs that have core meanings related to the contextually appropriate sense in the ambiguous sentence. If the wrong sense of the ambiguous verb is initially selected, reinterpretation would require retrieving the inhibited alternative sense. To do this requires time and processing resources [Tanenhaus, Burgess, D'Zmura, and Carlson, 1987]. Part of this garden-path recovery could involve accessing this alternative verb sense from the right hemisphere, since inhibition would have occurred in the left hemisphere. Accessing the alternative verb sense from the right hemisphere would circumvent the need to reactivate the already inhibited sense in the left hemisphere. On this view, it would be required that attention shifts to the right hemisphere at the point the language processor recognizes that a comprehension error has occurred. Accessing the right hemisphere, then, would provide the information needed for disambiguation.[9]

If this story is correct, one would expect to find greater right hemisphere involvement at the point in online comprehension at which the language processor notices the semantic incongruity. While this discussion of right hemisphere involvement in garden-path recovery is, at this point, speculative, it appears that the right hemisphere is involved in processing semantic incongruity. Kutas and Hillyard [1982] presented subjects with sentences, some of which ended with a semantically anomalous word. They recorded event related potentials as subjects read these sentences and found that a semantically anomalous word evoked a negative component (N400) in both hemispheres. However, this

---

9 It seems intuitively clear that the verb sense ambiguity results in more of a garden-path than does the noun sense ambiguity. The reason may be that the verb is more strongly intertwined in sentential understanding.

negativity associated with the semantic anomaly was stronger in the right hemisphere than in the left hemisphere. While Kutas and Hillyard did not evaluate the cognitive processes involved in garden-path recovery, their results suggest that the right hemisphere seems particularly sensitive to the sort of semantic anomaly that may be associated with garden-paths that result when subjects initially assign the inappropriate sense to a verb.

We are suggesting that the role of the right hemisphere is to provide the less frequent meaning when needed by context after inhibitory processes in the left hemisphere have caused activation for the subordinate meaning to decline. This discussion answers the questions concerning the point in language processing at which the left hemisphere would access information from the right, and the question about the nature of the information the right hemisphere provides in this circumstance, that is to say, the less frequent meaning. There is, in addition, a respectable amount of clinical research that bears on the question of ambiguity resolution.

3.2 *Reviewing the Clinical Evidence*

Before reviewing the clinical literature on the retrieval of ambiguous word meanings, we should recapitulate what we would expect from patients with left or right hemisphere damage. The results of our visual field study would suggest that patients with left or right hemisphere damage would have access to the dominant meaning. The dominant meaning showed priming at the short and long SOA in both hemispheres,[10] leading us to think this meaning would be available. The subordinate meaning is quickly inhibited in the left hemisphere, but activation builds more slowly in the right hemisphere. Left hemisphere damaged patients should have the subordinate meaning available. Right hemisphere damaged patients may not have access to the subordinate meaning, except for the brief period of time it would be available in the left hemisphere prior to inhibition. This discussion, then, concerns the availability of word meanings in semantic memory. It is quite another question whether a patient can access and/or integrate word meanings.

3.2.1 *Ambiguity Resolution*   Deloche and Seron [1981] found that subjects with left hemisphere damage (Broca's and Wernicke's aphasics) had difficulty writing sentences when the task was to incorporate a homograph (*BANK*) and a meaning that biased the sentence context (*MONEY* or *RIVER*). Specifically, less frequent meanings caused more errors. Pierce [1984] found similar results

---

10 It is theoretically possible that a left hemisphere damaged patient would not have access to a dominant meaning if enough time had elapsed for sufficient decay for that meaning to have occurred. However, this is unlikely since integration of a meaning into the discourse structure would likely have occurred by this time.

with aphasics using a different task. He had patients listen to (and read) an associate of an ambiguous word embedded in a phrase while having the ambiguous word in view throughout the trials. For example, a patient might have the ambiguous word *PASS* and be asked to decide if *A MOUNTAIN GAP* or *A FOOTBALL THROW* represented a meaning of the word. There were also distractor trials. Pierce found that aphasics had difficulty with the less frequently used meanings. Since our visual field results would suggest that left hemisphere damaged patients would have the less frequent meaning available, the Deloche and Seron [1981] and Pierce [1984] research appears to be counterevidence to our claim. It is difficult to know, however, if their results suggest a disruption in the semantic organization of ambiguous word meanings or difficulty in executing the processes necessary to retrieve and integrate the word meaning into a context. It must either be the case that we are wrong and these less frequent meanings are not available in the right hemisphere for left hemisphere damaged patients, or that the processes involved in integration are disrupted. These studies do not discriminate these two alternatives.

It seems reasonable to suggest that controlled processes might be involved in the integration of word meanings into a semantic context. We have found that controlled processing of ambiguous relationships (inhibition for subordinate meanings at the 750 msec SOA) occurred in the left hemisphere. Chiarello [1985] also found that controlled semantic processing was a left hemisphere phenomenon. It may be that the results of Deloche and Seron [1981] and Pierce [1984] reflect the disruption of controlled processing and not the underlying semantic organization.[11] If so, their work does not compromise our model.

Milberg and Blumstein [1981; Blumstein, Milberg, and Shrier, 1982] have shown that left hemisphere involvement is necessary for controlled semantic processing. In a lexical decision experiment, patients with left hemisphere damage showed a priming effect with semantically related words, but were unable to make reliable semantic judgements of word relatedness. This suggests that semantic tasks using lexical decision are sensitive to the semantic representation present with left hemisphere damaged patients, where judgment tasks that require higher-level cognitive processing are not.

An experiment that directly manipulated priming to meanings of ambiguous words with left hemisphere damaged patients was recently described by Gerratt and Jones [1987]. It has been observed that lexical decision latencies to ambiguous words are shorter than latencies for unambiguous words in normals

---

11 Deloche and Seron [1981] and Pierce [1984] all claim that their results suggest disruption in the mechanisms used to integrate the meanings once accessed from memory and not a disruption in semantic organization. However, since the left hemisphere damaged subjects in their studies could not show evidence that would lead one to believe that the less frequent meanings had been accessed or integrated, we do not think they can make this claim.

[Jastrzembski, 1981]. Gerratt and Jones reasoned that this effect should be evident with aphasics if the underlying semantic organization is maintained. They found that fluent and nonfluent aphasic subjects showed shorter latencies to ambiguous words, as did their non-brain-damaged controls. This suggests that the left hemisphere damaged subjects have access to more than just the more frequent meaning. Deloche and Seron [1981] and Pierce [1984] failed to find an effect for the less frequent meanings with left hemisphere damaged patients, but the Gerratt and Jones results (as well as [Milberg and Blumstein, 1981] suggest that this was because they were tapping higher level controlled processes, which made their procedure insensitive to lexical access patterns. Tasks that involve sentence construction [Deloche and Seron, 1981] or phrase matching to ambiguous words [Pierce, 1984] appear to involve sufficient higher level controlled processes that mask the left hemisphere brain damaged subjects' sensitivity to multiple meanings of words. This is all indirectly consistent with our proposal that the right hemisphere plays a role in ambiguity resolution.

There is an experiment that seems to test more directly the idea that left hemisphere damaged subjects would be more sensitive to subordinate meanings, while right hemisphere damaged subjects would be more sensitive to dominant meanings. Brownell, Potter, Michelow and Gardner [1984] had brain damaged subjects select the two words that were most similar in meaning (or went together best) from a set of three words. While their intent was to investigate sensitivity to connotative and denotative relationships between words, some of their items can be considered to be ambiguous.[12] For the purpose of this discussion, consider several of their stimuli in Table 1.

Table 1   Selected stimuli from the Brownell et al. experiment

Ambiguity	Dominant	Subordinate
WARM	COLD	LOVING
COLD	WARM	HATEFUL
DEEP	SHALLOW	WISE
SHALLOW	DEEP	FOOLISH

---

12 In ambiguity studies, not all homographs have distinct meanings or senses (refer to stimuli in [Onifer and Swinney, 1981; Tanenhaus et al., 1979]). For example, while MONEY and RIVER seem to be distinct senses of BANK, WAR as a sense of TANK seems almost metaphorical with CONTAINER. We must also point out that in the Brownell et al. stimuli we discuss here, the relationship between the ambiguous word and the subordinate meaning is more synonymous than just weakly associated. It is possible, then, that these data are consistent with our hypothesis for reasons other than we suspect.

The items we have defined as dominant were the most frequent associates to the item we are considering ambiguous [Shapiro and Palermo, 1968]. Brownell et al. [1984] found that left hemisphere damaged patients were sensitive to the subordinate relationship and showed a selective insensitivity to the dominant relationships. The reverse was found with right hemisphere damaged patients. They were sensitive to the dominant relationships and show a selective insensitivity to the subordinate relationships. The Brownell et al. results are consistent with the model for hemispheric specialization of ambiguity resolution that we are proposing. After rapid inhibition of the subordinate meaning in the left hemisphere, the right hemisphere provides the subordinate meaning. Decay is occurring for the dominant meaning in the right hemisphere, but activation for this meaning is maintained in the left hemisphere; thus right hemisphere damaged patients are more likely to make the connection with the dominant meaning.

3.2.2 *Indeterminacy of Meaning*

While our understanding of the neuropsychological processes involved in resolving indeterminacy is still quite tentative, several lines of research have been suggestive of the role of the right hemisphere in the resolution of indeterminacy.[13] In some ways, aspects of the model for cerebral hemispheric contributions to ambiguity resolution can be seen in other forms of indeterminate speech. The suggestion of a right hemisphere role in the resolution of indeterminacy receives some support from the clinical literature, which indicates a number of difficulties in comprehending figurative language that accompany right hemisphere lesions.

The research of Brownell et al. [1984] describes how patients with right hemisphere lesions are unlikely to make use of connotative relationships between words. This would imply that they would have difficulty in interpreting indirect speech acts where the speaker's intention is to convey the indirect meaning or request. Hirst, LeDoux, and Stein [1984] presented brain damaged patients with videotaped scenarios containing indirect speech acts. Right hemisphere damaged patients were unable to discriminate between appropriate and inappropriate responses, but they were able to interpret the literal request. Anterior aphasics understood the conveyed but not the literal meaning.

The role of context is crucial in understanding indeterminacy with brain damaged subjects as well as with intact subjects. Apparently, an elaborated context will allow brain damaged patients to comprehend indirectly presented ideas. Ideas that were indirectly presented, but preceded by a contextually relevant paragraph, were understood by left and right hemisphere damaged patients as well as the intact controls [Brookshire and Nicholas, 1984]. Yet, when the

---

13 See Simpson, Burgess and Peterson [in press] for a general review of indeterminacy of meaning.

context is only two sentences, right hemisphere patients prefer the literal interpretation of an idiom [Myers and Linebaugh, 1981]. This combination of results suggests that semantic integration processes involve the right hemisphere. It leaves unresolved, however, the locus of contextual effects, whether at the semantic level, or in the integration of semantic information into the discourse model.

3.3 The Nature of Inhibition

We are left with the need to discuss the role of inhibition in our model. Earlier we claimed that attentional mechanisms resulted in the inhibition of subordinate meanings and that this is a function of left hemisphere resources. Ordinarily, inhibition refers to the cost associated with limited capacity attentional mechanisms being consciously directed to a narrow range of semantic items [Neely, 1976]. Inhibition is calculated as the difference in reaction time between a set of unrelated trials and a set of neutral trials (i.e., *XXXXXs*). The cost in response latency is incurred when attention is directed to the word prime and is then redirected to the unrelated target. This cost is not incurred in the case of a neutral trial. In the present experiment, however, the neutral trials did not provide a reliable baseline against which to measure inhibition. What we found was that response latencies were slower for subordinate related meanings than for the unrelated trials at the 750 msec SOA in the left hemisphere. That the subordinate related trials were slower than the unrelated suggests to us that an active suppression mechanism is operating resulting in inhibition in the left hemisphere. This is in contrast to inhibition that results from the simple redirection of attention. While positing an active suppression mechanism may be controversial at this point, we are not the first to suggest it. MacKay [1970] first suggested that in order to see an alternative meaning of an ambiguity, the other meaning must be suppressed. Tanenhaus et al. [1979] proposed that active suppression is a plausible explanation for the rapid selection process that occurs for the contextually appropriate meaning of an ambiguous word. We are suggesting that the locus for this suppression mechanism is in the left hemisphere. The left hemisphere, then, shows automatic and controlled processing with these semantic relationships, while only automatic retrieval with no inhibition occurs in the right hemisphere. Similar conclusions were arrived at by Luria and Simernitskaya [1977] with a clinical sample. They found that word recall from a memorized list was severely impaired for left hemisphere lesioned patients. In a second experiment in which word recall was incidental to the memorization task, patients with right hemisphere lesions were severely impaired as compared to patients with left hemisphere lesions. A possible explanation for their results is that focused recall required additional attentional resources beyond what was required for the incidental recall task, resulting in the left hemisphere lesion patients' severe impairment.

There exists another role for inhibition in our model, although we now use inhibition in a different sense. An attentional control mechanism must exist, permitting the left hemisphere to access the right hemisphere's information. This must be a very precise gating mechanism, given the nature of language processing. With the two hemispheres functioning in parallel, information from both must converge in such a way as to avoid disruption of function. We view the nature of this interhemispheric relationship as unidirectional inhibition exerted by the left hemisphere, at least for the type of semantic information transfer being discussed here (see [Allen, 1983; Searleman, 1977], for reviews). However, we are a long way from having a clear idea of the performance characteristics of this gating mechanism.

4 *Summary*

The model presented here demonstrates that the divided visual field method can be used to explain in greater detail the word recognition processes that are involved in normal language comprehension. We have suggested that the two cerebral hemispheres operate in parallel, but that the time course of ambiguity processing differs for each hemisphere. We propose that the left hemisphere accesses the right hemisphere in order to make use of its semantic information in the disambiguation process. What we have discovered is consistent with, and advances our knowledge of lexical access with respect to single word priming and, presumably, sentence comprehension. In brief, we have seen that ambiguity resolution in the left hemisphere proceeds in a manner similar to such resolution when stimuli are projected centrally. The right hemisphere, however, shows (1) a lack of an inhibitory component for the subordinate meaning, (2) slower activation for the subordinate associate corresponding to when this meaning will be needed by comprehension processes after inhibition has occurred in the left hemisphere, and (3) slow decay of the dominant meaning.

The hemispheric differences in lexical access that have been described in this chapter are important to understand, moreover it is important to understand these differences in the context of how the hemispheres cooperate and integrate their information for normal language understanding. It is only with this thought in mind that divided visual field research can be useful to mainstream cognitive psychologists and psycholinguists and provide direction to those interested in modeling these processes.

Acknowledgments

We would like to thank Susan Garnsey, Mike Tanenhaus, Robert R. Peterson, Christine Chiarello, Thomas G. Bever, Lisa Greene, and four anonymous reviewers for their helpful comments and criticisms. Preparation of this manuscript was supported in part by a University of Rochester Rush Rhees Fellowship awarded to the first author and by a U.S. Department of Education Grant G008630072 to the Kansas Bureau of Child Research and the Learning Disabilities Institute of the University of Kansas, while the second author was a fellow in the Child Language Program of the University of Kansas.

References

Allen, M. 1983. Models of hemispheric specialization. *Psychological Bulletin* 93:73–104.

Blumstein, S. E., Milberg, W., and Shrier, R. 1982. Semantic processing in aphasia: Evidence from an auditory lexical decision task. *Brain and Language* 17:301–315.

Bradshaw, J. L., Nettleton, N. C., and Taylor, M. J. 1981. The use of laterally presented words in research into cerebral asymmetry: Is directional scanning likely to be a source of artifact? *Brain and Language* 14:1–14.

Brookshire, R. H., and Nicholas, L. E. 1984. Comprehension of directly and indirectly stated main ideas and details in discourse by brain-damaged and non-brain-damaged listeners. *Brain and Language* 21:21–36.

Brownell, H. H., Potter, H. H., Michelow, D., and Gardner, H. 1984. Sensitivity to lexical denotation and connotation in brain-damaged patients: A double dissociation? *Brain and Language* 22:253–265.

Burgess, C., and Simpson, G. B. In press. Cerebral hemispheric mechanisms in the retrieval of ambiguous word meanings. *Brain and Language.*

Carlson, G., and Tanenhaus, M. K. 1987. Thematic roles and language comprehension. To appear in W. Wilkens (ed.), *Thematic Relations.* New York: Academic Press.

Chiarello, C. 1985. Hemisphere dynamics in lexical access: Automatic and controlled priming. *Brain and Language* 26:146–172.

Cohen, G. 1982. Theoretical interpretations of lateral asymmetries. In J. G. Beaumont (ed.), *Divided Visual Field Studies of Cerebral Organisation.* London: Academic Press.

Cottrell, G.W. 1985. A connectionist approach to word sense disambiguation. Tech. Rep. No. TR154. Rochester: University of Rochester, Department of Computer Science.

Deloche, G., and Seron, X. 1981. Part of speech and phonological form implied in written-word comprehension: Evidence from homograph disambiguation by normal and aphasic subjects. *Brain and Language* 13:250–258.

Forster, K. I., and Bednall, E. S. 1976. Terminating and exhaustive search in lexical access. *Memory and Cognition* 4:53–61.

Gerratt, B.R., and Jone, D. 1987. Aphasic performance on a lexical decision task: Multiple meanings and word frequency. *Brain and Language* 30:106–115.

Glucksberg, S. 1984. How people use context to resolve ambiguity: Implications for an interactive model of language understanding. Invited address at the meeting of the Eastern Psychological Association, Baltimore, MD.

Glucksberg, S., Kreuz, R. J., and Rho, S. 1986. Context can constrain lexical access: Implications for models of language comprehension. *Journal of Experimental Psychology: Learning, Memory, and Cognition* 12:323–335.

Hardyck, C., Chiarello, C., Dronkers, N., and Simpson, G. V. 1985. Orienting attention within visual fields: How efficient is interhemispheric transfer? *Journal of Experimental Psychology: Human Perception and Performance* 11:650–666.

Hasher, L., and Zacks, R. T. 1979. Automatic and effortful processes in memory. *Journal of Experimental Psychology: General* 108:356–388.

Hirst, W., Le Doux, J., and Stein, S. 1984. Constraints on the processing of indirect speech acts: Evidence from aphasiology. *Brain and Language* 23:26–33.

Hogaboam, T. W., and Perfetti, C. A. 1975. Lexical ambiguity and sentence comprehension. *Journal of Verbal Learning and Verbal Behavior* 14:265–274.

Holley-Wilcox, P., and Blank, M. A. 1980. Evidence for multiple access in the processing of isolated words. *Journal of Experimental Psychology: Human Perception and Performance* 6:75–84.

Hudson, S. B., and Tanenhaus, M. K. 1984. Ambiguity resolution in the absence of contextual bias. *Proceedings of the Cognitive Science Society* 6.

Jastrzembski, J. E. 1981. Multiple meanings, number of related meanings, frequency of occurrence, and the lexicon. *Cognitive Psychology* 13:278–305.

Jonides, J., and Mack, R. 1984. On the cost and benefit of cost and benefit. *Psychological Bulletin* 96:29–44.

Krashen, S. D. 1976. Cerebral asymmetry. In H. Whitaker and H. Whitaker (eds.), *Studies in Neurolinguistics, Vol. 2*, pp. 157–191. New York: Academic Press.

Kutas, M., and Hillyard, S. A. 1982. The lateral distribution of event-related potentials during sentence processing. *Neuropsychologia* 20:579–590.

Luria, A. R., and Simernitskaya, E. G. 1977. Interhemispheric relations and the functions of the minor hemisphere. *Neuropsychologia* 15:175–178.

MacKay, D. G. 1970. Mental diplopia: Towards a model of speech perception at the semantic level. In G. B. Flores d'Arcais and S.M. Levelt (eds.), *Advances in Psycholinguistics*, pp. 76–100. New York: Elsevier.

Milberg, W., and Blumstein, S. E. 1981. Lexical decision and aphasia: Evidence for semantic processing. *Brain and Language* 14:371–385.

Myers, P. S., and Linebaugh, C. W. 1981. Comprehension of idiomatic expressions by right-hemisphere-damaged adults. In R. H. Brookshire (ed.), *Clinical Aphasiology: Conference Proceedings.* Minneapolis: BRK.

Neely, J. H. 1976. Semantic priming and retrieval from lexical memory: Evidence for facilitatory and inhibitory processes. *Memory and Cognition* 4:648–654.

Neely, J. H. 1977. Semantic priming and retrieval from lexical memory: Roles of inhibitionless spreading activation and limited-capacity attention. *Journal of Experimental Psychology: General* 106: 226–254.

Onifer, W., and Swinney, D. A. 1981. Accessing lexical ambiguities during sentence comprehension: Effects of frequency of meaning and contextual bias. *Memory and Cognition* 9:225–236.

Pierce, R. S. 1984. Comprehending homographs in aphasia. *Brain and Language* 22:339–349.

Posner, M. I. 1981. Cognition and neural systems. *Cognition* 10:261–266.

Posner, M. I., and Snyder, C.R.R. 1975. Attention and cognitive control. In R. L. Solso (ed.), *Information Processing and Cognition: The Loyola Symposium*, pp. 55–85. Hillsdale: Erlbaum.

Schvaneveldt, R. W., Meyer, D. E., and Becker, C. A. 1976. Lexical ambiguity, semantic context, and visual word recognition. *Journal of Experimental Psychology: Human Perception and Performance* 2:243–256.

Searleman, A. 1977. A review of right hemisphere linguistic capabilities. *Psychological Bulletin* 84:503–528.

Seidenberg, M. S., Tanenhaus, M. K., Leiman, J. M., and Bienkowski, M. 1982. Automatic access of the meanings of ambiguous words in context: Some limitations of knowledge-based processing. *Cognitive Psychology* 14:489–537.

Sergent, J. 1986. Prolegomena to the use of the tachistoscope in neuro-psychological research. *Brain and Cognition* 5:127–130.

Shapiro, S. I., and Palermo, D. S. 1968. An atlas of normative free association data. *Psychonomic Monograph Supplements* 2(28):219–250.

Simpson, G. B. 1981. Meaning dominance and semantic context in the processing of lexical ambiguity. *Journal of Verbal Learning and Verbal Behavior* 20:120–136.

Simpson, G. B. 1984. Lexical ambiguity and its role in models of word recognition. *Psychological Bulletin* 96:316–340.

Simpson, G. B., and Burgess, C. 1985. Activation and selection processes in the recognition of ambiguous words. *Journal of Experimental Psychology: Human Perception and Performance* 11:28–39.

Simpson, G. B., Burgess, C., and Peterson, R. R. In press. Comprehension processes and the indeterminacy of meaning. *Cognitive Systems.*

Stanovich, K. E., and West, R. F. 1979. Mechanisms of sentence context effects in reading: Automatic activation and conscious attention. *Memory and Cognition* 7:77–85.

Stanovich, K. E., and West, R. F. 1981. The effect of sentence context on ongoing word recognition: Tests of a two-process theory. *Journal of Experimental Psychology: Human Perception and Performance* 7:658–672.

Stanovich, K. E., and West, R. F. 1983. On priming by a sentence context. *Journal of Experimental Psychology: General* 112:1–36.

Tanenhaus, M. K., Leiman, J. M., and Seidenberg, M. S. 1979. Evidence for multiple stages in the processing of ambiguous words in syntactic contexts. *Journal of Verbal Learning and Verbal Behavior* 18:427–440.

Tanenhaus, M. K., Burgess, C., D'Zmura, S. H., and Carlson, G. 1987. Thematic roles in language processing. *Proceedings of the Cognitive Science Society*, pp. 587–596. Hillsdale: Erlbaum.

Wapner, W., Hamby, S., and Gardner, H. 1981. The role of the right hemisphere in the apprehension of complex linguistic materials. *Brain and Language* 14:15–33.

Young, A. W. 1982. Methodological and theoretical bases of visual hemifield studies. In J. G. Beaumont (ed.), *Divided Visual Field Studies of Cerebral Organisation*, pp. 11–27. London: Academic Press.

Zaidel, E. 1978. Lexical organization in the right hemisphere. In Buser and Rougeul-Buser (eds.), *Cerebral Correlates of Conscious Experience*, pp. 177–197. Amsterdam: Elsevier/North Holland Biomedical Press.

Zaidel, E. 1983. Disconnection syndrome as a model for laterality effects in the normal brain. In J. B. Hellige (ed.), *Cerebral Hemisphere Asymmetry: Method, Theory, and Application*, pp. 95–151. New York: Praeger.

Tracking the Time Course of Meaning Activation

Cyma Van Petten
Marta Kutas
Department of Neurosciences
University of California, San Diego

The comprehension of text or speech requires of the reader/listener several conceptually distinct levels of analysis: recognition of individual letters or phonemes, recognition of the words so created, syntactic parsing of each sentence to determine the structural relationships between individual words, comprehension sentence meaning, and finally, an attempt to integrate individual sentences into a coherent message. For over a century psychologists have been interested in how these levels of analysis are combined to yield the rapid and seemingly effortless comprehension of language [James, 1890]. Some theorists have taken the human language processing system to be strictly hierarchical in that each processing component accepts input from only the immediately preceding lower level [Fodor, 1983; Forster, 1981; Garrett, 1978] while others have proposed more interactive models in which different facets of the system have more latitude to influence the computations and/or input to others [Marslen-Wilson and Tyler, 1980; McClelland and Elman, 1986].

A great deal of research has focused on word-level recognition (lexical) and its relationship to both lower (letter/phoneme detection) and higher (syntactic and semantic constraint) levels of analysis. It has been known for some time that a response to a given word can be speeded if it is preceded by a semantically related word. This apparent interaction between sensory and semantic analyses can, however, be accomodated within an autonomous framework of word recognition by the argument that such semantic priming effects reflect memory organization rather than on-line comprehension effects [cf Fodor, 1983; Seidenberg, 1982]. In this view, word recognition still proceeds in a strictly bottom-up fashion but, as a consequence of having "accessed" a given lexical entry, activation spreads to highly associated entries in the mental word store via a mechanism such as that proposed by Collins and Loftus [1975]. Semantic priming of this sort would seem to have little utility in the comprehension of a sentence or of extended discourse since it arises out of stable long-lived connections between lexical entries. Single words can acquire many different shades of meaning or connotations depending on their immediate context whereas it is unlikely that structural connections between entries in the lexicon could be so modified on a moment-to-moment basis.

The results of a number of recent experiments on lexical ambiguity have been seen as presenting a strong case for models which postulate autonomous lexical processing and which consider the integration of individual words into larger semantic units to be a subsequent and separate process.

1 *Lexical Ambiguity*

The fact that ambiguous words have a single physical representation but two or more semantic representations makes them a useful tool for examining the balance between data-driven (bottom-up) and concept-driven (top-down) processes in word recognition. [Norman and Bobrow,1975]. Three mutually exclusive possibilities exist for the cognitive processes engaged when a reader/listener encounters a lexical ambiguity. (1) Only the semantic representation appropriate to the prior context is activated (selective access). (2) The most common or dominant meaning of the ambiguity is accessed first with the subordinate meaning accessed only if the dominant meaning proves inconsistent with the context (ordered access). (3) Both meanings of the ambiguity are, at least briefly, activated (multiple access).

Evidence of selective access would imply that word recognition includes top-down processing by which sensory input is analyzed in light of the preceding context. Evidence of multiple access, in contrast, would suggest the presence of automatic, data-driven processing that acts independently of context and derives all possible meanings from the sensory input regardless of their relevance to the text. The ordered-access model also involves an automatic process that invariantly selects a meaning for a word regardless of context.

1.1 *A Partial Review of Previous Lexical Ambiguity Experiments*

The majority of studies of ambiguity resolution have supported the multiple access model (for a review see [Simpson, 1984]). Two primary experimental measures have been used: reaction times (RTs) in a phoneme monitoring task, and RTs in priming paradigms with color naming, lexical decision, or word naming tasks.

The phoneme monitoring paradigm relies on the assumption that accessing multiple meanings of a word drains more cognitive resources than does accessing one meaning. Reaction times in the secondary task of phoneme monitoring are thus used as an index of the number of meanings that were accessed for a given word. Several investigators have presented auditory sentences and observed slower responses to target phonemes following ambiguous than unambiguous words [Foss,1970; Foss and Jenkins,1973; Cairns and Kamerman, 1975; Swinney and Hakes, 1976; Cairns and Hsu, 1980].

Recent reviews have emphasized difficulties in interpreting the results of lexical ambiguity studies which employed the phoneme monitoring task. Mehler, Segui and Carey [1978] noted that the comparison between ambiguous and unambiguous words was confounded by word length differences in some of the studies cited above. In addition, Newman and Dell [1978] pointed out that few of these studies controlled the degree of phonological similarity between the target phoneme and the initial phonemes of the ambiguous and unambiguous words. Simpson [1984] discussed these and other difficulties in the interpretation of phoneme monitoring studies.

Ambiguity studies using a priming paradigm have been less subject to methodological criticism and have, in addition, included a number of important variables such as the dominance of the sense of the lexical ambiguity used in the context, the strength of the context, and the temporal interval between words. A single trial in the priming studies to be discussed consisted of three stimuli: a semantic context biasing one sense of the ambiguity, the ambiguous word, and a target word which was related to one or the other meaning of the ambiguity or to neither.

Several investigators who have used a sentence fragment as the context have obtained evidence that targets related to both meanings of the ambiguity are primed relative to unrelated targets [Conrad, 1974; Onifer and Swinney, 1981; Oden and Spira, 1983; Seidenberg, Tanenhaus, Leiman and Bienkowski, 1982; Swinney, 1979]. Onifer and Swinney obtained this effect even when the sentence context biased the dominant meaning of the ambiguity and the target was related to the subordinate meaning, thus providing strong support for the multiple-access model versus either the selective- or ordered-access models. However, the results of Simpson [1981] are inconsistent with this conclusion in suggesting that dominance interacts with the strength of the sentence context. 'Strength of context' in Simpson's experiments was determined by having subjects rate the degree to which each sentence biased one of two possible interpretations of a sentence-terminal ambiguous word. With a weak biasing context, Simpson found that targets related to the dominant sense were always primed, whereas targets related to the subordinant sense were primed only if the sentence context biased this meaning. Given a stronger sentence context, only targets related to the contextually appropriate sense of the ambiguous words were primed, whether this was dominant or subordinate.

The importance of the 'strength of context' variable has also been examined in a series of experiments by Seidenberg et al. [1982] who contrasted sentences which were disambiguated only by syntactic or pragmatic information with sentences that also contained a semantic associate of the ambiguous word. It was found that neither syntactic nor pragmatic constraints (e.g., "He bought a rose" or "Go to the store and buy a spade") prevented multiple access. However, sentences containing semantic associates (e.g., "The bridge player trumped the spade") yielded evidence of selective access for ambiguities with two noun meanings, but not for ambiguities with a noun and a verb meaning. Based on these results, Seidenberg et al. argued that the influence of strength of context in determining lexical access can be reduced to a single factor, lexical priming or spreading-activation. These authors describe lexical priming as occurring *within* the same module that automatically derives candidate word meanings from the sensory input. According to this view, the finding of selective access under some circumstances does not necessarily implicate "top-down" context effects on lexical access. However, it is not clear how Seidenberg et al. [1982] determined that lexical priming alone was the important factor in producing selective access given that the various sentence types were not matched on other measures of contextual constraint such as cloze probability or a rating procedure like that used by Simpson [1981].

Existing data do not allow a clear statement as to the influence of strength of context on ambiguity resolution, in part because of the difficulty in comparing stimulus materials across different experiments. However, in its strongest form, the multiple access model holds that lexical access is context-independent. Thus, the more constraining the biasing context, the stronger will be the test of this model.

Another important factor in ambiguity resolution that can more easily be quantified is the temporal interval between the ambiguous word and its related targets. The multiple-access model holds that the two senses of an ambiguous word are only briefly activated until a slower process selects the contextually appropriate meaning. Studies which have manipulated the interval between the ambiguous and target words have shown that time is indeed an important variable [Kintsch and Mross, 1985; Onifer and Swinney, 1981; Seidenberg et al., 1982]. In general, a very short interval between the ambiguous word and the onset of the target word yields priming for targets related to both senses, whereas a longer interval yields priming for only targets related to the contextually appropriate sense.

In the experiments of Seidenberg et al. [1982], evidence of multiple access was obtained with zero delay between the offset of the ambiguity and the onset of the target word, but selective access was obtained with a delay of only 200 msec. These results suggest that, although it is slower than the presumably automatic process which derives all of the possible meanings from a single letter string, the selection process is still completed very rapidly. It is thus possible that Simpson's [1981] finding of selective access with strong context was due to the 120 msec delay between ambiguity and target.

The majority of ambiguity studies, then, are consistent with the idea that that all meanings of ambiguous words are simultaneously activated upon presentation, with the contextually irrelevant meaning being discarded at some later time. However, such conclusions do not strictly follow from the data.

2 An Alternative Interpretation of the Lexical Ambiguity Results

There is ample theoretical support for the idea that the human language processing system may utilize overlapping, cascaded or parallel processes to analyze more than one word at a time [Marslen-Wilson and Tyler, 1980; McClelland and Elman, 1986]. Empirical evidence also supports this concept; readers often do not fixate short function words in text but may gather information about these while fixating adjacent words [Rayner, 1983]. An overlap in the processing of individual words may be greatly encouraged if the words are related or similar along some dimension. When simultaneously presented with two words which are unrelated in meaning but share common letters, subjects may experience letter migration between the words and for instance, report having seen "lane" and "lice" rather than "line" and "lace" [Mozer, 1983]. Sanocki and colleagues [1985] have recently shown that the time required to find a nonword letter string embedded within a sentence is not only reduced by the presence of syntactic and semantic structure, but that the advantage of well-structured sentences over scrambled ones increased with the position of the target within the sentence. These results suggest that words in sentences are processed progressively faster as the syntactic and semantic constraints of the sentence develop. Marslen-Wilson and Tyler [1980] have reported similar findings in spoken word recognition.

The semantic priming literature also suggests that related words may be processed in an overlapping manner. There have been several demonstrations that lexical decisions are faster for pairs of simultaneously presented words if they are related than if they are not [Carroll and Kirsner, 1982; Fischler, 1977a; 1977b; Meyer and Schvaneveldt, 1971]. Moreover, Kiger and Glass [1983] have demonstrated that the *subsequent* presentation of a related word can result in faster lexical decision for a target word if the temporal interval between the two words is short.

The possibility that two words can be processed in an overlapping, cascaded manner has clear implications for the interpretation of lexical ambiguity results. Although all of the experiments to date have presented words in a serial manner, the experimental paradigm may be tapping into a system which is designed to begin analyzing a new word before the processing of the previous word is complete. It is thus possible that the finding of multiple access may be an artifact of the experimental paradigm designed to measure it. The target word, rather than serving as a neutral probe to determine how the preceding ambiguous word was processed, may itself serve as a source of context in the interpretation of the ambiguity. Although the sentence context may initially constrain access to a single meaning of the ambiguous word, the subsequent presentation of a word related to the alternate meaning could serve to activate this previously irrelevant meaning via a "backward priming" mechanism. The newly activated, irrelevant sense of the ambiguity would then be processed concurrently with its related target, leading to a shorter reaction time for this target.

The alternative interpretation of lexical ambiguity results offered above may prove experimentally difficult to distinguish from the multiple access model of ambiguity resolution. The critical issues in resolving the question are those of time.

One question is whether the SOAs (stimulus onset asynchrony) which produce multiple access are also those which lead to backward priming. Kiger and Glass [1983] observed backward priming in a word-pair lexical decision task at SOAs of less than 130 msec, while Seidenberg et al. [1982] observed multiple access in a sentence paradigm at delays of less than 200 msec. Allowing for the additional complexity of processing a sentence context over a single word context, these values are rather close to one another.

A second empirical question is whether backward priming acts quickly enough to influence the behavioral response being measured. Seidenberg and colleagues have argued that, unlike the lexical decision task, the naming task is not susceptible to backward priming effects [Seidenberg, Waters, Sanders, and Langer, 1984]. However, it is not clear that the "backward priming" discussed by Seidenberg et al. [1984; see also Koriat, 1981] is the same phenomenon as that observed by Kiger and Glass. Seidenberg measured both naming and lexical decision times for the second words of asymmetrically related word pairs, such as "stick-lip," which were highly related only in the "backward" direction. The SOA between the first and second word of a pair was 500 msec. So although the semantic relations between primes and targets were "backward," the temporal relations were "forward," in that the prime preceded the target. Given the relatively long SOA, it seems unlikely that prime and target recognition would have overlapped in time. The finding that naming latencies are unaffected by semantically backward priming may, then, have little or no bearing on the question of whether naming latencies may be affected by temporally backward priming.

In the sense that we will use the term, "backward priming" refers to temporal overlap in the processing of two words, and can be thought of as "mutual priming" analogous to that which occurs between two simultaneously presented words.

The experiment described below was designed to provide evidence about the time course of meaning activation via the recording of event-related brain potentials (ERPs). Before proceeding to the experimental details, a description of the technique and its relevance to the problem are in order.

3 *Event-Related Potentials*

Electrodes placed on the scalp can be used to record voltage fluctuations known as the electroencephalogram (EEG). It is generally believed that the electrical activity seen at the scalp is the summation of graded post-synaptic potentials (PSPs) generated by the depolarization and hyperpolarization of brain cells. (See [Wood and Allison, 1981] for a review of the neurophysiological basis of the EEG or [Nunez, 1981] for a treatise on the physics of EEG). At any given moment, the observed EEG is likely to reflect the activity of a number of functionally distinct neuronal populations. With the advent of computer averaging some two decades ago, it became possible to obtain an estimate of activity which is time-locked to some arbitrary point, such as the presentation of a stimulus. Averaging many epochs of EEG following the repetition of similar stimuli tends to result in the cancellation of the random background EEG, leaving a record of the evoked or event-related potentials (EPs or ERPs) which were synchronized to the stimulus presentation. The resulting waveform of voltage plotted against post-stimulus time typically contains a series of positive and negative peaks. Much ERP research has focused on the decomposition of these voltage fluctuations into experimentally dissociable "components" which can be linked to a given physiological and/or cognitive process. Attempts to identify a functionally distinct component may include manipulations of the physical (size, luminance, pitch, etc.) or psychological (task-relevance, meaningfulness, predictability, etc.) attributes of the stimuli, or the physiological state of the subject (drug administration, selecting a population with a particular type of brain damage, etc.). Polarity, latency, distribution across the scalp, and general waveshape are also factors in identifying a given component.

This sort of experimental logic has resulted in a heuristic division of ERP components into "exogenous" and "endogenous." (See [Donchin, Ritter, and McCallum, 1978; Hillyard and Kutas, 1983; Hillyard and Woods, 1979] for reviews.) Exogenous components are those which are mandatorily elicited by a given stimulus in a normal subject, regardless of the stimulus' "psychological" attributes. These are often referred to as the "early" (typically less than 200 msec post-stimulus onset) or "sensory" components of the ERP, in that they are tied to a particular stimulus modality, and their amplitude and latency are influenced by the intensity of the eliciting stimulus. Endogenous, "late," or "cognitive" ERP components are those which are not mandatorily elicited by a given physical stimulus but rather vary in amplitude and/or latency with the psychological attributes of the eliciting stimulus.

The identification of a given component as "cognitive" requires some care in that one must ensure that it is not due to some overlooked physical attribute of the stimuli. It is also desirable to attach some specificity to a given component, in that it can then be linked to some inferred cognitive process. Cognitive ERP researchers are currently engaged in this enterprise through the use of strategies similar to those used by other experimental psychologists to isolate inferred cognitive operations.

ERP components, exogenous and endogenous, are usually named by their polarity and peak latency (e.g., P100—a positivity peaking at 100 msec). For ease of comparison across experiments and conditions, however, this nomenclature has sometimes become frozen. For example, if a positive peak with the same scalp distribution occurs at 90 msec in response to bright flashes of light and a similar peak occurs at 108 msec in response to dim flashes, the experimenter might refer to both as a "P100" or simply a "P1." This discrepancy between nominal and observed latency is particularly apparent in the cognitive ERP literature where the observed latency of a component may vary widely with the timing of the underlying cognitive operation (see [Coles et al., in press; Kutas, McCarthy, and Donchin, 1977]). The peak latency of a positivity with maximum amplitude over central and parietal scalp may vary as much as three hundred msec depending on the difficulty of stimulus evaluation and the attendant reaction time, but it is generally referred to as a "P300" because the original experimental report of this component recorded a peak latency of 300 msec [Sutton et al., 1965].

3.1 *Event-Related Potentials and Semantic Priming*

Over the last few years a number of experimenters have recorded ERPs in semantic priming paradigms. In the experiments of Kutas and Hillyard, for example, simple sentences were presented one word at a time on a CRT screen. The final words of these sentences could either be sensible and predictable (as in "He mailed the letter without a *stamp*.") or nonsensical and unpredictable (as in "I take my coffee with cream and *dog*."). It was seen that the difference between sensible and nonsensical words consisted of a large negative wave beginning around 200 msec and peaking at 400 msec after the onset of the word. Thus the name "N400." Control experiments established that this response was specific to the meaningfulness (or lack thereof) of the terminal word, and was not a general "surprise" reaction. The presentation of a sensible word in a larger typeface, or a novel meaningless slide in the place of the final word did not elicit N400s but rather P300s, while the presentation of a nonsensical word in a larger typeface elicited both an N400 and a P300 [Kutas and Hillyard, 1980a, 1980b, 1980c, 1984]. The relative independence of the N400 response from the physical characteristics of the eliciting word was confirmed by experiments demonstrating that N400-like difference waves could be elicited by speech and American Sign Language [Holcomb, 1985; Kutas, Neville, and Holcomb, in press; McCallum, Farmer, and Pocock, 1984; Neville, 1985].

The sentence experiments described above incorporated rather crude psycholinguistic manipulations in that the sentence-terminal words were either quite predictable or wholly anomalous. Other work has shown that the amplitude of the N400 is quite sensitive to finer gradations of semantic priming and expectancy. One experiment used interpretable congruent sentences which varied in the degree to which the preceding sentence fragment constrained the final word. For example, the sentence fragment "The bill was due at the end of the ..." is of high contextual constraint in that most people will choose "month" as the appropriate final word, while the fragment "He was soothed by the gentle ..." is of low contextual constraint in that there are many equally acceptable endings [Bloom and Fischler, 1980]. Such fragments were terminated by words of varying cloze probability,[1] a measure of how predictable or expected a given word is in a given context [Taylor, 1953]. In the examples given, both fragments could be terminated by words of equal (low) cloze probability as in "The bill was due at the end of the *hour*." and "He was soothed by the gentle *wind*.". The results of this experiment showed that the amplitude of the N400 elicited by the terminal word was highly correlated with its cloze probability and generally independent of the contextual constraint of the preceding sentence fragment, indicating that the N400 response does not require semantic anomalies or extreme violations of semantic expectancies [Kutas and Hillyard, 1984; Kutas, Lindamood, and Hillyard, 1984]. These results parallel those obtained with the lexical decision task [Fischler and Bloom, 1979], in that words of low cloze probability elicit large N400s and prolonged lexical decision times.

A number of experiments have demonstrated that the relationship between the N400 and semantic variables is not restricted to sentence paradigms. In tasks requiring a speeded lexical decision, a relatedness judgement, or a delayed letter search (such as that used in the current ambiguity experiment),

---

1 In a cloze probability procedure, a large group of subjects is asked to fill in the missing terminal word of a sentence. A word's cloze probability is defined as the proportion of subjects using that word to complete the sentence. The measurement of cloze probability for a particular word is dependent on the contextual constraint of the sentence. For a highly constrained sentence such as "He mailed the letter without a _____", the word "stamp" might have a high cloze probability, while "address" would have a low cloze probability. In contrast, a low constraint sentence such as "There was nothing wrong with the _____" might have a number of equally acceptable endings, none of which would have an extremely high cloze probability.

larger N400s are elicited by the second word of unrelated pairs than related pairs [Bentin, McCarthy and Wood, 1985; Harbin, Marsh and Harvey, 1984, Kutas, 1985; Kutas and Van Petten, in press; Rugg, 1985].

A subtle variant of word-to-word priming effects was also observed in the Kutas and Hillyard sentence paradigms. Namely, anomalous sentence completions which were related to the predictable sensible ending elicited smaller N400s than did unrelated anomalous endings, i.e., words such as "umbrella" in the sentence "The game was called when it started to *umbrella*." elicited smaller N400s than words such as "dog" in "I take my coffee with cream and *dog*." [Kutas, Hillyard, and Lindamood, 1984]. These results indicate that the amplitude of the N400 reflects lexical associations even when one of the words is not physically present, but only suggested by a preceding context.

A similar indication that the N400 is sensitive to lexical priming even within the context of a sentence comes from the work of Fischler and his colleagues [Fischler, Bloom, Childers, Roucos, and Perry, 1983; Fischler, Childers, Achariyapaopan, and Perry, 1985; Fischler, Bloom, Childers, Arroyo, and Perry, 1984]. In an experiment using simple categorical statements which could be true or false and affirmative or negative (four combinations), these authors found that the amplitude of the N400 elicited by the final word of such sentences depended on the relationship between the subject and the object rather than the truth value of the sentence. Statements such as "A robin is a *bird*." and "A robin is not a *bird*." both yielded smaller N400s than statements such as "A robin is (is not) a *vehicle*." regardless of the overall truth or falsity of the statements.

More recent data collected by our laboratory in sentence paradigms has served to strengthen our supposition that the N400 is closely linked to some aspect of word processing which is influenced by semantic factors. First, it has become apparent that open-class or "content" words (nouns, verbs, adjectives, etc.) elicit larger N400s than do closed-class or "function words" (articles, conjunctions, prepositions, etc.) ([Kutas, Van Petten, and Besson, in press; see also Garnsey, 1985] for content/function ERPs in a single-word paradigm). Second, we have noted that the amplitude of the N400 elicited by content words is not invariant over the course of a sentence. We supposed that, given a series of isolated sentences (as opposed to connected text), the first content word in each sentence would, by definition, be semantically unprimed and that later content words, on the average, would have accrued some degree of semantic priming over the course of the sentence. It was found that, in fact, N400 amplitude for intermediate sentence words did vary with word position, in that the first content word yielded a larger negativity than did later content words [Kutas, Van Petten, and Besson, in press]. A more fine-grained analysis of N400 amplitude by word position is ongoing.

This brief and partial review of existing evidence suggests that a particular component of the event-related potential, the N400, can be used as an empirical measure of the process known as "semantic priming," much as reaction time to press a button or say a word is used. The N400 or a similar negative component in the same latency range has also been shown to be sensitive to phonological priming, at least in tasks such as rhyme-detection where subjects are encouraged to make use of words' phonological aspects [Rugg, 1984a, 1984b], and perhaps to orthographic priming as well [Kramer and Donchin, 1987].

Most empirical measures of inferred underlying cognitive processes such as "lexical access" or "semantic priming" bring with them some unwanted baggage and some technical difficulties. In the case of some commonly used psycholinguistic tasks, experimenters are well aware of the drawbacks of particular tasks, but continue to apply them because of their demonstrated utility (see [Balota and Chumbley, 1984, 1985] for discussions of the lexical decision and naming latency tasks). The event-related potential measure is no exception to this general rule. One experimental constraint in the recording of ERPs is a limit on concurrent motor activity that the subject can be allowed to engage in. Eye movements, activity of facial muscles, and tongue movements each produce electrical artifacts which may obscure the record of ongoing EEG [Grozinger et al., 1980; Stuss et al., 1983]. In fact, our laboratory has found it useful to try to circumscribe concurrent *cognitive* activity in order to avoid eliciting multiple endogenous ERP components which occur in the same latency range. For instance, a well-studied large positive ERP component named the P300 generally appears in any task in which the subject is required to make a binary decision, as in go/no-go tasks or cases where the subject must press one of two buttons (see [Donchin, 1981; Johnson, in press; Kutas and Van Petten, in press; Pritchard, 1981]). Thus, semantic priming paradigms which require an on-line decision of this type typically result in the elicitation of an overlapping P300 and N400 within the same latency window. While not insurmountable, we feel that the difficulties involved in disentangling these two components can be avoided by eliminating the necessity for a task-related decision within the post-stimulus epoch of interest. It is quite possible to record priming-related ERPs with no overt behavioral responses required of the subject. In the series of Kutas and Hillyard sentence experiments described above [1980a, 1980b, 1980c, 1983, 1984], the subjects were simply instructed to read for comprehension in order to answer questions about sentence content at the end of the experiment. We consider the possibility of obtaining data related to language processing without requiring additional task-related cognitive operations to be one of the advantages of the ERP technique.

3.2 *Application of ERPs to the Problem of Lexical Ambiguity Resolution*

A second opportunity/advantage offered by ERP recordings is the possibility of obtaining a dependent measure which is temporally continuous over whatever pre- and post-stimulus epoch the experimenter chooses to measure. This stands in contrast to the typical behavioral response which occurs at some discrete instant in time. It was this opportunity which we exploited in the present study.

Two experiments are reported. The first is similar to previous ambiguity studies in using naming latency as the dependent measure. The primary purpose of Experiment 1 was to to insure that the stimulus materials constructed for this study would produce the expected priming effects for both contextually appropriate and inappropriate semantic associates of ambiguous words relative to unrelated target words. In Experiment 2, ERPs were recorded to these same stimuli.

4 *Experiment 1*

4.1 *Methods*

4.1.1 *Stimulus Construction* One hundred and twenty words with two distinct and unrelated meanings were selected. Half of these homographs had both a noun sense and a verb sense, the other half had two noun meanings. Published norms were used to select the subordinate sense of the homographs [Geis and Winograd, 1974; Gorfein, Viviani and Leddo, 1982; Kausler and Kollasch, 1970; Nelson, McEnvoy, Walling, and Wheeler, 1980; Perfetti, Lindsey and Garson, 1971]. No published data could be found for 18 of the 120 homographs used; in these cases the authors chose what seemed to be the less common sense of the word.

Each homograph was used in its subordinate sense to complete a sentence fragment. Biasing the sentence contexts toward the less common meanings of the homographs ensured that the 'contextually appropriate' target words would be related to this subordinate sense, whereas 'contextually inappropriate' targets would be related to the more dominant meaning. This design thus allows a distinction between the selective access model on the one hand and the multiple and ordered access models on the other hand, without being able to distinguish between the predictions of the latter two models. Any priming of the contextually inappropriate targets could arise either from exhaustive access of all of the homographs' potential meanings, or from a tendency to access the dominant meaning regardless of context.

An attempt was made to construct moderate to highly constraining sentence fragments for which the ambiguous words were the most likely completions. The success of this attempt was assessed by asking a separate group of 20 subjects to complete each sentence fragment with a single word. Each sentence was completed with the appropriate homograph by an average of 11 out of these 20 subjects. Representative sentences are shown in Table 1.

Three target words were selected to follow each homographic sentence: one related to the sense of the homograph used in its sentence ('contextually appropriate'), one related to the other sense of the word ('contextually inappropriate') and one which was unrelated to either sense ('unrelated'). There were no significant differences among the three target types in frequency of usage [Kucera and Francis, 1967]: contextually appropriate targets, 99 + 157 (mean + standard deviation); contextually inappropriate targets, 108 + 148; unrelated targets, 109 + 141; $F(2,359) = 0.18$, N.S.) No attempt was made to match the initial phonemes of the different classes of target words. A list of the homographs and targets used appears in Appendix 1.

Table 1 Sample stimuli for Experiments 1 and 2

Homograph sentence	Contextually appropriate target	Contextually inappropriate target	Unrelated target
The gambler pulled an ace from the bottom of the deck.	cards	ship	parent
It is not legal for an employer to consider a person's religion or race.	color	run	art
The logger cut down the tree with a chain saw.	ax	look	proof
The bicycle mechanic fixed the flat tire and repaired the broken spoke.	wheel	talked	pill

Filler sentence	Related target	Unrelated target
He bought a quart of milk and a dozen eggs.	bacon	buckle
The sweater was knitted from blue and grey wool.	lamb	cigar

An additional one hundred and twenty sentences were completed with un-ambiguous words ('filler sentences'). Related and unrelated target words were chosen for each filler sentence.

Three separate stimulus lists were constructed. In each list, 40 of the homographic sentences were followed by a contextually appropriate target, 40 by a contextually inappropriate target, and 40 by an unrelated target. The type of target was counterbalanced so that, across lists, each homographic sentence was followed by each type of target. Half of the filler sentences in each list were followed by related targets, half by unrelated. Within each subject group, one-third of the subjects saw each list.

4.1.2 *Stimulus Presentation* Words were displayed in the form of brightened dot matrices on a CRT controlled by an Apple II microcomputer. The duration of each word was 200 msec. Each sentence was presented one word at a time with an SOA (the time from the onset of one word to onset of next) of 900 msec. Each sentence ended with a period such that subjects were aware of sentence terminations. Target words appeared at a location which was slightly below that of the sentence words to further differentiate target words from sentence words. For half of the subjects, target words appeared 16 msec after the offset of sentence terminal words to yield a total stimulus onset asynchrony (SOA) of 216 msec. For the other half of the subjects, sentence-target SOA was 700 msec.

Our 216 msec SOA condition is probably quite similar to the zero delay condition of previous ambiguity experiments which used cross-modal presentation [Onifer and Swinney, 1981; Seidenberg et al., 1982; Swinney, 1979]. The effective SOA in these experiments would have been equal to the duration of the auditorily presented ambiguity. Given a normal rate of speech, the SOA between ambiguity and target might then have been 200–300 msec.

4.1.3 *Subjects* Forty-two young adults, (age range 18–25 years, 22 male, 20 female) were paid for participating in the experiment. All had normal or corrected-to-normal vision.

4.1.4 *Procedure* Subjects were tested one at a time in a sound-attenuating chamber. They were instructed to read each sentence in order to complete a multiple-choice questionnaire about its contents at the end of the experiment, and to say each target word aloud as fast as possible. Each subject was given a practice run consisting of ten unambiguous sentences, five with related, and five with unrelated targets.

Assignment to SOA group and stimulus list was pseudorandom, with the constraint that 21 subjects were in each SOA group, and 7 subjects within each SOA saw a given stimulus list.

Table 2   Naming latencies in Experiment 1. SOA = stimulus onset asynchrony. Mean and standard deviation in msec. N=21 for both SOAs.

Target type	200 SOA	700 SOA
Filler related	602 (70)	542 (64)
Filler unrelated	627 (85)	569 (78)
Contextually appropriate	591 (73)	547 (71)
Contextually inappropriate	617 (77)	562 (69)
Homograph unrelated	635 (85)	571 (71)

Voice onset was recorded via a microphone and a voice-activated trigger. Together with stimulus codes, the responses were recorded by a PDP 11/34 computer.

4.1.5 *Data Analysis*   Incorrect responses and responses that failed to trigger the microphone were excluded from analysis, as were reaction times shorter than 400 msec or longer than 900 msec. Approximately 3.2% of the trials were lost due to these reasons.

4.2 *Results*

4.2.1 *Filler Targets*   The means of each subject were subjected to a 2 × 2 analysis of variance (ANOVA) with repeated measures, using SOA as a between-subjects variable and target type as a within-subjects variable. As seen by the mean naming latencies shown in Table 2, the long SOA group responded more quickly than the short SOA group for both target types, $F(1,40) = 6.69$, $p < .02$. Responses to related targets were faster than to unrelated targets, $F(1,40) = 61.0$, $p < .001$. There was no significant interaction between SOA and target type, $F(2,80) = 0.05$, N.S.

4.2.2 *Homograph Targets*   The means of each subject were subjected to an initial 2 times 3 ANOVA with SOA and target type as factors. As for the filler data, there were significant main effects of SOA, $F(1,40) = 5.62$, $p < .05$ and target type, $F(2,80) = 59.6$, $p < .001$. There was also a significant interaction of SOA by target type, $F(2,80) = 5.22$, $p < .01$. A more detailed analysis of the interaction was carried out using the Dunnett test for comparisons with the control (unrelated) condition [Keppel, 1982]. Responses to contextually appropriate targets were faster than to unrelated targets at both SOAs: long SOA, $F(1,20) = 21.0$, $p < .01$; short SOA, $F(1,20) = 65.6$, $p < .01$. Responses to the contextually inappropriate targets were faster than unrelated targets at the short

SOA but not at the long SOA: long SOA, $F(1,20) = 5.58, p < .05$; short SOA, $F(1,20) = 21.2$, $p < .01$. A *posthoc* comparison (Tukey test, [Keppel, 1973]) showed that, although faster than unrelated responses, contextually inappropriate responses were slower than contextual responses at the short SOA, $F(1,20) = 48.9$, $p < .01$.

4.3 *Discussion*

Our results replicate those of previous studies in showing that, despite a sentential context biasing one reading of an ambiguous word, targets related to both senses are primed if the temporal interval between the ambiguous prime and its target is short [Kintsch and Mross, 1985; Onifer and Swinney, 1981; Seidenberg, Tanenhaus, Leiman, and Bienkowski, 1982]. Note that, in the present study, the contextually inappropriate targets were related to the dominant, higher-frequency sense of the homographs used. The RT facilitation observed for these targets is thus consistent with either the "multiple access" or "ordered access" model of ambiguity resolution.

Although faster than the RTs to unrelated targets, the contextually inappropriate target RTs were slower than those to contextually appropriate targets. This effect has been reported in past studies [Onifer and Swinney, 1981; Simpson, 1981], although it has not always been statistically significant ([Seidenberg et al., 1982; Swinney, 1979]; see [Simpson, 1984]). A greater degree of priming for contextually appropriate targets over contextually inappropriate targets may reflect preferential processing of the biased meaning of ambiguous words. Alternatively, it may reflect direct priming of the contextually appropriate targets by the sentence contexts independent of the ambiguous words.

In the present study, many (76 out of 120) of the homograph sentence contexts contained words which were lexically associated with the contextually appropriate targets (e.g., "The gambler pulled an *ace* from the bottom of the *deck. cards*"). The RTs to the contextually appropriate probes may then have reflected priming by intermediate words in the sentence as well as by the terminal homographs, a benefit not enjoyed by the contextually inappropriate targets. However, these lexically associated intermediate words occurred, on the average, 5.7 words (or 5.2 seconds) prior to the target words. We do not know if a lexical priming mechanism, when extended over so many words, could account for the differential priming of contextually appropriate and contextually inappropriate targets. It has been reported that semantic priming drops off sharply with even a single intervening item in word lists [Dannenbring and Briand, 1982; Foss, 1982], but can be maintained over intervening material in prose passages [Foss, 1982]. The present case falls somewhere between a word list and a passage, and the question of priming between sentence intermediate words and targets remains open. This issue will be examined at greater length in Experiment 2.

The primary purpose of Experiment 1 was to validate this set of sentences and targets for producing reaction time priming of both contextually appropriate and inappropriate targets of homographs. This purpose achieved, we proceeded to record ERPs to the same set of stimulus materials.

5 Experiment 2

5.1 Methods

5.1.1 Subjects Eighteen paid volunteers were assigned to the short SOA group, fifteen to the long SOA group. All subjects had normal or corrected-to-normal vision, and were right-handed (5 with left-handed relatives). The age range was 18 to 25 years and 11 of the subjects were female. None of these subjects had participated in the previous experiment.

5.1.2 Stimuli The stimulus materials were the same as those in Experiment 1, with the following exception. ERP subjects were assigned a task other than naming because of the electrical artifacts associated with speech (electromyogram, glossokinetic potential, respiratory potentials, etc.; see [Grozinger, Kornhuber, Kriebel, Szirtes, and Westphal, 1980; Picton and Stuss, 1984] for reviews of these problems). This task was a letter search of the target word performed subsequent to its presentation. Single trials then consisted of the sentences and "target" words as before, but a single letter of the alphabet appeared 1500 msec after each target word. Letters were selected pseudorandomly with the constraint that 50% of each target type were followed by a letter that had been in the word, and 50% by a letter that had not been in the word. ERP responses to these target letters were not analyzed, rather the task was selected solely to insure that subjects attended to the "target" words. We will continue to refer to these words as "targets" for the sake of consistency with Experiment 1, but note that the ERP subjects were not required to make an overt response to these words. It has been shown in previous research that ERPs recorded during such a letter search task reliably discriminate between primed and unprimed words although no behavioral response is required to the words themselves ([Kutas, 1985; see Kutas and Van Petten, in press]). The specifics of stimulus presentation were as in Experiment 1.

5.1.3 Procedure Subjects were tested in one session that lasted three to three and a half hours, while reclining in a comfortable chair. They were instructed to read each sentence in order to answer a multiple-choice questionnaire at the end of the experiment, and to read each target word in order to decide if the subsequent letter appeared in the target word. Subjects pressed one of two buttons held in either hand on each trial to indicate "letter present" or "letter absent." Half of the subjects in each group used the right hand for "letter present" and the left for "letter absent," and the other half the reverse.

5.1.4 *Recording System*
EEG activity was recorded from ten scalp electrodes, each referred to an average of the left and right mastoids. Eight were placed according to the International 10-20 system at frontal (Fz), central (Cz), parietal (Pz) and occipital (Oz) midline locations, as well as at frontal and central lateral sites (F3, F4, C3, C4). Symmetrical temporoparietal electrodes were placed lateral (by 30% of the interaural distance) and 12.5% posterior to the vertex. Eye movements were monitored via an electrode placed below the right eye and referred to the mastoids for vertical movements and blinks, and via a right-to-left canthal bipolar montage for horizontal movements.

The midline and EOG recordings were amplified with Grass 7P122 preamplifiers (system bandpass 0.01 to 35 Hz, half-amplitude cutoff). The EEG from the lateral scalp leads was amplified with Grass 7P511 preamplifiers modified to have an 8 second time constant (high frequency half amplitude cutoff = 60 Hz).

5.1.4 *Data Analysis*
Analog-to-digital conversion of the EEG, EOG and stimulus trigger codes was performed online by a PDP 11/45 computer. A 2048 msec epoch of EEG, beginning 200 msec before the onset of sentence terminal words, was averaged at a sampling rate of 125 Hz. Trials characterized by excessive eye movement or amplifier blocking were rejected, approximately 15% of the trials.

ERPs were quantified by computer as the mean voltage within a latency range, relative to the 200 msec of activity preceding the sentence terminal words. Two latency windows were used to quantify the response to target words. A 300 to 700 msec post-target window was chosen to encompass the usual latency band of the N400 response [Fischler, Bloom, Childers, Roucos, and Perry, 1983; Kutas and Hillyard, 1980a,b,c; McCallum, Farmer, and Pocock, 1984]. A later latency band of 700 to 1100 msec post-target was also measured.

5.2 *Results*

5.2.1 *Filler-Target Responses*
The responses to unambiguous sentence completions and subsequent target words at both SOAs are shown in Figure 17.1. It can be seen that the overall waveshape of the response was quite

different at the different SOAs. At the 700 msec SOA, the N100 (negative peak at about 100 msec) and P200 (positive peak at about 200 msec) waves elicited by the terminal word of the sentence were followed by a negative-going anticipatory potential (i.e., contingent negative variation, CNV) before the presentation of the target word, which elicited then similar N100-P200 ERP components. The 200 msec SOA response, in contrast, was a compound ERP in which the responses to terminal and target words overlap.[2]

It is important to note, however, that where the ERP to the terminal words could be isolated, namely in the 700 msec SOA data, there were no differences between the various conditions before the presentation of the target words. This was to be expected since the different conditions included responses from the same sentences counterbalanced across subjects. Therefore, any ERP differences among conditions can be attributed to the target words. It can be seen that the difference between related and unrelated targets at the two SOAs was similar, consisting of greater negativity (an N400) to the unrelated targets. We will focus, therefore, on the relative difference between the ERPs to related and unrelated targets within each SOA.

Long SOA: Figure 17.1 shows that the unrelated targets elicited substantially larger N400s than the related targets. The negative difference between the two target types begins around 300 msec after the target and continues for several hundred milliseconds. The mean amplitudes of each subject's ERPs were subjected to a repeated measures ANOVA using target type (related and unrelated), latency window (300 to 700 msec post-target and 700 to 1100 msec post-target), and electrode site (10 levels) as factors. There was a main effect of target type, $F(1,14) = 8.05$, $p < .02$, reflecting the greater negativity for unrelated targets. There was also an interaction of target type by latency window, $F(1,14) = 5.97$, $p < .03$, reflecting the greater difference between related and unrelated targets in the early (300–700 msec post-target) portion of the waveform than in the late (700–1100 msec post-target). Separate ANOVAs were carried out to test the target type effect within each latency range; the significance of these F-values was evaluated by the Dunnett test. The relatedness effect was significant in both latency windows: early—$F(1,14) = 9.07$, $p < .05$; late—$F(1,14) = 7.03$, $p < .05$.

---

2 There are two factors which act to make the overall waveshape of the ERP different for the two SOAs. One is a simple superposition, or overlapping, of the ongoing ERPs to the terminal word of the sentence and the target word. An algebraic subtraction routine could, in principle, cancel this superposition effect. However, this is not a tenable procedure for obtaining the "true" ERP to a single word as there are also different physiological/cognitive processes at work in different SOAs. Much research has been devoted to the potentials which develop during the interval between two stimuli presented at a fixed rate (see [Rohrbaugh and Gaillard, 1983] for a review of the CNV). The waveshape and amplitude of these potentials are sensitive to the duration of the interval; we have thus confined our experimental comparisons to within-SOA data.

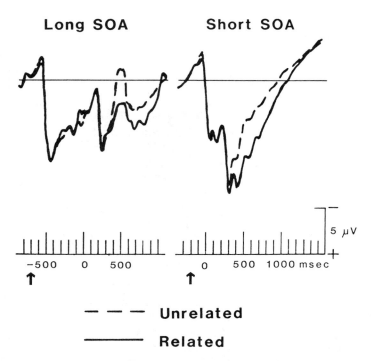

Figure 17.1 Grand average ERPs to unambiguous (filler) sentence terminal words and subsequent targets in the 700 and 200 msec SOA conditions. Onset of the sentence terminal words is indicated by an arrow. Onset of the targets is at 0 msec. The ERPs were recorded at a midline central site (Cz).

Short SOA: ERPs obtained at the 200 msec SOA were similar to those of the 700 msec SOA in that unrelated targets elicited more negativity than related targets beginning about 300 msec after the target word. The ERPs obtained at the 200 msec SOA were analyzed in the same manner as the 700 msec SOA waveforms. There was a main effect of target type, $F(1,17) = 43.9$, $p < .001$, and an interaction between target type and latency window, $F(1,17) = 16.0$, $p < .001$. Separate comparisons showed that unrelated targets elicited greater negativity in both the early, $F(1,17) = 53.6$, $p < .01$, and late, $F(1,17) = 22.9$, $p < .01$, portions of the ERP response.

5.2.2 *Homograph-Target Responses* *Long SOA*: As in the filler data, unrelated targets elicited a large N400 while the contextually appropriate targets (see Figure 17.2). elicited a much smaller N400. The ERP response to contextually inappropriate targets appears very similar to that for the unrelated targets. The mean amplitudes of each subject's ERP were subjected to a repeated-measures ANOVA with target type (3 levels), latency window (2 levels), and electrode site (10 levels) as factors. There was a main effect of target type, $F(2,14) = 8.13$, $p < .002$, but no significant interaction of target type by latency, $F(2,28) = 2.47$, N.S. The main effect of target type in this overall ANOVA is not very informative; the Dunnett test was used to compare the contextually appropriate and contextually inappropriate target responses to the unrelated response. This procedure showed that contextually appropriate target ERPs differed from unrelated target ERPs in both the early and late portions of the response: early—$F(1,14) = 11.3$, $p < .05$; late—$F(1,14) = 8.67$, $p < .05$. In contrast, the inappropriate target responses did not differ from the unrelated response in either portion of the waveform: early—$F(1,14) = 0.21$, n.s; late—$F(1,14) = 0.005$, N.S.

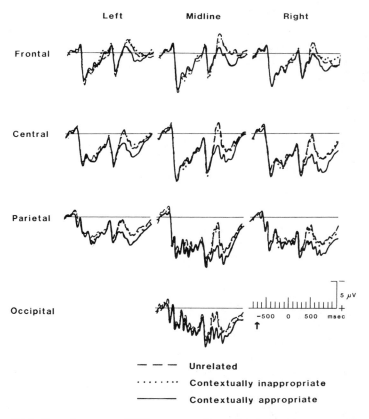

Figure 17.2 Grand average ERPs across electrode sites to homographic sentence terminal words and subsequent targets in the 700 msec SOA condition. Onset of the sentence terminal words is indicated by an arrow. Onset of the targets is at 0 msec.

Short SOA: As in the long SOA data, the unrelated targets elicited a larger N400 than did the contextually appropriate targets. Figure 17.3 shows that the responses to unrelated and contextually appropriate targets begin to separate as early as 300 msec after the target word. Unlike the long SOA data, the response to contextually inappropriate targets does not appear to be identical to the response to unrelated targets throughout the recording epoch. The contextually inappropriate target ERP initially resembles the response to unrelated targets, but subsequently becomes more positive and resembles the response to contextually appropriate targets.

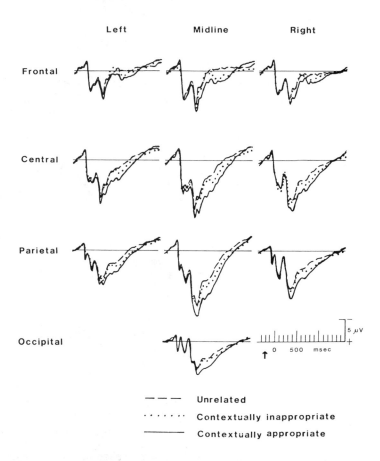

Figure 17.3 Grand average ERPs across electrode sites to homographic sentence terminal words and subsequent targets in the 200 msec SOA condition. Onset of the sentence terminal words is indicated by an arrow. Onset of the targets is at 0 msec.

The ERPs obtained at the 200 msec SOA were analyzed in the same manner as the long SOA ERPs. The overall ANOVA showed significant main effects of target type, $F(2,17) = 18.9$, $p < .001$, and latency, $F(1,17) = 46.5$, $p < .001$. There was also a significant interaction of target type by latency, $F(2,34) = 4.74$, $p < .02$. Pairwise comparisons showed that the contextually appropriate target responses differed from the unrelated in both early and late portions of the waveform: early—$F(1,17) = 52.8$, $p < .01$; late—$F(1,17) = 16.9$, $p < .01$. The contextually inappropriate target responses, in contrast, differed significantly from the unrelated responses in the late portion of the response, $F(1,17) = 13.2$, $p < .01$, but not in the early portion of the response, $F(1,17) = 1.27$, N.S.

Additional *posthoc* tests were conducted on the contextually inappropriate target ERP to further describe its similarity or dissimilarity to the contextually appropriate and unrelated response. Pairwise ANOVAs were computed; F-values evaluated via the Tukey test [Keppel, 1973]. The contextually inappropriate ERP was significantly different from the contextually biased ERP during the 300–700 msec portion of the response, $F(1,17) = 17.7$, $p < .01$. The difference between contextually appropriate and contextually inappropriate responses in the 700–1100 msec latency range, however, failed to reach significance, $F(1,17) = 4.05$, $p < .05$.

It is of some interest to track the time course of the brain responses to the three target types and, in particular, to determine when the contextually inappropriate response deviated from the unrelated response and took on the likeness of the contextually appropriate response. The ERPs averaged across subjects show that the contextually biased response diverges from those to the other two target types at about 300 msec after target onset. The contextually inappropriate response appears to diverge from the unrelated response at about 500 msec following the target. The latency windows originally selected for the analysis of individual subjects' data are, however, too broad to evaluate these impressions about the onset latencies of the experimental effects.

A more fine-grained analysis was provided by comparing successive 25 msec epochs of the responses following presentation of different target types. The 300 to 325 msec epoch was the earliest point at which the contextual target responses differed from the unrelated responses, $F(1,17) = 20.3$, $p < .001$. Similarly, the contextual target responses began to differ from the contextually inappropriate targets in this same time band, $F(1,17) = 9.77$, $p < .01$. This relationship also held for the comparisons between filler related and unrelated targets, $F(1,17) = 5.59$, $p < .05$.

In contrast, none of the comparisons between contextually inappropriate and unrelated target ERPs conducted within the 300 to 500 msec latency region revealed any significant effects due to the semantic relationship between homograph and target. Beginning with the 500 to 525 msec band (and in each 25 msec epoch in the 500 to 700 msec region) there was a significant interaction of relationship type with electrode site, $F(9,153) = 6.08$, $p < .001$. The interaction indicates that for this latency band, the unrelated/contextually inappropriate difference was significant at the three most posterior midline sites only: Cz—$F(1,17) = 5.10$, $p < .05$; Pz—$F(1,17) = 5.38$, $p < .05$; Oz—$F(1,17) = 5.35$, $p < .05$. A significant main effect of target type did not appear until the 700–725 msec band, $F(1,17) = 7.97$, $p < .05$.

In summary, the ERPs to contextually inappropriate targets and to unrelated targets were highly similar during the first 500 msec following the onset of the target. The contextually inappropriate target ERP became more like the contextually appropriate ERP between 500 and 700 msec after the target presentation, and became statistically indistinguishable from the contextually appropriate response in the 700–1100 msec epoch.

5.3 *Discussion*

The present results extend those of previous ERP experiments by demonstrating that the amplitude of the N400 reflects priming across a sentence boundary, as well as priming by a sentence fragment or single word [Bentin et al., 1985; Fischler et al., 1983; 1984; Harbin et al., 1984; Holcomb, in press; Kutas and Hillyard, 1980a,b,c; 1983; 1984; Rugg, 1985]. Targets with no semantic relationship to the final word of a sentence elicit a larger N400 component than do related target words. This relationship between N400 amplitude and priming held for targets following both ambiguous and unambiguous terminal words.

It should be noted that while we speak of fluctuations in the amplitude of a negative wave, the N400, the data can be described in terms of fluctuations in the amplitude of a positive wave in the same latency range. These descriptions are equivalent for our present purposes. The relationship between priming and positivity, or lack of priming and negativity, can be used to test two opposing models of ambiguity resolution. According to the selective access model, contextually inappropriate targets should be processed as if they were unrelated to the preceding ambiguity and so should elicit N400s of equal amplitude, latency, and duration to those elicited by completely unrelated targets at any SOA. The multiple access model, in contrast, predicts that the priming of contextually inappropriate targets is dependent on SOA. In this case, the contextually inappropriate target ERP should be identical to the contextually appropriate target ERP at the short SOA when both senses of the ambiguity are still activated, and identical to the unrelated ERP when a longer interval allows selection of the contextually appropriate meaning.

Our finding of equivalent N400s for contextually inappropriate and unrelated targets at the long SOA is compatible with either the multiple or selective access model. On the other hand, the ERPs obtained with the 200 msec SOA do not fit neatly into the pattern predicted by either model. We cannot accept the selective access model in its simplest form because the contextually inappropriate and unrelated ERPs at the short SOA do differ. The greater positivity of the contextually inappropriate ERP as compared to the unrelated one suggests that the contextually inappropriate targets were, at some point, processed in a manner similar to contextually appropriate targets. However, the ERPs to unrelated and contextually inappropriate targets do not differ until 500 msec have passed since the presentation of the target. In contrast, the ERPs to unrelated and contextually appropriate targets differ as early as 300 msec post-target. The 200 msec lag between the onset of these two effects is not consistent with the multiple access model of simultaneous and parallel activation of both senses of ambiguous word.

How can we account for the existence, but late onset, of the contextually inappropriate/unrelated target difference? Some possible interpretations must be discounted by the lack of any difference between unrelated and contextually inappropriate targets in the long SOA condition. For instance, if the late priming-related positivity was due to the delayed realization that the contextually inappropriate targets *were* related to the homographs, although not in the way originally expected, there should be a similar "double take" effect some 500 msec after the target in the long SOA condition. There was not. Similarly, one might suppose that the subjects engaged in a deliberate attempt to recover the contextually contextually inappropriate meanings of the homographs (after the experiment, several subjects in both SOA conditions reported noticing these), and that the late effect is the product of slow strategic priming of the sort described by Neely [1977]. Although subjects in the long SOA condition had more time to engage strategic or attentional processes, their brain responses did not differentiate between contextually inappropriate and unrelated targets. Thus, this explanation seems unlikely.

Finally, it has been suggested that the differing onset latencies of the priming effects we report for contextually appropriate and inappropriate targets reflect the targets' differential relationships to intermediate sentence words, rather than their relationships to the terminal homographs. Many of the contextually appropriate targets had semantic relationships to intermediate words while the contextually inappropriate targets did not.

In this view, the priming effect for contextually appropriate targets might be composed of two parts: an early part (onset at 300 msec post-target) due to direct priming by intermediate words, and a late part (onset at 500 msec) due to priming by the terminal homograph. The apparently different onset latencies for priming of contextually appropriate and inappropriate targets would only reflect the fact that contextually inappropriate targets lack the early, intermediate-word component of the priming effect. If this were true, the present results might reflect equal and simultaneous priming of both target types by the terminal homographs, thus supporting the multiple access hypothesis. We find this explanation unlikely, although logically possible, because 500 msec seems very long for the *onset* of a forward priming effect.

It is not possible to refute this proposal via analysis of the ERPs to homograph targets. The intermediate word—target relationships were a necessary consequence of our effort to construct constraining sentence contexts for the homographs. Note however, that this alternative explanation is not specific to sentences with ambiguous words, but makes general predictions about the onset latency of the ERP priming effect for targets which have been primed solely by the terminal word of a sentence. A substantial proportion of the filler sentences contained no intermediate words related to the filler targets (see Appendix 2). According to the proposal outlined above, the priming effect for the related targets of these sentences should onset at the same time as the priming effect for the contextually inappropriate targets of homograph sentences.

Filler sentences were thus split into two conditions, "high associative context" and "low associative context" and the ERPs to related targets following "low context" fillers averaged separately for the subjects in the short SOA group. For each subject, 38 of the original 60 related targets fell into this condition.[3] Figure 17.4 compares the ERP difference wave (priming effect) for "low associative context" fillers with those for contextually related and contextually inappropriate homograph targets. It can be seen that the "low context" filler effect substantially precedes the contextually inappropriate target effect, although it does begin slightly later than the priming effect for contextually appropriate targets. The onset latency of the "low context" filler priming effect was determined in the same manner as latencies in the other conditions (see Results). The first time window in which these related and unrelated targets differed was 350–375 msec post stimulus, $F(1,17) = 10.9$, $p < .004$. The 50 msec lag between the onset of this priming effect and that for the contextually appropriate targets of homographs may well be due to the lack of intermediate word priming. This small latency shift cannot, however, account for the much longer delay in priming of contextually inappropriate homograph targets. The 500 msec onset of this priming effect is clearly much later than the normal onset latency for priming by sentence terminal words.

The hypothesis most consistent with our results is that backward priming of the type reported by Kiger and Glass [1983] occurred in the 200 msec SOA but not in the 700 msec SOA condition. It seems reasonable to assume that there was greater temporal overlap between terminal word and target word processing in the short SOA condition than in the long SOA condition. Thus, target words presented shortly after the terminal words might have served as second sources of context in the as yet incomplete interpretation of these words. When the terminal words were ambiguous, contextually inappropriate targets

---

3 The remaining 22 trials constituting the "high associative context" condition were insufficient for an adequate signal-to-noise ratio in averaging the ongoing electroencephalogram to form an ERP. The "low associative context" condition is, however, of greater relevance here.

could have served to activate the sense of the word which had not been primed by the preceding sentence. The concurrent processing of this newly activated meaning and its related target would, in this view, have led to the observed priming effect for the contextually inappropriate targets. One would expect such mutual priming between the ambiguity and its contextually inappropriate target to lag behind priming between the ambiguity and its contextually appropriate target because the former requires *de novo* activation of a new meaning for the ambiguity while the latter can draw on the previously established sentence context.

200 SOA DIFFERENCE WAVES

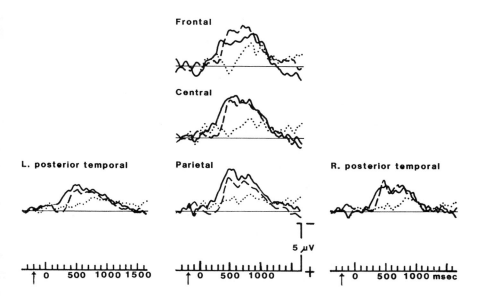

Figure 17.4 Grand average difference waves for the 200 msec SOA. Onset of the sentence terminal words is indicated by an arrow. Onset of the targets is at 0 msec. The solid line is the result of subtracting the ERP to contextually appropriate targets from the ERP to unrelated targets following homographs. The dotted line is the result of subtracting the ERP to contextually inappropriate targets from the ERP to unrelated targets following homographs. The dashed line is the result of subtracting the ERP to related targets following filler sentences of low associative context (see text) from the ERP to unrelated filler targets. Copyright © 1987 by Academic Press, reprinted by permission.

This interpretation of the present results is consistent with one tenet of the multiple access model of ambiguity resolution: it takes some time to process an ambiguous word. It is inconsistent with the tenet that one stage of such processing involves the simultaneous activation of both senses of the ambiguity. Rather, it suggests that there is an early stage of ambiguity resolution in which the ambiguity can be *reinterpreted* due to the additional context provided by a subsequent word. At some later time, a final interpretation has been found and the ambiguous word is immune to further context effects.

6 *Conclusions*

We believe that the backward priming interpretation of the ERP data obtained in Experiment 2 is also compatible with the naming latency data reported for Experiment 1. A direct comparison between the behavioral reaction time and ERP onset latencies is not feasible because these were obtained from different subjects. However, it is important to note that the first ERP indication of a differentiation between contextually inappropriate and unrelated targets in one group of subjects precedes the behavioral response of the other group of subjects. Naming latencies hovered around 600 msec in the short SOA condition of Experiment 1 (see Table 2). At this point in time, mutual priming between ambiguities and their contextually inappropriate targets may already have taken place so that the reaction time to such targets would reflect this benefit.

This backward, or mutual, priming interpretation of RT data which appear to reflect multiple access is supported by evidence obtained from a new reaction time technique which Glucksberg and his colleagues have recently applied to the problem of ambiguity resolution. These investigators have used a variant of the lexical decision task in which RT for nonwords rather than words is the dependent variable. Nonwords are constructed so as to be reminiscent of true words, such as "piamoe" and "kidnea" from "piano" and "kidney," respectively. In a simple word-pair task, subjects are slower to reject 'related' nonwords such as "piamo" or "kidnea" following "organ" than 'unrelated' nonword controls such as "moepia" or "nedika." This interference is, however, asymmetric. "Organ" influences reaction time for "piamoe," but the presentation of "piamoe" neither facilitates nor inhibits the lexical decision to "organ" [Gildea, 1984]. The unidirectional nature of this interference effect was used to construct a lexical ambiguity paradigm which was insensitive to backward priming effects. Reaction time interference was found for only the contextually 'related' nonword targets following ambiguous words in a biasing context [Glucksberg, Kreuz, and Rho, 1986].

Glucksberg's nonword version of the lexical decision paradigm appears to eliminate the possibility of backward priming even at short prime-target SOAs.

Since only real word targets were used in the experiments reported here backward priming was not eliminated. Instead we relied on the temporal resolution of the event-related potential measure to distinguish forward from backward priming by their different time courses. The study of this sort of backward (mutual) priming may, in the long run, reveal much about the nature and tem poral characteristics of the integration of single word meanings into discourse.

Acknowledgments

This work was supported by a grant from NSF (BNS83-09243). C. Van Petten is supported by an NSF Graduate Fellowship. M. Kutas is supported by a Research Scientist Development Award from NIH (MH 00322). We are grateful to Susan Garnsey for helpful comments on a previous version of this manuscript although only the authors can be held accountable for the opinions expressed. Portions of this article will appear in the *Journal of Memory and Language* [Van Petten and Kutas, in press] and are reprinted by permission of Academic Press.

Appendix 1

Homograph	Contextually Appropiate Target	Contextually Inappropriate Target
bail	bucket	money
bank	river	account
bats	vampire	baseball
bear	carry	grizzly
bill	beak	pay
bit	chew	piece
blues	rhythm	sky
bluff	cliff	fake
bow	stern	kneel
bowl	ball	soup

Homograph	Contextually Appropiate Target	Contextually Inappropriate Target
box	fight	cardboard
bridge	cards	river
bug	spy	insect
cabinet	president	cupboard
calf	leg	cow
can	tin	can't
capital	money	washington
change	alter	dollar
check	over	cash
chest	box	body
china	japan	dishes
club	group	hit
coach	carriage	football
coast	beach	roll
count	duke	ten
court	tennis	law
date	girl	day
deck	cards	ship
deed	title	act
draft	tap	army
draw	tie	sketch
fall	winter	down
fan	follower	cool
fence	sword	wall
file	nail	folder
gin	rummy	vodka
glasses	drinks	lenses

Homograph	Contextually Appropiate Target	Contextually Inappropriate Target
grate	grill	cheese
ground	grind	floor
hide	skin	seek
key	note	lock
leaves	goes	trees
litter	kittens	trash
lot	acre	plenty
march	april	walk
match	same	light
may	june	might
means	thinks	average
miss	hit	mrs
nag	horse	bitch
nails	fingers	hammer
nut	bolt	seed
organ	liver	piano
palm	tree	hand
park	car	bench
pass	mountain	fail
pen	pig	ink
pick	shovel	choose
pipe	smoke	water
pit	hole	peach
pitch	tone	throw
pitcher	beer	baseball
plant	factory	green
play	stage	game
plot	land	story

Homograph	Contextually Appropiate Target	Contextually Inappropriate Target
poker	fireplace	cards
pool	table	swim
port	wine	harbor
pot	soup	marijuana
pound	weigh	beat
present	give	future
press	news	push
punch	fruit	hit
pupils	eyes	students
race	color	run
refrain	chorus	stop
rest	remainder	sleep
ring	bell	finger
rose	stood	flower
row	line	paddle
ruler	measure	king
rung	rang	ladder
saw	ax	look
scales	fish	weigh
second	minute	third
sentence	prison	paragraph
shed	tool	fur
sink	swim	kitchen
slip	dress	slide
slugs	worms	hits
solution	mixture	problem
spade	ace	shovel

Homograph	Contextually Appropiate Target	Contextually Inappropriate Target
spoke	wheel	talked
spring	jump	summer
squash	racquet	vegetable
stall	delay	barn
star	movie	planet
sticks	stay	stones
stock	cattle	exchange
story	floor	read
straw	hay	sip
swallow	bird	drink
table	figure	chair
tank	gas	guns
temples	head	jewish
tick	flea	tock
tie	win	knot
till	soil	cash
tip	turn	waiter
tire	sleep	car
toast	drink	bread
toll	chime	fee
top	spin	bottom
train	practice	freight
volume	book	sound
wake	wave	sleep
watch	look	wrist
will	testament	won't
yard	inches	front
amount	art	call

Unrelated targets

chain	classic	curly
doll	echo	final
glad	glum	guru
held	honor	hope
keep	lips	mineral
modern	nature	never
parent	pie	pill
poetry	proof	quotes
risk	scare	school
score	sell	shine
shown	smile	soon
steam	threat	trigger
understood		

Note: the same 40 unrelated targets were used for each of the three stimulus lists.

Appendix 2

Low Associative Context Fillers and Related Target Words

He almost got lost driving home because it was so foggy.
clear

The interview went well and he got the job.
work

It was a dark and stormy night.
day

He admitted that he was wrong.
right

Low Associative Context Fillers and Related Target Words

He thought the most important issue in the election was peace.
war

She was afraid to walk alone after dark.
light

The library kept very short hours and seemed to usually be closed.
open

He glanced out the window and saw that it was a beautiful day outside.
inside

She wanted to find the owner of the dog she had found.
lost

They stayed home and watched an old movie on TV.
radio

She had lost her comb.
hair

The professor gave a surprise quiz.
test

She didn't want to travel in Mexico until she had learned Spanish.
language

The scientist had proven the old theory to be false.
true

They told him the check was in the mail.
letter

He was planning on winning the lottery and becoming rich.
poor

He had never learned to swim and tried to stay where the water was shallow.
deep

She made a point of arriving early.
late

The sun didn't set until ten in the evening.
morning

He wrote a note to himself so that he wouldn't forget.
remember

Low Associative Context Fillers and Related Target Words

He left yesterday.
today

He got paid twice a month.
week

The geese were flying south.
north

He painted his kitchen white.
black

He lifted weights but still thought he was weak.
strong

Most truck drivers belong to the Teamsters.
union

He had made many political enemies.
friends

His speech lasted only ten minutes.
hours

She let the phone ring six times but there was no answer.
question

He had trouble eating and sleeping when he was under pressure.
stress

The mountain is twelve thousand feet high.
low

She had always wanted to sail to Hawaii.
island

He was sorry to hear that the old man was dying.
dead

His uncle wanted to know why he hadn't settled down and gotten married.
single

He didn't believe that his friend would have told him a lie.
truth

She had moved to New York.
city

Low Associative Context Fillers and Related Target Words

The shepherd led his flock to the summer pasture.
field

The man looked very familiar but she couldn't remember his name.
face

The convict tried to get a special pardon from the governor.
state

You could tell by his accent that he had grown up in the east.
west

He wouldn't show his work to anyone until it was finished.
start

The little boy promised Santa Claus that he had been good.
bad

She bought a stuffed toy for her granddaughter.
grandson

He is always careful to wear his seat belt.
buckle

He took four aspirin.
headache

She was teaching her dog to beg.
plead

He thought the cake was too sweet.
sour

He wanted a roommate who would be quiet and neat.
sloppy

The first thing she reads in the Sunday paper is the comics.
cartoons

The airline had lost her suitcase.
luggage

Every muscle in his body ached.
sore

They made camp just before sunset.
sunrise

Low Associative Context Fillers and Related Target Words

He had forgotten the words to the song.
tune

They went to the zoo to watch the apes.
monkey

She never paid any attention to the gossip.
rumor

The kids had a great time at the circus.
clown

The usher was collecting tickets at the entrance.
exit

He bought a quart of milk and a dozen eggs.
bacon

He was wearing a down jacket and mittens.
gloves

They wouldn't let her into the restaurant because she wasn't wearing shoes.
socks

He ordered french fries with his hamburger.
hotdog

She spent many years with an Indian tribe and wrote down many of their stories
and legends.
myths

He bought a spool of thread and some needles.
pins

She was afraid of spiders.
web

The medical students had to memorize all of the major arteries.
veins

He got drenched walking in the rain.
umbrella

They couldn't agree on what kind of ice cream to buy and finally settled on vanilla.
chocolate

Low Associative Context Fillers and Related Target Words

The sweater was knitted from blue and grey wool.
lamb

He refused to clean the kitchen because it wasn't masculine.
feminine

He woke up screaming from a bad dream.
nightmare

Everything she owned was in a brown paper bag.
sack

The hunter dropped his rifle.
shotgun

Her car broke down in the desert and she had to hitchhike.
thumb

They were out of dish soap.
suds

They had a big family dinner every Thanksgiving.
turkey

When he cleaned his desk he threw most of his old notes into the trash.
garbage

References

Balota, D.A. and Chumbley, J.I. 1984. Are lexical decisions a good measure of lexical access? The role of word frequency in the neglected decision stage. *Journal of Experimental Psychology: Human Perception and Performance* 10:340–357.

Balota, D.A. and Chumbley, J.I. 1985. The locus of word-frequency effects in the prounciation task: Lexical and/or production frequency? *Journal of Memory and Language* 24:89–106.

Becker, C.A. 1979. Semantic context and word frequency effects in visual word recognition. *Journal of Experimental Psychology: Human Perception and Performance* 5:252–259.

Bentin, S., McCarthy,G., and Wood, C.C. 1985. Event-related potentials associated with semantic priming. *Electroencephalography and Clinical Neurophysiology* 60:343–355.

Bloom, P.A., and Fischler, I. 1980. Completion norms for 329 sentence contexts. *Memory and Cognition* 8:631–642.

Cairns, H.S., and Kamerman, J. 1975. Lexical information processing during sentence processing. *Journal of Verbal Learning and Verbal Behavior* 14:170–179.

Cairns, H.S., and Hsu, J.R. 1975. Effects of prior context upon lexical access during sentence comprehension: A replication and reinterpretation. *Journal of Psycholinguistic Research* 9:1–8.

Carroll, M., and Kirsner, K. 1982. Context and repetition effects in lexical decision and recognition memory. *Journal of Verbal Learning and Verbal Behavior* 21:55–69.

Coles, M.G.H., Gratton, G., Bashore, T.R., Eriksen, C.W. and Donchin, E. In press. A psychophysiological investigation of the continuous flow model of human information processing. *Journal of Experimental Psychology: Human Perception and Performance*.

Collins, A.M. and Loftus, E.F. 1975. A spreading activation theory of semantic processing. *Psychological Review* 82:407–428.

Conrad, C. 1974. Context effects in sentence comprehension: A study of the subjective lexicon. *Memory and Cognition* 2:130–138.

Dannenbring, G.L. and Briand, K. 1982. Semantic priming and the word repetition effect in a lexical decision task. *Canadian Journal of Psychology* 36:435–444.

Donchin, E. 1981. Suprise! . . . Suprise? *Psychophysiology* 18:493–513.

Donchin, E., Ritter, W., and McCallum, W.C. 1978. Cognitive psychophysiology: The endogenous components of the ERP. In E. Callaway, P. Tueting, and S. Koslow (eds), *Brain Event-Related Potentials in Man*, pp. 349–441. New York: Academic Press.

Fischler, I. 1977a. Associative facilitation without expectancy in a lexical decision task. *Journal of Experimental Psychology: Human Perception and Performance* 3:18–26.

Fischler, I. 1977b. Semantic facilitation without association in a lexical decision task. *Memory and Cognition* 5:335–339.

Fischler, I., and Bloom, P.A. 1979. Automatic and attentional processes in the effects of sentence contexts on word recognition. *Journal of Verbal Learning and Verbal Behavior* 18:1–20.

Fischler, I., Bloom, P.A., Childers, D.G., Arroyo, A.A., and Perry, N.W. 1984. Brain potentials during sentence verification: Late negativity and long-term memory strength. *Neuropsychologia* 22:559–568.

Fischler, I., Bloom, P.A., Childers, D.G., Roucos, S.E., and Perry, N.W. 1984. Brain potentials related to stages of sentence verification. *Psychophysiology* 20:400–409.

Fodor, J.A. 1983. *The Modularity of Mind.* Cambridge: MIT Press.

Forster, K. 1981. Priming and the effects of sentence and lexical contexts on naming time: Evidence for autonomous lexical processing. *Quarterly Journal of Experimental Psychology* 33A:465–495.

Foss, D.J. 1970. Some effects of ambiguity upon sentence comprehension. *Journal of Verbal Learning and Verbal Behavior* 9:699–706.

Foss, D.J. 1982. A discourse on semantic priming. *Cognitive Psychology* 14:590–607.

Foss, D.J., and Jenkins, C.M. 1973. Some effects of context on the comprehension of ambiguous sentences. *Journal of Verbal Learning and Verbal Behavior* 12:577–589.

Garnsey, S. 1985. Function words and content words: Reaction time and evoked potential measures of word recognition. Cognitive Science Technical Report No. URCS–29, University of Rochester, Rochester, NY.

Garrett, M. 1978. Word and sentence perception. In R. Held, H.W. Leibowity, and H.L. Teuber (eds.), *Handbook of Sensory Physiology Vol. VIII, Perception.* Berlin: Springer-Verlag.

Geis, M.F., and Winograd, E. 1984. Norms of semantic encoding variability for fifty homographs. *Bulletin of the Psychonomic Society* 3:429–431.

Gildea, P. 1984. *On Resolving Lexical Ambiguity: Can Context Constrain Lexical Access?* Unpublished Doctoral dissertation, Princeton University.

Glucksberg, S., Kreuz, R.J., and Rho, S. 1986. Context can constrain lexical access: Implications for models of language comprehension. *Journal of Experimental Psychology: Learning, Memory and Cognition* 12:323–335.

Gorfein, D.S., Viviani, J.M., and Leddo, J. 1982. Norms as a tool for the study of homography. *Memory and Cognition* 10:503–509.

Grozinger, B., Kornhuber, H.H., Kriebel, J., Szirtes, J., and Westphal, K.T.P. 1980. The Bereitschaftspotential preceding the act of speaking. Also an analysis of artifacts. In H.H. Kornhuber, and L. Deecke (eds.), *Motivation, Motor and Sensory Processes of the Brain: Electrical Potentials, Behavior, and Clinical Use, Progress in Brain Research* 54:798–804.

Harbin, T.J., Marsh, G.R. and Harvey M.T. 1984. Differences in the late components of the event-related potential due to age and to semantic and non-semantic tasks. *Electroencephalography and Clinical Neurophysiology* 59:489–496.

Hillyard, S.A. and Kutas, M. 1983. Electrophysiology of cognitive processing. *Annual Review of Psychology* 34:33–61.

Hillyard, S.A. and Woods, D.L. 1979. Electrophysiological analysis of human brain function. In M.S. Gazzaniga (ed.), *Handbook of Behavioral Neurobiology: Neuropsychology* Vol. 2, pp.345–378. New York: Plenum Press.

Holcomb, P.J. 1985. Unimodal and multimodal models of lexical memory: An ERP analysis. *Psychophysiology* 22:576. (Abstract).

James, W. 1890. *The Principles of Psychology.* New York: Holt.

Johnson, R., Jr. In press. The amplitude of the P300 component of the event-related potential: Review and synthesis. In P.K. Ackles, J.R. Jennings, and M.G.H. Coles (eds.), *Advances in Psychophysiology Vol. 3.* Greenwich: JAI Press. Greenwich, Connecticut.

Kausler, D.H., and Kollasch, S.F. 1970. Word associations to homographs. *Journal of Verbal Learning and Verbal Behavior* 9:444–449.

Keppel, G. 1973. *Design and Analysis, A Researcher's Handbook.* Englewood Cliffs: Prentice-Hall.

Keppel, G. 1982. *Design and Analysis, A Researcher's Handbook, Second Edition.* Englewood Cliffs: Prentice-Hall.

Kiger, J.I., and Glass, A.L. 1983. The facilitation of lexical decisions by a prime occurring after the target. *Memory and Cognition* 11:356–365.

Kintsch, W., and Mross, E.F. 1985. Context effects in word identification. *Journal of Memory and Language* 24:336–349.

Koriat, A. 1981. Semantic facilitation lexical decisions as a function of prime-target association. *Memory and Cognition* 9:587–598.

Kramer, A.F., and Donchin, E. 1987. Brain potentials as indices of orthographic and phonological interaction during word matching. *Journal of Experimental Psychology: Learning, Memory and Cognition* 13:76–86.

Kucera, H., and Francis, W.N. 1967. *Computational Analysis of Present-Day American English.* Providence: Brown University Press.

Kutas, M. 1985. ERP comparisons of the effects of single word and sentence contexts on word processing. *Psychophysiology* 22:575–576. (Abstract).

Kutas, M. 1986. Event-related brain potentials (ERPs) elicited during rapid serial visual presentation of congruous and incongruous sentences. In *Proceedings of the Eighth International Conference on Event-Related Potentials of the Brain (EPIC VIII),* Stanford, California.

Kutas M., and Hillyard, S.A. 1980a. Event-related brain potentials to semantically inappropriate and surprisingly large words. *Biological Psychology* 11:99–116.

Kutas M., and Hillyard S.A. 1980b. Reading senseless sentences: Brain potentials reflect semantic incongruity. *Science* 207:203–205.

Kutas M., and Hillyard, S.A. 1980c. Reading between the lines: Event related brain potentials during natural sentence processing. *Brain and Language* 11:354–373.

Kutas M., and Hillyard, S.A. 1983. Event-related brain potentials to grammatical errors and semantic anomalies. *Memory and Cognition* 11:539–550.

Kutas M., and Hillyard, S.A. 1984. Brain potentials during reading reflect word expectancy and semantic association. *Nature* 307:161–163.

Kutas, M., McCarthy, G., and Donchin, E. 1977. Augmenting mental chronometry: The P300 as an index of stimulus evaluation time. *Science* 197:792–795.

Kutas, M., Neville, H.J., and Holcomb, P.J. In press. A preliminary comparison of the N400 response to semantic anomalies during reading, listening, and signing. *Electroencephalography and Clinical Neurophysiology Supplement*.

Kutas, M., and Van Petten, C. In press. Event-related brain potential studies of language. In P.K. Ackles, J.R. Jennings, and M.G.H. Coles (eds.), *Advances in Psychophysiology, Vol. 3*. Greenwich: JAI Press.

Kutas, M., Van Petten, C. and Besson, M. In press. Event-related potential asymmetries during the reading of sentences. *Electroencephalography and Clinical Neurophysiology*.

Marslen-Wilson, W. and Tyler, L.K. 1980. The temporal structure of spoken language understanding. *Cognition* 8:1–71.

McCallum, W.C., Farmer, S.F., and Pocock, P.V. 1984. The effects of physical and semantic incongruities on auditory event-related potentials. *Electroencephalography and Clinical Neurophysiology* 59:477–488.

McClelland, J.L., and Elman, J.L. 1986. The TRACE model of speech perception. *Cognitive Psychology* 18:1–86.

Mehler, J., Segui, J., and Carey, P. 1978. Tails of words: Monitoring ambiguity. *Journal of Verbal Learning and Verbal Behavior* 17:29–35.

Meyer, D.E., and Schvaneveldt, R.W. 1971. Facilitation in recognizing pairs of words: Evidence of a dependence between retrieval operations. *Journal of Experimental Psychology* 90:227–243.

Mozer, M.C. Letter migration in word perception. *Journal of Experimental Psychology: Human Perception and Performance* 9:531–546.

Neely, J.H. 1977. Semantic priming and retrieval from lexical memory: Roles of inhibitionless spreading activation and limited-capacity attention. *Journal of Experimental Psychology: General* 106:226–254.

Nelson, D.L., McEnvoy, C.L., Walling, J.R., and Wheeler, J.W. 1980 The University of South Florida homograph norms. *Behavior Research Methods and Instrumentation* 12:16–37.

Neville, H. 1985. Biological constraints on semantic processing: A comparison of spoken and signed languages. *Psychophysiology* 22:576. (Abstract).

Newman, J.E., and Dell, G.S. 1978. The phonological nature of phoneme monitoring:a critique of some ambiguity studies. *Journal of Verbal Learning and Verbal Behavior* 17:359–374.

Norman, D.A. and Bobrow, D.G. 1975. On data-limited and resource-limited processes. *Cognitive Psychology* 7:44–64.

Nunez, P.L. 1981. *Electric Fields of the Brain: The Neurophysics of EEG.* New York: Oxford University Press.

Oden, G.L., and Spira, J.L. 1983. Influence of context on the activation and selection of ambiguous word senses. *Quarterly Journal of Experimental Psychology* 35A:51–64.

Onifer, W., and Swinney, D.A. 1981. Accessing lexical ambiguities during sentence comprehension: Effects of frequency of meaning and contextual bias. *Memory and Cognition* 9:225–236.

Perfetti, C.A., Lindsey, R., and Garson, B. 1971. *Association and Uncertainty: Norms of Association to Ambiguous Words.* Learning Research and Development Center, University of Pittsburgh.

Pritchard, W.S. 1981. The psychophysiology of P300. *Psychological Bulletin* 89:506–540.

Rayner, K. 1983. *Eye Movements in Reading.* Hillsdale: Erlbaum.

Rohrbaugh, J.W. and Gaillard, A.W.K. 1983. Sensory and motor aspects of the contingent negative variation. In A.W.K. Gaillard and W. Ritter (eds.), *Tutorials in ERP Research: Endogenous Components.* Amsterdam: North Holland.

Rugg, M.D. 1984a. Event-related potentials in phonological matching tasks. *Brain and Language* 23:225–240.

Rugg, M.D. 1984b. Event-related potentials and the phonological processing of words and non-words. *Neuropsychologia* 22:435–443.

Rugg, M.D. 1985. The effects of semantic priming and word repetition on event-related potentials. *Psychophysiology* 22:642–647.

Sanocki, T., Goldman, K., Waltz, J., Cook, C., Epstein, W. and Oden, G. 1985. Interaction of stimulus and contextual information during reading: Identifying words within sentences. *Memory and Cognition* 13:145–157.

Seidenberg, M.S., Tanenhaus, M.K., Lieman, J.M., and Bienkowski, M. Automatic access of the meanings of ambiguous words in context: Some limitations of knowledge-based processing. *Cognitive Psychology* 14:489–537.

Seidenberg, M.S., Waters, G.S. Sanders, M., and Langer, P.L. 1984. Pre- and postlexical loci of contextual effects on word recognition. *Memory and Cognition* 12:315–328.

Simpson, G.B. 1981. Meaning dominance and semantic context in the processing of lexical ambiguity. *Journal of Verbal Learning and Verbal Behavior* 20:120–136.

Simpson, G. 1984. Lexical ambiguity and its role in models of word recognition. *Psychological Bulletin* 96:316–340.

Stuss, D.T., Sarazin, F.F., Leech, E.E. and Picton, T.W. 1983. Event-related potentials during naming and mental rotation. *Electroencephalography and Clinical Neurophysiology* 56:133–146.

Sutton, S., Braren, M., Zubin, J. and John, E.R. 1965. Evoked-potential correlates of stimulus uncertainty. *Science* 150:1187–1188.

Swinney, D.A. 1979. Lexical access during sentence comprehension: (Re)consideration of context effects. *Journal of Verbal Learning and Verbal Behavior* 18:645–659.

Swinney, D.A., and Hakes, D.A. 1976. Effect of prior context upon lexical access during sentence comprehension. *Journal of Verbal Learning and Verbal Behavior* 15:681–689.

Taylor, W.L. 1953. Cloze procedure: A new tool for measuring readability. *Journalism Quarterly* 30:415–417.

Tulving, E. and Gold, C. 1963. Stimulus information and contextual information as determinants of tachistoscopic recognition of words. *Journal of Experimental Psychology* 66:319–327.

Van Petten, C., and Kutas, M. In press. Ambiguous words in context: An event-related potential analysis of the time course of meaning activation. *Journal of Memory and Language.*

Wood, C.C. and Allison, T. 1981. Interpretation of evoked potentials: A neurophysiological perspective. *Canadian Journal of Psychology* 35:113–135.

18

Cognitive Topology and Lexical Networks[1]

Claudia Brugman
George Lakoff
University of California, Berkeley

This article is a rather long and detailed study of a polysemous lexical item—the English word *over*—paying specific attention to the character of the relations among its senses. Polysemy is a subtype of lexical ambiguity, contrasting with homonymy, wherein a single lexical form is associated with more than one meaning, and those meanings are unrelated. In the case of polysemy, one word is taken as having senses which are related. The distinction is an important one for the resolution of lexical ambiguity, for, as we will show in the bulk of this article, the way semantic information is stored in a lexical entry may differ depending on whether that lexical entry is taken as reflecting homonymy or polysemy. We will show that the common practice of giving a list of meanings of ambiguous items is neither the only way, nor, for polysemous words, the most efficient way, of storing such semantic information. We will argue instead that a network-style mode of storage is cognitively real, and that

1 This paper is a shortened version of a discussion of polysemy and image-schemas that appears as case study 2 in Lakoff 1987. It is published here with permission of the University of Chicago Press. That study, in turn, was based on Brugman's University of California M.A. thesis [Brugman, 1981]. Portions of this work were supported by grant no. BNS-8310445 of the National Science Foundation and a grant by the Sloan Foundation to the Institute of Cognitive Studies at the University of California, Berkeley.

this allows for a maximum of shared, and otherwise related, information between senses.

Network-style representation is common in many areas of AI. But we use it here not by notational fiat but as part of a much more general conception of categorization, explored at length in [Lakoff, 1987]. That work provides detailed empirical evidence and theoretical argument against the classical view of categories as collections of objects characterized by lists of necessary-and-sufficient conditions, and in favor of an enriched view of categories. On that view, categories may contain a great deal of internal structure—for instance, that one member of a category should be more exemplary of that category than some other member; that the boundaries of the category are not always clear-cut; that categories may be characterized in part with respect to their contrast with other categories. The category structure utilized here is called a "radial" structure, with a central member and a network of links to other members. Each noncentral member of the category is either a variant of the central member or is a variant on a variant. The theoretical claim being made is that a polysemous lexical item is a radial category of senses.

What is important for our purposes is that the kind of network structure found here is not made up ad hoc to characterize this set of facts. Instead, this is a common category structure that occurs in domains other than the lexicon.

There is an important consequence of using the general theory of radial categories to characterize polysemy. In the general theory, the links between members of the network are not arbitrary. The theory of radial categories comes with a characterization of possible link types. In the case of polysemy, the link types are the types of relations linking the senses of the word. In general, some of the links may involve shared information, some may involve the relation between a general and a specific case, and some may be metaphoric. In the case under discussion, most of the links are what we have called "image-schema transformations." But overall there is only a small number of types of relations between senses of words, and this study is one of many that is being carried out in an attempt to figure out what they are.

Such studies are significant in a number of respects. They show that the relations between senses are not arbitrary, but are rather *principled, systematic,* and *recurrent* throughout the lexicon. Moreover, the relationships are natural, in the sense that they are either relationships that arise naturally within the cognitive system, or they are characterized by metaphors that have an independent existence in the conceptual system. From an explanatory point of view, the natural and independently motivated character of the links allows us to explain why polysemy should exist as a general phenomenon. From the point of view of language processing studies, it suggests that the lexicon has a structure that is made use of in processing.

1 *Cognitive Topology versus Semantic Features*

The traditional mode of representing lexical information, whether in linguistics or in cognitive science, has been the use of semantic features. Semantic features arise in general within the symbol manipulation paradigm in cognitive science: they are finitary symbols with no inherent meaning, but are to be made meaningful by being connected to things in the world. The features have no inherent structure, and any relationships among them are to be specified by a calculus characterizing permissible operations on the symbols.

One reason that we have chosen the example of *over* is that it demonstrates the inadequacy of feature analyses and shows the need for an oriented cognitive topology, which characterizes structures oriented relative to the human body that apply generally to spatial situations, structures like paths, bounded regions, tops, etc. Structures in a cognitive topology differ from semantic features in a number of ways: they are inherently meaningful (arising from sensory-motor operations), they have an inherent structure, they are analog rather than finitary, and the relationships among them arise naturally via the operation of the human sensory-motor system.

The evidence in this paper suggests that there are two respects in which cognitive topology is superior to feature analysis for *over*:

> The topological properties of the concepts are necessary to characterize "image-schema transformations" in terms that are cognitively natural, rather than in terms of an arbitrary calculus.

We will discuss this issue at the end of the paper. To facilitate the comparison between topological and feature analyses, we will use both types of representation in this paper. The drawings indicate the topological representation, while the names (such as 1.VX.C.E) indicate feature representations. We will demonstrate that, while feature representations might be useful in computer simulations, only topological representations characterize the cognitive reality of the meanings of words like *over*.

> Topological concepts are needed in order to account for how prepositions can be used to characterize an infinity of visual scenes.

The semantics of even the most basic spatial senses of *over* is such that a feature analysis simply will not do. Take, for example, the sense of *over* in *The ball went over the net*. Given a scene with a ball moving with respect to a net, there is an infinity of trajectories of the ball relative to the net that *over* will fit and another infinity that it will not fit. To characterize those two infinities, one needs concepts that generalize over possible trajectories and properties of the landscape: this sense of *over* requires two bounded regions, and a path from one to the other that is oriented vertically relative to the net. In short, what is needed is an oriented cognitive topology with elementary structures (paths, bounded regions), orientations (vertical), and means of fitting them together into an overall gestalt.

Our reason for going into this issue in such detail is as follows: It is sometimes claimed that the Symbol Manipulation Paradigm is necessary to account adequately for natural language. In fact, the reverse is true. The Symbol Manipulation Paradigm cannot account for natural language semantics. For a lengthy discussion, see [Langacker, 1987].

2 *Two Levels of Prototype Structure*

The lexical representation of *over* actually contains two levels of topological structure. First, each sense of *over* is a complex topological structure. Second, all the senses together form a radial category, which is itself a complex topological structure. It is crucial to distinguish these two levels: The first is the level of semantic content and the second is the level at which that content is structured in the lexicon.

Correspondingly, there are two levels of prototype structure—one at each level. At the second level, the level of lexical structure, the central sense in the radial category is the prototypical sense of *over*. But at the first level, the level of semantic content for each particular sense of *over*, the nature of prototypicality is quite different. At this level, prototypicality concerns the degree of fit of some real-world relation to an individual sense of the word. For example, consider "The plane flew over the mountain." The best fit is where the path goes right above the center of the mountain. As the path of flight moves away from the center of the mountain, the degree of fit lessens.

This introduction does not provide the whole story: we will not fully motivate the independent existence of all principles that relate senses, and we cannot do justice to the question of how contrasting lexical categories and the conventionalization of boundaries figure in a full semantic description of this item. The chief concern here is to provide a detailed example of how a lexical ambiguity of a specific kind can be given a reasonably complete description and to show the kinds of theoretical apparatus required for that description. To sum up: the critical features of this description are that feature-based descriptions are inadequate, that a topological representation appears to be needed, and that the senses of a polysemous item form a radially-structured lexical network.

3 *The Problem*

To get some sense of the problem, let us consider a handful of the senses of *over*:

The painting is *over* the mantel.

The plane is flying *over* the hill.

Sam is walking *over* the hill.

Sam lives *over* the hill.

The wall fell *over*.

Sam turned the page *over*.

Sam turned *over*.

She spread the tablecloth *over* the table.

The guards were posted all *over* the hill.

The play is *over*.

Do it *over*, but don't *over*do it.

Look *over* my corrections, and don't *over*look any of them.

You made *over* a hundred errors.

Even this small number of examples shows enormous complexity. The problem Brugman undertook was how to describe all these senses and the relations among them. The analysis we will be presenting is a minor refinement of the semantic aspect of the earlier analysis. Let us begin with what was found to be the central sense.

4 *The* Above-Across *Sense*

The central sense of *over* combines elements of both *above* and *across* (see Figure 18.1). In this example, the plane is understood as a trajector (TR) oriented relative to a landmark (LM). TR and LM are generalizations of the concepts figure and ground [Langacker, 1983; 1987]. In this case the landmark is unspecified. The arrow in the figure represents the PATH that the TR is moving along. The LM is what the plane is flying over. The PATH is *above* the LM. The dotted lines indicate the extreme boundaries of the landmark. The PATH goes all the way *across* the landmark from the boundary on one side to the boundary on the other. Although the figure indicates noncontact between the TR and LM, the central sense is neutral on the issue of contact. As we will see shortly, there are instances with contact and instances without contact. In this this respect the schema cannot be drawn with complete accuracy. Any drawing would have to indicate contact or the lack of it. The image-schema is neutral, and that is part of what makes it schematic. What we have here is an abstract schema that cannot itself be imaged concretely, but which structures images. We will return below to the question of what it means for an image-schema to structure an image.

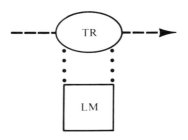

Figure 18.1 The plane flew over. Name: Schema 1

Let us now turn to some special cases of the schema in Figure 18.1. These are instances of the schema that are arrived at by adding information, in particular, by further specifying the nature of the landmark and by specifying whether or not there is contact. We will consider four kinds of landmark specifications: (1) LM is a point, that is, the landmark is viewed as a point with no internal structure. (2) LM is extended, that is, the landmark extends over a distance or area. (3) LM is vertical. (4) LM is both extended and vertical. For each such case, we will consider two further specifications: contact between TR and LM, and noncontact. Each schema will be named using the following abbreviations: X: extended, V: vertical, C: contact, NC: no contact. Thus, the schema name '1.VX.C' stands for the special case of schema 1 in which the landmark is both vertical and extended (VX) and there is contact (C) between the LM and TR.

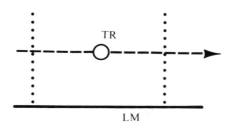

Figure 18.2 The bird flew over the yard. Name: Schema 1.X.NC

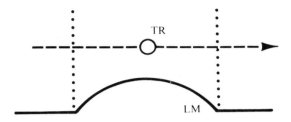

Figure 18.3 The plane flew over the hill. Name: Schema 1.VX.NC

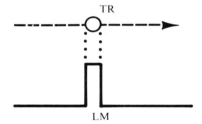

Figure 18.4 The bird flew over the wall. Name: Schema 1.V.NC

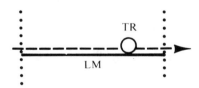

Figure 18.5 Sam drove over the bridge. Name: Schema 1.X.C

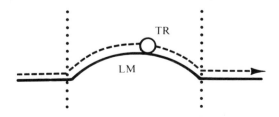

Figure 18.6 Sam walked over the hill. Name: Schema 1.VX.C

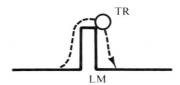

Figure 18.7 Sam climbed over the wall. Name: Schema 1.V.C

The schemas in Figures 18.2–18.7 can be related by a diagram in Figure 18.8.

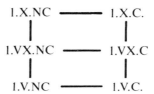

Figure 18.8 Links among schemas

These links indicate similarity. Thus, all the the schemas are linked, as are all the schemas that share noncontact. Moreover, each pair of schemas that share everything except for the contact parameter are linked. In addition, they are all linked to schema 1 (see Figure 18.1), since they are all instances of that schema.

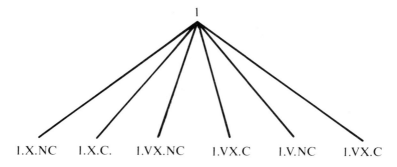

Figure 18.9

The schemas in Figures 18.2–18.7 can be viewed in two equivalent ways. Take, for example, a sentence like *Sam walked over the hill* in Figure 18.6. We can think of *over* in this sentence as being represented by the minimally-specified schema 1 of Figure 18.1, and we can think of the additional information as being added by the object and the verb. Thus, a hill is vertical and extended (VX) and walking requires contact (C) with the ground. Let us refer to this as the *minimal specification interpretation*. Equivalently, we can view the minimally-specified *over* of Figure 18.1 as generating all the fully-specified schemas of Figure 18.2–18.7. On this *full specification interpretation*, we can think of the *over* in *Sam walked over the hill* as having the full specification of schema 1.VX.C in Figure 18.7. The verb *walk* would then match the contact (C) specification, and the direct object *hill* would match the vertical extended (VX) specification. The difference is whether the verb and direct object *add* the VX and C information or whether they *match* it.

These two interpretations make slightly different claims about the lexical representation of *over* in these sentences. On the minimal specification interpretation, only schema 1 exists in the lexicon; the other schemas all result from information added by the verb and direct object. On the full specification interpretation, there is a lexical representation for all these schemas; the more specific schemas are generated by schema 1 plus the general parameters we have discussed: C-NC and X-VX-V.

On the basis of what we have said so far, these two interpretations are completely equivalent; there is no empirical difference between them, and no a priori reason to choose between them. There is, however, additional evidence that favors the full specification interpretation, and we will be citing it throughout the remainder of this case study. We will be arguing that the senses of *over* form a chain with schema 1 at the center. On the full specification interpretation, the schemas in Figures 18.2–18.7 are part of that chain. Some of those schemas form links to other senses. The existence of such links suggests that the full specification interpretation is correct. Consider the following case, where there is a focus on the end-point of the path. We will use the abbreviation E in naming schemas where there is end-point focus.

In Figure 18.10, there is an understood path that goes over the hill, and Sam lives at the end of that path. The end-point focus is not added by anything in the sentence, neither *hill*, nor *lives*, nor *Sam*. *Over* here has an additional sense which is one step away from schema 1.VX.C—a sense in which end-point focus (E) is added to yield schema 1.VX.C.E.

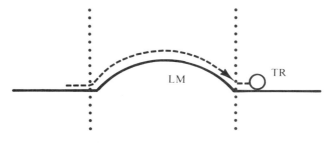

Figure 18.10 Sam lives over the hill. Name: Schema 1.VX.C.E

But end-point focus cannot be freely added to just any of the schemas in Figures 18.2–18.7. It can only be added to those with an extended landmark, as in Figure 18.11.

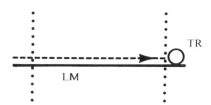

Figure 18.11 Sausalito is over the bridge. Name: Schema 1.X.C.E

In these cases, *over* has the sense of 'on the other side of' as a result of end-point focus. However, *over* does not in general mean 'on the other side of.' For example, sentences like *Sam lives over the wall* and *Sam is standing over the door*, if they occur at all, cannot mean that he lives, or is standing, on the other side of the door and the wall. And a sentence like *Sam is sitting over the spot*, can only mean that he is sitting *on* it, not that he is sitting on the other side of it. Thus there is no end-point focus schema corresponding to schema 1.V.C of Figure 18.6.

Assuming the full specification interpretation, we can extend the chain in Figure 18.8 to include the schemas in Figures 18.10 and 18.11, which is illustrated in Figure 18.12.

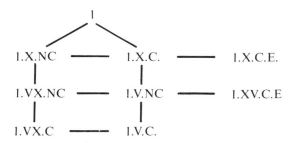

Figure 18.12 Links among schemas

So far, we have considered two types of links among schemas: *instance links* and *similarity links*. Here are examples, where '←' indicates an instance link and '↔' indicates a similarity link:

Instance link: 1 ← 1.V.C

Similarity links: 1.VX.NC ↔ 1.VX.C

Thus, the link between schema 1 and schema 1.V.C is an instance link, with 1.V.C being an instance of 1. And the link between schema 1.VX.NC and schema 1.VX.C is a similarity link, where 1.VX and C are shared.

So far, we have looked only at instances of the *above-across* sense. And we have only looked at the least interesting links between schemas. Let us now turn to other senses and more interesting kinds of links.

5 *The* Above *Sense*

Over has a stative sense, with no PATH. It is roughly equivalent in meaning to *above* (see Figure 18.13).

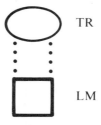

TR

LM

Figure 18.13 Hang the painting over the fireplace. Name: Schema 2

Schema 2 has no particular constraints on either the TR or LM. It is linked to schema 1 in that it has the TR above the LM. However, it differs from schema 1 in two respects: First, it has no PATH and no boundaries; in other words, the *across*-sense is missing. Second, it does not permit contact between the TR and LM. The no-contact requirement can be seen in examples like *The helicopter is hovering over the hill.* If the helicopter lands, it is no longer *over* the hill, it is *on* the hill.

From time to time, linguists have suggested that schema 2 is *the core meaning* of the preposition *over*, that is, that schema 2 is present in all the uses of *over* as a preposition. It should be clear from what we have seen so far that this is false. Since schema 2 requires no contact, it cannot be present in those cases where contact occurs, for example, in schema 1.X.C exemplified by *Sam drove over the bridge.* Schema 2 also does not occur in the cases of end-point focus, such as schema 1.VX.C.E, which is exemplified by *Sam lives over the hill.* In this case, the TR is not above the LM.

One of the instances of schema 2 is the case where the TR is one-dimensional (which we will abbreviate as 1DTR—see Figure 18.14).

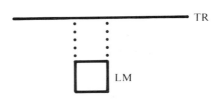

Figure 18.14 The power line stretches over the yard. Name: Schema 2.1DTR

This schema is a minimal variant of schema 1.X.NC, exemplified by *The bird flew over the yard*, as shown in Figure 18.2. The extended path in Figure 18.2 corresponds to the one-dimensional solid trajector in Figure 18.14. We will call this kind of link between schemas a *transformational link*. This particular link between an extended path (X.P) and a one-dimensional trajectory (1DTR) will be represented as:

X.P ↔ 1DTR

This relationship is not directly reflected in the naming system for schemas that we have adopted. However, we can state the relationship more systematically if we do a little renaming of a sort that reflects image-schema decompositions. Let us use ABV for the 'above' subschema. And let us use PATH (P) for the 'across' subschema. Schema 1 would be renamed ABV.P, and Schema 1.X.NC of Figure 18.2 would be renamed ABV.NC.X.P. This name would reflect the fact that in this schema the TR is moving above (ABV) the LM, along a path (P), where the landmark is extended (X) and there is no contact between TR and LM (NC). Correspondingly, schema 2 would be renamed ABV.NC, and schema 2.1DTR in Figure 18.15 would be renamed ABV.NC.1DTR.

Schema 1.X.NC = ABV.NC.X.P

Schema 2.1DTR = ABV.NC.1DTR

This decomposition displays the relationship between the schemas directly. The schemas are transforms of one another, given the transformational link X.P ↔ 1DTR.

It is important to bear in mind the difference between similarity links and transformational links. In the case of similarity links, the link is defined by shared subschemas. In the relationship described above, there are, indeed, shared subschemas: both schemas contain ABV.NC. But the transformational link is not a matter of *shared* subschemas, but of *related* subschemas.

The links among the schemas that we have described so far can be represented by the following diagram in Figure 18.15.

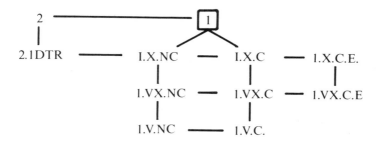

Figure 18.15 Links among schemas

6 *The* Covering *Senses*

There is a group of schemas for *over* that have to do with covering. This group is linked to the grid of Figure 18.15 in two ways. The basic covering schema is a variant of Schema 2, where the TR is at least 2-dimensional and extends across the boundaries of the LM.

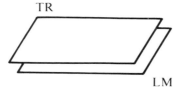

Figure 18.16 The board is over the hole. Name: Schema 3

There are two differences between schema 2 and schema 3. The first is that schema 2 is unspecified for the dimension of the trajector, while schema 3 must be at least 2-dimensional. But while schema 2 requires noncontact, schema 3 is neutral with respect to contact, allowing either contact or lack of it.

There is a minimal variant of schema 3 in which the TR moves to the position in schema 3. This schema is composed of schema 3 plus a path (P) indicating motion to the final position.

Schema 3.P.E (see Figure 18.17) is linked to schema 1. It shares motion of the TR above and across the LM. It also shares a lack of specification for contact. Schema 3.P.E differs from schema 1 in two ways. It is specified for the dimension of the trajector and it has end-point focus, which indicates that the final state is that of schema 3.

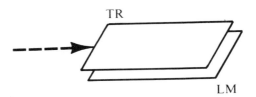

Figure 18.17 The city clouded over. Name: Schema 3.P.E

There are two covering schemas in which *over* is paired with a mass quantifier that quantifies regions of the landmark, e.g., *all, most, a lot of, entire*,etc. The quantifier *all* may combine with *over* in this sense to form the unit *all over*. The first of these two schemas has a *multiplex* (MX) trajector, that is, a trajector made up of many individuals.

> He has freckles over most of his body.
> There are specks of paint all over the rug.
> There is sagebrush over the entire valley floor.

In these cases, the individuals—the individual hairs, specks of paint, and bushes—don't completely cover the part of the landmark quantified over. Rather, the landmark has small regions which jointly cover its surface (or most of it), and there is at least one trajector in each region.

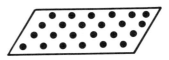

Figure 18.18 The guards were posted all over the hill. Name: Schema 3.MX

The relationship between schema 3 and schema 3.MX (see Figure 18.18) is the relationship between a continuous region (or mass) and a multiplex entity. Such relationships are very common in language. Compare *cows* (multiplex) and *cattle* (mass). Quantifiers like *all* and *most* can occur with either masses (*all gold, most wine*) or multiplex entities (*all ducks, most trees*). The relationship between multiplex entities and masses is a natural visual relationship. Imagine a large herd of cows up close—close enough to pick out the individual cows. Now imagine yourself moving back until you can no longer pick out the individual cows. What you perceive is a mass. There is a point at which you cease making out the individuals and start perceiving a mass. It is this perceptual experience upon which the relationship between multiplex entities and masses rests. The image transformation that relates multiplex entities and masses characterizes the link between schema 3 and schema 3.MX. We can characterize that transformational link as follows:

MX ↔ MS

There is a second covering schema for *over* in which *over* is associated with a mass quantifier. It is a minimal variant on schema 3.MX in which the points representing the multiplex entity of 3.MX are joined to form a path (P) which 'covers' the landmark. Examples are:

I walked all over the hill.

We've hiked over most of the Sierras.

I've hitchhiked over the entire country.

We can represent this schema in Figure 18.19. This schema is linked to schema 3.MX by an image transformation that forms a path through a collection of points. We will represent this transformational linkage as:

MX ↔ MX.P

Schema 3.MX.P is also minimally linked to schema 3.P. In schema 3.P, the landmark is gradually covered as the trajector moves along the path. This is also true in schema 3.MX.P.

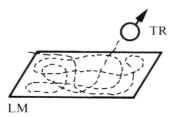

Figure 18.19 I walked all over the hill. Name: Schema 3.MX.P

The covering schemas all have variants in which the TR need not be above (that is, higher than) the LM. In all cases, however, there must be an understood viewpoint from which the TR is blocking accessibility of vision to at least some part of the landmark.

There was a veil over her face.

As the rain came down, it froze and ice spread all over the windshield.

There were flies all over the ceiling.

The spider had crawled all over the ceiling.

We will refer to these as *rotated* (RO) schemas, though with no suggestion that there is actual mental rotation degree-by-degree involved. One might suggest that instead of rotation from the vertical, there is simply a lack of specification of orientation. If there were, we would expect that the contact restrictions would be the same in all orientations. However, they are not. The rotated versions of the MX schemas—3.MX and 3.MX.P—require contact, while the unrotated versions do not. Here are some typical examples that illustrate the distinction:

Superman flew all over downtown Metropolis. (TR above LM, noncontact)

*Superman flew all over the canyon walls. (TR not above LM, noncontact)

Harry climbed all over the canyon walls. (TR not above LM, contact)

Thus, Superman's flying *alongside* the canyon walls does not constitute flying *over* them.

We will add 'RO' to the names of the unrotated covering schemas to yield names for the corresponding covering schemas. The rotated covering schemas have the following names: 3.RO, 3.P.RO, 3.MX.RO, and 3.MX.P.RO. Figure 18.20 is a diagram indicating the links among the covering schemas and the links to the other *over* schemas. And Figure 18.21 indicates the overall linkage among the schemas discussed so far.

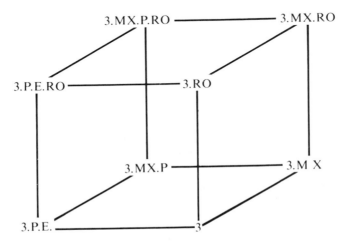

Figure 18.20 Links among covering schemas

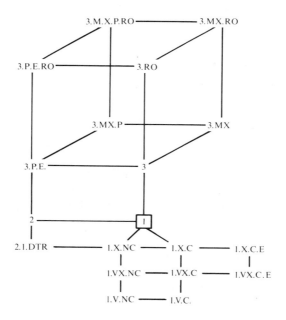

Figure 18.21 Links among schemas discussed so far

7 The Reflexive Schemas

Perhaps the most remarkable of the discoveries made by Lindner [1981, 1982] was the discovery of *reflexive trajectors*. The concept can be illustrated most simply using the example of *out*. The simplest use of *out* occurs in cases like *Harry ran out of the room*. We can represent this by the schema in Figure 18.22.

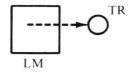

Figure 18.22 Harry ran out of the room.

In this diagram the container (the room) is the landmark, and the trajector (Harry) moves from the interior to the exterior of the room. But this schema won't do for cases of *out* like:

> The syrup spread out.
>
> The posse spread out.
>
> They stretched out the taffy.
>
> We rolled out the carpet.

Here the relevant trajectors are the syrup, the posse, the taffy, and the carpet. But they are not moving *out* with respect to any other landmark. Take the case of the syrup. Pour some syrup on a table. It will have a certain outer boundary at first; but the boundary moves. Some of the syrup that was inside the initial boundary is now outside that initial boundary. The syrup, or at least part of it, is moving 'out' relative to its own prior boundary. We can schematize this in Figure 18.23.

Figure 18.23 The syrup spread out.

In short, the syrup is its own landmark: TR = LM. Such a relation between a landmark and a trajector is called *reflexive*. Since there is only one entity under consideration, it is referred to as a *reflexive trajector*.

The '=' in 'TR = LM' is not strict identity; it is 'identity' of *part of* a bounded mass relative to itself as it *used to be* bounded. As we will see below, there are several ways in which 'TR = LM' can be realized. An important one is when parts of a single entity act as TR and other parts of the same entity act as LM. This kind of reflexive trajector occurs in the case of *over*. Consider examples like:

> Roll the log over.

Here a major part (roughly half) of the log is moving above and across the rest. That is, half the log is acting as landmark and the rest as trajector. The same is true in a case like

> Turn the paper over.

Both of these are variations on schema 1; they differ only in that LM = TR in the sense just described.

TR = LM

Figure 18.24 Roll the log over. Name: Schema 4

We can represent the schema for these cases in Figure 18.24. Schema 4 can be viewed as a transform of schema 1, with schema 4 adding the condition TR = LM. We will represent such a transformational link as

NRF ↔ RF

where 'NRF' means "nonreflexive" and 'RF' means "reflexive". If we had chosen to name schema 4 according to its status as a variant of schema 1, we would have called it 1.RF.

The path of *over* in schema 4 traces a semi-circle above and across other parts of the thing being moved. We will refer to this as a *reflexive path*. There is a variant on schema 4 in which no part of the thing moving moves above or across any other part; instead, the entity as a whole traces the reflexive path. This occurs in cases like

The fence fell over.

Sam knocked over the lamp.

These are cases where the TR is initially vertical and moves so as to follow the last half of a reflexive path (RFP). The schema represented is as in Figure 18.25. The relationship between schemas 4 and 4.RFP can be stated as follows: In schema 4, half of the TR follows the whole reflexive path; in schema 4.RPF, all of the TR follows the last half of the reflexive path.

TR = LM

Figure 18.25 The fence fell over. Name: Schema 4.RFP

This schema is not only a variant of schema 4. It is also a minimal variant of one of the most common instances of schema 1, the instance that characterizes *over* in *The dog jumped over the fence*. In this case, there is a vertical landmark and the path of the trajector both begins and ends on the ground (G). This results in a semi-circular path (see Figure 18.26). If we take the reflexive transform of this schema, letting TR = LM, we get the schema of Figure 18.25—schema 4.RFP. Thus, schema 4.RFP has close links to two other schemas.

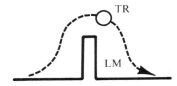

Figure 18.26 The dog jumped over the fence. Name: 1.V.NC.G

8 *The Excess Schema*

When *over* is used as a prefix, it can indicate excess, as in:

The bathtub overflowed.

I overate.

Don't overextend yourself.

The excess schema for *over* is a variation on one of the instances of schema 1, in particular, schema 1.X.C.E of Figure 18.11. In schema 1.X.C.E, there is an extended landmark; the trajector has moved across the boundaries of the landmark, and there is focus on the end-point, which is past the boundary. The excess schema has all these characteristics. It differs from schema 1.X.C.E in three respects. First, it is oriented vertically, with the end-point at the top. Second, it is understood as indicating amount via the MORE IS UP metaphor (see [Lakoff and Johnson, 1980]). Third, the path is taken as indicating the course of an activity, via the ACTIVITY IS A JOURNEY metaphor. Fourth, the boundary point is taken as the upper limit of what is normal for that activity. Thus, being beyond that boundary point indicates excess.

The excess schema is thus not merely an image-schema, but a complex image-schema that makes use of an image-schema (schema 1.X.C.E), an orientation transformation from horizontal to vertical, two metaphors (MORE IS UP and AN ACTIVITY IS A JOURNEY), and propositional information about what is normal. In link diagrams, we will refer to the excess schema as schema 5.

9 *The Repetition Schema*

One of the most common uses of *over* is to indicate repetition, as in

    Do it over.

Over here is used an an adverb. As in the case of the *over* of excess, the *over* of repetition makes use of a complex schema built on an instance of schema 1, namely, schema 1.X.C. This schema has an extended landmark, and indicates motion above and across it (see Figure 18.5). The repetition schema uses schema 1.X.C, and adds two metaphors to it. Again, the path is metaphorically understood as the course of the activity. This is via the very general ACTIV- ITY IS A JOURNEY metaphor. The landmark is understood metaphorically as an earlier completed performance of the activity. This is a special-purpose metaphor, which is, to my knowledge, used only in this complex schema. This is the part of the repetition schema for *over* that is *not motivated by an occur- rence elsewhere in the conceptual system.* It is what makes this sense of *over* somewhat idiosyncratic.

    At this point, we are in a position to give a link diagram that shows a good deal of the complexity of *over*. In that diagram, we will refer to the repetition schema as schema 6. Figure 18.27 displays all the links we have discussed so far. A number of additional metaphorical links will be discussed below.

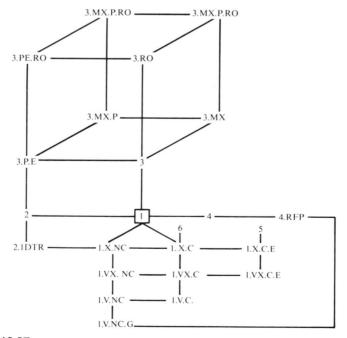

Figure 18.27

Figure 18.27 shows what is meant by a *radial* structure. schema 1 occupies a central position; it and its instances are of primary importance in the system of links. The links correspond to what Wittgenstein called 'family resemblances.' The links are sometimes defined by shared properties. But frequently they are defined not by shared properties, but by transforms or by metaphors.

10 *Some Metaphorical Senses*

It is extremely common for metaphors to apply to image-schemas. A great many metaphorical models use a spatial domain as their source domain. Among the most common source domains for metaphorical models are containers, orientations, journeys (with paths and goals), vertical impediments, etc. In this section, we will give a number of cases where *over* has a metaphorical sense based on an image-schema discussed above.

She has a strange power *over* me.

This is an instance of a very common metaphor: CONTROL IS UP; LACK OF CONTROL IS DOWN (see [Lakoff and Johnson, 1980]). *Over* in this sentence is an extension of schema 2 (Figure 18.14), where the trajector is simply above the landmark.

Sam was passed *over* for promotion.

Here we have an instance of schema 1 (Figure 18.1). Two metaphorical mappings apply to it. The first is CONTROL IS UP; LACK OF CONTROL IS DOWN. This entails that the person who passed over Sam was in control of Sam's status. The second metaphor the applies to this schema is another common one: CHOOSING IS TOUCHING. This occurs in such sentences as *He was tapped for service* and *The boss handpicked his successor.* Since the schema indicates that there is no contact, it is entailed that Sam was not chosen.

We are now in a position to make sense of the difference between *over-look* and *oversee.*

You've *over*looked his accomplishments.

We need to find someone who can *over*see this operation.

The *over* in *overlook* is based on schema 2.1DTR (Figure 18.5). There are two metaphors involved. The first is a metaphor for understanding vision: SEEING IS TOUCHING. This occurs in examples like *I couldn't take my eyes off of her, Her eyes picked out every detail of the pattern, He undressed her with his eyes,* and *He fixed his gaze on the entrance.* According to this metaphor, one's gaze goes from one's eyes to what one sees. You see whatever your gaze touches. Under the metaphorical mapping, the path in schema 2.1DTR is the gaze. Since there is no contact in schema 2.1DTR, the metaphorical gaze doesn't touch the landmark; thus the subject of *overlook* is *not* looking at, and therefore does *not* see, the landmark. The second metaphor is the general MIND-AS-BODY metaphor (see [Sweetser, 1984]). The relevant aspect of that metaphor is the part in which LOOKING AT SOMETHING IS TAKING IT INTO CONSIDERATION. Accordingly, *I'll take a look at it* normally entails *I'll consider it.* Therefore, to overlook someone's accomplishments is *not* to take them into consideration.

The *over* in *oversee* is based on schema 2 (Figure 18.15), in which the TR is above the LM. There are a metaphor and a metonymy that are relevant to this example. The metaphor is CONTROL IS UP. Thus, the one who does the overseeing has control over the persons overseen. The metonymy is SEEING SOMETHING DONE STANDS FOR MAKING SURE THAT IT IS DONE. This metonymy is based on an idealized model in which making sure of something typically involves seeing it. Because of this metonymic relation, *See that he gets his money* means *Make sure that he gets his money.* Thus, to *oversee* means to be in control and make sure that something is done.

We can now compare *overlook* to *look over.*

Look *over* my corrections, but don't *over*look any of them.

The *over* in *look over* is based on schema 3.MX.P (Figure 18.18), and the SEEING IS TOUCHING metaphor. The resulting complex schema is one in which the subject's gaze traces a path that 'covers' the direct object, *corrections.* In the resulting schema, the gaze does make contact with the landmark. The MIND-AS-BODY metaphor again yields a sense of *look* in which looking at something involves taking it into consideration. Thus, when one looks over X, one directs one's attention to a representative sampling that 'covers' X, and one takes into consideration each subpart that one directs attention to.

11 *Motivation*

Before we go on, it is worth commenting on what is and what is not being explained in these analyses. We are not explaining why *oversee, overlook,* and *look over* mean what they mean. Their meanings cannot be predicted from the meanings of *over, look,* and *see.* But their meanings are not completely arbitrary. Given the range of spatial meanings of *over,* and given the metaphors present in the conceptual system that English is based on, it *makes sense* for these words to have these meanings. We are explaining just why it makes sense and what kind of sense it makes.

In each of these cases, the metaphorical and metonymic models exist in the conceptual system independently of the given expression. For example, we understand seeing metaphorically in terms of a gaze that goes out of one's eyes and touches the object seen. This metaphorical understanding is present regardless of whether any of the expressions just discussed have those meanings. Similarly, the schemas for *over* exist for expressions in the spatial domain independently of the existence of *oversee, overlook,* and *look over.* What one learns when one learns these words is which of the independently existing components of their meaning are actually utilized. Each of these expressions is a specialized 'assembly' of independently existing parts. The only arbitrariness involved is the the knowledge that such an assembly exists.

The psychological claim being made here is that it is easier to learn, remember, and use such assemblies which use existing patterns than it is to learn, remember, and use words whose meaning is inconsistent with existing patterns. What is being explained is not why those expressions mean what they mean, but why those are natural meanings for them to have. Thus, if one is going to have a word that means 'to fail to take into consideration,' it is more natural to use *overlook* than to use an existing unrelated word like *sew,* or a complex word whose components are in conflict with the meaning, such as *underplan,* or *taste at,* or *rekick.* It is common sense that such expressions would not be used with such a meaning, and we are characterizing the nature of that 'common sense.'

As we have mentioned before, such an explanation requires going beyond the predictable/arbitrary dichotomy. It requires introducing the concept of *motivation.* Thus, the meaning of *overlook,* though not predictable, is motivated— motivated by one of the spatial schemas for *over* and by two metaphors in the conceptual system. Similarly, all of the noncentral schemas for *over* in the chain given in Figure 18.27 are motivated—motivated by other senses and by principles of linking.

12 *More Metaphorical Senses*

There are some additional common metaphorical senses of *over* that are worth discussing. Take *get over* in

Harry still hasn't gotten *over* his divorce.

This use of *over* is based on schema 1.VX.C (Figure 18.6), and two metaphors. In the first metaphor, obstacles are understood in terms of vertical landmarks—which may be extended or not. This metaphorical model is the basis for expressions such as *There is nothing standing in your way*. The second metaphorical model is one that understands LIFE as a JOURNEY. This occurs in sentences like *It's time to get on with your life*. In the above use, the divorce in an obstacle (metaphorically, a vertical extended landmark) on the path defined by life's journey.

Pete Rose is over the hill.

Over the hill makes use of schema 1.VX.C.E (Figure 18.10) and a metaphor for understanding a career in terms of a journey over a vertical extended landmark like a hill. In this metaphorical model of a career, one *starts at the bottom*, may *go all the way to the top*, and then *goes downhill*. Thus, *over the hill* means that one has already reached and passed the peak, or "high point," of one's career and will never have that high a stature again.

The rebels overthrew the government.

This is an instance of schema 4.RFP (Figure 18.25) and the CONTROL IS UP metaphor. Before the event takes place, the government is in control (metaphorically upright), and afterwards it is not in control (metaphorically down).

He turned the question over in his mind.

This is an instance of schema 4 (Figure 18.24), plus an instance of the MIND-AS-BODY metaphor in which THINKING ABOUT SOMETHING IS EXAMINING IT. This metaphorical model occurs in such sentences as *Let us now examine the question of factory chickens*. In examining a physical object, one turns it over in order to get a look at all sides of it. Questions are metaphorically understood as having sides, and when one turns a question over in one's mind, one is examining all sides of it.

The play is over.

Here we have an instance of schema 1.X.C.E (Figure 18.11). In general, activities with a prescribed structure are understood as extended landmarks, and performing such an activity is understood metaphorically as traveling along a prescribed path over that landmark. When one gets to the end, the activity is *over*. Thus, games, plays, and political campaigns can be characterized at their end as being *over*.

13 *Image-Schemas as Links between Perception and Reason*

Two of our major sources of information are vision and language. We can gain information through either perceiving something directly or being told it. And we can reason about that information, no matter what its source. We can even reason using information from both sources simultaneously, which suggests that it is possible for us to encode information from both sources in a single format. We would like to suggest that image-schemas provide such a format.

It is our guess that image-schemas play a central role in both perception and reason. We believe that they structure our perceptions and that their structure is made use of in reason. The analysis of *over* that we have just given is rich enough for us to discuss such questions in some detail. Let us begin with the following question. Are the image-schema transformations we have discussed natural, and if so, what is the source of their 'naturalness'?

14 *The Nature of Image-Schema Transformations*

There are certain very natural relationships among image-schemas, and these motivate polysemy, not just in one or two cases, but in case after case throughout the lexicon. Natural image-schema transformations play a central role in forming radial categories of senses. Take, for example, the end-point-focus transformation. It is common for words that have an image-schema with a path to also have the corresponding image-schema with a focus on the end-point of the path. We saw this in *over* in cases like

> Sam walked *over* the hill. (path)
> Sam lives *over* the hill. (end-of-path)

Pairs such as this are common.

> Harry walked *through* that doorway. (path)
> The passport office is *through* that doorway. (end-of-path)

> Sam walked *around* the corner. (path)
> Sam lives *around* the corner. (end-of-path)

> Harriet walked *across* the street. (path)
> Harriet lives *across* the street. (end-of-path)

Mary walked *down* the road. (path)
Mary lives *down* the road. (end-of-path)

Sam walked *past* the post office. (path)
Sam lives *past* the post office. (end-of-path)

It should be noted that although such pairs are common, they are not fully productive.

Sam walked *by* the post office. (path)
Sam lives *by* the post office. (= *near*; ≠ end-of-path)

Here, *by* has a path schema, but no corresponding end-point schema.

Sam ran *from* the house. (path)
Sam stood three feet *from* the house. (end-of-path)

Sam ran *to* the house. (path)
*Sam stood (three feet) *to* the house. (≠ end-of-path)

From allows both path and end-of-path schemas, but *to* only allows a path schema.

Path schemas are so naturally related to end-point schemas that people sometimes have to think twice to notice the difference. The same is true of the schema transformation that links multiplex and mass schemas. It is natural for words that have a mass schema to also have a multiplex schema.

All men are mortal. (MX)
All gold is yellow. (MS)

She bought *a lot of* earrings. (MX)
*She bought *a lot of* jewelry. (MS)

This schema transformation, of course, doesn't hold for all quantifiers:

She bought *two* earrings. (MX)
*She bought *two* jewelry. (MS)

There are also verbs which have both schemas:

He *poured* the juice through the sieve. (MS)
The fans *poured* through the gates. (MX)

This will also work for other verbs of liquid movement, such as *spill, flow,* etc.

The wine *spilled* out over the table. (MS)
The fans *spilled* out over the field. (MX)

There is a special case of the multiplex-mass transformation in which the multiplex entity is a sequence of points and the mass is a one-dimensional trajector. A variety of prepositions permit both schemas.

There are guards posted *along* the road. (MX)
There is a fence *along* the road. (1DTR)

He coughed *throughout* the concert. (MX)
He slept *throughout* the concert. (1DTR)

There were stains *down* his tie. (MX)
There were stripes *down* his tie. (1DTR)

There is a natural relationship not only between a one-dimensional trajector and a sequence of points. There is also a natural relationship between a one-dimensional trajector and a zero-dimensional moving trajector that traces a path.

Sam *went* to the top of the mountain. (0DMTR)
The road *went* to the top of the mountain. (1DTR)

Sam ran *through* the forest. (0DMTR)
There is a road *through* the forest. (1DTR)

Sam walked *across* the street. (0DMTR)
There was a rope stretched *across* the street. (1DTR)

Finally, there is a natural relationship between nonreflexive and reflexive trajectors. Here are some examples:

He stood *apart* from the crowd. (NRF)
The book fell *apart*. (RF)

She walked *up* to me. (NRF)
Let's cuddle *up*. (RF)

She poured the syrup *out* of the jar. (NRF)
The syrup spread *out* over the pancakes. (RF)

Let us consider for a moment what is natural about these image-schema transformations.

Path-focus/end-point-focus: It is a common experience to follow the path of a moving object until it comes to rest, and then to focus on where it is. This corresponds to the path-focus / end-point-focus transformation.

Multiplex/mass: As one moves further away, a group of individuals at a certain point begins to be seen as a mass. Similarly, a sequence of points is seen as a continuous line when viewed from a distance.

0DMTR/1DTR: When we perceive a continuously-moving object, we can mentally trace the path it is following. This capacity is reflected in the transformation linking zero-dimensional moving trajectors and a one-dimensional trajector.

NRF/RF: Given a perceived relationship between a TR and a LM which are two separate entities, it is possible to perceive the same relationship between (a) different parts of the same entity or (2) earlier and later locations of the same entity, where one part or location is considered LM and the other TR.

In short, these schema transformations are anything but arbitrary. They are direct reflections of our visual experiences.

The fact that image-schemas are a reflection of our sensory and general spatial experience is hardly surprising, yet it plays a very important role in the theory of image-schemas. Perhaps we can see that significance most easily by contrasting the image-schema transformations we have described with the names we have given to them. Take the transformation name 'MX $\leftrightarrow$ MS.' The names 'MX' and 'MS' are arbitrary relative to the character of what they name: a group of individual entities and a mass. The transformation is a natural relationship, but the name of the transformation is just a collection of arbitrary symbols.

This distinction is important because of certain versions of the Symbol Manipulation Paradigm. On one theory of image-representation—the 'propositional theory'—visual scenes are represented by arbitrary symbols which are linked together in network structures. Arbitrary symbols such as X and Y are taken as standing for some aspect of a scene, such as a point or an edge or a surface or an entire object. Other symbols are used to express relations among these symbols, for example, 'ABV(X,Y)' and 'C(X,Y)' might represent relations which are supposed to correspond to 'X is above Y' and 'X is in contact with Y,' but which, so far as the computer is concerned, are just symbols. Such a symbolization describes how various parts—points, edges, surfaces, etc.—are related to one another. Objects in a scene are described using such symbolizations.

According to the Symbol Manipulation Paradigm as applied to visual information and mental imagery [Pylyshyn, 1981], only such propositional representations are mentally real, while images are not real. This view stems from taking the Symbol Manipulation Paradigm *very* seriously. Since digital computers work by the manipulation of such arbitrary symbols, the strong version of the Symbol Manipulation Paradigm *requires* not only that visual perception and mental imagery be characterizable in such a 'propositional' form, but also that such symbolic representations, and only those, are mentally real.

The names that we have given to the image schemas, as well as to the image-schema transformations, are in keeping with feature representations. They have the properties that (1) they are arbitrary, in the sense that the internal structure of symbols plays no role in how the symbols interact or what they mean; (2) they are inherently meaningless, and have to be assigned meanings; and (3) they are finitary in nature. Such feature-style names are in these respects opposite from the corresponding image-schemas, which (1) are nonarbitrary, in the sense that they have an internal structure that plays a crucial role in what they mean and how they interact; (2) they are inherently meaningful; and (3) they are analog in nature.

Suppose that, instead of merely using such symbols as convenient names, we chose to take such a use of symbols seriously, as one would have to if one were to adopt the Symbol Manipulation Paradigm for Cognitive Science. According to that paradigm, topological representations such as image-schemas are not available as cognitive representations; all that is available are symbolic representations, which would look like the symbolic names we have given and would have their properties. The Symbol Manipulation Paradigm would thus make the implicit claim that the cognitively natural image-schema transformations of the sort we described did not exist. In their place would be arbitrary transformations relating the names we have given. Instead of a natural explanation of types of polysemy, we would have no explanation at all, but only an arbitrary description. We consider the lack of such explanatory force intolerable.

For instance, consider the relationship between the *over* of *The bird flew over the yard* and that of *The power line stretches over the yard*. These are adjacent senses in the network, linked by the natural relationship between a zero-dimensional moving trajector and a corresponding one-dimensional stationary trajector. If there were no such natural relation between the senses, they would not be adjacent in the network. Thus, the configuration of the network is anything but arbitrary; it is determined by an account of what constitutes a "natural" link type. Since it is the topological character of the representations that makes such relationships natural, it is that topological nature that makes the configurations of the networks nonarbitrary. If symbolic feature representations are substituted for the topological representations, then the naturalness of the relationships disappears and, with it, the explanation for what is linked to what. In short, there are natural reasons for the extensions of certain senses to other senses, and those reasons must be given in a cognitively adequate account of polysemy.

16 *Conclusion*

Systematic polysemy of the sort we have just seen is a pervasive phenomenon in language. It is so common and automatic that we often do not even notice it. Yet, as we have seen, simple basic processes like image-schema transformations and metaphors can interact to form rather large networks that characterize the natural relationships among the senses of polysemous words.

Our primary conclusion is that lists will not do; networks of the kind we have described are needed to characterize the relationships among the senses of polysemous words.

Our secondary conclusion is that features will not do. Oriented topological representations using image-schemas are necessary for two reasons: (1) to account for the range of scenes that concepts like *over* can fit, and (2) to account for the naturalness of image-schema transformations. This suggests that the Symbol Manipulation Paradigm, which cannot tolerate the existence of such representations using a cognitive topology, is inadequate for natural language semantics.

References

Brugman, Claudia. 1981. *Story of* Over. University of California, Berkeley M.A. Thesis. Available from the Indiana University Linguistics Club.

Lakoff, George. 1987. *Women, Fire, and Dangerous Things: What Categories Reveal about the Mind.* Chicago: University of Chicago Press.

Lakoff, George, and Mark Johnson. 1980. *Metaphors We Live By.* Chicago: University of Chicago Press.

Langacker, Ronald. 1983. Remarks on English aspect. In P. Hopper, (ed.), *Tense and Aspect: Between Semantics and Pragmatics,* pp. 265–304. Amsterdam: John Benjamins.

Langacker, Ronald W. 1987. *Foundations of Cognitive Grammar,* Vol. 1. Stanford: Stanford University Press.

Lindner, Susan. 1981. *A Lexico-Semantic Analysis of Verb-Particle Constructions with* Up *and* Out. University of California, San Diego Ph.D. Dissertation. Available from the Indiana University Linguistics Club.

Lindner, Susan. 1982. What goes up doesn't necessarily come down: The ins and outs of opposites. In *Papers from the Eighteenth Regional Meeting,* Chicago Linguistic Society, pp. 305–323.

Pylyshyn, Zenon. 1981. The imagery debate: Analogue media versus tacit knowledge. *Psychological Review* 87:16–45.

Sweetser, Eve E. 1984. *Semantic Structure and Semantic Change.* University of California, Berkeley Ph.D. Dissertation.

Index